All Crazee Now

DAVID TOSSELL

All Crazee Now

ENGLISH FOOTBALL AND FOOTBALLERS IN THE 1970s

pitch

First published by Pitch Publishing, 2021

Pitch Publishing
A2 Yeoman Gate
Yeoman Way
Worthing
Sussex
BN13 3QZ
www.pitchpublishing.co.uk
info@pitchpublishing.co.uk

A CIP catalogue record is available for this book from the British Library.

ISBN 978 1 78531 757 6

Typesetting and origination by Pitch Publishing

Printed and bound in India by Replika Press Pvt. Ltd.

CONTENTS

Introduction

THE DAY OF THE DAMNED

And this is just what English football did not want to see. Surely, we've got to get away from this ... Bremner is off as well. They are both throwing their shirts down and, really, this is a side of English football, a face of English football, we do not want to see. What do the players think they are doing?... We are seeing the unacceptable face of English football.

BBC commentator Barry Davies, FA Charity Shield, 1974

You're gonna get your fucking heads kicked in.

Leeds United and Liverpool fans underneath Davies's commentary

THE SIXTIES, many in America believe, was bisected by the moment when, on 25 July 1965, Bob Dylan and his band took the stage at the Newport Folk Festival in Rhode Island and, instead of their usual acoustic performance, plugged electric guitars into amplifiers and blasted out 'Like a Rolling Stone' to a chorus of boos from the audience. If English football in the Seventies had a similarly identifiable mid-point it was Saturday, 10 August 1974, the day when the FA Charity Shield announced its arrival at Wembley Stadium with an extraordinary contest between League champions Leeds United and FA Cup holders Liverpool.

Both teams travelled to north-west London facing life without their architects, Don Revie having accepted the England job after his second title triumph at Elland Road and Bill Shankly shocking a football community on Merseyside and beyond by announcing, only days before the match, that he was retiring from the job that appeared to define his very existence. The opposite directions in which the two clubs were about to head would shape the remainder of the decade; the mantle of 'team of the Seventies' passing from one to the other.

The symbolic nature of the occasion was made even richer, we know now, by the identities of the two men newly entrusted with guiding the fortunes of the two protagonists. Allowed to lead his team out one final time, thanks to the generosity of his successor, Bob Paisley, Shankly had made the same walk three months earlier before a 3-0 victory over Newcastle United in one of the most one-sided of Wembley finals. Captured by the television cameras seemingly conducting the moves with his hands from his seat on the touchline, there had been no hint that, after three League titles, a European trophy, and now a second FA Cup, Shankly was orchestrating a glorious farewell symphony. Nor did it seem likely on this disorientating August day that Paisley, the quiet assistant with nothing like Shankly's vibrant, overpowering personality, would have eclipsed his mentor's on-field achievements by the time the decade was up.

To Shankly's right strolled the unlikely figure of Brian Clough; the same man whose hatred of Revie's Leeds was legendary even before it was fictionalised and immortalised in book form and on celluloid by *The Damned United* three decades later. The appearance of a grinning Clough at the head of the bemused-looking line-up of Billy Bremner, Johnny Giles and the rest was as baffling as the sight of an electrified Dylan had been to the folkies in Newport. He'd already turned up several days late for pre-season training and then, in what would become an infamous first address, accused the players of having 'cheated' their way to their medals. The sense of trepidation around the club was reflected by Leeds fans being able to fill only three of the four chartered trains booked to carry them from Yorkshire to London.

The whole day had such an air of the surreal that it was hardly a surprise when the game, televised on that night's *Match of the Day* and accompanied by the horrified tones of commentator Barry Davies, degenerated into a punch-up. Bremner and Kevin Keegan threw their shirts to the turf as they marched towards their early baths, acts of rebellion for which they were subsequently suspended until the end of September.

With that punishment, English football seemed to be trying to draw a line. It was bad enough that the national team had been missing from the summer's World Cup in West Germany after failing to get out of a qualifying group that offered Poland and Wales as opposition. Now the new season was beginning with more of the nastiness that had become an increasingly visible blemish on the landscape over the past decade. There had been recent attempts to stamp it out, most notably three summers previously. Now it was time for an example to be made.

The climax of the match was entirely in keeping with the tone of the day. Following a 1-1 draw, Wembley's first penalty shoot-out was decided when Leeds goalkeeper David Harvey hit his team's sixth spot-kick over the bar. Despite Liverpool's eventual victory, it was an unsuitably shoddy final curtain on Shankly's career; a portent of the years ahead for Paisley only in the sense that Liverpool won; and a shambolic foretaste of what was to come at Leeds for Clough. His chaotic occupancy of Revie's old office would last for just 44 acrimonious days.

Events at Wembley can now be seen as a clear dividing line in the decade. Whether it was the reduced potency of Leeds – the team who for many epitomised the ugly realism of modern football – or a general turning of the tide, the Keegan–Bremner spat came to represent a low point in the game's on-field image. Liverpool under Paisley and, ironically, a Clough-led Nottingham Forest would dominate the latter years of the Seventies without attracting the kind of negativity with which Revie's Leeds were forever associated. Even the anti-establishment magazine, *Foul*, wrote in what was intended to be a farewell issue in June 1975, 'In spite of Norman Hunter winning the PFA Player of the Year award the season before last [and] the continuing presence of Storey and Chopper Harris ... the game has become a bit more civilised' and identified 'a trend towards better days'.

Under the more benevolent leadership of Jimmy Armfield, Leeds did manage to compensate for a stunted League campaign by reaching the European Cup Final. But, instead of it being a last crowning glory for the team that had dominated the psyche – if not the trophy cabinet – of English football over the previous decade, their controversial defeat by Bayern Munich, further marred by crowd violence, signalled the start of steady decline. Meanwhile, after one season of transition under Paisley, Liverpool were ready to launch themselves into successive League Championships, in 1976 and 1977, following up both with European Cup triumphs.

Clough, who had soared to unlikely heights with Derby County earlier in the decade, crawled back from the depths of his humiliation at Elland Road to create an even more remarkable narrative. Sticking two fingers up at those who had mocked his failure and defying those who thought this would finally knock the hubris out of the game's most outspoken character, he turned Second Division Nottingham Forest into the only team capable of regularly standing up to, and often overcoming, Paisley's Liverpool, both at home and in Europe.

This book, then, is presented in two parts. The first covers the period before Bremner and Keegan prompted Davies's lament for the state of the game; the years when Leeds, whom Revie had deliberately dressed up to look like Real Madrid, were the measuring stick for all of English football. The leitmotif of that period is the war that waged for the soul of the game; the battles between pragmatism and positive thinking, foul play and flair. The striving of the artist to find a home among the increasingly rigid science of winning matches.

The conflict was encapsulated by *Striker* magazine during the first year of the decade in a double-page feature headlined 'Method v Entertainment', in which it was stated, 'Even now Leeds find it hard to attract a crowd of over 38,000 at home. This is, no doubt, due to their past years of producing method football.'[1] The same article stated that

Manchester United and West Ham United 'believe in entertainment and good soccer, as opposed to results at the cost of total drabness' – an approach that would earn them only one FA Cup each during the 1970s and see both suffer relegation.

In the second section, it is Liverpool's dominance and the miracle of Nottingham Forest that take centre stage. And if the first part of the decade saw the sport preoccupied with what was happening within its own universe, then the latter years saw outside forces occupying a more prominent place in the storylines; much as the narcissistic glam rock of 1971–75 surrendered its place in the musical culture to a punk movement born largely of environmental reality. Football became a platform upon which to discuss race relations through the issues facing the increasing number of black players; the welcoming of foreigners as England opened it borders to overseas talent; and the contractual rights of the workforce – in this case, members of the Professional Footballers' Association. Clough, who would campaign on behalf of the miners and the Labour Party, had always argued that football could not be isolated from the society in which it operated. 'We are not morons playing on a little bit of green grass every week and shut away in ivory towers,' he said late in 1973. 'We have to deal with life seven days a week and 52 weeks out of the year. The decisions that people make in Parliament down the road are decisions that affect me, in football and sport. And we don't want to be typed as a thick, moronic, kicking-a-leather-ball-about lot.'[2]

Throughout, there was a lot more to the decade than wide-open championship races, shocking relegations, cup upsets and record-busting transfers. Escalating hooliganism was an omnipresent blight, while the growing media profile of the sport had a significant impact on the social and financial aspirations of its players. Some of the narrative will be necessarily subjective, tales that simply tickled my fancy. The cameo roles played by the Watney and Texaco Cups – tournaments that heralded the age of commercialism – get more prominence than certain FA Cup campaigns. The bizarre attempt of Clough to kidnap Ian Storey-Moore has greater space than some of the record transfer deals that actually took place. A man who could have been one of the decade's biggest stars, Peter Knowles, is as conspicuous as someone like Gerry Francis, who undoubtedly was.

Anyone attempting to tell the story of a decade within a solely chronological framework quickly finds themselves handcuffed, unable to send the keyboard down thematic routes that crisscross multiple years. I have tried to strike a logical balance, with broad discussions presented in a sequence that makes sense within the football events. Not that anyone should expect every trophy, every transfer detailed here. For that there are copies of *Rothmans Football Yearbook* widely available on eBay.

The chronicling of any sport is far less satisfying without historical and social context, which is why you'll find plenty of references to the people who helped create the backdrop against which football's narrative was written: Prime Ministers and pop stars, union leaders and sitcom characters. Harold Wilson, Ted Heath, Joe Gormley, Norman Stanley Fletcher, DI Jack Regan, Suzi Quatro, Mike Yarwood, James Callaghan, Noddy Holder, Terry Collier and Margaret Thatcher form an eleven as significant to the story of the decade as any who took the field at 3pm on a Saturday.

The parallels between Thatcher and Clough by the end of the decade, for example, are not so hard to discern. Having been installed in their respective positions, Leader of the Opposition and manager of Nottingham Forest, within a few weeks of each other early in 1975, both 'The Iron Lady' and 'Old Big 'ead' would achieve the pinnacle of their careers in May 1979: Prime Minister and European Cup winner. And for all their political polarity, it was not hard to see common characteristics. As divisive as Thatcher's rule would be for the country, many of the same personality traits that swept her to power on a wave of public support could be found in Clough, the 'people's choice' as England manager and the self-proclaimed greatest leader the national team never had. Both were charismatic orators; neither was afraid to reject consensus views. While Thatcher stood up and said 'no' to the trade unions, so Clough refused to concede to the stifling methodology that had become the hallmark of football in the 1970s, embodied most obviously in the Leeds teams of his nemesis, Revie.

The Seventies found a nation and its favourite sport advancing towards significant crossroads in their histories. As the last full season of the period concluded, the Labour Party was at the beginning of 18 years in the governmental wilderness, while football was about to enter its watershed decade. By the end of the 1980s, a new satellite television company would be waiting to sprinkle its stardust and money on a sport that had appeared close to ruin over the preceding years.

'With the passage of time, the 1970s begin to appear less like a sideshow and more like the main event,' wrote author Christian Caryl,[3] while historian Dominic Sandbrook argued, 'The Seventies is the tipping point for Britain. It really is the decade that I think made modern Britain, 21st century Britain. It is the watershed, where an old order, an old Britain – the bowler hat and the cloth cap, if you like – disappears and a new Britain came into being.'[4]

While both Caryl and Sandbrook refer to a world beyond football, their notion of the 1970s as a turning point is reflected on Britain's playing fields. Not merely a sandwich between two decades that brought English football its greatest global triumph on one hand and its descent towards apocalypse on the other, it can be viewed now as the last footballing decade that feels just as closely bound in its status and storylines to its immediate post-war past as to its corporate, big-money future. It was a decade when the sport was still played more in parks and on street corners than on live television and games consoles – even though consumption of the sport was heading more from the stadium to the living room. It was a division of eras. The months of the 1978-79 season, covering Jim Callaghan's 'Winter of Discontent', would resonate forever in Britain as a time of political and societal transformation, while, for football, the close of the decade would mark the beginning of the end of much that had been familiar and, at least in most instances, loved.

The experience of the players forms a key part of the 1970s narrative. It was the first decade in which they could be seen to be moving away from their fan base, yet it also saw them being left further behind by popular culture. By the end of the decade they bore little resemblance to the pop stars of the day – nor did their bank balances. Yet no longer were they living next door and riding to the games on the same buses as the man on the terrace. Stuck in the middle class with you, as Stealers Wheel might have sung.

There remains an affection for the 1970s, even as we get deeper into the 21st century. If you weren't there to witness it first hand, you are probably familiar with much that occurred. It might have been the last decade not to have featured live League football on television, but it is the first to have begun with cameras around to chronicle its weekly soap opera, most of which sits free for all to enjoy on YouTube. Over the years, shows such as BBC's *Match of the Seventies* and ITV's *The Big Match Revisited* have maintained the decade's presence on mainstream television, just as retro comedy channels have preserved, and renewed, shows such as *Porridge*, *Rising Damp* and *Fawlty Towers*. The decade has become a favourite old uncle; you can't recall him in his prime, but you enjoy his company, his memories of the old days and the Polaroids and cine films of him in flares and wide-lapelled jackets at family weddings.

If every book has its starting point then this one's, I admit, is the accident of my own conception, bequeathing to me an ever-present nostalgia for the Seventies, even though it was the dark era of hard men, hooligans and hopeless England teams. As Philip Cato wrote of the decade in his retrospective on glam rock, 'Try as I might, I really cannot remember any truly bad times.'[5] Which is at it should be with first love. So, while those older than me have waxed lyrical about Tom Finney and the fabulous Fifties, and relative youngsters will reach my age and look back through misty eyes at the birth of the Premier League and football coming home in the Nineties, here I am musing over Peter Osgood and the sideburned Seventies. While writing previous books, I have been fortunate enough to interview around 500 players, managers and coaches who were active in the decade. Virtually every conversation has been a delight and the memories and opinions shared have helped to inform much of my writing.

This was the decade in which I grew up. As I will propose in the first chapter, 1970s English football began with Leeds United's first title in 1968-69, the year I started junior school. I left secondary school after a Trevor Francis header won the European Cup Final of 1978-79 for Nottingham Forest. What happened in the intervening years has been burned into me like David Carradine getting his arms branded in the opening sequence of *Kung Fu*.

The 1968-69 season is the first of which I retain vivid memories. I recall going to work with my dad on the Monday after the first weekend of the season and, showing early journalistic flair, spending the day making my own hand-drawn football magazine. The front cover was my interpretation of the own goal with which Tottenham Hotspur's Phil Beal had helped Arsenal to victory two days earlier. I saw my debut First Division game a few weeks later (Arsenal 2, Queens Park Rangers 1 – a Terry Neill penalty won the game), and before the end of the season I had experienced the sour taste of an Arsenal defeat at Wembley. I was at least spared the ignominy of Don Rogers's decisive final goal in Swindon Town's 3-1 League Cup victory. My dad's friend was the assistant manager of Wembley FC and had arranged to pick us up near the stadium at 5.30, giving him time to do whatever the assistant manager of Wembley FC did after a game. My father, in a miscalculation that I found increasingly inexcusable as the years went by, forgot that the League Cup Final kicked off at 3.30 in those days, meaning we were on our way home before the end of extra-time. Even in my brief career as a fan, I had learned enough to understand the significance to the club of the occasion and I shudder to think what damage might have been done to our relationship had he dragged me off to his mate's car with Arsenal on the brink of winning their first trophy in 16 years.

Ten years later, just as I was about to sit my A-levels, my dad and I were back again at Wembley, where I had seen Arsenal beaten on two subsequent visits (missing out on the triumph of 1971). Two-nil up with five minutes to play, I was at last going to see my team parade a trophy around the old dog track. Four minutes and two Manchester United goals later, the ghosts of Rogers, Allan Clarke and Roger Osborne were dancing in front of my eyes. They moved aside just long enough for me to see Graham Rix's cross reach the far post for Alan Sunderland to score.

The embrace my father and I shared at that moment remains one of my most cherished memories of a man who died a further ten years on. He had seen it all before – losing his hat forever when he tossed it triumphantly during the Gunners' 1950 FA Cup win against Liverpool – but he held tight in the knowledge of how much it meant to me. Acknowledging that subsequent events have allowed me to romanticise the moment, I look back on it all as some kind of rite of passage; a day when fate chose to send me off to journalism college as a real man, childhood dreams duly fulfilled. I can even forgive my dad for wanting to make another early getaway from the stadium – the instant Pat Rice had lifted the trophy – which meant that we scurried the mile or so to our car accompanied entirely by disgruntled United fans, one of whom happily stuck his boot up my backside before I realised I had better hide my yellow and blue scarf beneath my jacket.

In between those two Wembley occasions, my footballing decade included the proud purchase of white boots; the elusive search for the final sticker in the collection; endless fully-formed Subbuteo leagues; the thrill of taking my place on the North Bank at Highbury; a dalliance with non-League Barnet; the frisson of travelling to away games; and a whole load of other milestones about which there is nothing unique. Every football fan will relate similar memories of their formative years; the names and places changing, but the passions and prejudices universal and timeless. If you experienced the 1970s for yourself, I hope you will find a piece of your story in this book. If you are a visitor from another era, perhaps there will be some historical context here to illuminate events that created your own experience.

Part One
GET IT ON

The Sixties teased us with trailers for a nicer planet – peace and love, guilt-free sex, equal rights for women, blacks and the young. The Seventies sloshed us with the cold flannel of cynicism.

Rob Steen, *The Mavericks* (Mainstream, 1994)

BARTHOLEMEW: The game was created to demonstrate the futility of individual effort.

***Rollerball* (William Harrison; United Artists, 1975)**

The guys were in the entertainment business – but only as hardened pros who happened to do something that millions of people wanted to watch. They didn't go out on the field to entertain. They went out to win.

Gordon Williams and Terry Venables, *They Used to Play on Grass* (Odhams, 1972)

Does anyone know the way? Did we hear someone say?
We just haven't got a clue what to do.

'Block Buster!', The Sweet
(Nicky Chinn, Mike Chapman; Chinnichap/RAK, 1973)

1

RAGE AGAINST THE MACHINE

DAVROS: Evil? No! No, I will not accept that. They are conditioned simply to survive. They can survive only by becoming the dominant species. When all other life forms are suppressed, when the Daleks are the supreme rulers of the universe, then you will have peace. Wars will end. They are the power not of evil, but of good.

Dr Who, 'Genesis of the Daleks' (Terry Nation, BBC TV, 1975)

THEIR REIGN of terror began in 1963. By the beginning of the Seventies, they had become a force so feared, so ruthless that a place behind the sofa was considered the safest place from which to watch their exploits on Saturday evening television. Yet they had vulnerabilities that their creator had not been able to entirely eradicate. Too often, an extraordinary force managed to halt their relentless quest to become masters of their universe.

Leeds United were human after all.

Since announcing their intent by winning the Second Division title in 1963-64, Don Revie's team had seen too many finals lost, too many titles snatched from them in the manner of the Doctor discovering the secret code to the Daleks' destruction in the final episode. But no longer, it seemed. As the first months of the new decade unfolded, Revie – football's crippled, one-eyed Davros, evil mastermind behind the enemy of the galaxy – was poised to see Leeds destroy everything in their path to win the League Championship, European Cup and FA Cup. It was his creation whose presence would define the first half of the 1970s in English football.

Events that characterise our decades rarely fit conveniently within the artificial boundaries of the calendar. Political historians might argue, for example, that the 1960s effectively began in 1956, when the Suez Canal crisis marked the decline of Britain as a global force. But social and cultural commentators are just as likely to contend that the decade only found its personality with the rise of The Beatles and the arrival of the contraceptive pill in the United Kingdom several years later. In the United States, they'll tell you that the transformation from Sixties idealism to Seventies cynicism was signalled by the resignation of Richard Nixon as president – in the wake of the Watergate scandal of 1972 – on the same 1974 weekend as the FA Charity Shield punch-up at Wembley.*

On the playing fields of English professional football, it is easy to argue that 1968 was the year when decades began to shift; the true fault line between a time when teams won mostly through talent and instinct and an age where the most successful formula was professionalism and method. Of course, no one will ever argue that Alf Ramsey's World Cup heroes of 1966 achieved their success with carefree football. But if you don't dig too deeply, Geoff Hurst's hat-trick, Kenneth Wolstenholme's commentary and Nobby Stiles's victory jig occupy the same place in popular memory as the club game's most powerful images of the Sixties: Tottenham Hotspur

---

* Historian Dominic Sandbrook suggests in *Mad As Hell* that the weekend of Nixon's departure signalled a shift in the decade in the US, much as the Don Revie departure from Leeds did in English football. It would be over-fanciful to go too far down the path of comparing Revie and Nixon, although their periods of hegemony did both span 1968–74 and both were famously suspicious to the point of paranoia, what with Nixon and his tapes and Revie and his dossiers on opponents. Both faced scandal within weeks of each other in 1972, Nixon with Watergate and Revie - although it would not be alleged for a few months - in supposedly attempting to bribe the Wolverhampton Wanderers players in a League title decider. Coincidentally, both men were depicted in movies (*Frost/Nixon* and *The Damned United*) in which their nemeses (David Frost and Brian Clough) were portrayed by Michael Sheen.

passing their way to the Double; George Best weaving spells at Old Trafford; Liverpool fans on the Kop serenading their title winners with Beatles songs. It was a decade given form by men such as Bobby Charlton, Jimmy Greaves, Denis Law and Ian St John, thrilling packed terraces and growing television audiences in matches that invariably seemed to finish 4-3.

The legacy of Ramsey's success, based on a team that placed functionality and formation before flair and flamboyance, was ready to quell the Corinthian spirit that still prevailed in the spring of 1968. Half of Manchester was revelling in the championship success of Joe Mercer and Malcolm Allison's City; the team of Francis Lee, Colin Bell and Mike Summerbee. Their triumph was clinched at Newcastle United on the final day of the campaign, 4-3 of course. A few weeks later, United beat Benfica 4-1 at Wembley to complete their emotional quest for the European Cup; a triumph for Matt Busby's steadfastness in recovering from his own serious injuries in the Munich air crash a decade earlier, and his insistence on leaving his team unencumbered by tactics.

But a force was emerging from south Yorkshire to cast the sport into the darker corners that Dr Who fans understood. Leeds, runners-up in League, FA Cup and Inter-Cities Fairs Cup since arriving in the top flight, had finally won a trophy, the 1968 League Cup. They were about to add a second, the Fairs Cup of 1968, whose final was played early the following season because of scheduling problems. By the end of 1968-69, the poster boys for pragmatism were League champions. The accumulation of silverware was personal vindication for Revie, whose methods made him one of the most divisive figures in the game. His supporters championed his principles of preparation, teamwork and team spirit. Detractors saw little beyond a combative, cynical edge that saw the likes of Billy Bremner and Johnny Giles dominating midfield with their dynamism and vision one moment, before raking studs down the opposition's leg the next.

The clash of cultures was captured in the 1969 release of Ken Loach's *Kes*, with Brian Glover's PE teacher imagining himself as Bobby Charlton in the film's famous games lesson scene. Charging into the penalty area in his scarlet No.9 shirt, Glover throws himself to the ground, awards himself a penalty and barks at the poor protesting pupil accused of a foul, 'Who do you think you are? Bremner?'

Whether they were responsible for initiating a whole era of dubious virtue or merely a product of a new age of realism, Revie's Leeds were clearly the identifiable enemy of those who longed for the days of the WM formation and seven-goal thrillers. As Giles noted, 'We've been called a Machine,' although he added, 'We take that as a compliment to our teamwork.'[6]

As a player, Revie's reputation was that of a thoughtful stylist, named Footballer of the Year in 1954-55 and capped six times by England. When Manchester City beat Birmingham City to win the FA Cup in 1956 they did so by employing the 'Revie Plan', which had been the basis of their game for a couple of seasons and was, essentially, a version of the Hungarian tactic that utterly bamboozled England in their 6-3 hammering at Wembley three years earlier. Revie played the role of Nándor Hidegkuti, the Hungarian No.9 who left the England defenders wandering around in a daze by the simple tactic of dropping deep to initiate moves from midfield. This was considered most unsporting in an age when the centre-forward was expected to stand obligingly with his back to goal waiting for the centre-half to kick him whenever the ball was near.

Born in Middlesbrough, the son of a frequently unemployed joiner, Revie had been brought up with an acute understanding of the power of money. Quite where his famously superstitious nature came from was a mystery, but one of his first acts upon being appointed Leeds player-manager in March 1961 was to shed the traditional blue and yellow strip, in which they'd never won a major honour, in favour of the imposing all-white of perennial European Cup winners Real Madrid. He also felt it would make it easier for players to find each other on the field. He later eliminated the figure of an owl from the club crest because he thought birds were unlucky. He declared his intention of turning a struggling Second Division club, based in a city that cared more about rugby league, into one of the best in Europe. You could hear the scoffs from Budapest to the Bernabéu.

'As a kid I remember how repressed the place was,' said Paul Madeley, an Elland Road lifer. 'It was awful.'[7] The atmosphere pervading the club was one of self-pity. Players who were sick of losing were looking for exit routes and training had long since become a chore. 'I was at [Revie] every day,' said Bremner, 'pleading, demanding, trying to convince him that it would be good for him and the club if he were to let me go back to Scotland.'[8]

Confidence had disappeared and relegation to the Third Division was a stark possibility. Discipline needed to be instilled, yet at the same time Revie insisted to club chairman Harry Reynolds that the players should be treated like champions, with new equipment, first-class travel and five-star accommodation. Numerous men would echo Jack Charlton's memory that Revie would 'bend over backwards to do anything to help the players'.[9] That included flowers to wives if they were sick and birthday cards to children. Bremner recalled Revie as 'a stickler for minor detail', explaining that 'the cleaners' birthdays were never forgotten, letters from fans were always answered – and, above all, he never criticised his players in public'.[10]

On one occasion, Revie told his charges, 'If you have financial problems, gambling problems, family problems or problems with your wife, come to see me. I don't want you worrying.'[11] Meanwhile, he ensured that his backroom staff got a weekend off on rotation every seven weeks, and even took care of the club's two laundry ladies, whom he nicknamed Omo and Daz after popular brands of washing powder. He would often tell them they had a pound each way riding on a horse and, if it came in, would return later that day with their winnings. 'People will walk through walls for a boss like,' said Fred Street, who heard such stories when he worked under Revie as England's physiotherapist. 'Call it psychology or whatever, but the great managers in sport or the military have it instinctively. He expected everyone to contribute fully and he also rewarded equally.'[12]

Revie wanted his team to be populated by men of character who understood 'that it was not sufficient merely to become champions; of equal importance ... was to behave like champions, off as well as on the field'.[13] That message was drummed into prospective Leeds players before they even signed. Promising schoolboys were presented with a glossy brochure designed to 'help you decide' whether to sign for the club. 'Obviously I am looking for boys with natural football ability, but it takes much more than this to make a first-class professional player,' began Revie's message. 'It takes, in addition, courage, loyalty, discipline and readiness to learn.' He went on to give examples of each of those traits. 'Show us that you have the other qualities and my staff and I myself will give everything in time, trouble, teaching and encouragement to get you to the top,' he concluded.[14]

By bringing through players from the club's youth system, Revie ensured an unquestioning loyalty to his views and to team-mates. Such methods would come to include the oft-derided practice of spending Friday nights before home games at the Craiglands Hotel in Ilkley, where he could occupy his players with games of carpet bowls and bingo rather than worrying about whether they were up to no good. It meant that, several years after finding that he was surplus to Revie's requirements, forward Jimmy Greenhoff was able to say, 'I went there at 15 and grew up with Sprake, Reaney, Hunter and the rest. I've never known people work for each other the way they did.'[15]

Revie owned up to some sleepless nights at the start of his reign, lying awake or getting up to make cups of tea and even promising wife Elsie he'd resign before the job killed him. But having survived the board's desire to give Bremner his wish and sell him for £25,000, a move that could have irrevocably changed the course of English football, he stuck around to build a team that, if it did not always reflect his grace as a player, epitomised the uncompromising, ruthless and thorough way in which he tackled the job of manager. As men like Norman Hunter and Paul Reaney progressed to the first team, Bremner was joined in midfield by Bobby Collins, a fierce competitor recruited from Everton in 1962, and Giles, signed the following year from Manchester United.

According to Bremner, Revie did not clutter his players' minds with tactics. 'He was probably one of the first to pioneer the idea of studying the opposition and being prepared for their tactics and individual skills, but he certainly did not tell us to play like robots and he didn't send anyone out to kick the opposition either. Don barely gave us any strong instructions at all. He knew he had a young intelligent side who could find their way.'[16]

Revie's approach brought Leeds the Second Division title in 1963-64. The following year they almost pulled off the League and FA Cup double, losing the championship to Manchester United on goal average and being beaten in extra-time by Liverpool at Wembley. Yet their accusers said they were prepared to strive for success at any price, resorting to the underhand tricks usually associated with teams of Latin origin, by whom English fans were used to being enthralled and appalled in equal measure. Even Giles, an artist with the ball at his feet, could quickly turn assassin. 'There was a new professionalism and a new approach in the game,' he said. 'It became more violent in the Sixties right through to the mid-Seventies.'[17] Charlton, who said that Giles 'used to do some awful things to players', even confronted him in the dressing-room one day. 'It was us he was putting at risk. John caused us a lot of hassle at Elland Road over the years.'[18]

Hunter conceded that 'we turned games into tough, physical games where we probably didn't have to',[19] while Eddie Gray, one of the era's artists, admitted that 'some of our tackling in those days made me cringe' and found himself thinking, 'How are they being allowed to get away with this?'[20] Even Bremner remembered, 'People must have thought we were wild animals.'[21]

Controversial, ugly games were strewn throughout the fixture list. If, over the years, Leeds and their followers felt they were frequently hard done to by referees, then perhaps it was because match officials found it impossible to approach games without preconceptions and previous convictions in mind. As Clive Thomas, one of the decade's most prominent referees, said, 'Innocuous? I suppose that nothing to do with Don Revie's Yorkshire team could be thus described.'[22] Their football was based on the philosophy of not losing; Revie's priorities being a solid, technically correct defence and a willingness to embrace the physical aspects of the game. There was also a shameless use of tactics that were attaching negative connotations to the word 'professionalism': time-wasting, intimidation of referees, crafty digs at opponents. 'The Bremners would be doing little things off the ball, the niggly things, and I found Allan Clarke similar,' said Thomas. 'Giles was also one of the players I watched very carefully.'[23]

Revie was not so much guilty of heresy against the gospel of carefree football, more accurately he was one of the first managers to recognise the game's harsh new reality. But, said many, Leeds took it too far. 'It wasn't just being stronger and stopping the other team, it was cynical,' remembered Malcolm Allison. 'There was no need for it. They were the best team in England, a great side, but greedy, greedy. That was the nub of it. A lot of what they did was pre-meditated.'[24]

League runners-up again, to Liverpool, in 1965-66 and beaten in the semi-finals of the Fairs Cup, they came close in two more competitions the following season, beaten by Dynamo Zagreb in their first European final and in the FA Cup semi-finals by Chelsea. The critics loved it. That Leeds, for all their professionalism, could not administer the final blow to their opponents was a sign that their methods were flawed, like the Daleks' inability to go upstairs. Good would ultimately prevail over evil; the natural order maintained.

The 1967-68 campaign saw a fourth-place finish in the League and an FA Cup semi-final defeat. But it was also the season of the great breakthrough, the capture of the Football League Cup and Fairs Cup. Inevitably, the first of those triumphs was wrapped in bitterness.

For a long while, Leeds' tactics at corners had angered opponents. Pursuing a plan hatched with brother Bobby and Jimmy Greaves at an England training session, Jack Charlton had begun positioning himself on the goal line. At almost 6ft 2in, but with hitched-up shorts over long legs making him appear even taller, the England defender was accused of standing on goalkeepers' feet, obstructing, shoving and generally making a bloody nuisance of himself. 'When he stands on the goal line he is there to try and score,' insisted Revie. 'There is nothing in the rules against it.'

Jim Finney, one of the most experienced referees of the time, took to standing off the field outside the goal posts so that he could look through the side netting in order to keep an eye on Charlton. Arsenal's Bob Wilson and his fellow goalkeepers had to be prepared for all kinds of abuse, physical and verbal – even from those who were viewed as the relative innocents in the team. 'I always remember Paul Madeley saying things about my wife or family. They would try anything. Leeds had a defining part in my growth as a goalie because they had those corner-kick tactics at the time I started in the first team.'[25]

Wilson was on standby for Arsenal against Leeds in the League Cup Final, missing out when Jim Furnell recovered from injury. Ironically, the only goal came via a first-half Terry Cooper volley from 10 yards while Furnell was looking up from his knees after encountering Charlton at the near post. Half a century later, Furnell was still insisting, 'He was all over me. It should have been a foul.'[26] Arsenal's frustration with opponents happy to sit on their lead boiled over in the second half when skipper Frank McLintock charged into goalkeeper Gary Sprake to spark a full-scale brawl.

'This League Cup Final will make history only as a game so bad it was little short of scandalous,' wrote Desmond Hackett in the *Daily Express*, while *Charles Buchan's Football Monthly* bracketed the game with the latest Scotland–England contest under the headline: 'Shabby and Squalid – What have we come to?' and accused Leeds and Arsenal of a 'complete and cynical disregard for the £90,000 paid by real football supporters'. Football League secretary Alan Hardaker would recall, 'If somebody had taken the ball from the pitch, the players of Arsenal and Leeds would have been the last to notice.'[27]

Leeds could not have cared less about such comments. So aware had they been of the importance of the match that Revie decided to stage an impromptu sports quiz in the dressing-room half an hour before kick-off to distract them from their nerves. 'You had to start somewhere,' said Hunter. 'You got the League Cup medal in your pocket and after that you were thinking "what's next?".'[28]

Arsenal took away a lesson that would hold them in good stead in the coming years. 'Leeds at that time were dominating and bullying people,' said striker John Radford. 'Losing to them in the League Cup was a good game for us in some ways because from then on we started to get a little bit like that ourselves and we were probably the first side to stand up to them.'[29]

It was only a matter of months before more silverware arrived at Elland Road, courtesy of a Mick Jones goal in the home leg against Hungary's Ferencvaros in the final of the Fairs Cup, a tie delayed until August. In the second leg, in front of 76,000, a typically staunch rearguard action in the absence of Giles and Gray secured a goalless draw. No one in Budapest was laughing at Leeds now.

They finished the 1968-69 season as they had started it, by winning a trophy. This time, it was the most treasured of all domestic honours, the League Championship. Revie's men finished with a record 67 points, six ahead of Liverpool, at whose ground they clinched the title on an evening of high emotion. Having secured a 0-0 draw to make the title safe, several Leeds players were moved to tears by the rousing chorus of 'Champions, Champions' that rolled off the Kop. That Liverpool (24 goals conceded), Leeds (26) and Arsenal (27) had all bettered Huddersfield Town's 44-year record for the best defence in a 42-game First Division season was proof that the 1970s had arrived a year early. And before long Tommy Docherty, manager of Aston Villa at the time, would warn, 'Too many teams are copying Leeds. Unfortunately, there is a tendency to produce rather dull games. We are supposed to be providing entertainment for the cash customer.'[30]

THE STYLE COUNCIL

LEWIS: Machines are gonna fail. And the system's gonna fail.

Deliverance **(James Dickey and John Boorman; Warner Bros., 1972)**

The 1968-69 season saw attendances in English football dip for the first time since the 1966 World Cup sent its revitalising shot through the game. Articles addressing the decline frequently presented somewhat simplistic headlines along the theme of, 'We Want Goals.' The issue was somewhat more nuanced than that. In his book, *Football and the English*, author David Russell noted a lack of direct correlation between goals and attendance, citing as a prime example the 1960-61 season, when crowds in the First Division suffered their biggest drop since the Second World War, even though the 1,724 goals represented the highest total since 1931-32.† Yet football, in the eyes of many, required a redeemer or two. Dr Who might have been too busy saving the universe, but two teams in blue, from opposite ends of the country, emerged in early 1970 to take on Revie's white forces of destruction.

The visit of Leeds to Goodison Park two months into the 1969-70 campaign proved portentous. Everton went into that game on the back of only a single loss in their 18 League matches, while Leeds were riding a 34-game unbeaten streak dating back to their championship season. It was Leeds who succumbed, Everton's 3-2 win marking them down as serious title contenders after threatening for a couple of seasons.

Manager Harry Catterick had been steadily rebuilding the team with which he'd won the First Division in 1963 and FA Cup in 1966. At the heart of his new side was a midfield trio that would become revered by Goodison Park fans as 'The Holy Trinity' and provided, in the eyes of the neutrals, an elegant antidote to Leeds. Colin Harvey, a local boy who came through Everton's youth system, had been joined by two important signings. Alan Ball, at 21 the youngest member of England's 1966 World Cup-winning team, had moved from Blackpool for a British record £110,000 in the days after his man-of-the-match performance in the final against West Germany. Howard Kendall, who also made his name at Wembley as the FA Cup's youngest finalist when he played for Preston North End against West Ham at the age of 17 in 1964, had followed later in that 1966-67 season.

Catterick, a grumpy old-school type who retained a suspicion of the media that Revie would have recognised, had a greater eye for talent than flair for coaching. He let his midfield trio figure out their own approach, sitting back to witness the sublime results. According to Kendall, 'Our brand of football was about retaining possession, passing quickly and incisively, and moving into space. It was largely intuitive, perfected over endless, joyous games of five-a-side.'[31] Ball was the fulcrum, a one-touch genius capable of 20 goals per season

† At the time of writing, no season of top-flight football has produced more goals since then.

from his advanced position; Kendall the tackler and runner on the right; Harvey the skilled schemer on the left. On the back of their collective contribution, Everton were FA Cup runners-up in 1968, top scorers in the First Division a year later, and were now poised to sweep the title from Revie's grasp.

'All three were great individuals,' said winger Jimmy Husband, 'but the balance was brilliant. Howard had no pace at all but was a great passer over long distances and a good tackler. Alan was everywhere; good, neat control and a great engine. He scored goals as well. Colin was a beautiful little neat player, hard to get the ball off. Give him a really hard pass and it was under control in a flash and he could turn quickly. Put the three of them together and you had a great combination.'[32]

Yet it said a lot for the quality throughout the Everton team in 1969-70 that they survived the absence, for several weeks each, of Harvey with an eye problem and Ball because of suspension. 'We had a goalkeeper and ten players who were good on the ball,' said centre-forward Joe Royle. 'Alan Ball used to say before games, "If you want to play, we'll play you; if you want to run us, we'll run you; and if you want to try to bully us, we will take it and bully you back." Whatever way you wanted to play that side we could handle it.'[33]

Six consecutive victories in March put Everton in an unassailable position in the table. 'I don't want a team of ballerinas,' Catterick had said, 'but I want a side which plays football above all else and that is what present Everton sides are trying to do. Unfortunately, the cloggers of the game will do their best to destroy this kind of play.' By the time Everton were in possession of the championship trophy, Catterick could boast, 'It has often been said that the end justifies the means – in other words it does not matter how you win as long as you win. But as far as I am concerned the way Everton achieve victory IS important.'[34]

Once Goodison Park had been identified as the probable destination of the title, Revie admitted defeat by sending out teams of understudies as Leeds attempted to fit varied commitments into a season squeezed by the forthcoming World Cup. He had resolved two things as the defence of their League title began. Firstly, the dual knockout targets of European Cup and FA Cup – the latter still the most glamorous of England's club prizes – were to be prioritised. And, to be fair to the man whose name became a byword for cynicism, he had also told his players that they were now free to express themselves a little more.

Revie had always been acutely aware of his team's image. When a game at Nottingham Forest during their title-winning campaign was abandoned because the main stand caught fire, Revie remarked to the *Yorkshire Evening Post*, 'At least no one is blaming us for the disaster, like they blame us for most things.' To his disappointment, the mud of the 1960s continue to stick to the white Leeds kits – literally, too, in this era of pitches ankle deep in sludge – and few observers had softened their attitude by the time a new decade was marked by the lowering of the official age of adulthood from 21 to 18 and the end of the half-crown coin.‡

The naming of Revie as recipient of an OBE in the New Year's Honours List spoke of his achievements in the game, but it was performances such as the one his team gave at Stamford Bridge on the second weekend of the decade that offered more compelling evidence of his team's unappreciated qualities. Despite an opportunistic piece of finishing by Clarke, a record £166,000 signing from Leicester City, Leeds fell 2-1 behind to Chelsea. Yet in a scintillating second-half performance, captured by *Match of the Day* cameras, they tore one of the country's finest teams to shreds, albeit one with a somewhat hapless reserve, Tommy Hughes, in goal instead of Peter Bonetti. Cooper finished a flowing move with an unexpected right-foot finish; Giles clipped in a penalty; Peter Lorimer added a fourth; and Jones was on hand at the far post to complete a 5-2 win. It was a statement game by Revie's team, had anyone been inclined to listen.

According to Bremner, 'I think the reputation we got of being hard and ruthless was earned for that first four or five years.'[35] But he also stressed that 'from '69 to '74 we [were] let off the leash a little'

‡ Worth two shillings and sixpence (two and a half pence once decimalisation was introduced the following year).

and claimed, 'We played some of the best football the country has seen for a long long time.'[36]

As for Chelsea, they were waiting in the FA Cup Final by the time Leeds had taken three games to get past Manchester United in the semis. The marathon contest featured only a goal by Bremner, the new Footballer of the Year, and exacerbated an already critical fixture situation. In an exhausting period from 21 March to 4 April – the Saturday before the FA Cup Final – Leeds played eight games in 15 days. This included the second and third instalments of the United epic and a 1-0 defeat at Elland Road in the first leg of their European semi-final against Scottish champions Celtic. On that same night, Everton were clinching the title by beating West Bromwich Albion. Within 24 hours, Leeds were back in action at West Ham. Madness.

Revie had already voiced concerns about the demands on his players. When he was warned by club doctors that some of them urgently needed a rest, he'd decided that with the title as good as gone he would field a half-strength team in a defeat to Southampton and then a complete reserve unit at Derby County, where they lost 4-1. While football fans of a certain vintage are able even now to reel off a Leeds first eleven made up entirely of internationals, it is doubtful that too many could recall a line-up at the Baseball Ground that read: David Harvey, Nigel Davey, Paul Peterson, Jimmy Lumsden, David Kennedy, Terry Yorath, Chris Galvin, Mick Bates, Rod Belfitt, Terry Hibbitt, Albert Johanneson. 'What is the point of employing the services of a fully qualified medical officer if you don't take his advice?' Revie asked. 'Our doctor declared that the players concerned were thoroughly tired, mentally and physically, and if they carried on there was no knowing what damage might be caused.'

The manager best qualified to comment on such issues was Revie's rival at Arsenal, Bertie Mee, who had been a leading physiotherapist in the outside world before going into football. 'We are now asking for many of our players to commit themselves to upwards of 60 games a season,' he would tell a sportswriters' lunch in 1972. 'I believe that from the physical aspect we are operating at a maximum … in terms of wear and tear and what we can ask the body to do.'

The martinets at the head of the Football League were having none of it. Prompted by the moaning of Bert Head, manager of Southampton's relegation rivals Crystal Palace, they fined Leeds £5,000. League president Len Shipman even added a veiled threat. 'The League can, after all, forbid clubs to take part in European competitions if they cannot fulfil commitments at home.' The episode highlighted Revie's strained relationship with the League. Hardaker called him 'a pain in the neck' and accused him of being 'obsessively concerned about injuries, international calls, the choice of referees, switching fixtures'. He added, 'Unless he could control everything, he seemed to feel the dice were being deliberately loaded against Leeds.' Hardaker claimed Revie could have avoided this pile-up of matches by accepting 'convenient early dates'.[37][§]

Revie's worst fears were realised at West Ham, where Leeds were playing their fifth game in eight days. There was no firm evidence that fatigue played a role, but when right-back Reaney went down early in the second half he knew immediately that his leg was broken. A member of Sir Alf Ramsey's provisional 28-man World Cup squad[¶] and hopeful of two major finals, Reaney lamented, 'Everything was there, but now it has gone.' If the same was not to be said of his club's season, then FA Cup Final victory on the unusually early date of 11 April looked like a game they had to win.

Nothing could have been more symbolic of what lay ahead in the 1970s. A match between two teams with philosophies as contrasting as their kits.

This was a decade in which the dominant on-field narrative was conflict over the way in which the game should be played. The 1970 FA Cup Final embodied the debate perfectly. Chelsea versus Leeds

---

§ According to Hardaker, Leeds were not only team to seek to manipulate the fixture list when it suited them. He described Arsenal attempting to get a 1973 game against Sheffield United postponed as late as 11am on the day of the match because of illness and injury. When permission was refused, they miraculously managed to field an unchanged side.

¶ Team-mate Paul Madeley turned down the chance to replace Reaney, citing his belief that he would end up not playing and therefore did not wish to travel after such a gruelling season. Arsenal's Bob McNab was chosen instead, failing to make the cut when the final squad of 22 was confirmed.

United. Flair against formula. Southern style versus northern grit. Maestros against the machine.

If Leeds personified the new pragmatism, then there was no team better than Chelsea to represent the romantics who still believed in the free-spirited nature of bygone years. With their billowing hair, long sideburns and discotheque-ready fashion, the Chelsea men might have looked more modern than Revie's neatly-styled bingo players, for whom long hair and moustaches were prohibited, but in football terms they were the throwbacks; Leeds the modernisers.

Leeds had scored 84 goals on their way to second place in the table; a total that might have acted as a battering ram against the prejudices of their critics. Chelsea scored only 70 in finishing one place lower, yet the manner of their progress to Wembley proved that image was more powerful than statistics, striking a greater chord with the capital-based media whose views went nationwide and shaped so much opinion. The northern backlash to that portrayal was expressed by the character of Terry Collier in *Whatever Happened to the Likely Lads?* 'I hate Chelsea,' he declared in a 1973 episode. 'They stand for everything I hate in football with all their showbiz supporters. They come out looking more like the Young Generation** than a football team.'[38]

Even their kit had a certain élan, with its flashy white stripe down the side of blue shorts. And when they had to change from white to yellow socks to avoid a clash, so the stripe and the shirt numbers changed colour too; everything coordinated. 'It was so modern,' former Chelsea forward Alan Birchenall recalled. 'I'd come from Sheffield United, where the fucking shirts were this thick. Great big fucking things. Horrible nylon shorts and nylon socks. I get to Chelsea and the first thing I thought when I put the kit on, fucking hell, I felt like an Italian … and the players liked to look the bollocks off the pitch.'[39]

Having scored three goals in each of their victories in the third and fourth rounds, against Birmingham and over Burnley in a replay,

** The troupe of young men and women who were the BBC's in-house dancers on many light entertainment shows in the late 1960s and early 1970s.

it was from the fifth round onwards that Chelsea really sparkled. They went south of the river to beat Crystal Palace 4-1 with a burst of second-half scoring. The quarter-final draw threw up another London derby at Queens Park Rangers, where they won 4-2 with a performance that defied the heavy surface. David Webb, a tough defender with a face that looked like it had been slammed with a dustbin lid, swept in a half-volley and Peter Osgood helped himself to a hat-trick. The victory felt a touch sweeter for the goal-scorers because they had been the only players not to pass an FA coaching course a few weeks earlier when QPR goalkeeper Mick Kelly had been one of the supervisors. Who needed to do things by the instruction manual anyway?

Chelsea stayed in the capital to face Watford in the semi-final on a White Hart Lane pitch whose sandy surface matched the amber shirts of their Second Division opposition. Putting aside the geographical convenience, it was surprising that the FA would place a showcase game at a ground then infamous for its terrible playing surface. When Tottenham went out in the fourth round after a replay at Crystal Palace, *Goal* wrote, 'Spurs' talented if erratic players still swear that it was the mud bank playing pitch that cost them their place in the FA Cup sun. Perhaps the time is near when the Football League will have to finance research into artificial surfaces.' After Webb's close-range finish was cancelled out, Chelsea strolled through the second half with four goals, including two typically neat finishes by Peter Houseman.

Chelsea and Leeds had recent history. The foundations of the team now led by Dave Sexton had been laid by Tommy Docherty, who turned them from a Second Division club earlier in the Sixties into a vibrant side capable of challenging for the title. 'Docherty's Diamonds', as the media named them, reached the FA Cup Final of 1967 by beating Leeds 1-0 in the semi-finals. Revie's men were convinced they were robbed of a late equaliser when Lorimer laced a free-kick into the top corner, only for referee Ken Burns to indicate he had not given permission for the game to restart. In this current season, Chelsea had also knocked Leeds out of the League Cup.

The son of an East End boxer, Sexton was a quiet, shy man with a love of jazz and magic tricks. He was destined for coaching once he joined West Ham United and became part of a group, led by team-mate Malcolm Allison, who would spend afternoons after training dissecting the game in a local café. It was Sexton who helped Docherty create his young, exciting Chelsea team before he left for a short spell as Orient manager and ended up, via Fulham, as Arsenal coach under Mee. His reputation was enhanced by his popularity with the Highbury players. 'Dave Sexton was a revelation,' said ex-Arsenal midfielder Jon Sammels. 'We would play a game on Saturday and he'd go over to Italy on Sunday to watch training sessions and games, and he'd bring back ideas. Doggies, a series of sprints, was one. We were down in Sussex before a cup game, staying in Hove, and seven o'clock in the morning he'd have us doing these doggies along the sea front. You didn't want a fried breakfast by the time you got back to the hotel.'[40]

The difference in his character from the outgoing, frequently outrageous, Docherty was reflected in the way in which he set about the job at Stamford Bridge. While Docherty tended towards headline-catching deals, like buying Millwall goalkeeper Alex Stepney when he already had Bonetti, Sexton built shrewdly, signing Webb from Southampton and John Dempsey from Fulham for £60,000 each to provide defensive stability. With the foundation of a disciplined back four, Chelsea became a well-drilled unit in addition to retaining the expression and artistry nurtured by Docherty. And no team containing Ron 'Chopper' Harris, the man from Hackney with an iron framework and the on-field personality of a nightclub bouncer, could be accused of being unafraid to mix it when the need arose.

Houseman, one of the less flamboyant members of the team and one of the few to refuse to allow his sideburns to creep down the side of his face,[††] said that Sexton's arrival had turned a group of individuals into a team. But for all the organisation, Chelsea were above all identified by the blend of brilliance of three men. The leader

†† On the official Chelsea team picture for 1973-74, Houseman's are the only ears visible among the 20 players.

of the pack was Osgood, a Windsor boy who had recovered from a broken leg in 1966 to lead the line as a multi-dimensional centre-forward. A converted wing-half, it is a sign of how good he had been before his injury that, for all he would go on to achieve, his output was a notch down from the level he had been expected to attain. 'His greatest asset was his supreme confidence,' according to Alan Hudson, who named his black poodle after his colleague. 'He didn't give a monkey's who he was playing against.'[41]

The focal point of much of Chelsea's attacking play was Charlie Cooke, the artistically inclined Scotland international who'd identified Stamford Bridge as his destination of choice even before Docherty signed him from Dundee. 'I didn't want to play for Manchester United or anybody like that,' he said. 'Chelsea were the team at the time. I knew the reputation they had as a young up-and-coming side – a busy team with young, quick boys; a team for the future.'[42]

A lover of literature who was sometimes accused of letting his mind wander during games, his promise had found form under Sexton and alongside Osgood. So much so that the duo, typically, were highlighted early in 1970 by Jimmy Hill, the game's foremost media pundit, in yet another article lamenting the flair missing from the English game. 'There is a distinct lack of glamour and personalities in British football,' Hill said. 'Sure enough, Manchester United have George Best, Chelsea have Peter Osgood and Charlie Cooke, Queens Park Rangers have Rodney Marsh and now Arsenal have Peter Marinello,[‡‡] but there aren't many others that will guarantee an extra 10,000 on the gate.'[43]

Chelsea's FA Cup run brought another player into that conversation. The suave midfield play of Hudson was the revelation of his club's campaign. A former youth-team captain who had been raised close to Chelsea's ground as a Fulham fan, he had been offered

‡‡ Signed from Hibernian from £100,000 just before Christmas, the frail, long-haired winger who worked on a building site to help add extra muscle was already being hailed as London's George Best even before he made the mistake of marking his Arsenal debut at Old Trafford with a clever individual goal. Bombarded by publicity and commercial opportunities, it was inevitable that he would never live up to expectations and was soon deposed in the Gunners team by the dependable, hard-working George Armstrong.

a professional contract just before his 17th birthday, despite knee problems that had kept him off the field and led to him piling on so much weight that Birchenall one day challenged his presence in the dressing-room, unaware he was a player. Fully fit, Hudson helped keep Birchenall out of the line-up and had Sexton purring during his first season in the team. 'He is a positive player and a fine organiser in midfield,' said his boss. 'He creates chances for other people with his running and intelligent use of the ball. He is quick to seize an opportunity.'[44]

Sir Alf Ramsey had shown up at Selhurst Park for the FA Cup fifth-round tie, by common consent to look at Osgood. But it was Hudson who was thrust to the forefront of his consciousness. ITV commentator Brian Moore noted in his report of that game in *The Times* that Hudson 'battled the length of the field, showing the resilience of one of his age and the guile of someone very much his senior'.

An energetic force, Hudson preferred to prompt with crisp, short passes rather than banging the ball on long diagonals. 'Sometimes Tony Currie's passes were fantastic,' he said of the Sheffield United midfielder, as he explained his methods. 'But by the time they got there they weren't always as dangerous as the little ones.'[45] And he was a dream for team-mates; animated and available, creative and dynamic in possession, eager to do his share of tackling. He had a swagger of cockiness – socks rolled around his ankles – that infected those around him.

After watching Hudson again, eclipsing Marsh and helping to take apart QPR, Ramsey named him in his preliminary squad of 40 for the Mexico World Cup, saying, 'Hudson looks like being one of the great players of the future. There is no limit to what he can achieve.'

Hudson's partnership with Osgood appeared destined to help his upward trajectory. 'I could always anticipate [Osgood's] runs, sense his presence,' he explained. 'At times it was as if we were telepathic.'[46] In turn, Osgood described his young team-mate as 'one of the greatest players I ever played with … even at 17, incredible skills, great brain, great stamina.'[47]

Yet Hudson would not be gracing the mud and sand of Wembley in April 1970, nor the sun-hardened Mexican fields that summer. Less than two weeks before the Cup final, he tore ankle ligaments at West Bromwich Albion, a victim of 'the biggest hole you've seen'. He even saw a faith healer in hope of being fit for Wembley. 'I felt like a kid who had gone to bed on Christmas Eve and seen all the toys wrapped up and then woke up in the morning and they had been taken away,' he recalled.[48] Cortisone injections would become a constant companion throughout his career. After a transfer to Stoke City, manager Tony Waddington would order the pitch to be watered before a game to keep it soft enough to reduce the stress on Hudson's ankle. It was 1975 before he made his debut for England.

WHEN WORLDS COLLIDE

Hate. No other word to describe it. They hated us and we hated them. Whenever we played, the two sets of supporters had pitched battles, home and away. On the pitch, oh dearie me. I've still got the scars. There was no love whatsoever.

Chelsea striker Ian Hutchinson[49]

There was little doubt in which direction public sentiment was flowing as the first FA Cup Final of the 1970s arrived. Chelsea, with their sense of adventure and whiff of romance, gave the impression of approaching the game in the untroubled manner with which most people wished they could approach life. 'We made everyone believe in us,' said Hudson.[50]

'We were flamboyant, we were happy-go-lucky,' said Osgood. '[Leeds] were a machine, if you like. I think that's basically where they fell down. Over a period of 42 games they were the best. There's no doubt about that. When it came to the one-off we were so much better than them because we went out to enjoy ourselves, but they stuck to the same rigid plan.'[51]

The Wembley match programme asked 18 leading national newspaper football writers to pick their winners. The vast majority tipped Chelsea, citing their flair and an ability to lift their game on the day. Those siding with Leeds did so because of professionalism and organisation.

The artisan talents of Tommy Baldwin were hardly a like-for-like replacement for Hudson, but the playing surface that greeted the teams was no inducement to skilful football. More suited to the cars that would set off from the stadium a week later in the *Daily Mirror*-sponsored London to Mexico World Cup Rally,[§§] the Wembley pitch had been a source of embarrassment for more than a year. The narrative that would extend over the ensuing decades whenever anyone referenced the poor state of the field around this time was 'they staged the Horse of the Year show there the week before'. In fact, it was another of the major British show-jumping festivals, the Royal International Horse Show, that was held at the stadium in the summers of 1968 and 1969. Yet even though no horse's hoof had been on the field for nine months before Chelsea and Leeds, the damage had been done. Tom Kneeshaw, an area manager of En-Tout Cas, the pitch providers, explained that large amounts of water had to be used to make new grass grow, before 'scorching sun' caused the top to grow too quickly, 'without the roots growing down'. It meant that the horses simply ripped the surface away from immature roots. 'As soon as horses are set on a pitch,' said Peter Ursell, described as a drainage and football-pitch expert, 'without the turves having time to settle, you are asking for trouble.'[52]

Preparation of the surface for the League Cup Final between Manchester City and West Bromwich Albion, a month before the FA Cup Final, had been particularly fraught. Having cleared away the snow that fell the day before the game, the ground-staff put down a layer of straw to protect the surface. No sooner had that been cleared, than it snowed again. Once that had been shifted, down went the sand. It was a swamp.

---

§§ Jimmy Greaves, recently transferred from Tottenham to West Ham United, was co-driver of one of the Ford Escorts in the field and would help his partner Tony Fall to a creditable sixth place.

At nine years old, the 1970 FA Cup Final was the first football match I had ever seen on colour television, as my dad and I went to a work colleague's house to watch it on his new set. The red tracksuit tops of Chelsea contrasted exotically with the light blue of Leeds, but the Wembley pitch offered only an occasional suggestion of green. More than 100 tonnes of sand had been applied to a playing surface that *The Times* described on the morning of the match as a 'dark stew'. The few breaks from the dull light brown before our eyes were the distinctive squares where replacement turves had clearly been the only option since the League Cup Final. Within minutes of kick-off, it was obvious that the surface was not up to the task, players leaving tracks like footsteps on the beach and the ball requiring a right old thump if anyone intended it to travel across the ground to a team-mate.

There had been a clear warning sign when Sprake attempted to bounce the ball on the red carpet as he lined up for the pre-match ceremonials and saw it die at his feet. Sure enough, when Charlton pulled away from under the Chelsea crossbar to meet Gray's corner after 20 minutes, his soft downward header flopped under the swinging boots of Harris and Eddie McCreadie and rolled barely a foot beyond the line. Five minutes before half-time, Houseman fired a first-time shot from outside the box and Sprake, diving to his left, allowed it to burrow under his body for an equaliser. It was a horrible mistake – the kind that made the berating of the goalkeeper by Charlton a regular sight – but on a better surface the ball might at least have bounced up and smacked Sprake in the face.

It was hardly a surprise that the Man of the Match would be a winger, Gray making the most of some semblance of grass close to the touchlines to torment Chelsea right-back Webb. He had demonstrated the kind of form he was in a week earlier in a home win against Burnley. Benefitting from the good fortune of the television cameras' presence, a nation was left breathless by his two stunning goals. The first-half effort, a nonchalant 30-yard chip over the goalkeeper, was special enough, but it was nothing compared to what he produced in the second half. There seemed little danger when he collected a loose ball on the byline, his back to goal ten yards from the left corner flag.

With a drag back almost too fast for the eye, he beat one man, swerved around another and found himself just inside the corner of the penalty area. He might have shot; instead he dummied his way inside one man, checked back past another, scraped the ball back towards him to beat one more diving defender and then poked a right-foot shot past keeper Peter Mellor from eight yards. Ten seconds from start to finish. No wonder it has been set to music on YouTube.

At Wembley, Gray's performance contained everything but a goal, although he slapped the ball against the bar when he cut inside to shoot late in the game. 'There can be no doubt who the Man of the Match is,' said ITV's Brian Moore. He was right, even though there was plenty of football still to play. Mick Jones restored the Leeds advantage with six minutes remaining and Ian Hutchinson equalised with a header. With Revie wearing his lucky suit and Sexton his talisman jacket with one missing button, it was perhaps inevitable that neither man would lose. Extra-time failed to prevent the first drawn FA Cup Final since 1912, and the demands of the Home Internationals meant it was not until Wednesday, 29 April that the teams reconvened at Old Trafford.

As a club-match record audience of 29 million took advantage of a choice of live viewing on BBC or ITV, Chelsea and Leeds contrived 120 minutes of pulsating, breathless pandemonium that ended with the FA Cup heading to Stamford Bridge for the first time.

Similar to the 'Horse of the Year show' recollection, something of an urban myth has grown up around the match in the ensuing half-century. Yes, it was fiercely contested and some of the challenges were not for the squeamish. Yet it has become categorised as a pitiless, clogging contest in which most players were lucky to remain on the field. The image has been reinforced by clips served up over the years of Charlton and Osgood and Hutchinson and Bremner in the kind of confrontations that would bring instant dismissal in later years. In fact, when Michael Oliver, one of the Premier League's top referees, was asked to reassess the match on its 50th anniversary, he concluded that he would have issued 11 red cards. It was an exercise, however, that served to illustrate the different interpretation and application of the laws in the modern era more than the brutality of the match.

Far more instructive is an attempt to view the game through the lens of the laws as practised at the time. Certainly, Stourbridge referee Eric Jennings, in his last professional match, was guilty of turning a blind eye too often, with only Hutchinson booked for intervening in Bremner's tussle with Osgood by shoving the Leeds captain to the ground. In *The Times*, Geoffrey Green described Jennings as 'a referee who would have a short life in Latin America'. But even applying the standards of the day, there were maybe only four others who could consider themselves fortunate not to be cautioned: Harris, for a knee-high assault on Cooper; Charlton, Osgood and Bremner for flare-ups. Cooke, usually on the receiving end, committed a series of cynical fouls to derail Leeds attacks – acts that in the 21st century would each be worthy of a yellow card and be justified as 'taking one for the team'. But no one at the time suggested he had got away with anything.

More accurate than the 'Battle of Old Trafford' handle perpetuated over time is Green's description in *The Times*. 'From the earliest stages, bush fires of anger flickered across the field – briefly, it is true, before they died,' he wrote, although adding that 'all the time there was a cauldron simmering just beneath the surface'.

What you really have, if you watch the full 120 minutes, is a match that offers a perfect snapshot of football of its time. The action began at a blistering pace, barely subsiding over the next two hours; no backward steps taken all night. And all set against an assault of noise that only standing terraces could generate. Viewers were sent to bed with ears ringing as though they'd been at a Black Sabbath concert.

As was so often the case in the era, it was hard to understand how another trophy had eluded Revie's men. Aided by an easier playing surface than at Wembley, Leeds dominated the replay with incisive and inventive play; sweeping attacks executed at pace. There was no better example than the goal with which they took a 35th-minute lead, Clarke starting off the move by turning inside Webb in his own half and surging forward, leaving three Chelsea men floundering on the floor. He pushed the ball forward to Jones, who burst between Hollins and Dempsey to flash a shot beyond Bonetti's right hand and into the netting halfway up. It was a stunningly executed goal.

Of course, there were typical moments of Leeds cynicism. Giles, while showing his usual luxuriant passing, was not slow to bring down an opponent threatening to break into attack. Jones was accused of recklessness in a challenge that left Bonetti limping on a bandaged left knee, an incident Charlton felt his team failed to fully capitalise upon. 'He is a friend of mine is Peter, but we ought to have whacked him again,' he argued. 'Not dirty like but got stuck into him. It might sound cruel, but that is what professional football is all about, being ruthless.'[53]

Yet, for all the elements of the good (Chelsea) versus evil (Leeds) story arc, it was not quite so straightforward. Chelsea seemed intent on ensuring that Leeds were unable to dominate the game and went to considerable lengths to do so, as evidenced by Cooke's frequency of offence. In the off-the-ball scuffles that have gained so much traction down the years, Chelsea shared equal billing with their opponents.

Harris's switch to right-back was an understandable move designed to spare Webb another ordeal after what he would call 'the worst day's work I ever did in my whole football career'.[54] Admitting he lacked the quickness to play full-back, he said, 'I take about 40 yards to get into my stride.'[55] Gray avoided Harris by drifting towards the middle, from where he was still able to pose problems, and that allowed Cooper to exploit the vacated space and display the full range of his attacking threat down the left. Even Hunter found himself foraging down that flank on occasion.

Chelsea's equaliser, against the run of play with only 12 minutes remaining, was characteristic of their more aesthetic side; Cooke's exquisitely clipped diagonal delivery into the box being met by Osgood at full flight, diving in front of his own fans in the Stretford End to head past goalkeeper David Harvey, who had replaced the injured Sprake. Osgood would describe the moment as 'an out-of-body experience', in which he could see the faces of individual fans behind the goal as he launched himself.[56] Even then, it was Leeds who looked likely to take the lead for the fourth time in the tie and it needed the sight of Hunter suffering from cramp in extra-time to bring the Chelsea fans among the 62,000 crowd back to full voice, sensing that the final match of a marathon season was about to bring Leeds to their knees. The winning goal, late in the first period of extra-time, went in off the side of Webb's face after a Hutchinson long throw. That it failed to match the narrative of Chelsea as saviours of flowing football mattered not a jot to their fans, or to history.

Revie blamed a lack of post-match organisation for his players leaving the arena without bothering to collect their losers' medals. Instead, cameras in the tunnel captured them stumbling back towards the dressing-room, the vacant stares and language of their stooped bodies speaking of shell shock. There was little sympathy from the masses. No one ever cried for the Daleks, either.

2

WHATEVER HAPPENED TO THE LIKELY LADS?

RIGSBY: Players today? Have you seen them? Prancing around the fields like a bunch of made models, kissing and cuddling. Listen, in my day when you scored a goal all you got was a brisk handshake. Now you get covered in love bites.

***Rising Damp*, 'A Body Like Mine' (Eric Chappell; Yorkshire TV, 1975)**

PLAYED IN the first summer of the decade, England's meeting with Brazil in the World Cup in Mexico remained one of their most iconic matches of the next ten years – partly because they would not qualify for the finals again until the 1970s were history.

With the sun at its full midday height, England, in specially designed aertex shirts, set aside the high tempo that characterised the national game and matched the tournament favourites throughout the first half. It did need a magnificent save by Gordon Banks to keep the game scoreless at half-time, launching himself across goal to claw away Pelé's bouncing downward header from a Jairzinho cross. But a diving header by Francis Lee forced a stop out of eccentric Brazilian keeper Felix and proved that England could threaten a defence renowned for its flakiness.

Brazil broke through after an hour. The little centre-forward, Tostao, weaved across the edge of the penalty area and sent a swivelled delivery to Pelé, who casually rolled the ball to his right for Jairzinho to slap a shot beyond Banks. Faced with substitutes in the World Cup for the first time, Alf Ramsey's response was to make a move that saw England revert to stereotype. His replacement of the tiring Bobby Charlton in midfield by Manchester City's energetic Colin Bell was fair enough. But the introduction of West Bromwich Albion centre-forward Jeff Astle signalled that their approach to finding a way back into the game would be the crude launching of long balls.

There was one great opportunity, squandered by Astle, when Brazil got in a flap after one such delivery, but overall one had to question whether an injection of flair and finesse rather than blunt force might have been more productive. For example, if Peter Osgood had been put in a position to bring his unique talent to bear. Wistfully, one wondered about his Chelsea team-mate, Alan Hudson. How exciting might it have been had he been fit to be considered for Mexico? Would Ramsey have included him in his 22 instead of picking three strikers – Astle, Osgood and Allan Clarke – to back up Lee and Geoff Hurst? That always felt like one too many, especially for a team that had no x-factor in midfield. Hudson was exactly the kind of player able to impose himself on the late stages of a tight game. Would Ramsey have dared drop him into the middle of such a theatre? Probably not.

There was another name that, as recently as a year earlier, England fans might have expected to feature in Ramsey's squad. Someone who, had he allowed his life to follow a different path, could have been made for a Mexican moment such as this. Yet as a tide of cynicism threatened to engulf English football, Peter Knowles had been unwilling to ride out that wave. He was gone before the decade even dawned.

Born in Fitzwilliam, the Yorkshire town that produced England cricketer Geoffrey Boycott, and with a father who played professional rugby league for Wakefield Trinity, Knowles might have been expected to favour those other sports. But it was football that took hold, as it had for older brother Cyril, who would play for Tottenham Hotspur and England. Offered a trial by Wolverhampton Wanderers, Knowles was given his Football League debut by manager Stan Cullis in October 1963, shortly after his 18th birthday. With his team relegated the following season, Knowles became one of the club's prime assets as they sought a swift return to the top flight, where they had won three titles in the 1950s. His balance, vision and effective right foot provoked interest among First Division clubs, which new manager Ronnie Allen exploited to bring the best out of his prodigy. 'Spurs are watching you today,' he would casually drop into conversation when Knowles appeared below his energetic best.

Knowles drove Wolves towards promotion in 1967. A thick mop of hair topping a frail figure, he gave the impression of a player out of his time; his skills seemingly of a different era as he skirted around the minefields of Second Division battles. In an article entitled 'The Wolverhampton Showman', Kenneth Wolstenholme wrote, 'Off the field he can be spotted by his long hair (mod styled, of course), his best boutique clothes and his flashy sports car. On the field he can be identified just as easily by the same long hair, his shirt hanging in a rather slovenly fashion outside his pants, and more especially by his brilliant football.'[57] In a 2-2 draw at Portsmouth, featured on *Match of the Day*, he earned a degree of notoriety after heading an equaliser and volleying the ball high over the stand in celebration, prompting Wolstenholme to claim that 'millions reacted' and 'wanted to know who the big-headed show-off was'.

In the First Division, where his skills had more room to flourish, Knowles's career appeared to be progressing towards England selection. But by the start of the 1969-70 season a greater influence than Ramsey had entered his life. Ken Fletcher, newly converted as a Jehovah's Witness, lived near Knowles in the Wolverhampton suburb of Oxley, but had been nervous about knocking at the door of a footballer. 'I took a couple of magazines, which he did not accept,' he recalled, 'but he asked me to call the following week to discuss the Bible.'[58] Fletcher came to describe Knowles as his first successful convert, but shed little light on the reasons for the player's wholehearted acceptance of his faith during 12 months of meetings.

On the first day of the new season, Wolves hosted Stoke City, although the *Wolverhampton Express and Star* appeared more excited about local girl Babs Lord appearing that night with Pan's People on ITV's *The Frankie Howerd Show.** A couple of Derek Dougan goals and several town-centre arrests later, Wolves were comfortable winners. By Thursday, 29 August, they were unbeaten in six matches, but the front page of the *Express and Star* carried the headline, 'Is Knowles near a career crisis?' The accompanying story stated that he faced 'a moral crisis, with his religious activities claiming more and more of his time'.

The following Monday, after Wolves' first defeat of the season, the retirement of Knowles was confirmed. 'I know the longer I play football the more I will drift away from being a Witness,' he told local reporter Phil Morgan. 'When Saturday comes and I put the football shirt on I am not a Christian. You have to be a Christian every day of your life.'

Knowles, the story explained, would play two more games before turning his back on a £100-a-week wage for door-to-door voluntary work for 'the sect'. Bill McGarry, Wolves manager since 1968, revealed that he'd attempted to talk Knowles out of his decision and suggested, 'My feeling is that he may have been ill-advised by people outside the game because I feel he could still serve his cause as a player.'

Supporting stories offered a mixture of shocked reaction – 'he is giving up what amounts to a part-time job', said one Wolves fan – eulogies for a lost talent, and suggestions that Knowles had been abducted by a sinister cult. His most complete explanation for his retirement was given to BBC's *Sportsnight With Coleman*. Watching the interview, it is hard to reconcile the naïve, stilted delivery and the often-clumsy framing of words with the apparent maturity of the sentiment expressed and resolve demonstrated.

'No matter how long I play football and no matter how near to perfection I come, I know that I could break somebody's leg,' he said.

* 'Beautiful Babs – dunno what her name is,' as Ronnie Barker's Fletch would comment wistfully in *Porridge* some years later.

He dreaded that someone could be crippled and said, 'I don't want this in my conscience, and I know the person I am, I could do this.' He added that games were 'dragging myself away from me wife and dragging myself away from religion' and that from Wednesday until Saturday he might as well not be married. 'But this is wrong because the Bible expects you to be a Christian seven days a week.'

Knowles signed off by expressing his concern about the violence that was increasingly surrounding football. 'There is so much at stake, anything can happen,' he said. 'There are people getting smashed over heads with bottles and I can see it is going to come to a big climax in one game.'

After Knowles had been mobbed by Molineux fans following a 1-0 League Cup win against Tottenham in his penultimate game, Morgan's report said Knowles had displayed 'talent I am convinced the good Lord never intended he should keep from his fellows.' Such appeals continued to fall on deaf ears. Even his mother, Jane, reportedly turned up at his house to say, 'I think you are stupid, lad.' But Knowles insisted that beyond the £5,000 house provided by the club and his £1,200 sports car 'ahead lies a greater life' – even if it meant taking a part-time job as a window-cleaner.

And so, on Saturday, 6 September, the day that ITV broadcast its first test colour transmission, Peter Knowles – a player seemingly born for football's conversion from monochrome broadcasts – appeared in his final professional game, a 3-3 draw against Nottingham Forest. Throughout the game, the Wolves fans mixed humour with pathos by singing his name to the tune of various hymns. The shock of Forest scoring three times in the final 30 minutes to snatch a draw seemed to stun the crowd, who forgot to charge the field at the full-time whistle, allowing Knowles an unmolested escape.

In one picture from the game, Knowles looked so happy in celebrating a goal that it was impossible to believe that he was about to walk away from a sport he seemingly still cared so much about. Yet, discarding his kit and shaking hands with his team-mates, he took one last walk across Molineux's changing room and exited. Waiting for wife Jean to meet him in their yellow sports car, he was surrounded by fans, some in tears. Two teenaged girls handed him a Bible in wrapping paper. 'The fans gave me a great reception, but if I could have gone off at half-time I would have done,' he explained. 'I have had enough of football. I wouldn't go back for a million pounds. There will be no comeback.'

The club had half-expected him to turn up for training on the Monday. 'One by one we all tried to talk Peter out of quitting,' said winger David Wagstaffe. 'But we also admired him for having his beliefs and sticking to them.'[59] A player who could have done much to shape his sport in the 1970s would never return.

The Peter Knowles story was an extreme example, but there were plenty of people who, while not understanding how someone could throw away his career for a religious mission, sympathised with his reservations about the cynicism of modern football. There was no disguising the weariness of Tottenham Hotspur manager Bill Nicholson when he said, 'Tactics are not new in football, but these days more and more teams are making an effort to use them.'[60]

The success of Everton and Chelsea in the spring of 1970 brought a glow of satisfaction to a large section of England's football public, but that was nothing compared to the rapture induced by events of the summer, more than 5,000 miles away. England might have got no further than the quarter-finals of the World Cup, but they played a part in two of the best games of the tournament and could reasonably argue that they had been significant contributors in Mexico – even if their football was born of Ramsey's pragmatism. Seven days after the enthralling contest against Brazil, England fans were back in front of their televisions to cheer their team to a two-goal lead early in the second half of their quarter-final against West Germany in Leon.

Alan Mullery and Martin Peters had scored and Alan Ball was squeaking, 'Goodnight. God bless. See you in Munich,' in the ears of opponents. In the stands, however, reserve Jack Charlton was nervous. 'Instead of closing the game up and making sure we kept it at 2-0, our defenders were flying into their half of the field,' he said. 'It's not the way I would have done it.'[61] Sure enough, with 20 minutes remaining, a shot by Franz Beckenbauer skimmed under the body of Peter Bonetti, a last-minute stand-in when Gordon Banks was confined to the team hotel with a stomach upset. Jack Charlton left his seat to wait anxiously in a café outside the ground and Ramsey sent on Bell for a tiring Charlton to shadow West Germany's scorer. Norman Hunter replaced Peters ten minutes from the end, taking with him the instruction to 'stop them playing'. But within a minute, a long ball into the England area plonked on to the back of Uwe Seeler's head and arced over Bonetti. Extra-time loomed and Ramsey's reputation for being hopeless when it came to substitutions was assured.

The tie was 11 minutes from being decided by the drawing of lots when German substitute Jürgen Grabowski's cross from the right was headed back across goal by Johannes Löhr and an unmarked Gerd Müller jumped to volley his eighth goal of the tournament. 'I can't believe we lost,' said forward Francis Lee. 'Germany had four or five world-class players and we made them look like selling-platers. Alf made a mistake when he picked Peter Bonetti. I think he should have picked Alex Stepney, who was more of a big-time player and had played really well in the European Cup Final.'[62]

Disappointment over the loss of its crown hurt English football deeply, but the manner of the tournament gave hope to those who believed that idealism was not yet dead in football's new age. Over the course of 22 wonderful days, Pelé and his Brazilian colleagues flashed across British screens twice a week, their yellow shirts shimmering vibrantly for those lucky enough to have access to a colour television. The somewhat hazy pictorial nature of live events arriving from across the globe – 'via satellite' as the captions proudly proclaimed – added an other-worldly aspect to the football. Reeling off six victories in which they scored 19 goals – England being the only team to hold them below three – they furnished a library of indelible images on their way to a third Jules Rimet trophy in 12 years.

There was Rivelino's free-kick against Czechoslovakia, a feat as luxuriant as his moustache; Pelé's attempt from halfway in the same match and his outrageous dummy of the goalkeeper in the semi-final against Uruguay – two of the most famous near-misses in World Cup history; Jairzinho, the team's lord of the dance, leading a prancing conga line whenever he scored; Gerson's majestic strike in the 4-1 defeat of Italy in the final. Best of all was the magnificent symphony with which they signed off, begun by Clodoaldo's fancy footwork outside his own penalty area and completed, after various team-mates' party pieces, by skipper Carlos Alberto's unequivocal finish.

Meanwhile, Italy and West Germany contrived one of the most thrilling games in World Cup history, a 4-3 victory for Italy that featured five goals in extra-time and the heroic sight of Beckenbauer playing with a dislocated shoulder. In all, 34 goals were scored in the tournament's seven knockout games (compared to 31 in the 15 sudden-death matches of 1990).

The mood of Mexico 70 pervaded talk of the new English season. Even the *Radio Times* ran an article headlined 'Can the ball-player come back?', in which it spoke to four of the game's more skilful players. Hudson, inevitably, was among them, suggesting that 'people around you must realise they must play to you all the time', while Arsenal's Peter Marinello insisted he would play his own game. Burnley midfielder Ralph Coates suggested sadly that his attacking instincts 'probably cost me a place in the World Cup side' and Eddie Gray warned, 'You can't play pretty-pretty stuff in three inches of mud and a howling wind.'[63]

Such comments reflected that those responsible for what happened on English fields were refusing to get carried away. For those concerned with negotiating the ankle-deep sludge of Derby County's Baseball Ground in February, there were only limited lessons to be taken from Guadalajara in June. Ramsey had even dismissed Brazil by saying, 'We have nothing to learn from these people.'

And if a whiff of South America had reached Elland Road it clearly had not got as far as Jack Charlton. Early in the new season he was interviewed by Fred Dinenage on Tyne Tees Television and asked about violence on the field. 'You do what is necessary,' he said, citing it as one of Ramsey's sayings. 'If I was playing in an international and saw someone getting away with the ball and I could not catch him, I would flatten him.'

The real controversy arose when Dinenage enquired about the 'worst foul' Charlton himself had suffered. 'I cannot mention names, but I have a little book with two names in it and if I get the chance to do them I will,' was the reply that would go down in football folklore; being remembered as his 'Little Black Book'. Explaining that some players had gone 'over the top' on him, he promised, 'There are two or three people who have done it to me and I will make them suffer before I pack this game up.' Charlton never did reveal those names, but over the years Everton winger Johnny Morrissey and at least one player from Chelsea were thought to be candidates. Re-run a week later on ITV's *World of Sport*, the interview was intended to convey pantomime-style villainy, but the FA charged Charlton with bringing the game into disrepute and excitable newspaper columnists called for him to be sacked by Leeds. The *Daily Mirror*'s Peter Wilson asked, 'Have these petulant, primping, over-paid, under-principled gladiators no responsibility?'

Revie couldn't see what all the fuss was about and the FA's disciplinary committee agreed. Admonishing Charlton for remarks that were 'ill-advised', they acknowledged that the interview had been intended to be light-hearted and let him off without punishment. Ian Wooldridge of the *Daily Mail* praised Charlton for breaking 'a conspiracy of silence', while Arsenal coach Don Howe acknowledged, 'There is more physical contact in our game and that hinders individual flair. Most managers will continue to do what will bring success.'

Alongside manager Bertie Mee, Howe intended to do exactly that. Victory in the Fairs Cup Final in April 1970, a two-legged win over Belgian side Anderlecht, had broken a 17-year trophy drought at Highbury, but it had hardly prompted observers to mark Arsenal down as serious First Division contenders. No more than the success of Newcastle United in the same competition a season earlier had precipitated a title challenge on Tyneside. Arsenal had finished only eighth and possessed a workmanlike team devoid of big names.

With Peter Marinello's goal-scoring debut becoming a distant memory, they appeared to lack players capable of game-changing individual feats – especially after precocious young forward Charlie George broke his foot in the opening match of the new campaign. What they did have, though, was Howe's tactical acumen; a deep sense of what it meant to represent Arsenal; a team spirit that ensured they would stand shoulder to shoulder in any type of battle; and a manager in Mee who was blessed with military organisational skills and a fierce pride in his club.

Even a 5-0 defeat at Stoke City in the autumn became the catalyst for a long unbeaten run that saw them locked in a title battle with Leeds as the spring of 1971 came around, although their points deficit made them clear outsiders. An emotional speech delivered by Mee challenged his players, who were also going well in the FA Cup, to go on and make history. 'I remember seeing his hands trembling and thinking how nervous he was,' said goalkeeper Bob Wilson. 'He said to us, "Look, you have a chance here to put your names into the history book for always. But to do so, you have got to make football the priority of your life, at the expense of your family, your wife and everything else. You have got to try to explain to them that this is your chance for glory."'[64]

It was exactly the challenge that a group of players who had largely come through the Arsenal system – complemented by shrewd signings such as Wilson, Frank McLintock, Bob McNab and George Graham – thrived upon. As Graham explained, 'You don't all have to sit and laugh and joke together at dinner, but in a good team you gel when you start training and playing. I have nothing but admiration for the way Bertie and Don built that team and had players and people who complemented each other.'[65]

As Leeds faltered, Arsenal kept on winning, although rarely by much. Their final four wins of the League campaign were all 1-0, meaning that no one was ever likely to compare them with Brazil. 'They lacked majesty,' said one report and leading sportswriter Patrick Collins commented, 'For the past season or three Arsenal's football has, to my mind, had all the wit and originality of ITV's Christmas programmes.'[66] The *Rothmans Football Yearbook* summed up the season of the Gunners' success by stating, 'The game in 1970-71 was, by and large, dull and negative; rugged and hard.' For those looking for statistical support, Arsenal had won the title by scoring 15 goals fewer than the 86 with which Newcastle had been relegated a decade earlier.

One of the lighter moments of the season occurred at Highfield Road early in October. Fortunately, *Match of the Day* cameras were present when Coventry City's Willie Carr placed the ball between his feet at a free-kick, lifted it into the air by flicking his heels up towards his knees and stood aside as Ernie Hunt volleyed the dropping ball beyond Everton goalkeeper Andy Rankin. It even caught the attention of *Daily Telegraph* TV critic Sean Day-Lewis. 'Television offered two memorable happenings over the weekend. On both there was a combination of superbly-trained professional skills and outstanding artistic inspiration,' he wrote. 'One was the performance of Donald Pleasence in *Tea Party*. The other was Coventry City's third goal against Everton.' FIFA responded by banning the move, clarifying that the ball had to be actually 'kicked' to restart the game.

Perhaps the greatest mitigation of some of the more functional football of the period was the playing surfaces. Rarely retaining much grass beyond the first leaf fall of autumn, they did not encourage South American artistry. Kevin Keegan reckoned he was forced to slow down his game on pitches where 'the mud pulls on the boot soles so much that you think the force of gravity has doubled' and matches became 'a 90-minute test of endurance'.[67]

'You had to have common sense,' said Arsenal full-back Bob McNab. 'The fields were diabolical so if we were playing a lower division team in the Cup we just knocked it down in their corner and said, "Right, you try to play with it." On those mud heaps, how could you contemplate knocking it around?' McNab also felt that the public never saw what the Double winners were truly capable of. 'I regret that they never filmed our games of one-touch in training,' he continued. 'Everyone criticised us because they thought we were defensive, but our two centre-backs were the key in people breaking forward. We were effectively playing three at the back even in those days because I would go down the wing and Peter Simpson would come out wide on the left, or he would go forward and I would cover him. People didn't understand it.'[68]

Whether or not onlookers were sufficiently sophisticated to appreciate such technical advancement can be debated as much as the methods of Revie's Leeds, but one important victory – 1-0 of course – illustrates McNab's point. On the first Saturday of February, Arsenal were being stifled by Manchester City until Simpson strode forward from inside his own half. Continuing purposefully until he was 25 yards from goal, he unleashed a low left-foot shot that keeper Joe Corrigan could only divert for John Radford to stab in the winning goal.

That game was additionally significant for the return of the mercurial George. He would give Arsenal the additional impetus, the dash of the unexpected, that drove them towards a dramatic and historic climax to the season. His mighty contributions included a double that won an FA Cup fifth-round tie at Manchester City and a header that beat Leicester City in a quarter-final replay. In the League, he thrashed the only goal against Newcastle United to send Arsenal to the top of the table on 17 April, celebrating in front of the same North Bank fans with whom he had stood during his younger years. The goal featured on *Match of the Day*, alongside referee Ray Tinkler allowing a contentious 'offside' goal by West Bromwich Albion's Jeff Astle to seal a shock victory over Leeds at Elland Road.†

According to Radford, the Cup performance at Maine Road was prompted by McLintock tapping into George's natural disposition towards confrontation, telling him that City coach Malcolm Allison had been calling him an 'upstart' who was not as good as everyone was claiming. 'I suppose, at the time, it does wind you up,' George admitted. 'After the game, you do say, "Fuck you." I didn't like people saying personal things. I played well and I scored the goals. I had a

† 'Leeds will go mad,' said Barry Davies on commentary. 'And they have every right to go mad.' The authorities didn't agree. The invasion of angry fans that followed the goal caused Leeds to be forced into playing their first two home games of 1971-72 on neutral venues. The two drawn games cost them decisive points, meaning Leeds fans argue to this day that Tinkler cost them two titles.

knack of scoring winning goals in the FA Cup games and in important League games. However important the game was, I felt I was capable of doing something.'[69]

Such self-assuredness had been obvious to team-mates from the outset. Wilson, as a part-time PE teacher at Holloway School, had coached young Charlie, who would greet him with, 'How you doin', Bob?' Wilson explained, 'Charlie was a free spirit. He was this precocious talent who could do anything. We used to wellie balls up into the air and Charlie would wait for it and just kill it. Plonk.'[70]

McNab continued, 'He used to call me "son" and I was in the England team. He was as gifted as anyone I have ever seen. His power was nothing short of extraordinary. If we had a free-kick we just used to tell him to hit it at the goalie as hard as he possibly could. I have seen Charlie stand on the halfway line at Highbury and kick it over the bar without a run-up, then do the same going the other way with his left foot.'[71]

Out of the spotlight of any television coverage, it was Ray Kennedy's header that secured Arsenal the title on a Monday night at Tottenham, in a game they needed to either win or draw 0-0 in order to deny Leeds. Yet it was George, with his grasp of the big occasion and his splash of showmanship, who grabbed the biggest stage of all to secure the Double five days later at Wembley. With the game locked at 1-1 with nine minutes of extra-time remaining, George accepted a return pass from Radford and, barely drawing back his right foot, fired off a shot that flew past Ray Clemence's right hand. He had done little else all afternoon, but with the game on the line had brought his brilliance to bear. 'A lot of people were tired,' he said, 'but I could always hit the ball from anywhere. I may have been the only one capable of scoring a goal like that.'[72]

As if the goal were not memorable enough, he lay on the Wembley grass, arms spread Messiah-like in one of Wembley's most iconic celebrations. Graham added, 'Only Charlie could have scored that goal. He had a thunderbolt of a shot; a short backswing and "Bang". I don't know if he lay down because of exhaustion or what, but we still have a laugh with him about that.'[73]

DANDIES IN THE UNDERWORLD

They were the Lairds of Laddism, disruptive influences one and all. Unclean, unclean. Not that they worked overtime to dispel that image. Hudson, Currie and Worthington liked a tipple. Bowles a flutter. George was the yobbo who scrapped with photographers and threw V-signs at spectators. Osgood fell in love once a week with women bearing scant resemblance to his wife. Marsh was a swank.

Rob Steen, *The Mavericks*
(Mainstream Publishing, 1994)

Playing it for laughs was not something that too many players had the self-assuredness to do in the early years of the 1970s. Those who dared to do so were quickly lost in the stampede of players eager to offer the sweat and toil that was valued more highly. It was why Eamon Dunphy made his sad observation that players had a 'feeling that they have got to go out and punish themselves for 90 minutes.' Writing in his diary of a season at Millwall, *Only A Game?*, he stated, 'It is one of the most important things in the game at the moment – the idea that you somehow have to suffer. This is what really distinguishes English football – the amount of people willing to do that. And that is also what destroys English football.'[74]

It was a rare player brave enough to display an affinity with the notion of sport as another branch of show business. Rodney Marsh was one such man. 'Footballers are a little like actors,' he said. 'Extroverts who want to be reminded that they have ability and are appreciated.'[75]

There was Hudson and Osgood and George; the Loftus Road rebels, Marsh and Stan Bowles; Elvis wannabe Frank Worthington and Sheffield United's artist, Tony Currie. Author Rob Steen had a name for this group: *The Mavericks*. They stood out like stack-heeled glam rockers on a *Top of the Pops* line-up featuring schoolgirl heart-throb David Cassidy, Eurovision Song Contest winner Vicky Leandros and the Pipes and Drums of the Military Band of the Royal Scots

Dragoon Guards.[‡] Steen told their story brilliantly in his ode to non-conformism, published two decades after they were giving it the old razzle-dazzle on a stage becoming more dominated by monochrome and monotony. It is an indictment of the prevailing mood of the early 1970s that his subjects were small enough in number to be contained within fewer than 200 pages. There were some others – Duncan McKenzie, Alan Birchenall[§] and Robin Friday,[¶] for example – who had the right attitude, but not the elite level of performance required for entry into Steen's club.

The spirit of George Best was the common denominator. 'George gave us the link between football and the world,' Marsh told Steen. 'There were so many players that had character and desire, but we didn't have a champion. George was the champion.'[76] Yet, unlike Best, these players left no great legacy of cups and caps. Charlie George was the only one of them to win the League Championship and their combined total of England caps was 46 – collectively eight fewer than Glen Johnson. None of them went into management. A four-day *Daily Mirror* series in 1978, featuring the sexual conquests of Marsh, Worthington and Bowles (and, of course, Best), was their kind of bequest; reinforcing reputations that constantly undermined their collective influence on the field. Happily, there exists a collection of images burned forever into the minds of fans of a certain age; given life on YouTube for those with a feeling for football history or a pushy parent bristling with tales of 'in my day'.

It was the often-rugged landscape upon which the mavericks added their own splash of colour that made their contribution so

‡ The top three in the UK charts on FA Cup Final day 1972 – until Marc Bolan's T. Rex knocked them off a week later.

§ Birchenall made the cover of *The Mavericks* via a famous picture of him and Currie exchanging a kiss while on their backsides in a First Division game. Birchenall told *Football Monthly* in June 1973, 'I think football takes itself too seriously at times.'

¶ Former Reading and Cardiff forward Friday was the subject of *The Greatest Footballer You Never Saw*, written by journalist Paolo Hewitt and Oasis bassist Paul McGuigan in 1998. Retired from the game at 25, he died from a heart attack aged 38 after years of drug and alcohol abuse. 'Blessed with awesome stamina, he ran riot outside football,' read the book's introduction. 'He danced naked in clubs, naked in pubs. He openly smoked spliff and dropped pills. He caroused until late at night and would then return to his flat and crank his beloved music up until dawn.'

vivid and enduring. 'The strong, rugged defensive player is king,' wrote journalist and broadcaster John Camkin in his introductory comments for the 1971-72 *Rothmans Football Yearbook*. 'He wears his crown in all too many cases by virtue of tactics which deceive even the most skilled and experienced of referees.' Which is not to say that the likes of Tommy Smith, Ron Harris, Peter Storey and Norman Hunter were merely a stain on the game. Not only were they in many cases far greater ball players than given credit for, but all were the kind of 'character' beloved of the terraces and press boxes, adding greater texture to the time. If the mavericks brought a touch of showbiz to the sport, then so did the hard men. After all, who bothers to cheer a baby-face if there is no heel?

Cloggers were no new phenomenon. Nor were they universally despised within dressing-rooms, most of which contained one or two of their own. When the stylists of Ron Greenwood's West Ham United failed to add to their successes of the mid-1960s, even Geoff Hurst was forced to lament that his team lacked an 'element of legitimate violence'.[77] After they managed to finish sixth in 1972-73, Bryan 'Pop' Robson, the First Division's leading scorer, echoed Hurst in saying, 'West Ham are easily the best footballing side I have ever played for, but perhaps we could do with a bit more aggression.'[78]

Hammers manager Greenwood belonged to a different age. His Corinthian values might help win him the England job later in the decade, but for now it meant that his team was simply out of step with the modern game. 'Six years of excuses – we've had enough,' read one banner at Upton Park early in 1971. Ruthless opponents saw them as 'a soft touch; that's why they never won anything' – in the words of McNab.[79] In 1973, Keegan, the prototype for the successful yet pragmatic Seventies superstar, asked the question at the heart of the argument. 'What is the point of being entertaining if you're not winning,' he wrote. 'I admire many aspects of West Ham's play, but they lack the overriding will to win.'[80]

Jimmy Hill ventured, 'Greenwood's passionate belief that pure football will eventually pay championship dividends is causing him headaches ... he has watched other, more ruthless managers prepare to fight with the fashionable weapons of the day and collect their medals.'[81]

Such a comment reflects that the greatest threat to the values of George, Hudson and the rest was the institutional, cynical stifling of flair that had become a tactical imperative for the majority. Sir Matt Busby had told *The Observer* in 1969, 'Hard men are nothing new in football. What is new and frightening about the present situation is that you have entire sides that have physical hardness as their main asset. They use strength and fitness to neutralise skill.'

McNab admitted as much when speaking about his successful Arsenal team. 'In the old days, the better team won. When you had the ball, you played – and when they had the ball they played. There was no pressuring. Arsenal were pressuring, hustling, knocking people down all over the field like ice hockey.'[82]

Teams might still go through the back of ankles to stop the flair players, but now it was possible to be negative without violence. And as early as the end of the 1960s it was no longer heresy to identify England's World Cup triumph as the moment where pragmatism became the sport's guiding principle. 'There is no doubt that the events of 1966 caused the pendulum throughout the land to swing rapidly towards defensive football,' Camkin's editorial continued. In the middle of the decade, England forward Mick Channon complained, 'Our football is run by frightened men. Managers are frightened of losing their jobs.'[83]

The debate, however, had greater nuance than was sometimes attributed to it. Joe Mercer agreed that 'there is too much fear in our game', but in the same breath he praised Ramsey for his willingness to 'get rid of the public's glamour boys who used to play at our expense, go through their party tricks and then drop somebody in it.'[84] And yet Mercer would make a point of picking Worthington when he became England's stand-in manager in 1974. Even a Revie disciple, Terry Yorath, would leave Leeds with fears that 'the modern game has far too many robot footballers'. Having become captain of Coventry City, he said, 'Managers insist that players should adhere to instructions at any cost, so the up-and-coming lads are afraid to go against orders for the fear of being dropped.'[85]

After the first FA Cup Final of the 1970s, *Goal* editor Alan Hughes lamented, 'The fear of defeat makes the risk of playing a bit of pure football a luxury most teams in big games would rather do without. We are squeezing out all the skill, all the colour, all the enterprise, all the entertainment. After that we haven't got a lot left. Except a lot of runners who go until they drop, and robot matches between press-button footballers.' And even Chelsea manager Dave Sexton, whose team's victory in that final was welcomed by many as positive for the game and who enjoyed the best years of Osgood, Hudson and Bowles, observed, 'It is fair to say that most managers in the Football League would settle for workers rather than talented individuals who are not prepared to contribute to the team effort.'

Bowles, who said he 'didn't have a clue about defending', would constantly be told by Sexton, when manager of Queens Park Rangers, to track back when his team lost possession. 'My idea was that I was up there to score and make goals,' he explained.[86] Before that, Sexton had left Osgood out of his Chelsea team early in the 1971-72 season, announcing after a home defeat against ten-man Manchester United** that his striker was available for transfer. 'I've not been satisfied with his effort or his performances. He's been doing less and less,' Sexton explained. At the time Osgood accepted the criticism publicly and was quickly reinstated. Looking back, he said, 'Just because you don't turn it on, doesn't mean you're not trying. It was a disgrace for him to say that.'[87]

Perhaps Slade had Osgood and Sexton in mind when they sung, 'So you think I have lazy time, well you should know better,' in their No.1 single 'Cum On Feel the Noize' a couple of years later. Osgood had, after all, by that time come to resemble lead singer Noddy Holder with his expanding curls and sideburns. All that was missing was the top hat with the mirrors.

Articles about Osgood in the early 1970s tended to veer between criticism of his attitude – 'Ossie is happy enough getting lost for long spells' charged *Shoot!* in 1971[88] – and pieces such as one in the

** George Best had been sent off for abusive language.

same publication, headlined 'The Chelsea Striker Who Never Stops Working', in which he admitted, 'I should never give it less than 100 per cent enthusiasm.'[89] Osgood's style even became fair game for his fellow professionals. Newcastle United's Malcolm Macdonald said on television late in 1973 that he would not want to partner Osgood for England because he would have to do all the work. Macdonald perhaps should have been more concerned about securing his own place in the team than suggesting who should play alongside him. Osgood described it as a 'sick comment to make'. He did concede, though, 'I do look lazy, but it's my style.'[90]

Currie was the maverick appreciated most by England managers, picked by Ramsey six times. Ignored for all but one game by Revie, a move to Elland Road put him back into England contention under Ron Greenwood, who selected him ten times late in the decade. But even his Leeds manager Jimmy Armfield demonstrated distrust, telling the man for whom he paid £250,000, 'Cut out the showmanship.' A generous Currie said, 'I could understand how he felt. He wanted to show the fans he'd bought an action man, not a playboy. I tried to fit into the Elland Road pattern. But, no matter how hard I tried, my instincts led me to let my hair down on the pitch. I was blowing kisses and waving to the fans.'[91]

The final phase of his international career included a memorable night when Brazil were outplayed in a 1-1 draw at Wembley, having 'disregarded their skills and used force' – according to *The Times* – against an England side in which Currie anchored the midfield. It was that kind of performance that added credibility when Currie concluded, 'Over the years I've been left out of the England side in favour of donkeys in terms of vision and skill.'[92]

The 1970s dawned with similar harsh lessons about the modern game delivered to players such as Bobby Gould, transferred out of the methodical environment at Arsenal. 'Everything was very disciplined,' he recalled. 'My work-rate improved a lot and I learned to play out wide, but I lost some of my sharpness as a striker around the penalty area.'[93]

Across town at White Hart Lane, a teenaged midfielder was about to learn that 'it was the era of work rate'. Steve Perryman recalled,

'Teams couldn't afford to be outworked and therefore the special talents suffered. I was known as a passer, but by the time I have played 50 games in the first team I am an "umper and dumper". I am work rate and winning tackles. My brother said to me, "Steve, I am not watching you play anymore. All you do is run about. You don't pass it; you don't play."'[94]

Perryman's manager, Bill Nicholson, who had led his 1960-61 stylists to the Double, was forced to admit, 'There was a time when the public came to be entertained. Now the only thing they are interested in is winning.'[95] Comments like that make it unsurprising that author Hunter Davies, having spent the 1971-72 season following Tottenham at close quarters for his book, *The Glory Game*, concluded gloomily that the pressures the players operated under meant they were 'getting such little pleasure out of playing football'. Busby offered the same observation on BBC TV late in 1973. 'The charm has gone out of the game,' he said. 'I very seldom see today anyone laugh on the field, unless a player scores a goal.'[96]

Jimmy Greaves had retired at the age of 31 in the summer of 1971, just as a teenager called Trevor Francis was completing a spectacular first season in the Birmingham City team. 'The pressures and tensions in football are now so great,' Greaves commented. 'I wouldn't like to be Trevor Francis, just breaking into the game. The demands on players are increasing every season. They don't get the chance to enjoy the game like when I first came into football.'[97]

It was all a far cry from the happy-go-lucky days of Stanley Matthews, who'd been excused defensive duties and offered space and time by respectful opposition. Harry Johnston, who had been Matthews's skipper when Blackpool won the FA Cup in 1953 and was the club's assistant manager as the 1970s dawned, spoke for many of his generation when he complained, 'Some of the games I have to watch nowadays almost give me nausea. Chiefly because there is so little skill in the present-day game.'[98]

What the likes of Osgood, Marsh, Bowles and a few others could do was create their own space within the mayhem; put their foot on the ball and invite the hatchet men to take their best shot. To watch

Marsh swaying away from a voracious defender, to marvel at the deft touch of Bowles or to see Currie find an angled pass through a crowded midfield was to witness the kind of imagination and improvisation that was supposed to have no home in 1970s English football.

Yet that quality could still require an iron fist to clear its path. Early in his Cup-winning 1969-70 season, Osgood had said, 'I don't feel I can cope with the pressure of playing in midfield. I'm not hard enough to do the job. You need a ruthless streak and I am not built that way.'[99] According to Marsh, Osgood did himself a disservice. 'What happened to people like me and Ossie is that we became the aggressors, getting in first,' Marsh said. 'Ossie was brutal.'[100]

George, who confessed admiration for the professionalism of Leeds, was never slow to fight his corner. That could take the form of getting stuck in against opponents or giving V-signs to rival fans, as he did in a 1971-72 FA Cup tie at Derby, nearly causing a riot. He put it down to coming from Holloway, where 'you learn from the pram to butt people who pick on you'.[101]

Frequently debated was whether the prevailing style of English professional football was becoming so ingrained within the structure of the entire game that teams could not change even if they wanted to. One theory went that there simply were not the gifted players emerging to steer the sport down a different path. An unnamed First Division manager was quoted in 1969 as saying, 'If we taught academic subjects the way football is taught in schools we should be breeding a nation of morons.'[102]

Malcolm Allison, the great romantic, felt that young players were being brainwashed into believing they lacked the requisite skill. 'I cannot accept that it is no longer possible for skilful players to hold their own in our leagues,' he argued. 'What we should be doing is revising the way we set about development. We pay too much attention to results at an age where it doesn't really matter.'[103] And Mee told journalist Ken Jones, 'We are getting physically higher developed boys, much better physical specimens. But there are few very highly skilled individuals.'[104]

That doesn't explain why, where that elevated level of skill did exist, it seemed to go with the apparent prerequisite of an unreliable, rebellious streak. There again, how effective would Worthington have been in a two-decade career without the conceit that saw him grinning from the cover of an autobiography entitled *One Hump or Two?* And would Bowles have been such a force on the field without the same 'life is for living' inner monologue that drove him to the bookies and had seen his career meander through Manchester City, Bury, Crewe Alexandra and Carlisle United before flourishing as the inheritor of Marsh's No.10 shirt at QPR?

The *Goal Annual* wrote an untypically empathetic article in its 1977 edition, although the heading of 'Soccer's Problem Boys' suggested the usual disapproval of the likes of Bowles, Hudson and Co. was on its way. 'Unfortunately, players of such rare talent, who are in essence the game's lifeblood, often become identified equally as its bad blood,' it began. But it went on to point out, 'The problem is not a new one. Perhaps the increased publicity surrounding the game gives the impression that the tantrums, flare-ups and walk-outs of this decade are a symptom of the times and the declining standards within the game. In fact, they are the symptoms of the unpredictability of the explosive inner fuse of the man who is blessed with a talent he struggles to come to terms with.'[105]

Bowles was certainly not about to apologise for any of his supposed character failings, as he demonstrated when interrogated by Brian Moore in *The Big Match* studio after scoring in a 2-2 draw at Arsenal early in the 1974-75 season, a campaign during which he had been suspended by QPR for the opening two games after reporting back late from a get-together of England players:

> MOORE: [People] are mystified as to how you have these little things in your career, where you don't turn up or miss training or whatever. *[Camera remains on Bowles smiling sheepishly].* Can you explain that?
>
> BOWLES: No. I can't really. At the time I think whatever I do is right, and I just do it.

MOORE: And yet it upsets people who want to support you, who want to say Stan Bowles is great, he is good for England, and yet they are worried about, you know, your behaviour in these sorts of matters. Are you putting this behind you now?

BOWLES: Yes, I think so … only time will tell.[106]

His international career was already under threat after he'd disappeared from the England camp after being substituted by Mercer in a Home International Championship game against Northern Ireland. Ironically, he had been replaced by Worthington, who proceeded to set up the only goal of the game. Bowles refused to travel with the squad to Scotland. 'I firmly believe that if I had not walked out I would have had many more caps for my country,' he said. 'I was playing very well at the time.'[107] Yet only three months after his interview on *The Big Match*, Bowles, angered at being substituted at West Ham, ended up in a dressing-room scuffle with skipper Gerry Francis and claimed he would never again speak to Sexton. This was not long after a training-ground fight with Frank McLintock.

Maybe the mavericks have been over-romanticised; their personalities more memorable than those of their equals on the field. Trevor Brooking and Glenn Hoddle hardly lacked natural gifts, but the fact that they steered clear of trouble on the field and controversy off it made them outsiders to Steen's squad – and may explain why they collected 100 caps between them, with one being knighted and the other serving a spell as England manager. Never would either of them have a manager wondering, as Sexton did of Bowles, 'How can you be so good at training and be fantastic on the field, when the rest of your life is just bedlam?'[108] Nor would they find a newspaper wondering whether they would have been a 'long, thin, lank-haired, loud-mouthed yob' if not for football, as the *Daily Express* did of George after the Baseball Ground incident.

That might have been part of the attraction of George's band of brothers. As Steen wrote, 'To my generation they embodied what we fondly imagined to be the spirit of our youth.'[109] The North Bank kids loved that Charlie had as little regard for Mee as they held for their headteachers. Playing only 133 League games for Arsenal in six seasons, he complained about wages, brushed regularly with authority and was banished to the sidelines by his disciplinarian manager as frequently as the classroom troublemakers found themselves in detention.

It was a sad moment when, towards the end of his playing days, he suggested, 'If there's a lesson from my career, it's don't join your favourite club. Just imagine growing up and going to school with a crowd of lads who are Arsenal daft and being there on the terraces with them on match days, then suddenly you're in that side as a teenager. I was at the centre of everything in football and it became increasingly difficult to remember the right things from the wrong. I don't regret playing for Arsenal but I'm sorry that certain things happened there.'[110]

Howe was aware enough to observe, 'It's a very special problem being a local boy making good with Arsenal … he's playing for the entire community in which he lives. It's a hell of a burden for any young player.'[111] Yet George was left to regret the coincidence of timing that meant Mee was his Arsenal manager. 'Bertie wasn't a great manager of flair players,' he said. 'At the end at Arsenal, Bert and I hardly spoke at all. Successful managing is about handling different types of people.'[112] It was a familiar lament of the mavericks.

Bobby Campbell, the last of George's Highbury coaches, said, 'If Charlie was to lend an ear now and then and discipline himself, he could be the greatest player in England. He could be England's answer to Johan Cruyff.' Asked what prevented him from doing that, Campbell responded, 'Charlie's character … his strength becomes a weakness.'[113]

Fans at Loftus Road idolised Marsh because he refused to conform. He had learned the professional game at Fulham, where a make-it-up-as-you-go-along approach was encouraged, and became the master of it after a spring 1966 transfer to QPR, where manager Alec Stock had assured him, 'You just play football and I'll have the others adjust around you.'[114]

'The vibe at Loftus Road was stunning, as was the reaction I got from the fans,' Marsh recalled. 'I would do things during games that only if you were there as a fan you would appreciate.'[115] The love affair was consummated by the wonderful individual effort with which he equalised as Third Division QPR came from 2-0 down to beat West Bromwich Albion in the 1967 League Cup Final, the first played at Wembley.

And he scored one of the 1970s' most memorable televised hat-tricks – a monstrous volley on the run, a towering header and a piece of penalty-box trickery – to demolish Birmingham City and declare his manifesto for the way the game should be played.

By the time he was ready to make a much-discussed transfer to Manchester City *(see Chapter 5)* he even had his own theme tune. It was entirely appropriate that the terraces took up the chant of 'Oh, Rodney, Rodney ... Rodney, Rodney, Rodney, Rodney, Rodney Marsh' to the tune of Chicory Tip's February 1972 No.1, 'Son of My Father' – a piece of glam-electronica written by Giorgio Moroder that would come to be recognised as an important forerunner of the synthesizer pop movement. Marsh was every bit the innovator himself.

Ramsey was more Mantovani than Moroder. Even when Marsh was given a run of seven starts in the England team, shortly after his 1972 transfer, it was hardly a surprise that he failed to replicate his club-level feats when asked to perform in the manner of Hurst, who was being phased out of the side. Marsh lived with the feeling that perhaps he should have told Ramsey to stuff it and done his own thing. Nor did he help his cause if the much repeated tale of an exchange with Ramsey actually happened. 'If you don't work hard I'm going to pull you off at half-time,' the England boss was said to have warned him. To which Marsh shot back, 'Blimey, Alf, at City all we get is a cup of tea and an orange.'

'It was the last time I ever got picked,' recalled Marsh, who at least appreciated being given a greater opportunity than many others of his ilk. 'I don't regret for one minute my attitude towards football,' he insisted, claiming that he was born 'a free spirit'. He concluded, 'Did that contribute to me only getting nine caps? Probably.'[116]

McLintock argued, 'All the rebels had a very fixed idea of the way the game should be played. Must be easy when you've got that much talent. They took liberties. If all these maverick characters had played anywhere else, they'd have all won more than 40 caps.'[117]

Worthington, meanwhile, came within a few heartbeats, literally, of joining Liverpool at the beginning of their first title-winning campaign of the decade. A fee of £150,000 was agreed with Huddersfield Town in June 1972, only for him to fail his medical because of what was said to be high blood pressure. He went on holiday to Majorca with the intention of unwinding but reported back with no change to his condition. Bill Shankly backed away. 'As I walked into Shanks's office I could already sense the change,' Worthington recalled. 'It was as if his mind was already made up.'[118]

Instead, Worthington ended up at Leicester City, playing a leading role in Jimmy Bloomfield's stylish side for the next five years. Quite how Shankly would have dealt with Worthington boggles the mind. It is hard to imagine him reacting with great joy to his new signing turning up for training wearing his signature black velvet Stetson in one of his flash sports cars, Isaac Hayes blaring from the stereo. Even Worthington's supposed rest in Majorca became the stuff of legend. He would claim to have bedded a fellow plane passenger and enjoyed a threesome with two Swedish girls before hooking up with 'a magnificently-built Belgian girl'. All of that after he suffered severe dizzy spells that he self-diagnosed as 'some sort of nervous breakdown'.

Despite the concerns of Liverpool's medical staff, Worthington's lifestyle had no detrimental effect on his longevity in the game. He was still playing League football for Stockport County in his 40th year. In the meantime, he performed well enough at Birmingham City in the early 1980s to be considered a candidate for England's World Cup squad in Spain and had scored one of the most memorable televised goals of the 1970s while at Bolton Wanderers.

Given a run in the England team under the temporary managership of the genial, fun-loving Mercer in 1974, Worthington was never likely to thrive among the neuroses and nervous tics that would characterise Don Revie's reign. Taken off in Revie's first game and given a couple of minutes as a substitute in the second, he was then discarded. But by the autumn of 1978, there was speculation that he might once again appear in an England shirt under the more open-minded Greenwood.

Despite playing for a Bolton team that would end up only 17th in the table, Worthington was on his way to finishing as the First Division's top scorer in 1978-79 with 24 goals. The best of them came at home against Ipswich Town. The ball dropped towards him, two yards inside the away team's box with his back to goal. A controlling header took the ball just beyond the boundary of the area, where he flicked it up twice with his left foot. A third touch sent it spinning back over his head, and those of the five Ipswich players advancing in formation to the edge of the box. Worthington span through 180 degrees and was the only one in position as the ball fell towards the earth about a foot inside the area. Before it could hit the floor, he swung his left boot to send a low shot skidding past the outstretched left arm of goalkeeper Paul Cooper. It takes considerably longer to read that description than it took for Worthington to execute his outrageous feat: one header, a three-part juggling trick, a shot buried just inside the post – all without the ball touching the ground. Even now, watching the goal on the Internet, it takes at least a couple of replays to fully appreciate what has just happened. On the day of his signature goal, the new issue of *Shoot!* had found him talking about England again. 'I'm good enough and scoring goals regularly enough to win further honours,' he insisted. 'Unfortunately, a lot of it has to do with whether you are playing for a successful club.'[119]

If only, in Majorca, he'd thought more about the Kop instead of copping off.

READ ALL ABOUT IT

As attendance levels fell, the media, in all its forms, took on an ever more important role in shaping public perceptions of the modern game

Dave Russell, *Football and the English* (Carnegie Publishing, 1997)

They might not have made it often enough on to the teamsheets of England managers, but the names of George, Marsh and the like featured frequently in the planning meetings of football's editorial boards. As Steen noted, 'The most staple strewn midriffs belonged to the mavericks, the fourth estate's bread and butter.'

Football's media market had always needed its pin-ups, from the artificially coloured posters of Brylcreemed stars who adorned the pages of *Charles Buchan's Football Monthly* in the 1950s. Now, with technology allowing for a more vivid representation of the game's heroes, here was a collection of stars bright, bold and beautiful enough that your sister could appreciate them, rather than the harsh-faced warriors of yesteryear whose image could frighten the children.

Launched in 1951 by the former Arsenal and Sunderland forward, who had become an influential journalist, *Charles Buchan's Football Monthly* established itself as the first modern magazine devoted to the sport. A year later, renowned midfielder Raich Carter put his name to a weekly publication, *Soccer Star*, which continued until being incorporated into *World Soccer* in 1970. *Jimmy Hill's Football Weekly*, which began printing in 1967, followed the template of a big-name endorsement for any new publication.

But by 1971 the market was dominated by two weekly publications that had recognised an appetite for personality-led reportage ahead of facts and figures, supported by photography that gave the featured players an added dimension. *Goal*, launched by IPC in 1968, was the first weekly magazine to make the posters that could be pinned on bedroom walls as important as the words. Even the text came with a little gloss, with Bobby Charlton signed as its lead columnist and – once his own titular product had ceased to print in April 1970 – Jimmy Hill offering the same forthright opinions that featured on *The Big Match*.

Goal, though, was still trying to find a balance between the familiar design of *Football Monthly*, the need to cater to a young audience eager for access to their heroes, and the desire to be considered an authoritative voice. Barely a week went by in the six years of the publication's existence without one of its columnists or opinion-givers writing in crusading terms about the lack of goals, skill or entertainment in the modern game.

Shoot!, dropped into the market by IPC in 1969, acknowledged no such tightrope or responsibility and approached its task unashamedly as cheerleader. It was 'aimed deliberately at the young', according to former editor Peter Stewart. More photographs, shorter features, greater emphasis on design, and content driven by personality rather than issues were its distinguishing features. Glamourising the game was its mission statement. Soon, the magazine boasted England captain Bobby Moore, fellow World Cup winner Alan Ball and George Best as its columnists – although it proved to be a cut-throat business. Best was quickly replaced by Kevin Keegan as their respective stars fell and rose, while neither Moore nor Ball survived transfers out of the First Division. Ghost writer Christopher Davies, who recalled that Ball was paid 'about £50 a week', added, 'I don't recall how much notice we gave him, maybe a month or so, and he was really pissed off about it.'[120] When deposed England captain Gerry Francis was replaced by Andy Gray in 1977 he acknowledged that the magazine 'felt I'd been out of the public eye and wanted a change'.[121]

Along with its star power, *Shoot!* featured the iconic 'You Are the Ref' series, which came to be drawn by Paul Trevillion; and its colourful cardboard 'League Ladders', borrowing an idea previously used by comics such as *Tiger*, *Valiant* and others. That particular offering is one of the features remembered most fondly by former readers, even though it became a test of will to still be bothered with slotting the team tabs into position by the middle of September.

By 1971, as noted by Soccerbilia – a website dedicated to the history and cataloguing of British football magazines – the two IPC products, *Shoot!* and *Goal* were each selling 220,000 copies per week. Such publications became as much of a weekly habit among boys my age as the delivery of the weekly local paper in the days when most households still desired such a connection to their community. I remember clearly the rush to the doorstep each weekend to retrieve my copy of *Shoot!*, beginning its consumption by flicking through the colour photos before reading the features. Often the bulk would have been read before *Grandstand* began. On a slow week, it might take until the following day's *The Big Match*. And the advantage of *Shoot!* over stablemate *Goal* was that the pages were collated via a lightweight glue rather than staples, meaning that if the centre spread was destined for your wall you didn't end up with annoying holes or tears as you released it from its moorings.

The success of *Shoot!* prompted IPC to seek an even younger readership with its 1970 launch of *Scorcher*, a comic dedicated purely to football stories, although the publishers insisted on calling it a 'paper' to distinguish it from the likes of *Dandy* and *The Beano*. The strips included 'Jack of United' and 'Jimmy of City' – interwoven tales about brothers at rival clubs – 'Billy's Boots' and 'Lags Eleven', about a prison football team. The publication incorporated *Score* between 1971 and 1974, before being swallowed by *Tiger*.

Also in 1970, *Striker* and *Inside Football* entered the fray. Published by City Magazines, *Striker* attempted to combine the style of *Shoot!* (big-name columnists in Colin Bell and Peter Osgood, for example), with the comic strip stories of *Scorcher* (which were quickly dropped). Hampered by long lead times that made its content feel dated,[††] it lasted only until early 1972. For a while its name survived on the masthead of *Inside Football*, a newspaper-format publication that featured many of the day's leading football writers and numbered Bill Shankly among its columnists. Aimed at 'people who really know the game', it folded in March 1974.

With *Goal* still clinging to an increasingly outdated design and philosophy, *Shoot!* would eventually smother its rival, which disappeared during the 1974 World Cup, briefly maintaining some form of life with *And Goal* being added to the *Shoot!* title until its owners recognised that it no longer mattered.[‡‡] *Goal*'s monthly counterpart, which had dropped the Buchan name and simply become *Football Monthly* in 1972, disappeared at the same time. From the

†† Peter Osgood, for example, did not mention Chelsea's FA Cup triumph against Leeds, achieved on 29 April, until the edition dated 13 June.

‡‡ *Goal*'s final-issue advert for readers to subscribe to *Shoot!* showed commendable foresight in featuring Billy Bremner and Kevin Keegan, who would be the headline-makers in the first big domestic game to be played after the merger.

start of the 1973-74 season it had undergone an even more radical rebrand, becoming pocket-sized and changing its name to *Football Monthly Digest* in an attempt to revamp its image. The first smaller issue claimed, 'It's exciting. It's new. It's different. And we've done it this way because Soccer in the Seventies needs an approach that's a bit special.' In reality, the approach was to trot out the same tired 'We Want Goals' and 'Win Back the Fans' pieces until it folded in June 1974, citing escalating printing and distribution costs.

Marshall Cavendish published two part-works series in the decade. Its *Book of Football* spanned 75 weeks in 1971 and 1972, forming a comprehensive, colourful encyclopaedia that covered the great players, games, incidents and strategies of the sport. It also launched a notable career in football journalism and broadcasting. 'While on the dole in the early 1970s, I was tipped off that a new part-work, *Book of Football*, was launching,' recalled Sky Sports' Martin Tyler. 'In May 1971 I started a month's trial. It was a fantastic first week to be in football journalism and it was love at first sight. I lived the perfect life for two years because not having to cover weekend matches ensured I could continue playing.'[122] The smaller, even brighter, *Football Handbook* was published for 63 weeks during 1978 and 1979, including tips from the stars – Phil Neal on the nutmeg, anyone? – player interviews and features on football around the world. The most exciting element was the coloured diagram reconstructing one of the top goals of the week, complete with analysis by future England manager Graham Taylor. In the days before YouTube, this opportunity to replay events whenever you liked was ridiculously satisfying. For anyone wanting a snapshot of English football at the beginning and end of the 1970s, the respective series are well worth searching for on eBay or at programme fairs.

By the start of the 1970s, most clubs had come to realise that their fans demanded more from their match programme than team line-ups and advertisements for local businesses. They wanted to see their players projected as others were in the national magazines. Thus, home lives, families and consumer tastes became part of features that made players more than just a name and number on the back page.

The *Football League Review* had launched in 1966, an in-house promotional journal for the governing body that was given away as a free supplement in approximately two-thirds of clubs' programmes. Dave Russell called it 'a sometimes patchy and awkward read which at times revealed as much about the Football League's self-perception as it did about the deeper social and economic realities of the game.'[123] The publication, which listed Hardaker as managing editor and public relations officer, specialised in long rants in response to the latest perceived slight or factual inaccuracy in the media. These would start off with comments such as 'despite wild statements by people who should know better' or 'the whole article presented a completely distorted view'. Even Hardaker eventually admitted that the publication was 'over-sensitive'.

Alongside the anger were long small-print articles on finances and the interpretation of the laws. By the time the name was changed to *League Football* in 1972 and colour pictures of star players were added, the magazine was dying a slow death. It might have stated an intention to leave behind accusations of 'being too reactionary, insular, a platform for outdated ideas and even conceited', but it could not save itself from passing away at the end of 1974, a year that had already seen the demise of *Goal*, *Score*, *Football Monthly* and *Inside Football*.

Football League Review had claimed to be 'covering aspects of the game not offered by more commercial publications'. But the lack of quality journalism among the periodicals clearly frustrated author Peter Douglas, who made little effort to hide his disdain in his 1973 book, *The Football Industry*. Having described magazine writers as being 'acutely conscious of their inferior status', he talked about a 'fairly illiterate readership' for their products. He added, 'The pity is that the magazines are in a unique position to explore some of the wider issues of football.'[124]

One writer given the opportunity to examine the game up close and in depth was Hunter Davies, biographer of The Beatles among other subjects. The Tottenham Hotspur players were taken aback when he and his notebook arrived in their dressing-room in August 1971 with the intention of writing the inside story of the season. 'It was bizarre that the club let Hunter have so much insider access,' recalled Steve Perryman. 'It hadn't been done before and for a club that was so keen on keeping things in-house and discreet it defied belief.'[125] The result was *The Glory Game*, a classic that no self-respecting sporting bookcase should be without.

For those needing a weekly antidote to the populist style of chronicling the game, there was *Foul*, set up in 1972 by a group of Cambridge undergraduates that included future mainstream football journalist Steve Tongue, TV producer Alan Stewart and script writers Stan Hey and Andrew Nickolds. They believed that the football media lacked depth or the guts to criticise players upon whom they might be relying for their next big interview and offered their publication as a response to a 'mountain of disgust' about the state of the game. In its inaugural issue, the editors argued that 'most football material is written for males with an undemanding intellect' and added 'far more fundamental is the nest of self-interest which surrounds the game'.[126]

Viewed as football's version of *Private Eye*,[§§] its publishers accepted that they lacked the readership to enjoy the influence of its political counterpart, but it was an important precursor to the culture of fanzines that would help revolutionise football fandom in the coming decades. In its unique style, it confronted some important issues.

'Who says we are just pretty boys?' said the speech bubble coming from Bobby Moore's mouth as he apparently elbowed an opponent on the inaugural cover. In March 1973, Arsenal physiotherapist Fred Street was pictured on the front page emerging from the Highbury tunnel with a football, saying, 'Bertie says try it with this, lads.' Hardaker was a frequent target, with one column declaring, 'His most durable reason for fame is his pig-headed stupidity on most of the big soccer controversies.'[127] And as well as a 'Foul of the Month' slot there was 'Spot the Brawl', with instructions that 'all you have to do is put an X where you think the next fist will land'. A total of 34 issues were published between 1972 and 1976, the last four spread

§§ *Private Eye* itself had been satirising events in English football through the misadventures of Neasden FC, managed by 'tight-lipped, ashen-faced supremo Ron Knee, 59'.

over a year or so. The funds ran out more quickly than the editorial inspiration. 'We wanted to try to introduce more radical writing with more of a satirical edge,' said Tongue. 'It's just a shame the world wasn't quite ready for us at the time.'[128]

The proliferation of football magazines in the early 1970s served to add words to the pocket-sized images that were an increasing part of playground life. Card collecting was no new phenomenon, but the traditional collections given away with packets of cigarettes had all but disappeared immediately after the Second World War because of paper shortages. In the late 1950s and early 1960s, however, the card collection returned – now in conjunction with bubble gum and covering the whole range of popular culture, from sport to movies to television.

The next phase, the one that impacted hundreds of thousands of schoolchildren of my vintage, was the launch of the FKS *Wonderful World of Soccer Stars* sticker collections – although the sticking we had to do ourselves by applying a thin line of glue to the top of the reverse of the player picture. Launched on a limited basis in 1967-68, the collection really took off a year later, when FKS used the same album cover (a Tottenham v Sheffield Wednesday action picture) and many of the same cards. Formats of photographs varied from year to year – headshots one season, action the next – and the stickers came in packets of seven (eight in the first year). Initially, they cost an old sixpence (2½p) from the local newsagent. The thrill of ripping open a new packet and going through the 'got, got, need' ritual remains a highlight of many a childhood, not to mention the excited rush home with Wyn Davies and David Wagstaffe in your blazer pocket ready to be stuck in place while you watched *Wacky Races*.

The fact that the manufacturers would often deal with deadline-busting transfers by plonking players' heads on conveniently-kitted bodies or employ primitive painting methods to re-colour shirts and skin tones, was obvious even to an eight-year-old eye. But it mattered not. In the allotted place for each card was a basic biography of the player, accessed by lifting up the card (if you had been careful enough in applying your glue), and when you tired of trying to find the last few elusive stickers, the album contained a form that allowed collectors to pester parents into purchasing the prized pieces needed to complete the book. At the time of writing completed albums were changing hands on eBay from anything between £50 and £100, with empty, mint-condition albums going for even more, and rare unopened packets of cards fetching up to £20. It would be a hardened soul who could buy one of them without resisting the temptation to transport themselves back to the pavement outside their local sweet shop by ripping off the top to see who lurked within.

The relegation of FKS to the second division of stickers would occur when Italian company Panini set up a UK division and launched its *Football 78* collection in January of that year via a free album given away with *Shoot!* Not only were the pictures of elevated quality, but the cards had a peel-away sticky backing which eliminated the need for time-consuming gluing. The template had been created that would define sticker collecting for the next half a century.

There were other opportunities to acquire football ephemera. For a couple of years, car-owning parents were persuaded by their offspring to fill up exclusively with Esso petrol, four gallons of which would earn a silver coin to be placed into a blue mounting board. In the build-up to the 1970 World Cup these coins featured the faces of the England footballers; prior to the Centenary FA Cup Final of 1972 it was the badges of clubs who'd won the tournament. Or you could persuade the family to exchange its traditional Robertson's in favour of Hartley's New Jam, whose lids featured 12 different British footballers.

The 1970s offered a significant publishing development for those who were looking for more than pages with which they could decorate bedrooms or pocket-sized faces to fill an album. Launched in the first summer of the decade, *Rothmans Football Yearbook* would offer a build-up of blue spines on sporting bookshelves to complement the yellow of the *Wisden Cricketers' Almanack*. It was a comparison that the publishers, Queen Anne Press, were happy to invite. 'For many years, *Wisden* has held pride of place among the many fine books annually written for and about cricket,' wrote FIFA president Sir

Stanley Rous in the first edition. 'I believe that *Rothmans Football Yearbook* could fill this gap in football literature each year.'

It proved to be no idle boast. Even the opening message by cigarette company Rothmans – whose name remained on the book until 2002 – proved difficult to argue with, capturing the essence of the publication's success. 'The facts and statistics of a game are not dry bones to be left mouldering,' said the sponsor's foreword. 'They are things that jog the memory.'

Pocket-sized handbooks such as the *Playfair Football Annual* and the *News of the World Football Annual* had long since offered recaps of previous seasons, but the defining feature of the new larger format publication would be its grid of player appearances for all the English and Scottish League teams – although that was absent from the first edition. Instead the book laboriously reproduced team line-ups for each match, a space consuming exercise that didn't make for easy fact-checking, especially considering the publication's argument that there was 'an urgent need for a reference book on the subject of soccer'. The book, with an editorial board that originally included former and future Sports Minister Denis Howell, Sir Matt Busby, David Coleman and Jimmy Hill, quickly settled into a format that became a must-have item for fans and journalists when each August came around, including historical international line-ups, details of European and global tournaments, amateur football and the popular daily diary of the previous season – a valuable tool for the book researchers of the future.

Then there was the complete fixture list for the season, vital if, like me, you intended to stage the entire First Division campaign on the Subbuteo pitch. Created in the late 1940s by Peter Adolph after being demobbed from the RAF, the tabletop game in which players were encouraged to 'flick to kick', was entering its peak years as the 1970s rolled around. The introduction of heavier three-dimensional 'OO scale' plastic figures rather than flat cardboard players had added a new dimension of skill, while moulded plastic rods replaced slot-in pieces of wire to make the goalkeepers more robust. A wider selection of teams was now available, offered in special presentation boxes, while a whole range of stadium paraphernalia could be purchased as accessories. Each season Subbuteo would release its team list, which grew from 81 in 1971-72 to 165 only two seasons later. At the end of the decade, there were 322 teams being manufactured, featuring sides from all corners of the globe.

An international tournament was staged in August 1970 at London's Savoy Hotel for the John Waddington World Cup trophy, with West Germany emerging victorious from the 13 competing teams. To celebrate its oversized and accessory-packed Munich World Series Edition in 1974, a second World Cup was staged, with England reaching the final. There was a limit to the game's realism, after all.

Inevitably, others looked to capitalise on the potential of tabletop football games, but Subbuteo spent the 1970s seeing them off. Table Association Football (TAF 4-2-4) was a stilted game, where players were moved into designated tactical positions on the field and passes were made by pushing or flicking the ball with the flat or angled surface of the hefty base. The game had been perfected over a period of 20 years by Guernsey signwriter Tom Waterman, who had already invented baseball, motor racing and war games. 'My claim is I can reproduce football tactics on the table more closely than any game yet invented,' he said. A good-looking game, my own version featured the England and Scotland teams, and when I wrote to the manufacturers to complain that they were more breakable than Subbuteo I was sent not only replacement players, but the new Arsenal Double-winning team, whose detail included one forward – obviously Charlie George – with long hair down his back.

The novelty of Striker – later known as Super Striker – quickly wore off. Introduced by Parker Games early in the decade, its distinctive feature was player figures who kicked the ball when you pressed down the heads, their moveable legs being operated by a rod and spring. Played on a pitch enclosed by a plastic fence, the lack of depth in a five-a-side game was never going to satisfy those nerds like me intent on constructing entire seasons with player bookings and injuries, all recorded on Rothmans-style grids. There was a similar 11-a-side version called Big League, produced by Chad Valley, but that required you to paint the players yourself and then pull back and release the leg to kick. Casdon Soccer involved twiddling knobs to make the players kick, but that quickly got old, too. There is a reason why Subbuteo kept us playing for hours on end and has survived into the high-definition exact-likeness video age.

Football consumerism in the early years of the decade also catered for those who wished to preserve memories of their favourite matches rather than recreate alternate realities. At the start of the Seventies, £2 would buy you a vinyl LP recording of the BBC Radio commentary of your team's FA Cup Final appearance, or other famous games, such as the 1966 World Cup Final and 1968 European Cup Final. If you were someone who was into home movies, you could acquire 8mm or 16mm cine films of big matches, ranging from £4.20 for a silent movie to £14.50 for Super 8 footage with sound. Or if your technology was more basic, approximately 50p would buy you a selection of colour slides of star players that you could project on to your living-room wall. It was 'the collecting craze that's sweeping Britain', according to its punchy advertising.

A further opportunity to relive some of the great moments in English football was presented by the opening in 1971 of the sport's first Hall of Fame, housed over two floors in a building in London's Baker Street. Along with the historical exhibits, a group of 24 men were elected by a panel to be the Football Hall of Fame's first inductees. Yet if it were not for personal memory of a visit and possession of the original promotional brochure, it would be difficult to prove existence of the place, which disappeared as quickly as it arrived.

A new Hall of Fame was established in 2002 – part of the National Football Museum based originally in Preston and later in Manchester. It managed to rewrite history by including only seven of those honoured back in 1971 on its list of founding inductees: Matt Busby, Dixie Dean, Duncan Edwards, Tom Finney, Stanley Matthews, Alf Ramsey and Billy Wright. Of the missing 17, seven have been subsequently inducted at the time of writing.

3

THE EMPIRE STRIKES BACK

REFEREE (ERIC ARMISTEAD): What we are about to witness is known as a football match – not the beginning of World War Three, not the destruction of the human race; a football match. In it, each team will attempt to score more goals than the other. That will be done by trying to kick the ball in the net, as opposed to kicking other people in the crotch.

***Another Sunday and Sweet FA* (Jack Rosenthal; Granada Television, 1972)**

THE REFEREES were the only ones aware of the ticking timebomb in their top pockets; the memo they'd received after the first weekend of the 1971-72 season. A day after the postman came calling, the first midweek fixtures of the new term marked the beginning of what the media quickly labelled 'The Refs' Revolution'. In an attempt to offer some protection to the ball players in danger of being kicked out of the game, match officials booked 32 players in 15 Tuesday night games – a ludicrously modest number by 21st-century standards, but enough to create talk of apocalypse at the time.

At Portman Road, six were cautioned in Ipswich Town's 3-1 win over Coventry City. 'The game won't continue if they keep booking people like this,' said Ipswich manager Bobby Robson. Wednesday night saw seven players booked as Tottenham Hotspur and Newcastle United drew 0-0 at White Hart Lane, after which Newcastle captain Bobby Moncur commented, 'We will be going out there with handbags soon. The referees are turning it into a game for cissies.' Elsewhere that night, three players were sent off and 38 more booked. Under a back-page headline that read, 'Soccer on the brink of revolt,' the *Daily Mirror* asked, 'What is football trying to do to itself?' and blamed the 'lunatic decision to operate football to the letter of the law'.

Spurs manager Bill Nicholson insisted, 'It is time we were told what was going on. It seems the Football League are giving the referees books and pencils and trying to get them to frighten the players. We have been told nothing.'

It was that which angered so many. There had been no warning from the Football League, no sharing the intention to apply laws more rigidly or any collective discussion of how all could operate more effectively within the new environment of 'zero tolerance'. The League's approach, well intentioned as it might have been, was akin to the police waiting on a blind corner with their radar guns without having published a new speed limit. All the clubs could find when they looked back through official correspondence was an apparently innocuous pre-season reminder from the FA about fair play and bookable offences, which they had been urged to pin on changing-room walls. Yet Football League secretary Alan Hardaker offered the justification that 'the impact on the game was far greater than if the directive had been announced months earlier and then watered down and conditioned by argument and criticism'.[129]

Newspaper headlines on the first Saturday of the season had warned of a desire to curb tackles from behind, the offence highlighted most often when referees had been canvassed during the summer. Hardaker had warned of a 'campaign' to come and there had been enough of a sense that something was afoot for renowned Liverpool hard man Tommy Smith to be asked for his opinion. 'If you're going to let forwards use their assets – speed and ball control – you must let defenders use theirs, hard tackling and strength,' he stated. 'If I started playing like a fairy – not tackling and showing off the old ball control – the Liverpool fans would soon have a go at me.'[130] No forward had endured greater physical punishment over the previous five years than World Cup winner Geoff Hurst, who felt that referees 'must show a greater awareness of the criminal tactics employed by some defenders'.[131]

The 'clean-up' operation, as it became known, took shape on that first Sunday when match officials were summoned to meetings all over the country and told to expect further instruction. It arrived 24 hours later when a memorandum, dated 16 August, dropped on the doormat of every referee and linesman. Along with guidelines on how to interpret offsides, offences against the goalkeeper and time-wasting, there were the following significant sections:

> DELIBERATE HANDLING OR CATCHING THE BALL
>
> If a player deliberately catches or handles the ball to prevent an opponent gaining an advantage which, in the referee's opinion, would reasonably have occurred in the normal pattern of play, then the referee shall deem it to be ungentlemanly conduct. And in addition to the direct free-kick... he shall caution the offending player.
>
> DELIBERATE OBSTRUCTION
>
> If a player deliberately interposes his body to prevent an opponent gaining an advantage... then the referee should deem it to be ungentlemanly conduct and he shall caution the offending player.
>
> DELIBERATE TRIPPING
>
> If a player deliberately trips an opponent to prevent him gaining an advantage... then the referee shall deem it to be ungentlemanly conduct and in addition to the direct free-kick (or penalty) which he shall award for the offence, he will caution the offending player. The above three offences are examples of what are being termed 'professional fouls.'

The memorandum highlighted a perceived tendency to favour the caution of players for dissent ahead of punishing them for acts of foul play, such as contact with the man when tackling with a raised foot or with both feet together. There was also a specific section on the tackle from behind:

> If the ball is played without the player first touching an opponent's legs, this is allowed. If the opponent's legs are touched first, a direct free-kick will be awarded... If there is no clear intention to play the ball, a direct free-kick will be awarded if the player is tripped. (Note: It is suggested that it is almost impossible to tackle fairly from behind *through a player's legs*). For this offence (d), a referee shall caution the player in addition to awarding the free-kick.

The measures were clearly intended to address the win-at-all-costs approach pervading the English game, although Norman Burtenshaw, who had refereed the latest FA Cup Final, felt it was games involving teams striving for the top level where intervention was most urgently required. 'The games I hated refereeing were those involving the top four clubs in the Second Division,' he said. 'Often those would be kicking matches.' And he was not afraid to cite culprits. 'I used to shudder when I saw big fellows like Duncan Forbes, the Norwich centre-half, go into tackles from behind. Most central defenders were at it. Bobby Bell when he was at Ipswich; Derek Jefferson, Ipswich and later Wolves; John McGrath of Southampton; John Roberts, Arsenal and later Birmingham; Denis Smith of Stoke. You couldn't blame them. They were doing their job.' He also praised Leeds left-back Terry Cooper and Peter Rodrigues of Sheffield Wednesday as men 'who could tackle from the side and pluck the ball away without first touching the players' legs'.[132]

Burtenshaw, who had reported the entire Benfica team for dissent during their 6-2 defeat at Arsenal in a pre-season challenge match, was sorry the referees had not initiated the new measures themselves, while Jack Taylor, the Wolverhampton butcher who would referee the 1974

World Cup Final, said the campaign was necessary 'not only to stop the bully and the cheat, but also to restore the referee as a meaningful representative of authority'. He admitted, 'Matches were getting out of hand. The clever players were being kicked to death and referees nailed to the wall every week.'[133]

Given his reluctance to brandish his notebook in the 1970 FA Cup Final, it was no surprise that the retired Eric Jennings was an opponent of the new methods. 'I am disgusted at the militant approach which League referees are being forced to adopt this season,' he said. 'I would never have carried out the present instructions.'[134]

By the middle of December, more than 1,000 players had been booked. When Brian Daniels failed to take a name in a Fulham–QPR match a fan sent him a 'Get Well' card. It was, suggested football historian David Russell, a reflection of a moral conversation that extended beyond the playing field. 'In an age in which many commentators demanded clear public displays of discipline in all public areas and where, in the football world, links between violence on and off the pitch were always likely to be made, officials were forced to make a more "formal" approach.'[135]

Such rigidity, however, was not welcomed by those who feared the erosion of the crunching tackle – a defining English characteristic that technically-advanced nations such as Holland and West Germany would have mocked. 'It seems to me that the game is rapidly becoming foreign to all we've ever known,' said Bobby Charlton. 'Physical contact is what makes our game the tremendous spectacle it is.'[136] Crystal Palace chairman Arthur Wait called for the resignation of Hardaker and the Football League management committee, arguing, 'If the people responsible for this policy want to watch continental stuff they should go there. I know some of the country's players, when you see the length of their hair, look like girls, but don't make them play like it.'

More modern thinkers suggested that the complaints were loudest from those with most to lose. 'It's the player who goes out to intimidate an opponent who will suffer,' said England forward Francis Lee, who would end the season as the First Division's leading scorer. 'I believe only the isolated few are moaning about it.'[137]

And *Goal* columnist Ken Jones, a former professional player turned journalist, noted, 'There are one or two who aren't capable of doing anything apart from kicking lumps off others. I think we all know who they are. It will be interesting to see how long they survive.'[138] Some of those players resorted to fighting against suspensions caused by the referees' new instructions, forcing Vernon Stokes, chairman of the FA's disciplinary commission, to promise, 'We will work through the night if necessary to get through all the appeals.'

Sheffield United's Trevor Hockey – once described by *Goal* as having 'Castro's beard, Geronimo's headband, McCartney's hair and Popeye's muscles' – would break ranks with the grievances of the hard men when he stated, 'You are still allowed to tackle – now you have to time your tackle accurately or get booked. This is a frightening thing and can inhibit players.'[139]

The refereeing debate at least served to divert the sporting public's attention away from the England cricket team's first-ever defeat on home soil by India and Virginia Wade's failure to win a vital match in tennis's Wightman Cup against a 16-year-old American schoolgirl called Chris Evert. And less than a week after the newspapers' hysterical response to the start of the referees' campaign, the *Daily Mirror* reported on an evening where seven games produced only four bookings by suggesting 'players have learned not to back-chat the referee, nor to trip up their fellow workers'.

It was a premature conclusion. On the last day of August, Wolves centre-forward and PFA chairman Derek Dougan reacted to having his name taken against Crystal Palace by saying, 'If this continues, we will have 85 minutes of stoppages and five minutes of football. It is imperative that we get around the table and talk with the League and FA as soon as possible.' Several weeks into the season it was, however, becoming clear that, like it or not, English football was a safer environment. As Brian James would write in *Rothmans Football Yearbook*'s summation of the season, 'It is impossible to doubt that a saner, more just, style of football began to evolve.'

The experience of West Bromwich Albion centre-forward Jeff Astle was that teams were simply packing the penalty area instead of kicking forwards, thus making goal-scoring even more difficult. But the majority view was reflected by Leeds United forward Peter Lorimer, who believed that 90 per cent of strikers had benefitted, and West Ham United's Trevor Brooking, who noticed defenders hesitating before trying to take the ball from him.

Watford manager George Kirby went as far as trying to entice Jimmy Greaves out of premature retirement. 'Jimmy's decision to retire was forced on him by the sort of tackling that was going on and the defensive tactics,' he said – although not entirely accurately. While Greaves would remain outside the game, battling far more serious personal problems than a boot up the backside as he slid into the grip of alcoholism, former England team-mate George Eastham, the slender midfielder, was enticed back to Stoke City from South Africa, where he had been player-manager of Hellenic.

Overall, there appeared to be acceptance that the aims of the clampdown were valid. Even Cliff Lloyd, secretary of the PFA, admitted that 'the game can only be better for the removal of the tackle from behind'. Most remained miffed, however, that they had not been party to the campaign from day one.

Meanwhile, some felt that the referees were milking their moment in the spotlight. The advent of regularly televised football had helped create personalities of the leading match officials, whose decisions were now debated on screen as well as in the pub. Arthur Ellis, the former referee now officiating BBC's *It's A Knockout*, was no longer the only instantly recognisable member of his profession. Viewers were familiar with characters such as the stout and balding Roger Kirkpatrick – frequently likened to Dickens's Mr Pickwick – who would sprint on to the field, usually to great cheers, and was prone to exaggerated mimicking of players' fouls when awarding free-kicks. A director in a women's hosiery and fashion business, another trademark was his burst of running backwards as fast as his little legs would carry him. On one such occasion Chelsea midfielder Alan Birchenall couldn't resist sticking out a foot to send him crashing to the ground. 'Managers have got to succeed, players have got to succeed,' Kirkpatrick said. 'The referee is caught in the cauldron.

I believe a referee's job is to get the game going in the best possible atmosphere.'[140]

Then there was the irritatingly flashy Clive 'The Book' Thomas; and Gordon Hill, renowned as the players' favourite – mostly, it seemed, because he swore at them as much as they did at him. Hill's preference for industrial language over the taking of names didn't always endear him to those running the game. Hardaker said that 'Hill's style was fine so far as his own matches were concerned, but he made life difficult for others who refereed according to the book'.[141] Thomas and Hill, along with Burtenshaw, Taylor and Pat Partridge were among the first referees to discover that their fame created a market for their autobiographies.

According to Eamon Dunphy, in his 1973-74 diary *Only a Game?*, 'It is one thing that everyone in the game agrees on – the inefficiency of the referees.' He believed that his fellow professionals shared a frustration that after all their hard work and preparation 'some man can come along and on some whim he just destroys everything'. Dunphy concluded, 'You have no respect for the man, you know he doesn't know the game, that he is basically not equipped technically to do the job he is doing.'[142]

The 108 referees on the Football League list for the controversial 1971-72 season included a wide range of mostly white-collar professionals, with an abundance of teachers, salesmen and engineers of various descriptions. Calls for these men to become full-time, and the recruitment of former players to join them, became loudly discussed themes. Alan Ball had said before the season, 'I wouldn't mind becoming a referee just as long as it was a professional occupation. Until that happens, I can't see professional footballers ever thinking of becoming referees.'[143]

Tommy Smith was among those who felt that 'we would have better understanding from ex-professionals'.[144] The trouble, he said, was that 'they're not part of this exclusive club of football players … they seem to want to treat you like kids.'[145] Peter Osgood, whose lengthy suspension early in 1971 prompted him to say that 'some referees are diabolical', offered a similar opinion. 'The trouble with referees today is they don't see enough of the game.'[146]

Jimmy Hill believed that events had 'brought into sharp relief the referees who can't control a game' because they were 'lacking leadership and personality'. His suggestion to the Football League was to 'recruit ex-professional players under the age of 40 and put them immediately on a refereeing course'.[147] Yet recently-retired official Jim Finney argued that the introduction of full-time referees would rob the role of those who ran their own businesses or enjoyed successful careers that they were not inclined to relinquish. It would result in diminishing standards, he said.

Ironically, an advocate for former players becoming full-time referees was Stoke City manager Tony Waddington, whose team would suffer when ex-Bolton Wanderers player Bob Mathewson was responsible for one of 1971-72's most disputed decisions. Stoke were drawing their FA Cup semi-final replay against Arsenal 1-1 at Goodison Park when Charlie George looked suspiciously offside in delivering a cross for John Radford to score the winner. The truth, according to Stoke fans, was that linesman Mathewson, who would go on to referee the infamous 1974 FA Charity Shield, mistook the white coat of a programme seller for a white-shirted Stoke defender. It was still being disputed in 2014, when the *Stoke Sentinel* said, 'There is conjecture on this claim, however. The bloke in the white coat might have been selling peanuts or ice cream.' Hardaker reckoned that Waddington never again pestered him about converting ex-players into match officials.

Few people ever bothered to ask the current referees what they wanted. It was not until 1974 that a magazine survey of four top officials – Taylor, Mathewson, Ken Burns and Gordon Kew – found unanimous opposition to becoming full-time professionals. And Mathewson said, 'I don't think [former players] necessarily make better referees. There is no substitute for experience at junior level.'[148]

The light at the end of autumn 1971's tunnel of threats and rhetoric appeared when FA secretary Denis Follows announced a summit meeting on 7 October. PFA representatives gathered in London with officials of the FA and Football League, the Association of Football League Referees and Linesmen and the Secretaries and Managers

Association. It was only the second time in 108 years of organised football in England that members of all those bodies had been brought together. A statement issued after two and a half hours of talks said there had been unanimous agreement that the bodies 'should consider a suggestion for a committee of study – without executive power – to examine such matters put forward for discussions by the parties concerned.' Not exactly the most stirring action plan. Meanwhile, players were denied the amnesty they had sought for their early-season bookings. But the meeting was harmonious enough to provoke a vast change in the attitude of Dougan, who described it as 'a marvellous step forward' and foresaw 'more understanding between players and referees'.

Hardaker remarked that the game had been given a much-needed cold shower, trumpeting, 'Somewhere, sometime the people who believe have got to stand up and be counted.' And, in the achievement of 35-year-old Eastham in the final of that season's League Cup, he would be offered the most perfect vindication of his stance.

The introduction of the League Cup had been one of the defining elements of Hardaker's 15 years in his post. A former Hull City reserve, he had worked as a mayoral secretary in Hull and Portsmouth, either side of a wartime spent as a naval officer, before he joined the Football League in 1951. Having been led to believe that the position of secretary would be his within six months, he had to wait until the early days of 1957 to move into the office previously occupied by Fred Howarth. He remained football's most dominant administrative figure throughout the 1970s, a man with a reputation for getting his own way and little regard for whom he fought to get it. Lord William Westwood, who became Football League president in 1974, described him as 'forthright, honest and sometimes blunt', but insisted, 'He is not a dictator.'[149]

Speaking in his own defence, Hardaker said, 'There are many people in football who do not like me but who still believe I am honest.' Describing himself as 'a paid servant' of the game, he admitted, 'It has never been part of my brief to please people.'[150]

Despite resistance, he had forced the League Cup into existence in 1960, partly to meet clubs' increasing demands to play floodlit football and also to compensate for what he and then-League president Joe Richards forecast would be a reduction in fixtures as part of their 'Pattern for Football'. The plan, which called for five divisions of 20 teams, was eventually voted out at the League's AGM in 1963.

The closing rounds of the 1971-72 competition would produce a thrilling series of matches that reflected perfectly the kind of football envisaged when the referees' memo was typed up in the Football League's art deco headquarters in Lytham St Annes, down the Fylde coast from Eastham's hometown of Blackpool. The semi-finalists were perhaps the four First Division teams who best embodied the 'spirit of the game' that administrators yearned for – which might have explained why none were serious title contenders.

Stoke were drawn to face West Ham United, teams whose respective managers, Waddington and Ron Greenwood, shared a philosophy that emphasised attack and aesthetics over structure and strategy. Meanwhile, Chelsea, bidding to win a third cup competition in three seasons,* and Tottenham, the League Cup holders, offered the often brilliant, rarely consistent, brand of football that made them more dangerous in one-off games than over the course of an arduous League programme. Between them all they produced an epic series of semi-final matches.

West Ham began what became a marathon series against Stoke by showing the kind of resilience and fortitude for which they were not exactly renowned in coming from behind to win the first leg 2-1 away from home. Such was their resolve that Bobby Moore was cautioned for a deliberate trip. At Upton Park a week later, Stoke centre-forward John Ritchie sent the tie into extra-time. With only four minutes of the night's two hours of action remaining, Hammers winger Harry Redknapp went down under a challenge from goalkeeper Gordon Banks and referee Keith Walker pointed to the penalty spot. Hurst, as usual, moved towards the ball with fierce intent and smashed it. Banks flung himself to his right, stuck up his left arm like a periscope

* Chelsea had beaten Real Madrid 2-1 in a replay in Athens to add the European Cup Winners' Cup to their FA Cup triumph. Many fans had slept on beaches while they waited 48 hours for goals by John Dempsey and Peter Osgood to overcome the six-time champions of Europe after an initial 1-1 draw.

and found enough strength in his wrist to keep Hurst's effort out of the net. Were it not for Guadalajara in the summer of 1970, it might have been the save of his career. Greenwood ended up suggesting that perhaps someone other than Hurst, who had beaten Banks with a penalty in the first leg, should have taken this one, to which Hurst countered, 'No one else could have taken it. As it was, half of them couldn't find the nerve to watch.'[151] That an exciting replay at Hillsborough ended goalless was in no small part due to more Banks brilliance.

The most dramatic action was yet to come. At Old Trafford three weeks later, Moore volunteered to take the goalkeeper's jersey when Bobby Ferguson was injured after 15 minutes, designated stand-in Clyde Best having told team-mates he could not face it. Moore survived Mike Bernard hitting the post and then had to face up to the same player's penalty kick. He flopped to his right and parried it, but Bernard netted the rebound. Bonds fired West Ham level from 25 yards and Ferguson ended his 20-minute recuperation by returning to the field. Brooking's sweeping volley put West Ham 2-1 up, only for Stoke skipper Peter Dobing to equalise before the end of a breathless first half. Five minutes after the break, Terry Conroy converted a cross and Stoke were in sight of the first major trophy in a century of existence.

Chelsea's progress past Tottenham into the final had been less protracted, but similarly dramatic. A late penalty by John Hollins earned them a 3-2 win at home, but that was nothing compared to the excitement two weeks later at White Hart Lane in a contest that, according to *The Times*, 'held a near 53,000 crowd in a hypnotized state of concentration'. Hudson remembered that it 'made the first encounter look like a reserve match'.[152] Chivers scored with a volley, his 30th goal of a season that was barely into January, and Chris Garland levelled with a long-range left-foot strike. Hudson's handball allowed Spurs to take a 2-1 lead via a Martin Peters penalty, levelling the tie at 4-4 on aggregate. Again, Chelsea scored inside the final seconds, earning a place in the final when Hudson's free-kick from the left was diverted into his own net by Cyril Knowles.

Enough people appeared sufficiently enraptured with Chelsea's progress to send their jolly singalong, 'Blue is The Colour', to No.5 in the UK charts. But two years on from playing the role of nation's sweethearts in the FA Cup Final, Chelsea now found themselves cast as villains. Even Osgood had once had a poster of Eastham on his bedroom wall. 'What sheltered housing they sprung him from I'll never know,' he would joke. 'I didn't even know he was still alive, let alone still playing.'[153]

'Any neutral in the stadium today must want something to happen for George Eastham,' said ITV commentator Brian Moore after Hardaker, Shipman, Burnley chairman Bob Lord and their overseas guests – each wearing a trilby or bowler hat – had greeted the teams to the field like members of the politburo lined up on the balcony of the Kremlin. More appropriate for the occasion was the way Hudson immediately looked at home on the field – lush and green this time – that he'd missed out on two years earlier.

Yet it was Stoke who took the lead after five minutes via Conroy's ginger head. Osgood swept the ball in while lying on the ground on the stroke of half-time, but with 17 minutes remaining Ritchie headed down, Jimmy Greenhoff forced a save from Peter Bonetti, and Eastham prodded in from inside the six-yard box. 'The old man has done it,' shouted Moore. 'And if that happens to be the winner it really is a storybook come true.' Stoke held on for the first trophy in their 108-year history, the game described by *The Times* as 'a triumph for emotion rather than justice'. Even Bill Shankly was moved to write, 'I fancied Chelsea yet was so pleased for Stoke when the result came through. There was a lot of sentiment on their side.'[154]

For Chelsea, defeat at Wembley one week after a surprising FA Cup exit at Second Division Orient marked the end of their spell as one of the most dangerous and exciting teams in the country. The break-up was on the way. Meanwhile, *Rothmans Football Yearbook* heralded Stoke's success as 'a significant omen of improving times' for the English game, while those going on holiday with that year's *Shoot! Summer Special* in their luggage were able to read that 'even if the game hasn't stepped all that far forward, it's certainly stopped taking disastrous steps back.'

But when the decade moved past its mid-point it was clear that the playing fields of England were not entirely free of the tackle from behind. At regular intervals, there were calls for a return to the unforgiving days of 1971. Early in 1977, Kevin Keegan feared that 'the curse of English soccer is back – worse than ever' and demanded 'a renewal of the campaign'.[155]

THE BEST YEARS OF OUR LIVES

BRIAN'S MUM: He's not the Messiah, he's a very naughty boy.

***Monty Python's Life of Brian* (HandMade Films, Python [Monty] Pictures, 1979)**

For observers desiring a return to the good old days of carefree football, the prospect in the first half of 1971-72 that Manchester United could be champions once more was exactly the sign they had been seeking. The club might have undergone all kinds of change since their last League title in 1967, but the name alone was enough to excite the romantics – especially with George Best offering a final extended reminder of the young man who took the game by storm through the mid and late 1960s.

Manager Frank O'Farrell, less prone to hysteria than some of his First Division counterparts, had spoken of 'rampant fear running through dressing-rooms', in the wake of the referees' clampdown, but added, 'There is no manager worth his salt who does not want the very few thugs weeded out and the game kept clean.' Of course, he possessed the most obvious beneficiary of a stricter approach to the application of the laws, which made it somewhat ironic that the biggest furore in the early days of the purge surrounded the sending off of Best.

On the first Wednesday of the season, Burtenshaw gave the managers of Chelsea and United his usual warning about foul language. 'Protests (by word or action) against referees will result in a caution,' the officials' memorandum had said. There was no dissent when United had an early goal disallowed, but they were not so forgiving when the home side scored in the 41st minute, claiming Osgood had fouled a United defender when setting up Tommy Baldwin. Willie Morgan protested at length, talking his way into the referee's book. As Morgan was walking away from the scene of his crime, leaving Burtenshaw standing in front of Stamford Bridge's main stand, Best approached with the words, 'You are a fucking disgrace.' Best's defence was that he had been talking to Morgan.

'Best was looking right at me,' Burtenshaw would argue. 'Morgan was some distance away, walking in the opposite direction. There was no doubt in my mind that Best was talking to me.'[156] Best looked astonished when Burtenshaw ordered him off. He sat down and held his head before being accompanied to the dressing-room by coach Malcolm Musgrave, an image that made the front page of *The Times.*

After United had achieved a commendable 3-2 win, O'Farrell felt Best's dismissal 'underlines the problems facing football'. He said, 'I'd seen the bruises and swellings on his feet. The fellows who had given Best those bumps and bruises were not booked.' With a suspended sentence still hanging over him from previous misdemeanours, Best prepared for an appearance before the FA hierarchy, but his possible ban was seen to be damaging to football at a time when it was taking dramatic steps to improve its product. When Best ran rings round the Crystal Palace defence two days before his hearing several weeks later, Palace chairman Arthur Wait pleaded, 'We cannot afford to have great entertainers like Best sitting on the sidelines. All I know is that we had 15,000 on the gate today. Best put them there.'

Enjoying his best spell of form for at least two years, Best had scored twice and set up another goal in a 3-1 win against West Bromwich Albion to give United three wins and a draw from their first four games. Gerry Harrison observed in *The Times* that 'such are the fruits of new leadership, the new referees' policy and the old George Best'.

'No one is getting the flags out yet,' warned O'Farrell. 'Our enthusiasm is tempered by the sobering thought that the knife which was thrown on to the pitch, causing Old Trafford to be closed, has cost the club £20,000.' Ordered by the League to play their first two home games at neutral venues because of that incident at the end of the previous season, United not only had to pay Liverpool and Stoke City to use their grounds, they had to compensate Everton because the Goodison Park crowd on the day after United beat Arsenal at Anfield fell below a pre-agreed figure of 46,000. 'It seems a bit harsh that clubs can be punished to this extent for the despicable act of some unknown idiot,' continued O'Farrell.

An articulate Irishman, strong-principled, honest and firm, O'Farrell had just masterminded Leicester City's Second Division title triumph when he was summoned to Old Trafford. He had been at Filbert Street since December 1968, having previously been in charge at Torquay United and, before that, Southern League Weymouth. At Leicester, he inherited a team that had won only four out of 22 League games, but by tightening up the defence he led them to the FA Cup Final. Avoiding relegation, however, proved beyond him. Their return to the First Division reaffirmed his credentials and he was appointed by United after a six-month spell in which Busby had taken over team affairs once more following the demotion of Wilf McGuinness.

McGuinness had been promoted from youth-team coach at the end of the 1968-69 season, at the age of 31. Busby, with his 60th birthday approaching, had chosen to 'move upstairs' after finding that administrative matters were taking him away from the club's training ground at The Cliff. No more was he able to rush though his paperwork by 11am and change into his tracksuit. At one point during their season as European champions, United had even been in danger of descending into a relegation struggle. Such a plight would have been unthinkable earlier in the club's 24 years under the genial son of a Scottish miner, a man who won five League Championships and made 'Manchester United' the two best-known words in the English language in some parts of the world.

Burnley's Jimmy Adamson, Celtic's Jock Stein and even Don Revie were touted for the United job before McGuinness was appointed, receiving confirmation of his new role only two hours before the scheduled media announcement. McGuinness had been at the club since signing as a 15-year-old schoolboy wing-half and had won two England caps before his career was ended by a broken leg. But most thought United would go for a personality to match the stature of the club, someone undaunted by the mighty trinity of Charlton, Best and Law.

McGuinness was never sure exactly where the demarcation line was drawn between the training ground and the office of general manager Busby, particularly in the area of transfers and player contracts. Nor was it always obvious to the fans who was in charge. When visitors to Old Trafford opened their match programmes, it was 'Sir Matt's Column' that greeted them. McGuinness had no voice in the publication.

McGuinness's first season brought a disappointing League position and semi-final defeats in both domestic cup competitions. United's FA Cup run featured a revenge victory over Manchester City, their conquerors in the League Cup, and an 8-2 victory over Northampton Town in the fifth round in which Best, in his first game back from a month's suspension after knocking the ball out of referee Jack Taylor's hands, scored six times.

There were signs of ambition leaking out of the club once the European Cup had been won. Instead of marking the beginning of a great new era, as would Liverpool's triumph in the competition nine years later, United's realisation of Busby's dream precipitated a slump. An injection of new players would have helped. World Cup hero Alan Ball and Wales centre-half Mike England might have ended up at Old Trafford rather than Everton and Spurs had United been more aggressive in the transfer market. Instead, the old guard of Busby's side, notably defenders like Bill Foulkes, Shay Brennan and Tony Dunne, saw their places going to untested youngsters like Paul Edwards and Steve James and former Arsenal centre-back Ian Ure, signed for £80,000. 'They were buying a pup,' admitted Ure, who was 'taking pills like sweeties' for an injured knee. 'You didn't advertise it if you weren't right, but Arsenal must have known and they kept quiet.'[157] The only significant signing in that period was Burnley winger Morgan, a talented player saddled forever with comparisons to Best.

McGuinness attempted to assign specific roles to players, rather than adopting the free-and-easy approach that had been the hallmark of Busby's teams. It was, of course, the modern way, but McGuinness's diagrams on blackboards proved less effective than Busby's ability to inspire players to give their best effort. At least he could not be accused of lacking bravery, dropping Charlton, Law and Foulkes three games into his reign. 'He dropped everybody,' recalled Morgan, 'to make a point. He was infantile in his approach. If you got caught with your hands in your pockets you had to do ten press-ups.' According to Morgan, it even applied to Charlton, dressed in a suit on a cold, muddy day. 'I think Wilf got sacked the day after.'[158]

By Boxing Day 1970, after a 4-4 draw against Derby County, United decided they had slipped far enough. McGuinness was informed that Busby was taking charge once more and the team duly climbed the table to finish eighth. As results improved, goalkeeper Alex Stepney, restored to the team after McGuinness had preferred Jimmy Rimmer, explained, 'The lads have so much respect for the boss that once he took over they had to pull out that bit extra.'

Such comments did not portend well for O'Farrell, who accepted the United position after Busby attempted to pay him less than the £15,000 per year chairman Louis Edwards confirmed was on offer. Admitting to being taken aback by the sheer size of Old Trafford, O'Farrell took a significant stand that McGuinness had never dared. Having shown O'Farrell to a small office at United's training ground at The Cliff, Busby announced that he was retaining the manager's office. 'Matt, that's not right and it's not going to look right,' O'Farrell fired back. 'The press have been speculating that nobody will come here while you are hanging on to the manager's office.'

'OK,' a reluctant Busby replied. 'I'll move my stuff out.'[159]

Yet O'Farrell was no tough guy. Stepney suggested, 'There were people who knew Frank well who felt that he was more cut out for the priesthood than for a career in football ... Frank was a very proper, circumspect man.'[160]

If the deeply religious O'Farrell needed divine assistance as he tackled his task, he received it in the play of Best. Collectively, United were performing better than for some time, but they had not suddenly gone from also-rans to the 1968 team re-born. Best's form was the big difference. Either side of United's defeat at Everton – their only loss in the first 13 League games – Best scored their only goals against Wolverhampton Wanderers and Ipswich Town and then came the game in which he tore Palace apart.

On 13 September, the FA disciplinary commission sat at the Great Western Hotel near Paddington and watched witnesses placing Subbuteo players on a field to indicate the positions of the relevant parties in the Stamford Bridge incident. 'The commission, after hearing all of the evidence, are not satisfied beyond all reasonable doubt that George Best directed the words complained of to the referee,' was the verdict. 'But they were contrary to Rule 12 and would call for severe punishment in view of the pre-match talk given by the referee.' The sending off was justified, they ruled, but no further punishment was required. A furious Burtenshaw felt the League had missed a chance to emphasise its commitment to better conduct. One unnamed referee was quoted as saying, 'The FA have let us down completely. It makes us look like complete mugs.'

Best promised to control his temper and returned to wreaking havoc on First Division defences. He celebrated his reprieve with a hat-trick against West Ham United, completing it with an emphatic finish after dummying and shimmying his way across the box. At one point, ITV commentator Gerald Sinstadt noted, 'George Best, these days without a defender stood on his heels, [is] really looking the player we have always known him to be and so rarely had the chance to see him being.'

Two weeks later, Old Trafford witnessed another much-replayed moment of Best genius in the home game against leaders Sheffield United, who had taken the First Division by storm by winning eight and drawing two of their first ten games after promotion.† A

† During Sheffield United's season, the club announced that their Bramall Lane ground would no longer double as a home for the Yorkshire cricket team after the summer of 1973. 'It's becoming too much of encumbrance,' said chairman Dick Wragg as plans were revealed to build a new South Stand over the cricket square, enclosing the football pitch on all four sides.

beneficiary of the referees' protection, Blades midfielder Tony Currie was not optimistic that 'a new attacking trend' was about to become permanent in English football. 'Sadly, I don't think it ever will,' he said. 'There are only three or four clubs who attempt real attacking football.'[161]

With many thousands locked outside the ground, Norman Fox of *The Times* noted of the surprise pacesetters, 'Any well-prepared team can be turned to stony inability when Best casts a sudden, hypnotic spell on a defence.' And with the home team a goal up inside the final ten minutes, Best gathered the ball just inside his opponents' half, turned to face downfield and began making tentative forward progress. The first hint of a challenge prompted him to accelerate, embarking on a diagonal run past two challengers and then between two others to drive into the right of the penalty area. Just when it looked as though his momentum would carry him into harmless territory, he clipped an impossibly angled shot from close to the corner of the six-yard box beyond keeper John Hope and in off the far post. His look skyward and broad grin suggested that he had managed to impress even himself. 'Television showed it three times,' gasped *The Times*, referring to *Match of the Day* later that night. That such an occurrence was deemed worthy of mention demonstrates that this was still the era of reluctance to over-analyse in the studio.

Best scored in the next three United games, all victories. His performance in the third of those games, at Newcastle, was even more remarkable given that he had received an anonymous threat that he would be killed if he played. After the run of wins ended in defeat at Leeds, Best scored another hat-trick at Southampton in the final game of November, a 5-2 victory. The residue of goodwill that existed towards Manchester United might be unfamiliar to a younger public used to the cynicism of non-believers who grew up during the all-conquering Alex Ferguson era. Yet United's revival under O'Farrell was generally seized upon as good for the game. For example, *The Times* was already set to crown new champions, gushing, 'United have developed a new, exciting form of attacking football that seems destined to take them back to the top in England, if not in Europe, again.'

When United defeated Nottingham Forest on the first weekend of December they were five points clear of Derby County, Manchester City and Leeds with 20 games played. And then they didn't win another match until the middle of March – 12 games later – when Best opened the scoring against Huddersfield Town. It was his first League goal since The Dell more than three months earlier and would be followed by only one more First Division goal from open play, although he did add two penalties and totalled five in United's run to the FA Cup quarter-finals. Despite finishing with 26 goals in all competitions, Best's form 'dissipated' in the second half of the season, according to *Rothmans*, as United slipped to eighth place, ten points off the lead.

That United should fall off the same cliff as Best's performance was no real surprise. Morgan might have said, 'It's not just an individual revival, it's a collective revival,'[162] but their First Division lead had been achieved almost exclusively because Best dragged his team-mates by the winged collars on their new shirts to heights that they had no reason to expect. He was fooling few people when he said, 'I'm as sick as anyone when I get the lion's share of the credit and know full well that there are other players who contributed more.'[163] As Pat Crerand observed, 'George had one of these subliminal four months or whatever and was banging them in left, right and centre and destroying everybody. He had a golden period in that time under Frank and then George just fell off the wagon, didn't he?'[164]

The modest talent O'Farrell had at his disposal is evidenced by the men he fielded during those early months. Of those who had not played in the European Cup Final, it is hard to argue that anyone other than Law, injured on the big night, and Morgan might have got into that team. Even Morgan would have struggled to match the magnificent career-defining performance that John Aston gave on the wing at Wembley. The likes of defenders Tom O'Neil, Francis Burns, James and Edwards were journeymen, while Sammy McIlroy was still a wet-behind-the-ears prodigy, despite a goal-scoring debut in the Manchester derby.

When, in February, Best confided in John Roberts, his ghost-writer at the *Daily Express*, that he was tempted to ask for a transfer, he cited on-field problems as the biggest motivation. 'I've got nothing against the management,' he said in a conversation that never made it into the newspaper. 'It's the team. It's just not good enough. It's just not going anywhere. I could go right through the team and find things wrong. People knock me when I'm not doing it, but when I'm not doing it, who is?'[165]

The ease of Best's pathway through the playing fields of the First Division appeared destined to be undermined by the chaotic diversions of his private life. By the middle of the season, a man who had once spoken of his envy at Law's ability to go home to his wife and children after training was growing weary of the people eager to write to O'Farrell whenever he was seen out with a drink in his hand or a girl on his arm.

Early in January, he missed two days of training and was dropped for the home defeat against Wolves. On the Monday, the club announced a fine of two weeks' wages, ordered extra training with the youth team, barred him from having days off for five weeks and told him to leave his custom-built luxury house and move back into digs with his original landlady, Mary Fullaway. The latter sanction was for show only and never seriously considered something to which Best would adhere.

As the season drew towards its disappointing close, Best continued to skip training. O'Farrell felt that Best would 'opt out' of facing up to any problems and used to send Crerand searching for him. But the Scot admitted, 'I knew every bolthole in Manchester, but I still couldn't find George.'[166]

Having played in 40 of United's 42 League games, Best reached the summer with his mind made up – for now. He'd had enough. According to Roberts, in his account of those turbulent months, *Fall of a Superstar*, Best had told O'Farrell that in order to stay at United he wanted £1,000 per week and for the club to buy his unloved house from him. Despite Best's belief that O'Farrell would ask the board for acceptance of such terms, United informed him that they did not want him on their summer trip to Majorca, telling him to join up with Northern Ireland for the Home Internationals instead.

Best had no such intention, instead boarding a flight to Marbella in southern Spain. 'My mind is made up about football,' he told the throng of reporters who took the first available flight after him. Posing for pictures juggling a football in a pink vest and brightly-patterned swimming shorts, he said, 'I'm sorry. It's all over.'

Except, as anyone with a passing familiarity with Best's story knows, it wasn't. A few weeks later, another beach (Majorca) and another announcement. 'A short time ago I went away to make a decision and now I realise it was the wrong decision. I would like to go back and play for Manchester United.' This time, United's welcome-back punishment was to move him in with Crerand – followed by another return to Mary Fullaway – and a two-week suspension. All the while, players such as Charlton and Kidd were growing increasingly frustrated, both with Best's behaviour and United's apparent indulgence of him. 'That was the dilemma,' O'Farrell explained. 'The team wasn't good enough without him.'[167]

Perhaps inevitably, Best would not see the end of 1972 at Old Trafford. More missed training sessions, more omissions from the team, more fines. By the beginning of December, he would be permanently absent without leave and on the transfer list for a sum of £300,000. And, by then, he would not even be top of the list of United's problems.

4

MIDDLE-CLASS HEROES

BOB: These streets are ugly, but they have a kind of beauty.

TERRY: Working-class sentiment is the indulgence of working people created through football and rock and roll or people like you who moved out to the Elm Lodge Housing Estate at the earliest opportunity.

BOB: Well, I didn't want my kids growing up on these streets.

***The Likely Lads* (Dick Clement and Ian La Frenais; Anglo-EMI, 1976)**

THERE IS a popular notion that from George Best onwards professional footballers all turned into Beatles-style pop stars. The Manchester United icon was certainly the first player who was closer to the Fab Four than the boy next door, and he helped more members of his profession cross over into the celebrity world, hastening a process that had begun with the end of the maximum wage. But even with profiles rising through television coverage, the post-1966 boom and more glossy magazines and sticker collections than ever before, footballers of the Seventies were a long way from occupying the same universe as Mick Jagger and Elton John.

It had been the threat of a national strike in 1961 that proved strong enough to bring about the abolition of the Football League's pay ceiling of £20 per week, £18 in the summer. At that time the players' maximum wage, which was earned by only those at the top of the game, had been merely £3 per week more than the national average. Yet even freedom from their shackles did not necessarily mean an explosion of salaries. Despite the much-publicised pay rise of Fulham's England captain Johnny Haynes to £100 per week – the fulfilment of a promise made by the club chairman, comedian Tommy Trinder – many had to be content with modest moves up the pay scale. And few would ever have the balls to demand an increase. 'I never once asked for a rise,' said England midfielder Ian Callaghan, who made his Liverpool debut before the abolition of the maximum wage and left for Swansea City during the 1978-79 season. 'The manager would come to you if he was going to give you more money. None of us had agents. The first time we came across one was when Kevin Keegan joined.'[168]

Yet even during the early part of the Seventies, when salaries were increasing at a glacial pace compared to the phone-number contracts of the new millennium, references to 'spiralling wages' were commonplace in any discussion of the state of the sport. 'Player wages are just too high,' argued Football League secretary Alan Hardaker. 'I said at the time the maximum wage was removed that if the players took all the money in the game there would be none left for those who followed them. So many football clubs are existing because of the goodwill of their bank managers.'[169]

The inaugural *Rothmans Football Yearbook*, published in 1970, spoke of an 'economical sickness which threatens the very existence of eight out of every ten Football League clubs' and essentially blamed that situation on the clubs pursuing success by outbidding each other for the best players. 'Instead of expansion founded on sound economic principles, logic was thrown overboard,' it said of the aftermath of the maximum wage. 'Transfer fees quadrupled and players' earnings increased at an even greater rate.'[170]

Embedded in such comment was an implication that the players' greed exacerbated the situation, with market forces rarely considered.

Forces, it should be noted, that saw the number of registered professionals at League clubs fall from 4,000 in the late 1940s to fewer than 1,600 by 1983.

Unsurprisingly, Professional Footballers' Association secretary Cliff Lloyd defended his members. 'It is nonsense to blame the players for the economic problems in the game,' he said. 'If clubs over-commit themselves financially it is bad management.'[171] Don Revie, a man whose own love of an earner would later acquire for him the nickname 'Don Readies', was another who spoke on the players' behalf. '[They] know now that the rewards are big, but their time in the game is getting shorter so they have to make the money as quickly as they can. I reckon that the present-day footballer is finished three years earlier than he would have been in my day.'[172]

Yet there was a sniffy implication in remarks by the likes of Hardaker that players were getting above their station; a patronising inference that it was somehow in their best interests to be kept in their place. 'Footballers have climbed a rung and a half up entertainment's social ladder,' he said. 'That is one of the problems, and one of the dangers, that modern players face. They have been swallowed up by their public image. They have got fact and fiction mixed up to the point where they believe they are something more than they are.'[173]

In their own defence, players were quick to express the view that they worked harder than their predecessors – and harder than they themselves had been made to earlier in their careers. When *Shoot!* asked in its 1972 annual about the 'most startling development' in the sport over the previous five years, Arsenal's George Graham noted that 'application and dedication to the game has improved', while Leeds United's Eddie Gray stated, 'Players' work rate has increased tremendously.'[174]

For all the economic and industrial challenges of the 1970s, the improving lot of the footballer was hardly out of step with the majority. As historian Dominic Sandbrook pointed out, 'The paradox, of course, was that despite rising prices and steadily mounting unemployment, most ordinary families led more comfortable lives than they had ten or 20 years earlier.'[175]

Of course, players were advancing at a more accelerated pace than most. But by 1976, according to research by the Sporting Intelligence group, weekly wages in the First Division were still running at only double that of the national average: £140 to £71.* Lower down the Football League there were only marginal gains over factory workers. It was enough to move the country's best footballers out of the terraced streets occupied by many of their fans, but millionaire lifestyles still belonged to Hollywood heroes, heavyweight champions and pop stars. 'We were earning good money, but not the extent that it caused the gulf between players and fans that I find today,' Alan Hudson noted in 2017.[176] It was why increased freedom to choose who paid their wages was a principle held so dearly by the PFA throughout the decade.

'At that time, you had done well if you'd paid for your house by the time you finished your career,' said Bob McNab, a Double-winning full-back with Arsenal, who also played for England four times during 13 years in League football. McNab had received £5,000 after his £50,000 move from Huddersfield Town in 1966, but explained, 'It worked out at £1,250 a year over four years – about £800 a year after tax. I had just bought a home in Huddersfield for £2,250 and after joining Arsenal I didn't have enough money to buy a house. In the end, I was able to buy the townhouse in New Southgate that Arsenal had found for me to rent.'[177]

A decade later, house prices had increased along with wages, so when goalkeeper George Wood moved from Blackpool to Everton for £150,000 in August 1977 he was far from debt-free. 'I was able to buy a four-bedroom detached house in Parbold for £75,000, though, of course, I had a mortgage on it,' he told author Brian Viner. 'And for my first year at Everton I drove a bashed up Morris Marina.'[178]

---

* A period of acceleration would exist between 1977 and 1985, driven partly by greater freedom of contract, the arrival of overseas stars, and the need to prevent the best British players following the route of Kevin Keegan, Liam Brady, Trevor Francis and others to European countries. By 1985, First Division wages were five times the national average and they stayed around that mark until the Premier League rewrote football's finances throughout the 1990s. Overall, however, 70 per cent of professional footballers were still earning less than £15,000, the salary of a well-paid head teacher.

So, no, England's footballers did not suddenly all turn into George Best. There were some who played and lived with something of his swagger, while the mavericks could easily have passed for glam rockers had they been inclined to slap on a bit of make-up. But by later in the 1970s, while the cool kids were listening either to punk, the perfect soundtrack for a decaying, divided Britain, or disco, the hedonistic import from America, footballers were decidedly more sober in their lifestyle tastes. The boys on the terraces might be into The Jam or Black Sabbath, while their sisters and more strait-laced friends bought the Bee Gees, but their heroes' preferred soundtrack was that of suburban dinner parties.

Football in the Seventies might well have 'joined the vanguard of English youth culture', as the cover blurb to *The Mavericks* contends, but the footballers themselves appeared keen to maintain a respectful distance. The weekly barometer of their tastes was *Shoot!*'s 'Focus On' series, where readers could discover, among other things, the favourite food (usually steak and chips) and TV shows (any football programme) of a different player each week.

Inexplicably, the most popular choices of favourite singer among these sporty 20-somethings in the early years of the decade were American crooners Andy Williams and Jack Jones (not the union leader, whom we'll come to later). Steve Perryman, who at age 19 might have been listening to Frank Zappa, plumped for Frank Sinatra. Unique was the revelation of Stoke City defender Alan Dodd in 1975 that he was into Wishbone Ash and Genesis, exactly the kind of bands that the older brothers of my friends all seemed to follow. Throughout the final full season of the decade, 1978-79, the names most frequently cited were Rod Stewart and Neil Diamond, with Stevie Wonder, Elton John, The Eagles and Fleetwood Mac receiving their share of votes. Only one player, Stoke City centre-forward Paul Randall, named one of the most influential rock acts of the decade, David Bowie, while Garry Birtles of Nottingham Forest displayed the most flamboyant taste with Alice Cooper and Bryan Ferry. One can only assume that Bolton Wanderers' Roy Greaves was messing with the questionnaire when he named Des O'Connor and Vera Lynn, but you can never be sure.

Not a single punk or new-wave act was given a mention. Punk's image as working-class protest music might have been reflective of the background of most players and those who watched them from behind the goals, but it did little to speak to the vast majority of professional footballers. Having been spared the battle with the dole queue by virtue of the ability in their feet, they wanted nothing to do with the anarchy or art-school posturing of the movement. Punk, although it perfectly reflected the times and remains a symbol of the era, was not so popular that it had crossed over into the mainstream. The players certainly felt no need to use it to project themselves as being down with the kids. The permed hairstyles that afflicted so many players in the latter part of the decade were more 10cc than The Damned.

In short, the footballers of the 1970s aspired to be middle class. While the players of the 21st century, removed from most people's reality by their Premier League millions, strive to create connections with their young social media followers by interacting with urban musical influencers or showing off their latest tattoo, the average 1970s player was desperate to join the social circles inhabited by the doctors and lawyers on the semi-rural housing estates to which they had gravitated.

Hunter Davies's *The Glory Game* features a chapter based around a house party thrown by Tottenham's Wales international centre-half, Mike England. Squeezing a mobile discotheque into his Hertfordshire home, among the Victorian *chaise longue*, louvre doors and deep pile carpets, England invites members of the local Round Table group to which he belongs. Noting the presence of most of England's team-mates, Davies adds that 'one or two of their ladies looked a bit nervous, watching their husbands for a lead, wanting to say and do the right thing, but not getting much help as the boys tended to talk to each other'.[179]

Around the same time, Peter Douglas highlighted the challenges faced by footballers' wives as their husbands embarked on their social climbing and had horizons broadened by their success. 'Meanwhile, the little wife is left at home surrounded by the material benefits of her husband's success, her only company usually the wives of other players bemoaning the absence of their mates,' he wrote in *The Football Industry*. 'They can only observe the changes occurring in their husbands, as they grow more confident, more worldly wise.' With increased travel and increased confidence came increased opportunities for extra-marital activity, with fears on that score hardly helped by tabloid exclusives. Acknowledging the simplistic view he was presenting, Douglas, who was working as public relations officer for Crystal Palace, concluded, 'Gradually a crack in their relationship will appear; the player has outgrown his wife, and another football marriage is heading for a breakdown.'[180]

Back in England's living room, Davies, whose research of the Spurs players identified most as Conservative Party voters, points out, 'The local middle classes hardly spoke to the footballers in their floral shirts, sticking mainly to their own groups.'[181] It is difficult to read the passage without thinking of BBC's 1977 screening of Mike Leigh's *Abigail's Party*, in which Beverly, an aspiring middle-class housewife, impresses her new neighbours, Ange and Tony, with everything from the kitchen tiles and rotisserie to the 'real' silver-plate candelabra and 'cheesy-pineapple' nibbles. Another neighbour, Sue, genuinely middle class, can barely hide her disdain, especially when Beverly accepts the bottle of Beaujolais she has offered and tells her, 'I'll just pop it in the fridge to chill.'

Tony turns out to be a former Palace footballer forced to retire at 20 because of injury and Beverly's husband, Laurence, delights in highlighting his lack of education. It was, of course, true that while footballers might share a postcode with their learned neighbours there was no common interest in, say, literature or current affairs. 'You don't have many conversations in football,' said former England physiotherapist Fred Street, who spent much of his working life around footballers. 'I know it sounds stupid but that is partly why I decided I had done long enough at Arsenal. I left a bigger world behind to go into football. It is a narrower world and you can find yourself becoming narrower in it. They are not broad people. They read the paper back to front and if World War Three happened they would be the last to know. I used to go to players' houses – affluent guys – and you wouldn't see a book around the house. I thought I would get arthritis of the brain if I stayed in too long.'[182]

University-educated Alan Gowling, one of the game's intellectuals, was not going to argue with Street's assessment. 'Footballers like to talk about football most. In this respect, their interest is total,' he observed. 'They will discuss topics in the news regarding football, they will discuss any matches that they may have seen on TV or live, covering details of their thoughts on the game, who played well, what they thought of the ref, or what they thought of the match commentator if the game is on TV. They will talk about players at other clubs, discussing their virtues or some incident involving them in the past. They will talk about managers and trainers, including their own. They will criticise or praise them in turn.' He said they could be serious about politics and 'other topics that are of concern to other groups of people', but concluded, 'They do find it difficult to maintain their serious conversation for long. There is always someone to turn the situation back to a more mundane level.'[183]

Most players would have admitted that, despite their social climbing, they remained more comfortable in the blokey atmosphere of post-match pubs than handing out the *vol-au-vents* in their lounges. The hard-drinking culture that gave rise to the anecdotes dotting footballers' autobiographies survived the game's migration to the suburbs. One of the most frequently cited badges of honour was the player who could have a skinful one night and be ready to sweat it out on the training ground the next morning. Former Queens Park Rangers and Arsenal defender Terry Mancini remembered, 'With no paparazzi around, no one taking pictures with a mobile phone, you could go out and have a good time. In our era many players would still have been under the influence at three o'clock on Saturday.'[184]

Douglas observed 'the lack of cultivation of the mind' among footballers and suggested, 'It cannot be easy for a young man in his late teens and early 20s to cope with the problems that come with newly acquired wealth and regional or national acclaim. What is surprising is that more players do not go off the rails.'[185] After arriving at Chelsea, Chris Garland noted, 'You would not believe how much they could put away.' When the squad performed 'Blue is the Colour' on *Top of the Pops,* they were required to be on site from early morning to early evening. 'By the evening there were several players who simply couldn't stand up they'd had so much to drink,' Garland recalled. 'We had to drag in some passers-by just to make up the numbers.'[186]

Former Tottenham winger Cliff Jones was far from unique in recalling that his team's motto was 'win or lose, on the booze'.[187] A writer who was close to the Spurs players socially, former *Daily Express* man Norman Giller, explained, 'Back in those days we had free access to the players. I have an old contacts book with telephone numbers of every major player and manager of the time.' Describing the time as 'heavy drinking days' he added, 'It was the culture in the game at the time; a good performance rewarded with a good drink. The writers used to drink with the players regularly after matches. The man who could really put it away was Alan Gilzean, who hardly said a word but got through his Bacardi and Cokes at a rate of knots.'[188]

Birmingham City and Everton centre-forward Bob Latchford admitted that the 1970s was 'an era where players garnered reputations as great socialisers', noting that for the first time they were 'relatively well paid and had lots of spare time'. Rather sadly, he also admitted that most players had no great desire to do much with that time, especially on the road. 'You travel a lot, you see lots of hotels and transit points, but very little of the towns and countries you visit,' he said. 'If I'm honest the only glamorous thing about being a professional footballer is actually playing the game. The rest is very mundane.'[189]

It meant that a player such as Steve Heighway, another graduate, was considered strange by his Liverpool team-mates when he displayed a preference for culture and sight-seeing on European trips rather than getting stuck into the local brew over a game of cards. There were even occasions when Brian Clough encouraged his players to get drunk together in the team hotel the night before a big game rather than having them going out or lying in their rooms fretting. It was hard to imagine Mike England's Round Table buddies taking a similar approach in preparation for an important board meeting.

Arguing that 'footballers have not quite made it socially', Douglas added, 'They may wear their hired tails and toppers in the best traditions of the society wedding, but they are still tied to their class'.[190] Yet football as a home for middle-class heroes was a narrative that many in and around the game were eager to perpetuate, especially against the backdrop of increased crowd trouble. With attendances falling, the game's authorities were determined to penetrate beyond the traditional working-class fan base and make the sport attractive to the sponsors who were now being welcomed into the boardrooms.

Stories about upwardly-mobile players and glamorous celebrity fans not only offered quirky and appealing storylines, they created on behalf of media outlets a more attractive playing field for potential advertisers. For example, the graduate-turned-footballer proved a rich seam of stories in the early part of the decade. Rarely were the Liverpool duo of Brian Hall and Heighway mentioned without reference to their science and politics degrees from Liverpool and Warwick universities respectively – which earned them the nicknames of 'Little Bamber' and 'Big Bamber' after *University Challenge* presenter Bamber Gascoigne. Any schoolboy knew that Manchester United midfielder Gowling had studied for an economics degree, although he later admitted that 'the pressures of this exacting double role almost led to my having a nervous breakdown'.[191] And Steve Coppell would arrive at Old Trafford a few years later while completing his economic history studies at Liverpool University.

But, as author Stephen Wagg argued in *The Football World: A Contemporary Social History*, 'The graduate invasion was always more publicity than serious assertion. It was a good selling line aimed at the potential middle-class supporter but also … to legitimate the game in the eyes of advertisers. In this context a cloth cap sport would have a narrower appeal.'[192]

Football was being portrayed as a sufficiently serious career option that BBC's educational programme *Scene* visited Liverpool to make an episode called 'It's a Tough Life'. Aired during the network's block of schools programming in January 1973, it showed the day-to-day life of an apprentice, with the aim of demonstrating that not everyone became a star overnight. 'We wanted to show there is far more hard work than glamour involved and far more frustration and disappointment than success,' said producer Tom Stanier.[193]

And there was an eagerness to celebrate famous football fans who might help carry the game further towards the gentrification many desired. It became well documented that Stamford Bridge in the late 1960s and early '70s was a regular home for the acting community; names such as Richard Attenborough, Michael Caine and Michael Crawford. Hairdresser to the stars, Vidal Sassoon, even promised Chelsea's players and wives a free trip to his salon if they reached the 1972 League Cup Final.

Interviews with Radio 1 presenter Ed 'Stewpot' Stewart (Everton) or Radio 2's Pete Murray (Arsenal) featured regularly in football publications, while Donny Osmond claimed to have donned a disguise to go and watch Tottenham, where he might have bumped into The Sweet's lead singer, Brian Connolly, who was also big pals with Sunderland's Billy Hughes. Alvin Stardust was a Liverpool fan and Les Gray of Mud followed Leeds United; comedians Mike and Bernie Winters were pictured training with Denis Law and told their agent not to book any shows that would clash with the 1974 World Cup finals; and the *Shoot! Annual* of 1976 featured 'The Sport of Showbiz Kings' – with Manchester City fans Little and Large and shots of singer Vince Hill training with Coventry City. And no FA Cup Final on television was complete without Jimmy Tarbuck (Liverpool) popping up with Wembley Way behind him. Then there were those who joined the board of their favourite teams, such as Elton John (Watford), Eric Morecambe (Luton Town), Mike Yarwood (Stockport County), Eric Sykes (Oldham Athletic) and prog rocker Rick Wakeman (Brentford).

All of which was doing little to change the demographic of the dressing-room. Wagg reported that the research he conducted in 1969, when he heard back from 220 professional footballers, had identified zero players from what would be considered middle-class backgrounds, defined as Social Class II on the registrar general's scale.† Therefore, the increase in photographic features in which players showed off their new saloon car – Wolves captain Mike Bailey boasted of an 'A40 with a flick switch for V8 power and mink-trimmed seats' – or were captured attending to the lawn in spacious gardens helped to further separate them from their roots. So, too, did the proliferation of autobiographies in which players spoke proudly of the new homes and holidays that their success had bought them. Players, according to Wagg, had 'become standard bearers for the new consumer capitalism, catapulted, many of them, far from their working-class origins into the wide, blue new-bourgeois yonder'.

Of course, that created its own set of problems. Unlike in earlier decades, dressing-rooms of the 1970s were increasingly likely to be riven by dissatisfaction at what the player on the next peg was earning. A prime example of that was the December 1971 signing of Alan Ball by Arsenal, who had just won the Double against the backdrop of what some felt was a prohibitive pay policy. Not only was the top weekly wage a mere £90, but a large percentage of bonus money on offer was determined by length of service. It meant that a long-tenured loyalist on the fringes of the squad could be earning considerably more than a recently-signed first-teamer or a valuable youngster. McNab, signed from Huddersfield, called it a 'very irritating situation' and 'fundamentally unfair'.[194] Charlie George threatened to take the club to court and spoke for the new generation of Arsenal stars when he said, 'It can't be right that we should be so far behind them because we are younger.'

When Arsenal agreed to loosen their financial grip to procure Ball from Everton for a British-record £220,000, the England player made no effort to disguise his comparatively generous deal. Future Arsenal signing Mancini recalled, 'You used to get your pay slip in a brown envelope on a Friday and he would open his up, stand in the middle of the dressing-room and read it and then leave it on the table for everyone to see. He didn't mean any harm by it, but people like

---

† Introduced in 1911, it was the standard measuring tool used for the remainder of the century and was based on the perceived standing in the community of different occupational groups.

John Radford, Peter Simpson and others would go fucking berserk. He was on £250 a week after tax, plus bonuses, and it drove a wedge between him and the other players.'[195]

When Garland joined Chelsea he was happy to hear he was achieving a pay rise to £80 per week from the £50 he'd earned at Bristol City. 'I was happy enough with that until I found out Peter Osgood was on between two and three hundred a week,' he said.[196] But as frustrating as those situations might be for some, the players hardly had cause for complaint when it was their own union that had fought for that state of affairs. As Wagg noted, 'Footballers had, because of the events of 1961, to be weaned off a working-class collectivist ethic to a middle-class one, stressing individualism and market forces.'[197] Conversely, at those clubs who retained an egalitarian salary system, it was the star players who were disgruntled. 'It's plain daft for the club to pay everybody the same money,' complained West Bromwich Albion's Jeff Astle. 'Surely you pay a player by the results he gets. I'm worth more than £60 a week.'[198]

By the early 1970s, though, there were still some players who had known the maximum wage era and longed for those simpler times. Announcing his retirement in 1973 because of recurring back problems, Stoke City captain Peter Dobing said he 'much preferred the game when there was a maximum wage of £20 a week', arguing, 'You used to play because you wanted to win something; now you play because winning something brings you a lot of cash.'

In the England team, World Cup-winning captain Bobby Moore was the personification of the increasing affluence and social status of the top footballer, with he and blonde wife Tina becoming sought-after party guests and photoshoot subjects. 'No one doubts the glamour of being a top-class player,' he said. 'The autograph hunters. The opportunities to travel and mix with celebrities. And the chance to earn money outside the game. There, too, can be pressures.'[199]

In *Football Monthly*, columnist Leslie Vernon argued that football's 'aura of show-biz phoniness is basically harmful.' He continued, 'Like canned music [football] is an ever-present companion – hence the stickers, the scarves and the giveaway gimmicks, whether one buys a gallon of petrol or packet of cornflakes or bubble gum for the kids. The star players have been elevated into the ranks of top-class entertainers and their private lives have become public property.'[200]

For a figure such as Moore, the pressure extended beyond being pestered to sign napkins during dinner. He became a target for something far more sinister in the build-up to the 1970 World Cup in Mexico, the result of a stopover in Colombia's capital city, Bogota, as the squad returned to Mexico from their final warm-up game in Ecuador. Killing time at the Hotel Tequendama, where they had stayed while playing Colombia a few days earlier, Moore was arrested for allegedly stealing a bracelet from one of the hotel stores. The original accusation, made shortly after Moore and Bobby Charlton had been into the shop on the earlier visit, had been dismissed as ludicrous. Now there were claims of a new eyewitness and Moore was placed under house arrest at the home of the head of the Colombian Football Federation. It was three days before the case was dismissed and Moore was freed to join his team-mates in Mexico. And with no contradictory evidence having emerged in the ensuing half-century, it appears safe to regard the whole bizarre episode as an attempt by forces unknown to undermine England's World Cup defence. If so, they picked the wrong target. Famously meticulous and unruffled on and off the field, Moore proceeded to use the tournament to cement his reputation as the best defender of his type in the world.

Like many players of his age – he turned 30 in the season after that World Cup – a greater concern to Moore than foreign espionage was the matter of securing his family's future beyond football. By 1973 he was estimated to be earning £20,000 a year outside the game, with a leatherwear company being one of his main sidelines, although an unsuccessful country-club venture would cost him most of his money.

Alongside a desire to rub shoulders with suburban professionals, footballers of the 1970s could not help becoming anxious about what happened when the cheering stopped. In *Only A Game?*, Eamon Dunphy described his 28th birthday as 'the age when insecurity like a slowly descending fog appears on the horizon'. He added, 'Of course, you reassure yourself that this is your prime. It's a shock to realise how rapid the descent is from pinnacle to valley.'[201] As Richard Harris's character, facing his professional football finale in the 1971 movie *Bloomfield*, cries, 'The last game – what comes after that?'‡

In the decades immediately following the Second World War, the most ambitious players aspired to high-street concerns such as the newsagent owned by Blackburn's England captain Ronnie Clayton or the Blackpool sports store of Stan Mortensen. By the 1960s and 1970s, the greater income and vision of players in a modern age saw Mike Summerbee selling trendy shirts; Manchester City clubmate Francis Lee establishing a waste-paper business that would amass a fortune and fund his entry into training racehorses; Crystal Palace defender John Sewell running a babywear shop; Manchester United's Willie Morgan operating a chain of launderettes; Arsenal's George Armstrong investing in flats; and Chelsea's Bill Garner running a sports trophy firm in Essex and reporting great demand for his items in the Middle East.

After signing for Liverpool from Nottingham Forest, midfielder Peter Cormack began 'dabbling at clothes design ideas' and modelled his own Cormack Creations products. 'It seemed like a great idea at the time,' he said. 'To complete the look, I grew a trendy moustache.'[202] And he released a single – a version of 'Route 66' that appears to have sold fewer copies than the number in its title.

Then there was 'The Clan', a collective of football figures who teamed up with leading photographer Terry O'Neill in 1972. Alan Hudson, Geoff Hurst, Terry Venables, Rodney Marsh, Malcolm Allison, Gordon Banks, Martin Buchan, Francis Lee, Martin Chivers, Phil Beal and Mancini were all involved, pictured modelling clothing or plugging restaurants. But it was little more than a social club, quickly fizzling out and leaving nothing but a fascinating archive of photographs. 'We would go out for lunch and stay all night,' said Mancini, struggling to remember any specific endeavours undertaken by the group.[203]

‡ Harris, who had played a professional rugby league player in the 1963 film *This Sporting Life*, co-directed the story of a 40-year-old former football star in Israel facing up to the final game of a successful career. The movie ends with Harris missing a vital penalty with the final kick of the game. Curiously, it is the voice of Brian Moore that is heard commentating.

Given footballers' love of the pub, it was no surprise that it became a post-retirement option for many. The image of the formerly fearsome centre-half as jovial landlord, his waist expanding along with his line in anecdotes, was a common one. Larry Lloyd, Willie Young and Jim Holton were among the Seventies stoppers that forwards were far happier to encounter in later years from the safety of the customer's side of the bar.

But the footballer-turned-tycoon was in a minority. Duncan McKenzie, who played for Belgian side Anderlecht as well as several English teams, recalled, 'The level of entrepreneurial activity was generally limited. Many players relied on a testimonial to provide for a rainy day, but that was not the attitude on the Continent. It was not uncommon for footballers to have outside business interests in a variety of areas and the Dutch lads, especially, embraced the revolution.'[204] McKenzie, incidentally, was honest enough to admit to his own financial motivation. 'Let's be brutally frank, I didn't join a club in Belgium simply for the sake of my health,' he said. 'I was going in search of … a crock of gold.'[205]

For the loquacious, a description that certainly applied to McKenzie, there was the after-dinner circuit – as Jack Charlton had discovered after the success of his impromptu acceptance speech at the Footballer of the Year dinner in 1967. Having gone on to make some 'expenses only' engagements at various venues, he found himself sharing the bill with Yorkshire cricket legend Fred Trueman, who advised him to always ask how many guests would be attending. 'When they say 200, I say, "OK, add an extra pound on the tickets and pay me 200 quid."'[206]

Others saw a route into broadcasting; Bob Wilson, for example, who was analysing games for BBC while still playing for Arsenal.[§]

§ Wilson was not the only goalkeeper of the age to go into TV. In August 1973, Hereford United's David Icke, who had helped the team to promotion in their first season in the Football League, was forced to retire because of an arthritic condition in his knees and ankles. After contemplating a career in cricket, he went into journalism and ended up as one of BBC's leading sports presenters until his life took an unexpected turn in 1990. Donning a turquoise tracksuit, he claimed to be receiving messages from the spiritual world and began writing and speaking about his increasingly unorthodox theories about life and the universe.

And BBC Radio Birmingham featured Derek Dougan as host of a Friday sports chat show, along with recently retired West Bromwich Albion goalkeeper John Osborne as a match reporter and Aston Villa keeper Jim Cumbes as a Sunday morning disc jockey. 'I try to keep away from football and reach as wide a family audience as possible,' Cumbes explained.

The versatile Cumbes was one of the last group of professional footballers who found additional employment in county cricket, achieving the double of appearing in a Lord's final and a Wembley final within the space of two years. Having opened the bowling in Worcestershire's Benson and Hedges Cup defeat to Kent in 1973, he was part of Villa's victorious League Cup team against Norwich City two years later. Sheffield United left-back Ted Hemsley regularly went in at No.3 for Worcestershire, while Carlisle United midfielder Chris Balderstone had been man of the match in the 1972 Benson and Hedges final for Leicestershire, one of five trophies he won in his summer sport. Among his county colleagues was Leicester City centre-back Graham Cross, another dual finalist (1969 FA Cup, 1975 Benson and Hedges Cup).

Balderstone's was perhaps the most notable dual career of the 1970s. In 1974, it was his penalty against Tottenham that put Carlisle top of the First Division after the first three games, and two years later, aged 35, he played two Test matches for England against West Indies. In 1975, he played in the County Championship and Football League on the same day. Ending the second day against Derbyshire on 51 not out, he took off his pads and drove 30 miles to play for Doncaster Rovers against Brentford. He completed his century the following morning to help Leicestershire towards their first championship triumph.

The chosen few, internationals at the leading clubs, were at least in position to cash in on commercial opportunities. The staples were magazine and newspaper columns; sportswear endorsements; themed annuals published by Pelham Books in the case of the likes of Best, Ball, Denis Law and Derek Dougan; and openings of car showrooms. Astle was a popular figure at the Shrewsbury Flower Show and one of a group of players crossing over into light entertainment with an appearance on the ITV game show, *The Golden Shot*. There were a handful of sitcom appearances, too, including Osgood in *Never Mind the Quality, Feel the Width*; McNab playing football with Reg Varney in *On the Buses*; Colin Bell in *The Dustbinmen* and Ball, Moore and Geoff Hurst alongside Alf Garnett in *Till Death Us Do Part*.¶

Best's agent at the time, Ken Stanley, said that his phone never stopped ringing, while another of his clients, Law, preferred to play football, go home to his family and leave the money-chasing to others. Stanley was also the agent given the task of maximising the earnings of England's 1970 World Cup squad, setting a target of putting £250,000 in the pot, but reportedly having to settle for around £2,000 a man. Defending his profession – a new phenomenon in the game – and his clients' rights, he spoke out against the 'pirates who make lots of money on other people's graft'. He claimed, 'There were many people making tens of thousands of pounds going around grounds selling pictures of players and rosettes. People thought this was official and willingly paid out. Back-street cameramen would join genuine press photographers at photographic sessions … and the next thing was the pictures of the players were sold without their permission and without them being paid a copyright.'[207]

Terry Venables, meanwhile, found his own creative pathway to the bank, teaming up with scriptwriter Gordon Williams to write a not-bad football novel, *They Used to Play on Grass*. It led to the duo collaborating on a series of books about a private detective, which was made into a TV series by Thames TV, *Hazell*, running for 24 episodes over two series.

Then, of course, there was the boot deal, with the less familiar manufacturers often the most aggressive in their pursuit of celebrity endorsement. To the tune of £20,000 plus five per cent royalties, Best

¶ Football references came thick and fast in popular shows at the time. Rare was the episode of *The Sweeney*, for example, that didn't mention the beautiful game; whether it was DI Regan and Sgt Carter asking each other, 'Are you going to QPR tonight?' or Carter bemoaning Saturday night duty because 'West Ham are on the box later', or Regan lamenting, 'Where are you now, Nobby, when we most need you?'

was the face of Stylo Matchmakers, the boot that dabbled for a while with laces on the side, and was later joined by Keegan, Heighway and Trevor Francis. Among other challenger brands, Kingswell signed up Gordon Banks and Peter Lorimer; Cheetah had Peter Shilton; and Simlam the less ambitious collection of David Cross, John Roberts and Jon Sammels, promoting boots that could be coloured for your favourite team.

As any fashion-conscious Sunday footballer knew, the trend for exotic footwear gained pace with Alan Ball in 1970. Brian Hewitt, a sales executive for Hummel, decided that the only way to take on the likes of Adidas and Puma was to try something different, hitting upon the idea of white boots. Having offered Ball £2,000 to endorse them, they were to be unveiled in the FA Charity Shield when Everton faced Chelsea at Stamford Bridge. Except that Ball had not received any boots to play in. 'We got a pair of his Adidas boots and I took them off to [the manufacturers in] Heckmondwike and said, "Spray those beggars white so it stays on and put chevrons on them." God knows how many times they sprayed them. They were absolutely gleaming. We got them out of the factory, put them on a Red Star train down to King's Cross on Saturday morning, got one of my guys to pick them up and Bally got them about an hour before kick-off.'[208]

BBC commentator Kenneth Wolstenholme could barely take his eyes off them, remarking on Ball's 'twinkle toes' multiple times during the game. More than 50,000 pairs of white Hummels were sold over the next two years, with players such as Alan Hinton and Colin Todd at Derby County, Arsenal captain Frank McLintock, Leeds United's Terry Cooper and Manchester United winger Ian Storey-Moore following the trend. Charlie George even wore red boots in the 1972 FA Cup Final. Ball, however, unhappy with the white Hummels that eventually arrived, would continue to play in painted Adidas footwear, which can be clearly discerned in a close study of pictures of the time. He discarded them completely after two seasons, but the iconic image would endure far beyond that.

Osgood was involved in a less conventional piece of publicity-grabbing when Hollywood sex symbol Raquel Welch was persuaded to say in an interview in *The Times* that she was a fan of English football, and Osgood in particular. That led to a sickening sequence on ITV's *The Big Match*, where Jimmy Hill took La Welch to Stamford Bridge and could barely stop himself dribbling down the front of her tight-fitting white blouse. In response, Raquel told her fawning chaperone, 'If women knew what the hell they were doing they'd be down here watching this game and enjoying it. Watching all these lovely men.'

A similar statement was made by Pan's People dancer Dee Dee Wilde, who confessed to having a Chelsea patch sewn on her hotpants. 'Football turns me on,' she declared. 'It's seeing all those lovely legs, and the way the boys tackle each other and bang themselves about.' All of which was typical of the portrayal of female involvement in the sport. They were either drooling sex maniacs; the object of male desire in competitions such as 'Goal Girl of the Year' – where contestants sent in glamorous portraits in order to qualify for a final in which they paraded in team kit; or the 'girl behind the man', as portrayed in magazine pictorials of cosy suburban homelife. Any reports of the women's game itself earned a fraction of the column inches of a blonde in a tight-fitting Liverpool shirt.

Goal felt it appropriate to run a full page early in the decade under the heading 'Women's football is no joke now' yet illustrate it, without a hint of irony, with a picture of the Reading players' wives and girlfriends in team jerseys, white hotpants and knee-high boots. And when a reader from Tooting wrote to *Shoot!* in June 1973 explaining that his dad was manager of Chelsea Ladies and that they didn't see enough women's football in print, the magazine's response was to publish a small team picture and a slavering response from the editor that said, 'After looking at this line-up of lovelies I'm inclined to agree with you.'

In 1972, after the FA belatedly gave official recognition to women's football, a full-page article in *Inside Football* declared, 'Petticoat Soccer will never catch on.' Writer Ken Houston said he was happy for the country's 5,000 female footballers, but announced, 'Come on, girls, you must realise that women's football has as much chance of catching on as I have becoming president of the Mothers' Union.'[209]

Meanwhile, when Raquel left Stamford Bridge she did so before the final whistle. She passed in front of the construction site for the new East Stand, which meant she was effectively strolling down the touchline, from where she insisted on yelling and waving goodbye to Osgood, an 'ill-mannered intrusion' according to watching journalist Ken Jones.

But not every English footballer of the Seventies had screen sirens lining up to meet them, boot manufacturers throwing product at them or even flower show organisers handing them tenners. For many, match tickets were the currency of additional income. In London, a key figure was the 'broker' Stan Flashman, later to become chairman of Barnet Football Club. Every major city had its characters to whom players could deliver spare tickets in exchange for cash in their pockets, and in the capital the best-known was 'Fat Stan'. *Shoot!* writer Christopher Davies remembered the occasions when he would meet Alan Ball outside Highbury to prepare the Arsenal man's weekly column. 'Before we did the interview we had to go and see Stan Flashman at Edward Bond House, just off Gray's Inn Road,' he said. 'I have never seen as many locks on a door. Bally would go there to do some transactions and then we would do the column.'[210]

Speaking in 1972, Flashman explained the hours he spent going around the country, keeping in touch with players and building up contacts. 'I can ring up any ground in the country and have tickets left for me,' he said. 'I pay out the players when I see them, which may be months later. They're all right about waiting, except for [one player]. If he's not had the readies in a week, he's on to you.'[211]

Depending on his club, a player reaching the FA Cup Final could find himself with up to 100 tickets in his possession. 'Players looked upon Stan as their big payday,' said Terry McDermott, who played in two finals in the decade. 'The wages weren't massive in those days. You were finished at 33 or 34 and there were a lot of years ahead.'[212] When Southampton got to Wembley in 1976, manager Lawrie McMenemy told his players that he needed the names of any third party receiving a ticket. 'These lists showed my players had wonderful imaginations and many unusual friends, such as D Duck and M Mouse,' he explained.[213]

Flashman became so much a part of the Wembley scene that when Arsenal won the FA Cup in 1979 many of the players left the team banquet at the Grosvenor House Hotel on Park Lane to attend his party down the road at the Hilton. Arsenal manager and former player Terry Neill felt that Flashman was indulged because he had a 'more genuine feeling' for football than many of its administrators. 'For the players who sell the tickets to touts it is a perk,' he said, 'but I concede that it has an unsavoury ring about it.' Admitting that directors at some clubs were in on it too, Neill conceded, 'How many in other jobs reject the chance of making extra cash if they can?'[214]

Another well-known tout, Johnny 'The Stick' Goldstein, was asked to attend an investigation on one of many occasions when the FA tried to stamp out the black-market sale of final tickets. 'Willingly,' legend has it he replied. 'Provided I am able to name the FA and League officials who have bought tickets from me for Sinatra concerts.'

According to Tommy Docherty, 'The players were selling tickets – but that was because the wages then weren't what they are like now. It was a chance to pick up an extra bonus. The players did it and I did it.'[215] But when Manchester United were looking for reasons to fire Docherty in the wake of a front-page scandal in 1977 *(see Chapter 11)*, the board held the selling of Wembley tickets against him, even though he claimed he had done so on behalf of the directors themselves. So open were his actions that he'd invited Flashman into the United boardroom.

But while the touts provided cash for visits to pubs, clubs and bookmakers, it was no annuity fund. And in the days before multiple media platforms offered new careers to any retired top-flight performer with an ounce of personality or insight, those concerns about making ends meet in the long term weighed heavy. The traditional safety net was the testimonial match, awarded to players after ten years with the same club; a vital windfall for most, either to buy that business or house, or to invest in a PFA pension. But it could sometimes be a source of acrimony. Nothing was guaranteed to create greater friction than when a player was off-loaded by his club with a testimonial on the horizon.

Not everyone was as fortunate as defender Ollie Burton, who was told in 1972 that Newcastle United would keep him on the books for a further season when a knee injury ended his career after nine years at the club, qualifying him for his testimonial. McLintock, for example, was a few months away from completing a decade at Highbury when he was sold to Queens Park Rangers for £25,000. He'd been described in a magazine article that year as enjoying the rewards of his success 'in a semi-detached four-bedroomed house in Winchmore Hill, where he can relax with his favourite records ... and set out for a round of golf when he is free'.[216] But before saying farewell to his Arsenal team-mates, McLintock asked manager Bertie Mee about a testimonial. 'He said he would put it before the board, but [then] he said that I had only been there nine years and six months,' McLintock explained. 'I felt I deserved better. They could have offered me one when I retired.'[217] Instead, McLintock was the beneficiary of an independently-organised benefit dinner at the Hilton in central London, from which he was reported to have earned £7,500.

Even when it was granted, the testimonial match came with no guarantees. The 56,214 crowd that packed Anfield for World Cup winner Roger Hunt's 1972 match was not typical. Nor was everyone as lucky in their timing as Southampton's Mick Channon, whose benefit game at The Dell turned out to be two days after the club shocked Manchester United to win the FA Cup in 1976, or Tommy Smith, who cashed in days after he'd scored a vital goal in the European Cup Final a year later.

For others, it was a gamble, as Chelsea's Eddie McCreadie discovered in 1974 when netting only £3,000 from a testimonial against Manchester United, granted after 12 years' service and attended by fewer than 7,000 spectators. QPR full-back Ian Gillard suffered a similar fate in 1979, when only 3,500 watched his testimonial against Tottenham. 'Diabolical, an absolute waste of time,' was how he described it. 'I wasn't expecting great crowds of people – maybe about 6,000 to 8,000. Spurs did me proud, turning up with a full side, and I can't thank them enough. But the fans stayed away. This meant I collected about £500 for ten years' loyal dedicated service. I had to pay all the expenses. I felt that in the circumstances the club would have done something for me, but they didn't. It just shows that loyalty is a one-sided arrangement. The testimonial system is wrong.' Suggesting clubs invested in an endowment that matured after ten years, Gillard concluded, 'The whole thing should be scrapped. No player should have to rely on this antiquated system.'[218]

Yet Billy Bremner might have thought twice before using his 1974 testimonial to launch an attack on the game's pay structure. 'To an extent football is like white slavery,' he wrote in the brochure for the match against Sunderland. 'Our earnings are unrelated to our crowd pulling power. Some of the stars of television, show business and the pop world get five-figure contracts for just a week.' The fact that Bremner was estimated in the press to have earned £40,000 from a crowd of 37,708 meant that his comments were hardly designed to illicit great support.

A couple of years later, he admitted, 'Thanks to a bumper testimonial, my family's future is secure. If any of my kids want to go on to a higher education I'll be able to provide for their studies and see they get a good start in life.' And while pointing out that many lower-division players were struggling to make ends meet, he returned to his argument that the elite were underpaid in comparison to entertainers.[219] There was support for that view from Elton John, who used the platform of his position as a director of Watford to argue, 'Look, do you think I could do a concert in Manchester every second week and pull in 30, 40 or even 50,000? Well, the players of Manchester United have been doing it for years and they are still underpaid.'[220]

Kevin Keegan adopted a similar tone to Bremner when his lucrative move away from Liverpool was being finalised. 'I wouldn't go so far as to call it slave labour, but it almost amounts to that,' he said, in the knowledge that he would get little sympathy. He did have a point, though, when he pointed out, 'If you compare the number of games we play and our wages with those of continental players in the top flight we come off strictly second best.'[221]

In that same year, 1977, Channon acknowledged that his annual salary of £25,000 made him one of the game's highest earners but reckoned there were only about 20 players picking up as much as £20,000. He echoed the comparison with other entertainment industries and added, 'I feel really sorry for the thousands of players who get very low wages who would be better off financially working on a building site.' Which is where many lower-division players, finishing their careers without qualifications or any opportunity to accrue savings, ended up. Often prematurely. PFA chairman Dougan felt the Football League should re-examine its provident fund for low-income players, who were able to invest a tenth of earnings into a pot that was paid back to them at the age of 35. He wanted anyone earning £3,000 or below to qualify, but had been turned down by the clubs, who wanted to restrict the scheme to those earning below £2,000.

When Venables and Williams wrote *They Used to Play on Grass*, set a few years on from the book's 1972 publication, the voice of the fretting professional footballer was easy to hear. 'It's a short life so they just get on with it. None of them go about with long faces thinking deep thoughts about capitalism and the law of the jungle – but deep down they know it is a jungle,' read one passage. 'Their lives are castles built on wet sand. No matter how good they are, or how fit or how dedicated, come 30 and they are getting old.'[222]

The voice may well have been that of Venables's own professional mortality. At QPR when the duo published the book, Venables was struggling with injury at Crystal Palace when manager Malcolm Allison told him, on New Year's Eve 1974, to quit playing and join him on the coaching staff. Venables was still a few days shy of his 32nd birthday.

'I am more than just a footballer, aren't I?' Harris's movie character – 'The King' – asked the board of his club. 'I mean, I have a future in the game, haven't I? Well, haven't I?'[223] Venables was lucky that he didn't have to plead in such a manner. A successful managerial career lay ahead. As he and Williams had written, 'I couldn't live outside the game, he told himself. Not like those men out there. To stay in the game – that was the player's dream. But only one in a hundred achieved it.'[224]

POWER TO THE PEOPLE

> *CLIVE LAWSON: I know how they treat these soccer stars; you see? You don't. You think it's all big money and swish night clubs, don't you? ... Yes, well, I happen to know it's different. It's not like that at all. They push them about from pillar to post. Do this, do that. Their lives aren't their own. It's not all beer and crumpet, believe you me.*
>
> ***Rooms* (Willis Hall; Thames Television, 1975)**

A shared dream of the players of the 1970s was the ability to truly control their own professional destinies. Aiming to make that a reality was a trade union determined to eliminate the biggest impediment to its members' ambitions.

In modern times, the omnipotence within the Professional Footballers' Association of long-time chief executive Gordon Taylor relegated the chairman to the margins of the union's activities. Most football followers since the turn of the century would have struggled to name the PFA chairman at any given time. That was certainly not the case in the 1960s, when Jimmy Hill wielded the threat of a strike in order to get rid of the £20-a-week pay limit, and into the next decade, when Derek Dougan took over from former Arsenal captain Terry Neill. Instead of a chief executive, there was a secretary, the stalwart Cliff Lloyd, happy to yield the position of front man to the individual the members had mandated to be their mouthpiece.

Belfast-born Dougan was more than willing to fulfil such duties. He was an iconoclast, frequently a mischief-maker, and an expert in self-publicity – to which a series of autobiographies, and even a football-based novel, bore convincing testimony. Yet he loved a cause and cared deeply about the plight of the professional footballer. Having begun his career in England at Portsmouth in the days of the maximum wage, he'd been shocked at the way experienced players were happy to keep their heads down and allow clubs to take advantage of them. So at the moment of his greatest on-field triumph, when Wolves won the League Cup in 1974, he said that it wasn't the highlight of his career: that had been bestowed four years earlier when he was voted in as chairman of the PFA.

'We trained a lot together and roomed together and you could see where he was going and how he was going to develop,' recalled Wolves colleague John Holsgrove. 'He had very strong views and felt that the players should have a strong union because we had gone through a period of doffing the cap. He felt that directors did not have a clue about football.'[225]

That such a man was leading football's professionals was entirely appropriate. Strong trade union leaders were part of the personality of Britain in the 1970s, loved and reviled in equal measure; the saviours of the workforce or the cause of the country's ills, depending on one's political viewpoint. In particular, there was a small group of superstar union figures who were rarely off television. If they were not appearing at the top of the nightly news bulletins, then Joe Gormley (National Union of Mineworkers), Hugh Scanlon (Amalgamated Engineering Union), Jack Jones (Transport and General Workers' Union) and Len Murray (successor to Vic Feather as leader of the Trades Union Congress) were being imitated by Mike Yarwood as part of primetime viewing; genuine media celebrities with the power to change history. There was even a 1973 hit single that became an unofficial anthem, 'Part of the Union' by The Strawbs, who declared, 'I say what I think, that the company stinks; Yes, I'm a union man.'

In a poll conducted by Gallup in 1977, 'Emperor Jones', as the docker's son from Liverpool became known, was named as the most powerful man in Britain by 54 per cent of the participants. During the double general election year of 1974, a famous graffito urged, 'Vote Jack Jones. Cut out the middle man.'

Gormley, a round-nosed Lancastrian who spoke through pursed lips and with one of his union's more moderate voices, was credited as the man who brought down Edward Heath's Conservative government in 1974. Indirectly, he also played havoc with football's schedules over the course of two industrial disputes and helped to hasten the introduction of Sunday football.

Early in 1972 the miners took their first official strike action since 1926 after the collapse of pay talks with the National Coal Board. Surprised by the doggedness of the miners, shocked at the violence on some of the picket lines, preoccupied by the escalation of the crisis in Northern Ireland and caught out by severe late-winter weather that tested existing coal stocks, the government declared a State of Emergency. Energy-saving measures included a three-day working week, scheduled power cuts of up to four hours per day, and instructions to householders to heat only one room and use as little lighting as possible. While not exactly a life-and-death matter compared to women having to give birth by candlelight in hospitals, football was ordered to cease the use of floodlights.

It meant that midweek games were staged in the afternoon. One such match, a fifth-round FA Cup replay between holders Arsenal and Derby that kicked off at 2.45pm on a Tuesday, attracted a crowd of more than Highbury's official capacity of 63,000, as workers and schoolchildren found excuses to play hooky. So packed was the ground that the action was halted briefly while fans spilt on to the pitch after a crush barrier collapsed. The game was played the day after the official end of the strike, following the miners' acceptance of an improved pay deal.

Yet by late 1973, the miners were unhappy at having slipped back down the league table of industrial sector pay. With oil prices soaring because of the Arab–Israeli conflict and Heath's government trying to plug a leaking economy with pay freezes, the miners saw their opportunity and demanded a seven per cent pay rise. When their demands were not met, an overtime ban led to an eventual strike. Another State of Emergency was declared, the three-day working week was reintroduced, and TV companies were ordered to cease broadcasts at 10.30pm on weekdays. It was little wonder that the Christmas charts were dominated by Slade's 'Merry Christmas Everybody', a raucous, knees-up of a tune that evoked family singalongs and offered three minutes of escapism.

Not only did football face up to another ban on floodlights, but the government encouraged clubs to look at playing games on Sundays, when energy usage was lower as factories and offices took a day off. Bolton Wanderers, Bradford City, Cambridge United and Nottingham Forest led the way by staging their third-round FA Cup ties on the Sabbath, circumventing Sunday Observance Laws by allowing fans in for free and charging them the usual admission for a compulsory programme purchase. All four teams recorded crowds twice as big as normal. 'Today's events are abundant proof that Sunday soccer as a general thing must surely come,' stated Bradford City chairman Robert Martin.

Sir Alf Ramsey, clinging on to his job as England manager, was critical of the FA for allowing such a turn of events, citing Sunday as the one day when he could be with his family. Referee Clive Thomas and Brian Clough, whose Brighton team had already gone out of the FA Cup to non-League Walton and Hersham, were among other dissenting voices. And Keegan reckoned that 'if the prospect facing me for the next 10 years in top-class football was being forced to play on Sunday, I'd seriously think about hanging up my boots.'[226] Which was nonsense, of course, but reflected the concerns of PFA secretary Lloyd, who argued, 'We should not commit players to Sunday football without having obtained their instructions. I would be surprised if the majority were in favour.'[227]

While a selection of Sunday games in League and FA Cup continued over the ensuing weeks, Heath had played his final card in his battle to beat the miners, calling a general election for the end of February. He was hopeful that victory would demonstrate the public's support of his stance. So much for that. Harold Wilson's Labour Party won a narrow victory and ended the miners' dispute by awarding them a 35 per cent pay rise, more than double the amount offered by Heath. Sunday football was discontinued. It had proved its viability, with 121 games bringing in an estimated 260,000 more fans than if those same contests had been staged on a Saturday. But it would have to wait almost a decade for its resurrection.

Football's Jack Jones – Dougan – had stood alongside his fellow-professionals when they voted for strike action in order to end the wage ceiling in 1961. Then he'd watched as George Eastham challenged Newcastle United's right to prevent him moving to another club as part of the old 'retain and transfer' system, which allowed a club to say that if someone didn't want to play for them anymore, he couldn't play for anyone. Eastham, whose dispute had ended when he eventually signed for Arsenal, went along with the PFA's proposal to take Newcastle to court and, in 1963, won an historic ruling from Justice Wilberforce, who described Newcastle's actions as 'restraint of trade'. It was not complete freedom of contract, but the PFA, with two big wins in the books, was content to take its boot off the Football League's throat. Dougan saw it as his calling, as much as getting on the end of crosses to score more than 200 goals in English football, to advance that cause as he prepared himself for office. As future PFA deputy chief executive Brendon Batson put it, 'Derek liked a good argument, particularly if he felt he was in the driving seat.'[228]

The Eastham ruling, for all its significance, had not allowed players to simply sell themselves to the highest bidder. Clubs still had the right to renew contracts at a salary at least equal to the original deal. An unhappy player could take his case to the League Management Committee and, if necessary, to a tribunal consisting of League and PFA representatives and an independent chairman. The tribunal would decide all aspects of the case, including any eventual transfer fee. It was that ability to seek arbitration that kept the union happy for a while. Yet Dougan insisted that 'the system we have accepted for far too long treats players as serfs'.

Bristol Rovers forward Bruce Bannister, who would sit on Dougan's PFA management committee, explained, 'Freedom of contract was the only place it could go. We suffered restraint of trade and it needed to be put right. A good step had been taken through George Eastham and eventually the Bosman case put it right completely, but there were myriad steps between them.'[229]

Lloyd argued that a well-managed club would have nothing to fear from freedom of contract. 'If a club has a good player on its books it should never allow his contract to run out,' he said. 'It should be negotiating a new one before the present one is due to expire.'[230] And shortly after becoming Leeds United manager in 1974, Jimmy Armfield would concede, 'Moralistically in this society of ours [contractual freedom] is a well-intentioned move,' although his fear was that it might encourage 'back-door approaches' that the traditional transfer system legislated against.[231]

In 1973, the Football League accepted the recommendation of the Commission on Industrial Relations to set up the Professional Football Negotiating Committee, which would have an independent chairman, and which, at its second meeting, recommended a four-point formula for player transfers: 1. the transfer system to remain for contracted players; 2. players to have the right to seek another club at the end of their contract; 3. clubs to be compensated for losing an out-of-contract player; 4. agreement that the compensation system should not hinder players in finding new employment.

Reaching accord on how that compensation would be determined was a whole different ball game. League secretary Hardaker proposed a Dutch-style 'multiplier', based on a player's wages, age and the level at which he played. The League suggested that the wage used in the multiplier should be that offered by the new club rather than the player's salary at his current team, a notion opposed by the PFA. Early in 1976, the League suggested scrapping the multiplier and going direct to tribunal, at which point the PFA declared it was happy to use a multiplier based on the wages being offered by the buying club.

Yet the League continued to reject the multiplier system it had once championed, with Hardaker warning that it was a deal-breaker. In the meantime, the PFA management committee received a mandate from its members to go all the way to a strike if necessary. 'Derek was fantastic as we moved towards freedom of contract in '78,' said Batson. 'I went to a regional meeting in Finsbury Park and the players suddenly realised that we could control our own destiny. There were a lot of doom and gloom merchants in the game saying it would be the death of the lower divisions and that players would be out of work, but I was one of those players at the lower levels and at Cambridge we said we would take our chances.'

Such a willingness for militancy was surprising among a PFA membership becoming increasingly comfortable with their lifestyles. Writing about the organisation in 1973, author Peter Douglas spoke of 'a distinct apathy among players generally about the affairs of the union' and described club delegates having to chase down team-mates in changing rooms for their subscriptions – which he felt were too low anyway. A small administrative staff also contributed to a situation where 'the players' union fails to be a completely effective voice'.[232]

Maybe that was why Dougan was bluffing in 1978, knowing that a strike would drive away spectators. However, he felt the threat was needed to break the deadlock. Meanwhile, the PFA management committee conceded that tribunals should be used to settle disputed transfer fees without any formula applied. Dougan, supported only by Bannister, would happily have fought on in pursuit of complete freedom of contract, but he conceded, 'I decided it would not have been circumspect to take on the rest of the committee, so a watered-down version of freedom of contract was agreed upon.' The PFA's annual meeting in the summer formally accepted the deal and even Dougan's disappointment at falling short of total victory could not erode the significance of the moment. The right of a player to leave his club at the end of his contract had been established.

Inevitably, the tribunal system itself was open to dispute and discussion. The first transfer to be settled by the new process was that of central defender John Lacy from Fulham to Tottenham; a transfer overshadowed by the north Londoners' shopping spree in South America in that same month *(see Chapter 14)*, but no less historic in its own way. Spurs offered £150,000, while Fulham held out for £250,000, excluding VAT and the 10 per cent levy that had to be split between the player and the Football League. Arbitrators representing the League, PFA and the Managers and Secretaries Association settled on £238,000 all in. John Bond, never slow to throw out an opinion from his manager's office at Norwich City, voiced fears about misuse of the system after being ordered to pay £110,000 for Orient centre-half Phil Hoadley, £40,000 more than he had offered. 'All they have done is split the difference,' he complained.

Whatever the merits of a tribunal system that could be easily manipulated by unrealistic opening gambits on either side, its installation acknowledged a new era of players' rights. 'In addition to freedom of contract,' Batson continued, 'there were things within that [deal], like the players' cash benefit scheme, which meant that as a player you would get something from the game irrespective of your earnings. While the modern-day player might not be fully aware of Derek's contribution it is there for people to read about. We should recognise the huge contribution he made to the wellbeing of players.'[233]

Dougan, in his own way, had ensured a place in trade union history alongside the likes of Gormley and Scanlon, the league leaders in industrial relations. And as he prepared to make way for incoming chairman Gordon Taylor, he could see the extra swagger that his members, with all their middle-class aspirations, would carry towards the end of the decade.

TWENTIETH-CENTURY BOY

Well you started off with nothing
And you're proud that you're a self-made man

'Stuck in the Middle with You', Stealers Wheel (Gerry Rafferty, Joe Egan; A&M Records, BMG Rights Management, 1973)

It was one hour before kick-off; excitement and anticipation spilling off the buses in Walton Breck Road, filling Kemlyn Road, Lothair Road and the surrounding streets. Strewn about the feet of the 50,000 or so making their way towards Anfield were discarded newspapers previewing the first day of the 1971-72 season. Down the road, the young man who would become symbolic of the successful 1970s footballer able to determine the course of his career without the help of a trade union sat fretting in his Ford Cortina. Kevin Keegan wasn't big-time enough yet to have advanced to a Capri, although he had added a garish yellow flash to the side of the maroon vehicle.

For the 20-year-old who was about to wear the red of Liverpool for the first time, the swell of humanity occupying the roads between his vehicle and the changing-rooms meant trouble. Inside the cramped car, a mood of panic jostled for prominence with various members of Keegan's family, several of whom had chipped in to raise £800 to buy the vehicle in which they were now trapped. Keegan, who should have been getting changed in readiness to run out against Nottingham Forest, pictured his manager, about to stake his reputation on an unknown talent who was nowhere to be seen. He'd left his digs at 1.55pm for what was a normally a five-minute journey. Until then, his experience of making his way to home games had been limited to the effortless journey to the Old Show Ground in Scunthorpe.

The local constabulary knew better than to assist a young stranger who looked as fear-struck as a joy rider pulled over without a licence. 'Playing for Liverpool today, son?' was the sarcastic response to Keegan's plight. 'And I've got to get my Forest kit on in a minute.' Forced to continue inching his car through the labyrinth of streets before talking his way past the stewards, having forgotten to acquire a car-park pass, Keegan stumbled into work 25 minutes late. Team-mates, grateful for an outlet for their pre-game tension, seized upon the opportunity to tease their unfortunate colleague. Hurrying to pull the No.7 shirt over his muscular 5ft 7in body, there was no time to get anxious. And instead of receiving a bollocking, he found Shankly at his shoulder as he left the dressing-room, saying in his ear, 'Go and enjoy yourself, son.'[234]

The petrol fumes were barely out of Keegan's nostrils when the Forest defence gave the ball away, allowing John Toshack to deliver a cross from the right wing. Keegan was on the end of it and, although mistiming his shot with his right foot, saw the ball squeeze inside the far post. A surging wave of bodies rolled down the Kop terracing. Keegan stood Canute-like in front of the sea of delirious humanity, arms aloft. A new king was born.

Before long he was wriggling his way into the Forest box to win a penalty. By the time Liverpool had completed a 3-1 victory, all the talk centred on the young man who had provided the Liverpool attack with the drive and direction missing in their FA Charity Shield defeat against Leicester City the week before.** For the fans on the Kop it was love at first sight. Here was a player who was not so removed from them. A player who would put in a hard day's graft. A player whose style owed as much to energy, enthusiasm and work ethic as pure skill on the ball. He was no Rodney Marsh. Better yet, he put many Liverpudlians in mind of their recently departed hero of the Sixties, Ian St John. 'I will never understand why the crowd are the way they are with me,' he said later in the decade. 'I do very, very ordinary things and the crowd will cheer and then someone else does something very exceptional and they don't do a damn thing about it.'[235]

A promising footballer at St Peter's Secondary School in Doncaster, Keegan had declined the opportunity to sign as an apprentice for Coventry City at the age of 15, persuaded by his father and headmaster to complete his O-levels. Playing for the reserve team at the brass foundry where he worked as a clerk, and for the Elmfield House Youth Club and a Sunday pub team, he was recommended to Scunthorpe United, signing for them on New Year's Day, 1968. In the spring of that year, Scunthorpe were relegated to the Fourth Division, but reorganisation of the team saw Keegan become a regular in midfield, scoring ten goals in the 1970-71 season. He was brought to Liverpool's attention by Andy Beattie, Shankly's former Preston North End team-mate, now working as an Anfield scout. Beattie couldn't believe that no one else had moved for Keegan and Liverpool bought him for £35,000 – a deal Shankly would describe in later years as 'robbery with violence'. Keegan signed five days before Liverpool's appearance in the FA Cup Final and had been as disappointed as anyone at their loss to Arsenal.

He wasted little time in staking a claim for the place that the underachieving £100,000 signing Alun Evans had been occupying. A player who would become renowned for working to make the most

** After Arsenal's 1970-71 Double, there began a sequence of three seasons in which the Charity Shield was contested by randomly chosen teams, in this case the FA Cup runners-up against the Division Two champions.

of every opportunity, he threw himself into pre-season training with passion and drive. 'He wanted to be bloody first at everything in training – sprinting, jumping over the hurdles, playing five-a-sides,' said Shankly. With the new season approaching, Keegan was surprised when he was selected for the first team against the reserves in the final practice game at the Melwood training ground. Upsetting the form book for that fixture, the first team won by a street and Keegan scored four times.

Having seen his faith repaid against Forest, Shankly said, 'If Keegan had only done half as much he would have done enough. It was a very satisfactory start for us. There was plenty happening. For instance, Keegan was happening.' And he was happening fast. By February of his first season at Anfield, Keegan had been selected for England's Under-23 team; by next November he had won his first full cap. And recorded his first single.

George Best had once said, 'If I could sing, I could have made a fortune.' Such considerations didn't appear to bother Keegan. 'It Ain't Easy' was released on the MAM label two days after he played in England's World Cup qualifier in Wales. It sounds like something most self-respecting floor-stomping glam rock bands would have rejected and tells the listener how difficult its singer is to live with – on this evidence, especially if he insisted on singing in the shower. 'Many people wrote saying they could not get hold of a copy,' Keegan said. 'And I wrote back saying how lucky they were.'[236] The record bombed as badly as England's World Cup campaign, although it didn't stop Keegan having another go in 1979 with 'Head Over Heels in Love'. Keegan's singing, ahem, career is an indication of the marketability of someone who combined a degree of talent with an unquestioned work ethic and, unlike Best, seemed like someone your daughter could bring home without worrying that he'd make a move on her mother.

He was aware enough to realise that not even winning the League title and the UEFA Cup in his second season at Liverpool was going to bring him the rewards he craved. 'Bitterly disappointed,' was how he described his reaction to a club bonus of £2,000, the majority of which he lost to the taxman. 'What hurt most and was especially depressing was that people assumed we had earned a fortune.'[237]

Money was not going to be in short supply, though. Keegan might not have topped the charts, but he was soon on primetime television cavorting in the locker-room and shower with national treasure Henry Cooper in adverts for Brut products, as he and the former heavyweight champion exhorted each other to 'splash it all over'. He would also go on to flog children's slippers, Grundig radios, Lyons Maid ice creams, Stylo and Patrick football boots, Mitre footballs, a 'KK' range of leisurewear, *Match* magazine, Sugar Puffs and an early electronic football game. He was the face of a Green Cross Code road safety campaign and even beat Gary Lineker into the potato-snack business when he signed up to promote Smith's crisps. Then there was his famous appearance in the 1976 edition of BBC's multi-sport *Superstars* programme, where he took the skin off his right side in a bicycle crash on a gravel track and had to spend four days in hospital.††

As Barney Ronay put it in his comparison to the David Beckham phenomenon, 'By 1979, [Keegan] had twice been voted European Footballer of the Year. Captain of England, cheerfully bilingual, a sartorial and hairstyling icon, he was the most recognisable footballer in the world – without the aid of replica shirts, satellite television or marrying a member of the Nolan Sisters.'[238]

When Keegan welcomed Brian Moore into his German home for a 1979 documentary, he explained, 'I am very aware it won't be every week they want to put Kevin Keegan on a tracksuit,' and said that having his money tied up in investments meant he expected to be better off when he retired. Most revealing, given Davies's discovery of the Spurs players' Conservative leanings several years earlier, is the moment in the programme when Keegan is told by his agent, Harry Swales, that Margaret Thatcher has invited him to attend a youth rally with her in Birmingham. 'Harry, if it was Jim Callaghan, okay,'

†† Footballers had mixed fortunes on the show. While Malcolm Macdonald won his 100-metres race in a time that many top track athletes would have been proud of, Stan Bowles entered the swimming race without being able to swim and was remembered by presenter David Vine as one of the worst competitors in series history.

Keegan replies. 'You know my feeling on this. If I went there with Margaret Thatcher my old dad would kill me, I tell you, if he was here.' Even at that moment, though, the image-conscious Keegan is aware of not upsetting anyone. 'I am thrilled she has asked me,' he adds. 'I know it's a European thing and nothing to do with politics. I don't mean that disrespectfully.'[239]

If Best had fallen somewhat haphazardly into the world of commercial endorsement, then Keegan sought to exploit it unashamedly. He set up a fan club – which was run out of an office in a Liverpool junk shop – and was quick to establish a limited company to handle his business interests: Nageek Enterprises. Geddit? As a non-drinker, alcohol was the only brand category he would not entertain. Acknowledging his role as commercial and cultural successor to Best, he said, 'The problem with George was that he rarely turned up to the events he was being paid to attend.'[240] Keegan also promised late in 1972, 'I know where I am going and I don't think George did.'[241]

Keegan's memory of taking over Best's *Daily Express* column – as he would in *Shoot!* – was that it earned him more than his salary at Liverpool. Such was the multitude of activities in which he was involved that Shankly had to quietly remind him that it was football where he needed to concentrate his efforts. But when Leeds forward Mick Jones was publicly cautioning that 'a young lad in the game today has to watch his step – with so much money in the game he could spoil himself',[242] it was the kind of warning superfluous to the level-headed Keegan, a player who recognised his own limitations and the way in which the game was heading. 'Everybody says skill is the most important part of a footballer's make-up,' he said. 'I say you can't beat 100 per cent effort.'[243] Spoken like a true poster boy for the age.

5

SWEET TALKIN' GUYS

[Revie] is a very talented man and I don't like him. His record is unsurpassable, but I don't like the way he goes about football.

Brian Clough

I didn't like the feud between Clough and Revie. They were two sour men.

Bill Shankly

That man Malcolm Allison is an embarrassment to the game.

Don Revie

I couldn't get along with Shankly. I recognise his tremendous strength, his freakish enthusiasm, but I couldn't see any point at which our thoughts would meet.

Malcolm Allison

THE PERIOD in English football between 1971 and 1974 was dominated by the personality, achievements and shortcomings of some of the most vivid managerial figures that the country has ever seen: Brian Clough, Don Revie, Bill Shankly, Malcolm Allison and Tommy Docherty – Cloughie, The Don, Shanks, Big Mal and The Doc.

Over the course of three seasons: Clough won the League Championship, left his club amid a wave of public protest, took over at his arch-rivals and got sacked after 44 days. Revie won the FA Cup, the League and a European trophy, suffered a series of agonising and controversial near-misses and took over as manager of his country. Shankly laid the foundation for a for almost two decades of dominance by winning the League, the FA Cup and UEFA Cup, before stunning the football world with sudden retirement. Allison went from the brink of adding a League title as manager to his list of coaching achievements to suffering relegation to the Third Division. Docherty revived his country and led them to the brink of World Cup qualification; took over at the biggest club in the world and, six years after they had been champions of Europe, oversaw their relegation to the Second Division. Rare was the day when one of them wasn't making headlines of one kind or another, either through the deeds of their team or, increasingly frequently, their own squabbles, opinions and character quirks.

Big personalities in the managerial offices of leading clubs were not entirely new. As far back as the 1930s, Herbert Chapman had redefined the role by introducing the alien notions of tactics and team talks. He also demonstrated an eye for public relations by getting London Transport to rename Gillespie Road station to Arsenal, the club he was turning into the dominant force of the decade after guiding Huddersfield Town to three League Championships.

Major Frank Buckley, who had survived wounding at the Somme during the First World War and whose wife even called him 'Major', excited the media by fuelling rumours that he was preparing his Wolverhampton Wanderers players with 'monkey gland treatment'. More importantly, he helped set his club on the way to becoming the nation's best side of the early 1950s under Stan Cullis. Champion manager three times, Cullis came to be acknowledged as one of the men who helped instigate European competition by boasting that his club should be acknowledged as 'world champions' after they beat Hungarian side Honved in a high-profile challenge match in 1954.

And Sir Matt Busby, survivor of the air crash that claimed the lives of eight of his championship-winning 'Busby Babes' side at Munich in 1958, was a revered figure beyond just Manchester United, thanks to his recovery and the dignified, empathetic way he had built another great team. When, ten years on from Munich, United beat Benfica to lift the European Cup, the tears he shed with his players also flowed in living rooms up and down the country. But now, in the early years of a new decade and with Busby finally retired to the boardroom, his quiet and statesmanlike manner had little in common with the methods of the rat pack now at the forefront of his former occupation.

Here we were with a group of managers born of the Busby era, but truly coming of age in a new world of celebrity. Whereas the players, despite being on pedestals to the fans, had previously never felt too far removed from them, a first generation of stars had come through who knew nothing other than uncomplicated hero worship. It was a situation with which old-school managers such as Bill Nicholson, Bertie Mee and Ron Greenwood were constantly uncomfortable. Not so these big-personality bosses. Little did they care that the players, with their own fattening pay packets and public profile, were no longer subservient in the manner of their maximum-wage predecessors. Clough, Allison and Docherty could trump any of them when it came to ego; Shankly employed his air of mysticism; while Revie's insistence on creating a 'family' might have been ridiculed by outsiders, but was pursued with pastoral integrity and allowed him to exert a Svengali-like influence over his men.

He meant it when he said, 'It might seem trite to say that I looked on my players as sons, but this is true. I had promised their mothers and fathers I would look after them.'[244] You only have to read or listen to comments of those who played under Shankly or Revie to know how they fitted the notion of the players' manager. This was perceived to be an increasingly important prerequisite because of what historian Stephen Wagg called 'the growing militancy of footballers in the matters of pay and conditions'.[245]

Importantly, these managers fed off a cultural environment that offered a feast for their egos and personalities. Author Mark

Garnett was referring to politics when he said that television in the 1970s meant that 'applicants for high office now had to be clever, conformist, charismatic and easy on the eye'.[246] But he could also have been talking about football management at the elite level.

The most modern of managers were ready to gorge themselves on the broadcast interviews that the 1970s required to be fulfilled, or the newspaper and magazine columns that had to be ghost-written. And while they stuffed themselves, their waistlines were further fattened by legend, anecdote and scrutiny. There was a new kind of reporting on football. In previous decades, opinions had been the preserve of the big-name writers; the likes of Geoffrey Green at *The Times* or Desmond Hackett, the town crier of the *Daily Express*. Views expressed by managers tended to offer journalists a foundation for contradiction; a lining with which to layer their own soap box. But since the 1960s, the managers had occupied a more central position in football reporting. Their views were increasingly the hooks on which match reports were hung; previews were built around opinions and insights given freely when reporters phoned or called at the training ground. Managers unwilling to give the reporters 'a line' were less likely to find supportive pieces written on their behalf in tough times. And the growing frequency with which television had taken their jobs into living rooms meant that the public cared more about what these now-familiar faces had to say than the men paid to report on it.

When it came to filling magazines with glossy posters or producing stickers and bubble gum cards, then the players, with their lengthening sideburns and feather cuts, offered a glamour that the previous generation of up-from-the-pits pros would have scoffed at. Their managers could not grow their hair or strut around the field like fancy dans, but when words – written or spoken – were demanded, then step forward Clough and company. In London, where I lived, *The Big Match* would often invite the star of the previous day's games into the studio. For every confident and relaxed Terry Venables chatting comfortably about Queens Park Rangers' latest game, there was a parade of painfully nervous, monosyllabic stars – usually shot in unforgiving close-up without effective make-up – whose eloquence clearly ended at the touchline.

They offered little other than reinforcement of a sketch in the final *Monty Python's Flying Circus* of 1969, when the interviewer, Eric Idle, sat across a studio from the cross-armed, lock-jawed John Cleese, playing Jarrow United's Jimmy Buzzard.

> PRESENTER: Jimmy, at least one ageing football commentator was gladdened las night by the sight of an English footballer breaking free of the limpet tentacles of packed Mediterranean defence.
>
> BUZZARD *(staring at interviewer)*: Good evening, Brian.
>
> PRESENTER: Were you surprised at the way the Italians ceded midfield dominance so early on in the game?
>
> BUZZARD: Well, Brian *(pause)* ... I'm opening a boutique.
>
> PRESENTER: This is, of course, symptomatic of a new breed of footballer. It is indeed symptomatic of your whole genre of player, is it not?
>
> BUZZARD: *(pause)* Good evening, Brian.
>
> PRESENTER: What I'm getting at, Jimmy, is that you seem to have discovered a new concept with the mode in which you dissected the Italian defence last night.
>
> BUZZARD *(looking around)*: I hit the ball first time and there it was in the back of the net.

Where the players might have to suffer a little ridicule in the name of light entertainment, for the managers, with all their idiosyncrasies, there was the flattery of imitation. If Mike Yarwood was not getting his material from union leaders, political heavyweights or Frank Spencer from *Some Mothers Do 'Ave 'Em*, then the likes of Clough and Revie offered a change in repertoire. When the nation's favourite impressionist pointed his finger and let the words 'young man' descend from his nasal passages on weekend television, you knew that thousands of schoolboys would be doing the same in playgrounds on Monday.

And while there might have been little in common between Revie's paranoia, Clough's braggadocio and Shankly's messianic quality, what did connect this managerial group was their fanatical self-belief. No one could tell Revie that his dossiers and superstitions were not the way to go about it; Clough would never worry that the force of personality that drove his methods might require deeper tactical thought. You couldn't ask Shankly to tone down the rabid passion for everything connected to Liverpool; and if Allison wanted to step – cigar and champagne in hand – out of the relative shadows of a brilliant coaching career into the managerial spotlight, well, pass him his Cuban. And you might as well have told Docherty to take a vow of silence as suggest that he cut out the gags and be seen to be taking a more solemn approach to his job. 'People who think I am not serious enough don't really know me,' he once said. 'If I didn't have a sense of humour I'd be dead by now.'

According to Barney Ronay, in his 2009 book, *The Manager*, 'Bill Shankly gave the manager his voice.'[247] Not that every manager wanted to use it. There were still suspicious souls, such as Bertie Mee, whose view was, 'if a manager says what he wants, he must allow his players to say what they want. The media are out to exploit them.'[248] And Jeremy Novick, in his study of the profession, *In a League of Their Own*, cited Shankly as linking the old guard of managers, such as Mee and Nicholson, with Clough and Allison. He described him as 'the man who developed the one-liner as a weapon when managers were only just coming into public perception'.[249]

With his buzz-cut hair and instantly recognisable, easily copied growl, Shankly had a powerful persona to complement his success at Liverpool, the club at which he arrived after a decade learning the managerial trade at Carlisle United, Grimsby Town, Workington and Huddersfield Town. Accompanying the image was a depth of instinct that perhaps no one since Chapman had shared.

He tapped into the sense of civic pride that was mounting in Liverpool with every hit recorded by The Beatles, Gerry and the Pacemakers and Billy J. Kramer; each television appearance by comedian Jimmy Tarbuck or singer Cilla Black. He turned the Anfield crowd into his team's 12th man, connecting The Kop with his players in a manner never previously witnessed at an English football ground. 'I loved the way he seemed to encapsulate everything I held close to my heart and aspired to be; a Liverpudlian, a football man and a socialist,' said fan and future journalist Brian Reade.[250] Long-time Liverpool defender Tommy Smith contended, 'He made the crowd part of the club and the club part of the side. He energised everything and made everyone pull together.'[251]

Mind games were everything with Shankly – whether it was the hypnotic spell he cast over the terraces; the manner in which he got inside players' heads by dismissing the opposition in team talks; or his attempts to intimidate faint-hearted visitors with the famous 'This Is Anfield' sign that was unavoidable as rivals entered the field of play. He understood the power of image, too. While Revie was putting his team in white to make them think they were Real Madrid, Shankly changed his team's shorts from white to red in 1964, getting his skipper Ron Yeats to model the new all-scarlet uniform and telling him, 'You look eight feet tall.'

He fostered team spirit by forcing the players to spend additional minutes with each other by making them arrive at Anfield every day before being taken by bus to the training ground. On a practical level, the return journey also ensured that they finished sweating before showering, a far healthier approach to personal hygiene, reducing the risk of fevers and muscle strains.

And Shankly could recognise talent. He built the team that won the Football League in 1964 and 1966 – and the FA Cup in between – by making shrewd cost-effective signings such as Ian St John, Ron Yeats, Geoff Strong and Willie Stevenson, and recognising the right time to introduce the likes of Roger Hunt, Ian Callaghan, Chris Lawler and Smith from the club's own development pathway. He also recognised when it was time to start again. Early in 1970, with

The Beatles only weeks away from dissolving, an FA Cup defeat at Second Division Watford told him that it was time to break up the band. The likes of Yeats, St John and Strong were on their way out.

Acknowledging that Shankly 'knew exactly when to replace you', Yeats admitted, 'I don't think anybody had any qualms about it.' As St John added, 'As a player you always felt that there was another season. Then you'd run out of seasons.'[252]

Goalkeeper Ray Clemence – a replacement for Tommy Lawrence – and Kevin Keegan arrived inexpensively at different times from Scunthorpe United; left-back Alec Lindsay from Bury; defender/midfielder Emlyn Hughes from Blackpool; and centre-back Larry Lloyd from Bristol Rovers. Midfielder Brian Hall and winger Steve Heighway came through the ranks, while Smith, Callaghan and Lawler were as good as ever. Meanwhile, six-figure signings John Toshack, the Welsh centre-forward signed from Cardiff City, and Scotland's Peter Cormack, the ex-Nottingham Forest midfielder, proved far more effective than Shankly's previous two big-money signings. Centre-forward Tony Hateley, who cost a club-record £96,000 from Chelsea in 1967, always seemed too statuesque for Shankly's system and lasted one season, while an uncharacteristic £100,000 gamble on teenage Wolves forward Alun Evans failed to live up to the promise of a goal-scoring debut. Shankly's move for the 19-year-old with the blond mop-top haircut and only 22 League appearances and four goals to his name prompted angry justification from the Liverpool manager. 'If a player is good, then he's worth a million pounds if that's what you have to pay for him,' he boomed. Even at a tenth of that price, Evans failed to deliver return on investment and never became a fixture in the team.

Cormack admitted that being called to see Shankly left him 'shitting myself though both fear and excitement'. Yet he also remembered, 'He had a simple philosophy to football and how the game should be played.'[253]

And he loved the sport. If one aspect of Shankly became the stuff of legend more than any other, it was his passion for football. He'd taken his wife, Nessie, to a match during their honeymoon, so the story went. When he said that football was more important than life or death, it came to characterise, for better or worse, his obsession with the sport. It was that quality that allowed him to feel greater empathy for Revie than other contemporaries could muster. His recollection of the man whose side emerged to battle his own across so many competitions was, 'We discussed the game together many times and possibly Don gave his opinions to me more than anyone else. I knew Don's approach. Perhaps I was the only one who did. You could say we were as thick as thieves.'[254]

What Revie lacked in charisma, he made up for in what he could offer amateur psychologists with his paranoiac tendencies. Shankly was hardly alone in believing Revie could have benefitted from some of the levity that he, Clough, Allison and Docherty were able to bring to their roles. 'I gave him a laugh,' Shankly said. 'He seemed to be a fellow who was short of laughs and when he was with me he laughed so hard that I thought, "Well, he hasn't had a laugh for two months."'[255]

There was never a shortage of humour in the managerial life of Malcolm Allison – the shame of it being that a considerable amount ended up being at his expense. A modestly talented half-back, his career at West Ham United had been halted when tuberculosis cost him a lung. Despite an attempt to fight his way back into a team that had just won promotion to the First Division, he succumbed to the inevitable when his protégé, Bobby Moore, was preferred to him when the club suffered a series of injuries.

Allison had a well-developed interest in the technical and tactical side of football; so much so that his first book, published in 1967, would be entitled *Soccer for Thinkers*. At West Ham, he'd found a responsive group of disciples – future managers such as Dave Sexton, John Bond, Frank O'Farrell, Jimmy Andrews and Malcolm Musgrave – who would spend afternoons with Allison in Cassettari's cafe close to Upton Park, pushing condiments around the table in search of their sport's winning formula. Under an indulgent manager, Ted Fenton, Allison had been a *de facto* coach, guiding training sessions and encouraging his club to adopt the lightweight kit of the Hungarian team who captured his imagination at Wembley in 1953.

Yet it was not towards formal, full-time coaching that Allison turned when his playing career ended. Instead, he became a professional gambler and nightclub manager, which says a lot about the lifestyle preferences that were as much a part of his DNA as an instinctive feel for what it took to win on the football pitch. Allison explained that it was seeing the anticipation of Jimmy Greaves at his impending transfer from Chelsea to AC Milan – an initial excitement that the player quickly misplaced – that reminded him what he was missing. Via managerial positions at Bath City and Plymouth Argyle, Allison arrived at Maine Road in 1965, accepting the role of coach under Joe Mercer, whose ill health during his previous role at Aston Villa convinced him that attempting to steer Manchester City back to the First Division was a two-man job.

Winning promotion, it turned out, was just the beginning. In three consecutive seasons, City won the 1967-68 League Championship; lifted the FA Cup a year later; and achieved the double of League Cup and European Cup Winners' Cup in 1969-70. The latter triumph, a 2-1 win against Poland's Gornik Zabrze in a rain-sodden and deserted stadium in Vienna, was denied the recognition it deserved by virtue of being played without live television coverage in Britain on the night of the epic Chelsea–Leeds FA Cup Final replay.*

Allison's innovation was the perfect foil for Mercer's benevolent nurturing of players and avuncular public relations persona. He introduced revolutionary science-based fitness training and recognised the need to create tactics to suit the situation. He was, for example, one of the first British coaches to regularly employ a sweeper when the need arose. And, like Shankly, he possessed the ability to make players perform above themselves. Colin Bell, whom Allison had pursued while at Bury and turned into – he believed – England's finest midfielder, explained, 'Malcolm was into eating the right things on match days, drinking the right drinks. He would bring in anyone or any little thing that improved your performance. At Salford

* 'It was a complete and utter disappointment,' said Colin Bell in his *Striker* column. 'The walk-out on to the field in this giant stadium was one of the greatest anti-climaxes ever experienced … I have been to non-League games that have commanded more attention.'

University, he would make us run around in a gas mask to make us breathe more economically.'[256]

He wanted teams to rely on more than fitness and stamina, however, and insisted that the introduction of a coached playing system did not mean that his teams had to follow what he felt was the cautious, rigid approach with which England won the World Cup. 'We played the system which suited us and did not conform to the "new age",' he once said. According to winger Mike Summerbee, 'The Dutch learned from us. We attacked quickly and could be shooting at goal in three passes. Our forwards were never in the same place, we could switch positions, and we played simple football at a fast pace. Teams were afraid of us. We never passed the ball square; the intention was to get the ball and run at people. We had Mike Doyle and Alan Oakes coming forward and Bell making his 40-yard runs. People ended up talking about [Francis] Lee, Bell and Summerbee because we were the forwards, but we had good players throughout the team.'[257]

Yet everything changed for Allison in the summer of 1970, when he was invited to sit alongside Derek Dougan, Pat Crerand and Bob McNab on ITV's revolutionary World Cup panel. While BBC carefully and cautiously placed the likes of Brian Clough and Bob Wilson into their coverage of events in Mexico, ITV head of sport John Bromley decided to stick all his experts in front of the camera at once. With the studio-bound Brian Moore and the usually-opinionated Jimmy Hill struggling to keep control, the result was television gold. The quartet, often dressed as though they were on their way to a nightclub – which they probably were – argued, joked, drank and smoked through three weeks in which the commercial network, for the first time ever, found its football ratings matching those of the BBC in a straight shoot-out. Allison was the undisputed leader of the pack, his views as loud as his shirts and as politically correct as a comedian in a working men's club.

'We suddenly realised we had hit the jackpot,' Moore recalled, describing the panel as 'attractive men with a knowledgeable, knockabout style'. He added, 'They gave football punditry a fresh, intoxicating sparkle ... we had passionate, controversial, confrontational discussion, sometimes outrageous, even bigoted.'[258] Quite. It was Allison's reference to Soviet and Romanian players as 'peasants' that brought calls of complaint to the ITV switchboard.

Yet the objectors were outnumbered by those who wrote fan letters and clamoured for autographs. 'Malcolm took to it like a duck to water,' said McNab. 'He loved going out and being recognised in restaurants. One night we went to eat in Mayfair and Michael Caine came in with a group of people and he came over and bought us a couple of bottles of champagne. He told his people to go and get themselves some drinks "while I have a drink with the lads". Malcolm took over then. He was the leader and Michael Caine seemed pleased just to be with us.'[259]

It turned out that Allison the coach had been merely a skin struggling to contain the larger-than-life celebrity that resided within; the alter ego that people came to remember ahead of the on-field innovator. A popular joke at the time went, 'They are making Malcolm Allison the England coach. They are fitting the seats in his mouth next week.' And the gentle, old-fashioned Alec Stock told *The Sun* that managers such as Allison and Docherty were popular 'because they are ready to say all the impolite things a real professional wouldn't say'. He warned, 'They'd better be good. The long knives are waiting for them.'

After winning so many trophies as a second-in-command, the additional jolt of energy his ego received from the World Cup panel had the same effect as someone making Dr Robert Banner angry. Instead of the green-skinned Hulk bursting out of Banner's ripping shirt, it was Big Mal, clad in a fedora and clinking jewellery, who emerged from the maroon tracksuit in which he was frequently photographed on the training ground.

Allison never made any secret of his preferred lifestyle, counting a former Miss United Kingdom, singer Dorothy Squires and the infamous Christine Keeler† among the many conquests on his road to

† Keeler was the former call-girl who created a national scandal at the height of the Cold War in 1963 when it transpired she had been sleeping with Defence Secretary John Profumo at the same time as conducting an affair with a Soviet diplomat.

a pair of divorces. 'He always had this swagger about him,' said Tony Book, the full-back whom Allison took from Bath City to Plymouth Argyle and then helped to become Footballer of the Year at City. 'He was a big, strong, good-looking fellow. In those days we had free-standing weights and once you had done your exercise he would just lift the weight off your shoulder and hand it to the next man. Easy as anything.'[260]

But after the summer of 1970 Allison began to lose his powers. 'Malcolm was probably one of the best coaches the game has ever seen and at that time he was probably the best in the world,' said Lee. 'But the moment he hit the big time and things started to go really well he wasn't happy to be the coach, he wanted to run everything.'[261]

Allison had masterminded various on-field successes and was a media darling. He believed he should be calling the shots at Manchester City, especially as Mercer had previously given him the impression that he intended to step aside. A proposal that Allison accept the title of team manager while Mercer, as general manager, maintained overall control was a matter of semantics, not the transfer of power he craved. Yet a struggle for boardroom power offered Allison an opportunity. He became an ally of new chairman Peter Swales, and early in 1971-72 was named as team manager with full responsibilities. Mercer was moved upstairs without any obvious portfolio.

Allison was free of Mercer and, according to many, free of the restraints that kept his ego in check. 'If there was one person Malcolm would listen to it was Joe,' Bell recalled. 'He let him do his own thing most of the time, but if Malcolm went off the straight and narrow, Joe was there.'[262] Not anymore. The beast had been unleashed.

While Allison had been an average player with big ideas, Clough had been a genuine star. Had it not been for the fact that he scored his goals for Middlesbrough and Sunderland in the Second Division he would likely have earned more than two England caps. Yet his managerial origins shared one defining element with the story of Allison; the need to prove himself after a playing career ended prematurely. At the age of 27, three years younger than Allison when he lost his lung, Clough tore up his knee in a collision with Bury goalkeeper Chris Harker on a muddy Boxing Day pitch at Roker Park. Like Allison, he made an unsuccessful comeback attempt. But where Allison took to the racetrack, Clough found salvation from depression in an offer to coach Sunderland's youth team. With that simple appointment, football history was changed forever.

After gaining his FA coaching certificate and helping Sunderland to the semi-finals of the FA Youth Cup, he was named manager of Fourth Division Hartlepools United, taking his close friend, former Middlesbrough goalkeeper Peter Taylor, as assistant manager. John McGovern, whose career would become inextricably linked with Clough, first met the new manager when he addressed a group of triallists. 'Stand up straight, get your shoulders back and your hair cut. You look like a girl,' Clough told McGovern, who cycled home to tell his mother that 'the bogeyman has arrived'. Yet McGovern, whose father had died when he was 11, had been introduced to the man who was to dominate his working life. 'Brian probably represented that senior dominant male figure I never had at home,' he said, 'and I listened intently to this fascinating man who had suddenly come into my life.'[263]

When Clough wasn't doing his own DIY work on the ground or gaining a licence to drive the team bus, the youngest manager in the League was making shrewd signings, earning his club a bigger name within the game and, of course, promoting his own abilities. 'I am better than the 500 or so managers who have been sacked since the war,' he said.

Inevitably, a bigger opportunity awaited, although the Derby County at which he arrived in 1967 had won nothing since lifting the FA Cup immediately after the war and were stuck in the Second Division. Having taken Taylor with him – much to the surprise of chairman Sam Longson and his bank account – he grabbed a bargain in signing the influential Dave Mackay from Tottenham for £5,000 in the summer of 1968. The former Scotland half-back might have been bearing a little more weight than when helping Spurs win the Double, but with the resolve that had seen him battle back from two broken legs, he carried Derby's combination of youngsters and small-team signings to the Second Division title, and a share of the Footballer-of-the-Year award with Book. Mackay became mentor to Roy McFarland, a stylish young centre-half signed from Tranmere Rovers after Clough's midnight visit to his home and promises of turning him into an England player; and he helped to inspire forward John O'Hare and midfielder McGovern, signed from Sunderland and Hartlepools respectively.

Once up in the top flight, Clough went to Nottingham Forest – from where he had signed left-winger Alan Hinton in his early weeks at the Baseball Ground – to secure experienced Wales half-back Terry Hennessey. His team finished fourth, but were denied the place they had earned in Europe and fined £10,000 after being charged with 'gross negligence' in administrative matters – including a payment of £2,000 to Mackay for writing programme articles. They picked up another trophy in the summer of 1970 when they thrashed Manchester United in the first final of the pre-season Watney Cup *(see Chapter 6)*.

The 1970-71 season saw them finish an unremarkable ninth but pull off the eye-catching British record £170,000 signing of Colin Todd, a defender in the Bobby Moore mould whom Clough had coached at Sunderland. What made it more audacious was that he completed the deal without bothering to tell Longson, who was on a Caribbean holiday.

There always seemed to be a story around Clough's transfers. At the start of 1971-72 he decided that Archie Gemmill, a little bundle of energy in Preston North End's midfield, was what he needed to strengthen his team. Knowing that Everton were also interested, Clough refused to accept Gemmill's initial reticence, declaring that he would sleep in his car outside the player's house so that they could talk again in the morning. Instead, Gemmill's wife offered him the couch for the night and legend has it that agreement was reached over a fried breakfast.

But that was nothing compared to the strangeness that ensued as the season approached its exciting climax. Looking to make a signing that could provide vital impetus over the final weeks, Clough set his heart upon Nottingham Forest's Ian Storey-Moore, a beautifully balanced forward who could play wide or at inside-forward, scored a goal every other game, and who might have won more than one England cap under a more daring manager than Sir Alf Ramsey. Someone like Clough, for example. The brilliant individual effort with which he had scored against Arsenal in December 1971, overshadowing Alan Ball's Gunners debut, was voted the City Ground's greatest goal decades later.

That kind of skill meant that Manchester United saw him as the ideal successor to an apparently uninterested George Best. Forest manager Matt Gillies agreed a fee of £200,000 with United's Frank O'Farrell, inviting him to discuss personal terms with the player. When no immediate agreement was reached, Clough was allowed to try his luck and the player was told to wait at Nottingham's Edwalton Hotel, where he had met O'Farrell, for Derby's managerial duo. 'Peter and Brian arrived with their big coats and all and basically told me that I was going to Derby County,' he recalled. 'It was intimidating. Like most players and people in the game, you were in awe of the two of them.'[264]

Agreement was reached and Clough told his apparent recruit that he had sorted things out with Forest. He then effectively kidnapped Storey-Moore, taking him to the Midland Hotel in Derby. He refused to allow him contact with anyone until he had taken him on to the Baseball Ground pitch before kick-off against Wolverhampton Wanderers and staged a contract signing. 'He is a Derby player and has been a Derby player since seven o'clock last night,' Clough told reporters as they entered the stadium. Asked why it was being suggested that he would be joining United, a confused-looking Storey-Moore responded, 'I don't know anything about it. All I know is I have joined a great club.'

But which club? Those same reporters were still outside the ground after the game. 'Not again,' sighed Clough when confronted by the microphones. He was informed that the Forest board were saying there had been no deal with Derby. 'I am not interested in what the Notts Forest committee has to say at all,' he replied, clearly agitated. 'I told you earlier he signed for Derby last night. Please do not waste my time asking the same question.'

For all Clough's bravado, Storey-Moore recalled, 'I didn't know, but they were trying to bluff it and the [Forest] chairman phoned my wife and said there was no way Forest would allow me to go to Derby.'[265] Forest argued that whatever Storey-Moore had signed was worthless. That he ended up joining United for £200,000 was, according to a BBC news report, down to his wife, Carol. Interviewed at home on an orange armchair in front of crimson wallpaper – this was the 1970s, don't forget – she explained that this was a rare occasion on which she had put her foot down. 'I don't interfere with his football in any way,' she said apologetically, 'but where our personal happiness is concerned I felt it was my duty as his wife to have him here and give him a chance to think clearly and decide what he wanted to do.'

Publicly, Clough shrugged and got on with the title race. Privately, he never forgave Storey-Moore and when they crossed paths at a function many years later, Clough barked at him, 'Oh, it's you. They tell me you're not as big a shithouse as you used to be.' No one emerged from the episode with any credit, Storey-Moore admitting he ended up being 'embarrassed and disorientated by the whole thing'.[266] *Inside Football* columnist Bob Dawbarn summed it up by saying that Clough 'ended up looking like the guy with custard pie on his face', while his verdict on Storey-Moore was, 'Thank God he shows more decisiveness on the field than he does off it.'[267] It was one of the rare occasions when Clough, whose actions were described as 'crass' by journalist Patrick Collins, did not get his own way.

FIGHT TO THE FINISH

Take me on a roller coaster, take me on an airplane ride

'Virginia Plain', Roxy Music (Bryan Ferry; Universal Music, 1972)

Having emerged into public consciousness in the 1960s, the managerial personalities of Shankly, Revie, Clough and Allison were fully formed by the early 1970s. And now fate threw them together in a 1971-72 League Championship race in which the top four teams finished separated by a single point, something that had not happened before or since. When the final Saturday of the League season was concluded, three of them were still in with a chance of winning the title. To demonstrate how close things were, Manchester City, who had assumed top spot with a superb 2-0 win against Derby, were the only one of the top four who were unable to take the title, due to the various games in hand that their rivals still had to fulfil.

Once Manchester United began to falter and George Best's unpredictability ensured that they wouldn't recover, it became merely a question of time before the pack swept past the pacemaker. Quite who would emerge on top, though, was anyone's guess. Leeds and Liverpool beat Derby, who beat Manchester City, who beat Liverpool, who lost against Leeds. As 1972 arrived, and Leeds beat Liverpool for a second time, the table showed United's lead down to two points.

United and City had shared six goals in one of the games of the season at Maine Road in November, but now it was City who made the first major move as United slipped out of contention. With Lee on his way to 33 League goals, City boasted a five-point lead by the middle of March. Leeds still had games in hand, but they had seen in previous campaigns that quick-fire fixtures at the back end of the season had less currency than points in the bank. Allison, though, was taking no chances. Or was he? In a move still debated by City fans – even after the club eventually became champions of England again in 2012 after a gap of 44 years – Allison decided that Queens Park Rangers forward Rodney Marsh could provide the stimulus to carry them through the final weeks of the campaign.

On one hand, Marsh fitted the Allison ideal perfectly, having established himself unequivocally as one of the most gifted footballers of his generation. Allison's long-time pursuit of Marsh had been one reason why he'd fallen out with the more cautious Mercer. But with the freedom to disregard sound counsel, Allison seemed to have forgotten that Marsh was used to playing as an individual. QPR fitted their game around him. City's essence, meanwhile, was movement and fluidity, their speed of passing. What they didn't need was someone to stop the ball in its tracks, flick it up and indulge in a bit of juggling while his team-mates raced into position for a pass that never arrived.

Some believed that Allison felt he'd needed to match the impact of neighbours United signing Storey-Moore. It was an identical £200,000 that Allison committed to the purchase of a man who had scored 17 Second Division goals for QPR that season and who, he believed, 'could blossom in to English football's biggest crowd puller'. But after a 1-0 victory over Chelsea on his debut, City won only three of their final eight games and Marsh was dropped for failing to meet Allison's fitness demands. By the time he cut Derby to shreds with a virtuoso first goal in a 2-0 win in City's last match, the title was a mathematical impossibility. Marsh would come to be remembered unfairly as the man who cost City the title. The fault was Allison's. 'If [Rodney] was going to come,' said Bell, 'I couldn't understand why he didn't come in the summer instead of when we were sailing on quite nicely. It was too much to expect to bring in a player and get him used to your formation and your team in a few games.'[268]

In the middle of February, it had appeared that Leeds, despite having already lost six League matches and been involved in their own transfer saga,[‡] were in the kind of form that gave them the best chance to threaten City's aspirations. First, they demolished the previously high-flying Manchester United, who conceded all five goals in the second half. Two weeks later, after reaching the FA Cup quarter-finals in the meantime, Leeds stuck seven past Southampton. It was the television viewers' good fortune that BBC's cameras had been in place to record both victories. In the second, they captured one of the most famous televised sequences in an entire decade of football as the Leeds players flicked, volleyed and stroked the ball around among themselves. More than 20 passes were completed, most in the

‡ In November 1971, Don Revie agreed a £177,000 deal to sign West Bromwich Albion's 21-year-old midfielder Asa Hartford. A press conference was staged and, before heading into his medical examination, Hartford was informed he would be making his debut that Saturday against Leicester City. Without hesitation, he told the Leeds doctors he had been diagnosed with a heart murmur as a child, but it had never affected him. An electro-cardiograph test was duly carried out and, the following morning, Revie told him there would be no debut and that he needed to see another specialist. Later, Revie informed him, 'We cannot sign you. It's your heart.' Tests had revealed a small hole. Two days later, another specialist gave him clearance to continue his career with West Brom. He was still playing professionally at the age of 40, having appeared in two World Cups.

Southampton half, as the ball swung from one touchline to the other. 'To say that Leeds are toying with Southampton is the understatement of the season,' purred Barry Davies in the commentary position. 'Poor Southampton don't know what day it is. Every man jack of this Leeds side is now turning it on.' As Giles curled his left leg around right to deliver a first-time 'Rabona' pass to Clarke, Davies exclaimed, 'Oh, look at that. It is almost cruel … for the second home match running Leeds United are turning on a brilliant show and the other team are just not on the park.' Even Bremner was forced to admit years later, 'Certainly Southampton players took exception to it at the time and rightly so.'[269]

When Nottingham Forest were beaten 6-1 three weeks later, *Sunday Express* writer Alan Hoby exclaimed, 'I used to think in their golden heyday that Real Madrid, Manchester United, Celtic and Spurs represented poetic perfection in soccer … but I am beginning to wonder if Leeds, with their advanced tactics, their exciting elegance and flair, may outstrip them all.'

Revie might have been the least 'show-business' of the title-chasing managers, but it was he who struck up an unlikely alliance with Paul Trevillion, who, as well as making a name for himself as a football artist, was a stand-up comedian and marketing ideas man. Having approached Bill Nicholson with his notions of adding some razzmatazz to Tottenham's presentation, he was encouraged by the Spurs boss to speak with Revie, whom he knew craved a brighter public image for his team. Trevillion's ideas were revealed before a home tie against Tottenham in the FA Cup quarter-finals. Long before kick-off, wearing tracksuit tops bearing their names, the players took the field for an elaborate, choreographed warm-up routine. They were also sporting numbered sock tags, with the idea of handing them to children at the end of the match. When they re-emerged prior to kick-off, they waved to all four sides of the ground and kicked plastic footballs into the crowd before backing up the showmanship with a 2-1 victory.

Not everyone approved of such an ostentatious display. Noting that Leeds might never be widely loved, *Inside Football*'s Patrick Collins suggested, 'They might offset some of the resentment if only they would stop trying so hard. They could start by scrapping the gimmicks. They're far too obvious, too transparent and, anyway, people go to Elland Road to watch a match, not to collect stocking tags.'[270]

The eventual progress of Leeds to a Cup final against holders Arsenal meant the usual distractions to their title challenge, but after they had beaten Spurs *The Times* ventured, 'They are playing so well it is difficult to visualise them ever losing again.' Yet when they were beaten 2-0 by Derby on 1 April – Gemmill, Alan Durban and McGovern having overpowered Bremner and Giles in midfield – the same publication was quick to write them off with a headline that announced, 'Leeds heading for their usual disappointment.' Manchester City's home defeat by Stoke City meant it was Derby's turn to sit on top of the table, although Clough warned, 'We are only there until the next match.' Clough should have been proved right when Derby promptly lost 1-0 at home to Newcastle United on Easter Monday, but they remained as leaders when City went down at Southampton. And with the games coming thick and fast – a product of the magnificent, crazy holiday football schedules of yore – Derby were held two days later at West Bromwich Albion. Meanwhile, Leeds climbed over Liverpool into second place with a laboured 3-1 home win against Huddersfield Town, meaning that only two points separated the top four. Bookmakers clearly disagreed with *The Times*'s dismissal of Leeds, making them 6-4 favourites, with Derby 5-2, Liverpool 7-2 and Manchester City 9-2. Yet in the very next set of games, it was Derby who played like champions in a 4-0 win at Sheffield United, while Leeds lost left-back Terry Cooper to a broken leg in their win against Stoke, haunting echoes of Paul Reaney two years earlier.

With only one full Saturday of the League season remaining, it was Liverpool who had made the quietest progress into contention. Their efficient 2-0 win at West Ham was their 12th in 13 games. A title challenge had appeared a long way off when they won only five of their first 12, and by the time they kicked off 1972 with defeats against Leeds and Leicester they had lost three straight games and eight overall. Stuck in ninth place, a swift end to the miners' strike appeared more realistic than another Liverpool title. A 0-0 draw against Wolves meant they had not scored in five League games and when Keegan netted the fourth goal against Crystal Palace on the last Saturday of January it rounded off their first League victory for seven weeks. But what followed was a run of seven games in which they didn't concede a single goal and racked up six wins.

On the final Saturday, John Toshack's two goals against Ipswich Town made it 13 wins out of 14, although they now had tough trips to Derby and Arsenal in their last two games. Derby had been beaten at Manchester City, while Leeds won at West Bromwich, against whom their hopes had exploded in controversy a year earlier.

Now came the additional games that would decide the title, all played beyond the glare of the television cameras and without national radio commentary. The detailed urgency of Peter Jones and the unhurried delivery of Maurice Edelston on BBC Radio 2 could only be heard during the second half of one Saturday afternoon League game per week. Midweek radio football was confined to cup competitions. It meant that Arsenal's dramatic title decider a year earlier could only be followed via occasional score flashes. Such would be the case for the key games that remained in the current season, and for the various other times throughout the decade when the eventual champions were unable to cooperate by earning their decisive points at the weekend.

With the days after the final Saturday of the League season being kept free for England to prepare for their European Nations Cup quarter-final against West Germany, it was the Monday before the FA Cup Final when Leeds beat Chelsea by two goals and Liverpool travelled to the Baseball Ground. Only victory would be enough for a Derby team who had begun the season with a 12-game unbeaten run but then had their fixture schedule punctuated by frequent defeats. Never were they considered title favourites, certainly not until they concluded a run of seven wins in eight games during spring with that win against Leeds at the beginning of April.

Always unpredictable, Clough threw 16-year-old midfielder Steve Powell into potentially the biggest match in the club's history in place of injured right-back Ron Webster. He watched him perform with maturity and confidence in the frenzied atmosphere created by a crowd of almost 40,000. Derby scored the only goal after 20 minutes of the second half, McGovern shooting high past Clemence to complete a flowing team move. Top of the league with 58 points from their completed schedule of 42 games, all they could do now was head off on a club holiday to Majorca and await further news.

Seven days later, it was Leeds who had the destination of the title in their own hands. Having had 48 hours to patch themselves up after Allan Clarke's diving header against Arsenal won them their first FA Cup – at the cost of Mick Jones's dislocated elbow late in the game – a draw at Wolves would see them replicate the Gunners' Double of the season before. If Leeds lost, Liverpool would be able to steal top spot if they could win at Highbury. A Derby triumph was rated third in the line of probable outcomes.

Events at Molineux, in front of more than 53,000, would resonate over the years, the subject of controversy and court action. 'Leeds died like heroes,' according to *The Times* after a game that Clarke and Giles could only play in once injuries had been heavily strapped and in which they were denied two legitimate penalty appeals for handball. They fell two goals behind either side of half-time, the second after 67 minutes by Derek Dougan, who described the night as 'the most dramatic match I ever played in'. Within a minute, Billy Bremner pulled a goal back, but Revie's fatigued troops could not force another breakthrough in a frantic final 20 minutes.

Liverpool's bid to snatch a title that had seemed beyond them at the mid-point of the season ended when they were denied a winning goal inside the last five minutes at Arsenal, referee Roger Kirkpatrick ruling that Toshack was offside when putting the ball in the net. 'I was there because I had reacted quicker than anybody else,' Toshack argued,[271] while Shankly complained that the linesman had not flagged. The decision was toasted by the Derby players in their seaside bar and by Clough, who was holidaying separately with his family in the Scilly Isles. He promptly bought champagne for everyone in his hotel restaurant. With Derby champions of England for the first time and Leeds having to settle for their fifth runners-up slot in eight seasons, Clough announced, 'For a team and a town like Derby to win the title is a credit to all concerned.'[§]

Yet the real drama surrounding the night's events was not over. In September that year, the *Sunday People* ran a story suggesting that three Wolves players had been offered £1,000 each by Revie to let Leeds win, allegations that both the police and the FA dismissed after their investigations. Revie had already made himself an easy target with his dubious tactical approach to some games, but by the time he had abandoned the job of England manager for a relative fortune in Arab money five years later, it appeared to be open season. Again, accusations were made about that Monday night at Molineux, this time in the *Daily Mirror* by Wolves players Frank Munro, scorer of his team's first goal, and Danny Hegan, who claimed they had been encouraged to give away penalties in return for cash. On this occasion, one of Revie's own men, goalkeeper Gary Sprake, supported such claims. Historical allegations of attempted match-fixing were also made, dating back to the early 1960s.

Revie was apparently too wrapped up in trying to overturn the ten-year ban the FA had imposed after his defection to take legal action, but when the *Sunday People* reported further claims by Hegan aimed at Bremner in 1982, the former Leeds captain called his lawyers. Hegan, by then suffering from alcoholism, was unable to give evidence and Sprake said he could not recall making his accusations, but Munro stuck to his guns. Meanwhile, Dougan, no great fan of Bremner, spoke on the Leeds man's behalf, saying he was unaware of any skulduggery. 'If there had been any attempts to get the game fixed, I would surely have known about it,' he argued. 'Surely you nobble the guys who might score goals for a start?' The jury took two hours to award Bremner £100,000 in damages. Revie's decision not to take legal action had been against the advice of those close to him. Leeds United president, the Earl of Harewood, told Revie's

§ A few weeks earlier Clough had stated, 'This town isn't big enough for the championship,' after fewer than 27,000 turned up for a vital home game against Ipswich Town. It was a theme he would return to while at Nottingham Forest.

biographer, Richard Sutcliffe, 'He would have won. I am certain of that. Why he didn't, I never found out. It would have helped his reputation.'[272]

It is hard not to view the Molineux episode through the lens of Johnny Giles, who described it as 'typical of some of the madder notions that have attached themselves to Leeds over the years, put about by those who seek any explanation for our success apart from the blatantly obvious one that, for a long time, we were just better than anyone else.'[273] It was, however, a suitably contentious and sensational way to conclude a top-flight season that, for all the Premier League's 'Super Sundays', may never have been beaten for its dramatic content.

WHAT'S UP, DOC?

> *REGAN: Get on with the job, to hell with tomorrow, to hell with the consequences. Because once you stop to think, once you stop to consider the ifs, the buts, the maybes, you've blown it.*
>
> ***The Sweeney*, 'Trust Red' (Richard Harris; Thames Television, 1978)**

While the League title race was playing out in a way that secured the legend of Clough, began the dismantling of Allison's reputation and narrowly failed to add to the lore of Revie and Shankly, Tommy Docherty was rebuilding his own managerial career.

Scotland team manager Bobby Brown had stumbled through the 1970-71 season in the wake of failure to qualify for the Mexico World Cup. When defeats against Belgium and Portugal quickly scuppered any hopes of qualification for the quarter-finals of the European Nations Cup, Brown criticised his players for lack of effort and accused the Scottish Football Association of lethargic efforts to secure the release of English-based players. The SFA's response was to end Brown's four-year reign during July of 1971.

By early September, the post was still vacant, although Allison was floating his name as a candidate. A more popular choice among the Scottish population was, inevitably, Celtic manager Jock Stein. But, having paid Brown an annual salary of £4,000, the SFA were scared off by the £15,000 he reportedly earned at the Scottish champions. Two days after Allison's declaration of interest, the job was handed to someone no less outspoken, although at least he was a Scot. Docherty, a former international wing-half, was offered the job on a trial basis for three matches. If he proved himself in that time, the £8,000-a-year position would be his. Perhaps only someone as self-confident as Docherty, at the time working as assistant manager at Hull City, would have accepted those terms. 'I'm the best man for the job,' he said in his usual blunt manner. 'If I didn't think so I would not have taken it.'

Docherty had taken his first steps in management when he joined Chelsea as coach in the spring of 1961, at the age of 32, after a distinguished club career with Celtic, Preston North End and Arsenal. Promoted when Ted Drake was sacked, Docherty's team played with flair and daring, and it soon became apparent that one of his greatest assets was identifying young talent. Chelsea quickly regained the First Division status they lost in the first season under new management and finished fifth, third and fifth in successive seasons. They won the League Cup in 1965 and were beaten by Tottenham Hotspur in the 1967 FA Cup Final.

Irrepressible and outspoken, with a mischievous sense of humour, Docherty was also a firm believer in discipline. He proved as much after discovering that eight players had broken a midnight curfew before a vital game against Burnley in 1965, staying out until 4am in Blackpool, where the team was lodging. The next day, skipper Terry Venables, George Graham, John Hollins, Barry Bridges, Eddie McCreadie, Bert Murray, Marvin Hinton and Joe Fascione were put on a train back to London and a depleted Chelsea side lost 6-2, derailing their title hopes.

The board backed Docherty on that occasion, but after the death of chairman Joe Mears there was a series of clashes with new chairman Charles Pratt. The incident that finally led to Docherty's departure occurred on a club tour to Bermuda, where he told a match official, 'You should be swinging from a tree, not refereeing.' The remark earned him a one-month ban from football and in October of 1967, depressed at the direction in which his career was heading, he resigned.

After a 12-month term of office at Rotherham United, where he was unable to prevent relegation to the Third Division, he was appointed in November 1968 as manager of Queens Park Rangers, who had just sacked Alec Stock following a disastrous start to their first season in the top division. Docherty approached chairman Jim Gregory to request £100,000 to sign Brian Tiler from his previous club. Gregory refused and, 28 days after his appointment, Docherty resigned again.

He was not unemployed for long. With his club struggling near the foot of the Second Division, new Aston Villa chairman Doug Ellis handed Docherty his third managerial post of the season. Relegation was avoided, but relations with Ellis never ran smoothly. Midway through another season of struggle, Docherty was fired. Next stop was Portugal, where he fulfilled a one-year contract as coach of Oporto.

His stock had plummeted over the previous three years and the man who was once lining up opposite the likes of Revie and Shankly in the biggest games in the country, now returned to England to accept the job of assistant manager at Second Division Hull City under player-manager Terry Neill, a former Arsenal team-mate. When the Scottish FA came calling, Docherty grabbed the chance to achieve the notable landmark of having captained and managed his country.

If his tongue had got him into trouble before, he still believed it was communication that was an important element of his managerial rehabilitation. There were many who felt he had blown his career at the highest levels of the game, but Docherty, rather than hitting out, went on a charm offensive. He had been 'appalled by England's breakdown in public relations in Mexico' and observed 'an atmosphere of hate and hostility towards [the media]'.

One of the great skills Docherty maintained throughout his career was getting the media to deliver stories in the way he desired. 'I always knew that in the journalism world you have got a job to do as well as I have,' he explained. 'The better the relationship we have, the better for both of us. I appreciate the fact that the editor will tell a reporter to go and check out a story and if the reporter doesn't have a good relationship with the manager then he gets agitated.'[274]

With a squad that showed a bias toward English-based players – he even picked former England Schoolboys goalkeeper Bob Wilson – and included only three players from Celtic and Rangers, Scotland beat Portugal 2-1 in Docherty's opening game, driven from midfield by Gemmill and Arsenal's George Graham. 'Some managers are thoughtful and quiet and others, like Tommy, are brash and up front,' said Graham, one of the Chelsea players Docherty had banished six years earlier. 'He was great fun, but he was very black and white. He would either bawl you out or you were the best player in Europe. And what a sense of humour. You could never take him on with one-liners.'[275]

Victory over Belgium and a brave performance in defeat in Holland confirmed Docherty as Scotland's full-time manager. 'No country in the world possesses as much natural talent as we do,' he said. 'Possibly Brazil, but that's all.' There would be a chance to prove Docherty right in a summer tournament in the world champions' backyard, but first there was the annual grudge game against England to negotiate. After Alan Ball scored the only goal at Hampden Park, there was more gnashing of teeth over the state of the British game, the excitement of the end of the English season already a distant memory. The headline in *Goal* was, 'Britain's prestige hits rock bottom in Hampden's SOCCER SAVAGERY', while editor Alan Hughes wrote of the 'disgraceful actions of a dozen or so thugs in football shirts'. Even Docherty's boss, SFA chairman Hugh Nelson stated, 'If that was international football, it is a shame. The public have a right to be entertained.'

Untroubled by such comments, Docherty took his team to Brazil, where they drew with Czechoslovakia and Yugoslavia before facing the host nation in front of 130,000 at the Maracana Stadium. Docherty at his best was, like Allison, Shankly and the others, able to convince his players that they could perform beyond what they might have thought themselves capable of. 'He gave you a lot of confidence,' said Aberdeen goalkeeper Bobby Clark. 'We felt we were as good as any opponent, even Brazil. You know in a game like that you are going to have to pick their pocket, but we didn't give them a lot of opportunities. We worked very hard.'[276]

Only in the final ten minutes did Brazil win the game, Rivelino's low diagonal cross being met by Jairzinho's diving header. According to Scotland defender Martin Buchan, 'It was a shell of a cross from Rivelino; tremendous speed. If you got on the end of it you were as liable to score an own goal as clear it.'[277]

Docherty claimed, 'The World Cup is coming up and we could not be better prepared,' and was proved correct with a pair of victories over Denmark in their opening qualifying games. With Christmas 1972 approaching and his reputation within the game reignited, Docherty was in a relaxed mood when he visited Selhurst Park to watch Crystal Palace play Manchester United. Taking his seat in the directors' box, primarily to watch Palace's Glaswegian left-back Tony Taylor, he did not have to look along too many seats to find United manager Frank O'Farrell sitting with club chairman Louis Edwards and the imposing figure of Sir Matt Busby. Lying 20th in the table, United were torn apart 5-0 by one of the two clubs below them in the table. ITV commentator Brian Moore noted their state of 'total and utter confusion'.

In the directors' lounge after the game, Docherty was astonished when Busby approached him to say, 'There's a lot of trouble in the camp. Fancy the job?'

'You've got a manager,' Docherty replied.

'We won't have by Wednesday.'

O'Farrell had gone down with the sinking ship of George Best's United career. When things had been going well in the manager's early months at Old Trafford, Denis Law had said 'he has given United back its faith and self-respect'.[278] Yet Bobby Charlton greeted his dismissal by saying, 'The team weren't fully receptive to his ideas. I don't think anyone could accuse us of lack of effort, but there just wasn't the rapport we needed.'[279]

Docherty was a former Preston team-mate of O'Farrell and the men were godfathers to each other's children. He felt compelled to share what he had been told. 'I am not surprised,' said O'Farrell, who urged his friend to accept the position when the offer was formalised. By the time *Football Monthly*'s January 1973 issue was on sale and spotlighting O'Farrell across two pages as 'the man with the most glamorous – and difficult – job in football' that challenge was now Docherty's. As much as he had loved managing his country, he could not resist the lure of Old Trafford. Besides, when he looked at the calendar, he saw that it was almost a year before Scotland played their next two qualifiers against Czechoslovakia. 'That's what I didn't like about international management; the gaps between games,' he said. 'If you didn't do something very well then you had to wait until the next training session in a few weeks to put it right. At a club you could put it right on Monday.'[280]

There was a lot to put right at Old Trafford. And it would take a lot longer than the following Monday to achieve it.

6

GAMES WITHOUT FRONTIERS

SIR HUMPHREY APPLEBY: Minister, Britain has had the same foreign policy objective for at least the last 500 years; to create a disunited Europe. In our cause we have fought with the Dutch against the Spanish, with the Germans against the French, with the French and Italians against the Germans, and with the French against the Italians and the Germans. Divide and rule, you see. Why should we change now when it's worked so well?

Yes Minister, 'The Writing on The Wall'
(Antony Jay and Jonathan Lynn; BBC TV, 1980)

'I WILL not speak to cheating bastards.' Brian Clough's words hung in the air; their meaning clear to those Italian journalists who possessed only the most basic understanding of English. For those in any doubt, Brian Glanville, the Italian-speaking English writer, was instructed to translate.

Derby County had just lost 3-1 at Juventus in the first leg of the 1973 European Cup semi-final and Clough was fuming. The result was bad enough. The actions of the German referee Gerhard Schulenburg were what really had him at boiling point. 'We had two key players booked well before half-time,' he recalled later. 'Their only crime was to stand somewhere adjacent to an opponent who flung himself to the floor.'[281] The fact that the men in question, Roy McFarland and Archie Gemmill, would now be suspended for the second leg was, Clough believed, no coincidence. Peter Taylor had seen Juventus's German midfielder, Helmut Haller, trailing the referee towards his dressing-room at half-time – and had been manhandled by security officers when he tried to intervene. No wonder Clough felt that 'the whole episode stank the place out'.[282] John McGovern left the field with tears in his eyes, 'astonished that such favouritism could happen during a televised game at which UEFA officials were present'.[283]

Clough would claim, 'Juventus bought the referee. Of that there is no shadow of doubt. I was cheated, Taylor was nearly arrested, and two players were booked for next to nothing. What surprised me is that Juventus were good enough without that. They were the better side, but we could have reached the final if Gemmill and McFarland had played at Derby.'[284] The comment column in *Goal* satisfied its nationalistic self by declaring that 'no English referee would have handled the game in such a fashion. They have far too much character for that.'[285]

Derby could only draw the second leg 0-0, Alan Hinton missing a penalty and Roger Davies being sent off for an attempted headbutt on defender Francesco Morini, who ended up sprawled in the back of the goal. 'I'd given him a good right hook earlier on which I'd got away with,' admitted Davies, who'd grown weary of the shirt pulling and holding. 'I actually missed Morini with the headbutt, but he made the most of it.'[286] It also emerged later that the Portuguese referee, Francisco Marques Lobo, was offered $5,000 and a car if Juventus won, although a UEFA investigation found that the Italian club had not been the instigators of the alleged bribery.

A few weeks later, Leeds United, who had set out to achieve in the Cup Winners' Cup what Derby were denied in the premier European competition, were left feeling equally aggrieved. Again it was Italian opposition, AC Milan, that aroused suspicion. Sidelined because of injury, Johnny Giles had attended a pre-match press conference and heard talk among journalists that Leeds 'can't win this game'. A goal resulting from a dubious free-kick award by Greek referee Christos Michas and the refusal of two Leeds appeals for penalties left the fans in Salonica jeering the referee at the final whistle and halting the winning team's lap of honour with a barrage of missiles. Although nothing could be proved in relation to this match – which came days after Leeds had been stunned by Second Division Sunderland in the FA Cup Final – UEFA subsequently banned Michas from officiating in their competitions. Meanwhile, the request of Leeds for the game to be replayed was turned down.*

As bitter as the feeling induced by both those incidents was, neither were particularly new or unexpected when it came to matches between English and Italian opposition in these still relatively early years of European competition. *Goal*'s European football correspondent Leslie Vernon had written, 'The distressing European Cup Winners' Cup Final has confirmed my long-held belief that if there are two countries which shouldn't meet on a football pitch it surely must be England and Italy. Their written and unwritten rules create a practically unbridgeable gap.'[287]

Without the widespread televising of international leagues that would become commonplace in the 21st century, foreign opposition was still viewed with suspicion, being largely unknown to all but the best-travelled journalists. Trips to away games were treated as ventures into war zones; tactics and methods that were common in overseas domestic competitions considered underhand.

When Britain had entered the European Economic Community – the Common Market – on the first day of 1973,† it was supposed to have brought its people closer to their continental counterparts. Yet a month later, the prevailing mistrust of foreigners was reflected in the

* Decades later, in 2009, the incident still rankled enough for Richard Corbett, MEP for Yorkshire and Humber, to present a 15,000-signature petition to UEFA demanding a re-examination of the match.

† Football offered a symbol of the UK, Ireland and Denmark's entry into the European community by the staging of 'The Three versus The Six' match in front of 36,000 at Wembley Stadium. Sir Alf Ramsey's team won 2-0 against a side selected from the six incumbent Common Market countries, managed by West Germany's Helmut Schoen. Denmark's Henning Jensen and Scotland's Colin Stein scored the goals. The greater symbolism of the night, though, was Bobby Charlton being made captain in his final representative game at Wembley in his last season of top-flight football.

'No Hiding Place' episode of *Whatever Happened to the Likely Lads?*, in which James Bolam's character, Terry, shares his views on various nationalities with his more liberal-thinking friend, Bob, played by Rodney Bewes. Offering the wisdom of his years in the army, Terry reels off a list of perceived national characteristics that were probably a closer reflection of popular opinion than Bob's mocking response. Russians, says Terry, are 'sinister'; Italians 'greasy – not as greasy as the French, mind'; Germans 'arrogant'; and the Spanish 'lazy'. He concludes, 'God didn't make this country an island by accident.'

Such suspicions had long been voiced, in less direct terms perhaps, in relation to football. Tottenham forward Alan Gilzean had written an illustrated column in the *Sunday People*, offering his guide to the 'Dirty Dodges' of European teams, including shirt pulling, time wasting and hair tugging (not that the latter was much of a concern for the balding Scot). Team-mate Phil Beal complained, 'If the European players can't have it their own way out on the park, they give up and resort to childish tactics like feigning injuries. The continental footballers must be the best actors in the world.'[288]

For years, the story of Anglo-Italian football had been one of mutual antipathy. 'In those days, the difference between Italian football and English football was remarkable,' said Arsenal captain Frank McLintock. 'In our opinion they would be sly. They would fall over looking for free-kicks and spit on you – all that stuff. We would tackle from behind and go in with big crunching tackles that they thought were unfair, so the ideologies of the two camps were poles apart.'[289]

Tommy Docherty articulated a similar view when saying, 'When these foreign sides come over here they are greeted with the tackle. And that frightens them to death. When they get back home they howl about the rough handling they have had in England. You would think we had been chopping their legs off with meat axes.' Bobby Charlton had played enough football around the world, however, to hint that prejudice was the real problem. 'There seems to be a feeling among English clubs that Italians are not to be trusted,' he said, 'and this is something we hold against them whenever we meet.'[290]

In the early 1970s, there were still plenty of fans who remembered the 1934 'Battle of Highbury'. On that occasion, England beat recent World Cup winners Italy 3-2 in a game that began with visiting centre-half Luis Monti having his foot broken in a challenge by Ted Drake after only two minutes. Retaliation was swift and repeated. Eddie Hapgood's nose was broken, Eric Brook suffered a fractured arm, Drake was punched. All before half-time. Reduced to ten men, Italy almost fought back from three goals down and returned home as heroes. The Football Association, meanwhile, considered withdrawing the England team from future international matches.

Anglo-Italian competition continued along a course of rancour, mistrust and outright violence, not helped by the unhappy tales of British players such as Denis Law and Jimmy Greaves, who returned home with horror stories after brief and unhappy transfers to Italian teams in the early 1960s. In a scenario that Clough and Don Revie would come to recognise, Liverpool took a 3-1 European Cup lead to the San Siro Stadium in 1965, only to lose 3-0 to Inter Milan when Spanish referee José María Ortiz de Mendíbil allowed two disputed goals, while ruling out a valid-looking effort by Ian St John. Glanville recalled Tommy Smith being so incensed that he kicked the referee 'all the way to the dressing-room'. Working at Inter at that time was Italo Allodi, who would be general manager of Juventus by the time they played Derby in 1973.

The following season, Chelsea beat AS Roma 4-1 at Stamford Bridge in the Fairs Cup, despite having full-back Eddie McCreadie sent off for retaliating after being grabbed by the throat. Even before kick-off in Rome, Chelsea chairman Joe Mears was struck by a tomato thrown from the crowd. The missiles became more dangerous during the game – coins, stones, cans, bottles of urine. The Roma players elbowed, stamped and pinched; John Boyle was felled by a bottle; and George Graham narrowly missed being impaled by an iron railing. Chelsea advanced with a goalless draw, while Roma were left facing a three-year ban from European competition.

Another year, another battle. This time it was Burnley who came through a bruising first leg to take a 3-0 lead to Napoli in the Fairs

Cup. Again, the English team achieved a 0-0 draw, but then the real contest began. 'Run for your lives,' ordered Burnley manager Harry Potts as home fans set fire to seat cushions and skimmed them towards the field. Reserve goalkeeper Adam Blacklaw was thrown down the steps leading to the dressing-room and the Burnley players had to hold suitcases against coach windows to protect themselves from objects thrown by Italian fans.

You might think that this manner of mayhem would discourage football contact between the two nations. Far from it. As the conflicts raged into the 1970s, they were instead given their own formal battle theatre in the shape of the Anglo-Italian Cup. Conceived in the spirit of goodwill and friendly competition, it quickly became home to festering bitterness that merely reflected what was going on in the bigger competitions. The tournament had its genesis in Swindon Town's 3-1 upset of Arsenal in the final of the 1969 League Cup. Denied entry into the Fairs Cup because they were a third-tier team, a compensatory challenge was set up against Coppa Italia winners Roma, which was duly won over two legs by the English underdogs.

The renowned Italian football agent Gigi Peronace, who had helped broker the transfer of John Charles from Leeds to Juventus and Greaves from Chelsea to AC Milan, was convinced that an expanded Anglo-Italian Cup deserved a place in the calendar. So, while the challenge between cup winners would be played over the next two seasons – and make a brief comeback in the middle of the decade – the summer of 1970 saw six teams from each country engaged in Peronace's new brainchild. Split into three groups, with two teams from each country in each, home and away contests were staged between the opposing nation's sides. With every team having played four matches, the best English and Italian teams were awarded a place in the final, points having been awarded for each goal scored in addition to the usual two for a victory.

Middlesbrough, Sheffield Wednesday, Sunderland, Swindon, West Bromwich Albion and Wolverhampton Wanderers were the first English entries. A taste of what the competition would offer came when West Brom travelled to face Lanerossi Vicenza. With the scores level at 1-1 and 15 minutes remaining, Asa Hartford's foul on home captain Roberto Di Petri set off a brawl between the players. When many of the 12,000 crowd decided it would be good fun to join in, English referee Kevin Howley abandoned the match and the competition organisers awarded a 2-0 defeat to both teams. Wolves, meanwhile, found themselves engaged in a game against Lazio in Rome that was described as a 'fight to the death' by Derek Dougan, who admitted thinking, 'If they want it that badly they can have it.'

What was needed was a showcase final. Swindon, clearly at their ease against Italian opposition, qualified to face Napoli in front of 55,000 in the Stadio San Paolo. Goals by Peter Noble gave them a 2-0 lead and when Arthur Horsfield added a third after 62 minutes the home fans had seen enough. Concrete benches were smashed and thrown, along with bottles. Fires were ignited in the stands. With 11 minutes left, and with his linesman almost struck by a missile from the crowd, Austrian referee Paul Schiller called the whole thing off and the game was awarded to Swindon. Bizarrely, the trophy presentation went ahead amid the mayhem. Swindon manager Fred Ford thought misguidedly that it might help to calm the most frenzied section of the crowd if he walked over and showed them the trophy they had failed to win. He was soon running for cover under another barrage of rubble.

Undeterred, the organisers planned for 1971, although Lanerossi, Lazio and Napoli would all be absent. By that time, Lazio – coached by Uruguayan Juan Carlos Lorenzo, who led the Argentina team referred to as 'animals' by England manager Alf Ramsey during the 1966 World Cup – had left their mark again in one of the most incredible episodes in the history of Anglo-Italian football. Arsenal had begun their defence of the Fairs Cup by drawing a bad-tempered game in Rome 2-2. 'They were treading on us and elbowing, and they would spit in your face at a corner,' recalled goalkeeper Bob Wilson. 'And they went up to the younger ones and pulled their hair. It really was horrible stuff.'[291]

It was nothing compared to what transpired at the post-match banquet, where Arsenal's less worldly squad members provoked matters by sniggering when they were presented with the kind of leather man-bags fashionable in Italy. The gifts were tossed around during the formal speeches. When striker Ray Kennedy, accompanied by full-back Sammy Nelson, ventured outside to escape the stuffy restaurant, one of the Lazio players walked past, made a derogatory comment and attempted to knee Kennedy. 'Ray just went "Smack!" and splattered him,' said Nelson. 'The other lads were coming out and there was shouting and screaming. It was like a comedy film, with people being thrown over Fiat 500s.'[292]

Bob McNab almost ended up through a plate-glass window, George Armstrong was slammed against the team bus and Peter Marinello was thrown over a car. When manager Bertie Mee attempted to restore order, he was lifted by his lapels by his opposite number. It needed the arrival of armed police to bring things to a halt. One Lazio official accepted his club's culpability, but only because 'with the dinner we provided some excellent wine'.

Mee adopted a rather more serious tone. 'It was asking too much of any group of men to resist defending themselves when they were provoked again and more seriously after the match,' he said. Arsenal's players would cite the incident as being one of those shared experiences that engendered greater team spirit as their season advanced towards the League and FA Cup double.

By the time the dust had settled on the 1970-71 season – and Leeds had beaten Italian opposition Juventus on away goals in an untypically good-natured Fairs Cup Final – six English teams were embarking on a new Anglo-Italian Cup adventure. This time the referees managed to keep the teams on the field for the duration of all the games, with Blackpool, just relegated from the First Division, finishing as the leading English representative. 'You could always feel an undercurrent,' said midfielder Alan Ainscow, who played his first games for Blackpool during the tournament. 'There was something in the air that did not feel right, something sinister. I remember one night, after a match, we got involved in an altercation. It ended with one of our players punching an Italian.'[293]

The status of the competition had grown enough for BBC to show the final, played in Bologna, live on *Grandstand*. It was a rare bonus in the days when live games were strictly rationed. The host team were held to one first-half goal by the brilliance of 19-year-old goalkeeper John Burridge and Blackpool levelled the game after 62 minutes through John Craven. Nine minutes into extra-time, the small group of travelling fans in the 40,000 crowd were sent into raptures by winger Micky Burns, who cut across the face of the penalty area from the left and lashed in the game's winning goal. With Chelsea having lifted that season's Cup Winners' Cup and Leeds the Fairs Cup, the *Blackpool Gazette* heralded its team's victory as England's third European trophy of the season. Burns explained, 'When we got back to Blackpool there was a civic reception, an open-top bus tour. It was definitely seen as an achievement.'[294]

Burns scored four goals in a 10-0 win against Lanerossi Vicenza as Blackpool made their way to the final the following year, the only English team to win all four group games. This time they went down 3-1 to Roma in front of 75,000 at the Stadio Olimpico. The tournament had featured a Stoke–Roma match in which three players were sent off.

By 1973, the fourth year of the tournament, the organisers felt obliged to address the elephant of bad blood that was not so much in the room as forcing all other occupants out into the corridor. Admitting to 'teething troubles' when writing in the souvenir brochure, Italian League president Aldo Stacchi said, 'It was inevitable that these would occur. It was no small thing to introduce a competition between peoples who needed time to understand each other.' Football League president Len Shipman sounded relieved when writing of the previous year's event, 'With one or two exceptions, the competition was played in the sporting manner we all hoped for.' It had, however, been deemed necessary to introduce a 'Good Behaviour Award', whereby the club whose players and supporters were judged to have best exemplified the notion of sportsmanship would have the team's travelling expenses to its two away games covered by a sponsor, the Fiat car company.

Having expanded to eight teams per country, the tournament was spread over the closing months of the season, rather than jammed into the summer break, and no longer featured points for goals. There was also a semi-final for the two most successful teams from each country.

In England's case, it meant Newcastle United scoring five in the second leg against Crystal Palace to ease through. Manchester United had been one of the English also-rans, with their game at Verona in May seeing Bobby Charlton score two goals in his last competitive appearance in a United shirt.

Newcastle travelled to Italy to beat Fiorentina 2-1 in the final, something midfielder Terry McDermott referred to as 'no mean feat with all the tricks the Italian teams got up to'.[295] Skipper Bobby Moncur was presented with the trophy and then saw it dented when winger Terry Hibbitt fell down some steps. There was no rush to get it fixed. Diminishing interest meant the tournament was scrapped – although it would be resurrected as a competition for non-League teams later in the decade and tried again as a professional event for a further four years in the early 1990s.

There was a reminder of why the tournament had always appeared ill-conceived a few months later when Ipswich Town beat the notorious Lazio over two legs in the UEFA Cup after Trevor Whymark's four goals had given them a 4-0 lead to take to Rome. They ended up with a 6-4 aggregate victory, but midfielder Bryan Hamilton called it 'an unsavoury night, where we just wanted to get the match over with and go home'. Angered by refereeing decisions, the home crowd 'went crazy' – according to Lazio forward Giorgio Chinaglia – and the Ipswich players were forced to shelter in their dressing-room for two hours for safety. 'No team should ever be asked to come here again,' said Ipswich manager Bobby Robson. 'Night of shame,' read the local newspaper headline, although Lazio's record suggested they might have had that one on permanent standby. On their way to winning the Serie A title, Lazio would be banned from contesting the European Cup the following season.

THERE'S A NEW SENSATION; A FABULOUS CREATION

MR SMOKETOOMUCH: Then once a week
there's an excursion to the local Roman ruins where

you can buy cherryade and melted ice cream and
bleedin' Watney's Red Barrel.

***Monty Python's Flying Circus* (BBC TV, 1972)**

In the beginning was the FA Cup, followed in relatively short order by the Football League. Not until another 70-odd years had passed did the Football League Cup arrive on the scene in the early 1960s. Now the 1970s was spawning new competitions as rapidly as Marc Bolan was churning out hits as lead singer and songwriter for the decade's first new pop sensation, T. Rex.

While the Anglo-Italian Cup had apparently been born of a desire to capitalise upon national rivalry, the new tournament that became a feature of the pre-season of 1970-71 was driven by one thing – money. 'I believe sponsorship in football has now arrived,' said Football League secretary Alan Hardaker when announcing details of the Watney Mann Invitation Cup, a competition in which the two highest-scoring teams from each division not to have qualified for Europe or been promoted would play in a knockout tournament over the course of a week. As well as a share of ticket revenue, clubs would receive £4,000 for participating in what quickly became abbreviated to the Watney Cup. There was also the award of £500 for wins in the first round and semi-finals and a further £1,000 for winning the tournament. For Manchester United, who entered the first two competitions, it was hardly a life-changing amount, but for the likes of Halifax Town it could make a significant difference. Meanwhile, the Football Association and Football League shared £50,000 from the brewery company.

It all seemed innocuous enough, but it had taken three years of negotiation and persuasion to bring the event to life. 'A company entering the field of sponsorship in football cannot hope to achieve its object simply by using the game to advertise its product,' Hardaker assured those who felt that the sport was selling its soul. This was a time when many major clubs still refused to allow advertising around their pitches. 'There has to be a genuine interest in the welfare of the game,' Hardaker continued.

His view of sponsorship was that 'its financial influence could well revolutionise football during the next decade, but it must … never be sold cheaply to a sponsor just for the sake of financial gain.' He dismissed the idea of 'the kind of advertising prevalent on the Continent where one team's shirts endorse a certain brand of alcohol, while another team carries plugs urging male supporters to use a particular brand of eau de Cologne'.

Football League Review spelled out that for a commercial deal to be considered it had to benefit the game, the spectators and the sponsors. 'There have been other approaches from industry which have been engendered by a desire by industry to use football for its own ends,' it explained. 'The League have refused to entertain any of these suggestions.'[296] And the authoritarian voice of Bobby Charlton warned, 'I don't think anyone would like to see his favourite team trotting out for a big game with a foaming pint of bitter painted on his shirt and a slogan underneath.'[297]

Coming off the back of the vibrant World Cup in Mexico, the timing for the sponsors could not have been better. Average attendance throughout the inaugural Watney Cup was more than 21,000, proving that fans were eager to see some sun-kissed football of their own – even if Peterborough United v Hull City at London Road contained only the merest whiff of Guadalajara's Jalisco Stadium. Manchester United fans took it seriously enough to queue overnight outside Elm Park before their 3-2 first-round victory at Reading, while ITV gave their highlights shows the full World Cup panel treatment and introduced them with their Mexico 70 theme tune, 'The World at Their Feet', performed by the John Shakespeare Orchestra. United's Pat Crerand, a man who had fought considerably more important battles during his career, could not quite share the gravity that Brian Moore and Jimmy Hill attempted to bring to the studio, resting his chin on his hand as he insisted that no one could read anything into games this early in the season.

The second round saw history made with the first penalty shoot-out in English football after Hull held United 1-1 at Boothferry Park. George Best achieved the distinction of being the first scorer and

Denis Law the first to fail – although Hull keeper Ian McKechnie, who had saved from Law, shaved the crossbar with his own spot-kick to send United into the final against Derby County. The *Daily Mail*'s Brian Taylor was sufficiently impressed to report that 'the penalty-taking session which settled this pulsating game was one of the most exciting and dramatic features I have ever seen on a soccer field'.

On the same day that Alan Ball was running around in white boots in the FA Charity Shield, 32,049 turned up at the Baseball Ground for the first Watney Cup Final. It may only have been a pre-season competition, but it offered the clearest possible picture of two clubs heading in different directions. Derby took advantage of the statuesque United defence to sweep to a 4-1 victory. Both teams played their strongest side for the third time in a week – no thought of preserving legs for the beginning of the League season or giving fringe players an opportunity – but the most fight displayed by United was in a feisty spell in the first half, ending with Crerand hurling the ball into the face of Alan Hinton, who dropped like a murder victim on an amateur dramatics night. 'In one week the Watney Cup has made an astonishing impact,' said Moore, 'no doubt about that.'

Having waited so long for this sponsored competition, more were on their way. Once the pre-season Watney shindig was out of the way, it was time for the Texaco Cup to make an entrance. A European-style tournament featuring 16 English, Scottish, Irish League and League of Ireland teams who had not qualified for mainstream continental competition, the tournament regularly produced crowds in excess of 20,000. When Wolverhampton Wanderers beat Hearts to win the inaugural trophy, the two matches attracted 51,000 fans.

The sponsors, keen to create brand recognition after taking over the Regent chain of filling stations, put up £100,000. The Football League banked £22,500; the Scottish League £17,500; the Irish League £5,000; and the League of Ireland £3,000. Other payments included £1,000 per competing team, plus £1,500 for first-round winners; £2,000 for second-round winners; and £2,500 for the winning semi-finalists. Renewing the event for a second year, assistant Football League secretary Eric Howarth assured everyone, 'Texaco have not interfered at all. Some people feared a sponsor would insist on gimmicks. They have left us alone to run the competition.'[298]

The Watney Cup continued for three further summers. The 1971 event offered proof of Manchester United's problems – beaten at Third Division Halifax Town – and Colchester United's ability on the big occasion. A few months after upsetting Leeds United in the FA Cup, the Fourth Division side beat Luton Town and Carlisle United, both two tiers above them, to reach the final. Luton boss Alec Stock had not been thrilled about having to start pre-season training early, but admitted, 'There's a few bob involved, which is what soccer's all about.'

Against West Bromwich Albion in front of a crowd of 19,000 at The Hawthorns, a remarkable match saw Colchester fall behind 3-2 at half-time, before hitting back to lead 4-3 and then conceding a last-minute equaliser to Jeff Astle. As the scorer disappeared among the fans behind the goal and the ground swayed and surged with the kind of excitement that might seem unthinkable to those reading about a long-discarded manufactured tournament, BBC commentator Barry Davies exclaimed, 'He and everybody else in this town will believe in fairies.' It was Colchester who enjoyed the magic ending when Len Cantello's ballooned effort proved fatal in the penalty shoot-out. It was exactly the kind of match that was envisioned with the introduction of an experimental law whereby players could only be offside if inside or level with the penalty area. 'How about that then?' beamed Hardaker.

Manchester United declined their invitation to enter a 1972 tournament won by Second Division Bristol Rovers, who beat Sheffield United on penalties following a 0-0 draw, and Watney Mann's decision not to renew the sponsorship meant only one more year remained. A pair of Jimmy Greenhoff goals saw Stoke City beat Hull in front of their own fans to become the last winners.

The Texaco Cup lasted one year longer. Derby won the competition in its second year, beating Scotland's Airdrieonians over two legs separated by exactly three months because of bad weather. On 26 January 1972, they drew 0-0 in Scotland, but not until the final days of April did they beat Airdrie 2-1 in front of 25,201 at the Baseball Ground – where Texaco, as it happened, had become the dominant stadium advertiser. '[It] may not have had the appeal and clout of the FA Cup, but we took the competition seriously,' said Rams forward Roger Davies, 'and the atmosphere that night was unbelievable.'[299] As in the case of the Watney Cup, Clough was happy to commit his first team to the task in hand, even with the League title on the line.‡

The political climate meant that Irish clubs were excluded from the competition's third season, which, intriguingly, brought East Anglian rivals Ipswich and Norwich City together in the final. Ipswich showed evidence of their development under Bobby Robson by winning both legs 2-1. They would be frequent qualifiers for European competition in subsequent seasons, building towards trophy success in the 1978 FA Cup and 1981 UEFA Cup.

Having won the final Anglo-Italian Cup of the era in 1973, Newcastle went on to win the last two Texaco Cup tournaments, beating Burnley 2-1 at St James' Park in the one-off final of 1973-74 and Southampton 3-1 over two legs the following season. The first of those campaigns featured a bizarre quarter-final tie against Birmingham City. With the second leg kicking off at 2pm because of the ban on using floodlights during the miners' dispute, the match ran into trouble when the scores finished level on aggregate. Only ten minutes of extra-time could be played before the November daylight disappeared and the game was abandoned. When the match was replayed, in front of the BBC cameras, only 53 seconds had elapsed when Newcastle's Jimmy Smith, a skilful midfielder with a ruthless streak as dark as his hair, went into a challenge with Tony Want and left the Birmingham defender with a broken leg. Smith was sent off.

It appeared to be a case of familiarity breeding contempt, this being the fifth of six meetings between the teams in little more than

‡ Clough's commitment to second-tier competitions was significant. He would cite his Nottingham Forest team's success in the 1976-77 edition of the Anglo-Scottish Cup, the Texaco Cup's successor, as an important landmark on their way to national and European prominence. Under Clough, Forest would also win two of the seven editions of the Full Members' Cup, staged between 1985 and 1992 as a make-good for English teams' suspension from European competition after the Heysel Stadium disaster.

six weeks – two League Cup matches, three in the Texaco Cup and then a League game three days later at St Andrew's. In the final contest, Newcastle had four men booked and Birmingham one, while two visiting players, Frank Clark and Irving Nattrass, were carried off. Geoffrey Green in *The Times* called it a display of 'the truly dark side of football', while Newcastle chairman and future Football League president Lord Westwood said, 'The players, by this type of behaviour, are putting the livelihood of their colleagues in jeopardy.'

It was precisely what the third of the sponsored competitions introduced in 1970-71 had been designed to eradicate. The Ford Motor Company Sporting League sought to promote fair and attacking play by offering prize money to be spent on facilities. Over the course of the season – or the first 42 games in the case of Divisions Three and Four – teams were awarded one point for a home goal and two for an away goal, with the loss of five points per booking and ten for a dismissal. Oldham Athletic were the first winners, picking up £50,000 after receiving only four bookings all season. They also won all eight monthly prizes of £2,500 each, a nice windfall for a team that was in the process of winning promotion from the Fourth Division, enabling them to build a new stand at Boundary Park. Crewe Alexandra earned £30,000 for their second place. Both teams suffered the deduction of only 15 points all season. Belying the notion that only bad guys could be successful in the top flight, the two top-rated First Division teams were League Champions Arsenal and runners-up Leeds United, who finished fifteenth and eighth respectively. Southampton's reputation as one of the most physical teams in the League was confirmed by them finishing as the lowest-placed top-tier club, with a final total of minus one point.

The good intentions of the tournament prompted Sports Minister Denis Howell to describe it as 'an interesting example of how sponsorship can be intelligently used to further developments in sport that need to be encouraged'.[300] Yet there was opposition to the competition from those clubs who felt they were being embarrassed by the exposure of their crimes. And Ford, mired in industrial conflict, decided it had more important matters requiring its attention than fulfilling its original pledge to Hardaker of a £750,000 investment over five years. The new league never saw a second season.

BEG, STEAL OR BORROW

Money, it's a gas. Grab that cash with both hands
and make a stash
New car, caviar, four-star daydream. Think I'll buy me a
football team

'Money', Pink Floyd (Roger Waters; Sony/ATV Music Publishing, Warner Chappell Music, BMG Rights Management, 1973)

After a flurry of currency and good intentions, English football reached the middle of the 1970s without major visible commercial support. This after journalistic giant Ian Wooldridge had said of the Texaco Cup, 'Soccer struck oil in its own goalmouth.'

Reports published after the 1969-70 season had shown that only 12 League clubs made a profit, with *Football League Review* blaming the fact that almost £5 million was being spent by the game on players' wages, out of gate receipts of only £7 million. 'The margin is too small,' it said. 'Not enough to pay managers, staff, running expenses and ground improvements. What is upsetting the balance? The struggle for success.'[301]

In 1977, Hardaker described the game's reluctance to fully embrace sponsorship as a solution as 'one of my chief regrets' and 'something which angers and baffles me at the same time'.[302] Chelsea chairman Brian Mears saw increased sponsorship as 'only a question of time', but warned, 'Frankly, I can't see many firms wanting to put a lot of cash into clubs with small gates and no publicity value.'[303] Meanwhile, Blackburn Rovers winger Gordon Taylor, becoming a more influential voice within the PFA, suggested, 'There must be a way to get the money going to the clubs who need it the most,' even though he spoke for the majority of his profession when he objected to the idea of corporate names adorning the players themselves. [304]

Hardaker had foreseen 'sponsors coming in with all manner of offers and ideas' but had reckoned without the economic pit into which the country slipped. So deep, in fact, that 1976 would see the UK go to the International Monetary Fund for the biggest loan it had ever granted, $3.9 billion, in return for cutting its own spending.

Historian Alwyn W. Turner pointed out, 'The deal was the kind more normally associated with Third-World countries, allowing domestic policy to be determined by international bankers.'[305] Or, as stated by Professor Maurice Peston, chief economic adviser to Labour minister Roy Hattersley, 'If the IMF had said the entire Cabinet had to jump off Westminster Bridge, you would have had to jump off Westminster Bridge.'[306]

Such was the nation's growing number of creditors that US Secretary of State Henry Kissinger had observed to President Gerald Ford, 'Britain is a tragedy. It has sunk to begging, borrowing, stealing ... that Britain has become such a scrounger is a disgrace.'[307] Offering a little less in the way of political credibility, *Opportunity Knocks* presenter Hughie Green closed his final show of the year by asking viewers, 'In your farewell to 1976, did you see Britain as old and worn, on the brink of ruin, bankrupt in all but heritage and hope, and even those were in pawn?' He ranted for several minutes, for which he was reprimanded by his bosses at Thames Television, although that did not stop him putting out his outburst as a single.

Even *Shoot!* had begun the decade with an uncharacteristically serious article in which it pointed out the low number of clubs turning a profit. Those such as Manchester United, reckoned to have made a net £130,000 in a year in which they won nothing, were few and far between. Sponsorship, the magazine suggested, was one of the keys to a healthier financial future for the sport. Other proposed measures included staggered kick-offs so that lower-division clubs were not competing with high-flying neighbours.

Hardaker's dismay was not just because of the delayed realisation of his logo-branded vision of the future. It represented the overall concern about the finances of the clubs in the grip of such a challenging environment. '[They] have been in a mess for years,' he said. Dependency on what they could drive through the gate meant that Hardaker reckoned League clubs were collectively £15 million in debt (the equivalent of almost £100 million in 2020). 'To me this represents nothing less than insanity,' he said, describing many directors as 'wrongly motivated, greedy, impatient, unqualified, short-righted and rather confused'.[308]

Clubs' major outlay was the cost of getting a competitive team on the field. The most visible manifestation of that was the transfer fee, an element of the game that League president Shipman had argued was becoming 'too ridiculous for words' when Tottenham paid Southampton £125,000 for centre-forward Martin Chivers early in 1968. 'I was talking recently to a club director who visualises fees reaching £250,000 within the next six years,' Shipman added. That unnamed director underestimated the market's acceleration.

Tottenham opened the 1970s by making Martin Peters the first £200,000 player in British football in a deal that sent Jimmy Greaves to West Ham as a chunk of the fee. The 1971-72 season saw another 1966 hero breaking that record when Arsenal pulled off the £220,000 signing of Alan Ball from Everton, a move that no one had seen coming and which Goodison Park fans would still be mourning half a century later. Striker Joe Royle struggled to understand why the man he described as 'the best player ever to wear a blue shirt' was sold by Harry Catterick only a season and a half after Everton's title triumph. 'We always thought Harry would build a new team around Bally,' he explained. 'There were all kinds of rumours that Alan had wanted to move, that there were financial problems and this, that and the other. But we were all surprised when he went.'[309]

The same season saw significant transactions in the same bracket: Ralph Coates, sold by Burnley to Tottenham in the summer for £190,000; Malcolm Macdonald, who scored a hat-trick for Newcastle on his home debut against Liverpool after a £180,000 pre-season move from Luton Town; the previously discussed £200,000 arrivals in Manchester of City's Rodney Marsh and United's Ian Storey-Moore. In that same month, United manager Frank O'Farrell also paid £150,000 for Martin Buchan from Aberdeen.

Ironically, it was O'Farrell who a few weeks later voiced fears over the money being spent on players. He even suggested restricting all transfers to the summer months. 'It's sheer urgency which creates huge fees – and urgency is the mood of the playing season,' he argued. 'Clubs panic if things go wrong and consequently are obliged to pay out more than they would like – and probably can afford.' O'Farrell might have foreseen the eventual introduction of formal transfer windows, but he failed to predict that the greater pressure applied by such windows would force prices up even more. An alternative regulation suggested by Stoke City chairman Albert Henshall in 1973 was a £250,000 spending limit per club. Looking at the lower end of the First Division, he argued, 'I don't think the wealth of clubs should enable them to keep out of trouble at the expense of two clubs who eventually go down. It is grossly unfair that the cheque book rules the game.'[310]

In the meantime, by the time our anonymous director's six-year timeline had concluded, his £250,000 vision had been surpassed by centre-forward Bob Latchford's £350,000 transfer from Birmingham City to Everton. Yet the economic challenges the country faced were evident in the fact that it would be three years before an English club paid more than that, when Liverpool spent £440,000 on Kenny Dalglish in 1977.

At that time, on top of the income they generated themselves, Football League clubs were sharing the £750,000 that BBC and ITV jointly paid for television rights. The League also redistributed the 4 per cent levy on all gate money (20 per cent for League Cup ties, worth around £300,000 per season); one third of FA Cup gate money from the third round onwards; and a quarter of the untaxed profits from international matches, worth approximately £750,000 a year. Important additional income had been earned by the League's successful legal fight to copyright its fixtures, allowing it to receive 0.5 per cent of the stakes bet on the football pools. What began as a £250,000 per year windfall rose in value to almost £2 million by the later years of the 1970s, a quarter of the money going to the Scottish League. The Pools Promoters' Association kicked in another

£1 million each year through its 'Spot the Ball' competition, money earmarked specifically for ground improvements.

Even the bigger clubs sought imaginative fiscal solutions. Volunteers selling raffle tickets on behalf of the Manchester United Development Association had, it was reported in 1972, allowed the club to bank £500,000 for stadium upgrades in the previous ten years. Everton's equivalent group was selling 40,000 bingo tickets per week, reaching as far as Jersey, and producing profits of £100,000 per year. Meanwhile, the club's annual income from programmes – around £14,000 as the decade began – was greater than some gate revenue in the Fourth Division, where players' wages could often total twice the money generated through the turnstiles.

Colchester had been among the first to follow Hardaker's preaching on commercialism and introduce match sponsors. The princely sum of £250 per game could, the club hoped, add up to a valuable £5,750 per season. But others had to count pennies rather than bring in the pounds. Scunthorpe United manager Ron Ashman explained that undertaking trips to places such as Swansea, Bristol and Bournemouth by coach rather than the relative luxury of a train was a valuable economy. 'It's four o'clock in the morning by the time we arrive back in Scunthorpe,' he said, 'We save about £100. For a club like Scunthorpe that's a lot of money.'[311]

Outside the Football League, Kettering Town manager Ron Atkinson was proud of a 1973 arrangement with Golden Wonder crisps to provide team tracksuits and help publicise the club's long road trips to destinations such as Yeovil and Weymouth in the hope of attracting additional funding. The same club would be the first in major English football to put a brand name on its shirts when chief executive Derek Dougan fell foul of FA regulations by plastering Kettering Tyres on their maroon and white kit in January 1976, a deal reportedly worth £2,500. Despite being told not to do it again, Kettering's players found the offending shirts laid out for them at a Southern League Cup tie at Weymouth. 'Doog had negotiated a deal and I don't know how much the chairman knew about it,' said goalkeeper Gordon Livsey. 'We thought we'd been told we couldn't wear it, but Doog said, "Nobody tells us what we wear. I am the one who tells you."'[312] Dougan's attempt to compromise by changing the logo to 'Kettering T' fared no better and Vernon Stokes, head of the FA's disciplinary committee, warned him, 'Do you know we could close down your ground?' Kettering were let off with a warning, but in June 1977 the FA would announce its decision to allow clubs to carry a small logo on their shirts; no more than 2.5 inches high and wide and not to be 'detrimental to the image of the game'. Ironically, Kettering were unable to find a sponsor.

By the end of the decade, many leading clubs were maximising the value of their kit by wearing shirts featuring garish trim made up of multiple repeats of the manufacturers' logo. Umbro's distinctive diamond might only appear on the right breast of Liverpool and Arsenal's players, but on the kits of Manchester City, Everton, Chelsea and others it created a pattern that ran down the sleeves and the outside of the shorts. Admiral, who made their mark with distinctive redesigns of England, Manchester United, Leicester City, Southampton and Coventry City kits, among others, introduced a similar sleeve-long device for clubs including Leeds United, Tottenham Hotspur and Crystal Palace.

Meanwhile, television, for all the financial importance it already had within the game, was still a relatively untapped revenue stream. In fact, the history of televised League football had been characterised by constant soul searching about the real extent of its benefits. By the mid-1970s, as *Match of the Day* celebrated its tenth anniversary of bringing highlights to the nation, there were still many who felt the money was not worth the aggravation. Even Jimmy Armfield, who became a major media figure after his playing and management career, told the *Blackpool Gazette* in 1972, 'Television is killing the game, and solely because of this medium I can see wholesale bankruptcy in the game unless something is done.'

The earliest football to appear on television screens had been a game between Arsenal and Arsenal Reserves that aired as an experiment on BBC in 1937, paving the way for the first televised FA Cup Final a year later. A sign of BBC's uncertainty about such an opportunity was the fact that only one outside broadcast unit was assigned to the match, while two had been booked for the Derby at Epsom a few weeks later.

One year after the launch of the ITV network in 1955, attempts to get the Football League to permit the televising of its games reached a point of serious negotiation when Associated Television (ATV) offered £50,000 – plus compensation for any lost gate revenue – to screen the second half of one game live each Saturday at 6.15pm. The League Management committee recommended acceptance of the deal, but the clubs voted against it. 'They began to worry, as always, about shadows around the corner,' Hardaker recalled.[313] Eventually, one game, Blackpool versus Bolton Wanderers, was shown live as a one-off experiment in 1960. By the early 1960s, more than 90 per cent of UK households contained a TV set and commercial television companies were the first to bring weekly highlights to the screen in 1962, with Tyne-Tees producing *Shoot!* on Saturday evenings and Anglia putting out *Match of the Week* on Sunday evenings.

But it was when *Match of the Day* aired for the first time in 1964, with Liverpool playing Arsenal at Anfield, that the TV landscape was changed. All it had cost the BBC was £20,000 and an agreement not to reveal its choice of game until 4pm on Saturday, a rule that stayed in place throughout the 1970s. Yet it was not until the post-World Cup boom of 1966 that the show was moved to BBC1, having begun its life on selected regional broadcasts on BBC2. The ITV network was given the green light for Sunday afternoon highlights in 1965, although only after the redistribution of the franchises in 1968 did the familiar regional line-up become established, including London Weekend Television's *The Big Match*.§ The show endured a slow and painful labour, with industrial action among technicians meaning LWT was forced to air re-runs of that year's European Cup Final and the execrable 1968 League Cup Final on the first two weeks of the League season. It was not until the third weekend that Brian Moore and Jimmy Hill, now the head of sport at LWT, had the chance to introduce a show billed by the *TV Times* as 'football's busiest and best

§ London's televised football had previously been provided by ATV's *Star Soccer*.

informed programme, bringing you action and controversy that sets you up for those Monday morning arguments'.

The BBC had made an unsuccessful attempt in 1967 to get live games aired on Thursday evenings. Instead, the corporation had to be content with a system of sharing highlights with ITV that began with a coin toss each season to determine first choice of games in August. When BBC had the honour, it would select its top game, after which the three big ITV regions (London, the North-West and the Midlands) would each nominate its preferred game. Then the BBC would identify a second match. When ITV was picking first, the three regions would all select before BBC had a choice. The system was further complicated by *Match of the Day* being prohibited to visit one ground more than three times per season for League games, while being compelled to air five Second Division matches and two from the Third and Fourth. All matches were picked a month in advance. 'The comforting thought about football audiences on television,' said BBC football editor Sam Leitch, 'is that they are not glamour snobs. Second and Third Division games manage to hold on to 90 per cent of that regular audience.'[314] Such was the relative scarcity of football on the television in an era when the FA Cup Final and a smattering of European finals and internationals were the only games shown live. Outside of World Cup summers, the month of May was the only time fans could bank on seeing regular live football.

For a typical game, *Match of the Day* employed five cameras, including one on the touchline for 'personality' close-ups and one high up on a crane for the panoramic stadium shots. It seems like nothing compared to the 20-plus used by Sky Sports in the modern age, especially as they could not always be relied on. 'You lose cameras; cameras break down,' said producer Alec Weeks in a behind-the-scenes film, 'but the viewers wouldn't miss anything.'[315]

In the mid-1970s, *Match of the Day* was attracting around 14 million viewers per week, while ITV's various regional offerings on Sunday afternoons accumulated 10 million. 'While the new scourge of hooliganism in the 1970s put many people off attending matches, the parallel universe of televised football achieved a new realism,' Joe

Moran wrote in his history of British television. 'Electronic cameras meant matches could be snappily edited, and on a colour set you could see everything beautifully, from churned up goalmouths to the grass changing colour from late summer to spring.'[316]

Such appeal was apparently considered a threat by the Football League. In *Football League Review* it spoke early in the decade of 'danger signals' and suggested that 'while filmed matches on television play a major image-building role for the game, football must beware that is does not become just another television progamme'. That was fair enough, but there was blind paranoia in its conclusion: 'Weekend television audiences of nearly 25 million on both channels compared with live attendances of three-quarters of a million a week suggest that a new type of football supporter is being bred, the armchair fan.' Nonsense, of course. The 'armchair fan' population might well have been booming, but every ground could have been full every Saturday and live crowds would still only have totalled a fraction of the on-screen audience.

It was symptomatic of the fears that had been around since the first strains of the original *Match of the Day* theme, 'Drum Majorette' – replaced by Barry Stoller's familiar refrain in 1970 – reached the airwaves. Everton manager Harry Catterick had taken three years to allow the cameras into Goodison Park for fear of giving away tactical secrets, although the club's attempt to get their neighbours to join them in a Merseyside boycott was scuppered by Liverpool's greater belief in the promotional benefits of regular exposure. Some feared that discovering the reality of periods of tedium in a live game would deter those accustomed to seeing only edited highlights. Leicester City secretary John Smith complained that games were 'edited to show the best parts', which meant, he said, 'A lot of people are happy to sit back at home and watch the box.'[317]

Such a view received unlikely support from Jimmy Hill, who became perhaps the best-known face in TV coverage in the 1970s. In a questionable analogy with politics, he argued, 'Football has suffered at the lenses of its discerning medium in the same way. Like our raped and de-bagged politicians (for how many of them have been caught by the cameras with their trousers down, metaphorically speaking of course?), soccer has not been strong enough to withstand the pressures of this intense observation.' His point was that edited highlights had 'introduced all soccer fans to the highest standards of the game available', which he believed meant that fans of lower-division teams were sat at home trying to take in this revelation.

Author Dave Russell agreed in his social history of the sport that TV coverage 'shaped perceptions, loyalties and attitudes in a number of crucial ways', including giving the top teams 'an increasingly glamorous image and a growing band of adherents'.[318] Yet he might not have been so quick to agree with Hill's claim that, for a fan of a smaller club, 'the game at his local club will be further impoverished by the lack of enlightening comment made available on the screen'. Such was Hill's ego that you assume that comment was made without irony.[319]

Leading journalist Brian Glanville wrote that 'TV is the Moloch of the age, into whose vast, undifferentiated maw anything and everything can disappear'. He said that editing was turning football into something 'vulgar' and voiced support for an idea floated by Danny Blanchflower that games should follow an editorial lead. Therefore, 'a poor game should be edited to look like a poor game'.[320] Yet that somewhat missed the point of televised football as an entertainment medium. As John Fiske and John Hartley noted in their 1978 study, '*Match of the Day* is not football, in the way that *Come Dancing* is not dancing.'[321]

Despite frequently voiced concerns about television's threat to attendance, crowd numbers were established on a downward curve long before *Match of the Day* came along. Only the excitement of the World Cup victory was able to offer a temporary reversal of that trend. Hill stated the overriding benefit of small-screen football when pointing out, 'At peak time, it would be £144,000 for 45 minutes' advertising. Don't anybody tell me that exposure on television is bad for future live gates.'[322]

The debate was reinvigorated when Tottenham announced a disappointing attendance of 24,000 for a 1972 UEFA Cup tie against Red Star Belgrade, televised later that night on BBC. 'How can we be blamed for falling gates when the British internationals – the only games we are allowed to name before we show them – have not been affected?' said Leitch.¶ 'The game itself must take some measure of action, for it is lacking in entertainment.' Support came from John Bromley at ITV, who argued, 'People are taking the easy way out by blaming TV. You can never over-publicise this game.'[323]

West Ham United chairman Reg Pratt likened televised football to 'building a cinema with glass walls – people stop paying to go in',[324] and as late as 1978 it was still being called 'a controversial subject' by England goalkeeper Ray Clemence. He at least cited the benefit to those who could not attend matches because of 'working unsocial hours, illness or living too far from the ground'.[325] The *Soccer Monthly Annual* saw in the 1980s with a feature entitled 'Television – a tool or a tyrant?' BBC commentator John Motson had the good sense to point out that without coverage of games, television stations would air far less of the news and soap opera elements that helped create the theatre and narrative surrounding the game. 'Every day football makes news and every time a preview or an interview goes on the screen somebody somewhere is being persuaded to go to a match,' he argued.[326]

As the 1970s began, Catterick had requested £5,000 per game compensation for accommodating the TV companies, instead of the standard £1,000 at that time. Such claims were typical of those who regularly quoted the low cost of producing an hour of sport compared to the sums involved in a major drama series, especially costumed epics such as BBC's *The Onedin Line* and ITV's *Upstairs, Downstairs*, both of which launched in 1971 and became staples of the weekend schedules for several years. A grumpy Hardaker complained of some clubs that they had a 'psychological fear' of television and 'if they had their way they just wouldn't entertain it at all'.[327] Burnley chairman Bob Lord was close to falling into that category, refusing coverage of

¶ That was debatable. When the Home Internationals were first condensed into a made-for-TV week at the end of the 1968-69 season, live broadcast was held responsible for the turnout of only 7,483 to see Northern Ireland's midweek visit to Hampden Park to play Scotland. *Charles Buchan's Football Monthly* also complained that England's 7.30 kick-offs on successive Saturdays meant fans having to 'do away with tradition and the Saturday night out with the missus'.

his team's FA Cup quarter-final against Wrexham in 1974 when the BBC refused to pay £10,000 per team.

The nature of the coverage itself had its detractors, including those who appeared to resent the opportunity for others to critique their performance. In 1973, Gordon Banks was among those who seemed to think that the job of anyone covering the game was to be a cheerleader. 'I have been on TV panels to talk about international games and it seemed to me that it was a case of knock, knock, knock. We now have so many critics of football that they are harming the game,' he argued. 'All this knocking doesn't do anything to lift players' confidence.'

The next demand by Catterick, clearly not an early adopter when it came to TV, was a ban on action replays 'because they are doing the game a lot of harm'. He had support from on high, with the edition of *Football League Review* that accompanied the 1970 League Cup Final going on one of its tirades. 'The playback continues to be exploited by TV football personnel,' began its opinion piece. Addressing the BBC's claim that 90 per cent of replays of controversial incidents proved referees right, it continued, 'We suggest it is no justification at all. It is surely wrong that the men who have to make split-second decisions out there on the pitch, in situations super-charged with tension, should be faced with the inquisition of a Magic Eye.' ITV, the article went on, re-ran incidents at normal speed, but said, 'It is no better.' Even the one in ten mistake ratio 'serves to disenchant a public which forgets the other nine'.[328]

For a while, there was a clause in the TV contracts prohibiting the vilification of match officials, while Hardaker once had to veto a *Match of the Day* opening sequence showing a montage of overly physical challenges. 'I think we are getting to the stage where the commentators are the star of the show while the footballers are just the chorus,' Hardaker said in 1972. 'I think harm can be done by their playbacks and criticism.' The response of Brian Moore was that, 'Everyone in football is far too sensitive. It is an unhealthy state of affairs if anyone is above criticism.'[329]

Hardaker, who led television negotiations for the Football League, continued to discount the possibility of live televised games, stating in

1977 that 'opinion now is very firm that regular live football would undermine the game's health'.[330] That view was softening enough, however, that live League action would only be six more years away.

In the meantime, light entertainment shows would have to meet viewers' demands for additional football content. In the second half of the 1960s, there had been *Quiz Ball*, a game where teams representing football clubs scored goals by answering general knowledge questions. The choice of taking four easy questions to score or one tough one brought the phrase 'route one' into the lexicon of the sport. Teams consisted of four members; three players (or sometimes the manager) and a celebrity fan. As an Arsenal fan, I was aware that the show had provided the big Scottish centre-half Ian Ure with his finest moment as a representative of the club, scoring bucketloads of goals as Bertie Mee, Terry Neill and radio disc jockey Jimmy Young carried off the first trophy.

By the late 1970s, though, TV producers decided that instead of asking footballers to answer questions or ride bicycles in the name of entertainment, they should ask them to do what they were trained to do: play football. *All in The Game*, a skills contest between League clubs, was dreamt up in the bath by Bristol City commercial director Graham Griffiths as a way of generating extra revenue for his club. Club manager Alan Dicks took the idea to some ITV contacts and the game ended up being aired across the network.

The competition, staged at Ashton Gate and aired in the summers of 1976 and 1977, was contested by clubs in a knockout format, featuring games designed to test players' ability to shoot, dribble, chip, head and bend the ball. Big names such as Frank Worthington, Gerry Francis, Brian Kidd, Eddie Gray and Stan Bowles took part and Wolves goalkeeper Gary Pierce even suffered a broken wrist stopping a shot by Ipswich's Kevin Beattie. When Derby veteran Alan Hinton led a young team to the £2,000 prize with victory over Norwich in the first final it made the top ten in that week's TV ratings. It was a sad indictment of the state of English football, though, when Don Howe observed, 'There were some excellent tests of skill and some of the players were furious they couldn't do them better.'

The reach of television had come to the rescue of QPR in February 1972 when a hastily arranged Friday-night friendly against West Brom had sold only 12 tickets three days before the game. Claiming 'a bit of soccer history', Rangers paid for an advert to be aired at 6.55pm on the eve of the match. Thus, viewers of *Crossroads* had their latest dose of drama in the life of Meg Richardson interrupted by an invitation to see 'the one and only Rodney Marsh in action' – for what proved to be one of the final occasions in a QPR shirt. A crowd of 7,087 turned up, justifying the £192.50 cost of the advert that the two clubs shared.

One of the biggest rows around on-screen football broke shortly afterwards, caused by a desire to show England's European Championship quarter-final first leg against West Germany live from Wembley on a Saturday evening in late April. This time, it was less a case of football versus television than a fight between administrative bodies. 'There now seems to be a state of war between the League and the Football Association,' Hardaker announced to the press after they could not agree the size of the fee to be charged to show the game. Hardaker felt the League and FA's joint television committee should be asking for £100,000 and was shocked when the FA unilaterally cut a deal with the BBC for £60,000. FA secretary Denis Follows said they had been 'motivated by the desire to ensure that the enormous public interest in the match should be satisfied', although the League did not see why that precluded holding out for more money and including Hardaker in the negotiations. The League even threatened a boycott of the FA Cup or a demand that the FA should pay them £100,000 for their clubs' participation. Toys were eventually returned to the pram and no such threats were ever followed through.

Then there was a near-blackout of League football in the autumn of 1974, after BBC and ITV's combined offer of £750,000 was rejected by the clubs in a 28-16 vote. The players disagreed with that position and PFA chairman Derek Dougan said they might refuse to play if the cameras were not present – the kind of stance Kim Kardashian would have appreciated decades later. While the TV companies threatened to show Bundesliga games instead, *Goal*'s comment column warned, 'Whatever the pros and cons of soccer on television, and there does seem to be a case for limiting the number of matches screened, we must not lose coverage completely. That would be a tragedy.'[331] When the clubs consulted industry expert Harold Davidson and were advised that the deal on the table was the best possible, they duly voted 36-13 to accept.

There was still some griping ahead. New FA secretary Ted Croker was angered by the BBC's decision to re-air the Muhammad Ali–George Foreman 'Rumble in the Jungle' on a Saturday afternoon. 'The BBC pay lip service to having the best interests of football at heart,' he complained. 'But when they make decisions like this, one can only wonder about their sincerity.' That, however, was a minor skirmish compared to the heavyweight battle for the future of televised football that lay ahead later in the decade.

7

THE YEAR OF LIVING DANGEROUSLY

TERRY: I didn't see the score. I only saw 'England F'.

BOB: Pardon?

TERRY: 'England F'. I saw the first word and the first letter of the second word – F. England F. See?

BOB: Oh, my God. Well that's it, isn't it? It's obvious. England flop.

***Whatever Happened to the Likely Lads?* 'No Hiding Place'**
(Dick Clement and Ian La Frenais; BBC TV, 1973)

THE EVENTS of 1966 and 1968 always seemed bound by some mythical, mystical thread, especially to those like me for whom the events happened in our formative years of football fandom. England's first World Cup and European Cup successes; the tears of Bobby Charlton; Sir Alf and Sir Matt; the myths, facts and images converged to create what we believed to be the truth of the sport: that England and Manchester United ruled the waves. Had any vestige of the invincibility of those teams survived within our maturing consciousness, the 1973-74 season destroyed it for good.

In terms of personnel, both teams were unrecognisable from their glory days. On the opening day of the season at Arsenal, goalkeeper

Alex Stepney was the only survivor of United's victory over Benfica. When England played their first game of the campaign, Martin Peters was the one World Cup winner on the field. Several months later, United had been relegated and England were at home watching the World Cup. As shocking as both events were, the warning signs had been there since the start of the decade.

Harold Wilson, Britain's Prime Minister since 1964, had always been quick to associate himself with his nation's football team. His second general election victory had come in England's *annus mirabilis* of 1966 and Chancellor of the Exchequer Roy Jenkins would come to speak of Wilson's 'theory of almost mystical symbiosis between the fortunes of the Labour Party and the England football eleven'. Perhaps Wilson should have remembered that when the polling booths closed across Britain on 18 June 1970. Sat in his constituency headquarters in the Liverpool suburb of Huyton and buoyed by opinion polls that had given him a cushion over Conservative leader Edward Heath, Wilson felt as confident as, well, a football manager holding a two-goal lead with 20 minutes remaining in a quarter-final.

Within a few hours, the Conservative Party had emerged as a clear winner, going on to achieve a 31-seat majority. The Tories had promised 'A Better Tomorrow' in their election manifesto, but Wilson was believed by some to have been a hapless victim of a national depression that had suddenly made its people feel more inclined to look for a change of government; a mood that had settled following events in the Mexican city of Leon four days earlier. Alf Ramsey had appeared comfortably on course to repeat his victory of four years earlier against West Germany. Yet, from a position of apparent impregnability, both Ramsey and Wilson had lost. Perhaps there really was something in that theory.*

* The same game had a pivotal place in one of the decade's great sit-coms, *Whatever Happened to the Likely Lads?*, when Terry tells Bob that separation from his German wife was sealed on 'June 14th, 1970'. Asked what happened, he replies, 'I thought that date was imprinted on every true Englishman's mind! England two, West Germany three! That's what happened!' He adds, 'I was on the sideboard singing *Rule Britannia*. Then the shame! The humiliation!'

After the loss of his team's world title, Ramsey began planning a European Championship campaign, just as the nation, under Heath, prepared for its entry into the European Economic Community on the first day of 1973. Ramsey, unlike Heath, would never make it through to his completion date – dumped out in the quarter-finals after winning an easy qualification section against Greece, Malta and Switzerland.

England began their group with a 1-0 win in Malta that was notable mostly for the debuts of Derby County's Roy McFarland, Tottenham Hotspur centre-forward Martin Chivers and Everton duo Colin Harvey and Joe Royle, along with the absence of Bobby Moore, out of favour at West Ham after a late-night visit to a Blackpool nightclub on the eve of an FA Cup defeat at Blackpool.† But, despite those enforced changes, Ramsey was a long way from being ready to tear down the foundations of World Cup success. The likes of Moore, Gordon Banks, Geoff Hurst, Martin Peters, Alan Ball and Norman Hunter from the 1966 squad still had important roles to play. 'It was very homely,' said McFarland. 'Alf had a love for those older players because of what they had done for him. Maybe in the long term he did hang on a little bit too long to some.'[332]

'It seemed like the 1966 team was a family,' said Arsenal centre-forward John Radford, who earned a pair of caps without breaking in on a regular basis. 'I remember watching one game on film and someone like Bobby Moore actually fell asleep. Alf had to go up and shake him and say, "Would you mind?" It was, "Right. Sorry, Alf," and we'd carry on.'[333]

A 3-0 home win against Greece saw Arsenal's Peter Storey awarded the first of his 19 caps, an amount that supporters of men such as Rodney Marsh and Peter Osgood saw as a blight. Storey appeared in most England games over a two-year period, either at right-back or in the midfield enforcer role he was now known for at Highbury. 'He didn't like doing it,' said team-mate Bob McNab. 'He would be

† Believing that a frozen pitch would cause the game to be postponed, Moore joined Jimmy Greaves, Clyde Best and Brian Dear in visiting the 007 club, owned by former British heavyweight boxing champion Brian London. Although they stayed only for a short while, their attendance was reported by fans to manager Ron Greenwood in the wake of a 4-0 defeat.

swearing under his breath and snarling. He hated it that much it made it worse for the poor bastard he was marking.'[334] His club captain, Frank McLintock, called him 'a head case, a loony – but you wanted him in your side'.[335] As did Ramsey, evidently seeing him as a natural successor to Nobby Stiles.

A three-man attack of Chivers, Hurst and Francis Lee all found the net against Greece, and Chivers scored two more when Malta were beaten 5-0 at Wembley. Another double by the Spurs man was the highlight of the 3-1 win over Scotland with which England wrapped up an unbeaten campaign in the Home International Championship. The victory meant that England were undefeated in seven games since the World Cup, although *The Times*'s Geoffrey Green said their final week of matches 'wore the label of all work and precious little play'. Green did enthuse, though, about the contribution of Chivers, arguing that he offered England 'the kind of ramrod they need to finish much of their elaborate approach play'.

It was an appropriate way for Chivers to end a season in which he had changed perception of him as fragile and injury-prone; someone unable to pack the punch his physique promised. He had come a long way from the man once dropped by Bill Nicholson for a game against West Ham and told to study the way Hurst played. He was now into a three-season stretch in which he was undoubtedly the most feared No.9 in the country, the sight of him collecting the ball, charging into the penalty area and finding the net becoming a staple of the weekly highlights. His 34 first-team goals in 1970-71 included both in Tottenham's 2-0 win against Third Division Aston Villa in the League Cup Final; and in the following two seasons he would find the net 44 and 33 times respectively in all Spurs games. It was a scoring rate of which Jimmy Greaves, the man he effectively succeeded at White Hart Lane, would have been proud.

Chivers had arrived in north London during 1967-68, signed from Southampton for £125,000 a few weeks after scoring a hat-trick for the Football League against the Irish League.‡ He scored on his Spurs

‡ Games played by the Football League team against other representative sides were a regular occurrence until the mid-1970s. Featuring only English players, the team was often used by Sir Alf Ramsey to trial players on the fringes of his full squad.

debut, but in September 1968 tore up his knee and was sidelined for almost a year. When he returned in the 1969-70 season, he managed only 11 goals in 31 League games. 'I used to think he was a bit of a joke,' an unnamed international defender was quoted as saying midway through Chivers's breakthrough season. 'He had all the muscle and skill, yet he never looked as though he wanted to put it to use.'[336]

During 1971-72, Chivers scored in England's victories in Switzerland and Greece and bagged eight in Tottenham's successful UEFA Cup campaign, including both in the 2-1 first-leg win against Wolverhampton Wanderers in the final.[§] It was his new-found appetite for the robust that had made the difference. 'We were always trying to get Martin to use his physique properly,' said his former Southampton manager Ted Bates. 'In those days a big, strong centre-half could swallow him.'[337] The television analysts' approval was provided by Jimmy Hill, who said, 'Chivers has everything a footballer needs – the physique of a giant, the control of a juggler, speed to burn, he can head and shoot and has a football brain to boot.'[338]

Chivers felt blessed to have joined a club that gave his talent the opportunity to flourish, especially as he could have ended up across north London in a more functional Arsenal unit. 'We were a good side,' he recalled. 'We won the League Cup and were at the start of a sequence of four finals in four years. I could never imagine playing the Arsenal way. It was very successful for them, but they did build on a strong defence, whereas we tended to play more attacking football.'[339]

England's European Championship quarter-final was a two-legged affair that would send the winners into the final four in Belgium. It saw them renew rivalry with West Germany, who had followed their third place in Mexico by constructing a team that drew upon the Total Football principles of Holland and its European Cup holders, Ajax Amsterdam. It was poignant that the West Germans always seemed to be standing in the way on England's most significant recent occasions: 1966, 1970, 1972. Memories, first-hand experience and

§ The Spurs players' wives had been promised an all-expenses paid trip to the away leg of the final and had been growing excited about possible visits to Milan, Turin or Budapest once the tournament reached the quarter-final stage. A couple of midweek nights in Wolverhampton were not exactly what they'd had in mind.

bestowed tales of more serious conflict were still too fresh for the public to treat these games in isolation from global history. Happily, the weight of such things did not seem likely to result in the same negative on-field approach that one witnessed in contests between, for example, India and Pakistan on the cricket field, where 13 consecutive Test matches between 1952 and 1978 were drawn. 'We have come here to play football, not just to defend,' German manager Helmut Schoen promised.

Ramsey might have been better served by adopting more of a bunker mentality. Uncharacteristically, he opted to field an attacking line-up that eschewed a defensive midfielder, even though his squad included both Storey and Alan Mullery, whose tale was one of the most romantic of the season. Loaned to Fulham after losing his place in the first team, the Spurs skipper was recalled before the UEFA Cup semi-final against AC Milan and proceeded to score important goals in the semi-final and final before lifting the trophy. Behind the midfield trio, Ramsey's selection of the left-footed Hunter in the absence of McFarland forced Moore to play on the right of the centre-back pairing. He was so unused to playing there that newspapers had predicted that Liverpool's Larry Lloyd would partner the England captain. Neither full-back, Paul Madeley or Emlyn Hughes, played there regularly for their clubs, although Madeley famously had no set position in the Leeds team and was understudy for everyone except the goalkeeper. In summary, Ramsey selected a back four in which only one man was playing in his week-in, week-out position and offered them no midfield protection. This was his line-up: Banks – Madeley, Moore, Hunter, Hughes – Bell, Ball, Peters – Lee, Chivers, Hurst.

To say that England were caught unawares would be an understatement. Borussia Moenchengladbach midfielder Günter Netzer was 27 years old and had made his international debut in 1965. Yet his absence from two subsequent World Cups meant that few expected him to turn in one of the finest individual performances in the history of the stadium. 'We hadn't been told a thing about him,' Moore lamented, while Ramsey admitted being 'surprised at the way the Germans came at us'. Netzer strolled around Wembley as though he owned the place, his long blond hair adding to his regal air, orchestrating the fluent movements of colleagues whose versatility and speed of thought embarrassed the home team. England's efforts looked outmoded and pedestrian. 'Netzer had the game of his life,' said Chivers. 'But he was never the same again as he was on that night. They took us to the cleaners.'[340]

If the Germans played with arrogance it was justified by their superiority. And they considered it further payback for the attitude England had displayed towards them in Mexico two years earlier. 'Just after England scored their second goal they started rolling the ball around as though it was all over,' Gerd Müller recalled of the World Cup game. 'This made me mad and I think all our team hitched up their shorts and got on with the game.'[341] There was no chance of the German team allowing this game to slip away from them. A 3-1 victory was fully merited, Lee's equaliser merely a temporary distraction.

In fairness to Ramsey, plenty of observers had been calling for more adventurous team selection. 'It is the mood as much as the mechanics which must be more adventurous this time,' writer Pat Collins had urged. 'The accent must be on scorers more than stoppers.'[342] The timing for such a development could have been better, however. It would now take a miracle in Berlin two weeks later to keep England in the tie, but Ramsey was disinclined to try for one. He opted for damage limitation, naming Hunter and Storey in a four-man midfield. It was what John Anthony, writing in *Football Monthly Digest*, called 'the selection above all else that persuaded most of us that Ramsey was not the manager we once believed him to be'.[343]

Picking the mercurial Marsh instead of Hurst – his England career now over – was fooling no one. England's line-up, and subsequent tactics, suggested that a 0-0 draw was the extent of their ambition. And that is what they got. 'Embarrassing, third rate,' was the resulting description of the England team by *Goal* editor Alan Hughes, while Green described them in *The Times* as 'like a train stuck to the same straight lines'. Schoen, revelling in the *Schadenfreude* of it all, said,

'I don't think you have moved forward. In Germany we have been trying to restore the balance between attack and defence and I think we are succeeding. We now put more emphasis on technique, but I don't think this is so in England.'

The Home Internationals failed to bring much relief. True, Marsh scored his first England goal in a 3-0 win in Cardiff, before Scotland were beaten at Hampden Park, but it was what happened at Wembley in between that defined England's tournament.

The Troubles in Northern Ireland had been raging since 1969, when increasing violence between the Protestant and Catholic communities – torn over whether the province should remain within the United Kingdom or be part of a united Ireland – led to the deployment of British troops. Nationalists, loyalists and British forces formed three points of an intricate, tragic triangle that saw more than 3,500 people killed over almost four decades of conflict. The year 1972 would come to be recognised as the worst of all, with 497 people dead, more than half of them non-combatants. In January, the 'Bloody Sunday' massacre saw 13 unarmed civilians shot dead by troops in Derry during a banned civil-rights march, with a 14th dying later. Reprisals would include the nationalist IRA's bombing of the Aldershot army barracks, killing seven, and a 'Bloody Friday' in Belfast in July, when more than 20 bombs were detonated in little more than an hour, killing nine and wounding approximately 130.

In March, home rule had been introduced, Westminster taking over Northern Irish affairs after the suspension of the Stormont parliament. And on the sporting front, the year's Five Nations Championship in rugby union had been left uncompleted when Scotland and Wales refused, on safety grounds, to fulfil their fixtures against Ireland in Dublin. In February, Northern Ireland were forced to stage a European Championship qualifier against Spain at Boothferry Park, where their player-manager, Terry Neill, fulfilled that same dual role for Hull City. It was Neill who prodded home the only goal after 34 minutes when the Irish visited Wembley in May, giving his country its second victory over England and the first since 1957.

'I happened to be leaning against the post,' recalled Neill, who believed that the opportunity to give their countrymen a brief respite from the atrocities of life fired his team's resolve to hang on to the lead. 'The Troubles were at their worst and at Wembley that night we all felt that it might have given the little province of Northern Ireland a bit of a lift,' he said. 'Our centre-half, Allan Hunter, epitomised the spirit. Alf Ramsey threw on Martin Chivers with about 20 minutes to go. Big Chiv had pace and skill and we are on our knees because we have grafted like mad. Chiv trots on and says to me, "Your boys are playing terrific tonight," Allan Hunter is a couple of yards away and says, "Kick the bastard." Chiv spent the last 20 minutes out on the right wing somewhere. It certainly was a sweet moment.'[344]

Appreciation of what the result meant in the streets, pubs and workplaces of Belfast was all well and good as far as English fans and media were concerned. What was of greater import to them was exactly where the events of these spring weeks had left their team in football's pecking order. Not since Hungary waltzed around them in 1953 had the national team appeared so irrelevant and out of touch, so removed from what was happening in the chemistry labs of the sport's development. According to Italy manager Ferruccio Valcareggi, 'England's great weakness is their lack of flexibility. They are extremely limited in some of the skills of the game.' While most people in English football liked to refer to Madeley as a 'Rolls-Royce', he called the Leeds man 'a robot'.[345]

English clubs might have won the UEFA Cup for the fourth consecutive season, but the method and teamwork that had become the foundation of successful teams, both at home and abroad, clearly didn't translate to international football – or, indeed, to the elite level of club competition. On the way to winning the second of three straight European Cups with a fluid style that saw players interchanging positions at will, Ajax had beaten Arsenal home and away, after which head coach Stefan Kovacs observed, 'I was a little surprised that Arsenal seemed to have so few ideas. All they did was concentrate on the long ball down the middle.' It was another damning indictment of the English game.

So were the comments of Bertie Mee after he, Dave Sexton, Ron Greenwood and Don Howe watched Ajax put four past Bayern Munich in the quarter-finals one season later. 'English sides don't give the opposition time to play, nor do they give them the space in which to play,' he said dismissively. *Football Monthly* reacted by writing, 'What makes Mee's statement so regrettable is not that it lacks sanity or purpose, but that he should assess the sum total of English soccer aspirations in these negative, barren terms.'[346]

THE END OF THE WORLD

> *ALF GARNETT: Cor blimey, that's the trouble with this country today. It's like being on a boat with no captain – and no crew*
>
> ***Till Death Us Do Part*, 'Three-Day Week'**
> **(Johnny Speight; BBC TV, 1974)**

The prioritisation of the national team became a talking point that would dominate the sport as thoughts turned to the 1974 World Cup. Malcolm Allison went as far as suggesting that the FA Cup be cancelled for a year to create more breathing space in the season's suffocating schedule.

'Responsibility for defeat was laid firmly at the feet of Sir Alf Ramsey,' wrote Ken Jones of the Wembley nightmare against West Germany, 'but how much of it should have been accepted by a system which permits such a critical match to be okayed in ludicrous circumstances?' Referring to the withdrawal of McFarland and Colin Todd because of Derby's important League game two days later, Jones cited a 'League system which has become ridiculously unwieldy and almost unmanageable. There is no doubt in my mind that there were at least seven England players at Wembley who were not entirely committed to the action. It could be disastrous if England are unable to qualify for the World Cup in two years' time. Let's not overlook that possibility.'[347]

Even Ramsey was eventually forced to concede that some of his players in the West Germany game had been distracted. 'I felt the game against the Germans would be enough in itself to motivate them,' he said, with justification. 'I should have done more to make them aware of their responsibilities.'[348]

Jones, whose work for the *Mirror* group and *Goal* magazine made him one of the country's most influential football writers, was not letting up, although his next blast conflated the problems of the England team with the lack of open, entertaining football on offer most Saturdays. 'A negative attitude has become so common to the experience of spectators throughout the Football League,' he observed, suggesting that the First Division was so competitive that it produced 'too many matches of a critical nature'. Bill Nicholson contributed his complaint that there was no time in the diary to practise technical skills, while Jones concluded, 'Overwhelming interest has created a situation where we now watch sub-standard football. It is reflected in the inadequacies of the England team and the failure of English clubs to make a lasting impression in the European Cup.'[349]

This wrapping up of national team results with a lack of exciting football tended to reflect the writer's overall lament for English football rather than offering a robust critique of the deficiencies of Ramsey's side. After all, its greatest achievement had not exactly been a triumph of flamboyance. When, at the end of September, FA chairman Sir Andrew Stephen suggested that 'the time is ripe to have a long look at the state of the game' it was not so much the performance of the England team that concerned him as it was three elements that he felt were forcing attendances down: too much competitive football – presumably a dig at the Football League; too much television coverage – ditto; and 'the madness that takes place on the terraces'.

Yet any fears the country was feeling about England in the 1974 World Cup still centred mostly on what would happen when they arrived for the finals in West Germany, not on the formality of winning a three-team group against Poland and Wales. Had it not been so, maybe the FA might have thought twice about its decision, two days after Stephens's pronouncement, to ban two of England's most talented young footballers, Todd and Alan Hudson, from two years of international football. Their crime was to withdraw from the England Under-23 team's tour of East

Germany, Poland and the Soviet Union in order to give themselves a full summer's rest.

So much for the apparent sympathy of the FA chairman, who'd felt that there was 'too much football'. Instead FA secretary Denis Follows announced, 'They have been told they are not wanted by England for two years.' And so much for consistency. Madeley had told England he did not want to go the World Cup in Mexico, but was in the full squad the following season. In the *Sunday Express*, Danny Blanchflower reflected the general astonishment at the punishment for Hudson and Todd by writing, 'This is good news for the Great Train Robbers. They can feel relieved now they were not confronted by the FA Committee.'

Hudson had been bitterly disappointed not to have made his full England debut that spring against Northern Ireland after Bobby Moore told him that Ramsey was going to play him. Meanwhile, Todd – described by Kenny Dalglish as 'the most difficult defender I ever played against'[350] – argued that his loyalties lay with his family. 'I honestly didn't expect any disciplinary action,' he said. 'I just did what I thought was right, which was to take my wife Jenny and our son away for a holiday. I was honest about it. I could have pretended to be injured.'[351]

With the fates, and the FA, conspiring to keep Hudson well away from the England team, it was another rising star, Kevin Keegan, who made his debut when a new World Cup campaign began with a narrow win in Cardiff. The warning signs of a disappointing 1-1 draw in the return against Wales at Wembley were then disregarded in the wake of a 5-0 thrashing of Scotland in Glasgow early in 1973. The Scottish FA's centenary celebrations were dumped on by England's strike force of Mick Channon, Allan Clarke and Chivers. And then a clean sweep of the Home Internationals sent England off in a confident frame of mind to eastern Europe, the centrepiece of the trip being the World Cup contest against Poland. According to Jimmy Hill, defeat and subsequent failure to qualify would 'have a disastrous effect on English football for a number of years'.[352] For once, he wasn't exaggerating.

After drawing in Czechoslovakia, England arrived at the Slaski Stadium in Chorzow, part of the mining city of Katowice. Maybe it was the dark, forbidding environment that persuaded Ramsey that there was tough, unforgiving work to be done and this was no place for the frivolity of three up front. The day before the game he approached Channon to tell him, 'I'm leaving you out tomorrow. I'm going to put in a destructive player in your place.' Storey was back in a line-up that would be wearing unfamiliar yellow shirts. 'I was stunned,' said Channon. 'To me, it was the biggest crime in the world that he left me out – an attacker – for Peter Storey, a midfield defending player.'[353]

Ramsey, who had misread the selection needs against West Germany a year earlier, was immediately questioned in the BBC's *World Cup Grandstand* studio for his apparent timidity. 'Despite everything, he still picks a side to stop him losing,' argued Brian Clough, who would shortly be transferring his opinions to ITV. Clough's view of Poland was that they were 'amateurs' and, 'I don't think they would grace the finals of the World Cup.' Yet, he continued, 'This is still not good enough for Alf. He has still selected a side which is cautious.'

A near-post mix-up involving Moore allowed Poland a seventh-minute lead and, immediately after half-time, the captain was caught in possession by Wlodzimierz Lubanski, who went on to beat Peter Shilton. Moore owned up to an 'unforgiveable error' but said that his attempt to get clear of his opponent and pick out a pass was 'a move I've done thousands of times'.[354]

'After such a magnificent career, Bobby had a bad game,' said Chivers. 'For all the great games that he had, that was one of his worst.'[355] Maybe it was finally time to consider the man widely regarded as Moore's natural successor, Colin Todd. Oh, hang on …

England's response in Katowice was delivered by Alan Ball, who fouled Leslaw Cmikiewicz with 11 minutes remaining and then grabbed his opponent by the throat and attempted to knee him in the region of his red shorts, believing that the Polish player had tried to put his boot in the face of Peters. Ball was shown a red card – joining Mullery as the only men sent off on full England duty – and had to be restrained and ushered away by trainer Harold Shepherdson. Earlier, Lubanski had been carried from the field – and out of Poland's World Cup campaign – after a challenge by McFarland, which journalist Brian Glanville saw as a metaphor. 'When Roy McFarland dragged down the Polish forward … as he broke clean through the English defence, something, I think, died in our football.'[356]

Once more, the result left Ramsey exposed to criticism. Even former disciple Jack Charlton was forced to admit to 'big doubts about the way he is tackling things now'. Recalling the aftermath of the game, McFarland revealed Ramsey's own feelings of culpability. 'The only thing you could drink out there was beer, so we ordered a couple of crates. We were all disappointed and sat in Bally and Bobby's room talking about how poorly we had performed. There was a knock and Alf came in and said, "Can I join you boys?" and then said, "It was my fault. We didn't get that near post sorted out." He drank his beer, persuaded everyone he was to blame and walked out.'[357]

Concerns quickly arose over England's ability to prepare properly for the must-win return game against Poland at Wembley on 17 October, a match described by Mike Langley in the *Sunday People* as 'the thundercloud hanging over the new season'. Failure, he said, would be 'a cataclysm'. Rodney Marsh, meanwhile, felt that the English game was in such a sorry state that 'it will be almost non-existent in 10 years' if England failed to qualify.

The typical timeline for an England home game was that players would make their way to the team hotel during the Sunday after a full League programme and be checked over by the team's medical staff. 'We used to sit by the phone on Sunday afternoons and Sunday nights waiting for the pull-outs,' said Fred Street, who inherited those anxious waits when he became the England team physiotherapist in 1974. 'Out of a squad of 22 you would get four most games who would pull out, and then you would have to call up the stand-bys. And that had often upset a player, knowing he was only a stand-by. They see themselves as a makeweight and they are probably not going to get a game anyway. So here we are on Monday with a squad of 22 and of those I would probably keep half a dozen out of training. If anyone had turned up on a Sunday night really suffering, I would send them back to the club to get ready for the following Saturday.'[358]

Players who were fit enough could look forward to a maximum of two full training sessions in which to reacquaint themselves with team-mates and develop enough understanding to achieve victory. The military-trained 'amateurs' of Poland, the English press delighted in pointing out, would have been together for months by the time they kicked off at Wembley.

With no prospect of the Football League agreeing to postpone the First Division programme on Saturday 13 October, a compromise suggested by many was for the League Cup games scheduled in the previous midweek to be played on Monday night, allowing Ramsey to have a few additional days with his squad before players returned to their clubs for the weekend. It did nothing to lessen the risk of injury right before England's most critical game for years, but it could aid the cause of cohesiveness. 'Everything possible must be done to help Sir Alf,' Clough suggested, correctly noting that the reputation of the entire English game was at stake. Yet Manchester City manager John Hart, while promising to do all he could to help England qualify, added, 'But I also want Manchester City to win the League Cup.' After all, the outcome of City's second-round tie against Walsall had a far greater impact on Hart's employment than England's result. That the onus should be on the clubs to 'do the right thing' was both unfair and, frankly, unrealistic, especially when there were managers such as Newcastle United's Joe Harvey, who said, 'I am getting fed up to the teeth with Sir Alf Ramsey's perpetual moaning. He should know his players by now and they in turn should know each other.'

The fact that, only a few weeks before the Poland game, the Football League management committee spent their time examining ways of cashing in on a new 'Spot the Ball' competition rather than debating ways of assisting the England team was greeted by the *Daily Express*'s David Miller thus: 'While the League fiddles, football burns. Why not go the whole hog, Mr Hardaker, cancel the players' contracts and have bingo on Saturday afternoons like the derelict cinemas?'

Finally, Hardaker's men instructed clubs to implement the League Cup compromise. After which, England went out and thrashed Austria 7-0 at Wembley, a result that seemed to lend weight to the arguments of those such as Harvey and eased the nation's nerves about the more important events of three weeks later. The pessimists were given ammunition when Poland's Under-23s held their English counterparts to a goalless draw at Plymouth the night before the real thing, and Green warned his readers in *The Times*, '[England] may well require one special virtue. It is patience.' More common, though, was the view expressed by Channon that 'the Poles just didn't compare in skill, flair or method and I can't see them being so fortunate again'.[359]

An unchanged line-up from the Austria game saw England field Channon, Chivers and Clarke up front, while Hunter was preferred to Moore at the back. Yet the men supposedly carrying the country's hopes all the way to West Germany got no further than the Wembley penalty area before being mugged by the 6ft 4in Polish goalkeeper. Jan Tomaszewski's brilliance might not have deterred Clough from telling his new ITV audience that he was merely 'a clown' – a comment Brian Moore was man enough to challenge – but it was sufficient to ensure that England would be absent from the World Cup finals for the first time since they deigned to enter the 1950 tournament. Having recovered from near disaster when he almost rolled the ball to the feet of Clarke, Tomaszewski – like Netzer – chose Wembley as the venue for the game of his life.

The entire match appeared to be played out in a flurry of mayhem in the Poland penalty area. Bodies flew everywhere to block shots; the ball bounced back off the woodwork; and the goalkeeper – when not flapping like an overworked traffic cop – pulled off a series of miraculous saves. None was better than the low parry to his right to deny Bell, shortly before stretching towards his left post to keep out Clarke's header. 'This is the most incredible first half of football I have seen for a very, very long time,' gasped commentator Hugh Johns, before describing another leaping save against Channon.

'If I could turn the clock back and play that game again, I'd want virtually everything to be the same again,' said Bell. 'We absolutely paralysed them that night and it was the most one-sided international I ever played in.'[360] In the dressing-room at half-time, Ramsey assured his players to keep playing as they were and a goal would come. It was impossible, on the evidence of the first 45 minutes, to believe anything else.

Into the second half. A Currie blockbuster pushed away; a Channon volley into the side netting; and then … disaster. Hunter lost a tackle on the touchline. 'The ball should have ended up down the North Circular Road,' he said. 'Like an idiot, instead of putting it out of play, I … tried to lift it over with my right foot. Well I must have had a brain seizure at that moment because I never did that.'[361] Hunter allowed a break that ended with Jan Domarski shooting under Shilton's body. 'It went too quickly for me to get down and save,' the keeper explained,[362] while Hunter recalled, 'He could have thrown his cap on it.'[363]

Now there was a disallowed effort by Channon to add to the drama and, finally, an England goal by Clarke from the penalty spot, with Shilton unable to watch at the other end of the field. But there were no more goals; just more saves, against Currie, against Clarke, against Channon, against everyone, it seemed. Ramsey's caution delayed any substitution until the introduction of Kevin Hector with a couple of minutes left, an inertia described by Miller in the *Daily Express* as 'the most inexplicable tactical blunder of his controversial career'. According to Ramsey's biographer, Leo McKinstry, *Daily Mirror* journalist Nigel Clarke was told later by Sir Alf that his watch had stopped and he didn't realise how little time was left.

Hector had been constantly asking an official near the England bench how much time remained and was taken by surprise when Ramsey ordered him to get ready for action. He ripped off the two tracksuits he was wearing for warmth, while Keegan did the same in the belief that he was the 'Kevin' for whom Ramsey had called. Hector stumbled on without instruction or warm-up and immediately had a header blocked from point-blank range. 'I headed it well, but the defender was on the line and it just hit him on the knee,' said the previously uncapped Derby forward. 'I could have been an overnight hero.'[364] After one further goal-line clearance from Bell's shot, with Tomaszewski again flailing around like, dare it be said, a clown, the whistle blew on what Johns called 'one of the blackest days' for English football.

The matter-of-fact headline in *The Times* – 'England fail to qualify for World Cup finals' – was as stark and damning as the statistics that England had failed to convert 31 goal attempts and 20-odd corners into victory. Green's observation that 'what England truly lacked this night was some guiding star' was a little harsh in light of such dominance, while Ramsey's public acceptance that 'in life one has many disappointments' demonstrated the same kind of equanimity with which he greeted his greatest triumph.

Others were less guarded about their emotions. 'Losing that game hurt me more than anything else I have ever experienced in football,' Chivers recalled, significantly referring to a drawn game as a defeat. 'In the dressing-room all the players were devastated and in tears.'[365] Hunter agreed that he was 'devastated', but would not admit to tears, while Clarke was too depressed to turn up to film an advert for NatWest the following day.

Much would be made in the 21st century of the 'golden generation' of English footballers unable to win the World Cup: Beckham, Lampard, Gerrard, Rooney, Cole and Ferdinand. For the likes of Bell, Chivers, McFarland and Channon, the cream of their own era, the chance of merely appearing in the tournament finals at the peak of their powers had been denied them. 'World Cups only come around every four years and I'd mainly been a substitute in Mexico, so this had been my big chance,' said Bell, perhaps the most complete English footballer of the early 1970s. 'I remember Alf telling us that the squad of 1974 was better than the one that had won it in 1966.'[366]

England's failure gave observers further freedom to air the dissatisfaction with Ramsey that had been building for three years. According to different analysts' views he had followed a 'grey groove of predictability' and wasted the years since 1970 with 'an over-cautious approach'. And it was now safe to lambast the manager on light entertainment shows. 'I think we've got three main problems with the England team,' said Mike Yarwood in the guise of Brian Clough on *Parkinson*. 'Sir. Alf. Ramsey. I'd blame him for the Test matches if I could.'

Joe Mercer said England were now 'a third-rate nation' but suggested that Ramsey's biggest problem was that he was 'a bad public relations officer' – an area of strength that Mercer would soon be bringing to the role on a temporary basis.[367] Mercer would certainly never have dreamt of undermining the football knowledge of the fourth estate in the abrasive manner of Ramsey when he told reporters in 1973, 'I was interviewed by a news man this morning and he seemed to think there were millions of people who think that the type of football I encourage England to play was dull, lacked flair. The word flair keeps cropping up and other words that infer you know absolutely nothing about the game of football.'

England's failure meant the state of the national game being exposed to scrutiny. To make matters worse, Liverpool would soon be beaten in the second round of the European Cup by Red Star Belgrade. Bill Shankly's dismissive 'would our public watch the sort of football they play on the Continent?' was not a response designed to challenge anyone to look seriously at any problems, but privately he'd made some important notes for the future direction of his team. Bobby Charlton's optimistic assertion that this was 'the start of a brave new world for English football' didn't find many supporters, although David Gregory, editor of the drum-banging *Shoot!*, urged readers to 'take pride in their heart-rending battle' against Poland. Yet when the magazine had run a recent article on Britain's teams in Europe, it seemed appropriate that the union flag that had formed the background graphic to the page had been printed upside down, the universally recognised signal of distress.

Many observers blamed the managers who perpetuated the unimaginative nature of League football, discouraging the free thinking that might have solved the problem of Poland. Ajax coach Kovacs, a frequent critic, said, 'When I watch an English team all I see are 11 faceless gladiators chasing around as though the clubhouse was on fire.'[368] West Ham's Ron Greenwood, who remained endearingly out of step with most of his peers, asked, 'Can you blame [Ramsey] if the players don't have sufficient intelligence?' Yet Ken Jones wrote of the 'pomposity' of leading managers, adding 'If they feel that professional footballers are incapable of thinking for themselves then it is high time that they did something about it. Unless they do we shall continue to witness the inadequacy which infests our technique when it is set against foreign opposition.' English football was breeding 'moronic athletes', he concluded.[369]

Even Hardaker was forced to admit that it was time to examine the structure of League football and perhaps reduce the strain on the top players. Rotation in this age was merely something farmers did with their crops, not an option for First Division managers. Ted Croker, who could have chosen an easier week to be taking over from Denis Follows as secretary of the Football Association, spoke of 'fundamental problems to be tackled' and agreed with Hardaker when he said, 'We are asking our leading players to be both artists and artisans. It could be that when it matters most there are not too many reserves of strength to draw upon.'

Such apparent appetite for revolution did not signify immediate change. Hardaker's dismissive comment on BBC Radio in the game's build-up that failure to win would be 'a terrible thing for six weeks and then everyone will forget about it' proved to be not far off the mark when it came to the game's administrators. It would not be until the end of the 1980s that the Football League lessened the burden on the leading teams by reducing the top division over the course of two seasons from 22 to 20 teams.

An opinion poll by the Harris Organisation, commissioned the day after the Poland game, showed that only 21 per cent of fans thought that the 'heavy League programme' was the chief cause of England's omission from the World Cup finals. And while modern times might have seen #RamseyOut trending on social media, a mere 15 per cent blamed the manager.

Don Revie believed there was 'no need for Alf to go', while Ramsey loyalist Alan Ball turned the blame on an apathetic football public that was continuing to desert the League game and pick and choose its internationals. 'It was a disgrace to see only 60,000 turn up for the World Cup tie against Wales,' he said. 'Oh yes, the fans turned out when we played Poland, but we needed them more against Wales. The English public don't deserve a successful national team and if they haven't got one at present, it's only fitting.'[370]

Yet Ball's Arsenal team-mate Bob McNab was among those who felt Ramsey, considered a tactical innovator in leading an underwhelming Ipswich Town team to the League title, had been left behind by the demands of an evolving game since 1966 and allowed his team to become complacent. McNab, whose own England career was fleeting, recalled seeing warning signs four years earlier. '[England] training was Mickey Mouse. We went to Mexico and South America for several weeks in the summer of 1969 and it was the biggest waste of time of my life. I had never seen such amateurish training since I was at Huddersfield. It was like a pub trip. Not that we were drinking, but we never trained properly. The other players didn't notice it because they were part of it. They would be leaning on the post and talking. It was a joke.'[371]

The Football Association appeared undecided about Ramsey's level of culpability. After an initial statement expressing the FA Council senior committee's 'unanimous support and confidence' in the manager, FA vice-chairman Sir Harold Thompson, a bullying character who had a low opinion of managers,[¶] insisted at a later meeting that such sentiments 'did not represent the feeling of all members of the Council'.

With his contract up for renewal in June 1974, and a desire to increase a £7,200 annual salary that paled against the wages of other leading managers, Ramsey was in no mood to offer his resignation. He remained in charge for a home defeat against Italy in November and when he spoke early in 1974 about the conflict between the country's interest and the priorities of the clubs, he said, 'I have lived with these difficulties for ten years and I shall go on living with them.' Ironically, a friendly in Portugal in April further highlighted those issues. Having

¶ 'Harold Thompson was a bastard,' Alan Odell, secretary of the FA's international section, told author Leo McKinstry. 'He treated the staff like shit.'

already named Stan Bowles, Frank Worthington and Trevor Brooking in a new-look squad, he lost his Liverpool and Leicester players – including both goalkeepers, Ray Clemence and Peter Shilton – to an FA Cup semi-final replay and saw Revie withdraw Leeds duo Hunter and Madeley the day before departure. Complaining that clubs 'should be punished', he included six debutants in a rewritten teamsheet,** before witnessing a lifeless 0-0 draw. He then got on with naming 20 players for the summer Home Internationals and European tour.

Yet, as Croker would later reveal, a decision had been taken in February to sack him. 'We had to bow to popular opinion,' he explained.[372] Croker, who had a sharper commercial brain than most at FA headquarters, also saw the traditionalist Ramsey as an impediment to his desire to monetise the England team through kit sponsorship and the like. The FA's international committee approved Ramsey's departure by a narrow vote at its April meeting and the executive committee applied its rubber stamp. On 1 May, the public were told that Ramsey had been fired.

Stoke City full-back Mike Pejic, a young player recently introduced by Ramsey to the England squad, was brought to tears by the news, while Allan Clarke recalled the sacking as 'diabolical', adding, 'There is not another country in the world who have got rid of such a brilliant manager' – which was certainly not true but reflected Clarke's view that 'we would go through walls for him'.[373]

The contrary element of human nature meant that those who had spent years criticising Ramsey now mourned for the only manager to win England the World Cup and attacked the FA for its callousness. The fact that Ramsey was apparently offered no opportunity to publicly resign was disrespectful, many felt, of his contribution to English football. Even Ball, with an eye on his own England future, could not hold back. 'I'll have to watch what I write otherwise I'll be in trouble with the authorities,' he told his readers in *Shoot!*. 'I must confess I have lost a little faith in the men who rule our football.'

** Full marks if you identified Phil Parkes, Mike Pejic, Dave Watson, Martin Dobson, Stan Bowles and Trevor Brooking.

FA chairman Stephen explained, 'We had to look at the quality of our game and we realised we had been falling behind the rest of the world, particularly since 1970.' After 113 games in charge of England, Ramsey was given no offer of a future role with the FA or an official testimonial match. Instead he left with a mere £8,000 pay-off, a £1,200 annual pension and 'a feeling of despair, sadness and terrific disappointment'.

DEEPER AND DOWN

I want all the world to see
To see you're laughing and you're laughing at me

'Down Down', Status Quo (Francis Rossi, Bob Young; Sony/ATV Music Publishing LLC, Universal Music Publishing Group, 1974)

Brian Moore could see it coming. 'Certainly, it would be futile to condemn Manchester United on this one performance on the opening day of the season,' he told viewers of *The Big Match*, 'but there were people last season who said that rather than their troubles being over when they avoided relegation it could be that they were just beginning. They might be fairly near the truth.'

But one didn't need to be sitting on an elevated commentary gantry to see that United's defeat at Highbury on the first day of the 1973-74 season was symptomatic of a chronic malaise, not an opening-day hiccup. Tommy Docherty had lifted United up to 18th place after taking over for the second half of the previous season but had been forced to abandon any romantic residue of the Busby era. 'I got a shock when I joined how many poor players there were in the first team,' recalled defender Martin Buchan, who had arrived at Old Trafford shortly before Docherty. 'The squad was a curious mixture of superstars and lads who would not have got a game in Aberdeen reserves.'[374]

Docherty's only option, especially after going without victory in his first six weeks in charge, was to turn an ugly face to the world. It did not take long for David Meek to warn his *Manchester Evening News* readers, 'Manchester United's fight for their First Division lives is going to be a rugged one. It's going to upset the purists.'

'The Doc did the best with what he had,' said Buchan. 'Defensively, we weren't one of the worst and you worked on things during the week with the intention of scoring more goals than the opposition, but we didn't do it often enough.'[375] Writing in *Goal* during the summer, Ken Jones would lament United's unattractive image, revealing that two testimonial committees had recently chosen not to have United as opponents for their players. 'What we are forced to accept is a different Manchester United,' he concluded.[376]

Docherty's rebuilding efforts at Old Trafford revolved around signing several players who had made his Scotland team; men such as Arsenal's George Graham and Celtic's Lou Macari. Now, with George Best absent and Bobby Charlton retired, United's third superstar of the Sixties, Denis Law, found himself beginning the new season across the city at Maine Road after Docherty deemed him surplus to requirements. It was the fact that the Scotland striker heard that news on television rather than from his manager that so angered him. With a new house in the Manchester area and a testimonial game against European champions Ajax coming up, Law had been considering retirement. Instead, feeling betrayed by a man who had once claimed he had a job for life at Old Trafford, he signed for Manchester City.

United followed their defeat at Arsenal with wins against Stoke City and Queens Park Rangers, but Stan Bowles claimed, 'They're the worst team we've ever met.' And when goalkeeper Alex Stepney scored from the penalty spot against Birmingham City five weeks later, it was a sign of the disarray enveloping Old Trafford. Even more so when he still held the position of joint-top scorer with two goals as the final game of 1973 arrived. Even Stepney claimed that it was a poor reflection on Docherty's management.

Docherty and Busby extended an olive branch to George Best, whom they had visited in hospital during the summer when he was recovering from a thrombosis in his leg. 'We weren't blessed with too many good players,' Docherty would admit. 'Matt and I had a chat one day and it was it was on his suggestion; he thought it would be a good idea to bring George back. I was trying anything because we were a bit desperate.'[377]

Bearded and bloated, Best experienced two victories during a 12-game comeback, scoring twice and performing capably enough. But only rarely did he evoke memories of even two years previously. After a 3-0 defeat at QPR on New Year's Day, he failed to turn up for training on the Thursday before an FA Cup tie against Plymouth Argyle. Such absences, he claimed, would be indulged in his new agreement with Docherty, but when he turned up at Old Trafford on Saturday he was told he was not playing. He would not do so for United again. 'I think Tommy handled the George Best situation very well,' said Graham. 'Everyone knew George had a problem, but everybody thought that his ability would overcome everything. It was a brave decision, but that was Tommy. He didn't shy away from it.'[378] Docherty admitted, 'I wanted to be the man who handled George Best, but I couldn't.'[379]

United entered 1974 in the relegation places – increased to three that season – and never escaped them. Secure enough at the back, they scored only 38 goals. At one point, Busby told Docherty, 'Let's go out with dignity.' By the time of their final home game, United needed to beat neighbours City to have a chance of staying up, although it would need Norwich City to take points off Birmingham City to carry those hopes into their last match at Stoke. Anxiety and aggression were the dominant forces in a crowd of 56,996, with news that Birmingham had hit back to lead 2-1 at half-time adding to the incendiary atmosphere. With seven minutes to play Francis Lee scuffed a shot across goal and Law, with nonchalance bordering on reluctance, back-heeled the ball into the net. Far from enjoying any kind of revenge over the people who had discarded him, the faraway look on Law's face betrayed his horror at having perpetrated such an act on the club he still loved.

Scores of fans, displaying more disorientation than violent intent, entered the field of play from both ends of the ground. Referee David Smith met both managers before the game resumed – without Law, who had allowed himself to be substituted.†† As smoke rose from the

†† Jimmy Greenhoff, who signed for United from Stoke, believed Docherty demonstrated his empathy with Law's predicament late in the 1976-77 season. When United visited relegation-bound Stoke, Docherty left Greenhoff out of the team, telling him, 'You are not sending them down.'

Stretford End, United full-back Stewart Houston was almost tackled by a lone spectator in black Oxford bags and grey jacket. Emboldened, a few more intruders emerged and before long the field was engulfed, forcing the players to run for cover. An appeal to the fans, notably from Busby rather than Docherty, was a waste of breath and the game was abandoned. The Football League rightly allowed the result to stand. Even if United had won, or had the game been replayed, they were down, thanks to Birmingham's victory.

In the post-Alex Ferguson era, Manchester United managers have been dismissed for far lesser crimes than relegation. Louis van Gaal was even dispensed with only hours after winning the FA Cup. But there was something about Docherty, especially after the struggles of McGuinness and O'Farrell, that meant he still felt like the right man in the right place at the right time. As Richard Kurt and Chris Nickeas put it so neatly in *The Red Army Years*, 'A Seventies Old Trafford was surely no place for an O'Farrell – but it was made for the Doc, Seventies Man incarnate. Put him in a kipper tie, in *Man About the House*, next to a Party Seven or behind the wheel of a Capri – does he not fit perfectly within your mental image?'[380]

Busby announced, 'I believe in Tommy Docherty; that he's capable of making the club great again.' You could have made a baseball cap in United red out of such a statement.

8

SATURDAY NIGHT'S ALRIGHT FOR FIGHTING

I throw house bricks for the Arsenal, I chuck lead pipe for West Ham

I kick and maim for Chelsea, I kill for Tottenham

I drop bottles for United on the crowd from up above

Yes, football is the game that we all love

Rutland Weekend Television **(Eric Idle and Neil Innes; BBC TV, 1975)**

SHORTLY BEFORE midday on a late November Saturday in 1976, a Thames Valley Police officer received a telephone call from a coach driver transporting West Ham fans from Essex to that day's game at Manchester United. He was at the M1 service station at Newport Pagnall, where, during a break in the journey, he had seen various weapons in the possession of his passengers. He asked that this information be passed to the Greater Manchester Police.

By 2.30pm, the coach was in the vicinity of Old Trafford and was boarded by a sergeant, who was confronted by fans wearing United colours and claiming to be followers of the home team. All were searched and one arrested for being in possession of a flick knife, a wooden stave and a small razor. When officers took a closer look on board they found a meat cleaver, a sword, four wooden batons, two daggers and two flick knives. And the passengers' true West Ham colours.

If the intention had been to infiltrate United territory and create mayhem with their varied weaponry, then the Hammers fans were hardly alone in their desire to knock United from their perch at the pinnacle of England's hooligan hierarchy; one perpetuated by the media and dominated by United due to the activities of its fans over recent years.

The place of certain United followers in the infamy of 1970s English football had been confirmed with that pitch invasion on Old Trafford's relegation day and during the club's rollicking tour of Second Division outposts during 1974-75. While a vibrant team enjoying a rebirth under Tommy Docherty swaggered to the title, the self-styled 'Red Army' who followed them intimidated and terrorised their way on to the front pages and into discussions in the House of Commons.

On the first day of the season they descended on east London, fresh from wreaking havoc around a pre-season friendly in the Belgian town of Ostend, where magistrate Marcel Laurens fined five fans and told them, 'During the summer we have had lots of trouble, but only from the English, never from the Germans and never from the French.' Those who lived close to Orient's ground woke on Saturday morning to find United fans sleeping in their gardens and doorways. The day featured a two-goal United victory; a battle with Arsenal supporters at Euston station; pitch invasions and fighting inside Brisbane Road; and glass thrown into the goalmouth. By the end of it, 27 United fans had been arrested, two policemen injured and a London Underground train damaged. 'This football madness must be stamped out and quickly,' declared Hector Monro, the Conservative Party's spokesman for sport. 'With jail sentences if necessary.'

Authors Richard Kurt and Chris Nickeas referred to this season as 'the greatest period of off-the-field anarchy' in United's history.[381] In major cities such as Sheffield, opposing fans refused to back down, creating major battles on the streets and terraces – 106 arrests and 51 injuries when United visited Wednesday – while the smaller towns boarded up shops and took shelter. 'The troublemakers are a minority,' Docherty insisted. However, United historian Michael Crick, who attended every United away game at that time, argued, 'I don't think it was really true that the hooligan element was very small,' suggesting that it was 'perhaps a majority of away fans'.[382]

When United visited Cardiff City early in the season, *The Times* devoted a full page to Gavin Scott's first-hand account of the fans' experience, a report that got off to a somewhat Dickensian opening. 'They wheeled the cripples in their wheelchairs along the side of the pitch,' Scott wrote. 'The turf was silent, undisturbed, like a quiet green pool; the grey sky looked as though it had been clamped over the afternoon. On the terraces all hell was breaking loose.'

Scott's observation of fans having 'filed through the slots in the grubby concrete walls, handed their 5p pieces, and clicked through the rusty turnstiles' was hardly complimentary to Ninian Park – an international ground – but could have described the majority of League grounds in the mid-1970s. Earlier in the day, Scott had seen United fans arriving at Cardiff's train station to find that 'the reception committee had not let them down: lines of police, dogs, ambulances, vans ... and on the route to the football ground, through the defeated streets full of the smells of Saturday afternoon, there was more satisfaction; not only police every 25 yards, but shop windows boarded up and fearful householders peering from behind lace curtains'.

During the game, as well as hearing fans trading insulting chants relating to the Aberfan colliery disaster of 1966 and the Munich air crash of 1958, he noted instances where a lone assailant would charge opposing fans, 'splitting a head, bloodying a nose'. Referring to 'the futility of it all', Scott continued, 'The fans wanted nothing more than to get at each other and prove there was a point to each affair.'

United's response was to invite their fans to Old Trafford on a Sunday morning to meet the squad and foster, so they hoped, a feeling of communal responsibility. 'They are bad news,' said captain Willie Morgan. 'It is getting us a bit down now. If they won't stop we want them to go away and support somebody else.' Sir Matt Busby wished he could 'find them and throw them in the river'.

There was at least in this case an acknowledgement of the strong link between the club and the fans who were besmirching its name. The more common response from clubs afflicted by hooliganism was to imply that the perpetrators were nothing to do with them; that they attached themselves as an excuse for a punch-up. That was reflected by Football League boss Alan Hardaker, who said during United's season in the Second Division, 'They are not football supporters.' He would repeat that opinion in his 1977 autobiography, claiming, 'A "football" hooligan is simply a hooligan who happens to have chosen football as his main area of mischief.'[383]

During the first season of the decade, Hardaker's mouthpiece, *Football League Review*, claimed that football clubs were 'gradually winning' the war on hooliganism inside grounds – as evidenced by the fact that most arrests were now outside or while fans were in transit. So that was all right, then. There was also the usual attempt at distancing. 'Bad behaviour among a minority of adolescent football followers is but one manifestation of unrest and anti-authoritarianism which has spread though all stratas *(sic)* and types in the younger generations.'[384]

It was contrary to the findings of the Harrington Report in 1968, when the authors admitted being impressed by how knowledgeable trouble-making fans were about their teams and how closely they identified with them. It was not what those who claimed the hooligans were not 'real' fans wanted to hear.

One of the rare occasions when a club official spoke out in defence of misbehaving fans came after one of the 1970s' most infamous pitch invasions, at Elland Road in 1971. Leeds United chairman Percy Woodward attracted widespread criticism for his sympathy with those who charged the field when referee Ray Tinkler allowed a contentious West Bromwich Albion goal. 'They were incensed beyond measure,' he argued. 'I am not blaming the spectators. There was every justification for it.' Woodward, a local councillor, defended his comments by pointing out the advanced age of some of the invaders.

But it was not just his local political opponents who seized upon the inappropriateness of his comments. A police statement pointed out, 'Perhaps Alderman Woodward, football managers and others would do well to avoid remarks which could be interpreted as condoning irresponsible conduct. The problem of keeping soccer violence in check is difficult enough without the impression being given that crowds have a right in protesting violently against an unpopular decision.'

Players were inevitably circumspect about voicing support for the more boisterous fans. 'Obviously we didn't like it, but I forgave them because of the way they supported us,' Peter Osgood would say of Chelsea's fans, who rivalled United when it came to notoriety. 'There was an element of hooliganism, but in all fairness they were a fabulous crowd.'[385]

Manchester United's army duly announced its return to the First Division in August 1975 by helping to create mayhem at Wolverhampton Wanderers. The majority of the 86 arrested at Molineux on a day that saw 14 people stabbed were away supporters. 'We've seen nothing like it,' said a police spokesman. 'It must have been bottling up inside them all through the long, hot summer.' A few weeks later, *The Big Match* cameras captured the chaos inside Upton Park when United visited West Ham. Players were taken back to the changing rooms after fans spilled on to the pitch. What the cameras didn't see was the London Underground workers who had gone on strike rather than transport the United fans, or the full extent of fighting that was reported to have left 100 injured.

At least commentator Brian Moore chose not to adopt the tone of *The Sun*, which took glee in a headline describing 'The Day the Terrace Terrors Were Hunted Like Animals and *Hammered*' and offered an account of how United fans were 'nursing their wounds ... after a savage hammering from their West Ham rivals.' Such was the prevalence of violence on the terraces that the media, it appeared, were now presenting it like a match report in terms of winners and losers.

The battles continued. Derby South MP Walter Johnson said that 'these disgraceful, degrading and vicious scenes must be stamped out' after United fans injured three policemen in his town at the start of the 1976-77 season. 'These louts support each other and pay their fines collectively. They have got to be sent to prison.' One of United's most infamous encounters came at Norwich City later that season and was described by Manchester United Supporters' Club chairman David Smith as 'the worst exhibition of wanton, all-out destruction I have seen'. A stand at Carrow Road was damaged; missiles were thrown at police and rival supporters; windows were smashed around the city; and cars were dumped in the river. An emergency Parliamentary session banned United fans from buying terrace tickets at away grounds.

In 1976, the Association of Chief Police Officers listed the offences 'most commonly committed' in the vicinity of football grounds as 'robbery, theft, criminal damage, possessing offensive weapons, threatening behaviour, insulting behaviour, woundings, assault on police, minor assaults, drunkenness'.

United fans might have been the highest-profile perpetrators of such deeds during the decade, but there were groups everywhere working their way through that check-list on an average Saturday afternoon – at all levels of the game. And crowd violence around football matches was not an entirely new phenomenon. The term 'hooligan' is accepted as having appeared in police reports relating to street gangs in the late 19th century, around the same time that coverage of football matches frequently referred to supporters attacking rival groups, and even players and match officials.

Those incidents became less common in the first half of the 20th century, especially between the two world wars. Yet by the mid-1950s, reports were appearing of fans wrecking 'football excursion' trains and launching missiles at players and officials. And by the start of the next decade 'football hooliganism' was being acknowledged as a problem; one related to, yet sitting outside, the more violent aspects of life that had already been observed in the growth of youth culture. The increased wages of young workers in the early 1950s – with half as much spending money again as their pre-war counterparts – had created a specific teenage movement, most visible in the musical tastes and fashion choices of groups such as 'Teddy Boys' and, before long, 'mods and rockers'. Public sensitivity over the assertive behaviour of such groups, especially Bank Holiday battles in seaside towns, duly extended into the narrative that accompanied disturbances at football matches.

With the sport becoming more conscious of its image because of competition from other leisure activities, and with fears building about national image as the 1966 World Cup approached, minor incidents assumed great importance in the press. Sociologists Eric Dunning, Patrick Murphy and John Williams described the years leading up to the tournament as the period when football hooliganism 'became a self-perpetuating social problem with the actions of the youths and [mainly] young men who were centrally involved and the media and official reactions to what they did feeding each other in a vicious spiral'.[386]

As early as 1963, Everton put up fences behind the goal and created curved terracing to combat objects being thrown into the goalmouth, although some publications felt such measures were unnecessary, and the *Daily Mail* even offered a preference for 'hooliganism rather than indifference'. Yet a joint report by the FA and Football League in 1964 cited 'soccer rowdyism' as the game's biggest problem and the Chester Report of 1966, an investigation into the state of the game, noted an increase in violent incidents at football grounds. The sport and its stadia offered a cultural environment and a theatre for violence to grow and thrive, the report suggested.

It was around this time, according to one commentator, that 'gangs emerged, staking their claims to certain "territories" within football grounds, and strong "tribal" loyalties grew up, intermingling gang mentality and support for particular teams'.[387] One of the first acknowledged examples of one group of fans staking claim to rival territory was Manchester United's late-season visit to West Ham in 1967, a game that clinched them the First Division title. Fighting inside and outside the ground left 20 people hospitalised and had the *News of the World* reporting on 'Soccer's Day of Shame'.

In the very first month of the 1970s, Stoke City's home game against Leeds United saw 61 people taken to hospital after a crush barrier collapsed during fighting at the Boothen End of the Victoria Ground. Stoke chairman Albert Henshall reported that 'when [Stoke fans] found their usual places taken by Leeds fans there was resentment'. By October 1970, the FA was advising Football League clubs of new ground standards, including smaller self-contained enclosures to make invasion of opponents' terrain more difficult.

Only a few weeks later, Scottish football suffered a disaster that, even though unrelated to hooliganism, highlighted in the most tragic manner possible the perilous state of the nation's football grounds. On New Year's Day, 66 people died at Glasgow's Ibrox Park after Rangers supporters among an 80,000 crowd for the game against Celtic attempted to get back inside the stadium when roars signalled an equaliser by their team. It only took the slip of one person to create panic. The resulting human avalanche caused steel railings on the seven-lane exit stairway on Terrace 13 to buckle. 'I remember going down,' said one survivor. 'People were flailing their arms and screaming hysterically, kicking and pushing. All they did was end up with the rest of us. I passed out and my legs had been crushed. I rolled over to ease the pain and looked straight into the face of a dead man.' Within two weeks, one in five Football League clubs in England reported that they had made safety-related improvements at their grounds, including the addition of new handrails at Old Trafford.

Football hooliganism, however, was proving that it did not require rival fans or rickety grounds to provide it with opportunity. Trains offering cheap fares and often only the most basic of passenger amenities – the 'football specials' – presented an invitation for vandalism that was frequently seized upon by more aggressive fans. Comedian Ian Stone, who travelled to watch Arsenal in the 1970s, recalled, 'We'd pile on to the football special and we'd be whisked (well, rarely whisked; trundled perhaps or limped) to our destination. Sadly, the world "special" denoted the fact that the train was not part of the regular timetable rather than signifying a high level of on-board facilities. There was very little in the way of comforts. Most of the light bulbs didn't work. The toilet facilities were basic. There was never a buffet car.'[388]

And in the 1971-72 season, a new phenomenon was further tarnishing the image of the football fan. Newspapers spoke of 'motorway madness', which consisted of fans hitching lifts to games; although not just the odd hopeful thumb on the slip road. Instead, hundreds at a time would skip among the traffic, hopping on and off the central reservation in the hope of flagging down a free ride. When the Home Office called for the sport's governing bodies to help stamp out the practice, the *Football League Review* carried a warning to fans: 'What matters is that lives are at stake and for the sake of saving a few pennies. It is not worth the risk.' Which was clearly the opposite of what those hitch-hiking fans believed.

Dip into any newspaper archive of the 1970s and it doesn't take long to find a story of one kind of football disturbance or another, whether at home or when English teams travelled abroad. 'Crowd behaviour has improved enormously over the past couple of years,' Bobby Charlton claimed in 1972. 'You still get the occasional toilet roll thrown on the pitch, of course, but the far more dangerous missiles like bottles and knives now seem to be a thing of the past.'[389] He'd not been as wrong since thinking, 'Yes, combing this bit over there will work.'

The ubiquity of the sport's biggest problem was even evident in popular culture, where football could not be separated from its violent backdrop. In a *Morecambe and Wise* sketch, Eric explains that he doesn't like cricket. 'No, I like the straight left, the right hook, the uppercut.'

'Boxing,' Ernie nods knowingly.

'Football,' Eric corrects him.

And in the opening episode of Peter Tinniswood's BBC sit-com *I Didn't Know You Cared* in 1975, the character of Uncle Mort is reminded that 'Abide With Me' was sung at his wedding, 'Oh, aye,' he says. 'It were just like t'Cup final. We even had a bit of hooliganism at reception and all.'

It was rare that a football season during the decade began without discussion of what measures might be taken to curb its greatest problem. Leicester City were among the clubs that introduced a family section; Leeds United and others printed warnings in the match programme about bad language and anti-social behaviour. After becoming England captain, Gerry Francis urged more strict parenting, while winger Gordon Hill, who played his career in front of Millwall and Manchester United fans, suggested sentences in 'a special punishment unit staffed by army personnel'.[390]

After a wave of violence during pre-season, League president Len Shipman welcomed the 1973-74 campaign by saying, 'Violence on the terraces must be strangled at birth early this season. The League, police and local authorities must get together to work out a plan to stop this type of behaviour.' Harder to put into practice than to say, although he did have a suggestion a few days later when he said, 'Fines will not stop the violence. The time has come for the return of the birch.'

Alan Hardaker was among those who had the more humane suggestion of creating all-seater stadia, conceding that clubs would need financial help for that to become a reality. Various police forces, meanwhile, spoke about filming fans in and around grounds, while Alan Ball suggested doubling terrace prices at Arsenal to £1 'to keep the unruly element from our grounds'[391] – an idea, in effect, two decades ahead of its time.

While manager at QPR, Gordon Jago, a forward thinker in on-field matters, suggested that a solution for the game's problems was to make all matches 'an event'. Among his proposals were that females could be tempted along by 'a mannequin parade of all the latest fashions shown in one of the ladies lounges ... even a cooking demonstration. I wish I could get Graham Kerr or Fanny Craddock* along for us.'[392]

More pointedly, calls for courts to impose harsher sentences were common, a typical example being Sports Minister Denis Howell's anger that no one was fined more than £40 after Chelsea fans created fires in the ground, damaged the social club and turnstiles, and smashed the windows of cars and houses after a 4-0 defeat at

* The two leading TV chefs of the day.

Charlton Athletic in 1977. Howell had been suggesting fines of up to £1,000.

Among the Chelsea fans that day was Graham 'Suggs' McPherson, who would soon be known as the lead singer of Madness. He recalled his friend's description of going to matches at that time as, 'You wake up nervous and you go to bed fucking nervous.' Remembering the Charlton game, he said, '[We] went in their end. You'd hope that someone was going to start singing Chelsea songs and at the same time you'd hope there'd be enough of you not to get beaten up. There was enough of us, so much so that some of them got bored and set fire to the stand. By the time I left, the ground was on fire.'[393]

The early days of the 1974-75 season saw more than the usual amount of column inches devoted to crowd trouble, especially when – two days after United's violent visit to Orient – 135 arrests were made at Bristol City's League Cup game against Cardiff City. 'At this rate, football will die the death in Bristol,' warned local MP Michael Cocks. A death was indeed coming. The inevitable instance of a fan being killed at a game arrived only five days later when 17-year-old Blackpool supporter Kevin Olsson was stabbed during a home match against Bolton Wanderers – a crime for which no one was ever convicted. The editorial column in *The Times* suggested, 'The motives which all at once impel hundreds of young people to resort to violence in different parts of the country are inarticulate and perhaps hardly conscious. But if football as a spectator sport is not to decline, it is essential that the season should not go on in the way it has begun.'

One early-season Saturday saw a train completely wrecked by Chelsea supporters, while another had a carriage burned out when Liverpool fans used mail bags stolen from the platform at Leicester to start a fire. Howell called for ticket sales to visiting fans to be controlled by the away team and delivered only to trusted supporters, while the British Railways Board proposed that the clubs should be responsible for the trains upon which fans travelled to matches. 'Our aim is to instil into the supporter that any damage he does will harm the club as opposed to British Rail,' said an optimistic statement. British Rail's method of making that happen was to discontinue cheap day-return tickets before 3pm on Saturdays. Hardaker argued that the company should have taken the step four years earlier, adding, 'But it was making a profit out of these trips and that was that.'

Another short-lived attempt to reduce damage on trains was the 'League Liner', which stripped the seating out of its carriages in order to stage a disco for travelling fans. Between 1973 and 1976, clubs were able to hire the train in the hope, according to Hardaker, that 'the added touch of luxury, together with its unusual and novel facilities, will encourage supporters to bring their wives and families – and girlfriends – with them.' The intention was that travelling fans would pay their £3.50 and set aside thoughts of violence for the chance to shuffle around to the likes of Suzi Quatro or Eurovision winners Abba. When Burnley hired the train for a game at QPR, 2,500 cans of beer, 600 cooked chickens, 1,000 sandwiches and 500 supporters were on board. But 15-year-old Burnley fan Alison Crowther complained, 'The chaps came in and all stood at one end of the coach watching us dance. They were all too shy to ask us for a dance.' Some clubs put their players on board for the return journeys, but vandalism soon proved more popular than doing the 'Juke Box Jive'† and the beaten-up train was discontinued.

Howell, meanwhile, proposed the introduction of identity cards for those attending football matches and supported the idea that magistrates be given the power to force offenders to attend detention centres on Saturday afternoons. By 1977, there would be 40 such centres established for those aged 14 to 16, although only two for 17- to 21-year-olds. Yet a report in *The Times* quoted research that said only two per cent of those attending were sent there for football-related incidents. The age limit on the juvenile group was subsequently raised to 18 in an attempt to make greater use of the centres for those causing trouble at games.

The 1974-75 season, which had got off to its ugly opening at Orient, reached a suitably violent climax, with a series of high-profile incidents. Tottenham Hotspur and Chelsea spent the season

† A hit for The Rubettes in 1974, co-written by Tony Waddington. Not *that* Tony Waddington.

fighting against relegation and when the two met on the penultimate Saturday, the White Hart Lane pitch became a battleground for the two armies of supporters. 'I really thought I might die,' policeman Ted Garrington told the *Daily Express*. 'They just went bloody wild. I was defenceless and scared as they just kept battering into me.' Fellow officer Keith Hayes added, 'It seems a lot to go through for the £4 overtime money.'

On the same day, while United were clinching the Second Division title at Notts County, local police reported the confiscation of numerous homemade 'kung-fu stars' – knife-sharp metallic weapons popularised by the television show *Kung Fu*. One of the objects had struck the helmeted head of a policeman, three of whose colleagues ended up in hospital after the day's violence.

And then, for the second season running, Europe experienced the worst of English fans' behaviour at a major final. In 1974, it had been Tottenham whose supporters demonstrated their dark side after a decisive second-leg defeat in the final of the UEFA Cup against Feyenoord. 'Bottle-throwing Tottenham Hotspur fans ran riot in Rotterdam last night as their team crashed to defeat,' read the front page of the *Express*, ironically next to a story relating US Secretary of State Henry Kissinger's peace-keeping efforts in the Middle East. 'They left 200 injured – many of them badly – and 50 more cooling off in the cells. The drunken fans, who had been on an orgy of destruction in the city all day long, finally ran completely out of control.' Spurs fans used their elevated position in the stadium to direct broken seats and bottles at rival fans before running battles broke out on the perilously steep terracing. 'You hooligans are a disgrace to Tottenham Hotspur,' announced manager Bill Nicholson. 'This is a football game – not a war.' One policeman commented, 'Half of them were so drunk that we could have half killed them and they wouldn't even have felt it.' Steve Perryman recalled the Spurs players being distracted by worries about family members being caught up in the trouble and regretted Nicholson having to spend half-time trying to calm the fans rather than helping his team plan a way back into the game.

A year later, the scene shifted to Paris, where Leeds were beaten 2-0 by Bayern Munich in a European Cup blighted by poor refereeing decisions. After an apparently legitimate Leeds goal was disallowed, a section of their fans began a sequence of violence that continued long after the match had concluded. Reports spoke of a German television operator having lost an eye, a photographer suffering a broken arm and £50,000 worth of damage to TV equipment as a result of seats being ripped from their mooring in the Parc des Princes and, according to *The Times*, 'launched like flying saucers'. Trouble continued outside the ground after the match, with damage to property.

The stadium director said the violence was 'no surprise to us; we have come to expect it from English people' and added, 'Over the last three days Leeds followers have attempted to break in and damage our premises.' UEFA banned the club from Europe for four years, reduced to two on appeal.

Not to be outdone, Manchester United fans marked their club's entry into the European Cup Winners' Cup in the autumn of 1977 by creating such havoc in France that the second leg of their tie against St Etienne was ordered to be played 200 kilometres from Old Trafford, at Plymouth Argyle's Home Park as it turned out. United fans claimed to have been provoked by missiles thrown by home fans, but *The Times* reported that visiting spectators started a fight behind the goal – 'armed with bottles, sticks and knives'. It took three baton charges by police to halt the trouble, although not before a barrier collapsed and French fans climbed the wire fence around the pitch to escape. St Etienne chairman Roger Roche described the United fans as 'the worst hooligans I have ever seen. This ground had been without a blemish until these gangsters came here.' On this occasion, Howell spoke up in support of the Red Army, supporting their claims of provocation, whereas the *Daily Mail* likened their punishment to 'rapping Jack the Ripper across the knuckles'.

Back in England, Parliament had been given an estimated cost to the taxpayer of £750,000‡ over the course of 1974-75 for the additional police presence outside football grounds – the cost of police inside

‡ The equivalent of almost £8 million in 2020.

the stadium being the responsibility of the home teams. Manchester United were said to have spent £26,400 during their promotion campaign, although that was thought to be less than the combined additional costs borne by the clubs they visited.

United had also erected fences behind the goals. Caged like cattle and with League president Shipman likening football hooligans to 'wild animals', the United fans delighted in a new chant: 'We hate humans!' The *Observer*'s view was that the fences had turned the Stretford End into 'a kind of academy of violence, where promising young fans can study the arts of intimidation'. The effect of the 'cage' had been to 'make the Stretford terraces even more exclusive and to turn the occupants into an elite'.

FA chairman Sir Andrew Stephen recalled seeing a game in Brazil where 'it was only the moat and fence that prevented possible murder' and added, 'I never dreamed the day might come when we would have to consider such things in England.'[394] Yet Tyneside police had to call for fences to 'at least delay' pitch invasions after Newcastle United fans raced on to the field during their 1974 FA Cup sixth-round game against Nottingham Forest at St James' Park. Forest were leading 3-1 before the interruption and ended up losing 4-3 after referee Gordon Kew restarted the game once police and their dogs had cleared the playing area. The FA ordered a replay at Goodison Park, but Newcastle – after one drawn game – won again on their way to the final.[§] A total of 126 people were injured in fighting at the original match, including 23 who were hospitalised; two with fractured skulls. One fan was charged for an assault on Forest midfielder David Serella, who suffered a cut lip. 'It certainly wasn't pleasant for the Forest players,' Newcastle's Terry McDermott recalled. 'Many of them looked frightened to death.'[395]

It was after that incident that Chris Lightbown, writing in *Foul*, pointed out the futility of attempting to appeal to the fans' missing sense of social responsibility. 'This is the Maggie May generation,' he

§ Bizarrely, over the course of three games, Forest – arguably the wronged party – never got the opportunity to play at home, which even Newcastle players said they could not understand.

wrote, 'the kids that got so fed up with school that they just walked out, with truancy rates of 30 and 40 per cent. These kids have lost the fear of authority, and there is no barrier that they won't walk through. The pitch was sacrosanct to my generation, whatever we did off it, but to these kids invading the pitch is peanuts.'[396]

It was why many could see no alternative to fences. At Elland Road, Leeds directors would decide to erect them in the wake of an FA Cup tie against Manchester City early in 1978, when home fans went on to the field with their team losing. Referee Colin Seel grabbed the public address microphone to announce, 'This game will not be abandoned. It will be finished if we have to play until midnight in an empty stadium.'¶

THE MORAL PANIC

> *VIC LEE: Everything's changed around here in eight years. It's changed a bloody lot. Everything's violence, no class.*
>
> ***Out* (Trevor Preston; Thames Television, 1978)**

Sports Minister Denis Howell at least acknowledged the need to look a little deeper than working out what height of fencing was required when he called for greater investigation into the social causes of football hooliganism. Alan Hardaker, however, was less interested in hearing theories about the disintegration of traditional working-class life or the erosion of family values. 'Listening to someone saying that the trouble with hooligans is that they had the wrong potty training when they were babies is not my idea of getting things done,' he said.[397]

Theories, therefore, were more abundant than valid research. The dismissal, of Kevin Keegan and Billy Bremner at Wembley in August 1974 was an example of the kind of on-field behaviour that some felt

¶ The same match saw Leeds goalkeeper David Harvey and centre-back Gordon McQueen scuffling in the six-yard box as they waited for City to take a corner. After an exchange of words, Harvey shoved McQueen, who responded with a right hook. The Scotland defender was sold to Manchester United the following month for £495,000.

influenced what happened on the terraces, especially now that the game was considered more cut-throat and cynical – and, by extension, violent – than at any time since the shin-kicking 1800s. Labour peer Manny Shinwell said it would help if 'prominent footballers exercised more discretion and indulged in civilised behaviour themselves'. More fears about the setting of bad examples were voiced when England internationals Norman Hunter and Francis Lee were shown swinging terrace-style roundhouses at each other on their way to an early bath when *Match of the Day* featured Derby County's game against Leeds in the autumn of 1975.

In the wake of Alan Ball's dismissal in England's World Cup game in Poland in 1973, the *Police Federation Journal* had posed the question, 'When an England player in an international match is seen by millions of TV viewers to spend most of the first half trying to intimidate the referee and gets himself sent off after attacking an opponent, what happens? He is picked again and only prevented from playing again by higher authority. Can we wonder at the behaviour of young hooligans, who after all are not paid large sums for playing the game?'

Laying the problem of hooliganism at the feet of a World Cup winner might have seemed harsh, but Tom Stoppard took up the theme in his 1977 BBC television play, *Professional Foul*, in which one character, the academic McKendrick, argues, 'It's no use expecting them to be little gentlemen when their heroes behave like yobs. If you've got yobs on the pitch you are going to have yobs on the terraces.'[398] There was little evidence to back up such an argument. Manchester United played some of the country's most entertaining and non-violent football at the time when their fans' behaviour was at its worst. They even won the reinstated Fair Play League in 1976-77 as the cleanest team in the First Division. PFA chairman Derek Dougan had long been saying things like, 'Some go on the rampage before the game even starts. How can you logically blame the players for that?'[399]

The theories and proposed remedies kept coming. It needed the combined brains of the Social Science Research Council, the Sports

Council, the Home Office and the Department of the Environment to suggest in 1977 that opposing fans should be positioned so that throwing things at each other was impossible. The group also aired concerns that attempts at crowd control were 'bringing together elements looking for trouble instead of dispersing them among the sobering influences of other groups'. FA secretary Ted Croker read that report and announced, 'I don't think it will contribute one scrap to the prevention of football violence.' What was needed, he said, was to 'hammer' offenders. It is doubtful, either, that Croker thought much of the report of the Medical Council on Alcohol, which came up with the revelation that teenagers who had been drinking were more likely to cause trouble at football matches.

Meanwhile, Louis Blom-Cooper, QC, the chairman of the Howard League for Penal Reform, suggested, 'The invasion of soccer pitches is an outward expression of the public's desire to feel part of the premises from which they have in the past been excluded … If people are standing cheek by jowl, jostling each other for a better vantage point to see the game, it is hardly surprising that physical assaults take place.' Because, of course, the very reason why rival fans might want to 'take' the Stretford End at Old Trafford was so they could see the game more clearly.

Scott's conclusion in his article in *The Times* on the Cardiff – Manchester United match might have been much closer to the truth. 'The point that is too often missed in discussing football hooliganism is that it is immensely enjoyable. It is something to look forward to throughout the week; it is a source of friendship, it is a genuine adventure,' he wrote. 'In short, anyone who wants to end violence at football matches had better think up something pretty good to replace it.'

In *The Glory Game*, Hunter Davies illustrated the same point in describing a conversation he had with a Coventry policeman when he travelled with some of Tottenham's rowdier fans. 'I said it was the crowd excitement,' he wrote. 'I'd already felt it when they were stampeding off the train. In the middle of all the noise and shouting, you really did feel you'd taken over the city. I said they were all in rotten jobs, from rotten homes, all the usual things. There was no other excitement or meaning in their lives.'[400]

Things had not changed much by 1977 when a *Daily Mirror* editorial, talking about the motivation for punk rock, admitted, 'It's not much fun to be young today … 104,000 school leavers have gone straight from their classroom to an ideal and purposeless life on the dole. Is it any wonder youngsters feel disillusioned and betrayed?' One of those youngsters was Boy George, who chose music rather than football as his escape. 'In the 1970s, teachers just didn't like kids. If you came from a certain type of family you were marked the minute you went into school,' he explained. 'They don't want you to have a personality, they don't want you to be an individual, they want you to shut up.'[401]

Throughout the decade, author and sociobiologist Desmond Morris prepared his book, *The Soccer Tribe*, published in 1981. Devoting a large section to the make-up and behaviour of fans of the sport, he wrote, 'Sociologists studying the background of the offenders have found that, time and again, it is the young men from the more deprived areas of the city or town, living out their daily lives in crowded slums or boring soulless housing estates who are the typical offenders.' The sport, he suggested, 'merely acts as a dramatic stage on which they can perform'.[402] This was coupled, according to Dunning, Murphy and Williams, with 'greater assertiveness in public on the part of working-class youths, an assertiveness which showed itself in demonstrative support for a football team'.[403]

Morris argued that football crowds could be split into two, based on age. The older group contained seven behavioural types and the younger set consisted of ten, three of which formed the trouble-making elements. The 'hooligans', as Morris called them, joined in the threats and posturing, but 'rarely come to blows'. He added, 'Being particularly "showy" in their aggressive displays, they appear more dangerous than they in fact are.' Then there were the 'toughs', who were older, eschewed club colours and were 'most likely to take their aggressive rituals over into real fighting', although such action was planned and 'by no means out of control'. These men had 'graduated from the colourful-display stage to an older grouping where, on their past record, they are *known* to be important and carry their hardness and loyalty with them as a personal reputation rather than as a form of dress'.[404]

It was the 'nutters' who would lose control, commit serious violent acts and often carry weapons. Even the hooligans and toughs preferred not to be associated with the nutters, although it was this latter group who created the general public's largely unchallenged image of young football fans as brawling societal pariahs. Author Stuart Hall (not the BBC broadcaster) pointed out, 'There must be reasons for their behaviour which aren't adequately accounted for by reducing them to the status of wild animals.'[405]

Morris suggested of someone bracketed unjustly with the most antisocial of football followers, 'Pushed far enough, he may even begin to adopt this role with which society has unjustly saddled him.'[406] And there existed, of course, the parallel argument that the media's reportage of football violence might be glamorising it and encouraging greater participation.

When the *Daily Mirror* published its 1974 'League of Violence' and crowned Manchester United champions, based on the amount of arrests at their games, the intention – if we choose to be generous to the publishers – might have been an attempt to shame fans of the teams near the top. Perhaps that was what the *Daily Mail* had in mind in its 'Thugs League of London', in which Chelsea emerged victorious. Yet the impact was to create a pecking order in which any self-respecting 'firm' would wish to be pre-eminent. 'Hooligan fans began to fight increasingly for reputations which, as they saw it, were "celebrated" by the media,' wrote Dunning, Williams and Murphy.[407]

The tabloid newspapers themselves had long ago found out that sensationalist headlines concerning any topic were valuable tools in such an intensely competitive industry. Invoking terms of war in reference to trouble at football grounds not only caught the eye on the newsstand, but provided a call to action for many. 'Through the use of military rhetoric, football grounds began, in effect, to be "advertised" as places where fighting and not just football regularly takes place,' noted the above authors. 'Fans were also told of the likelihood of trouble at particular matches.'[408]

As well as being previewed on the sports pages, it became common for big matches to be preceded by stories of shopkeepers barricading windows and local police and transport workers preparing for combat. Typical was the *Daily Express* stating concerns before the 1976 FA Cup Final – due to the involvement of the feared Manchester United fans and the attendance of the reigning monarch. 'The Queen will be in the middle of the biggest security operation ever mounted for any British sporting event,' the newspaper reported. 'All police leave has been cancelled and they will be helped by a force of ex-Commandos as a 60,000-strong Red Army invades London. Wembley was like a town under siege last night.' The union leader for London's Tube train drivers warned of a work stoppage if any of his members were assaulted.

Top-class football was now being played in such an atmosphere of fear that a St John Ambulance Brigade member was photographed a year later wearing a riot helmet at Birmingham City's home game against Manchester United. After 30 arrests were made at the match, Brigade area commissioner Tom Hurley warned, 'There were instructions that these helmets were not to be worn', although a local Brigade chief pointed out that his members had been assaulted in the past. Such in-fighting among health workers offered a new and quirky angle for newspaper coverage of trouble on the terraces.

One of the most infamous pieces of 1970s journalism about football hooliganism was the 1977 documentary made by the BBC and aired on *Panorama*. Millwall's association with the more violent aspects of football had been confirmed by several incidents in the 1960s; for example, during a defeat at QPR, where Millwall fans sat on the pitch in an attempt to get the game abandoned,** and after a loss at The Den against Aston Villa that saw referee Norman Burtenshaw knocked unconscious by home supporters. At a home

** The incident was unwittingly prompted by the response to Rangers fans repeatedly rushing on to the pitch to celebrate their goals in a 6-1 victory. When the crowd was warned that any further invasions would force the game to be abandoned, the Millwall followers seized upon it as a possible way of avoiding defeat.

game against Brentford, a dead hand grenade had been tossed on to the pitch, an act more symbolic than threatening.

By the mid-1970s, even the club's location, Cold Blow Lane, could strike icy fear into the toughest of visiting teams – to the point where new manager Gordon Jago suggested changing the name to Montego Bay. Yet, having been relatively trouble free for a few years, the club saw the opportunity to change some perceptions and welcomed the BBC's cameras for what they believed would be a positive portrayal.

When Jago and club chairman Herbert Burnige viewed the programme that was to be shown they were horrified at what they saw as an attempt by the producers to push their own storyline about the horrors of hooliganism rather than offer an honest – less sexy – picture of a club striving to combat the problem. Of particular concern were shots of National Front organisers distributing racist literature and looking for recruits outside the ground; an occurrence that no one at the club recalled having seen before the TV cameras rolled up.

Charles Wheeler introduced David Taylor's report by warning that an endeavour to look at the game through the fans' eyes had led to language that viewers would not be accustomed to on television. The programme then opened by introducing Billy Plummer, who had at that time accumulated £300 worth of fines for disorderly behaviour at football matches. Other characters followed, such as Bobby The Wolf, Mad Pat and Harry The Dog, with his introductory declaration that Millwall was all about 'a good game of football, a good punch-up, a good piss-up'.

Various groups, broadly fitting into Morris's categories, were presented on screen, including the teenaged Halfway Liners; the surgical mask-wearing Treatment; and the hard cases of F-Troop, described by the reporter as 'self-confessed loonies'. F-Troop were shown travelling to neighbours Charlton Athletic to pick a fight with visiting Tottenham fans rather than following their own club to Sunderland. A terrace disturbance was explained by Taylor as having been caused by '12 nutters' charging at 2,000 Spurs fans, an achievement the protagonists were seen celebrating in the pub.

Describing it as a 'warm-up' for Tottenham's impending visit to The Den, they toasted 'one of the best days for years'.

There ensued much boasting about past battles; justification of violence through provocation by opposing fans; and descriptions of lifestyles where marriage would be an impediment to watching Millwall and prison merely an occupational hazard. A rare visiting Blackburn Rovers supporter told the cameras that home fans had just 'hammered the hell out of me' outside The Den before kick-off, while Millwall fans were shown attending a National Front march for the sole purpose of fighting with anti-NF protestors. Shots of the club's open days for fans, its Sunday community market and supporters' club meetings did little to soften the jarring impact of the piece. Nor did one fan's comment that 'we've got standards' and his assurance that women and children would be helped out of the way if they found themselves caught up in a fight.

'It was a disgraceful programme,' said Jago, manager of Millwall since 1975. 'That killed it for me. We had worked so hard to try to change the image of Millwall, with identification cards, supporters' trains, open days for the fans to meet players, a Sunday morning market, going to clubs and schools. I was in the New Cross area virtually every night because it was all part of changing the image. *Panorama* asked if they could do a feature on what we were trying to do.

'I got an inkling they had produced a concocted programme. I heard that they took people to a pub in Catford and got them drunk and interviewed them. That was F-Troop. We had one problem against Chelsea around that time, but we were winning the battle. It was a carve-up job. I knew then that no one would come to Millwall to see their team play, which would hurt us. Instead of 15,000 with visiting fans we would get 10,000. We needed the extra revenue to make the club run. We went to see the BBC. Ted Croker, the FA secretary, was there, so was the producer of the show, a head guy from the BBC and Denis Howell. Between the BBC guy and the minister, I have never heard two people insult each other so well with their use of the English language. The chairman turned around at the end of the meeting and said, "Your programme has cost me my manager and if I could I would resign." The club let me out of a year and a half of my contract to go to the Tampa Bay Rowdies.'[409]

Howell called the programme 'irresponsible' and there were questions raised in the House of Commons when it emerged that the key contributors among the fans were paid between £15 and £30 each for their cooperation. BBC chairman Sir Michael Swann responded that football was, in effect, attempting to shoot the conveyer of an unwanted message.

The outrage of those who felt that the thugs should not be publicised on national television was mixed with the envy of those rival fans who resented Millwall being given the star treatment. There was also a fear that the documentary had served as a recruitment film for hooligan groups around the country, with Labour MP Walter Johnson calling it 'virtually an incitement to violence'.

There was indeed an element of self-fulfilment at work. When Ipswich Town visited The Den in the sixth round of the FA Cup a few weeks later, fights overflowed from the terraces on to the field and in the streets around the ground, with all manner of weaponry being deployed. With Ipswich a goal up, referee Bill Gow took the players from the field for almost 20 minutes but made sure that a message was relayed that the game would finish regardless. The eventual FA Cup winners were able to complete a 6-1 cruise to the semi-finals. The equally significant scoreline was: 30 arrests and 45 injuries, including 11 police officers.

'To think that we fought in the war so that hooligans like this could survive,' said Ipswich manager Bobby Robson. He even made headlines by suggesting the use of a flamethrower against the miscreants, although he argued that it was an off-the-cuff, over-the-top comment overheard by reporters in the boardroom and not intended to be taken literally. 'It proved to be one of the most embarrassing moments of my life,' he recalled.[410] One MP, Nicholas Fairbairn, called for short and rigorous sentences that would include food rationing. The initial report by the Department of the Environment said Millwall were to blame for failing to effectively segregate supporters, a finding supported by the FA when they fined the club £1,500, closed the ground for two weeks and banned them from staging FA Cup games for two seasons.

Once again, the public were left with the impression that no game was complete without heads being split and collars being felt. Comments like those from Alan Hudson in *Titbits* didn't help. 'How any mother could let her young children go alone beats me,' he said. 'You see them every Saturday at every ground. Kids of ten and under with flick knives and bottles.'[411] Even a moderate voice such as Trevor Brooking's, in calling for a return of the cane in schools, said that the terraces 'are no longer safe places'.[412]

Morris sounded a note of restraint when he wrote, 'Nobody would deny that in rare cases there are savagely violent moments, but the way these are sometimes reported makes it sound as though they are a common occurrence.'[413] When *The Times* sent Robert Parker to watch the 1977 FA Cup semi-final between Manchester United and Leeds United from the Hillsborough terraces, he described 'the frightening tyranny of virtually uncontrollable youths' – after what police had told him had been a 'relatively quiet' afternoon.

No one can deny the blight of football hooliganism in the 1970s, but there was certainly at play here an element of the phenomenon identified by sociologist Stanley Cohen in 1972 when he wrote about the public's outraged response to fights between mods and rockers. 'Societies appear to be subject every now and then to periods of moral panic,' he suggested. 'A condition, episode, person or group of persons emerges to become defined as a threat to societal values and interests; its nature is presented in a stylised and stereotypical fashion by the mass media.'[414]

When a group of six individuals sent a list of anti-hooligan ideas – none of them new or revolutionary – to the government in 1978, it was enough to provide a page-lead news story talking about 'the Silent Six' and their 'beat-the-hooligans charter'. It is difficult to think of another subject so emotive that a simple letter from six well-wishers would receive such elevated projection. The same year's Report on Public Disorder and Sporting Events, written by the Sports Council and Social Science Research Council, argued that the amount of press coverage for football hooliganism was 'remarkable' in light of more serious issues impacting the country. 'The events are certainly dramatic, and frightening for the bystander,' it stated, 'but the outcome in terms of people arrested and convicted, people hurt, or property destroyed is negligible compared with the number of people potentially involved.'

Wagg wrote that the issue of football hooliganism 'refracted through the typewriters of Fleet Street football correspondents, rapidly became in the minds of many members of an indignant public just one more social cancer among the nation's young which needed to be stamped out by tough and uncompromising measures'.[415]

Morris referenced a Public Opinion Poll late in the 1970s in which ten per cent of people said they stayed away from football because of the threat of violence. A Marplan survey published in *The Sun* in 1976 stated that a 'high proportion' of fans *believed* that fear of crowd trouble was keeping others away. According to historian Dominic Sandbrook, 'What made football hooliganism so deeply disturbing was that it was such a public, unashamed exhibition of raw tribal aggression. Britain was supposed to be the country of the stiff upper lip, a land where youngsters obeyed the law, the streets were safe, and a spirit of quiet moderation ruled our daily lives.'[416]

In 1978, Albert Gibbon, whose son Richard almost lost a leg after being injured during trouble on a train after a match at Portsmouth, spoke for many when he warned, 'My immediate reaction is to plead with any parent that if they value their children's lives, don't send them to football matches.' Later that year Vernon Brown, whose Chelsea-supporting son of the same name died after being pushed under the wheels of a bus during fighting in Birmingham, said, 'I often tried to persuade my son not to go to football because of the violence.' Yet when psychologist Peter Marsh published his studies into crowds at Oxford United, during which he had asked about people injured in crowd trouble over the course of a season, he revealed, 'Out of those involving deliberate violence it was impossible to find any cases of "innocent bystanders" being hurt.'[417] As Russell noted in *Football and the English*, 'Hooliganism, as both myth and reality, was a damaging phenomenon.'[418]

As the atmosphere of intimidation and obscenity in football grounds began to alienate older spectators it combined with a cultural development that was at least as prevalent as fear in influencing the demographics of the 1970s football crowd. In the BBC TV series based on his written history of the 1970s, Sandbrook noted a 1977 government-commissioned survey into Britain's favourite hobbies. It highlighted pastimes such as DIY and fishing as rivals to football for the adult male's attention. 'For the ordinary British bloke, Saturday afternoons no longer revolved around the beautiful game,' Sandbrook noted.[419] Writers Dick Clement and Ian La Frenais observed as much in *Whatever Happened to the Likely Lads?* in 1973 when they had Terry challenging the increasingly middle-class Bob with, 'You'll stop going to football soon, won't you? Because Saturday afternoon will be golf.'[420]

Sandbrook explained, 'For decades, generations of men, young and old, had watched the local team side by side. But in the mid-Seventies, as men developed new interests and wider responsibilities, that tradition broke down … Without the role models in the stands, without the disapproving looks of dads and granddads to keep the troublemakers in line, the dynamic of the football crowd shifted.'[421]

Attendance at League football had begun its decline long before football hooliganism was identified as a major problem. From the peak of 40 million during the 1949-50 season, the 1950s had seen an average of around 33 million per season, falling to below 25 million in the 1970s. The one period of upturn had been after the 1966 World Cup, a time when hooliganism was on the increase. As crowd numbers dropped – through a combination of alternate pursuits and dissatisfaction at the state of the game on and off the field – Sandbrook suggested, 'It wasn't just that people were staying away from football because of hooliganism. It was the fact that people were staying away from football that allowed hooliganism to thrive. And, once established, the momentum towards greater violence and greater bloodshed became self-reinforcing. This wasn't just a story about football. This seems to capture so much of what was wrong with Britain. The scenes of appalling violence suggested that the nation was tearing itself apart and that traditional moral values, respected for generations, had simply collapsed.'[422]

The growing leisure options of the 1970s, especially the appeal of sitting in front of the colour television, meant that many forms of entertainment were having to present a new, brighter public face, leaving football as a last bastion of machismo. 'The smartening up of many pubs and clubs increasingly discouraged the masculine existence of hard drinking and hard knocks which had usually gone hand in hand with tough, unrewarding work,' noted Wagg. 'In many areas only the football ground remained – stark, dirty, exposed to the elements – as a traditional gathering for working-class lads.'[423]

The final year of the decade arrived with *Shoot!* asking six figures within the game to voice their hopes for the coming 12 months. Half of them highlighted the issue of crowd behaviour, including Coventry City manager Gordon Milne, who said, 'Too many people are lost to football because they are unwilling to risk contact with the violent element who rampage through the streets and lay siege to railway stations.' Manchester City chairman Peter Swales wished for 'a crackdown on hooligans in 1979' and suggested that 'the man who comes up with the answer deserves a knighthood'.[424]

One group hoped the solution might be found in music. In April 1979, a single called 'Peace' – written by TV theme composer Brian Wade – was released by WEA Records under the name of The Peace Band, who ostensibly consisted of a bunch of footballers. Huddled together in team kit on the picture disc version of the single were Dave Watson (Manchester City), Gordon McQueen (Manchester United), Phil Parkes (West Ham United), Ricardo Villa, Osvaldo Ardiles and Steve Perryman (Tottenham Hotspur), Paul Reaney (Bradford City), Peter Withe (Newcastle United), Bob Latchford (Everton), Viv Anderson (Nottingham Forest) and John Hollins (QPR), who had assembled at Bradford's Valley Parade for a photoshoot to promote the 'Hand of Peace' glove.

Urging listeners to 'take your brother by the hand', the song contained the global hope for 'peace throughout the world', but its positioning with the football public made it clear that fraternal love on the terraces was a goal. Such a line-up of talent would have made more impact on the field than it did on the charts, though. The decade had seen ten club or national teams make it into the top 50, but the dirge that was 'Peace' – featuring Kenny Lynch in a reggae version on the B side – sunk without trace. To be fair, it was no less effective in its attempt to bring harmony to the sport than most other measures put forward throughout the decade.

It was clear to many by the close of the 1970s that all-seater stadia offered the most likely deterrent to violence in football grounds – even though it would take the unspeakable tragedy of Hillsborough[††] ten years later to bring it to pass. With the dark decade of the 1980s beginning, Morris noted a desire among many that 'match-day events become more of a happy family outing, with gentle applause and the singing of cheerful club songs, like some school outing or boy-scout jamboree ... But such ideas disturb even those supporters who are the most vociferous opponents of soccer fan aggro. They suddenly realise how much excitement the pent-up tension of the typically belligerent soccer crowd gives to the sport.'

He concluded, 'The trick for the future, clearly, is to retain this tension, this intensity of involvement of the tribesmen, but at the same time to dispense with its most extreme and destructive forms of expression.'[425] Arguments rage into the 21st century about whether that balance has ever been achieved. Mercifully, no publishers find it necessary to print league tables of hooligans. Yet seek out YouTube footage of, for example, Manchester United's home fixture against Sunderland in 1974-75 – a Second Division game, let us remember – and it's impossible not to miss the visceral energy of football crowds in 1970s that explodes from your browser.

---

†† At the start of the decade, Sheffield Wednesday's home was actually the English ground with the most seats, 23,000

Part Two

SOMETHING BETTER CHANGE

When they studied their copies of the Telegraph, *the* Mail *or* Express *every morning middle-class Tories saw a breakdown of politeness and public order, a collapse of discipline and self-restraint, a mounting sense of vandalism, greed and self-interest, embodied by individuals from Arthur Scargill to George Best.*

Dominic Sandbrook, *Seasons in the Sun* (Allen Lane, 2010)

Bill Shankly and Don Revie have left behind not only 1exceptional football teams but several players who have been encouraged to believe they are entitled to exact their own kind of physical 'justice' if they disagree with the referee.

David Miller, *Daily Express*, 1974

This country's at war, Mr Dunford. The government and the unions, the Left and the Right, the rich and the poor.

David Peace, *Nineteen Seventy-Four* (Serpent's Tail, 2000)

Music's fallow period in the early '70s – all heavy metal and pablum – was echoed by the dreadful rut English football got itself into when fear ruled the game. In 1976, something happened. In music it was instant. In football more gradual. But the progress made in Europe by Liverpool and now Nottingham Forest, and the return of stability to the England side by Ron Greenwood, seem to herald some kind of renaissance.

Monty Smith, *New Musical Express*, 1979

9

TAKE ME TO YOUR LEADER

When you see 85 per cent of chairmen talking, I believe just the sight of them brings the game into disrepute. And when they open their mouths, it kills it. The very thing they have given me a lot of stick about over the years – talking too much – these are the very people who can't put two words together.

Brian Clough, *Parkinson* (BBC TV, 1973)

NAMED AS manager of Leeds United in the final week of July 1974, Brian Clough's 44-day spell at Elland Road remains one of the defining episodes of the decade. Yet the roots of the story had been embedded exactly a year earlier, just as Gary Glitter was knocking Peters and Lee* off the top of the charts with 'I'm The Leader of the Gang (I Am!)'.

Brian Clough was a man who preferred the scruffy sweatshirt of the training ground to the spandex and six-inch platforms of the *Top of the Pops* studio, but if anyone in English football was apt to declare, 'There's no one like the man I am,' then it was the manager of Derby County. Opinionated and brash, but with a League Championship triumph to back it up, Clough rarely missed a chance for self-

* The duo of blind singer Lenny Peters and Dianne Lee who had won *Opportunity Knocks*, not the England duo of Martin and Francis.

promotion. Eager for headlines, he would happily hijack someone else's story if it meant getting his own name in 144-point capitals.

Such an opportunity was presented to him by the Football Association. While England's cricketers were preparing for the First Test against the West Indies at The Oval, football snatched back the spotlight when members of the FA disciplinary committee emerged from a hearing a few miles away in Lancaster Gate. The subject of their debate had been Leeds United's 'persistent misconduct on the field'. Vernon Stokes announced that, along with Birmingham City, the Yorkshire side were being fined £3,000 because of their poor record. The sentence was suspended for a year and could be revised depending on the club's future conduct. Relieved Leeds manager Don Revie said, 'We are well satisfied. We have a good, hard attacking team and this will not affect our style of play next season.'

Clough seized upon these events like Clive Lloyd pouncing on the English bowlers' long-hops on the way to his match-winning Test century. Ten days after the FA's judgement, he launched an attack in the *Sunday Express*. 'Leeds should have been instantly relegated after being branded one of the dirtiest clubs in Britain,' he declared. 'I strongly feel that the tuppence ha'penny suspended fine is the most misguided piece of woolly thinking ever perpetrated by the FA.' It was, he said, 'like breathalysing a drunken driver, getting a positive reading, giving him his keys back and telling him to watch it on the way home.' Revie should also have been fined, he argued, concluding, 'The men who run soccer have missed the most marvellous chance of cleaning up the game.'

Somewhere in Yorkshire, Revie was probably smirking over his cornflakes. He knew he would have no trouble in motivating his team for a difficult trip to the Baseball Ground in late November. What no one knew, however, was that Clough would not be around to see that game.

Sam Longson, the Derby chairman, read Clough's comments with a combination of anger and embarrassment. His relationship with his manager had been strained for some time, even though he had originally defended him in front of board members who felt

Clough was too much of a showman and who questioned the role of Peter Taylor. Increasingly, Longson was wearying of Clough's outbursts and now the situation appeared likely to get worse. ITV had just lost their resident expert, Jimmy Hill, to front BBC's *Match of the Day* and had offered the post to Clough, who had been a BBC analyst since the 1970 World Cup. Although turning down a full-time ITV role worth a reported £18,000 a year, Clough agreed to air his forthright opinions every Saturday lunchtime on *On the Ball*, as well as becoming a contributor to *The Big Match*.

Meanwhile, there had been arguments about members of the Clough family being allowed on pre-season trips and Longson had questioned transfer deals for Terry Hennessey, Roger Davies and Colin Todd. A millionaire in the haulage business who owed his increasing prominence in the game to Clough's managerial skills, Longson was aware that his ambition of increasing influence in football would be undermined unless he was seen to be able to control his manager. The *Sunday Express* article implied that he could not.

Longson felt the transfer episode involving Ian Storey-Moore had embarrassed the club, a situation made worse when Clough wrote an angry letter to Football League secretary Alan Hardaker. As well as having to apologise to Hardaker for Clough's rage, Longson had to stomach a £5,000 club fine for breach of transfer regulations.

It was becoming harder for the chairman to be liked when he had a manager so many people seemed to despise. For example, recalling Clough's television appearances during the 1970 World Cup, journalist Patrick Collins wrote, 'He appeared to treat a fairly distinguished panel of players and managers like ground-staff boys and established a reputation for arrogance which may not have yet passed from the public mind.'[426] And former Arsenal captain Frank McLintock said, 'You wanted to shut a guy like Brian Clough up. You have to have great confidence to not care if you are liked, and he didn't give a monkey's.'[427]

Clough had lost much respect for Derby's executives following the Fairs Cup ban of two years earlier and relationships deteriorated further when he and Taylor told the board they were considering an offer to replace the sacked Noel Cantwell at Coventry City, but would stay for more money. The board agreed, only to find out that Coventry had no intention of meeting Clough's demands.

When the 1973-74 season kicked off, with his attack on Leeds still hanging in the air, Clough turned on Derby's fans after his team came from behind to beat Liverpool 2-1. 'They started chanting only near the end when we were a goal in front,' he complained. 'I want to hear them when we are losing. They are a disgraceful lot.' Once again, Longson felt compelled to say sorry for his manager's behaviour, disassociating the board from the remarks.

Clough and Taylor wrote to each director, asking for advice on how to resolve their ongoing problems with Longson. According to Taylor, the most significant response was that they found that their drinks cupboard was suddenly emptied. Publicly, Clough presented a happy face as Kevin Hector celebrated an England call-up with a hat-trick against Southampton and Henry Newton, the Mediterranean-looking midfielder, arrived for £100,000 after three less than happy years at Everton after moving from Nottingham Forest.

Meanwhile, Longson decided that Clough's publicity drive had to be stopped, issuing an ultimatum that all media work must be cleared by the board. Taylor, in his book *With Clough, By Taylor*, revealed Longson's blunt orders: 'Stop engaging in literary work by writing articles in the press and stop entering into commitments with radio and television.'[428] Fat chance. 'Brian thrives on the publicity,' said Taylor, who preferred to do his talking in the dressing-room and on the training ground. 'I don't subscribe to all Brian's views. We talk a lot before he goes on television and if he's done fine, well I tell him. But if he hasn't I let him know in no uncertain terms.'[429]

While Clough considered his next move, another confrontation arose on 13 October, when Derby remained unbeaten with a 1-0 win at Manchester United. Director Jack Kirkland, to whom Clough and Taylor had taken an instant dislike, pulled Taylor aside in the Old Trafford boardroom and demanded to see him on Monday morning. Instructed to explain his role to the director, an outraged Taylor kept the appointment, but later the same day Clough and Taylor were back in front of the directors, telling them they were quitting. A majority vote of the directors accepted their resignation, with Longson making it clear there would be no compensation. At opposite ends of the Baseball Ground's executive lounge, Clough told reporters, 'I'll tell you why I'm going,' while Longson stuttered his own explanation of a fight between 'right and wrong'.

Clough continued, 'My knees and elbows are sore from all the crawling that Peter and I have been forced to do these last three months.' And outside the ground he told a news crew there was not enough time to go into the 'million reasons' for their resignation. Clough, one year into a five-year contract, later admitted he should have made the board sack him to ensure a handsome pay-off. According to Taylor, Longson's parting shot to the pair was, 'Hand in your club-car keys on your way out.'[430]

If anyone thought that the affair would end with the repossession of a couple of saloons, they were quickly proved wrong. Derby's first game after Clough's resignation was five days later, at home to Leicester City. Knowing it would cause a stir, Clough borrowed a ticket and sat a few seats away from the directors' box. As he got to his feet to acknowledge the cheers of a 32,203 crowd, he saw banners saying 'Brian, We Support You Evermore' and 'Longson Out, Clough In'. It was a particularly galling sight for the chairman, especially after he had spoken up for the fans in the face of Clough's earlier attack. He did his best to pretend the cheers were for him rather than his nemesis. Derby achieved a 2-1 victory, but Clough, his point made, was long gone – on his way to London to be a guest on the BBC's *Parkinson*.

The undoubted king of chat-show hosts, Michael Parkinson's programmes enjoyed the feeling of a big event, unlike the modern era of multi-channels and daytime TV, when minor celebrities have any number of outlets upon which to plug their products. Parky, two years into an 11-year Saturday-night stint that made him a national institution, was *the* man by whom to be interviewed. Relaxed, well-groomed and content to sit back and allow his guests to shine, the Yorkshireman – born a week after Clough in 1935 and only a few miles away – was the perfect person to coax some outrageous comments from a more-than-willing guest. Around six million viewers tuned in to the show, aired after Derby's victory on *Match of the Day*, and lapped it up as Clough, wearing a grey suit, lilac tie and a schoolboy's look of mischief, discussed the importance of football, its impact on society and his refusal to be silenced on issues beyond the sport. 'Miners are beautiful people,' he declared at one point.†

The comparison between the glib Clough and the public persona of Longson could not have been starker. Speaking to a news crew, Longson looked like a character from the comedy series the BBC would launch a few days later, *Last of the Summer Wine*. Slightly-too-small pork pie hat perched on his head, he said, 'I think [Clough] has made the mistake of going on TV and the biggest mistake he has made is criticising and insulting the personnel of the football world.'

As well as dealing with the attack from Clough, Longson had the task of placating angry fans who had now formed a movement to reinstate Clough, coordinated by TV script writer Don Shaw. All while he was looking for a new manager. On an eventful day on 22 October, Ipswich Town's Bobby Robson informed Derby he was not interested in leaving Portman Road and club captain Roy McFarland handed the board a letter, signed by all the players, demanding the return of Clough and Taylor. After they'd met their former bosses at a local hotel, emotions were running high. Players were worried about careers and the loss of the men most likely to help achieve dreams of cups and medals. In an unprecedented show of player power, the Derby team's statement read:

> During the events of last week, we, the undersigned players, have kept our feelings within the dressing-room. However, at this time, we are unanimous in our support and respect for Mr Clough and Mr Taylor and ask that they be re-instated as manager and assistant manager of the club. It was absolutely vital that we won against Leicester on Saturday for ourselves,

† As Nottingham Forest manager, Clough would have his players crawling through narrow coal seams at Calverton Colliery to 'say hello to some of the people who saw you at work'.

> as well as for the club and fans. Now that match is out of the way, nobody can say that we have acted on the spur of the moment and are just being emotional. We called the meeting of first-teamers and it was emphasised that nobody was under obligation to attend. But everybody was there. We then decided to write this letter and again nobody was under pressure to sign. But again, everybody did.

Passing almost unnoticed that day, but to prove significant, was the sacking of Brighton and Hove Albion manager Pat Saward. And the next day, the Derby board turned to Baseball Ground favourite Dave Mackay, who had left the club to become player-manager of Swindon Town and was now in charge at Nottingham Forest. If the club thought that the announcement of an old pal as manager would placate the players, they were wrong. As the squad gathered in Archie Gemmill's house, McFarland contacted Mackay and urged him to turn down the job. Mackay had no intention of doing so, but did at least acknowledge that had he been a Derby player at that time he would probably have signed their letter as well.

Seeking a reasoned discussion, McFarland and other players went looking for the directors at the Baseball Ground, only to find the boardroom locked, although – according to Taylor – Kirkland and Stuart Webb were hiding inside. By now, talk among the players had turned to not playing, but common sense prevailed a couple of days later when they agreed to honour their contracts by turning out at West Ham. Mackay praised their attitude after a 0-0 draw, although Longson did nothing to endear himself to his new employee by announcing, 'I could manage this lot.'

While all this was going on, Clough announced he was taking the vacant job at Brighton for £15,000 a year, taking Taylor with him. He still harboured hopes of a return to the Baseball Ground and, two days before Revie was due to bring Leeds to town, Derby's players notified the club they would not train any longer under Mackay and would turn up 75 minutes before kick-off. Mackay countered with a threat to play his reserves, while PFA secretary Cliff Lloyd warned his members that they would be in breach of contract. It was the beginning of the end of the rebellion, especially when Clough himself reminded the players of their duty. 'I think we went too far,' McFarland eventually admitted. 'We knew the success we'd had and the success we would have had if he had stayed.'[431]

In his book about the fans' protest, Shaw pondered on a potentially different outcome had the players had a skipper like Billy Bremner who would have gone through with the strike threat. He also felt the fans could have done more, although these were the days when effective protest meant a commitment of time and effort; not simply using a hashtag or clicking an online petition. Britain was also entering a winter when too many people's own jobs and livelihoods were at stake. Shaw, who signed up 800 members of the protest, conceded, 'Maybe the majority were too concerned with their own lives to take up the cudgels on behalf of a football manager.'[432]

Clough might have cut his teeth in the lower divisions, but he now seemed no less out of place at Third Division Brighton than he did on the south coast, where he never set up permanent home. Suddenly, he was in a world where his team could be knocked out of the FA Cup 4-0 at home by non-League Walton and Hersham and, three days later, lose 8-2 against Bristol Rovers. And it was no private purgatory; not with journalists following every move and *The Big Match* cameras at the Goldstone Ground to capture his eight-goal humiliation.

Improved form early in 1974 lifted his team to mid-table and eased relegation fears. There was a big enough cushion to protect them from poor late-season results, but the final Third Division table showed Brighton in 19th place. Sixty-two positions higher, Revie, the man Clough had argued should have been relegated because of his team's behaviour, was a League champion once again. And destined for higher office.

PRESSURE POINTS

REG: I just don't understand what's happening any more.
Everything I was taught as a child seems to have gone by

the board. It's like living in no-man's land, except you can't see the enemy and you don't even know where your comrades are.

***Rooms* (Robert Holles; Thames Television, 1975)**

Loved in Yorkshire since the early 1960s and admired around the country – although hardly considered national treasures – Geoffrey Boycott and Don Revie were occupying the thoughts of those determining the fortunes of England's national teams in the summer of 1974. Boycott had been dropped as England's opening batsman after a couple of failures against India and even the riposte of a big unbeaten hundred in the County Championship could not force the selectors to bring him back for the third Test. While Boycott, already a veteran at 33, was seeing his place go to David Lloyd, a man seven years his junior, it appeared that age might also be a factor in the identity of the next England football manager.

Joe Mercer, at 64, was considered sprightly enough to take temporary charge of England in the seven end-of-season games that followed the dismissal of Sir Alf Ramsey, but when it came to a full-time successor, reporters seemed hung up on the idea that the new man would have to be recently retired as a player to properly meet the nation's demand for exciting and revolutionary change. Recently-departed FA secretary Denis Follows, who might have been expected to possess some insight into the selection process, had stated, 'I omit Don Revie because I believe England now need a man under 40, a tracksuit man, possibly more able to identify with the younger players.'

It was a strange corner to risk being backed into, especially as the defining characteristic of old man Mercer's interim reign was his close bond with the players. 'Joe came breezing in and everything was done for a laugh,' said Emlyn Hughes, who was chosen to captain the side. 'He was just what the team needed.'[433]

While Revie was waiting in the wings with his near-obsessional need to know and document everything about the opposition, Mercer was more like CJ, the bluff boss in BBC's *The Fall and Rise of Reginald Perrin*, whose attitude was, 'I didn't get where I am today by knowing the difference between one country and another.'[434] Mercer had even told the players before his first game, 'I didn't want this bloody job in the first place. We are all going to have a laugh and a joke.'‡

Revie was dismissed as a candidate by many early reports because, heaven forbid, he would be 50 by the time of the next World Cup finals. Meanwhile, Bobby Robson, Coventry's Gordon Milne, Queens Park Rangers' Gordon Jago and Bolton Wanderers' Jimmy Armfield might not have any trophies, but the numbers on their birth certificates were apparently more palatable. Brian Clough, of course, was young enough and, according to most newspapers, the most popular choice among the football public. But his future buddy Boycott was as likely to get the job as he was.

Yet the newspaper speculation proved incorrect. A six-man committee, plus secretary Ted Croker, decided that a resumé of two League Championships, the FA Cup, League Cup and two European trophies counted for more than the ability to talk about pop music with the junior members of the squad. Now there was talk of a £25,000 annual salary and the demand by Leeds of anything up to £200,000 from the FA in compensation. On 4 July, Revie was formally appointed, prompting what goalkeeper David Harvey described as a 'mood of desolation' at Elland Road. Any disbelief the Leeds players felt was because of the great bond between Revie and their club; not because they didn't think he was right for his country. According to centre-forward Joe Jordan, 'The shock element comes with the realisation that you have lost your manager and the accompanying consternation about who his replacement might be.'[435]

The *Daily Express* spoke for most of football, it seemed, when it tossed into one of its reports that 'heir apparent, Johnny Giles,

‡ For the most part, it was a fun interlude for the England team; with one defeat in a seven-game schedule that included a 2-2 Wembley draw against Argentina and an unbeaten three-match tour of Eastern Europe. The one unsavoury incident was on arrival in Belgrade for the game against Yugoslavia. A jovial Kevin Keegan 'began to fool around' on the baggage carousel and was dragged to a side room by security personnel, who punched and kicked him and accused him of sexually assaulting a Bulgarian air stewardess, before being told the identity of their prisoner and letting him go.

waits to begin his first job in management'. When Leeds reported back for pre-season training with the manager's office vacant, most players expected Giles's name to appear on the door, as Revie had recommended. Yet things would not be quite so straightforward. The board wanted to look externally as well, with Bobby Robson considered among the favourites for the position. The candidacy of many of those other England hopefuls was also reassigned to what had now become the most-coveted job in football.

With back pages to fill, the World Cup finished and an uninspiring, rain-affected summer of Test cricket plodding along, sports editors were offered a further unexpected gift on 12 July when Bill Shankly made a bombshell of an announcement. Barely had he completed the surprise £200,000 signing of Arsenal forward Ray Kennedy, the apparent heir to John Toshack in the Liverpool attack, than it was announced he was leaving his job.

'It is with great regret that Mr Shankly has intimated that he wishes to retire from active participation in League football,' John Smith read to assembled reporters as Shankly looked at the piece of paper in front of the club chairman as though he was about to interject with 'hang on a minute'. On footage of the press conference – at which someone's trilby on a windowsill is the backdrop rather than sponsors' logos – the unmistakeable voice of Granada TV's Tony Wilson asks, 'Don't you think there are still things to win?' Shankly's confused reply is, 'Oh, I think so because I was the best manager in the game and I should have won more.'

Only five months earlier, Smith had said that 'we want Bill to be with us forever'. Even though Shankly had conceded that retirement was on the horizon and predicted that it would be 'an abrupt break', he'd also indicated, 'It may be another year or two or even three.'

The Times began its account of events by stating, 'The bulldozers that have razed so much of the old Liverpool could not have torn the heart any more devastatingly than yesterday's news.' Kevin Keegan heard it on his return from a break in Spain and said, 'It was like visiting a city in mourning. I even saw people crying.'[436] Emlyn Hughes called it a 'shot in the head' and thought the billboards must be referring to a different Shankly.[437] News cameras captured the disbelief of a young ginger-haired boy when they told him the news. 'You're having me on, aren't yer?' he gasped. 'Who says?'

So what if he was 60 years old? This was a man for whom football was a life force. A recent headline in *Goal* magazine had described him as 'The Greatest Enthusiast of the Lot'. According to his former skipper Tommy Smith, 'Shanks ate, drank and slept football and expected his players to do the same. He never seemed to have a break from it. He related everything to football.'[438]

Even Shankly had to admit, 'I never thought I would give up football until a coffin came into the house,' but he had not allowed the club to talk him out of his decision. 'My wife and I both felt I needed a rest. I have felt tired and the pressures are intense. It's like being in a ship in a minefield.'

Those around him were left to guess at his real motives. 'In subsequent talks I had with him, I can see that there was some bitterness regarding something or other,' Toshack would speculate.[439] But even Shankly's own reflections years later left room for conjecture. 'When I sat down with my tea and pie my mind was made up,' he said of the moments after the 1974 FA Cup Final. 'I knew I was going to finish.' It was not an instant course of action, however. 'Weeks and weeks went by and I was not enjoying life at all until I could get it sorted out.'[440]

First the national team, then the League champions, and now the FA Cup holders had been forced to seek new managers. Former Prime Minister Edward Heath might have fought the February general election under the banner of 'Who Governs?' – referring to the battle between government and unions – but now it could equally be applied to the elite of the national sport.

Robson disappeared from Elland Road contention, happy to remain at an improving Ipswich, and Clough emerged as one of three being interviewed for the position, along with Ian St John, manager at Motherwell, and Armfield. As midnight arrived on 21 July, Clough and Leeds came to an agreement on a contract said to be worth £30,000 for each of five years. Whatever he had felt about Leeds in the past, the fact was that this job offered him an immediate opportunity for another assault on the European Cup. Yet Taylor would not be playing a part in that quest, committing himself to Brighton. Publicly, Clough said he felt 'comforted by the quality of the backroom staff' at Leeds, but Taylor's absence would be significant.

The Leeds players wondered what was about to hit them. They had recent memories of Clough calling Peter Lorimer 'a cheat' while presenting him the award as Yorkshire Sports Personality of the Year and there was a hint at what was ahead when he announced, 'This is a great team and already I am asking myself how I can improve upon the best. Perhaps I could hope to win the League in better style.'

The squad was kept waiting to meet the new boss, whose appointment was not allowed to get in the way of his family holiday in Majorca. There might have been a title defence and European Cup campaign to prepare for, but it was August before Clough turned up at Elland Road. The players' incredulity was now laced with resentment over what they saw as a lack of respect. On his first day, Clough's blue training top, yellow shorts and suntan combined to give him the appearance of someone heading for a set or two of holiday tennis rather than a man embarking on the top job in club football. He might have said to the hordes of press present, 'I have got work to do; will you please let me get on with my work?' but that didn't stop him posing a little longer for the cameras.

What happened when Clough first spoke to his squad has become the stuff of legend, recounted in all manner of media over the decades. While some of what is portrayed in *The Damned United* is understandably questioned for its accuracy, there has been little dispute that the gist of Clough's opening address was spot on. 'You lot may all be internationals and have won all the domestic honours there are to win under Don Revie,' begins Martin Sheen, playing Clough in the movie version, 'but as far as I'm concerned, the first thing you can do for me is chuck all your medals and all your caps and all your pots and all your pans into the biggest fucking dustbin you can find. Because you've never won any of them fairly. You've done it all by cheating.'

Clough then went around individuals, throwing insults at them in what Giles perceived as an attempt to assert his authority. Eddie Gray, with his history of battles for fitness, was told that if he'd been a racehorse he would have been shot.§ It didn't need a trained psychologist to sense someone intimidated by being surrounded by such a successful group, men who had found their own way in the game instead of being reliant on Clough. 'I am not sure he had as much confidence in himself as he sometimes portrayed,' Giles would venture. 'He had to dominate you and you had to defer to him. And once you deferred to him he started to build you up in his own image.'[441] It was Paul Madeley who responded first by telling Clough that he felt insulted.

When Clough showed up two hours late at the traditional pre-season gathering of players and wives, he handed Harvey the award as the club's best player with the words, 'How the fuck you won this, I will never know.' Little wonder that the Scotland goalkeeper insisted, 'Anybody, anybody at all, would have been better than Clough.'[442]

Clough told anyone who would listen that he wanted to bring 'a little more honesty' into the set-up at Leeds. His programme notes for the first home game of the season called upon the fans to demand more from their side. 'I do not think that Leeds United have ever received their just reward in terms of image,' he began. 'For the first time ever I want them to be fully accepted for the skill, ability and brilliance they so obviously have. To be the best side in the country is not enough.' Banging on about how his Derby side had been 'a breath of fresh air for the game', he challenged the Leeds supporters with, 'Are people really proud deep down?' It was safe to assume they were, despite Clough's stated intention to turn 'idealism into fact'.[443]

Giles recalled, 'Clough's attitude to football was the complete opposite of the attitude that was there at the club at the time. There was a clash that neither of us could understand.'[444] As for Clough's desire to bring 'a little more of me' into Elland Road, the first obvious

§ Ironically, Gray broke down at the start of the new season. Having been dropped to the reserves to play Stoke one week after featuring in the FA Charity Shield, Gray re-injured a thigh and would be absent for much of the campaign.

manifestation was signing Derby's John McGovern and John O'Hare, solid players who had been vital components of what he'd built at the Baseball Ground. They appeared to be mere comforters for Clough among an all-star squad at Elland Road, especially as they faced uncertain futures at Derby. Both were waiting to travel to a reserve match when Mackay informed them of their new destination. 'I was stunned,' said 27-year-old O'Hare, who was being kept out of Derby's line-up by Roger Davies and new signing Francis Lee. 'I'm at an age where you don't expect to take a step up the ladder.'[445]

McGovern had previously declined an offer to join Clough at Brighton, but could not refuse an opportunity with the League champions, although on his first day he realised, 'I'm in the shit here.' He explained, 'It wasn't the open hostility you see in the film. It was the Leeds lads being baffled why Peter Taylor hadn't come too and asking me and John O'Hare what [Clough] was good at.'[446]

The £240,000 signing of the flamboyant Nottingham Forest forward Duncan McKenzie, whose party piece was jumping over a Mini, felt more like a statement of on-field intent. It was hard to imagine Revie considering any of that trio to be suitable members of his Leeds family. While McKenzie felt that O'Hare and McGovern had performed well enough over the years for their new team-mates not to think of them as 'scrubbers' he would remember trainer Syd Owen, a Revie loyalist, taking against the new men almost as much as he 'despised' Clough.

Meanwhile, McKenzie, who had it tough enough already as an outsider in the dressing-room and had annoyed his team-mates with his elaborate tricks in training, was put in an even more invidious position when Clough asked him to report what the players were saying about him. Clough, whose previous and future success at Derby and Nottingham Forest would be built largely on the inspirational effect he had on his charges, had now managed to create discomfort not only for the established Leeds players but also his big-money acquisition.

Driving up the M1 to Leeds – sometimes with Jimmy Gordon, the trainer he had taken to Elland Road from Derby – Clough slipped into a pattern of late arrival at training. When he was there, he seemed content to supervise and take part in games of five-a-side, with little of Revie's meticulous preparation. Meanwhile, the players struggled with what they should call their new manager. 'Boss' or 'Gaffer' were titles forever attached to Revie.

And so, to the FA Charity Shield at Wembley, on a day that began with newspapers showing Gerald Ford being sworn in as the new president of the United States after Richard Nixon's resignation. Clough tried to avoid his own inauguration by asking Revie to walk out at the head of the Leeds team, an attempt perhaps to distance himself from the League Championship achievement that had secured their place in this fixture. Revie declined and when the teams arrived in the centre of the field to await presentation to the dignitaries, the space between Clough and skipper Bremner as they lined up was enough to have given Revie palpitations if he'd witnessed it between his defenders at a corner kick. The Leeds players, meanwhile, must have been the most miserable-looking ever to have marched out for a showcase game at the home of football.

There had been no attempt by Clough to address the specific challenge posed by Liverpool, as O'Hare and McGovern might have warned them and as Derby defender Colin Todd had explained previously. 'He rarely talks about the opposition team or individual players. Its's us, us, us – what are we going to do?'[447]

BBC would only be showing highlights on *Match of the Day*,¶ but that could not diminish the perceived significance of the match. Not only was it the first time the FA had placed the contest at Wembley, it was an opportunity for the country's leading clubs to draw a line under England's non-appearance at the World Cup and send fans into the new season with optimism about what lay in store. A chance to move on from descriptions of the previous campaign such as this one in *Football Monthly Digest*. 'Our football, battered and bruised but still very much alive, has just come through a combine harvester

¶ Another popular mis-memory is that BBC showed the game live. Instead, *Grandstand* was flitting between racing from Haydock Park, the European Championship of women's golf and England's Test match against Pakistan.

called season 1973-74,' it said. 'It suffered by its dual control at the top pursuing self interest in differing directions ... And it was made tatty once more by the mindless morons who ravish and ransack, whose behaviour sickens decent, ordinary people.'[448]

In the *Daily Express*, David Miller wrote, 'Clough and Paisley between them hold immense influence in the English game at the moment. It is an influence they can exert for the good. They can show us at Wembley today they have concern above all for the paying public.' Miller concluded, 'Only an exhibition of enterprising football will justify the FA's decision to give the derelict Charity Shield a Wembley backcloth and at Wembley prices. If Leeds and Liverpool cannot entertain, then who can?'

Clough and Paisley, whose promotion from within the Anfield coaching ranks had been confirmed at the end of July, certainly had the kind of approach to the sport that ought to have brought the writer's wishes to fruition. But even though this was supposedly a showcase occasion, maybe the confluence of so many of the decade's epic storylines made it inevitable that the fabric of the day would be torn asunder. The controversial nature of Leeds and their triumphs; their long rivalry with Liverpool; the failure of Ramsey's England and the appointment of Revie; the constant battle for the game's soul; Shankly, Clough and the cult of the manager – all were whipping around the Twin Towers like an angry tornado waiting to unleash disorder and destruction. A bad tackle in the early moments by Allan Clarke on Phil Thompson and the revenge exacted by Tommy Smith brought the vortex right over the field.

'On the pitch, [Clarke's] like an arsonist,' said Smith, booked for hacking down the Leeds man from behind. 'He sparks off the blaze then retires to a safe distance to watch the fire.'[449] And Keegan would admit, 'I do not hate many players and though I don't dislike Clarkie as a person I cannot stand him as a player.'[450]

With almost an hour played, the storm struck. Phil Boersma, who had hooked in a goal from close range to give Liverpool a half-time lead, forced a block from Harvey and then fired the rebound across the goal area. When the ball arrived back from the right wing to Emlyn Hughes just outside the box, he found Giles and Bremner snarling towards him, boots raised, from opposite directions – more like a Saturday afternoon wrestling tag team than two of the game's finest midfielders. As the ball ran loose, Keegan and Bremner both briefly had possession before clashing in a flurry of swinging legs. Keegan, blood apparently boiling, looked like a pinball as he bounced off Bremner and charged towards Gray, who now had the ball inside the penalty area. His pathway blocked, Keegan ran into the back of Giles, who turned and threw a punch with his right hand, sending Keegan to the grass. Bremner was quickly on the scene, showing his shin to the Liverpool man as if to remind him that he had merely suffered retribution for what had just occurred between them. Referee Bob Mathewson, the former professional player, led Giles away and booked him.

Liverpool's resulting free-kick came to nothing. But as the television cameras followed the Leeds clearance into the Liverpool half, voices in the 67,000 crowd rose excitedly in the manner indicative of only one thing; trouble off the ball. 'And now what?' asked an exasperated-sounding Barry Davies in the commentary box as pictures showed Hunter and McQueen confronting Keegan, while Bremner, from a pace or two way, stalked towards him with arms tensed. What the cameras had missed was Keegan and Bremner aiming punches at each other. 'And this is just what English football didn't want to see,' Davies continued as more agitated red and white shirts arrived on the scene. 'Surely we have got to get away from this.'

Mathewson separated Keegan and Bremner from the melee. The angry reaction of the England player soon made it apparent that he had been sent off, only days after being dismissed in a midweek friendly in Kaiserslautern – albeit in a reported case of mistaken identity.** Having shrugged off the attempts of Steve Heighway to comfort him, Keegan began his angry march from the field, taking off his shirt and tossing it towards the touchline.

** In his foreword to Peter Cormack's autobiography, Keegan admitted that the mistaken identity story had been concocted by the club to save him from further punishment. Cormack, similar in build and hairstyle, offered himself up as the man who had struck a German opponent in retaliation for a foul on Ray Kennedy.

'And Bremner is off as well,' announced Davies. Unafraid of comparison with the welterweight's six-pack and shoulders possessed by his opponent, Bremner followed Keegan's lead, exposing a pale-skinned midriff as his top was discarded, leaving linesman Murray Jesson to kick it away. 'To dismiss the referee's authority in such a manner cannot be good for the game,' Davies said of the first two British players to be sent off at Wembley Stadium. Keegan's march to the tunnel was halted briefly as he avoided a fan who had run to the field and appeared to be offering him a shirt. 'We are seeing the unacceptable face of English football,' Davies concluded sadly.

It was Mathewson's manner that had apparently so angered Keegan, as much as his decision to send him off. 'It's a good game. It's going well and you two are spoiling it,' the referee had told them, 'so go and get a bath.' According to Keegan, who would be bound for his uncle's in Doncaster before the end of the match, 'He treated us like a couple of schoolchildren.'[451]

Trevor Cherry's subsequent headed equaliser, and Liverpool's victory celebrations with the departing Shankly after winning the penalty shoot-out, merely delayed the repercussions of the day's events. Any failure by the FA to take severe action would be seen as condoning violence – on and off the field. Keegan and Bremner's shirt tossing was considered a more harmful image than the punches they had traded.

The high stakes involved in a game that was, ostensibly, a fundraising exhibition were thought by some to have contributed to what transpired. 'There's so much pride at stake,' Keegan had written before the game. 'Both teams feel there's a chance to prove they're the best in the country.'[452] After the events at Wembley he admitted to 'ill-feeling' between the teams and added, 'I can't explain why there was so much needle.'[453] In order to bring the top clubs back to the fixture after three seasons without the champions or Cup holders, each team had been promised £15,000 to participate, while players were reported to be on a £200 bonus to win instead of the game's previous £5 appearance fee. Mathewson, too, was criticised for not taking stronger earlier action when Giles thumped Keegan. 'Mathewson, no less than the FA, the Football League, his referee colleagues, the press and the public have become conditioned to an underlying mood of cynical intimidation often bordering on violence,' read Miller's report in the *Express*. And when the League season kicked off a week later, Roy Ullyett's cartoon in the same newspaper depicted fans behind a fence looking at a grimacing muscle-bound footballer, with one of them saying, 'I feel a lot safer this season behind a fence. There's no danger of the players getting at us.'

Already facing automatic three-match suspensions for their dismissals, Keegan and Bremner learned quickly that they were being charged by the FA with bringing the game into disrepute. A couple of weeks later, the FA fined them each £500 and extended their bans until the end of September – meaning an 11-game suspension in total – although injury would delay Bremner's return to League action for a further month.

A furious Paisley, who claimed his team had been 'blackmailed into playing the game', felt that Keegan and Bremner had been dealt with too harshly because of the FA's need to set an example after the violent start to the League season off the field. 'If they get this for throwing off their jerseys, what is there left for some of the things that happen in the game?' Forced to defend his players in public, privately Clough could not believe they'd approached the game in exactly the manner for which he had demonstrated such contempt. Bremner had been intent on kicking Keegan off the field, he believed.

What happened at Wembley was viewed as a symptom of a sick sport. 'One way or another, a solution has to be found if the game is to survive as a respectable spectacle,' Geoffrey Green wrote in *The Times*. 'The final solution may be for all reasonable people simply to stay away and let ritual violence destroy itself.'

One such reasonable person was Tottenham Hostpur's Bill Nicholson, the longest-serving manager in League football. Barely had the fate of Keegan and Bremner been announced when he declared he'd had enough, resigning the position he had held since 1958. 'Players have become impossible,' he said, his season blighted by pay disputes with several players. 'They talk all the time about security, but they are not prepared to work for it. I am abused by players when they come to see me. There is no longer respect.'

The *Daily Express* was grieving that 'the most honest man in football has finally had his spirit broken by the rampant dishonesty, selfishness, and cynicism in the game'. Nicholson would add in later years, 'The crowd trouble at the Feyenoord stadium undoubtedly contributed to my decision to retire. The increase in soccer hooliganism sickened me.'[454]

At Chelsea, meanwhile, Dave Sexton had become isolated from star players such as Peter Osgood and Alan Hudson since the trophies of the early decade. 'Huddy and I both felt we'd had enough of the guy,' Osgood recalled. 'His moods were always changing.'[455] Hudson thought Sexton failed to recognise the benefits of the social side of the game and appeared to be in a constant state of agitation. '[He] couldn't handle the fact that we conducted our team talks [in the pub] without him,' Hudson said. 'If it had been Tony Waddington, he'd have been in there drinking with us.'[456] There were few more revealing team pictures taken in the 1970s than the Chelsea version of 1972-73. Shot from an elevated position, with the players in a loosely-formed pyramid shape, Hudson stands on the right behind Steve Kember – the player he felt Sexton had signed from Crystal Palace to replace him – firing a death stare half towards the camera and half into the rear of Kember's skull. On the left of the picture, Osgood wears a loose-fitting shirt he appears to have slept in and has his socks around his ankles; the look of a man who couldn't be arsed with the whole thing and had probably turned up late.

Waddington ended up taking Hudson to Stoke for £240,000 early in 1974, two months before Osgood left for Southampton for £275,000. With the fans' favourites gone and a huge new East Stand to pay for, Sexton needed his team to make a fast start to the 1974-75 season. Instead, they won only two of their first ten League games and Chelsea announced that Sexton was being 'relieved from his contract'. Chairman Brian Mears blamed 'two years in which we have had very little success' and stated that the club had to 'look beyond survival and a place in the middle of the table'. By the end of the season they would indeed be able to plan for a title challenge – in the Second Division.

Sexton was soon appointed to replace Gordon Jago, sacked after a poor start to the season at QPR, where Stan Bowles felt 'the strain seemed too much for [Jago], what with me and other players getting on to him'.[457] It was another part of the season's managerial manoeuvring, which had also seen Ron Greenwood relinquish first-team management of West Ham United after 13 years in favour of an administrative role.

The pressure faced by managers in this new must-win age had been discussed frequently in the media, although the advice for coping during troubled times offered to managers by Jimmy Hill in 1970 would not stand the test of time. 'To let off steam publicly never won a point,' he wrote. 'Go home, shout at the dog, or beat the wife. I'm sure they'll understand your problem and have sympathy.'[458]

Not only had Shankly cited pressure as a reason for his resignation, but Nicholson blamed himself for being unable to relieve it by sharing the burden of the job. 'I was burned out. I resigned because I sensed I needed a long rest. I had no more to offer,' he explained. 'No one asked me to work all day and every day. But I ran the club and wouldn't trust the smallest job to anyone else.'[459]

Towards the end of his period as Southampton manager, Ted Bates had said, 'Tension is something you live with all the time, night and day. There is the travelling for a start. If my wife ever divorced me it would be for desertion.'[460] Before Sunderland's appearance in the 1973 FA Cup Final, manager Bob Stokoe told the *Radio Times*, 'I know I'm a poor husband and an inadequate father. I provide for my family to the very best of my ability, but I know I am remote from them. We've lived in 12 different houses and my daughter has been to five different schools.'[461]

And shortly before his resignation from Stoke in 1977, Waddington – by then the longest-serving top-flight manager at 17 years – announced that 'being a football manager is a daft way of making a living'. He added, 'I wouldn't recommend it to anyone. It demands 24 hours a day and I am never home before midnight. There is no way you can win. You are on show all the time and the press headlines are never far away. There is no job like that – except perhaps the Prime Minister's.'[462] Or maybe not. Even Harold Wilson had once said, 'If I were a football manager I would be more worried about job security than I am as Prime Minister.'[463]

Goal reporter Peter Barnard described spending 45 minutes in the office of a First Division manager, who answered 21 calls, 'swore viciously' each time the phone rang, half-smoked his way through a ten-pack of cigarettes and opened and shut the window four times. Yet such comments and observations were dismissed by others in the profession, notably Ron Saunders, the dour, no-nonsense former striker who had the distinction of leading three different teams to consecutive League Cup finals between 1973 and 1975 – Norwich City, Manchester City and Aston Villa – before guiding the latter to the League title in 1981. 'As for the pressures,' he stated, 'that is something that goes with the job of manager. If a manager doesn't like it, he should get out.'[464]

Alan Hardaker, who spent much of his time battling with managers over one thing or another, concurred. 'I have little time for the modern obsession with the word "pressure",' he said. 'It seems to me to be an excuse for laziness or lack of ability. Everybody has pressures and if a man is not big enough to carry them then he is not big enough for his job.'[465]

These were the days before the concept of mental health and wellbeing entered the vocabulary of professional sport, but it was still not the most enlightened outlook from a man who demonstrated considerable capacity for modern thinking when it came to practical issues such as all-seater stadia, sponsored football, and the need for managers to be relieved of the burden of transfers and player contracts. It was, however, typical of his view of the managerial profession, which seemed to range from suspicion to outright hostility. 'This small and special breed are, very nearly to a man, devious and ruthless and selfish,' he stated. 'I believe these qualities are fundamental to success in football management ... other qualities such as honesty and willingness to trust can be a handicap.'[466]

In 1977, Johnny Giles would resign as manager of West Bromwich Albion, saying, 'Football management under the current system is a precarious profession. It seems that the only thing certain is the sack.'[467] But there was little sympathy forthcoming from England captain Gerry Francis, a future manager himself, who said, 'I find it hard to feel very sorry for most managers who are fired. Getting the sack with a £12,000 pay-off is not the end of the world, is it?'[468]

LAST OF THE SUMMER WINE

You got a bad reputation; that's the word out on the town
It gives a certain fascination; but it can only bring you down

Bad Reputation, Thin Lizzy (Scott Gorham, Brian Downey, Phil Lynott; Pippin the Friendly Ranger Music Co. Ltd, 1977)

All the talk around the state of the game only occasionally diverted attention from the biggest narrative of the closing weeks of the summer of 1974. Clough was sinking at Leeds. Forced to start the season without the suspended Hunter and Clarke and with Bremner joining them after the opening game – all of which tended to add weight to Clough's point about the team's ill-disciplined approach – Leeds lost 3-0 at Stoke and 1-0 at home to Queens Park Rangers in their opening two First Division games.

After the first of those matches a smiling Clough, relaxed in a royal blue zip-up tennis shirt, appeared on *The Big Match* to tell Brian Moore, 'It's a long time since I was involved in a match where we have been whacked 3-0 and I have come away thinking, well, if we play like that we'll not only win the League, we'll walk it.' A one-goal home win against Birmingham City and a point in the return game at QPR eased the crisis temporarily, before defeat at Manchester City and a dropped home point against newly-promoted and winless Luton Town left them 21st in the table, inspiring chants of Revie's name from the Elland Road crowd. 'The boss is already being missed at Elland Road,' said Bremner, echoing the terrace sentiment. 'He was an institution.'[469] McGovern, wearing Bremner's No.4 shirt, was the target of much abuse from the crowd, and the Leeds players felt sympathy for him and O'Hare. The majority view in the dressing-room was that neither was good enough, even though they got on well with both on a personal level.

Clough argued that all his team lacked was confidence, although, in a moment of self-awareness, he conceded, 'I instil it or destroy it.' He might have added that he had managed, from day one, to demotivate his team, although there is no evidence that any player ever deliberately gave less than maximum effort in the hope of undermining the manager. It was simply not in the DNA of players who had been raised to pursue victory, often at any cost. McKenzie, the outsider, did observe, however, that 'some players refused to accept responsibility for our predicament'.[470]

Chairman Manny Cussins chose to announce, 'There is no unhappiness among the players.' But he knew better, especially once he and fellow director Sam Bolton had called them together for a meeting in which they were able to air their opinions on Clough's leadership – once the manager had left the room. As the players unburdened themselves, McGovern and Paul Reaney exchanged the view that 'this isn't right'. Clough returned and was told what his squad had been saying about him; that he had misjudged his first speech and that his team questioned his methods. Clough was shocked when it was again Madeley who told him, 'We just don't think you're any good as a manager.'[471] What was difficult to dispute was that Clough was not the right manager for this team. Even so, some players were uncomfortable that they were being manoeuvred into a position where they could be accused of having forced his dismissal. Giles, who felt he was beginning to strike up an unlikely rapport with Clough, argued, 'They hadn't consulted the players when making the appointment, but rather than admit they had screwed up, they were now attempting to shift the responsibility on to us.'[472]

After a late Lorimer penalty scraped a 1-1 draw in the League Cup at Third Division Huddersfield Town a day later, the Leeds board told

Clough that he was being fired after spending only 44 days at the club – although it was 53 days since his appointment. Cussins insisted he had personally been against such a move, but that the board was a democracy in which he had been outvoted.

'I'm shattered,' announced Clough. Accusing the directors of having become scared after not winning the first six matches, he denied that the players' influence had been the overriding factor in his dismissal. Cussins, too, said that conjecture about player power was 'grossly inaccurate', although he didn't do much to dispel that notion when he added, 'The directors detected from the feelings of the players a certain amount of unrest and apprehension. No club can be successful if the players are not happy.'[473]

Not for the first time, a group of players felt compelled to issue a statement after Clough's departure. But rather than the message of support delivered by the Derby squad, this was in defence of themselves:

> We wish it to be known that from the moment Brian Clough was appointed team manager he received 100 per cent effort and the same effort on the field as we gave for Don Revie. The players deplore the suggestion that 'player power' was responsible for Mr Clough's dismissal. Nothing could be further from the truth ... It is unfortunate that in recent weeks rumour and speculation have caused anxieties and pressures on those who have served the club loyally and firmly for so many years. Mr Clough had our wholehearted support.

Decades later, Cherry proposed a theory that 'history could have been very different' if Jimmy Armfield had succeeded Revie and paved the way for Clough to join the club later. 'Clough was a great manager, his record shows that,' he said, 'but we got him at the wrong time. He came in to confront the players he had criticised in the past and it was never going to work.'[474]

Clough would eventually acknowledge his lack of surprise at being fired, accepting that changing the culture of the club was a long-

The functional cover for the 1974 FA Charity Shield programme, offering no hint of what would play out on one of the defining days of English football in the 1970s. It ended up as a clear dividing line in the decade.

Brian Clough was an unlikely figure to be leading out Leeds at Wembley, while Bill Shankly was fulfilling his final duty for Liverpool after shocking football with his sudden resignation. (Empics/ PA Images)

The 1970 FA Cup Final had everything: a classic rivalry of styles and geography; dramatic and often brutal action over two matches; and a Wembley mudheap. As tempers flare, referee Eric Jennings is confronted by Leeds captain Billy Bremner while Chelsea's Charlie Cooke, Peter Osgood and Peter Houseman do their best to look innocent. (Empics/PA Images)

Wolves midfielder Peter Knowles could have been one of the biggest stars of English football in the 1970s. Instead, he spent the decade spreading the word of the Bible as a Jehovah's Witness. (Empics/PA Images)

The way football treated maverick talent like that of Manchester City's Rodney Marsh and Chelsea's Alan Hudson was one of the ongoing storylines of the decade. Neither man played as many England games as their fans demanded. John Dempsey is the Chelsea man watching them fight for the ball. (Bob Thomas/ Getty Images)

A&BC bubble gum cards and the FKS sticker collections became a permanent presence in school playgrounds as football's multi-media presence grew throughout the decade.

New saloon cars and fashionable, yet safe, clothing – as modelled by West Ham and England's Geoff Hurst and Bobby Moore – were symbolic of the professional footballer's arrival among the middle classes during the 1970s. (Empics/PA Images)

A momentous day for Liverpool and English football as Kevin Keegan poses at Anfield with Bill Shankly after his transfer from Scunthorpe United in 1971. (Empics/PA Images)

Derby captain Dave Mackay lifts the first Watney Cup after victory against Manchester United in the late summer of 1970. The competition was short-lived but an important milestone in the commercialisation of football. (Empics/PA Images)

Tony Currie, Paul Madeley, Martin Peters, Mick Channon and Roy McFarland show the nation's dejection and disbelief after failure to beat Poland at Wembley meant England would miss the 1974 World Cup finals. (PA Images)

Manchester United fans invade the Old Trafford pitch as relegation becomes an inevitability, forcing their game against Manchester City to be abandoned. The 'Red Army' would celebrate their team's successful Division Two campaign by terrorising provincial towns around the country. (PA Images)

Kevin Keegan and Billy Bremner discard their shirts after being sent off for fighting in the 1974 FA Charity Shield, an act that outraged the authorities and earned them lengthy suspensions. (PA Images)

Sunderland goalkeeper Jim Montgomery is congratulated by manager Bob Stokoe after one of the most famous saves in Wembley history helped to secure a shock victory over Leeds in the 1973 FA Cup Final. (Bob Thomas/Getty Images)

Sporting England's branded training gear, captain Emlyn Hughes and Don Revie share a rare happy moment. Hughes would fall out with Revie over money and selection, among other things, before Revie's defection to the United Arab Emirates. (Empics/PA Images)

Debutant Ade Coker lines up alongside Clyde Best as West Ham visit Crystal Palace in October 1971. Within minutes, Coker was on the scoresheet, prompting more talk of the growing role of black players in the English game. (Mirrorpix/Getty Images)

Laurie Cunningham, a standard bearer for black players in English football, helped make West Bromwich Albion one of the most exciting teams in the country. (Empics/PA Images)

Kenny Dalglish moves on to Graeme Souness's pass to score the winning goal against FC Bruges at Wembley, giving Liverpool their second successive European Cup victory. (Bob Thomas/Getty Images)

Tottenham Hotspur manager Keith Burkinshaw welcomes Argentina's World Cup duo Ricardo Villa and Ossie Ardiles to White Hart Lane after his club's historic transfer coup. (PA Images)

Million-pound hero Trevor Francis and reformed bad boy Kenny Burns lift the European Cup after Nottingham Forest's victory over Malmo in Munich. (Bob Thomas/Getty Images)

Brian Clough, giving his trademark 'well done' sign, enjoys the greatest triumph of his and Peter Taylor's career, taking Nottingham Forest from Division Two to European Cup triumph in Munich in the space of two years. (Bob Thomas/Getty Images)

term project rather than something to be attempted within minutes of meeting his players. With an estimated £100,000 pay-off, with which he immediately paid off his mortgage, and the keys to his company Mercedes in his pocket, Clough departed Elland Road. He was soon pulling into the car park at Yorkshire Television, where journalist Austin Mitchell was waiting to interview him. Revie was also in the studio. It was a remarkable heist on behalf of the producers of the *Calendar* show to get the two men sat together at such a time. It became a Clough versus Revie showdown and was predictably compelling.

Clough, with his dapper appearance in a light grey suit and his made-for-TV personality – heightened by several glasses of champagne – appeared more at ease than the less ostentatious Revie, who wore a voluminous blue blazer and the look of someone with indigestion. For the most part, Clough directed his answers down the camera, but on occasions his boasts in the face of Revie's interrogation lacked substance. 'It just went like magic from the moment they came in,' Mitchell remembered. 'Revie was there to put Clough in his place.' But the interviewer also conceded that Revie 'could have put a little warmth in it'.[475] It's well worth a watch on YouTube and is described in blow-by-blow detail by author Jonathan Wilson in his Clough biography, *Nobody Ever Says Thank You*. Here are some highlights:

Revie on the players' so-called vote of no confidence in Clough: 'They must have had a very good reason to do that.'

Clough on the antipathy with Revie: 'Naturally I didn't get on with him because invariably they were above us. That's the flippant answer. I believe in a different concept of football to Don. I believe it can be played slightly differently to the way Don plays it ... now that might be aiming for Utopia.'

Clough, answering Revie's question on why he had taken the job: 'I said, I want to win the League, but I want to win it better.'

Revie, after Clough accused him of being cold: 'A cold man? Don't ask our players that or they'll laugh their socks off.'

During the show's 25 minutes, Revie asked Clough why he had not given the squad members an opportunity rather than signing new players; and why he had not met all the club staff on his first day in charge. At times, Clough's uncharacteristically disjointed answers suggested a man intimidated by the role he had accepted and the man he had succeeded. He fired back by accusing the Leeds board of sending football 'back to the Dark Ages' by firing him so rapidly and argued, 'I do not think six weeks is long enough to learn where the butcher's shop is.' He concluded by suggesting he might now apply to Revie for the chance to coach the England youth team.[††]

'It would have been better if they hadn't gone on television together,' Bill Shankly observed. 'It was an unfortunate episode which both men could have done without.'[476] But it took more than an uncomfortable half-hour to deter Clough from putting himself back under the scrutiny of the TV studio lights. This time it was the political interrogator supreme, David Frost, with whom Clough happily jousted in November on *The Frost Interview*, referring to Revie throughout the show as 'the other guy'.

'I am loath to mention him, you know, and if we can refrain from doing it we'll do so,' he said with a mischievous smile. 'He's a very talented man and I don't like him. His record is unsurpassable, but I don't like the way he goes about football.' When Frost pressed Clough to share his true feelings about Revie, the reply was, 'I can't tell you, it's impossible. We'd get closed down, David.'

Clough's exile from the dugout to the chat-show circuit meant that, in the space of a few months, English football's managerial landscape had been redrawn dramatically. Ramsey, Shankly, Revie, Clough, Nicholson, Greenwood and Sexton were no longer in the same jobs. Docherty and Allison had suffered the indignity of relegation. Terry Neill, the youngest captain in Arsenal's history, had been appointed manager at arch-rivals Tottenham, against the wishes of Nicholson. Armfield, originally thought to be ahead of Revie as an England candidate and then overlooked for the Leeds job, had accepted the task of clearing up the post-Clough mess at Elland Road.

†† A role he and Peter Taylor filled for a brief period under Ron Greenwood.

It was hardly surprising that the season never settled into any definable pattern. Early in March, any one of nine teams had a chance of winning the First Division. Separated by only five points were Everton, Burnley, Stoke, Ipswich, Liverpool, Leeds, Derby, Manchester City and Middlesbrough. For parts of the season London's big three of Arsenal, Chelsea and Tottenham occupied the bottom places in the table.‡‡ Meanwhile, no First Division teams made the last four of the League Cup, which was won by Aston Villa with a 1-0 victory over Norwich City; while a Second Division club, Fulham, contested the FA Cup Final against a West Ham side who finished in the bottom half of the First Division.

Everton, beaten eight times, ended up as the only top-flight team to lose fewer than ten games, but failure to win more than two of their final ten left them in fourth place. Manager Billy Bingham said he never felt his team were good enough, although Bob Latchford said, 'I look back on that season with such regret. We weren't the finished article, but rarely will you get so many chances of winning a League title.'[477] Despite having three leading players out with broken legs, Stoke were leading the table with three games to play, but failed to win any of them. 'I blame Shilton,' was Hudson's blunt assessment, recalling Easter draws at West Ham and Arsenal that prevented them developing more of a cushion, 'He cost us in each game. I was struck by how much the back four loved and respected Gordon Banks. It wasn't like that with Shilton.'[478]

Champions with only 53 points were Clough's old charges at Derby; mostly the same players who had almost gone on strike for Mackay's first game. Having won only one of their first seven matches,

‡‡ There was an annual narrative in the 1970s around the 'London challenge' – clearly the product of the capital-based media as followers of London clubs never considered themselves part of a collective movement or felt any cross-town affinity. On a practical level, the weakness of the London challenge meant that after Arsenal's 1971 efforts, London fans spent most of the decade settling for mediocre mid-table derby games as the main action on *The Big Match*, knowing that the really meaningful action would be the five minutes they were shown from the most important game of the day, usually from Granada in the north-west.

a team that had Francis Lee[§§] up front and was led in goal-scoring by midfielder Bruce Rioch remained unbeaten over the last ten games. It meant they finished two points ahead of Paisley's Liverpool, despite failing to record most wins, fewest defeats, most goals or fewest conceded in the division. It had taken a season of consolidation before Mackay had felt fully in charge, a perspective he could have offered to Clough at Elland Road. 'When I arrived at Derby, I liked the way Clough did some things,' he said. 'There were others I didn't like. Obviously, I had to change those. Players need time to adjust, to adapt.'[479]

As the patient Mackay ended the season planning a European Cup campaign, Clough – who had gone to Elland Road for exactly that opportunity – was trying to work out how he could get Nottingham Forest, Mackay's former club, out of the Second Division. Clough's experiences at Brighton and Leeds had seriously dented his reputation and elicited little sympathy. 'There would have been a lot of managers who would have disliked the fact that Brian had won the First Division,' said McFarland. 'If he had a big head before it was ten times bigger afterwards.'[480] Now those same people had reason to snigger. Clough might not quite have made himself untouchable by the top clubs, but he was clearly a risky appointment.

Forest were not a club known for making flashy gestures, but when they sacked Allan Brown early in 1975 they decided to take a chance on Clough, who was not only dealing with failure but was most closely associated with a close geographical rival. The man who stood in front of the cameras welcoming Clough to his club certainly appeared to have doubts. As chairman Jim Wilmer shook a beaming Clough by the hand outside the City Ground, he offered a smile that turned into a grimace and squeezed the new manager's shirt-sleeved bicep in what looked like a Vulcan death grip. The

§§ Lee's £100,000 transfer from Manchester City produced another of the decade's great TV moments, with Barry Davies once more on the microphone. On his return to Maine Road, with the game tied 1-1, Lee turned inside two defenders on the edge of the City box. 'Interesting,' said Davies expecting something spectacular. 'Very interesting!' he exclaimed as Lee fired the ball into the top corner. And then, his voice cracking with excitement as a delighted Lee ran towards the bench, 'Look at his face. Just look at his face!'

message appeared to be less 'welcome to Forest' and more 'don't you try anything with me'.

The scene might have been played out 14 months earlier had Forest had the balls to attempt to acquire Clough to replace Mackay. But instead of a headline-grabbing job swap, Forest appointed Bury manager Brown, a man far less likely to disrupt the boardroom or steal the keys to the cocktail cabinet. 'I have heard it said that there could be a clash of personalities,' said Wilmer. 'I can't see how anyone can say that. The longest conversation I have had with him was when we sold Duncan McKenzie to Leeds and we had about a three-minute talk on the phone.' Yet it had been committee member Stuart Dryden who had led the drive to hire Clough.

The team lying 14th in the Second Division after appointing five managers in seven years might not have been the obvious choice for Clough, but he was hardly in a position to be selective. 'There is only one thing in the club's favour,' he said. 'And that's me.' Midfielder Martin O'Neill remembered the shock among the players when Clough walked in. 'I know celebrity status is easily attained these days, but he was a major celebrity,' he said. 'He was on *Parkinson* nearly every other week.'[481]

Undeterred by his disastrous first address to the Leeds squad, Clough gathered Forest's motley group of players together and told them, 'You're hopeless.' Full-back Viv Anderson remembered, 'He went on to say that we could do well or we could be also-rans.' The key, Clough told them, was to follow his instructions. 'If he had been in any way humbled by his time at Leeds it didn't show,' Anderson added. 'He was mesmerising.'[482]

Victory at Tottenham in an FA Cup replay – a game Clough described as 'utopia' – was a greater indication of Spurs' troubles than a Forest revolution and, having already hired coach Jimmy Gordon, favoured players McGovern and O'Hare were quickly summoned. Clough felt the Leeds directors 'didn't know what they had in their possession with those two',[483] and explained that he'd spent £70,000 on them 'to teach the others how to play'. Gordon, sacked by Leeds, felt his most important role was to stop Clough scaring the players too much.

Typically, Clough had told McGovern, 'You should be paying me to leave Leeds,'[484] but the player found his manager more subdued than he'd ever known. An eventual finishing position of 16th was scarcely cause for strutting around, especially when Clough looked west along the A52 and saw Derby on top of the English game; or north up the M1 to Leeds, who had earned a place in the European Cup Final against holders Bayern Munich.

The Leeds semi-final against Barcelona brought back memories of Wembley several months earlier with its flashpoints of violence. With Leeds leading 2-1 after the first leg, Brian Moore introduced his ITV commentary in the Nou Camp by saying, 'This really is a night for strong nerves.' Strong limbs, strong chins, too, as it turned out, especially after Leeds riled the home team by scoring through a typical Lorimer blast after seven minutes. 'I hope the Austrian referee is a little more severe on that sort of challenge,' Moore ventured after Francisco Gallego got away with a tackle from behind on Clarke. That was a mere sighter for the full-back, who was booked after half-time for wiping out Bremner. The Leeds captain was hauled off the field by the home players, prompting pushes and shoves all round, but he returned to exact some sort of revenge on Johan Cruyff, who was looking for a further European triumph in Spain after his three winners' medals at Ajax.

With a little over 20 minutes remaining, Manuel Clares headed a goal for Barcelona. The 110,00 fans were worked into an even greater state of frenzy moments later when Gordon McQueen, feeling his shirt being tugged by Clares, turned and swung his left fist. Unsurprisingly, he was sent off. Yet Leeds, with goalkeeper David Stewart often risking his head at the feet of Barcelona's snarling pack of forwards, held on to win 3-2 on aggregate.

The final at the Parc des Princes in Paris would be remembered – as referenced previously – for its off-field violence more than events on the pitch. But it has become accepted that one begat the other. In the first half, French referee Michel Kitabdijan failed to give Leeds an obvious penalty when Franz Beckenbauer brought down Clarke. Leeds were the better team, but midway through the second half

Lorimer's apparent goal was ruled out when the referee was intercepted by Beckenbauer on his way back to the half way line. Quite what the German captain said to him has never been established, but suddenly the goal was disallowed.

The best guess was that Bremner had been offside, but the decision not only incensed the Leeds fans but seemed to distract their players. Franz Roth and Gerd Müller scored for Bayern and all Leeds could offer in response were the missiles of their supporters. Those same fans would, for decades, chant, 'We are Champions. Champions of Europe.' But the record book stated otherwise. The final legacy of Revie's team was a wave of national sympathy, the like of which they had rarely experienced over the previous decade.

If the country's sudden affection for Leeds was a sign of football's strange days of the mid-1970s, then there were equally seismic changes taking place in the wider narrative of the country. In April 1975, Britain recorded an inflation rate of 33 per cent, five times more than any other European country. Meanwhile, unemployment had doubled in 12 months and was close to one million. 'Britain was trapped in a vicious circle,' according to Dominic Sandbrook, 'as prices rose, ordinary households howled with pain, the unions pressed for wage increases, profits fell, businesses buckled under the strain and prices inevitably rose again.'[485]

While Clough had been recovering from events at Leeds late in 1974, Edward Heath, beaten over both legs of the previous year's general election, found himself in a battle for the Conservative Party leadership. The general view was that if he had instigated a vote in the hours immediately after his October defeat to Harold Wilson, he would have been safe, or at least seen an ally like William Whitelaw take over, thus assuring him of continued political prominence.

Instead, a delay allowed Sir Keith Joseph, with former education minister Margaret Thatcher as a trusted aide, to emerge as a viable alternative. Until, that was, he spoke in Birmingham about the perils of the permissive society and said that the 'human stock is threatened' by children being born to unfit mothers. The NHS, he suggested, should extend birth control to 'these classes of people'. It was as well-judged as Clough's address to his new Leeds players. The overtones of the Third Reich put paid to Joseph's leadership hopes, at which point Thatcher, believing that his views – the economic ones at least – needed representing, opted to run for the leadership.

The first ballot was held on 4 February, as Clough's Forest were locked in an epic four-match FA Cup battle with Fulham, and saw Thatcher accrue more votes than Heath, although short of an overall majority. Unlike Forest and Fulham, Thatcher needed only one further attempt to achieve a result. Heath and Hugh Fraser withdrew from the contest, their places in a second ballot taken by Whitelaw, Geoffrey Howe, Jim Prior and James Peyton, all former Cabinet ministers. Between them they could not prevent Thatcher winning 146 votes (53 per cent).

Thatcher was now leader of the Tories and Clough manager of Forest. Thatcher, who would later describe her manner of dealing with cabinet members as, 'I don't mind how much my ministers talk, as long as they do what I say.' And Clough, whose method of discussion with players was, 'We talk about it for about 20 minutes and then we decide I was right.'

The Iron Lady and Old Big 'ead were ready to make history.

10

WE CAN BE HEROES

UNCLE MORT: Reality? It's all a con is that. If there were any reality in this world, there'd be no keg bitter, there'd be no Doberman pinschers, there'd be no bent collar studs, and United would hold the FA Cup in perpetuity.

***I Didn't Know You Cared*, 'After the Ball Was Over' (Peter Tinniswood; BBC TV, 1975)**

THE FA Cup was always more about dreams than reality. Never more so than in the 1970s, a time when the competition seemed to matter more than in any period before or since.

It was the first complete decade in which the final was an all-day experience shared by the whole country, with hours of build-up to the game on both major stations rather than coverage of the game only. It was an age of egalitarianism; still the only decade where the first nine finals were won by nine different teams, including two from outside the First Division.* It was a time when it was unthinkable that a television station would one day have to promote games with slogans such as 'Don't Mug off the Cup', as BT Sport did in the 2018-19

* The 1970s, which finished with Arsenal repeating their 1971 triumph, is one of only three decades, along with the 1900s and 1930s, to feature as many as nine different winners.

season. That was a stark acknowledgement that much of football had come to think of the competition as an irrelevance. Finishing fourth in the Premier League had become of greater import than winning what used to be the most venerated tournament in the world; and while a non-League team might still enjoy the day of their lives if drawn against a top-flight club, the rest of the nation either shrugs or fails to notice.

The FA Cup of the 1970s represented more than dreams of Wembley and the potential of lifting a trophy. The real reward of a Cup run extending into May was the idea of seeing your team live on television. Even for neutrals, that thrill of watching a complete club game while it was actually happening is impossible to convey to anyone brought up in the era of daily live matches from all corners of the globe. The yearning for a late equaliser to send the game to extra-time so that we could watch an additional 30 minutes was universal.

On the day of the first FA Cup Final of the 1960s, BBC had aired a brief 'How They Got There' piece before showing Wolverhampton Wanderers' victory over Blackburn Rovers. Meanwhile, ITV, which did not have outside broadcast facilities available after covering Princess Margaret's wedding the previous day, instead featured amateur boxing, professional wrestling and the Moscow State Circus on its *Let's Go* programme.

By the time the Football Association was celebrating 100 years of the tournament at the 1972 final between holders Arsenal and Leeds United, the Wembley television schedules had expanded to the hours of two-channel entertainment that makes those of a certain age go misty-eyed. 'I remember as a kid it was always a special day, no matter who was playing,' said Jimmy Case, a young Liverpool fan who would score for his favourite team on the sport's biggest day before the decade was done. 'FA Cup Final day was a television ritual: watching the teams at their hotels, interviews on the bus, *It's a Knockout*, wrestling ...'[486]

In 1972, Frank Bough introduced BBC's viewers to Wembley at 10.45am, with Brian Clough, Bobby Charlton and injured Arsenal and Leeds players Bob Wilson and Terry Cooper to help him through the next few hours. Segments such as 'The Wembley Scene', the history of the FA Cup and profiles of the players and managers filled the time until Stuart Hall and Eddie Waring introduced *Cup Final It's A Knockout*. Teams of Arsenal and Leeds supporters were joined by Bremner, Johnny Giles, Gordon Banks, George Eastham and DJ Pete Murray in a specially recorded version of the game show made famous by the antics of participants in padded costumes, pools of water, elasticated harnesses and the like. After 45 minutes of that frivolity it was back to Wembley for the players' arrival and the first look at the pitch; then the Royal Marines' marching band; a parade celebrating previous winners; Tommy Steele leading the crowd in 'Abide With Me'; and, at last, the introduction of the teams to the Queen followed by David Coleman's match commentary.

Over on ITV, presenter Dickie Davies and commentator Brian Moore went on air at 11.15 and were backed up by Jimmy Hill and World Cup panel stalwarts Malcolm Allison, Derek Dougan and Pat Crerand. The early part of the show featured interviews with children of the star players before it was off to St Albans for professional wrestling. The FA Cup theme was provided by two London versus Yorkshire contests featuring some of the sport's most recognisable figures: Mick McManus against Jeff Kaye, and Steve Logan versus Les Kellett. A burst of athletics from Crystal Palace, where Olympic middle-distance hope David Bedford was the main attraction, was followed by *Cup Final Comedians*, a special edition of the popular show where veterans of the working men's club circuit – including Bernard Manning, ex-player Charlie Williams, Frank Carson and Mike Reid – reeled off football-related jokes. Back inside the stadium, experts, old goals, celebrities and the on-field pageantry took viewers through to kick-off.

In the commentary box, Moore, Coleman and, later, John Motson,[†] understood the importance of their words and, like the players, felt the pressure of the event. 'You've got to try and make it

† Kenneth Wolstenholme commentated for the BBC on the 1970 and 1971 finals; Coleman 1972 to 1976 and again in 1978; while Motson took the microphone in 1977 and 1979.

sound like the great occasions it is,' said Moore. 'You must capture the mood and the action as well. If you are concentrating on all three, it's impossible to look at the game as a tactical exercise. That's why I always have an expert sitting alongside me. It's 90 minutes of live television and you know there is no chance of rubbing out any mistakes.'[487]

Apart from its year off in 1960, ITV had been covering the FA Cup alongside BBC since 1958. But it was in 1969, Moore's first year on the microphone for them, that Wembley literally became a battleground for the two networks. With Jimmy Hill as head of sport on London Weekend Television, the ITV network was becoming increasingly self-assured and set out to beat its rival to the big-name interviews when Manchester City took on Leicester City. This included Paul Doherty, a Granada TV producer, taking advantage of City coach Malcolm Allison being banned from the touchline by grabbing a seat close to him in the stands and secreting a microphone up his sleeve. Meanwhile, Peter Lorenzo hovered close to Leicester manager Frank O'Farrell to get comments during the game.

The most cunning part of the plan was to put production assistants into Manchester City tracksuits so that they could position themselves in the tunnel and be the first to grab players after the final whistle. Yet the BBC believed they had an exclusive contract worth £1,850 to ensure that they got the first Manchester City interviews, which became more imperative once they won the game. As ITV's troops scrambled to get their men, BBC producer Alec Weeks sent out a war cry of 'Stop those bastards'.[488] What transpired was little short of a brawl as rival broadcast crew members pushed, punched and kicked, with players looking on incredulously. LWT outside broadcast manager David Yallop, later to become a renowned writer, was among those who lost teeth.

Both sides proclaimed their innocence, with BBC head of sport Brian Cowgill calling events 'a rather undignified attempt to break the contract which had been genuinely given to the BBC'. The response from Hill was a claim that ITV had their own contract with Manchester City and went on to accuse BBC workers of 'physically interfering with and manhandling our operators – pulling out plugs and trying to grab players away from us'. FA secretary Denis Follows condemned both networks and described it as a 'shameful exhibition'. The romance of the FA Cup, indeed.

At the Centenary Final, the greater fears were about what people might see inside the 90 minutes. 'I think I'll go to the pictures,' *Goal* writer Eric Nicholls said when the semi-finals threw up the likelihood of a rematch of the Arsenal–Leeds 1968 League Cup Final. 'Anything – just ANYTHING – must be better than that,' he said. 'More fans are likely to be carried out suffering from boredom than all other sundry injuries put together.' Nicholls wasn't that far off the mark. The first foul was committed before the ball had left the centre circle; the first booking arrived inside two minutes. When Alan Ball and Billy Bremner weren't kicking lumps out of each other, or when Allan Clarke wasn't yanking Charlie George's hair in a defensive wall, there was just enough football for Clarke's diving header to win the game. BBC Radio commentator Peter Jones captured the nature of proceedings by describing Peter Storey going in for a tackle like an 'earth remover'. The image that fitted more appropriately into the lore of the FA Cup was Leeds centre-forward Mick Jones being helped up the steps in agony to collect his medal after the elbow he dislocated in the closing seconds had been strapped to his side. Even in the midst of banality, the Cup could deliver a moment of romance.

It was why the weekend in early January when the third round rolled around was truly one of the highlights of the sporting calendar – 32 matches, all kicking off at 3pm on Saturday; the sense that anything could happen. Modern-day efforts by broadcasters to perpetuate that sense of anticipation have been undermined by the dilution of the Cup itself and the spread of matches over multiple time slots across four days. When George Best said, 'The FA Cup is something special – even the most battle-hardened professionals get keyed up about it,' it was not just a soundbite designed to promote a live game on TV.[489] *Goal* magazine wrote, 'The FA Cup is something special. Under its banner you could play two teams of monkeys on the side of a mountain and still get a good crowd.'[490]

What other competition could feature – as the 1974 final did – Brendan Foster winning a pre-match 3,000 metres race before Bruce Forsyth pranced on to the field and booted the ball into the goal in front of the Liverpool fans before conducting the pre-match community singing?

When journalist Brian James wrote his classic book about the 1976-77 competition, *Journey to Wembley*, he said in his introduction, 'In the past 105 years, the Cup has evolved from almost casual roots to the very essence of intense competition. In England, it is established as *the* competition. For the world, it has been the model for them all.'[491]

Even Bremner could not help but admit that 'there's nothing to match the spellbinding magic of the competition',[492] although his Leeds team were on the wrong side of some of most memorable FA Cup storylines of the 1970s. And the epic duel against Chelsea in the first final of the decade was not even one of them.

Colchester v Leeds, Layer Road, 1971

The air of invincibility that Leeds carried – at least up until the final step of too many journeys – made it unthinkable that Colchester United, a middling Fourth Division side, could pose any serious threat to the First Division leaders when they arrived for their fifth-round tie in the 1970-71 competition. Previously in charge at Crystal Palace and Orient, manager Dick Graham had put together a team that relied on organisation and experience, with six of them over the age of 30; men Graham said he had 'resurrected'. His close-cropped grey hair gave him a look of the parade ground that was not totally out of place, but along with a firm approach to discipline was a strategic mind. Not that you needed to be a tactical genius to recognise that if Leeds had a weakness it was their goalkeeper. In the days approaching the game, Graham had his forwards working on ways of placing Gary Sprake under pressure via high balls into the box.

Among the men hoping to capitalise was Ray Crawford, part of Alf Ramsey's championship-winning team at Ipswich Town a decade earlier and owner of two England caps. At 34, Crawford had been at Southern League Kettering Town and looking for one last shot at

League football when Graham came calling. 'Dick was good enough to have managed at a higher level,' Crawford remembered. 'He was a great motivator and his training was hard but brilliant.'[493]

A crowd of more than 16,000 squeezed into the ground for a match that Leeds chairman Percy Woodward felt should not even have been necessary, having suggested to a reporter that lower-division teams should not be allowed in the FA Cup. In *The Times*, Geoffrey Green described it as 'the sort of match that is sure to attract all the vultures sharpening their claws and their pencils in the hopes of an upheaval'.

After an hour, those pencils had been worn down to nubs. Colchester were three goals up and no one could get it down on paper quickly enough. Crawford, who had pointed out that he 'always' scored against Jack Charlton, had headed the first after Sprake flapped at Brian Lewis's delivery. Just inside the half-hour mark, he found the net again while on the deck. Ten minutes into the second half, Dave Simmons headed the third goal when Sprake failed to deal with a long bouncing ball. At this point Colchester fans were almost falling off their perches in the trees outside the ground in their excitement. Revie's men had allowed themselves to get sucked into a physical battle and Simmons and Crawford had unsettled the Leeds defence to the point where Green observed that they 'reduced the lanky Charlton to a dithering novice'.

Leeds began to look like their true selves when Hunter headed in from a corner. A finish from Giles left Colchester with 15 minutes to survive, and a late save by Graham Smith to deny Jones was the final action.

While the nation processed its shock, Graham fulfilled a pre-game promise to scale the walls of Colchester Castle if his team won. They were duly dispatched 5-0 at Everton in the quarter-final, but Graham's boys were not done yet, winning the Watney Cup in late summer. By the end of that season, however, the fairytale was over. Graham resigned, claiming to be 'the victim of a witch hunt led by a shareholder who had won five shares in a raffle'. He decided that his 'lousy job' was not worth the strain on his family and complained that he was working for 'people who expected miracles without any thought of the professional and financial limitations I was working under'. When you beat Leeds in the FA Cup, people come to expect miracles.

Leeds v Sunderland, Wembley, 1973

If there is one day that encapsulates all that the FA Cup represented in the 1970s it is the meeting of Leeds and Sunderland in the 1973 final. The team of the era showing their infamous vulnerability; a massive upset; a stadium backdrop of passion and urgency propelling the players into 90 minutes of unrelenting, breakneck action; and iconic images that would endure for decades. As Sunderland fan and author Jonathan Wilson asserted, 'It's the best example of the golden age of the FA Cup when shocks were shocks and this was the big event that everybody watched and everybody cared about.'[494]

Having at last won the trophy the previous season, Leeds were back for their third final in four years. The mental hurdle of previous disappointments was behind them, which meant that they were expected to meet with little resistance. Meanwhile, Sunderland's four-month odyssey to Wembley represented an unforeseen turnaround in the club's fortunes; a journey that began with the appointment of 42-year-old Bob Stokoe as manager in November 1972. A north-easterner who had won the FA Cup as a Newcastle United player and now looked 20 years older than he was, Stokoe replaced Alan Brown, whose second spell as Roker Park boss had seen the club relegated from the First Division. 'We Geordies are a clannish lot,' Stokoe said as he launched his new role. 'That's why this job is a bit special.' Having managed at Bury, Charlton, Rochdale, Carlisle and Blackpool, where he won the Anglo-Italian Cup, he declared, 'I've earned the right to come home. I went away to learn my trade.'[495] So confident was he that he could get Sunderland into the First Division in two years that he'd refused the offer of a five-year contract.

Replay victories over Notts County and Reading did nothing to suggest that Manchester City had anything to worry about at Maine Road in the fifth round, especially when Tony Towers gave them the lead. Yet after goalkeeper Joe Corrigan gifted Mick Horswill an equaliser, a marauding Billy Hughes scored a fine solo goal to give Sunderland the lead. Hughes called it one of the most important goals he ever scored, giving Sunderland a belief that they could win the tie, even after City forced a replay when Jim Montgomery knocked Mike Summerbee's corner into his own goal. Montgomery, regularly described by media as the country's best uncapped goalkeeper, would make amends later in the tournament.

On a night that went down in Roker Park legend, Vic Halom gave Sunderland the lead in the replay by completing a slick passing move with a fierce shot from wide on the right, catching Corrigan unawares. 'Even through the din, I could hear Corrigan scream at his defenders to leave it,' recalled Dennis Tueart. 'He got a right mouthful from his team-mates afterwards. He probably didn't think Vic would do a whole lot of damage from out there.'[496] It was Hughes who administered the further damage, his two goals sending Sunderland through 3-1. Coach Arthur Cox praised the patience Hughes displayed to score the second goal and called him 'unplayable'.

Aged 24 and hailing from the Lanarkshire town of Coatbridge, Hughes's dark hair and features made him look like a younger version of Alex Harvey, the singer who'd grown up only a few miles down the road and whose Sensational Alex Harvey Band were at the start of a period of commercial success in the glam rock genre. Hughes, who was friends with chart-toppers The Sweet, shared something of Harvey's penchant for the theatrical, attacking from wide with enough pace, verve and skill to have Tommy Docherty describing him in 1974 as 'the most exciting forward in the country' and making himself a cult hero at Roker Park.

After the game, Stokoe went home and watched the highlights – broadcast in black and white on ITV – before walking his black Labrador, Jed. Malcolm Allison, meanwhile, faced up to the end of his first spell at Manchester City. Struggling to reproduce the title challenge of a season earlier, he looked back on the defeat at Roker Park and admitted, 'That, I suppose, brought the curtain down on me.'[497] A few weeks later he had one argument too many with the

City directors over their reluctance to spend any more money and departed for Crystal Palace.

Meanwhile, Sunderland faced a home quarter-final against Luton Town, although Halom, up against his former team only weeks after being signed by Stokoe, dismissed fears of complacency by promising, 'If we were playing a Presbyterian Boys club we wouldn't take them lightly.' Defenders Dave Watson and Ron Guthrie scored from set pieces to give Sunderland a 2-0 win. Watson, a giant figure whose heavily-fringed dark hair framed features that looked like they'd been shaped in the boxing ring, displayed enough ability in front of goal that his career had featured various spells spent as a centre-forward. Stokoe was done with all of that. 'He is like a steeple among defenders,' Stokoe argued. 'I saw him as a platform on which to build the defence when I came here.'[498]

Arsenal, pursuing a second Double in the space of three seasons and eyeing a Wembley rematch against Leeds, would have loved Watson in their side for the semi-final at Hillsborough. Instead, Frank McLintock's injury meant the reinstatement of Jeff Blockley, the £200,000 signing from Coventry City, who himself had been injured. 'He wouldn't have played if Frank had been fit,' Gunners coach Steve Burtenshaw admitted. 'Jeff wasn't at his fittest.'[499] Blockley's lack of sharpness was exposed after 19 minutes when he fluffed a back-pass to Bob Wilson, allowing Halom to steal in and score. Blockley was substituted after 56 minutes. 'It was my fault,' the defender admitted of his blunder. 'I was probably wrong in offering to play.' At the other end, Montgomery made a save every bit as brilliant as the one that would bring him fame a few weeks later, an instinctive change of direction to keep out a George Armstrong shot that took a deflection. A second-half header by Hughes during more Arsenal defensive confusion increased Sunderland's lead and George's reply was too little to keep Sunderland from Wembley.

For ten minutes after the final whistle, the Sunderland fans chanted for Stokoe to appear. When he emerged, his tears made it clear what victory, and such a reception, meant to him. He had to depart before he broke down completely. While his players adored him and the Sunderland fans saw him as 'The Messiah', the cameras had now captured enough to turn Stokoe into a national treasure. The desire of the country to see Sunderland win at Wembley ran deeper than the fact that Leeds would be the opponents. 'This unashamed reaction summed up Stokoe,' wrote author Lance Hardy in *Sunderland, Stokoe and '73*. 'Those who saw it later on national television – regardless of which team they supported – could only warm to the man. Football neutrals got completely caught up in it. From this moment until the Cup Final four weeks later, Stokoe was a popular hero throughout the country.'[500]

Stokoe had beaten Don Revie at Wembley once before, when they were players for Newcastle and Manchester City respectively in 1955. Now he had a personal reason for welcoming the opportunity to put one over on him again. When Leeds had been fighting relegation late in the 1961-62 season, two of their final four games were against Stokoe's Bury. As part of the *Daily Mirror*'s investigation into Revie in 1977, Stokoe would claim his rival manager offered £500 for Bury to throw one of the games. In the run-up to the 1973 final, Stokoe contented himself with trying to make sure referee Ken Burns was not influenced by players renowned for their haranguing of match officials. 'I was staggered during the semi-final at the way Bremner went the whole 90 minutes disputing every decision,' Stokoe said. 'I don't want any favours … just a fair crack of the whip.'

Stokoe's players had no grudges to bear – if you discount the broken leg Bobby Kerr suffered against Norman Hunter six years earlier. They were too busy doing what all Cup final teams of the era did; enjoying their moment of celebrity and watching the cash mount up. Along with the great unsaid, unofficial act of selling their spare match tickets, the 'players' pool' into which appearance fees were deposited was the annual windfall for those bound for Wembley.

The previous year it had been the injured Wilson's duty to arrange the Arsenal finances. Charging between £50 and £350 for interviews and appearances and £2,000 from Adidas and Umbro for boots and kit, the Gunners fell a few thousand short of their £17,000 target and ended up making about £650 per man.

Twelve months on, the traditional Cup final record, 'Sunderland All the Way', failed to trouble the charts, but a *Top of the Pops* audience invite was still forthcoming for squad members, along with modelling photoshoots in London and promotions for the Milk Marketing Board. The traditional practice was that whatever was earned was shared, whichever players fulfilled an engagement. With Tueart and Ian Porterfield taking care of the accounts, Sunderland's pool accrued around £19,000, plus a set of pots and pans for each player from a local manufacturer. 'I remember one of the shipbuilders on Wearside put £800 into the pool,' said Tueart. 'They were just delighted we'd got there. It was money well spent by their management as during the Cup run they had the highest work attendance ever.'[501]

According to Tueart, Sunderland's players were so busy enjoying their 'surreal bubble' that they were unaware of the soft spot they occupied in the nation's affections. As guests at the Footballer of the Year dinner two days before the final, they were taken aback when people such as actor Michael Crawford, a Chelsea fan, visited their table to tell them how much they were behind them.

The morning of the game found British trawlers being threatened with arrest for fishing in waters claimed by Iceland, and US President Richard Nixon trying to restrict colleagues' testimony on Watergate before a grand jury. English television viewers, meanwhile, were captivated by a group of Sunderland players who clearly had not a care in the world. They joked their way through hotel interviews with Barry Davies, interrupted by Hughes's introduction of a 'laughing policeman' toy, and then hammed it up for the ITV cameras on the team bus. Even as they marched out for kick-off, grinning in tracksuits emblazoned with their names, it all seemed like one glorious giggle to them, not a suggestion of pressure. After all, no team without a single international player had won the FA Cup since Barnsley in 1912. ITV's panel of experts had all picked Leeds to win on Friday night and Frank McGhee in the *Daily Mirror* was typical of those who felt Eddie Gray would be the match-winner. Interestingly, a dissenting survey was buried at the bottom of the preview in *The Times*, where a panel of their own writers and TV commentators had come out six to three in favour of an upset.

Leeds looked uneasy. Within a few minutes, the usually reliable Hunter, Giles, Bremner and Madeley had all misplaced passes, as though the combination of pouring rain and a gold-coloured ball had made them queasy. In attack, they were restricted to Giles's hopeful diagonal crosses from the right. 'We knew we had to snap at them and suffocate them – get in their faces, and not allow them to boss the game,' Tueart recalled. 'If we could swamp the midfield we could also cut off the supply line to Jones and Clarke.'[502] Revie would be forced to admit, 'They never allowed us to settle. We have no excuses.'

With just over half an hour played, Hughes swung in Sunderland's first corner from the left. Watson and Halom jumped and when the ball dropped to Porterfield he cushioned it with his thigh and lashed it into the goal with his right foot from eight yards. The left-footed Porterfield never scored with his right. But this rare goal was no more than the underdogs deserved. As half-time approached, Sunderland's fans taunted their opponents with chants of 'easy, easy', while Hughes used the back of his heel to find his team-mates in the manner of Leeds at their arrogant best. 'These flicks and touches have caused trouble in the Leeds defence,' Coleman observed of the man whose older brother John had helped Celtic beat Leeds in the European Cup three years earlier.

Leeds emerged from half-time with fresh resolve to match the clean, dry shirts several of them had put on. Curiously, though, the round-neck short-sleeved jerseys now worn by Bremner and several others didn't match the collared long-sleeved versions in which the team had begun the match. Apparently even the best club in the land could only run to one set of first-choice kit. For a while, there was more uniformity in their play, but then three attempts on goal by Sunderland left-back Guthrie was evidence that the underdogs were some way from throwing their backs against the wall.

The second signature moment of the match came 20 minutes into the second half. Leeds left-back Trevor Cherry arrived with a late run into the box and connected with a diving header that Montgomery pushed away. The ball fell to Lorimer with the goal at his mercy from five yards.

'And Lorimer makes it one each,' cried Coleman.

'And a goal,' echoed Moore on the rival station.

'It must be a goal – it's a goal,' Jones told Radio 2 listeners.

Yet their eyes deceived them. Montgomery had somehow lifted himself from the grass to fling himself back and to his left and diverted the ball against the underside of the bar.

'No. Astonishing,' barked Coleman as the ball bounced away from Cherry's attempt to flick a heel at it as he lay flat on his stomach.

'I knew I had to get off the ground as quickly as I could,' said Montgomery, who on a dry day would have tried to hold the ball after Cherry's header. 'I've seen him hit it and I stick my hands up to make a save and fortunately the ball hits my arm. As I turn around off the floor I see the ball come down off the crossbar. I trained to make saves life that.'[503]

Clarke was probably correct in his assertion that 'had we scored at that point we would have won. Sunderland were legless and they knew it.'[504] Montgomery didn't realise the significance of it at the time, 'but later, talking to players, the people and the supporters, that was the time they felt we are going to do it.'[505] After another 25 minutes of intermittent, although never overwhelming, Leeds pressure, they had indeed done it.

As the final whistle blew, ITV's director, Bob Gardam, made the inspired decision to keep a camera focused on an ecstatic Stokoe. It meant that his camera captured the Sunderland manager, in red tracksuit, brown mac and, according to Jones, 'a sporty trilby', racing on to the field and going directly to hug his hero goalkeeper. 'He was the kind of guy who was always going to do something at the end, so we had to follow him,' Gardam explained. 'It was a glorious moment.'[506]

Meanwhile, Revie went and stood among his players, their faraway stares betraying their disbelief. Kerr, Sunderland's little captain who often joked that he was mistaken for the mascot, collected his front teeth from one of the reserve players and headed towards the Royal

Box. 'Ha'wa the lads,' Moore intoned unconvincingly in his Home Counties voice as Kerr lifted the trophy. While the nation settled to watch *The Pink Panther Show*, the residents of the victorious town took to the streets or started parties in living rooms, community halls and working men's clubs – all captured by Tyne-Tees Television for its revealing piece, *Meanwhile Back in Sunderland*. 'The town's been brought back to life since Stokoe came to Sunderland,' one celebrating fan told the cameras. 'Not just the football club, the town itself.'

The football club would not do badly either. In the first year of Stokoe's arrival at Roker Park, they reckoned to have made £1 million in gate money, advance season-ticket sales, FA Cup cash and additional revenue from European football. 'There is nothing like the Cup,' said Stokoe. 'It has resurrected Sunderland.'[507]

Leeds v Wimbledon, Elland Road, 1975

One season after the trauma of Sunderland, Leeds – on their way to winning the League – were beaten at home by Second Division Bristol City in a fifth-round replay. You might have thought that all these FA Cup mishaps would have dissuaded Bremner from hasty predictions. But when Leeds prepared to welcome Southern League Wimbledon to Elland Road in the fourth round in February 1975 he announced, 'There is no question of Wimbledon beating Leeds on Saturday – none whatsoever.'[508]

The players of Burnley had probably felt the same in the third round a few weeks earlier. Above Leeds in the table and semi-finalists in the competition a few months earlier, they knew that no top-flight team had lost at home to non-Leaguers since before the Football League was reorganised beyond two divisions in 1920. Meanwhile, the borough of Wimbledon, chiefly synonymous with tennis, had added only the existence of furry, long-nosed rubbish collectors, The Wombles,‡ to its resumé. But beyond the view of the nation –

‡ Created by Elisabeth Beresford and living on Wimbledon Common, the Wombles moved from books to BBC children's television in 1973. They graduated to *Top of the Pops* when songwriter Mike Batt started churning out hits in their name and appearing on stage in full costume, along with noted rock guitarist Chris Spedding. The Wombles were the best-selling British singles act of 1974.

Burnley chairman Bob Lord having again banned the TV cameras – Wimbledon's footballers created their own identity.

'We really did not fear anybody,' said goalkeeper Dickie Guy of a team constructed by Allen Batsford, who had won the FA Amateur Cup in 1973 as manager of Walton and Hersham and taken several of his players with him to Plough Lane. Early in the second half, skipper Ian Cooke forced a save and the ball was put into the net by Mick Mahon, who had been a member of Colchester's giant-killers four years earlier. Guy made several saves to keep Burnley out and by the time Wimbledon were on their way back to London the fourth-round draw had paired them with Leeds. Paul Wilcox reported in *The Guardian*, 'The expected Wombling taunts from the crowd faded with Burnley's reputation … the only rubbish Wimbledon picked up on Saturday were the First Division team's errors.'

'We applied our skills to the best effect – Burnley didn't,' was the simple verdict of Batsford, who had prepared a 15-page dossier on the opposition. 'They were complacent in the first 20 minutes and when they got behind they panicked.' The same day had seen Everton come within a last-minute penalty of losing at home to Northern Premier League Altrincham; while Isthmian League duo Wycombe Wanderers and Leatherhead held First Division Middlesbrough and beat Third Division Brighton and Hove Albion respectively. It was enough to prompt *The Times* to print its round-up of events under the headline, 'The Cup that revives a nation's gaiety'.

Leatherhead's goal-scorer that day was centre-forward Chris Kelly, who was to make a national name for himself later in the evening. Having been out to celebrate and become 'a bit inebriated' he was tracked down to appear on *Match of the Day*. Responding to his team-mates' urging to 'wind them all up', he confidently predicted victory against Leicester City in the next round. 'I almost needed a prop up my back to stop me falling over,' he recalled. 'I just said some ridiculously stupid things.'[509] The tabloids quickly dubbed him 'The Leatherhead Lip'. Even after the non-Leaguers conceded home advantage for a bigger pay-day, Kelly almost lived up to his boast when scoring a goal to help his team to a 2-0 lead at Filbert Street, before the Division One side came back to win by the odd goal.

It was further support for Batsford's argument that 'the League sides think that skill alone is enough to beat a non-League side, but this season they have been taught a lesson'.[510] The most shocking reinforcement of that was very nearly delivered at the expense of Leeds, who were frustrated to find themselves held goalless at half-time by Wimbledon. Clad in all green, the bearded Guy made a series of saves, but seemed destined to have his clean sheet spoiled when future Dons manager Dave Bassett brought down Gray to concede a penalty. Guy kicked the post in frustration as he waited for Lorimer to place the ball; then dived to his right to push away a tame spot-kick from the man with the hardest shot in the game. 'Dicky Guy can have the freedom of Wimbledon this weekend,' called Yorkshire Television commentator Keith Macklin. Every headline in the Sunday newspapers belonged to the man who worked as a tally clerk in London's docks and who had the final touch of the game in making another remarkable save from Terry Yorath's header.

Bremner managed to compliment his own team on not falling into the trap that befell Burnley, that of chasing the game – which seemed a strange piece of self-congratulation from the League champions at home to non-League opposition. And he complained, 'A little too much credit was given to [Guy] for saving Peter Lorimer's penalty. The ball almost gave itself up to him.'[511] Even Guy was forced to admit, 'He scuffed it, and I just had to get my hand under my body to knock it away.'[512]

Guy was no less outstanding in the replay two weeks later, staged in front of 45,701 at Crystal Palace's Selhurst Park. But with 50 minutes played, a hopeful long shot by Giles took an enormous deflection off Bassett, leaving the keeper stranded and the underdogs out of the Cup.

Leeds went on to lose a third replay against Ipswich Town in the quarter-final, before falling victims to lower-division opponents for the fourth time in six years the following season. This time it was Third Division Crystal Palace, led by a fedora-wearing Malcolm Allison. Palace's successive relegations under Allison's leadership had done nothing to repress his ego. In fact, when his girlfriend Serena Williams presented him with some new headwear and he unveiled it for the third-round game at Scarborough, Allison was back in the spotlight he craved. 'We're going to win the Cup with this hat,' he told his players. Palace's Northern Premier League opponents were less than enamoured. 'The one chance we get of some publicity,' one Scarborough player was heard to observe as the photographers focused on Allison, 'and he wears that fucking hat.'

According to winger Peter Taylor, 'Leeds were such a good team that we said to Mal, "Let's not give it the big 'un. We believe we can beat them, but let's keep it low key." We woke up in Leeds on the morning of the game, picked up the paper and there's Malcolm saying we will win 3-0!'[513] Allison was wrong. It was only 1-0, a goal scored in the first half by the head of striker David Swindlehurst. But Leeds were so outplayed that Palace defender Stewart Jump was miming smoking a cigar as the final minutes elapsed. 'That is a special memory,' he said. 'I just wanted to portray to the bench how very, very easy it was for us. They didn't even come close to scoring.'[514]

PART-TIME LOVE

That Ronnie Radford goal gets brought out on the old video every time the FA Cup comes around. So there was I, a young and inexperienced commentator with an opportunity to cover a goal I never expected to be doing so.

BBC commentator John Motson[515]

It was perhaps the greatest FA Cup goal of the decade. The iconic crowd scenes marked one of the most unlikely upsets in the competition's history. And it kick-started one of the nation's most celebrated broadcasting careers. Saturday, 5 February 1972 holds a significant place in the history of English football. So much so that in 2007 readers of *The Observer* voted the third-round replay between Southern League Hereford United and First Division Newcastle United as the greatest Cup tie ever played.

It should have been the day on which all the fourth-round matches were staged, but a series of postponements meant that Edgar Street was still waiting to host the replay Hereford had earned with a 2-2 result at St James' Park. They had drawn level with a goal by Colin Addison, who had become the player-manager a couple of months earlier following the dismissal of Welsh football legend John Charles.

Unable to gain a place in the Sheffield United side that had surprisingly been challenging at the top of the First Division table, former Arsenal midfielder Addison had accepted a drop of four levels in order to take his first steps in management. 'Hereford had good facilities and a nice little ground,' he remembered. 'I could see the League potential.'[516]

Even through his inexperience, Addison could sense the agitation of opposite number Joe Harvey when bad weather forced repeated postponements and a series of wasted 500-mile round trips. 'When the match was called off again – this was the second occasion – Joe was absolutely distraught. I took [him] to my house. Joe had a whisky and I thought, "They're having to go home again, this will help us." They absolutely did not fancy it at Edgar Street.'[517] Newcastle waited so long to get the game played that Malcolm Macdonald recalled them stuck in their hotel for days in dirty clothes before the Cecil Gee menswear store in Worcester enjoyed a windfall of custom.

Addison had told his men to keep their heads up, look confident and prove that they belonged in a sport that some might have felt had dealt them a bad hand. With eight minutes remaining on Hereford's muddy field, they were still matching a club with a rich FA Cup heritage. Then Macdonald headed Newcastle into the lead. 'That's it,' said BBC's John Motson in a fatalistic tone.

But urged on by a crowd that was officially recorded at 14,313, but was thought to be underestimated and certainly didn't include those on vantage points outside the ground, Hereford weren't done. Three minutes later, Ronnie Radford, a signing from Newport County, won the ball in midfield, just as Motson was praising the 'tremendous spirit' in the home team. Radford pushed the ball forward – a miracle it reached its target in the cloying mud – found the ball laid back into his path and let fly from more than 30 yards. His shot sailed beyond goalkeeper Iam McFaul's right arm and into the top corner. 'I was four yards behind him,' said Macdonald. 'The ball sat up on a divot. He didn't know that was going to happen. Without that, it would've been a mishit and a throw-in.' Even Radford admitted, 'It could have finished in the car park, but as soon as it left my foot I knew it was going for the top corner.'[518]

What has enabled that game, that goal, to stamp such an indelible hallmark on the FA Cup is not just the strike, or its significance, but the scenes of spontaneous, unbridled, innocent joy as fans of all ages raced to the field to pursue the scorer as he ran off with arms aloft. One of the duty policemen on the day, Hereford fan PC Grenville Smith, was at the head of the charge until catching himself and shouting, 'Off the pitch!' at his fellow celebrants. And Motson's commentary has accompanied the goal into history. 'I often shudder when thinking about if I'd got the scorer wrong,' he said. 'You wouldn't spot it, but when I say, "What a goal!" there's a pause between the "a" and "goal" so that I could say "shot".'[519]

Ironically, when another hero emerged in extra-time, it was one of Motson's best friends from his hometown of Barnet, Ricky George. A regular substitute because of ankle problems, George had been sent on after Macdonald's goal to replace right-back Roger Griffiths, who would discover that he'd been playing since the early minutes with a broken leg. George had been up in the hotel bar later than some on the eve of the game, bumping into Newcastle legend Jackie Milburn in the hotel lift. Milburn, who was there to report on the game, told George off for not being in bed and telling him it was such indiscipline among players that had made him give up football management. Milburn departed by telling George he'd probably go on to score the winning goal.[520]

With 13 minutes of extra-time played, George gathered Dudley Tyler's low ball into the penalty area, turned towards goal and shot low beyond McFaul. 'I tried to cushion it, but it popped up in the air to my left. I followed it, turning all the time towards goal,' George explained. 'My brain said "shoot" and I struck the ball right-footed.'

The delighted goal-scorer was not on screen for long. Within moments he had disappeared within a swarm of Hereford fans. 'The elation is immediate. Your reaction is spontaneous,' he continued. 'For a moment, this was *my* moment. But the glory for all time will be the team's.'[521]

There was more of that glory to come four days later when Hereford drew 0-0 against West Ham United in the fourth round, causing Jeff Powell to tell *Daily Mail* readers, 'Hereford blew a rich, ripe, agricultural raspberry at West Ham and all the football aristocracy they represent.' West Ham manager Ron Greenwood, who visited Hereford's dressing-room and admitted his team was lucky to still be in the competition, was impressed enough to sign midfielder Tyler for £25,000. A Geoff Hurst hat-trick in the replay meant the end of a Cup run that was said to have earned them £27,000, but Hereford's real ambition – a place in the Football League – was now within their reach.

These were the days when the League operated as a closed shop, with an ambitious non-League club having to win a vote of the membership if they were to be admitted at the expense of one of the 92. It happened so rarely that Cambridge United's election to the League in 1970 was the first for a full decade. 'No one has a right to be in the League and we don't say we should be in,' said Addison. 'We have proved our playing abilities against League clubs; we have good support; our spectator and ground facilities are extremely good; the nearest League club, Newport, is 42 miles away; and we have a forward-looking chairman and board of directors.'[522]

Hereford, runners-up in the Southern League, won enough votes to replace Barrow, even though chairman Frank Miles admitted, 'We had to convince them that Hereford deserved a place in the League on overall merit and we did that by travelling thousands of miles spreading the word.'[523]

As if to prove a point, Hereford immediately won promotion from the Fourth Division and then beat West Ham 2-1 in another memorable FA Cup replay at Edgar Street the following season. It is the Newcastle game that endures, though. 'For me to regard the experience as less than the greatest moment of my life would be insulting to the dreams of millions of school kids,' said George, who would add joint-ownership of 1998 Grand National winner Earth Summit to his sporting achievements. 'It changed my life.'[524]

During a bleak 1977-78 season that ended in Newcastle United's relegation, one occasion at St James' Park was bathed in light. It was the night when the longest FA Cup run of any non-League team during the 1970s ended when Blyth Spartans of the Northern League lost to Wrexham. Victory would have made them the first non-Leaguers since 1914 to reach the quarter-finals. The game ended up being a final hurrah for the stadium's giant Leazes End, demolished at the end of the season. While Blyth attracted 42,617 to their temporary home on the penultimate night of February – their own fans standing shoulder to shoulder with Newcastle and Sunderland supporters – their tenants never once achieved that level of attendance in their own dismal season.

Based in a Northumberland port town, the very name of Blyth Spartans sounded romantic, the kind of moniker – like Bishop Auckland or Corinthian-Casuals – synonymous with football outside the professional ranks. Starting out in the first qualifying round, Blyth won seven ties to reach the fourth round proper, only one of which had been against League opposition. After beating Third Division Chesterfield at home in the second round, they had the disappointment of being drawn against another part-time side, Isthmian League Enfield, in the third. A header by Alan Shoulder earned them a visit to Stoke City, by now relegated to the Second Division in the wake of a financial crisis created by storm damage to an uninsured Butler Street Stand roof. In place of names such as Peter Shilton, Alan Hudson, Jimmy Greenhoff and Mike Pejic, the club were recycling the likes of Howard Kendall and Alec Lindsay, alongside a young striker called Garth Crooks.

After taking a tenth-minute lead via the prolific Terry Johnson, Blyth were 2-1 down with ten minutes to play when a free-kick by Sunderland's Cup-winning left-back, Ron Guthrie, deflected against a post. In the melee, Shoulder headed against the other post before

Steve Carney netted the equaliser. Their winner came in the final minute when Johnson fired home. True to non-League trope, coach Jack Marks recalled, 'Even after we beat Stoke we were all back at work at seven o'clock the next morning.'[525]

Blyth, whose players used to take the field with a shot of whisky still stinging their tongues, were denied a dream date with Newcastle by the First Division team's surprise defeat to Wrexham. Instead, they found themselves at the Racecourse Ground, where they conceded a last-minute equaliser by Dixie McNeil after the home team were twice allowed to retake a corner because the flag had fallen over. Consolation for missing out on a home quarter-final against Arsenal was their night at St James' Park. Despite Johnson pulling a goal back after they conceded two inside 20 minutes, Spartans' run came to a glorious end after 11 matches.

For defender Carney and forward Shoulder there were contract offers from Newcastle, the latter teaming up in attack with Peter Withe, who had been winning the League with Nottingham Forest during Blyth's Cup run. The rest of their team-mates, who earned around £7 a week to play for the team, had to content themselves with £350 worth of bedroom furniture from a local store and a lifetime of memories. 'I still remember going out and being amazed at the uproar and support that we got from a full stadium [at Newcastle],' said skipper John Waterson more than three decades later. 'It makes the hairs on the back of your neck stand up just thinking about it.'[526]

While Blyth went on to finish as runners-up in the Northern League, it was the second-placed team in the Northern Premier League, Wigan Athletic, who became the fourth team in the decade to break into the Football League, following Cambridge United's replacement of Bradford Park Avenue in 1970, Hereford in 1972 and Wimbledon's elevation in place of Workington in 1977. Wigan, who took the place of Southport, had been hopeful of election seven years earlier, having seen Cambridge campaign hard for their place the previous year. But after spending heavily on a promotional campaign, Wigan secretary Frank Postlethwaite said on that occasion, 'Public relations cannot help sell a football club.' When Wigan had rounded off their campaign by giving an expensive pen set to each club chairman at the Football League's decisive meeting, one of the recipients called it 'nothing short of bribery' and claimed, 'That little stunt cost them a stack of votes.'[527]

After Wigan eventually succeeded, it would be another nine seasons before the League welcomed another new entrant, when Scarborough became the first Football Conference champions to win automatic promotion.

FIRST AMONG EQUALS

Hey Mister Dream Seller, where have you been?
Tell me, have you dreams I can see?

***Meet Me on The Corner*, Lindisfarne (Rod Clements; Warner Chappell Music Inc., Universal Publishing Group, 1971)**

Nothing speaks more eloquently of the egalitarianism of 1970s English football than the FA Cups of the decade's middle years. As if to prove that Second Division Sunderland's triumph in 1973 was no anomaly, West Ham United won in 1975 from a position of 13th in the First Division; Southampton did so from the Second Division; and Ipswich Town won in 1978 after finishing only three points from relegation in 18th place in the top flight.

Fulham provided further Second Division representation at Wembley in 1975 after upsetting First Division Everton, Carlisle United and Birmingham City. And what made their story fit even more perfectly into the mystique and magic of the FA Cup was the fact that in their ranks was none other than Bobby Moore, returning to Wembley at the age of 34 and finding himself facing his former West Ham team-mates.

Upton Park's favourite son had moved across London in the spring of 1974, his final game for the Hammers having been an FA Cup game against Hereford in which he was injured. 'There I was,' he said. 'One moment on top of the world, captain of club and country, the next leading out West Ham's reserves.'[528] As the last of the club's trio of World Cup winners to depart, it also meant the termination of any connection to the team that had won domestic and European trophies in the 1960s. Ron Greenwood was no longer in charge as the Hammers began their 1974-75 FA Cup campaign, replaced as team manager by John Lyall, a prematurely retired player who had risen through the club's coaching staff.

Things had changed so much that after West Ham beat Leeds in mid-season, Bremner had the audacity to complain, 'They seem to have sacrificed all their traditional skill for aggression. I didn't like their provocative tactics one bit. West Ham were always respected in football in the past for their attractive style and sportsmanship.'[529] Easy to love a team who were always pushovers, of course.

Fulham's path to the final was personified by Moore and the emergence of an unlikely goal-scoring hero in John Mitchell, who netted the winner in the last minute of extra-time in the semi-final replay against Birmingham. Meanwhile, it was a previously unknown forward called Alan Taylor who emerged as the principal character in the West Ham story. Signed from Fourth Division Rochdale for £40,000 late in 1974, Taylor shot to national fame in one of his earliest games for his new club, a quarter-final played on a Highbury mud heap. Selected by Lyall in order to exploit what he perceived as a lack of speed on the left of the Arsenal defence, Taylor, who was awake with excitement in the early hours, scored both West Ham goals in a 2-0 win. The second, built down the Hammers' right flank with Brooking, was exactly the kind of execution Lyall had envisioned.

Brooking was a man who could make light of even the heaviest surface, with ball-winning colleague Billy Bonds saying, 'I always thought Trevor was better at playing in the mud. He was physically strong … he would stick his backside into people and hold them off.'[530]

Having taken a little time to establish a regular place in the first team of the club he supported as a boy – he had even asked for a transfer in March 1971 – there was now nobody in the English game who had better perfected the art of allowing the ball to run at his feet and do his work for him. Former team-mate Bryan Robson called him 'the most creative player I ever played with' and recalled, 'He did the same thing every time from our throw-ins, but no one could stop him from letting the ball run across his body before turning to build up the play.'[531] It was a sign of the times, though, that in identifying his main ambition of delivering 'killer balls', Brooking noted that packed defences meant that 'if I can pull off two or three of these passes in a match I am doing pretty well'.[532]

In front of Brooking, Taylor, pale and frail, appeared no match for the bruisers who patrolled First Division defences. Yet he seemed to have been sprinkled with the Cup's stardust, scoring West Ham's goals in their 2-1 semi-final replay win against Ipswich at Stamford Bridge. And it was the same in the final. Denying Moore and Fulham captain Alan Mullery their end-of-career bonus, Taylor twice pounced on shots that had been parried by goalkeeper Peter Mellor to give his team the trophy 2-0.

The human storylines were a counterpoint to one of the decade's blandest finals. In the *Daily Mirror*, Frank McGhee even complained that the low total of 17 fouls indicated a lack of passion in the game – a sign that a few lumps being taken out of opposing players had become accepted as part of the beautiful game in England.

Crystal Palace's hopes of representing the Third Division in the following season's final ended at Stamford Bridge, where winger Peter Taylor had inspired them to a memorable 3-2 win against Chelsea in the fifth round. Back there for a semi-final against Southampton, the prospect of a Wembley visit offered redemption to Allison after six years in which his career had been in steady freefall. Yet with Taylor, newly capped by England, unable to fire, Southampton were comfortable 2-0 winners. 'Everyone expected Peter to do more,' said Palace forward Alan Whittle. 'But he was tied up by Peter Rodrigues and it didn't happen. Malcolm probably put too much on the boy.'[533]

Rodrigues was a story in himself. A former Wales right-back, he'd played in the 1969 final for Leicester before five years at Sheffield Wednesday had ended with a free transfer in the summer of 1975. Even though only 31, his reaction had been to go on a pub crawl for several weeks – not to drown his sorrows, but to make notes in preparation for a career as a landlord. Yet before he got his name above the door, Southampton manager Lawrie McMenemy gave him the chance to continue his playing career. By the time the Saints began their FA Cup campaign early in 1976, he'd become club captain.

At Wembley, Rodrigues was up against Gordon Hill, whose signing from Millwall had allowed Tommy Docherty to complete the attacking 4-4-2 formation that characterised Manchester United's exciting return to the First Division. It might have sounded crass, but Docherty spoke for the majority when he looked forward to United's semi-final meeting with Derby County by saying, 'This is the first time the FA Cup Final will have been played at Hillsborough.' Both teams were chasing Liverpool for the League title and it was two long-range goals by Hill that won the day. The first, a brilliant curling finish after a swift build-up showcased the best of Docherty's side. 'This match summed up Manchester United under the Doc for me,' said Lou Macari. 'Great football played on the deck at good pace with a pair of wingers causing havoc. Gordon Hill never played a better game in a red shirt.'[534]

At Wembley, United were almost as heavy favourites as Leeds had been three years earlier, although – unlike Sunderland – McMenemy's Southampton could boast a handful of players with experience at the highest level. England forward Mick Channon was partnered by Peter Osgood, scorer in every FA Cup round in 1970, and their midfield support came from Scotland international Jim McCalliog, who had scored in a final for Sheffield Wednesday and twice been sold by Docherty. McMenemy, the former guardsman, would make a feature of signing established England players – the likes of Alan Ball, Mick Mills, Peter Shilton and Dave Watson would follow – and was unafraid of the challenges it presented. According to David Peach, 'Lawrie had to prove that signing these players wasn't just for fun. But he was a great man manager and he got respect from those players. Players like Osgood and Ball came, a bit of devilment in them, and they just needed a little bit of slack that they probably didn't get in other places. He gave them that and they would cross rivers for him.'[535]

McMenemy recalled that 'Ossie was irritating me' and suggested, 'He did not feel he fitted into second-tier football and in that I agreed with him … there was more than a touch of the diva about him.' But unlike some managers confronted with the mavericks of the period, he added with acceptance, 'You get that with players who are different because they possess outstanding talent and know it.'[536]

United knew it, too. 'When you looked at the Southampton team you saw a lot of good players,' said defender Brian Greenhoff. 'As a defender, you know you're going to have a hard game against Osgood and Channon. We did think that if we got into them for 15 minutes and scored we would win, but the longer the game goes on you get nervous about it. It only takes one deflected shot.'[537] Or even one controversial decision.

In a game that was a colourful triumph for the emerging Admiral sportswear firm – who kitted out both teams – referee Clive Thomas ruled that the yellow shirt of Bobby Stokes was in an onside position when, seven minutes from time, he latched on to a bouncing ball and beat Alex Stepney from the edge of the penalty area. United could complain all they liked but they'd hardly deserved to win the game. Hill had been so subdued by Rodrigues that he'd been taken off midway through the second half. 'I was having an absolute nightmare,' he admitted. 'They held the card up with my number and I looked at the boss and said, "Me?" and he said, "No, all fucking 11 of you!" Even then he was able to have a joke.'[538]

A joke that went too far provided a fatal footnote to the 1976 FA Cup campaign for Allison. At the end of one day's training, a Rolls-Royce pulled up and out stepped Fiona Richmond, star of Britain's mid-1970s soft-porn film industry. As the Palace players sunk into their communal bath they were shocked to find Allison and Richmond stripping off to join them, with a photographer on hand to capture the moment. Allison would explain that Richmond had said, 'Do you mind if I get in?' and he'd replied 'Yeah, why not?' – an inexplicable response for a manager with an eye on his reputation and career, but totally in keeping with the character of Big Mal. The Palace board had seen enough. After a series of clashes over Allison's reluctance to sell

Taylor, there was now an FA disrepute charge to face. Having failed to make himself unsackable by winning the Cup, Allison was gone.

Docherty, meanwhile, created a happier next chapter. Having gone around the Wembley dressing-room telling his players they would win the trophy the next year, he repeated his promise to 20,000 fans in Albert Square the following day. 'It was tongue in cheek,' Docherty admitted. 'That was hope rather than expectation. But I felt I had to say it. Some people probably thought, "Big mouth twat."'[539] Steve Coppell remembered thinking, 'Blimey, fancy putting that expectation on us, but Doc made a commitment and the crowd loved it.'[540] Sure enough, a year later Manchester United beat Liverpool 2-1 at Wembley and Docherty was about to hit the front pages *(see next chapter).*

The smallest town to boast an FA Cup winner in the 1970s was Ipswich, whose team were champions in the early 1960s and spent the next decade mounting a steady climb back towards the top of the table. Ironically, that expedition stalled in 1977-78. Starting with 1972-73, they had finished fourth, fourth, third, sixth and third in consecutive seasons. Manager Bobby Robson admitted that 'it may be strange to see Ipswich sitting up there with Leeds and Liverpool' but, without repeating Alf Ramsey's out-of-the-blue title success of 1961-62, they achieved a consistency that made it a surprise when they suddenly plummeted down the table again.

Robson cited a 3-3 draw at Leeds in August 1972 as one of the matches that persuaded his players that they belonged in elevated circles and proved a point to the football world. 'It does annoy me to keep hearing that Ipswich are in the backwaters,' he said. 'That sort of publicity has been very unfair to the club.'[541] It meant, he believed, that he had to rely even more on developing young players in order to make up for the stars' reluctance to move to Portman Road, despite the support of an ambitious board under chairman John Cobbold. In the summer of 1971, even Arsenal's out-of-favour midfielder Jon Sammels had declined a move to his hometown team and chosen Leicester instead. 'We have our £100-a-week players, our ground and our facilities,' Robson had said after succeeding Bill McGarry in 1969.

'Certainly, no player need be afraid of coming to Ipswich and getting less in any way than he might elsewhere.'[542]

Yet Robson's time at Ipswich was, by necessity, characterised by bargain purchases and bringing through players from a development system that earned them the FA Youth Cup in 1973 and 1975. Men such as Scots John Wark, converted from full-back to midfield, and George Burley, a stylish right-back; energetic England midfielder Brian Talbot; and Kevin Beattie, the powerful and skilful defender who put Robson in mind of Duncan Edwards. 'It was distressing to me when Beattie had to retire because of his knee injury,' Robson said. 'I ranked him as the finest player ever produced by Ipswich, one of the best British players in post-war British football. He had so much pace and power, and in the air there was no one in the world to match him.'[543] Leading them was defender Mick Mills, who had moved east when Portsmouth scrapped their youth system.

And while Ramsey's Ipswich, for all their strategic pragmatism, were never that easy on the eye, the rise of Robson's team was welcomed by those who longed for the return of greater ascetics. An attacking midfielder capped 20 times by England, Robson saw his team evolve from the scrappy style that ensured First Division survival in his early years to an eye-pleasing team who moved forward with pace and intent. At the end of the 1973-74 season, *Foul* magazine predicted, 'Ipswich look two years away from being the most dominating side in the game. And if they make it, and establish this domination, it will represent a complete turn of the tide back to skilful football rather than the negativity which has been prevalent since the mid-Sixties.'[544]

Along with the consistency of performance and elevation of players into international football, a sign of Ipswich's progress was when, in November 1976, they won a battle for one of the game's hottest properties, Plymouth Argyle centre-forward Paul Mariner, who was signed in an exchange deal worth £220,000. Mariner took the No.9 shirt that had previously belonged to David Johnson, an intelligent player considered by Robson to have been one of his best acquisitions when he arrived from Everton. Johnson had now gone back to

Merseyside to join champions Liverpool, but Robson described his replacement as another 'young, brave, smart' player.[545]

Such was Mariner's impact that by the spring of 1977, his strike partner, Trevor Whymark – who had scored four goals against West Bromwich Albion in Mariner's second game – was talking credibly about the club's title challenge and had the confidence to suggest, 'I don't rate Liverpool as the biggest danger to us. I still have a sneaky feeling that Manchester City will be the team who run us closest.'[546] Four defeats in their final six matches put paid to that, but it was a surprise when Ipswich stumbled through the next League campaign, winning only one match away from Portman Road. Yet it was a season that would go down in club history, thanks to an FA Cup run that reached the semi-final stage before they encountered another top-flight team in West Bromwich Albion. Mariner scored seven goals, including a hat-trick at Millwall, in helping his team to the last four.

Talbot's brave diving header gave his team the lead at Highbury after eight minutes, an act that left both the scorer and Albion skipper John Wile bloodied with head wounds. While Talbot was stitched and substituted, Wile played on with a red-stained bandage, but was unable to prevent Mills adding a second goal in a goalmouth scramble. Ipswich were on their way to a 3-1 victory and their first Cup final appearance.

Facing them would be an Arsenal team in its second season under Terry Neill's management and featuring some of the most significant names of the footballing decade. Most notably, Pat Jennings had followed his manager's path across north London after Tottenham's relegation, an unthinkable development that Jennings's reputation at White Hart Lane would survive, making him a rare beloved figure on both sides of that divide. 'I would have been willing to stay on,' he said after leaving Spurs for a four-year contract at Arsenal. 'The prospect of the Second Division didn't frighten me.' Yet at 32 and with Spurs believing Barry Daines to be a worthy successor, Jennings was sold for £45,000. Ironically, it could have been Ipswich that he joined, preferring a move that allowed him to stay in his home in the Hertfordshire town of Hoddesdon. Declaring himself 'fit and healthy' and 'sure I can last the pace',[547] Jennings would end up playing for Arsenal for eight years and appearing in two World Cups for Northern Ireland.

His new team-mates included Alan Hudson, hitting a rich vein of form in the second half of the season after struggling to settle following his transfer from Stoke, and Malcolm Macdonald, whose £333,333 transfer from Newcastle had marked Neill's arrival at Highbury after Bertie Mee's retirement in the summer of 1976. With the languid left feet of Liam Brady and Graham Rix helping Macdonald to 26 goals during the season, Arsenal advanced to the final during a period of attacking football that was barely recognisable to those who identified them with the functional methods of the Double winners and expected more of the same after Don Howe's return as first-team coach. Once again, Wembley featured a heavy favourite.

Macdonald had scored five goals in a single Wembley game for England after his disappointing performance for Newcastle in the 1974 final, yet those hoping for him to repeat such feats on this occasion might have found warning signs in his retrospective comments about that previous FA Cup Final experience. Sounding like a man daunted rather than excited by the occasion, he'd spoken a year earlier about the pressure that followed victory in the semi-final and the 'agony' of the bus ride to Wembley. 'No other word can sum up the feeling,' he said. 'Bad jokes, badly played card hands, loud and unreal laughter. To the ultra-sensitive person, the whole scene is almost nightmarish.' He went on to describe 'the dreaded knock' on the dressing-room door, the 'long and draining wait' for kick-off and 'iron butterflies'.[548] Doubtless that was an experience shared by many players over many years, but his honesty hardly inspired confidence that he would continue his record of scoring in every round of the competition.

Neill had his own worries – about the fitness of forward Alan Sunderland, Brady and Macdonald, whose knees were close to bringing his career to a premature end – and made the mistake of sharing his nerves with his players. The Gunners camp, meanwhile, felt that Robson was making too much of his own injury concerns, specifically around his beloved Beattie and defensive partner Allan Hunter. Neill concluded that 'Bobby can be a moaner at times'.[549]

Robson was reluctantly forced to admit that there was no place for his South African-born England midfielder Colin Viljoen, who had been injured for three months. Hoping to play him at Wembley, Robson brought him back for the last game before the final, at Aston Villa, moving Talbot to the right as part of a reshuffle. 'I knew the players didn't like Viljoen, but I failed to sense how deep their resentment had become about his attitude,' Robson would write, recalling a 6-1 defeat and his belief that Talbot was unhappy about being displaced. Angry and powerless, Robson felt he had to leave Viljoen out of his Wembley line-up, with Talbot back on the left, Wark in the centre and Roger Osborne recalled on the right of the midfield three. Robson at least felt that the episode had 'cleared the air'.[550]

After all that, it was Arsenal who looked disjointed and afraid of their status as favourites. Ipswich were dominant enough for Macdonald to admit they could have won by five goals. 'Their team outplayed, outran and outwitted mighty Arsenal in a triumph for the good things that football these days tends to forget,' said *The Times*. Blond forward David Geddis, playing instead of the injured Whymark, stretched the Arsenal defence by following instructions to drift out to the right. So impressive was he that even guest of honour Margaret Thatcher singled him out in a radio interview, although – taking her cue from the match programme – she identified him as Whymark. Meanwhile, Mariner tormented Wille Young, the giant accident-prone cult hero of the North Bank. The surprise was that it was only when Young failed to clear the ball 13 minutes from time that Ipswich eventually scored through Osborne. Such were the exertions of his celebration and his efforts in subduing Brady that Osborne – a Suffolk boy who had 11 close family members in the stands – was immediately substituted after almost fainting under a pile of happy team-mates.

In the manner of Docherty, Neill attempted to lift his men by assuring them they would return next year. And once they had survived an epic five-match third-round tie against Sheffield Wednesday,[§] they

§ Writing in his *Diaries 1969-1979: The Python Years*, Sheffield-born Michael Palin recalled the series of matches as a 'golden ring of light' during a winter of terrible weather and industrial chaos.

did indeed fight their way back. Opposing them at Wembley were Manchester United, led by Dave Sexton, winner of the decade's first final and successor to Docherty. Arsenal now had Talbot in their team and Frank Stapleton as undisputed leader of the attack with Macdonald crocked. They each scored a first-half goal to give their team a lead they still held with 85 minutes played. To most observers it appeared that Neill had sent on substitute Steve Walford in place of midfield worker David Price in order to give him the experience of playing in the final, although Neill would insist, 'That was untrue. David was fading fast.'[551]

And then 'The Five-Minute Final' began. It started with Gordon McQueen swinging a lazy left boot at the ball after Arsenal failed to deal with a free-kick into the box. And then, a minute later, Coppell knocked a hopeful pass forward to Sammy McIlroy on the right edge of the penalty area. 'And McIlroy's through,' Motson told BBC viewers, his voice rising in excitement as yellow-shirted David O'Leary hit the floor. 'McIlroy's through,' he repeated as United's long-serving Irishman cut inside Walford. 'And McIlroy,' he continued, pausing as a left-foot shot slid under Jennings, 'has done it!'

With United getting substitute Brian Greenhoff ready to play a role in extra-time, PFA Player of the Year Brady, as influential in this game as he had been disappointing a year earlier, put his head down and ran at the United defence. He nudged the ball to his left; Rix connected with a clipped cross just before two United defenders could get to him; and the ball dipped into the six-yard box just beyond the far post, where Sunderland stuck out a leg to score. United's players dropped to their knees, Sunderland sprinted away with eyes closed and team-mates in pursuit, and Talbot was caught by the cameras offering thanks to the heavens.

The FA Cup had signed off for the decade in the way it had begun: a good old north versus south ding-dong at Wembley, with high drama, heroes and heartbreak. And, this time, not a horse's hoofmark to be seen.

11

ENGLAND'S DREAMING

Where are we? Rock bottom. Tragedies? We got 'em.
Remedy? Why don't we rub it out and start it again?

'Rock Bottom', Lynsey De Paul and Mike Moran
(Warner/Chappell Music Ltd, 1977)

BETRAYAL. THE word hung over the early months of the summer of 1977 as clearly as if the letters had been spelled out in the bunting that fluttered above England's streets in celebration of Queen Elizabeth's Silver Jubilee. First, it had been Tony Greig's revelation in early May that he had been using his position as captain of the nation's cricket team to recruit players for Australian businessman Kerry Packer, who was setting up a series of games in direct opposition to established Test matches. Then Tommy Docherty, in the days after leading Manchester United to victory in the FA Cup Final, was removed from his role at Old Trafford after admitting that he and Mary Brown, the wife of the club physiotherapist, had an affair. Before long, the Sex Pistols, a symbol to many of all that was wrong with modern society, hijacked the royal celebrations by taking 'God Save The Queen' up the UK singles charts – despite the record being banned by the BBC*

* While the *NME* recorded the Sex Pistols at No.1, the BBC's charts, compiled by the British Market Research Bureau, had the song stuck behind Rod Stewart at No.2. While most in the industry seemed to acknowledge that some kind of fix was taking place, the official reason offered by the BMRB was that sales in Virgin stores of a record released on the Virgin record label could not be counted.

– and got themselves arrested on the official Jubilee Bank Holiday for an unauthorised performance on a Thames riverboat called the *Queen Elizabeth*.

Yet the outrage of Lord's, the titillation of the tabloid readers and the horror felt by royalists was nothing compared to the national indignation that erupted when Don Revie, the man entrusted with making England a great and respected football power again, announced he was buggering off to the desert. He was abandoning ship midway through a World Cup qualifying campaign for a small fortune in petro-dollars. For God's sake, the only two previous men to have held the role permanently were either knights of the realm (Alf Ramsey) or about to be made one (Walter Winterbottom in 1978). Revie seemed destined to go down in history as a snivelling traitor.

This was not the ending that had been envisaged three years earlier. While Harold Wilson's minority Labour government had spent 1974 hunting the corridors of Westminster to find the support it needed to remain in power, there had been few people around football – apart from the Brian Clough fan club – who were not fully behind the FA's decision to name the manager of the reigning League champions to take charge of the England team. After all, things had not worked out too badly when Ramsey had been given the national job on the strength of his own First Division title.

Revie appeared a sound appointment; his stock never higher. Having been close to signing a reported £30,000-a-year deal with Everton a year earlier,† he'd remained at Leeds to guide them to their second title. Their performance made a mockery of the article entitled 'Will Leeds Struggle Next Season?' that appeared in *Shoot!* in late summer, when it was suggested 'there's widespread feeling that Leeds have now reached the stage where they can only go one way – down'. For all of Clough's snarky comments, perhaps even driven by them, Leeds had done it in some style, especially during an unbeaten 29-game start to the League season, one short of what was then a record. Two goals up at Stoke

† Revie had been so close to joining Everton that reports of his anticipated salary prompted Labour MP Dennis Skinner to ask in the House of Commons whether the Pay Board would investigate under the terms of the 1972 Pay and Prices Code, which forbade anyone taking a job being paid more than the previous incumbent.

City, they were beaten 3-2, but maintained an eight-point advantage over Liverpool. Three successive defeats, including 4-1 at home against Burnley, narrowed the gap and fed Revie's inbuilt insecurity. 'The terrible thought had crossed my mind,' he admitted, 'that we might miss out again in the final furlong.'[552] Yet Leeds had enough in hand to withstand the Anfield challenge and take the title by five points.

'I think we are playing better now than we have ever done,' Billy Bremner said early in the season. 'We're entertaining the public. We have decided to attack from the start.'[553] The Leeds captain also appeared most proud that his team were apparently shedding their reputation for surliness on the field. 'I can see now what people were getting at when they complained about dissent,' he said. 'I know that I was perhaps the biggest culprit … I've talked to one or two players at other clubs this season and they all seem to agree with me – now that Leeds United have cut out dissent completely, we're much better for it.'[554] While subsequent events would prove that Bremner had not experienced a behavioural epiphany, a more clean-cut Leeds image did their manager no harm when suitable candidates for the England job were assessed.

Having been searching for three years for a replacement for Jack Charlton – who was now managing Middlesbrough to the Second Division title – the most significant part of the team's evolution was the establishment of blond former St Mirren stopper Gordon McQueen, bought for £40,000. Previously in his search for a long-term successor to Charlton, Revie had tried Sutton United centre-half John Faulkner, whom he signed after a 6-0 FA Cup win over the Isthmian League team in 1970. Faulkner scored an own goal in his first game for the club and broke his kneecap in his second before moving on to Luton Town. Then there was ex-Huddersfield Town man Roy Ellam, who only ever seemed like a stop-gap. When Charlton was injured for much of the 1972-73 season it was Madeley who filled in. Now Revie was able to say of McQueen, 'I waited 18 months to sign him and it was worth every minute.'[555]

Madeley's role had now become to fill the No.11 shirt of Eddie Gray, injured for most of the season. Meanwhile, Johnny Giles was absent for months and Terry Cooper for the entire season, his place taken by another ex-Huddersfield man, Trevor Cherry. Both Allan Clarke and Mick Jones missed a significant number of matches, allowing another young Scot, centre-forward Joe Jordan, to claim a place. It was why Revie called it 'the greatest season the club has ever had. Even for me who knows their character so well, it has been amazing they have been able to soldier on.'

Revie for once had no other competitions to fatigue his players at the business end of the League season. 'The problem was that while Don would say he had 16 internationals in his squad, the reality was he wanted to play the same 11 every week,' said Peter Lorimer.[556] Revie had finally taken a fatalistic approach in the UEFA Cup, notably against Hibernian in the second round, when he followed a 0-0 home draw by sending out the inexperienced John Shaw to play in goal in the second leg. Shaw played so well that Revie had to substitute him at half-time, but replacement Glan Letheren was not to be beaten either. As the penalty shoot-out began, Revie told his men, 'You might as well win it now. We'll just have to go out in the next round.'[557] Leeds duly lost to Vitoria Setubal, with Revie banned from dressing-room and touchline for being on the field illegally during the Hibs shoot-out. It seemed to be no coincidence that the last time Leeds had failed to reach a major final was in their previous championship season of 1968-69.

It was the triumphs rather than the collapses that the Football Association weighed up when naming Revie national manager, a post he took with the intent to 'build England on club lines'. As well as an ambition to replicate the close-knit environment of Elland Road, he wanted to see greater links between the various age-group England teams, with a common playing style and shared objectives. He also wanted to break down the kind of barriers he had erected in his previous role. 'I am paid by Leeds United to get results,' he'd said in 1972. 'I would like to help Alf Ramsey, but I always put Leeds first.'[558] Admitting that 'nobody had been more guilty' of prioritising club over country, he now hoped for greater cooperation from managers.

Revie named Les Cocker, his long-time assistant at Leeds, to help with the coaching – a role he had fulfilled under Ramsey – and appointed Arsenal's Fred Street as physiotherapist. 'I was one of the first in the game to be fully qualified to do the job,' Street explained. 'At that time, it was still largely ex-players who were acting as old-fashioned sponge men.' Revie had worked with Cocker long enough to recognise a passion that could be a liability in international football. 'Les was someone he could trust,' Street continued. 'But Don explained that they had been playing in Europe in a semi-final and there was a fracas on the pitch. Les ran on the field and he was getting in the players' faces, wanting to sort them out.' Knowing that an unfavourable referee's report about the incident could have landed the team in trouble, Revie told Street, 'I picked you because you don't get involved. You don't get emotional and let that affect the way you do your job. You are not going to tell me whether you think a player is playing well or badly.'[559]

Another element being transplanted to Lancaster Gate from Elland Road was a greater commercial focus. Admiral, in whose kit Leeds had just won the championship, would now be producing England's uniform, complete with red and blue trim on the previously all-white shirts; red and white stripes down the slightly lighter blue shorts; and the company name emblazoned across the team's blue training tops. The exact extent of the new manager's involvement in brokering the deal was never fully revealed, although secretary Ted Croker was unaware of Revie having benefitted personally. The FA were waking up to the value of the England brand anyway, but it is difficult to imagine such a happy arrangement had Ramsey still been in charge. For Revie, putting aside financial issues, it meant that his England had a clear identity of its own.

Revie's desire to have the players share in the FA's greater fortune became, unfairly, another stick with which to beat him once his financially-driven exit from the role came to pass. The players, who had previously been paid £60 per match, were to get a £100 appearance fee (including, at Revie's insistence, non-playing substitutes), plus £200 for a win or £100 for a draw. There were reports of a potential £6,000 per man for winning the forthcoming European Championship and £2,000 each just for qualifying for the finals. 'Don was a great one for getting everyone the same,' said Street, who even recalled him demanding additional gifts from opposition football associations if they handed out, say, 22 of a certain item. 'We have 30 players and staff,' Revie would inform them.[560]

Emlyn Hughes, who would end up with plenty of reasons for his low opinion of Revie, said a couple of decades later, 'If you were picked for England, you'd pay three million quid to play for your country. [Don] said, "I have got you three hundred quid, lads." I've looked at Ballie and Ballie has looked at me and I've gone, "I don't believe what he has just said." And I think he was virtually money-ruled.'[561]

A more reasonable response was that of Stan Bowles, who 'respected Don most of all because he was the first manager to make sure England internationals got paid a decent amount of appearance money'. Bowles recalled responding to Hughes's comment that 'I don't need to be paid a penny' by telling him, 'In that case, Emlyn, I'll have yours.'[562]

Revie, already missing daily contact with players and in the knowledge that his first game was not until the end of October, convened an overnight get-together of 81 potential England men in Manchester on 21 September. It proved memorable only to those for whom it would be the closest they ever got to representing their country – 47 of them never played under Revie. The event broke up with Revie declaring that 'these players have left here today with the promise that they will apply themselves to improving our game', but Bowles recalled, 'The general consensus was that it was a waste of time.'[563] The QPR man instead made the most of visiting his former hometown and ended up being suspended by his club for two weeks for failing to make it back in time for training.

According to Frank Worthington, Revie had taken him, Bowles, Alan Hudson and Tony Currie to one side to tell them that they had plenty of skill 'but there was something missing'. Worthington continued, 'His intentions were crystal clear. In effect it was two fingers to skill and up the workhorses.'[564]

England were considered strong favourites to win a European Championship quarter-final place from a qualifying group that matched them with Czechoslovakia, Portugal and Cyprus. The Czechs, considered the strongest opposition, provided Revie's first opponents. The game represented more than just the start of a new managerial era. The sport, and the country, needed something to lift it from the malaise into which it had descended in the past year. 'It appeared that the nation had lost faith in itself,' wrote historian Alwyn W. Turner. 'The events of the winter of 1973-74 and the background to them, were so traumatic that they had shaken confidence in the future of Britain, and there was a fear that disaster still lurked around the corner, a suspicion of crisis postponed.'[565]

On the football front, a party of 20 English managers had attended the final rounds of the World Cup in West Germany. Wolverhampton Wanderers' Bill McGarry felt he'd learned little because 'the continentals have always been able to control and pass better than us … our technique simply isn't good enough'.

Even as big an optimist as Alan Ball was forced to speak for the realistic majority. 'There is an air of depression hanging over the game right now, with too many bad things and not enough good things happening. Our soccer needs a shot in the arm and a win over the Czechs is just the right medicine,' he wrote in his weekly missive to the nation. 'Some people have lost interest in the game and it is up to the players to rekindle it.'[566]

Revie's first England starting line-up read: Clemence – Madeley, Watson, Hunter, Hughes – Dobson, Bell, Francis – Keegan, Worthington, Channon. It meant that only five players survived from Alf Ramsey's final competitive match a year earlier. Hughes retained the captaincy he had held under Mercer, despite a rebuke from the interim manager for 'doing exactly what I had told the players not to do' when he became involved in a scuffle during the friendly against Argentina.

As the players took the field, physiotherapist Street had his first experience of Revie's superstitions. 'Don had done all the preparation and analysis,' he said, 'and we had "Land of Hope and Glory" playing, which Don brought in. He came up to my side as we walked round the track and said, "We'll be all right, Fred. I've got my lucky suit on." I said, "We've done all this preparation and training and you've got the lucky suit on? Why didn't we just turn up now?"'[567]

It needed the second-half introduction of Trevor Brooking and Dave Thomas to break the deadlock, with Channon heading in a cross from Thomas. Bell then scored twice with typically well-timed runs into the box to meet deliveries from Channon. England's 3-0 win had to share the headlines with Muhammad Ali, who in the early hours had regained the world heavyweight title by knocking out George Foreman in Zaire, and Geoffrey Green warned in *The Times*, 'Unlike Muhammad Ali they still have some way to go before recapturing their football crown.'

Kevin Keegan, demonstrating the emotional manner that he would carry into his managerial career, was quick to declare that the victory 'flashed a warning to the world that England under new manager Don Revie are on their way back to greatness. He's completely won me over. In fact, I'd put him on a par with Shanks.' Big words on the evidence of 90 minutes. But even Revie was not convinced. Looking around for the likes of Bremner and Giles in his midfield, he admitted to himself, 'We haven't got the players.'[568] A goalless draw three weeks later at home to Portugal exposed his worst fears.

Inactivity is the biggest enemy of many international managers. Tommy Docherty, who resorted to feeding the pigeons outside his office at Scottish FA headquarters, admitted he might even have turned down Manchester United if not for the long periods without matches. Revie had to wait almost four months for another match. The consistently frantic schedule of club management at his overworked Leeds had protected him from some of the more damaging elements of his own personality; the caution, the self-doubt, the superstition bordering on paranoia. But he had no Sunday or Monday matches to fill his diary as modern managers do; and the satellite-age opportunity to watch overseas games from Milan to Monterrey was still years away. With weeks to brood, he had little else to do than second-guess his strategies, rethink his selections and build up his dossiers on opponents to almost unmanageable proportions.

A vehicle of ridicule once his England reign had gone south – or, more accurately, east – the documents that he distributed among his squad were used by some as scorepads for their card games. Yet, Revie was, in effect, an early adopter of modern methods of preparation. He simply had to use reams of paper instead of having his players fire up their iPads. Colin Todd, who as a manager would make use of any available computerised analysis tool, recalled Revie as thorough rather than obsessive, an opinion shared by Keegan, who said, 'Imagine the criticism if he didn't do his homework. It's the manager's business to know who we will be up against and what we will be up against.'[569]

The opposing view was expressed by Trevor Brooking, who felt that the dossiers 'cast us in the position of having to worry about the opposition and it may have proved psychologically harmful for some players' – not a glowing endorsement of the flexibility of thought of England's leading professionals of the age.[570]

Revie's free time was also thought to have contributed to him listening too much to uninvited opinions about selection. Several of those who played for Revie believed they were picked either so that the manager could satisfy newspaper critics, or for the express purpose of failing so that Revie could silence the amateur selectors. Newcastle United centre-forward Malcolm Macdonald, who had failed to score in seven previous England appearances, was greeted by Revie before the home friendly against world champions West Germany in March 1975 with the information that he'd been chosen because of media pressure. 'If you don't score I'll never pick you again,' he was told.[571]

Revie sprang another surprise for that match by selecting Alan Hudson, who had recovered from the shock of exchanging the King's Road for the Potteries and was playing out of his skin for a Stoke City side mounting a serious title challenge. 'When I arrived in Stoke it was pouring with rain and blowing a gale – not exactly picture postcard stuff,' he admitted, before realising the need to 'knuckle down and show I could play'.[572] Enjoying the free role he had been given by Tony Waddington, Hudson was highlighted by *Titbits* as a man 'set to become captain of the full England side one day'.[573] The excitable celebrity and lifestyle magazine was not known for its insightful football analysis, but at least Hudson would now win a first England cap five years after being named in Ramsey's 40-man World Cup squad. Convinced that Revie was prejudiced against players from the south, especially those with a Chelsea connection, he recalled, 'I always said Revie put me in against the Germans hoping I would fail.'[574]

Hudson did anything but. Looking at home in his new environment, he, Colin Bell and Alan Ball, recalled as captain, dominated the middle of the field to the extent that German captain Franz Beckenbauer admitted, '[England] were a revelation, playing a new and exciting style that we were not prepared for.' Bell turned home a 27th-minute free-kick from Hudson, who, Ball said, 'had as good an international debut as I have ever seen'. After 66 minutes, Ball received a quickly-taken free-kick and crossed from the right for Macdonald to head home. Keegan clipped the crossbar with the last action of a memorable match, although neither the impressive Hudson nor the goal-scoring Macdonald received a word of praise from Revie.

When Cyprus arrived for their European Championship qualifier at Wembley a month later, Macdonald was again given a score-or-else ultimatum. Ball announced to team-mates, 'Tonight, this man is going to break score six', telling Macdonald to 'keep making your runs and leave the rest to us'.[575] Ball was one out. Macdonald had to settle for five goals in a 5-0 victory.

DANCING WITH THE CAPTAIN

FLETCHER: A captain, Godber, has to possess certain attributes which set him apart from the rest of his team. That is why I have chosen Light Fingered Larry.

GODBER: Urquart? What attributes has he got?

FLETCHER: 'Alf an ounce of snout, which he's now given to me, all right?

***Porridge* (Dick Clement and Ian La Frenais; Black Lion Films/Witzend Productions, 1979)**

Spoilt by the unique bond he'd enjoyed with Bremner, Revie had been eager to find someone to play that same role of on-field proxy. Hughes, he'd decided after two games, wasn't that man and sent him a letter telling him so rather than informing him in person. Ball, however, was a man cast from the same clay as Bremner, right down to the red hair and fiery nature. Suspension and injuries meant it had been two years since he'd been an England starter, but when Revie picked him to face West Germany he also informed him he would be captain.

Ball's last major act for England had been to get himself sent off in a World Cup game, which meant he was not everyone's idea of the shining example the England captain was expected to be. Walter Johnson, MP for Derby South, raised it as a matter of national concern in the House of Commons. Never mind the industrial disputes, IRA bombs, soaring inflation or sinking pound, what was Revie doing putting his faith in a man Ramsey had pointedly ignored for the captaincy during Bobby Moore's absences?

If, as Alwyn W. Turner would remark, Revie's was 'an appointment that seemed somehow symbolic of a coarsening of public life in Britain',[576] then Ball's emergence as captain belonged, in the opinion of many, in the same category. Days after his appointment, he admitted, 'As a professional I must condone rugby tackles and even though they might not admit it in public, other players will agree with me. It's dog eat dog and I would expect a team-mate to bring down an opponent if he was in a goal-scoring position.'[577]

It was not the kind of comment that those at polite dinner parties expected of someone whose role was supposed to be to uphold traditional English values of fair play and sportsmanship. It was, however, the kind of brutal honesty the public saw demonstrated on a weekly basis. Tom Stoppard's character McKendrick addressed it in the play *Professional Foul*, mocking a group of England footballers in a foreign hotel with, 'Roy here is sensitive because he gave away a penalty today by a deliberate foul. To stop a certain goal, he hacked a chap down. After all, a penalty might be saved, broken legs are quite rare … No, no, no, it's perfectly all right. You were simply adopting the utilitarian values of the game for the good of the side.'[578]

After two victories in two games, Ball led the team again in Cyprus. Without the injured Hudson, whose England career was now over, they won by a single goal and then got the Home International Championship off to a stuttering start with draws against Northern Ireland and Wales. In light of the ongoing Troubles, the FA had agreed only a month previously to fulfil the fixture in Belfast. The game passed without incident, but what happened in its aftermath created headlines, Keegan abandoning the England camp after being omitted for the Wales game. He had thought he was being restricted to away games, where work-rate was paramount, and being sacrificed in home matches, where the forwards would have more freedom. Not for the first or last time, Revie's communication was at fault, having failed to explain to Keegan that he was simply being rested for one game to give someone else an opportunity. For all the praise he received from his Leeds players for his caring and thoughtful nature, Revie seemed to find the England environment less conducive to effective discourse with his men.

He did, however, visit one Liverpool player prior to the Wales game. 'I am not picking you for tomorrow's game and I will not be needing you in future,' he told a stunned Hughes. 'I'm going to build around certain players. You are not one of them.'[579] Inevitably, Revie would end up changing his mind.

Keegan was back in the team against Scotland at Wembley, with no hard feelings from Revie, who had eventually phoned him, or from skipper Ball, who 'took the mickey and said, "Welcome back, we didn't miss you."'[580] The usual hordes of travelling Scottish fans were stunned by two England goals inside the first six minutes; a shot on the run by Gerry Francis and a header from Kevin Beattie, the powerful centre-half Revie favoured at left-back. Bell and Francis advanced from midfield to fire in the third and fourth goals either side of a Scotland penalty just before half-time and Ipswich's David Johnson, who'd scored twice against Wales, completed a 5-1 thumping that sent England fans into the summer with dreams of a bright future.

By the time the new season came around, Ball, despite being in dispute with Arsenal, had reason to think he would be at the forefront of making those dreams come true. Instead, he awoke one August morning to a telephone call from a reporter asking for his reaction to being dropped. Once again, Revie's least concern in imparting the news had been the man immediately affected. He had allowed word to get to the press before a letter – which he did not even bother to sign – arrived on Ball's doorstep, informing him, 'I have not selected you for the Squad for the Switzerland match, and I will be making Gerry Francis captain. I have not discarded you completely, and I only hope that you will, if recalled for any special match, play for me.' Revie signed off with, 'I am letting you know first the complete position.' Of course, he was doing no such thing. He'd even acknowledged as much by expressing the hope that his letter arrived before the morning papers.

'I felt that Ball was out too soon,' said Brooking. 'He was still one of the top midfield players in the country. Maybe it was a personality clash. Hudson, too, had gone.'[581] Even Francis, made captain after only four games for his country, was uncomfortable over the jettisoning of a player who was only 30 and would still be playing in the First Division seven years later. 'His ability, his enthusiasm, his one-touch football was outstanding,' he recalled. 'He was obviously a very confident, experienced international. I don't think people realise the pressure on you when you play for England, so somebody like Alan was really important because he had been there, seen it, done it and won the World Cup. We had a good unbeaten run going and he was an excellent captain. To be honest, when I spoke to Don when I was made captain, I wasn't happy about Alan not being in the team.'[582]

To some, Francis seemed an unlikely choice for Revie to have made. One of Revie's old Leeds players, Trevor Cherry, recalled Francis telling team-mates to ignore a curfew imposed by the manager because 'we're grown men', something Bremner would never have countenanced. 'Gerry was not [Don]'s type of player and he certainly didn't believe in Don like Billy Bremner had,' Cherry explained. Yet QPR colleague Bowles recalled a ruthless streak that might well have appealed to Revie. 'Dave Sexton used to say that if you tried to intimidate Gerry, you'd wish you hadn't, because he would never let you get away with it.'[583]

England began the new season by beating Switzerland 2-1 in a friendly in Basle, a game that demonstrated the nervous nature of Revie. His cunning plan was to send out his men in unfamiliar squad numbers in the hope of confusing any Czechoslovakian spies; Channon and Keegan in 3 and 15 respectively, for example, while defenders Todd and Beattie wore 7 and 8.

In Bratislava, England faced the game that would determine their European Championship fate. A day after fog forced the original contest to be abandoned after 17 minutes – echoes of the famous *Whatever Happened to the Likely Lads?* episode – England went down 2-1 after Channon had given them the lead. While Czechoslovakia were criticised by the English press for their aggressive approach, Revie was accused of being reckless in having selected a three-man forward line and using Keegan in a midfield role that he rarely filled for Liverpool. Any lingering hopes of qualification disappeared in a 1-1 draw in Portugal three weeks later, a match that marked the end of Macdonald and Clarke's international careers. Bell's was also over, having ripped up his knee when tackled by Martin Buchan in a League Cup game against Manchester United a week earlier.‡

By the time England played again five months later in a match to mark the centenary of the Welsh FA, Revie was handing first caps to eight players, six of whom started the 2-1 victory, and had another new temporary captain, Keegan. On this occasion, Revie was hampered by injuries and a rearranged League game between Derby County and Stoke City, but it was this kind of selection that helped create the overriding impression of Revie's reign being one of uncertainty and inconsistency. When the teams met again two months later in Cardiff, there were three more debutants in a line-up featuring only three men who'd played more than two previous internationals.

‡ Despite an emotional return against Newcastle United on Boxing Day 1977, Bell was effectively finished as a professional footballer, formally retiring a further two years later.

By the time England had lost to Scotland in the climax of the Home Internationals – Clemence letting Kenny Dalglish's winning goal slip between his legs – and played Brazil and Italy in the summer's Bicentennial Tournament in the United States, Revie had awarded first caps to 15 players in 1976. 'The close team spirit he worked so hard to create was impossible to generate as the faces changed so much,' said Todd.[584] No wonder Brooking wished for a run of four or five games with the same line-up and Trevor Francis added, 'The players are judged very much on one performance and that can inhibit them.'[585] Macdonald called international selection 'the ultimate frightener' and said that 'to blow it all by playing badly on the night is that nightmare'.[586]

At least the performances in America were encouraging, a meritorious 1-0 defeat against Brazil and a 3-2 win against Italy after being two down at half-time in a game that saw Arsenal's Jimmy Rimmer and Manchester City's Joe Corrigan play 45 minutes each in goal. Channon, Revie's latest captain, scored two of the goals. After beating 'Team America' – a North American Soccer League all-star team that included Bobby Moore and Pelé – they began their World Cup qualifying campaign with a 4-1 win in Finland. Revie's satisfaction with that result was matched by his sense that he could feel the team bonding during their extended period together.

And, for all the fun his players might poke at the dossiers and the games of bingo – and for all the money some made by smirking about him in the press once he had gone – Revie, despite his frequent communication cock-ups, quietly demonstrated his protective attitude towards his players in Helsinki. After a party was staged by the FA in the team's hotel – with Elton John helping to provide the entertainment – Street had the task of making sure the players caught the bus to the airport the next morning. 'The doors of one of the rooms had been completely battered down,' he recalled. 'The two players were dead to the world. They'd been drunk and lost their keys and even though they could have got another, they just kicked the door in. The press were on the next floor.'

Street went to Revie's room and told him, 'We've got a problem. No names at the moment, unless we have to, but we have got a door kicked in.'

'Right,' Revie replied. 'See the manager of the hotel. Get it put right and see if they can lose the cost as "food" on the bill.'

The incident was never made public. 'You could argue that it was collusion,' added Street, 'but it solved the problem. I said to the players, "Look, it has been sorted out, but if it happens again Don will have to know. I am marking your cards."'[587]

The 1976-77 season would see a step forward in the England team's preparation, with the Football League agreeing to postpone First Division matches on the Saturday before World Cup qualifying games. Before the return match against Finland, though, was a friendly against the Republic of Ireland, a 1-1 draw memorable for providing Charlie George with the entire 65 minutes of his international career. Having enjoyed a successful first season at Derby County, including a European Cup hat-trick against Real Madrid, George had become the latest player promoted by the media for an international call-up. Starting in a position behind strikers Stuart Pearson and Keegan, George was told at half-time to play wide on the left. After 20 minutes of that, Revie replaced him with a proper winger, Gordon Hill. As Revie approached him to shake hands, George snarled 'fuck you' and disappeared towards the tunnel, never to be seen in the England team again. 'It was a farce,' George would recall. 'He played me, a right footer, on the left-hand side ... I felt I was picked to fail.'[588]

After Joe Royle's second-half goal earned a 2-1 win against Finland – but failed to prevent 92,000 Wembley fans chanting 'what a load of rubbish' – Revie went looking for another forward solution for the qualifier against Italy in Rome. This time he appeared to have been listening to the rave reviews for Bowles, who had been out of England favour while helping QPR come within minutes of beating Liverpool to the League title and had begun the new season by scoring nine goals in the first four games of their UEFA Cup campaign. The *Daily Mirror*'s suggestion that 'there is too much at stake to overlook his outstanding ability yet again' appeared to hit home. Another new face in the squad, Ipswich Town's Brian Talbot, also acknowledged that 'the press were very good to me'.[589] Keegan condemned the media for exerting pressure in such situations more than he blamed Revie for listening to them. 'I believe the press forced [Revie] to pick certain players,' he said. 'For instance, they had the flags out for Charlie George … the press boys dropped him quicker than they picked him up.'[590]

Recovering from flu, Bowles was given Royle's place in the starting line-up, Revie having been unimpressed with Pearson when Manchester United faced Italian opposition, Juventus, in Europe. No less surprising was the reappearance of Hughes as part of a back four who had never previously played together – Clement, McFarland, Hughes, Mills – and none of whom had played in England's previous match. The first inclination of Hughes when he discovered Revie on the end of the telephone line was to berate him for discarding him more than a year earlier.

Keegan had felt of Hughes that 'his attitude was not helping his cause' after being dropped by Revie and 'wondered if he had the character to right that disappointment'. He claimed, 'He was just crying about it, saying he should have been in the squad when I think he should have been doing something more positive about it.'[591] Now that Revie had seen enough to being him back, Hughes needed Bill Shankly to persuade him to bury the hatchet. Even so, the Liverpool captain would insist, 'I will never have any real respect for the man again. There has never been any explanation about why he had left me out or why, indeed, he brought me back.'[592]

What was the point of extended preparation time, it was tempting to wonder, when the manager was going into the most critical game of his reign with six changes from his previous line-up and no sense of a cogent strategy? His selection displayed the kind of inconsistency he would never have contemplated at Leeds; the product, it appeared, of a cluttered mind and too many empty days. Any sense of adventure indicated by the selection of Bowles was negated by the presence of two defenders, Cherry and Brian Greenhoff, in midfield.

A goal in each half didn't truly reflect the dominance of the Italians, whose own surprising nervousness prevented them inflicting a heavier defeat. The second goal, finished by the diving Roberto

Bettega, rounded off the kind of slick move that appeared well beyond England. That Revie said 'we played as well as could be expected' was a sad reflection on the national team. According to home captain Giacinto Facchetti, 'They were disorganised, confused, had only modest ability and, most surprising of all for a team from England, they seemed to have little heart for the battle.'

In *The Times*, Norman Fox pointed out, 'It has taken many people ten years to admit what was often obvious but stubbornly denied. England are not good enough to challenge the best teams in the world because they cannot stand comparison with those who fall short of the best, notably Italy.'

Such a verdict was emphasised early in 1977 when a brilliant Holland side, with Johan Cruyff and Johan Neeskens imperious, won 2-0 at Wembley. Bowles played again, his final England cap, and this time it was Paul Madeley and Greenhoff who were overwhelmed in the centre of midfield. 'The match was a disaster,' Brooking admitted. 'The Dutch concept of Total Football of creating space and then filling it with dramatic success was the opposite of [Revie's] rigid idea of how to play the game.'[593]

Dutch manager Jan Zwartkruis became the latest observer to condemn English football. 'They did a lot of huffing and puffing, but there was no thought behind their play,' he said. 'There was no brain behind all the bustle.' From within England's own managerial community, Manchester City's Tony Book said he didn't know how Revie could continue to pick skilful players who lacked consistency and sound temperament, while Leicester's Jimmy Bloomfield mourned a lack of technique.

Victories at home to Luxembourg in the World Cup a month later and in Northern Ireland in the opening game of the Home Internationals did little to raise spirits. England were made to wait until the final half-hour to score four of their five goals against a poor Luxembourg team, and needed an 86th-minute winner by Dennis Tueart in Belfast after going behind early on. And then they allowed Wales to secure their first victory at Wembley, a penalty by Leighton James giving them a deserved success.

A win against Scotland could provide a salve to England's wounds. But it was a day that would go down in the infamy of the decade for inflicting further scarring, both on Revie's reputation and on the Wembley pitch. As the final whistle sounded on the visitors' 2-1 victory, an estimated 10,000 blue and tartan-clad fans from a predominantly Scottish crowd charged the field. Once they had done with carrying off victorious captain Bruce Rioch, they set about tearing up pieces of turf as souvenirs, bringing down the goalposts and snapping the crossbar.

Among them was singer and arch-Scotland fan Rod Stewart, who was initially stopped by a policeman but allowed to enter the field when he recognised him. 'Great to feel the fabled turf beneath one's feet,' he recalled, 'although, to be honest, once you were on there, there wasn't a lot to do except bounce around with some blokes who were possibly even more pissed than you were. However, mid-bounce, I suddenly found myself grabbed and hoisted upwards, and the next I knew I was on somebody's shoulders, being carried aloft in triumph.'[594]

These were not exactly the images the nation wished to send around the world as it began its official week of celebration of the Queen's Silver Jubilee, although *The Times* was cruel in its put-down of England by describing Scotland's win as 'a hollow victory that was not worth the cost of the destruction of the pitch'.

Scotland striker Andy Gray, working for ITV because of an ankle injury, defended his countrymen, calling them 'the heart and soul of football'. He continued, 'What happened at Wembley was no more than a display of unashamed emotion,' and offered a conclusion that 'the only thing most of the Scots can hurt you with is kindness'.[595]

The FA had already announced plans to erect eight-foot fences around Wembley, but it appeared that it would take more than that to protect Revie from the inevitable consequences of four defeats in his past six matches. When, on the Monday after the game, bonfires were lit along the length of the country to celebrate Her Majesty's reign, it was surprising not to see effigies of the England manager thrown upon them.

Revie's biggest enemy came from within: the man who had been chairman of the FA since 1976, Sir Harold Thompson. A renowned chemist and Oxford University footballer, Thompson was described by journalist Brian Glanville as 'an Etonian buffoon … completely paranoid'.[596] He had taken against Ramsey when the England manager told him not to smoke his cigar while his players were eating breakfast, and had famously told Ramsey's successor, 'Revie, when I get you know you better I shall call you Don.' To which Revie replied, 'When I get to know you better I shall call you Thompson.'

WHEN TWO SEVENS CLASH

There's one thing you could never accuse Don Revie of – and that's being a quitter. So you can take it from SHOOT! that the England manager will never resign from his post.

***Shoot!* 17 March 1977**

As the English summer arrived, the punky reggae parties taking place in Brixton, Bristol and Birmingham were playing 'Two Sevens Clash', an album by Jamaican band Culture that drew on political activist and writer Marcus Garvey's prediction of chaotic events on 7 July 1977. In the end, despite many Jamaicans spending the day indoors, nothing bad happened, while in London the day was most notable for the premiere of the James Bond movie, *The Spy Who Loved Me*. The opening sequence had people on its feet in patriotic fervour when Bond (Roger Moore) was saved from plummeting to an early end by the opening of a Union Jack parachute.

Unknown to all but a handful of confidants, Revie spent the day working on a plan that he'd been hatching for a few weeks and which he would reveal five days later. It would create the kind of disorder that would have satisfied Garvey's prophecy.

England's footballers missed the street parties and parades that marked the Queen's 25 years on the throne; an achievement that would appear to have inspired some of the country's sporting endeavours as Virginia Wade became an unlikely winner of the ladies' singles at Wimbledon and England's cricket team regained the Ashes. As Revie's men slunk away from Wembley and flew off to three games in South America, most newspapers carried an innocuous paragraph stating that the manager would be absent from the first match in Brazil because he wanted to watch the World Cup game between Finland and Italy. 'We were not aware that he was planning anything,' said Street,[597] although many found it unusual that a control freak like Revie would leave the fate of such a prestigious game in the hands of Les Cocker, even if he had selected the team for him. Revie did see Italy's 3-0 victory, but not before he had flown to Dubai to discuss the possibility of becoming manager of the United Arab Emirates.

On arrival in Helsinki, Revie sought out Dick Wragg, chairman of the FA's international committee. He was aware, he told Wragg, that there were influential people within the organisation who would like to see him removed from his job. Revie had even been made aware by his old ally, Lord Harewood, the Leeds United president and former FA chairman, of rumours that Bobby Robson had already been sounded out about the role. Revie suggested to Wragg that he would go quietly if the final two years of his contract, worth £50,000, were paid up, although Wragg responded by assuring him that his job was secure for the time being.

Revie reconnected in Buenos Aires with a squad who had held their hosts to a 0-0 draw in Rio de Janeiro, having had plenty of their own chances in the first half. No one suspected anything other than his entire absence had been spent focusing on Italy. And no one expected anything other than the physical battle that ensued in a 1-1 draw in England's first visit to Argentina since Ramsey had called them 'animals'. According to Street, 'We were out on the pitch before the game, walking around in our blazers, and they were screaming at us. We had two fellows with machine guns in the dugout with us. They were young kids you wouldn't trust to post a letter. I remember thinking, "I hope those triggers are on a safety catch."'[598] When Cherry lost two teeth when being punched by Daniel Bertoni, he was astonished to be sent off along with his opponent. 'It was a political decision,' said Cherry, believing that the Uruguayan referee dare not banish an Argentina player without evening things out.[599]

Ironically, after all his tinkering with his team, Revie named his first unchanged side for what would be his final game as England manager, a lifeless 0-0 draw in Uruguay. The result left Revie with only 14 wins in 29 matches and an unbeaten tour had done little to change the perception of the public and media about his likely longevity in the position. Even the usually positive *Shoot!* was getting ready to summarise Revie's reign in damning terms. 'He showed both a lack of fresh ideas and the ability to select players who would complement each other,' the magazine would conclude a few weeks later.[600]

As Kenny Dalglish was declaring that 'I can't believe a man of his football knowledge will let his country down',[601] Revie set about finalising his UAE deal and planning his exit from the England job. For the latter he enlisted the help of long-time confidant Jeff Powell of the *Daily Mail.* On 11 July, the day after Revie's 50th birthday, they departed for Dubai, via a route that would take them through Zurich and Athens. Having received assurances in Switzerland that everything was in order at the Arab end, Powell instructed his office to run the first of two stories he had already written. 'Revie Quits Over Aggro', was the headline that arrived in the office of rival publications when the first editions landed late that night and was seen by millions the next morning.

'I sat down with my wife Elsie one night and we agreed that the England job was no longer worth the aggravation,' Revie had told Powell. 'It was bringing too much heartache to those nearest to us. Nearly everyone in the country wants me out. So I am giving them what they want. I know people will accuse me of running away and it does sicken me that I cannot finish the job by taking England to the World Cup finals in Argentina next year, but the situation has become impossible.'

His resignation had been delivered by hand to FA headquarters, but with no one there to receive it the letter sat unopened until after the newspapers had been read. 'The worst part of this miserable business was learning about it from reporters,' said Wragg. But he was wrong. There was worse to come in the eyes of many. After a day of searching for Revie, the *Mail*'s rivals were scooped again when the second part of the story was revealed; Revie was accepting a £240,00 four-year deal – plus a £100,000 bonus – to manage the UAE national team. 'This is an offer I cannot refuse,' he explained. 'If everything goes through OK it is an unbelievable opportunity to secure my family's future. I had many offers to stay in England but the tax structure, let alone the salaries available, make it impossible to earn this kind of money at home.'

As well as the wages, there was a luxury lifestyle on offer, as experienced by Frank O'Farrell when he had made a similar journey to become manager of Iran, leading them to their first Asian Games title in 1974. 'It's quite fantastic over there,' he said. 'My life has become an open-air way of living – roast sheep barbecues, pool parties. I have almost forgotten what it feels like to wear a suit. I've got a taste for caviar.'[602]

Conversely, Bill McGarry had a warning for Revie on the evidence of his own year in charge of Saudi Arabia. 'There's no way Don will last his four-year contract. A lot of things will surprise him – first, the quality of the players. They are amateurs and they think and behave like amateurs.' The former Wolves manager added, 'I still think it's worth the money, but the social life is almost non-existent.'[603]

Revie's statement of his motivation was poorly received, especially when it emerged he had been paid another £20,000 for giving the *Mail* its exclusives. 'If there was one thing Dad would have changed had he been able to have his time again it was his decision to sell the story to one newspaper,' his son Duncan would reveal. 'It meant the knives were out for him elsewhere.'[604] One of the sharpest belonged to long-time enemy Alan Hardaker, who chirped, 'Don Revie's decision does not surprise me in the slightest. Now I can only hope he can quickly learn to call out the bingo numbers in Arabic.'

Revie had left himself wide open to those who had never been disciples of his methods. Hughes called his actions 'underhand and pathetic' and said he had enjoyed the absence of bingo in Rio. 'He tried to create within the England squad the atmosphere that prevailed at Leeds. That is fine when you are with the same group of players every day but taking lads from all over the country for brief periods does not always draw the same response.'[605]

A more forgiving colleague, Street, felt that 'the nuts and bolts of the way he did it and selling the story to the newspapers were wrong', but added, 'He was a realist. He had created enemies at the top level. He knew if he didn't get success he was out, so he found another job. That is par for the course in any walk of life. And I think the fact that it was a job that made him rich for the rest of his life attracted more criticism than it merited.'[606]

Street's final comment touches on an important element that made Revie's duplicity so despicable in the eyes of the nation. The financial component of his decision led to a repeat of the reaction to Greig's lucrative defection to World Series Cricket. Kerry Packer, head of Australia's Channel 9, had been unable to prise the rights to Australian Test cricket out of the Australian Cricket Board and had promised Greig a job for life in return for becoming captain of his World XI and helping him take on the established game. To quote my own biography of Greig, 'In the 1970s, significant financial reward tended to be tolerated as long as it was a by-product of prodigious performance; it was not yet viewed as a worthy goal in its own right. Greig's unashamed assertion that he and his fellow professionals had money as their first priority was seen as grubby and unbecoming. This was, after all, still the television age of *The Brothers* – a sub-*Dallas* British drama about a road haulage business – rather than *Big Brother*, where pursuit of instant fame and fortune became an acceptable aspiration.'[607]

Then there was the question of basic loyalty. The mood of the Jubilee had added to – and fed off – the apparent longing for a simpler, more honourable, age; a time when allegiance and duty counted for more than Revie and Greig appeared to believe. While the Sex Pistols were singing about 'no future', the country seemed content to look to the past as an escape from the social and economic ills afflicting it. It was why many of the most popular television series of time were historical: *The Onedin Line*, *When The Boat Comes In*,

A Family at War, *The Duchess of Duke Street* and *Upstairs, Downstairs* among them.

Chronicling the 1970s, Turner noted the increase in turnover from £300,000 to £25 million of Laura Ashley, with its selling of 'rustic romanticism',[608] while author and presenter Lloyd Grossman would remember, 'Immediately people rush into nostalgia. You get the unbelievable popularity of the *Diary of an Edwardian Lady*[§] and suddenly every tea cosy, every table mat, has to have Edwardian illustrations of flowers on it. The feeling to nostalgia was quite an incredible phenomenon in the Seventies. Just when you thought people were about to fall in love with modernity they raced to go to 1910 and even earlier.'[609] Writing at the end of the decade, Christopher Booker stated, 'Never before in history had there been an age so distrustful of the present, so fearful of the future and so enamoured of the past. Therein lay the true significance of the Seventies.'[610]

It was why Revie's messenger, Powell, felt justified in arguing years later, 'The criticism that came Don's way was over the top. I don't think it would happen now because the world has moved on.'[611]

In the weeks following his departure, *Shoot!* explained that 75 per cent of its mailbag concerned Revie and offered the £3 prize for its 'Star Letter' to a reader from Tipperary who was thought to best sum up the sentiment of the masses. 'He, who preached loyalty and devotion to duty, chose to run away from his job in such a cowardly fashion that I am left wondering how he ever became manager of England in the first place. I am furious when I think he can get away with such a dreadful example of so-called loyalty.'[612]

Another form of loyalty – matrimonial fidelity – had already put football on the front pages during the summer of 1977. Four weeks after Manchester United won the FA Cup Final against Liverpool, and a month before Revie's revelations, the *Sunday People* of 19 June declared, 'THE DOC RUNS OFF WITH TEAM WIFE'. Manager Tommy Docherty had been having an affair with Mary Brown, 18 years his junior and the wife of club physiotherapist Laurie Brown.

---

§ Published in 1977, the facsimile reproduction of Edith Holden's naturalist's diary for 1906 sold one million copies inside a year.

'We are in love,' Docherty explained, having agreed to cooperate with the newspaper after discovering that it was publishing the story regardless. 'The bond has grown between us over the last three years and we've decided to bring our relationship into the open rather than live a lie. I believe that what has happened between Mary and me will be understood and accepted.'

But even Docherty, who had left his wife, Agnes, and come clean with the Manchester United board, harboured doubts about what this meant for his future career. 'I knew that Mary and I were going to be together,' he explained. 'I didn't know what would happen. Even after winning the Cup I never thought of life continuing the same at Old Trafford.'[613]

The initial reaction within United was one of simple surprise; much the same as in any workplace when two unlikely candidates turn out to be in a relationship. 'I was shocked,' said captain Martin Buchan. 'I thought I knew most of the things that were happening in and around the club.'[614] Steve Coppell recalled, 'Let's be fair, Doc is rough and ready at the best of times. I had met Mary a few times. Laurie was a good bloke, put upon sometimes and a different character to the Doc. Mary looked distant and I knew she was into horses. Football wasn't really her world, she just tolerated it. I burst out laughing. It couldn't be.'[615]

Docherty claimed he was given initial assurances that everything would be viewed as a 'private matter', but on 29 June he was summoned to a meeting at the home of chairman Louis Edwards. 'Under the circumstances we think it would be in the best interests of everyone concerned if you resigned,' Edwards told Docherty, citing a breach of the club's 'moral code'. Docherty, who'd never heard of such a code, argued that he should be judged on his ability to do the job, but was realistic enough to know that his energies were best directed towards ensuring a decent pay-off, which would end up in the region of £50,000. On 4 July, the club announced, 'A meeting of the directors has decided unanimously that Mr Docherty is in breach of the terms of his contract and his engagement is terminated forthwith.'

Docherty responded, 'During the past two weeks I have been treated like an animal. I have been punished for falling in love. It's as simple as that.' Many had thought pragmatism would prevail, Docherty having just delivered the FA Cup, while Lou Macari believed it would be the bond between manager and chairman that saved him.

Some newspapers suggested that the response of the Old Trafford wives was a major consideration for the board, although Docherty suggested that the spouses knew little of what really went on. 'I had seen a lot of things while I had been on tour,' he said. The club's strong Catholic background and its powerful public image of morality was another major factor. 'I think Matt Busby had a big say, being a Catholic,' Docherty suggested. 'I think maybe he was disappointed in me, being a Catholic as well.'[616]

Yet former United player Eamon Dunphy suggested in his examination of Busby's Old Trafford, 'The myth of United's integrity suited Matt Busby.'[617] And although United felt they needed to show support for the wronged man, Laurie Brown, they may also have feared him releasing all kinds of skeletons from closets if he was forced into leaving. Docherty, for instance, would claim after Busby's death that he had a 'lady friend' whom he visited on trips to London.

What Docherty had not realised was the strength of other forces amassing against him, including a group of wealthy hangers-on who became known as 'the junior board'. As early as his third month in the job, a group of seven men, including an MP and a QC, had proposed a takeover of the club in which Frank O'Farrell would be reinstated as manager. Within days of Docherty's dismissal, it emerged that private detectives had been compiling a dossier on his activities for two years. It included accounts of Cup final tickets finding their way on to the black market – an activity he engaged in quite openly – and incidents in hotels during tours. Chris Moore, director of a Stockport-based detective agency, said, 'I can't deny an investigation was made. These investigations were into a lot of things. I'm not going to break confidences.' According to the *News of the World,* the operation was carried out on behalf of local businessmen, not the directors.

Docherty believed that he had lost vital support by the way he had moved some of Busby's favourites out of the club; Denis Law, Willie Morgan and Pat Crerand, for example. 'Maybe some of the players I had got rid of had said things and had been stirring things up and there were repercussions,' he suggested. 'I know Matt wasn't happy when Pat was no longer assistant manager.'[618] O'Farrell had even written to Docherty, his old friend, warning him about 'the Knight', suggesting, 'He must be suffering torment at not being able to get rid of you as is rumoured he had been trying to do.'[619]

Ultimately, the weight of Docherty's faults and failed relationships became too heavy a burden for the club. They were riding high in the First Division and had won the FA Cup. The ship had been steadied; the skipper could be tossed overboard. The Mary Brown affair not only provided a final justification, it allowed United to ride that wave of moral indignation that was sweeping the country in the wake of Greig and the Sex Pistols. 'The hypocrisy of Docherty's years at Old Trafford, ironically reflected in the furore surrounding his demise, is extraordinary by any standards,' Dunphy concluded. 'When United's board of directors – the same men now lauded for upholding decent standards – had sacked [Wilf] McGuinness and O'Farrell nobody mentioned integrity and tradition.'[620]

Buchan reflected the thoughts of the bemused United fans when he said, 'I will go to my grave wondering what would have happened if the Doc had stayed. We had a decent team and the confidence of winning a major trophy. You never know who he might have been able to bring in. We'll never know how good that team could have been.'

12

YOUNG, GIFTED AND BLACK

SAMMY: You put a nice dinner jacket on. You've got a few associates with you. You're doing business; a nice meal, a bottle of brandy on the table. You've spent a few bob, put yourself out. You don't want to see a nigger knock the shit out of a nice white boy, do you? Other way round it's different. It's nothing to do with prejudice.

***Dinner at The Sporting Club* (Leon Griffiths; BBC TV, 1978)**

SATURDAY, 30 October 1971, was already memorable for 17-year-old Ade Coker. Given the chance to ride with the West Ham United first team to Selhurst Park, home of Crystal Palace, the apprentice from Lagos, Nigeria, was happy to help unload the skip containing his club's stylish change kit of light blue shirts with two claret hoops. Coker laid out the white-numbered jerseys and was wondering to whom he should hand the 12th when Ron Greenwood entered the changing-room and told everyone to sit down. 'Geoff Hurst's back injury means he can't play today,' the manager began. 'We have to bring in a new face. Get changed, Ade.'

Hurst handed his No.9 shirt to the stunned-looking teenager, who sat with eyes wide and head spinning. 'The shock was so great my legs turned to jelly,' he admitted. 'I could hardly speak.' Skipper Bobby

Moore, who remembered making his West Ham debut in similar circumstances, made a point of speaking quietly into Coker's ear as they headed to the field. 'Don't worry about a thing. Just get a goal in the first couple of minutes and everything will be fine.'

It took longer than that – but not much. Seven minutes had elapsed when Harry Redknapp's right-wing corner drifted beyond the granite figure of Palace centre-half John McCormick, before thumping off the thigh of defender Mel Blyth and bouncing across goal towards Coker's left foot. 'I'll never forget that moment,' he said. 'I hit it instinctively and it went into the net like a bullet.' Coker celebrated with the broadest of grins. 'What a smile,' London's television viewers heard commentator Brian Moore chuckle as the moment lit up their screens the following afternoon. Coker, of course, was among those watching. 'It took the television replay to prove to me that it was real,' he said. West Ham went on to win 3-0, Bermudan striker Clyde Best netting the third. Coker attracted further approval by using the sole of his boot to twice leave McCormick floundering, a show of skill that had Jimmy Hill 'thinking how coloured lads like Ade, with their negro athleticism and grace, could change the face of English League football'.[621]

Coker had moved to England with his parents at the age of 11, leaving behind two brothers and a sister. Because of that, the attention his goal attracted was undoubtedly greater than had it been scored by David Llewellyn, the other Hammers teenager who'd travelled to Palace. Coker was not just a young debutant, he enjoyed novelty status; a black player in the days when very few existed in the Football League.

Best, whose congratulatory hug after Coker's goal had been the tightest and longest, had been a regular in the Hammers squad since the 1969-70 season, while full-back John Charles, born in Canning Town and whose father was a merchant seaman from Grenada, had been a sporadic presence in the first team since 1963. Charles's younger brother, Clive, was now also in the squad. 'I've never felt conscious of my colour at Upton Park,' said Coker as reporters gathered around this curiosity. 'Perhaps having Clyde Best paving the way ahead of me has helped. We get along well because we've both had to work hard to adjust to English conditions.'

Best, who'd played football by the docks with visiting sailors and represented his country at the age of 15, had been recommended by national coach Graham Adams. West Ham paid the airfare to fly the 18-year-old from Bermuda without ever having seen him play, and then forgot to meet him at the airport. Instead, he made his way to Upton Park, where – it being a Sunday – there was no one around. Fortunately a passer-by knew where the Charles brothers lived and directed him to their house.

Aged 20 in the early stages of 1971-72, Best had never been more important to his team, leading the attack when Hurst was dropped after the Hammers failed to score in their opening two games. Hurst, who had bet Malcolm Allison £100 that he would score 15 goals during the season, was recalled after one game, but was initially condemned to playing in a deeper and wider position behind Best and Bryan 'Pop' Robson, the prolific scorer signed from Newcastle United.

Best's goal against Palace was his ninth in 11 games, with Greenwood prophesying, 'Clyde could make as big an impact on the game as other coloured players like Pelé and Eusébio.' It was a sign of less enlightened times that any achievement Best might enjoy was contextualised in terms of skin pigmentation. 'The colourful tale of the few who did make it,' was a typical headline in *Football League Review* above an article that said black players were 'bringing their own colourful characteristics to the game'.[622] It was a rare occurrence when, in February 1972, *Goal* ran a feature on Best without once specifically mentioning that he was black, although it did reference a fan who described him looking like a cross between Pelé and former heavyweight champion Sonny Liston.

That same week, both *Goal* and *Shoot!* published pieces about Ipswich Town winger John Miller, whose family were from Jamaica. Asked by the former about the possibility of being the first 'coloured' England player, he replied, 'There could be a lot playing for England in years to come.'[623] The article was indicative of the media's obsession with the narrative of a black player representing England. With due respect to Miller, had he been white he would not have figured in any conversation about national selection. He played little more than 50 games over six years at Ipswich before moving to Norwich City and into the lower divisions.

Greenwood's boast about Best had been evidence of him getting similarly carried away. For all Best's honesty and bravery, along with a sharp turn of speed for a six-footer with a broad backside, even the most committed West Ham fan would have struggled to make a convincing case for him being bracketed with the Brazilian and Portuguese legends. Greenwood also sounded somewhat patronising when he explained that the club put any money Best made outside of football into an account to pay for flights home. Yet Best welcomed the care, referring to his manager as a father figure.

Apocryphally, Best had been tempted to return home for good after his first game in West Ham's claret and blue, a reserve match in which the presence of Moore and Hurst created an attendance of 5,000 and which was played in snow and ice. Even he could not ignore the fact that his geographical background was newsworthy, saying in an early interview, 'I really miss the sun and I find it hard to get used to the cold. I had never seen snow before I arrived here, and I had never encountered the muddy conditions.'[624]

A small number of black players had performed in England before. They included West African Arthur Wharton, who played in goal for Preston North End and Rotherham United in the 1880s, and Walter Tull, who represented Tottenham Hotspur and Northampton Town before being killed in the First World War. Jack Leslie's Plymouth Argyle career spanned the 1920s and 1930s* and there were a few more around the lower divisions in the 1950s, including Middlesbrough's Jamaican forward Lindy Delapenha, frequently referred to as 'the coffee-coloured king of the wing', and future TV comedian Charlie Williams at Doncaster Rovers. South African winger Albert Johanneson became the first black player

* A campaign developed in 2020 for Leslie to be given a statue in Plymouth, along with revelations that he had been earmarked to play for England in 1925 before being left out when the selectors realised he was black.

to feature in the FA Cup Final when he played in 1965 for Leeds United, who had also featured fellow-countryman Gerry Francis earlier in the decade.

Yet the new generation, led by Best, were the first group to be seen regularly by the nation. 'Before televised games started, nobody except those who went to games knew that black players were involved,' he said. 'Once television coverage exploded, people like myself were given exposure. A lot of players over the years have come up to me and thanked me for making it possible for them to get somewhere.'[625] One such player was Viv Anderson, who Greenwood would make the first black player to win a full England cap before the decade was out. He remembered Best as 'the first black person I ever saw on TV'.[626]

Greenwood also created history on Easter Saturday in 1972, when Best, Coker and Clive Charles lined up against Tottenham; the first time three black players had appeared together in the First Division. According to Charles, 'I am not even sure we noticed it. Looking back, you think you must have done but I certainly don't remember thinking, "Oh there are three black blokes in our team." It was never really like that. I was just glad I was playing.'[627]

By 1972-73, the *Wonderful World of Soccer Stars* football stickers – featuring the First Division squad members – still numbered only two black faces in its collection, Coker and Best, with the former unable to get on the field in a top-flight game beyond the first four matches of the season. They were still part of a rare enough breed that any racist abuse directed at them was too isolated to attract national attention or to feel like part of a concerted movement. So much so that Jimmy Hill was able to blithely state in 1970, 'At a time when so much racial discrimination exists within sport, how good it is to see coloured players accepted within our own sport of football.'[628]

It was a picture of football that Best might not have recognised. Early in the 1970-71 season, he received an anonymous letter. '[It] made my blood run cold,' he remembered. 'It warned me that as soon as I emerged from the tunnel and took the field the next day, I would have acid thrown in my face.' What made it more frightening was that

Best had felt safe in the warm, respectful environment of West Ham. 'I couldn't imagine anyone could be so prejudiced as to threaten me in that way,' he said.[629] Yet Harry Redknapp recalled, 'Everywhere he went, he took abuse. What he had to go through was hurtful to all of us because he was such a special, special fellow, a laid-back guy who didn't have a bad bone in him.'[630]

Miller, meanwhile, admitted having been racially abused by 'one player from a Midlands club', but shrugged it off by explaining that his opponent apologised later.[631] After all, there was not much to be gained by going to the tabloids with the story. They would have thought little of it in an age where Alf Garnett was regularly abusing 'coons' on BBC television in *Till Death Us Do Part*.

It was clear that the potential for more displays of hatred would grow as second-generation British immigrants followed the trail blazed by the West Ham players. 'Boys who come here are bound to make a place for themselves in our game,' said Greenwood in 1971. 'Schoolboy football in London already has a lot of youngsters from immigrant families, sons of West Indians and Nigerians. We have seven or eight coloured boys training with us at schoolboy level. They have tremendous natural aptitude.' Once again, the racial stereotype that frequently populated such conversation was never far away, with Greenwood adding, 'They are loose-limbed players that I describe as athletic gymnasts.'

Arsenal manager Bertie Mee, who had black defender Brendon Batson in his squad, said at that time, 'Five years ago, out of a hundred boys we invited to Highbury for a trial only one would be coloured. Today, five out of a hundred are coloured and the number is growing. I can visualise a situation by the end of the Seventies when clubs from the big industrial centres of England are fielding teams that are 50 per cent coloured.'

Mee, an eminent NHS physiotherapist, knew enough about life beyond football to have been correct in the gist of his message, if somewhat premature in his timeline. At the end of the decade there would be approximately 50 black professional footballers in a total of 2,000, but in 1975-76, with both Best and Coker's Hammers careers having petered out, there was not a single black player being swapped by schoolboys in the nation's playgrounds.†

It reflected the general condition of the Caribbean diaspora in Britain at that time. Identifiable heroes were scarce, which was why the visits of the West Indies cricketers to England in 1973, 1975 and 1976 were seized upon as opportunities for an unabashed celebration of the Caribbean experience. Whether it was cheering their team's World Cup triumph of 1975 or banging out a victory rhythm on beer cans as Viv Richards and Michael Holding made England captain Tony Greig choke on the 'make them grovel' declaration he'd made before the Test series a year later, here was a chance for West Indians to celebrate the roots from which they were becoming increasingly disconnected; in a country in which they had yet to establish their own identity.

The converted troopship, HMT *Empire Windrush*, had docked at Tilbury in 1948 to signal the real beginning of the post-war migration of large numbers of Caribbean citizens to the British Isles. A decade later the number of West Indians in Britain had grown to approach 200,000. As Britain headed into economic recession in the late 1950s, racial tension was exacerbated, leading to discrimination when it came to finding jobs and housing and escalating into the Nottingham and Notting Hill riots of 1958.

The imminent Commonwealth Immigrants Act, introduced in 1962 to limit the rights of citizens of Commonwealth countries to permanent entry into the United Kingdom, meant a rush of new arrivals before the barriers came down. When Harold Wilson became Prime Minister for the first time in 1964 it was at the end of an election campaign in which both major parties had made the limitation of immigration a major issue, a reversal of Labour's earlier policy of opposing such controls. Even though annual immigration from Commonwealth countries plummeted from around 75,000 in 1963 to fewer than 4,000 in 1967, the Caribbean and Asian communities continued to find themselves blamed for all manner

† Both left England to pursue long careers in the outdoor and indoor leagues of the United States.

of the country's problems, including unemployment and increased crime rates.

Yet it was the immigrant population that suffered more than any, with government figures in 1975 showing unemployment running at twice the national average. Meanwhile, black Londoners were shown to be 15 times more likely to be arrested for petty theft, even though, as Dominic Sandbrook noted, 'few people seriously thought they were 15 times more likely to commit them'.[632]

And there had been the Saturday lunchtime in Birmingham in 1968 when Enoch Powell, then MP for Wolverhampton South West and considered a viable Conservative Party leadership candidate, made a speech prompted by the potential of an influx of Kenyan Asians. With a new Race Relations Bill intended to end discrimination in housing and employment about to be debated, he told his audience that a constituent had expressed a fear that 'in 15 or 20 years' time the black man will have the whip hand over the white man'. A classical scholar, he delivered in Latin the line, 'As I look ahead, I am filled with foreboding. Like the Roman I seem to see the River Tiber foaming with much blood.' The press translation was a prediction of seeing 'rivers of blood' because of racial conflict.

Edward Heath promptly sacked him from the Conservative front bench, but Powell had given a voice to many. When Heath's party won the 1970 election, Powell doubled his own majority and 'Powellism' was forecast to be a prominent feature of the country's politics. On election night, the BBC's Desmond Wilcox, who found revellers standing in the Trafalgar Square fountains chanting Powell's name, tentatively asked an observer, 'Can I have a word with you, sir? You're an immigrant. How did you feel about the increased majority?' The middle-aged Asian interviewee replied, 'I hope it's not a national trend throughout the country. But it's just clear, indicative of one fact: that the people's attitudes have changed over this period and it's a very dangerous sign.'[633]

Trevor Nelson, a future broadcaster who had emigrated from St Lucia, recalled, 'Even at a young age, we were aware of people like Enoch Powell. Our parents would tell us that we had been invited to come to Britain, but in the news we heard that people wanted the blacks out. It was very unnerving and strange.'[634] It was cricket, therefore, that offered Britain's Caribbean community a haven from such an environment.

Remembering England's Test match against the West Indies at The Oval in 1976, Nelson continued, 'I hadn't ever been to Notting Hill Carnival, but it was how I expected it to be, noisy and raucous. And I had probably never seen that number of black faces in one place. I was amazed by the feeling of pride from my dad and his friends. They were dancing and shouting. I had never seen them act like that before. They weren't behaving the way I had been brought up to behave; it was like they were back in the Caribbean. You can't understate how tough it must have been for a lot of them at that time.'[635]

At a time when youngsters from immigrant families needed their own heroes alongside those of their parents, football, along with the wider culture of British life, was taking its time in providing them. 'When a black person appeared on television it caused a flurry of excitement in our flat,' author Colin Babb remembered. 'Whoever was at home would scamper to get to the living room in time.'[636] Television's tea-time soap opera, *Crossroads*, introduced a recurring black character in 1974, the garage mechanic Mac; and the same year saw Don Warrington's character of Phil, a student of African descent, first get the better of Leonard Rossiter's Rigsby in *Rising Damp*. A teenaged Lenny Henry won the *New Faces* talent show in 1975 with impressions that he introduced by saying, 'You've seen them before, but not in colour.' And *The Fosters*, also featuring Henry, would become Britain's first sitcom to focus solely on a black family in 1976. But these were not exactly revolutionary times. In 1978, the BBC ran the first of two series of *Empire Road*, a drama series set in the Handsworth district of Birmingham and the first to be written, acted and directed predominantly by black artists. Yet in the same year, the corporation was still airing *The Black and White Minstrel Show*, featuring male singers in caricature blackface make-up, to millions of viewers. And BBC switchboards remained undisturbed when dialogue such as that at the head of this chapter made it to the screen.

Launched on ITV in 1972, *Love Thy Neighbour* – which at least gave leading roles to black actors – presented schoolchildren and factory workers with a new lexicon of racial insults. And, of course, Garnett had been spitting them out on *Till Death Us Do Part* since 1965. Any nuance in which the bigoted characters of Garnett and *Love Thy Neighbour*'s Eddie Booth were intended as the butt of the joke went over the heads of the average terrace bigot, who was about to develop a much louder voice as more black players emerged in the later years of the decade to unsettle his environment of white supremacy.

Meanwhile, very few of the black artists occupying the highest places in the UK music charts were likely to excite young British black males. For example, it was left to The Three Degrees, The Drifters, The Stylistics and George McCrae (all American) and Ken Boothe (Jamaican) to fill slots in the 20 best-selling singles of 1974. The only black British singers in the top 100 of the year were Sweet Sensation, a Manchester-based soul band, and Hot Chocolate, a multi-racial group who featured Errol Brown, a Jamaican immigrant, as lead singer.

It was 1974 that saw the senior football debut of a London teenager who would become a key cultural figure of the second half of the decade. On 3 August, with McCrae at No.1 with 'Rock Your Baby', 18-year-old Laurie Cunningham was included in the Orient team to face West Ham in the Texaco Cup. Two months later, he was given a first League game against Nottingham Forest, whose team on occasions in that season included Viv Anderson, a locally-born full-back previously discarded by Manchester United.

Cunningham, raised in Finsbury Park by parents who arrived from Jamaica in the 1950s, had also suffered rejection by a big club. He had signed as an apprentice for Orient in 1972 after two years of training with Arsenal. Robert Johnson, a young team-mate who also tried his luck at Highbury, told biographer Dermot Kavanagh, 'I didn't like how they treated us. You had the white and the black separate.' Johnson also recalled hearing comments such as, 'Those niggers are showing off again.'[637]

A winger with pace, skill and an attitude that valued the beating of three or four defenders over the placement of a well-timed pass,

Cunningham's swagger did not exactly fit the mould of a typical Arsenal player in the Mee era, regardless of skin colour. He was not around, therefore, to witness the ten appearances Batson would make as Highbury's first black player, although their paths would cross soon enough.

At Orient, Cunningham found a manager in George Petchey who saw what his individual talent could bring to a team capable of flirting with either end of the Second Division. 'He did a lot of things that you wouldn't expect a kid to do,' Petchey said of Cunningham's trial.[638] Petchey was also colour blind. Mixed race full-back Bobby Fisher and Indian-born midfielder Ricky Heppolette were already at Brisbane Road, and Nigerian winger John Chiedoze would soon join them. There was even an occasion when a local newspaper reporter clashed with Petchey, telling him he was signing too many black players.

It was a view that opposing fans were eager to express. One of Cunningham's earliest games was at Millwall, where bananas and verbal abuse were hurled at Orient's players. After Cunningham scored a late equaliser, he and Fisher left the field giving the Black Power salute to the crowd, an action for which they were castigated by the police. 'Some of the crowds we went to were diabolical in those days,' Petchey recalled. 'If you were black, you didn't half get some stick.'[639]

In his first two seasons in the Orient team, Cunningham played 51 League games and scored nine goals. At one point he even inspired Arthur Mitchell, founder of The Dance Theatre of Harlem, to write a letter to Orient describing him as 'the best athletic mover I have seen in ten to 15 years teaching dance'. Cunningham, a fan of the golden age of Hollywood musicals, would have been prouder of that comment than the rave reviews coming his way for his on-field achievements.

During 1976, while London's sport-mad black population was cheering on Clive Lloyd's West Indies team, Cunningham was emerging as an icon for a new generation. His play captured the imagination in a way that was impossible for Clyde Best, a battering ram of a forward in the traditional English style. 'Laurie played how we saw black guys playing football, anywhere, on any level: Sunday morning, at school, in a scrimmage game, down on the rec,' future

England striker Ian Wright would write in the foreword to Kavanagh's biography of Cunningham. 'He had the skills, but most importantly he had that swagger, he had that "vibe".' According to Wright, 11 when Cunningham made his League debut, he was 'the guy we all wanted to be like; a proper representation of how a London black guy is and how he should be playing football'.[640]

In March, *The Sunday Times Magazine* made Cunningham its cover star, pictured in Orient's second kit of yellow and green next to the heading, 'THE BLACK GOAL: Will Laurie Cunningham be the first coloured footballer to play for England?' The estimable Brian Glanville wrote the piece inside, although he had to be content with talking to Cunningham's mother after the absent-minded subject failed to show for the interview – just as he could often be late for, or even miss, training.

Glanville was a clear convert to the 'cause' of black players. Noting his conversation with Millwall duo Trevor Lee and Phil Walker, he wrote, 'Our football today is pathetically plodding, full of sweat and effort and predictability. Millwall's two young black players, Lee and Walker, say they can't even bear to watch it when they're not playing in it. For them, the way to play is the Brazilian way, with its jaguar jumps and bursts.'

The writer believed that the 'revolution' had been retarded by prejudice rather than performance. 'A few years ago, when a club like West Ham United seemed to swarm with exotic names and black faces, it appeared to be imminent; and why not? West Indian children were here in large number … they seemed to peer out in droves from photographs of junior school teams all over the country.' He continued, 'There was, meanwhile, a groundswell of dissent.'[641]

It was a view supported by Cyrille Regis, who was in non-League football around this time. 'There was a whole generation of black guys who came up in the early Seventies and who never made it into the game,' he said. 'Why? It was because of racism and the idea that they lacked bottle or couldn't stand the cold.'[642]

When ITV children's show *Magpie* profiled Cunningham, viewers heard him complain, 'The attitude managers have is that black kids are dainty on the ball and tend not to be physical.' Petchey addressed this by suggesting, 'I think why some of the coloured players tend to be timid is they're apprehensive of football in this country.' He believed that Cunningham's refusal to be intimidated – along with his natural ability, of course – was what differentiated him. 'If everyone called him a black bastard we'd be all right,' he said. 'The spark comes into his eyes and it makes him play.'[643]

Early in the 1976-77 season, Petchey challenged the *News of the World* to 'name me a better right-winger'. There was a growing clamour for Cunningham to be named as the 'first' black player to represent England at any level. Most media seemed to have overlooked that both John and Clive Charles played for the England Youth team and Nigerian-born Ben Odeje had represented England at schoolboy level at the age of 15 in 1971, thanks to FIFA basing qualification on the country in which the player studied rather than strict nationality. And there were others who had played England representative football before Cunningham, such as Wolves' Bob Hazell and Luton Town's Ricky Hill in the youth team and Godfrey Ingram, a future Luton forward, in the schoolboys' side. After Ingram scored twice in a victory in Dortmund, West German manager Helmut Schoen – being complimentary and sadly predictable at the same time – called him 'the next Pelé', and German club Schalke 04 offered him a contract.

That group were overlooked in the narrative of Cunningham, who would eventually become the first black England player at professional level. Odeje, incidentally, might have found himself in opposition to Cunningham had he managed to progress from Charlton Athletic's youth team. Instead, he ended up in the non-League game and would become an overlooked character in English football, his place in history needing reaffirmation by the FA in 2013 when they officially acknowledged him as the first black player to represent England, a well-intentioned act that managed to forget about John Charles.

It was clear how challenged Cunningham and others would be in reaching the very top. Not long before resigning as England manager, Don Revie had demonstrated his own blinkered view that black players found it hard to break through because 'they would be happier on dry, hard grounds'. No wonder they felt they were victims of institutional racism when the man at the pinnacle of the English game could subscribe to such a lazy stereotype. Cunningham admitted that he 'believed to be a black in this country was to be a loser'.[644]

Or, as film and music maker Don Letts put it, 'To most we were black bastards. We were like a lost tribe. It was something new in the Seventies and we were struggling to work out what this was.'[645]

There were by now a few more black faces in the Football League, among the most notable being Lee and Walker; Anderson and Chiedozie; Hill and the emerging Ingram at Luton; Notts County defender Pedro Richards; and young Stoke City forward Garth Crooks. *Shoot!* insisted on asking, 'How did Garth develop his skills?' as if it expected an exotic, other-worldly answer from a boy born and raised in Stoke-on-Trent simply because he had dark skin.

But it was Cunningham who remained the chief flag-bearer. And as his elevation to an England shirt became inevitable, so did a transfer to the First Division. With Orient in debt and battling relegation, Cunningham was sold to West Bromwich Albion for £110,000 in March 1977, two days before his 21st birthday. 'I don't give a damn whether a boy is black, red or green,' said manager Johnny Giles. 'If he can play then I am interested.' After helping his team to a 2-0 win at Tottenham on his top-flight debut, Cunningham said he thought the pace 'would be much quicker'. The following month he played his historic first game for England Under-21s, heading the only goal against Scotland at Bramall Lane.

DEGREES OF DIFFICULTY

Yes, this is the year; To open up your mind

'Year of Decision', The Three Degrees
(Kenny Gamble, Leon Huff; Gamble-Huff Music, 1973)

Tottenham's defeat on Cunningham's West Brom debut hastened them towards relegation from the First Division. Heading the other way were Nottingham Forest, whose elevation brought the long-limbed Anderson to national prominence. By now an established first-team member, he'd been given an early introduction to the reality ahead when, in his second Forest game, he went in front of Newcastle United's hostile crowd. 'What I experienced that night went way beyond the boundaries of acceptable behaviour,' he recalled.[646]

It was a pattern familiar to abuse victims such as Anderson, but still scattered too sparsely to attract the attention of anyone who might have been able to do anything about it. His manager at the time, Dave Mackay, told that him in order to be a professional footballer his only option was to put up with it. With supportive team-mates, Anderson felt he was able to use it as a motivating force. He had little choice. Any black player who had dared to speak up against his treatment would have been considered a trouble-maker and made himself even more of a target. Anderson said his experience at Newcastle was typical of most grounds – if louder than most.[647]

After Forest swept to an unlikely championship triumph in their first season after promotion, it was Anderson who claimed the achievement most had assumed would be Cunningham's; the first black player to win a full England cap. And when Greenwood named him for the friendly against Switzerland at Wembley in November 1978, it was no mere tokenism. Anderson had been a vibrant influence on Brian Clough's side, his careering runs forward a key part of their identity. There was no more valid candidate to challenge Liverpool's Phil Neal for the right-back position he'd held since the last matches of Don Revie's reign.

Kevin Keegan attempted to settle Anderson's nerves by reminding him, 'You wouldn't be playing if you weren't good enough,'[648] and as if to test the old theory of black players being unable to perform in extremes of weather, England's new cap ran out on to a field dusted with snow. It was Forest team-mate Peter Shilton to whom the home team owed a clean sheet in a 1-0 win, although *The Times* noted that Anderson was 'confident and safe' and observed, 'One's attention was drawn to the fact that only Anderson was displaying true club form at international level – the criterion of a good player in Mr Greenwood's mind.'

Anderson would play only two more England games before the end of the decade, but that did not mean that momentum had been lost. The year of his international debut, 1978-79, was among the most significant in the journey of the black player in English football. The season's *Football 79* sticker collection by Panini still only featured five black faces among the sweep of players from England and Scotland's top flights, but while West Brom's Batson was a journeyman and Hazell a young Wolves hopeful, Anderson and West Brom duo Cunningham and Regis were all contending for representative honours. And the fact that Albion always picked all three of their black players and made a stylish challenge for the League title meant that there was more for the bigots to feel uncomfortable about. 'Three black players in one team was just too much for some supporters,' Regis recalled. 'Nothing was being done by clubs, police or the football authorities to curb this behaviour, which had frankly been going on far too long to be dismissed as a passing fad. The racism spread to most grounds after Brendon came on board.'[649]

The rise of the black player now felt, unintentionally, like a movement, especially when set against the backdrop of events in Britain's wider society. West Brom's signing of Regis, born in French Guiana and brought to England aged five, advanced the story of England's black footballers considerably. It was chief scout Ronnie Allen who recommended that Albion pay £5,000 – doubling after 20 first-team appearances – to Isthmian League side Hayes for their 19-year-old centre-forward in May 1977. And it was Regis's good fortune that by the time the new season began Allen would be in charge following the resignation of Giles. Regis, a chiselled specimen with thighs like oversized hams, had to wait only until the end of August to make his debut in a League Cup tie against Gillingham, scoring twice in a 4-0 win. His first goal came when regular penalty-taker Tony Brown stepped aside to satisfy the crowd's chants for the debutant.

Regis, like Anderson, remembered Newcastle as the first League ground on which he heard racial abuse, although it was a quirk of the fixture list rather than evidence of a trait unique to that club. The first fans from whom he heard the particularly distasteful 'nigger, nigger, lick my boots' were those of local rivals Wolves after they'd occupied the Smethwick End of Albion's home ground. Author Dave Bowler recalled, 'At the back of terraces are corrugated iron sheets. Throughout the game, the Wolves supporters drum on these in jungle rhythm, and thousands of voices chant, "Nigger, nigger, lick my boots" or "Pull that trigger, shoot that nigger."'[650] The logic of such action was lost on Hazell, soon to earn a place in the Wolves defence alongside the luxurious Afro haircut of George Berry. Throughout a career that took him to QPR, Leicester and Port Vale he wondered how fans of his team could chant abuse at opposition black players one moment and sing his name the next. Berry would remember Albion fans screaming 'golliwog' at him while he was standing next to Regis at a corner.

Regis was a fixture in West Brom's team by the time Allen left the club in December 1977 – with Albion fourth in the table – to oversee the Saudi Arabian national side. In his place came Ron Atkinson, whose managerial style had all the flamboyance lacking in his unspectacular career as a wing-half for Oxford United, where he'd been known as 'The Tank'. On his way to reinvention as 'Big Ron' he had progressed from player-manager of Kettering Town to a successful spell at Cambridge United, leading the Football League newcomers to the Fourth Division title and putting them in a challenging position for promotion to the Second Division. The West Brom players got an idea of what to expect when he turned up for his first day wearing a full-length black leather coat. 'A flash bugger' was how he was described by winger Willie Johnston, who would soon be supplying Atkinson with showy pieces of jewellery through a dealer friend.[651]

The new manager urged a high-tempo game in which the ball reached the front men as soon as possible, a tactic that saw Regis score a goal that brought him further to the nation's attention. Having eliminated holders Manchester United in the fourth round of the FA Cup – Regis scoring twice in a replay – West Brom went on to host League leaders Forest in the quarter-finals. With the home side one up but under pressure in the early moments of the second half, a hoofed clearance by Paddy Mulligan found Regis sprinting behind the Forest backline. As the ball dropped, he drove it past Shilton's right hand with a low half-volley that almost scorched the ground as it left his right foot.

Regis was denied an appearance in the final when Ipswich beat West Brom 3-1 at Highbury. Embarrassingly, Atkinson had allowed himself to be filmed walking up the Wembley steps to pick up the trophy, believing that Bobby Robson had agreed to do the same. Albion finished sixth in the First Division, qualifying for Europe, and after a ground-breaking and eye-opening summer trip to China they were ready to embark on a season that would combine, according to Regis, 'sublime football with rancid racism'.[652]

A few weeks after arriving at The Hawthorns, Atkinson had paid £30,000 for Batson, his skipper at Cambridge United, believing he was better than the player he had in the right-back position, Republic of Ireland international Mulligan. 'I didn't like Ron,' said Mulligan years later. 'He tended to look down his nose at you and assumed he knew all there was to know about football.'[653]

Batson, born on Grenada and raised in Trinidad, arrived in England in 1962, sent by his parents to live with family in Tilbury in Essex. By the beginning of 1978-79, Batson was a first choice; Cunningham was ready to start every week after spells on the substitute's bench; and Regis was, well, bloody frightening. 'He was an absolute beast,' said Anderson. 'Challenging him was like hitting a brick wall. He was so powerful: great in the air, very quick, with two good feet and an eye for goal.'[654] Atkinson told author Paul Rees that only one Albion player had ever voiced any concern about the team's composition, complaining that 'you had to be black to get in' – to which Atkinson replied, 'Well it makes a change from being Scottish and Irish.'[655]

The idea of Regis, Cunningham and Batson as football's 'Three Degrees' became fixed in the nation's consciousness when Atkinson, discovering that the American soul-singing trio of that name were performing in Birmingham, invited the ladies to the club for a photoshoot, explaining to the press that Albion had 'our own Three Degrees'. The pictures of the singers in the club's striped shirts and the boys wrapped in the girls' fur coats appeared everywhere. It was intended as a harmless piece of fun and generally accepted as such, although Derrick Campbell, a local civil-rights activist, told Ross, 'I suppose there was a perverse sense that the "Three Degrees" was used as a term of endearment. But in the black community, we saw it as an act of ridicule.'[656] Batson would quickly come to see it as contrived and a potential source of resentment among the other players. When Cunningham and Regis accepted an invitation to join the group at a nightclub after they had been to a West Brom game, Batson opted to go home to his wife.

Whatever the appropriateness of the stunt – especially when viewed through a 21st-century lens – it was indicative of the increased presence of the black footballer. According to Regis, his concern was keeping his place in the team and 'the thought of being a role model for other black players didn't enter my head'.[657] Cunningham reluctantly accepted that he was a symbol of hope when *Shoot!* proposed that 'success for Laurie Cunningham could inspire countless other black youngsters to reach the top'. His response was 'I suppose that's true' and 'I know there are responsibilities on me'.[658]

It is impossible to reflect now without seeing the significance of the moment. It was no overstatement when Rees wrote of West Brom's black players, 'They empowered a generation of disenfranchised black youths, bringing to it a sense of hope and inspiration. They were agents of change as well and helped set in motion a domino effect that would allow a new order to assert itself in the British game.'[659]

Anderson would come to acknowledge as much, writing in 2010, 'I can say now that I am proud of the role I played. It helped pave the way for the huge improvements in football that have occurred since then. I'm also pleased to have helped the game move away from the prejudices that stood in the way of black footballers when I started.'[660]

The fact that much of this was happening a few miles up the road from Birmingham made it more poignant. Not only had England's second city been the scene of Enoch Powell's 'Rivers of Blood' speech, it had also, in effect, given birth to the Rock Against Racism movement when Eric Clapton, in a state of drunkenness, made a no less infamous declaration during a 1976 concert at Birmingham Odeon. Stating that Britain was 'overcrowded', he called for people to vote for Powell in order to prevent the formation of a 'black colony'. And then he became even more offensive. 'This is England, this is a white country,' he said. 'Throw the wogs out.' Clapton, a supposed champion of black music who'd had a hit with Bob Marley's 'I Shot the Sheriff', would apologise in later years, saying he was 'ashamed' of the person he'd become at that time through drink and drugs.[‡]

Clapton's incendiary outburst no doubt excited the likes of National Front chairman John Tyndall and his growing number of followers. But it was also enough to inspire a group led by photographer Red Saunders to go ahead with their idea of forming Rock Against Racism. It was, in effect, launched via an open letter of disapproval to Clapton that appeared in the major music papers and the *Socialist Worker*. Its founding members were closely aligned to the Socialist Workers Party, which had launched the Anti-Nazi League. Before long, no self-respecting sixth-former or college student would be seen without a Rock Against Racism or Anti-Nazi League lapel badge, although journalist Paul Foot was among those who noted that few young blacks or Asians joined because of the left-wing intellectual overtones of the organisations.

RAR and ANL stood alongside each other to protest against racism in general and the growth of the National Front in particular. One year after the NF had achieved more than 120,000 votes in the 1977 Greater London Election – surpassing its nationwide total in the previous general election – more than 80,000 turned up in Victoria Park in Hackney for an RAR concert headlined by The Clash, Steel Pulse and the Tom Robinson Band. 'That was the first time I felt something had changed in Britain forever,' said an Asian fan, Gurinder Chadha.[661] David Hinds of Steel Pulse, one of a group of multi-racial bands emerging from the same Midlands environment as

‡ When *New Musical Express* visited Cunningham's home in 1979, the writer was surprised to find an Eric Clapton gold disc on the wall. Cunningham said he had never heard of the Birmingham Odeon incident. 'Maybe I'd better burn it then,' he told his visitor.

Regis and company,[§] reflected, 'The show galvanized all the cultures that were happening in Britain at the time. It turned on the head the idea that Britain was racially divided.'[662] Yet such views were easily formed from within the bubble of such events. Less harmonic had been the 'Battle of Lewisham' in August 1977 when National Front supporters – reportedly bolstered by Millwall fans – clashed with SWP followers in south London, where 134 people needed hospital treatment and 214 were arrested.

Historians suggest that the National Front could have grown more quickly had it not been for Margaret Thatcher's own stance against immigration, which offered a mainstream voice to those who might otherwise have gravitated towards the NF. Appearing on ITV's *World in Action* in January 1978, the Leader of the Opposition said, 'People are really rather afraid that this country might be swamped by people with a different culture.'

Later that month, Hazell was subjected to a particularly nasty outburst from the Highbury crowd. Wolves were holding Arsenal 1-1 in the fourth round of the FA Cup when, late in the game, Hazell struck out at Graham Rix within touching distance of fans in the corner of the North Bank. Duly sent off, Hazell was virtually pushed from the field by the referee while spectators close to the incident screamed for blood. Within seconds, Malcolm Macdonald, who had been marked by Hazell, scored a winning goal for the home team. 'The letters came from everywhere, all over England, and it was really horrible stuff,' Hazell recalled of this period of his career. '"Go home, nigger. Get out of our country." My wife, bless her, kept a lot of them, and many that I never saw.'[663] It hardly helped Hazell and his peers when Labour's Home Secretary, Merlyn Rees, was asked on television that year, 'What you really mean is that immigration control is a device to keep out coloured people?' and he responded, 'That is what it is.'[664]

---

§ Also soon to hit the charts were the likes of Birmingham bands UB40, Dexys Midnight Runners and The Beat; and Coventry's The Specials and The Selecter. All of them featured large multi-racial line-ups and all took their influences from black music, including reggae, soul and ska.

This was the environment in which Anderson was making his England debut and Regis, Cunningham and Batson were helping West Brom challenge for the First Division title. Albion might have got closer than third had they not run out of steam in April, failing to win in six tightly-packed games after winter snow wreaked havoc on the fixture list. They beat Valencia on their way to the last eight of the UEFA Cup, but their most memorable performance of the season came at Manchester United in the final match of 1978, winning 5-3 to maintain their place at the top of the table. Batson would describe it as a 'seminal game'. During a thrilling first half that ended 3-3, the dancer's footwork of Cunningham and a back heel by Regis set up a fierce Len Cantello drive for one of West Brom's goals. In the second half, Cunningham ran on to Regis's header to score a fourth, and Regis completed the scoring with a sweeping finish after Cunningham launched an attack by running from deep inside his own half.

At the final whistle, Granada TV commentator Gerald Sinstadt's summary was, 'The magic that black footballers are bringing to the League [was] completely in evidence.' More pointedly, he had earlier called out the 'unsavoury barracking of the black players from certain sections of the crowd, which says nothing for their sportsmanship at all'. Despite the unavoidable racial tension that existed in the country, it was uncommon for it to be mentioned in relation to football, however audible the monkey chants from the terraces. The media were quick enough to refer to skin colour when reporting the action, but reluctant to dig any deeper. Regis generously suggested that perhaps there was a hope that 'if racist jeers weren't mentioned the idiots doing this kind of thing wouldn't be given any attention and it would wither away. But how can you fail to see bananas being thrown on to the pitch?'[665] What enabled him to grit his teeth and carry on was that 'it was confined to the arena'. He said, 'If it had spilt out on to my children at school, my wife walking down the street, bricks through the window, it would have been a totally different ball game.'[666] Clyde Best made the same relieved observation.

Atkinson counselled quiet pragmatism to his players, believing that the abuse was 'an issue that should be approached with mellowed understanding and humour'.[667] Perhaps not the kind of humour proposed by Millwall manager Gordon Jago when he said of Trevor Lee, 'He has his own way of dealing with opponents who give him abuse because of his colour – he threatens to move in next door to them.'[668]

Albion defender Ally Robertson encouraged Regis and the others to shrug off the abuse. 'If people call you a black so and so, then so what? How many times have I been told I'm a Scottish twat?' But even he saw a line that should not be crossed. 'We never allowed anyone to call them "nigger". That's derogative. Anyone did that, I'd be the first to punch them.'[669]

Yet Hazell admitted, 'I wanted to make a stand, but nobody would listen. Instead I was told to say stupid things about the abuse, like it did not worry me. The clubs just did not want to talk about it. Those in charge of football then, the real power brokers, they didn't care one jot.'[670]

As with hooliganism, football apparently preferred to disassociate itself from the issue. Rather than creating a need to protect anyone, black meant novelty value. And nowhere was that more evident than in the testimonial match staged for West Brom midfielder Cantello at the end of the season. Billed as a West Brom XI versus a Cyrille Regis and Laurie Cunningham XI it was, in fact, whites versus blacks. The latter side's starting line-up was: Derek Richardson (QPR); Batson, Berry, Larry May (Leicester), Hazell; Winston White (Hereford United), Vernon Hodgson (West Brom), Remi Moses (West Brom); Regis, Crooks, Cunningham.

The concept of the match is unthinkable to a modern audience, and even then community leaders opposed it because they feared it could be a vehicle for crowd trouble and racial abuse. Yet Batson recalled, 'We thought it was a great idea and we never once thought about the social aspects of it. We didn't hear any dissenting voices.'[671] In the end, a modest crowd of 7,000 watched a game that passed off without incident. Few can recall without recourse to the record books that Cunningham's team won 3-2.

As the new decade dawned, a far more significant date was approaching for Regis. Many were surprised that it was not until

February 1982 that Ron Greenwood gave him an England debut against Northern Ireland, perhaps three years after he had been at his raw and frightening best. Yet there were some who would rather the day had not come at all. Regis received a bullet in the post, with an accompanying note that said, 'If you put your foot on our Wembley turf, you'll get one of these for your knees.'

Cunningham was gone from West Brom shortly after the Cantello testimonial, sold for £900,000 to Real Madrid, becoming the first British player to play for the famous Spanish club. At West Brom, the promotion of Moses to the first team kept the 'Three Degrees' motif alive, while Cunningham helped Real to a league and cup double in his first season and played in the 1981 European Cup Final defeat by Liverpool.¶

By then it was almost a decade since Best, Coker and Clive Charles had become English football's first triple act. Things had changed more slowly than they might have hoped but a foundation for the modern multi-racial game had been laid. At the time of writing it is brutally clear that not all elements of prejudice within football have been eradicated, but no one can fail to recognise some progress. For that, the modern player owes a debt to the pioneers of the 1970s who faced – uncomplaining and unacknowledged by authority – levels of abuse and opposition that only their peers can truly appreciate. Some have never forgiven. 'I am bitter and angry when we talk about the past racist things we had to go through,' concluded Hazell, 'in what was the best time of my life.'[672]

¶ Afflicted by a thigh injury, Cunningham ended up bouncing around various clubs in Europe and England, winning an FA Cup winner's medal at Wimbledon in 1988, a year after his great friend Regis had been an FA Cup winner with Coventry. Back in Spain, at Rayo Vallecano, Cunningham died in a car crash in Madrid in July 1989, aged 33.

13

THE LIVERPOOL WAY

We can do, we can do it, we can really move

We're ahead right now and we just can't lose

'We Can Do It', Liverpool FC (Tony Waddington, Wayne Bickerton; Sony/ATV Music Publishing, 1977)*

LEANING HIS back against the wall of the Melwood training ground dressing-room as though needing support, a nervous-looking Bob Paisley told the players at his first team meeting, 'I never wanted this job.' The men 'upstairs' had forced him into it, he said.[673] After a few minutes he was gone, headed to the training pitch. Steve Heighway broke the silence. 'Listen,' he told his team-mates, 'unless we pull together and make this work this could all fall down like a pack of cards.'[674]

How could you follow the architect of the modern Liverpool Football Club? The man who'd created a bond between fans and manager that his sport had never previously witnessed. A character who loved to shove his club and himself into the limelight. 'I can go down the street and if nobody recognises me, I'm delighted,' Paisley

* Liverpool reached No.15 in the UK charts before the 1977 FA Cup Final with a version of The Rubettes' 1975 hit 'I Can Do It'. As well as rewriting the lyrics and slowing the tempo to make it more manageable for a communal singalong, they also lost the original's falsetto backing vocals. Perhaps it was too difficult to imagine Tommy Smith miming that part on *Top of the Pops*.

admitted. 'And, let's face it, Bill didn't do that. Bill always wore steel tips on his shoes so that people could hear him coming.' Paisley was the quiet companion, happiest in the shadows. Shankly was the ruddy Messiah.

A product of the mining community of Hetton-le-Hole in Co Durham, Paisley won an FA Amateur Cup with Bishop Auckland, the north-eastern powerhouse of non-League football, before joining Liverpool in 1939. A tough-tackling left-half with a dangerous long throw, he won a League title and ended up as club captain. Retiring in 1954, he became the club's physiotherapist and reserve-team coach. Shankly promoted him to work with the first team, and now he was being charged with building on his old boss's achievements. Paisley was aware that it had been a task beyond Wilf McGuinness at a post-Busby Manchester United. And he was not best pleased with Shankly's timing. 'I felt it would be better if he'd resigned at the end of last season,' he said a few months later. 'Taking over the reins when I did made it difficult.'[675]

Shankly had stepped down two months after one of the most memorable team displays of the decade; the 3-0 dismantling of Newcastle United at Wembley. Liverpool had won the League Championship and UEFA Cup the season before, but – given the rationing of live televised football – it was the 1974 FA Cup Final that showcased to the nation the team Shankly had built to continue the legacy of his dual champions of the 1960s.

After taking the majority of the first half to find their rhythm, Liverpool's performance became one of panache and ruthlessness. For Newcastle, it was like being carved into pieces by a silk scarf. Phil Thompson and Emlyn Hughes tied up Malcolm Macdonald, who had been boasting of what he would do to Liverpool's defence. Full-backs Tommy Smith and Alec Lindsay were able to express their creativity, the latter having a blistering first-time finish ruled out for offside. 'Shanks's pre-match team talk was brief and to the point,' Peter Cormack recalled. 'Clem was to try to feed the two full-backs early and their job was to get up and down the wing.'[676] Smith, delivering thoughtful passes, was more visible as an attacking force than defensive enforcer, while Footballer of the Year Ian Callaghan prompted busily from midfield. Wave after wave of Liverpool pass-and-move attacks could have produced more than three goals and at times the linesman's flag was the key Newcastle defender.

Liverpool's patience was rewarded in the 58th minute when Keegan teed up the ball and volleyed it to the left of goalkeeper Iam McFaul. 'Goals pay the rent,' exclaimed BBC commentator David Coleman … [pause while he realised the dead end his words had led him down] … 'and Keegan does his share.' While viewers pondered one of the great non-sequiturs of 1970s football commentary, Liverpool became even more dominant, with John Toshack flicking on a header and Heighway turning the ball back past McFaul for the second goal.

Directly alongside Newcastle manager Joe Harvey on the bench – a delicious quirk of the period's seating arrangements at Wembley – Shankly had been directing operations with a bookmaker's hand gestures. Now those movements seemed to sync joyously with the rhythm of the crowd's chants, a celebration of the near-perfect execution of Shankly's vision. 'The policy of the new team was the same as the old,' he said, comparing his two great sides. 'We played to our strengths. We pressurised everybody and made them run.'[677] And, as Coleman would have appreciated, everyone did their share. 'The team played in sections of the field, like a relay,' Shankly explained. 'We didn't want players running the length of the field, stretching themselves unnecessarily, so our back men played in one area, and then passed on to the midfield men in their area, and so on to the front men. So while there was always room for individuals within our system, the work was shared out.'[678]

When the fans turned 'Amazing Grace' into a chorus of 'Shankly, Shankly, Shankly, Shankly', Alan Thompson was moved to write in the *Daily Express* that 'men will kiss his feet' and asked, 'Has there ever been another man in any sport who so captured the hearts of the people?'

If Harvey experienced any awkwardness sat next to a rival whose name resounded around Wembley, it was no less than he would have felt at the end of the previous night's joint television interview between the managers from their respective team hotels. As things wrapped up, Shankly turned to someone out of camera shot to say, 'Jesus Christ, Joe's a bag of nerves.' The watching Liverpool players burst out laughing, knowing that an apparent off-the-cuff comment had been carefully designed to undermine the confidence of their opponents. It was classic Shankly.

And so was Liverpool's third goal: Keegan's crossfield ball from the left; Smith's cushioned pass to Hall without letting the ball drop; Hall's first-time return pass to Smith; his one-two with Heighway and driven pass across the six-yard box; Keegan's simple stabbed finish. Coleman was on the mark when he declared, 'And Newcastle were undressed.' Perhaps it was not surprising that Shankly decided to step down after that. How could it get any better? Keegan wondered whether he could see only decline for his team.

There were signs of evolution in the shape of the team that overwhelmed Newcastle; a significant change from the line-up that had won the 1972-73 title and beaten Borussia Moenchengladbach over two legs in the UEFA Cup Final.[†] It was a tactical advancement that straddled the passing of the managerial baton from Shankly to Paisley; one born partly of necessity and partly of a harsh lesson in the European Cup.

In the second round of the 1973-74 tournament, Liverpool were drawn against Yugoslavia's Red Star Belgrade,[‡] who won the first leg 2-1. Expected to overturn that deficit with some comfort at Anfield, Liverpool were frustrated by a team who fulfilled coach Miljan Miljanić's plan to keep the ball away from them. The visitors played in triangles, attacked with purpose and repeated their 2-1 victory.

† After the first leg at Anfield was abandoned after 27 minutes due to incessant rain, Shankly took the opportunity to reinstate John Toshack to the starting line-up in place of Brian Hall for the rearranged game a day later, although the Wales striker believed it was only because of an angry exchange of words between the two earlier in the day. Toshack's dominance in the air helped Liverpool to a 3-0 victory, twice heading down for Keegan to score. His presence also contributed to Larry Lloyd being left unmarked to head the third goal. Despite conceding two first-half goals in Germany, Liverpool hung on to become the first English club to win the League and a European trophy in the same season.

‡ Commonly referred to in modern times as Crvena Zvedza, use of anything other than the English translation of Red Star was unheard of in the 1970s.

The Red Star defenders' ability to play the ball on the ground made Liverpool's long balls appear primitive. 'It was a learning experience that was not lost on Shanks,' Cormack observed.[679]

And the game taught Paisley that 'it was no use winning the ball if you finished up on your backside'. He continued, 'The top Europeans showed us how to break out of defence effectively. The pace of their movement was dictated by their first pass. We had to learn how to be patient like that and think about the next two or three moves when we had the ball.'[680]

Shankly might have been dismissive publicly of the victors' methods, but in the Anfield boot-room, where rows of players' footwear shared the walls with old photographs, a vision of a new Liverpool took shape. Shankly had always loved a stopper. When he saw that his skipper of the 1960s, Ron Yeats, was approaching the end of his career he went out and signed another brickhouse to replace him, Larry Lloyd. Within two years, Lloyd had worn Liverpool's No.5 shirt at Wembley and played for England. When Liverpool won the League in 1972-73, he played every single minute.

But when Lloyd suffered a hamstring injury in the spring of 1974, Shankly and Paisley decided to pull Thompson back from midfield to partner Emlyn Hughes in the back four rather than find a like-for-like replacement. With two centre-backs able to play with the ball at their feet, the model for Paisley's Liverpool had been formed. Even *Goal*, whose tactical insight rarely extended beyond pleas for more goals, recognised a significant development – although the comment of Alan Hughes that 'centre-halves, as they weigh in at over 13 stones with a height of six feet upwards, are as obsolete as the boots Bill Shankly used to wear' might have been over-stating it somewhat.[681] Lloyd was not quite ready for the scrapheap.

A practical problem posed by Liverpool's new approach was that neither Thompson nor Hughes wanted the No.5 shirt. Cormack volunteered for it, believing that it couldn't harm his chances of retaining his place. And so was established a Liverpool numerical tradition that continued until the advent of squad numbering in the 1990s.

Any successful side will tell you that team spirit is a contributory factor. It's easy to be blind to conflict and be all pals together when the points are piling up and win bonuses are hitting the bank accounts. 'There is no jealousy, no bickering, no backbiting,' said Phil Neal, whose 11-year career at Anfield was a tale of unrelenting triumph – four European Cups, eight League titles, four League Cups and a UEFA Cup.[682]

But Liverpool's dressing-room was as prone to tension as any other. Toshack, for example, had reason for nerves when Paisley took over. 'I had always found him a strange sort of character,' the Wales striker recalled, adding that 'I had never been Bob's favourite player and the introduction of Ray Kennedy seemed to me to say that the writing was on the wall.'[683] David Fairclough, who would feel something of an outsider as perennial substitute under Paisley, recalled that the idea of all-for-one was a 'romantic notion'.[684]

Then there was the issue of the club captaincy, which had passed from Smith to Hughes in the 1973-74 season. Smith had always been the dominant personality in the dressing-room, the one to whom new signings looked for approval. Cormack had been told by Smith on his first day at Melwood that 'you run like a fucking poof' and had breathed easily when the skipper ended training with, 'You'll do for me, lad.'[685]

Cormack continued, 'Emlyn and Smithy never got on and that must have made it doubly painful for [Emlyn],' he explained. 'Whilst I respected him as an exceptional footballer, his people skills left a lot to be desired. I was not the only player at Liverpool that wasn't a member of the Emlyn Hughes fan club.'[686]

Smith, who felt he had become a better player with the responsibility of leadership, believed 'Emlyn takes care of number one' and took pride that 'the players still respected me a lot more than they respected Emlyn'. Despite all that, Liverpool never became a team whose performance was undermined by factional rivalry. Kenny Dalglish, who would arrive at Anfield to find that 'other people didn't like [Emlyn], but he was always all right to me' said, 'No Liverpool player ever carried a grudge out on to the pitch. Emlyn must have disliked people within the dressing-room too, as well as they him, so it was to his credit that he never let grudges show on the pitch.'[687]

Keen to ensure continuity, Paisley elevated Joe Fagan and Ronnie Moran rather than introducing outsiders to the coaching staff. And he encouraged greater participation from players in team meetings than Shankly had ever done. After a 1974-75 season that saw Liverpool achieve second place in the League, they were ready to resume their place at the top. Although not before opening-day drama at Loftus Road, where they lost 2-0 to a Queens Park Rangers team who would take the title race to the wire. In a further act of evolution, the full-back positions were filled by men capable of the offensive duties Paisley now required. Neal, signed a couple of years earlier from Northampton Town, and Joey Jones, a new £100,000 purchase from Wrexham, wore the shirts that once belonged to Smith and Lindsay. The problem in this game was that Hughes went wandering in the middle. 'Everyone charged off to do someone else's job, including selling the programmes,' was the comment to reporters by Paisley, who told Hughes in the privacy of the dressing-room, 'So that's how you thank me, is it? I got you the two faster full-backs you said I should buy.'[688] That didn't sit well with the listening Smith, who now felt Hughes had been plotting to get him out of the team.

Liverpool's response was to lose only once more in the next 16 games. They took revenge over QPR just before Christmas and, after a run of three winless games in the spring, powered their way back with five consecutive victories. The unlikely hero in that sequence was the tall, orange-haired striker Fairclough, a local 19-year-old, who scored all of Liverpool's goals in three successive victories. In two matches, he scored three goals when coming off the bench – including a late winner against Everton – ensuring the 'Supersub' nickname that would both bring him to national prominence and weigh heavily on his career. 'With the exception of the first few months of being a first-team member I honestly hated being a substitute,' he admitted.[689] His team-mates, however, felt differently. 'It was good to have someone with an eye for goal coming on as a substitute,' said Terry McDermott.[690]

Meanwhile, the man who had been earmarked to lead the Liverpool attack was being reinvented as one of the best left-sided midfield players in the country. 'I was struggling up front and Bob suggested I could be more effective coming from deep,' Ray Kennedy explained. 'We tried it and bingo.'[691] A target man at Arsenal, those who had seen him in training and played alongside him were unsurprised by his subsequent success.

'What a footballer Ray Kennedy was,' said Gunners team-mate Bob McNab. 'He never mis-controlled a ball in his life. Ray was so brave. I would be stuck in a corner being pressured and Ray would let me roll him a little under-weighted ball. He used to stick his great big backside in and the centre-half would be kicking him and Ray would win a throw or flick it back to me. And he'd look at me and go, "All right, little man?" I would have sold the North Bank before I sold Ray Kennedy.'

Having always struggled with his weight, Kennedy had made little impression as a Liverpool forward, even though Shankly, who said he reminded him of Rocky Marciano, had signed him to 'do the donkey work and take the knocks'. Where Arsenal's method had been to have him hold the ball up, Liverpool were used to Toshack moving the ball on. Kennedy found it increasingly difficult to motivate himself in the knowledge that Toshack was better than him. But when Cormack suffered a knee injury, it created an opportunity that would take Kennedy into the England team.

It wasn't quite the instant 'bingo' Kennedy proclaimed, but his skilful left foot, vision, and a lovely sense of how to time his runs into the box compensated for positional inexperience. 'Because he comes so late, it baffles defenders,' team-mate McDermott observed after exactly such a finish against Derby that would be named BBC's Goal of the Season in 1978-79. 'They don't know if they're coming or going.'[692] Kennedy's determination to lose weight also helped. 'I have never seen a player work so hard at rectifying that handicap,' Clemence recalled. 'It was as though his life was at stake.'[693] The result, according to Smith, was that 'he became one of the best midfielders we've ever had'.[694]

Alongside him, Callaghan kept on going as his 34th birthday came and went, and Paisley cleverly introduced Jimmy Case, another local boy, whose competitiveness and fierce shot would make him one of England's best uncapped midfield men. An unhappy footnote to Kennedy's conversion was early signs of the Parkinson's disease that would afflict him after his career. Although he could get through the 90 minutes, he was exhausted by the effort and became aware of a lack of coordination in certain training exercises.

Meanwhile, having seen off the challenge of Kennedy, Toshack's partnership with Keegan achieved even greater potency. The media loved it, filming Toshack reciting an embarrassing self-penned ode to his partner and at one point attempting to dress them up as Batman and Robin. In truth, they looked like outfits cobbled together from the contents of grandma's wardrobe for a school project. Keegan's Boy Wonder get-up was nothing more than red jacket, green shorts and tights, black eye mask and a black cape (which, of course, was the wrong colour).

Comic-book pedantry aside, there was no doubting the dynamism of the duo, who combined for 39 goals in 1975-76, although Toshack felt that Heighway's contribution as provider was overlooked. And for all their on-field empathy, Keegan did not perhaps fully reciprocate Toshack's poetic affection. 'Tosh and I are not even great friends off the field,' he explained, although he did 'find his occasional cockiness endearing'.[695]

The tactical development of the Liverpool team, the bold personnel moves and the resulting title challenge ensured that Paisley was established as his own man; spared the fate of McGuinness. 'Technically, Bob always knew a great deal about the game, but that side of him did not come into full view until he took the manager's job,' Keegan confirmed.[696] And while McGuinness had never been allowed to move into Busby's old office at United, Paisley had made an important stand to ensure that he would not have to operate in Shankly's shadow. When Shankly began showing up at Melwood every day in full training kit – with the players nodding 'morning, Boss' – Paisley had the balls to tell his old governor that it undermined him and would not be tolerated.[§] Lloyd also experienced the cold edge of Paisley's pragmatism. Surplus to the new Liverpool vision, he was sold to Coventry City within a week of the regime change.

When Keegan's goal against Leicester City achieved his team's fifth straight win early in April, Liverpool still only found themselves in second place in the table. Ahead of them on goal average, QPR were playing like blue-hooped cavaliers, carrying on from where they had begun on the first day of the campaign. An 11th-place finish the previous season – during which Dave Sexton became manager – gave little indication of the Rangers challenge in store. Nor did a line-up that featured a retread defensive pairing of Frank McLintock and David Webb, who was joined by another ex-Chelsea man, John Hollins, in time for the new season. But no one could fail to be excited by an attack that had the precocity of Stan Bowles teaming up with the talented Don Givens, fed by new England captain Gerry Francis from midfield and Dave Thomas from out wide. Few wingers of the era could deliver a cross at full speed as accurately as the ankle-socked speedster, who had arrived from Burnley for £165,000 in October 1972 – a record fee between Second Division clubs.

The victory over Liverpool had been a statement of intent, with Rangers' first goal ending up as BBC's Goal of the Season. Don Masson pushed the ball from deep to Bowles, who rolled it first time into the path of Francis. After a couple of touches, Francis played a one-two with Givens and advanced into the penalty area, through the channel Hughes had vacated, and calmly scored with a low finish. The second came when Mick Leach, the loyal squad player, found another seam in the Liverpool defence to net a diving header. No wonder Paisley was livid.

None of this had been unexpected to Sexton, who had told his players during pre-season that they possessed the ability to be champions. 'We knew something special was on the cards,' Bowles remembered. 'We reckoned if we could beat Liverpool we could beat anybody.' Rangers proved the veracity of that by hammering

§ Instead, Shankly began showing up at Everton's Bellfield training ground. Bob Latchford recalled him talking a lot with physiotherapist Jim McGregor. 'He'd be taking Liverpool to task, slagging them off,' he said. 'He was a bitter man.'

champions Derby County 5-1 at the Baseball Ground a week later. 'It was pure *Alice in Wonderland* stuff,' wrote Geoffrey Green in *The Times* of a performance that was part of a ten-match unbeaten start. Bowles recalled that there was 'no feeling of euphoria in the dressing-room', just a reaffirmation of the team's self-belief.[697]

As he had at Chelsea, Sexton put the emphasis on positive football. Bowles and Francis could express themselves and Thomas had freedom to roam in the knowledge that full-backs Dave Clement and Ian Gillard, both awarded England caps, would fill in when he drifted inside. 'Gerry and I were playing the best football of our lives. We had this uncanny understanding, which is hard to describe,' said Bowles, despite admitting that they were not close off the field. 'Gerry could play the ball blind to me, and I could backheel the ball to him knowing that he would be there.'[698]

McLintock, who had been a Sexton disciple since their days together at Arsenal, said, 'Some people struggled with Dave because he just wanted to talk about football all the time, but I loved him. At Arsenal his idea was always to keep your team up and down the pitch, no more than about 45 yards apart. If you can do that – and Liverpool did it for years – your midfield players are always in support of your forwards and always in support of your back four. At QPR, Dave was playing the Total Football of the Dutch and the Germans, with a lot of short passing.'[699]

Amid the torrent of points, Bowles's lifestyle was afforded greater tolerance, although he was dropped at Manchester City for arriving late. He had often been to chairman Jim Gregory for hand-outs to cover gambling debts and now, with the championship within reach, Bowles claimed he was being indulged to the extent of £200 a week. He would turn up late for games, direct from the bookmaker. 'No wonder Dave went grey,' he said. 'But when I was on that pitch, that was my stage, and I was relieved to be out there.'[700]

Often overlooked in tales of his unorthodox lifestyle is the fact that Bowles was a keen worker. 'I'd never seen anyone train harder,' said goalkeeper Phil Parkes. 'He'd be one of the first in and one of the last to leave.' Parkes also felt that Bowles offered more to the team collective than his predecessor, Rodney Marsh. 'Rodney was more of an individual while Stan was a real team player and formed a tremendous understanding with Gerry Francis. Their partnership was almost telepathic.'[701] And Bowles was brave, with McLintock observing, 'They'd kick him from pillar to post. But he rarely lost his temper. He was very resilient.'[702]

A mild winter helped the cause of Rangers' attacking football, while their defence would concede only two more goals than Liverpool. When QPR arrived at Norwich City on the penultimate Saturday of the campaign they had won 11 and drawn one of the previous 12 games and not conceded more than two goals in any League game. They promptly lost 3-2. Meanwhile, Liverpool were beating Stoke City 5-3 at Anfield. What a *Match of the Day* that was. *The Best of Upstairs, Downstairs* on ITV didn't stand a chance.

QPR won their last two matches, meaning that Liverpool needed a low-scoring draw or a win at Wolves in a final game that would not take place for a further two weeks. In the meantime, they found themselves two goals down at Anfield in the first leg of the UEFA Cup Final against FC Bruges. A disappointed Toshack was sacrificed at half-time to allow Case to bolster the midfield, and within 20 minutes the home side had a 3-2 lead to take to Belgium.

A week later, Liverpool went to Molineux while the QPR players gathered in a BBC studio to watch a game that, as usual for midweek League contests, was not broadcast to the country. They were on their feet after 13 minutes when Steve Kindon charged through to score for Wolves, who needed a result to maintain a chance of avoiding relegation. That lead lasted until the final 15 minutes, when Keegan got on the end of Toshack's flick and dug the ball from under his feet to equalise. Toshack and Kennedy executed further neat finishes inside the final five minutes and Liverpool's fans charged the field to celebrate the club's ninth League title.[¶] 'I'm proud to be a Liverpudlian tonight,' Paisley announced.

¶ There was no on-field presentation of medals to the players. They received them months later at the training ground, where they had to sort through the boxes dumped in Paisley's office to find one with their name written on it.

A further two weeks on, he emulated the feat of his predecessor in adding the UEFA Cup to the title when Liverpool drew 1-1 in Bruges. They conceded early, but Keegan made sure of the trophy by scoring minutes later. While Paisley was just getting started at Anfield, Keegan could see things coming to an end. The manager's greatest moment was coming, and it would be his star player's farewell.

DO ANYTHING YOU WANNA DO

> *I left England and became a tax exile [in 1975]. This didn't go down particularly well with the British press, who thought I was betraying the land of my birth. It didn't go down especially well with Elton John, either.*
>
> **Rod Stewart, *Rod: The Autobiography* (Century, 2012)**

'Obviously you can never see what is in the future, Colin,' Keegan told his television interviewer. Except that he could. 'This will be my last season at Liverpool because quite simply I can't afford for it not to be.' Rumours that Liverpool had turned down a £750,000 approach from Real Madrid had awoken him to possibilities across the water. '[It] unsettled me and hardened my resolve to leave,' he said, adding that he relished a 'fresh challenge'.[703]

Not to mention that seeing the taxman help himself to 83 per cent of his earnings had lost its appeal. 'At first climbing the ladder is exciting, because we live in a society which thankfully does not feel it is wrong to better oneself,' he would explain. 'Then it becomes noticeable how much the government is taking.'[704]

Keegan went to club chairman John Smith and told him, 'I think it's a chance of a lifetime and I think I should go.'

'I can't really let you go this year because we are in the European Cup,' was the response. 'But if you stay this year, without kicking up a fuss about it, I promise you faithfully that at the end of next season, you will go.'[705]

Satisfied, Keegan set about helping Liverpool towards the twin ambition of retaining their title and becoming England's first European Cup winners since Manchester United in 1968, although he would end up wishing he'd not gone public with his intentions. 'We eventually fell out of love,' said journalist and lifelong Liverpool follower Brian Reade. 'No fan could understand it. It had never happened before. The deal back then was that the club squeezed the life out of the players, discarding them like old dishcloths when time caught up with their knees, and the fans wished them well as they went off to run a pub or sell insurance. But *we* were never dumped.' Liverpool fans, Reade recalled, 'concluded he was an ungrateful, money-grabbing little git'.[706]

Smith believed that Keegan annoyed some team-mates by persisting with his insistence that he would be moving for greater footballing experience. It was 'just so much smokescreen', he said, feeling that an admission of financial motive would have been respected and accepted. 'He acted as though he was ashamed of it.'[707]

When Keegan spoke to Brian Moore for a documentary towards the end of his second season away from Anfield he continued to be guarded over his motives. 'Ambition drove me away,' was still his default position on his transfer to Hamburg, but he was happy to admit, 'Now we have found out that the grass is greener on the other side. We have got a quality of life here and we are being able to keep more of what we earn. My last contract was worth £22,000 a year and when I came to Hamburg I signed for £122,000.'[708] Such a prospect meant that Hughes felt that Keegan's 'mind was elsewhere' during his last season at Liverpool.[709]

Keegan felt the pressure to bring something else to his game; partly to justify the kind of transfer fees being spoken about, but also to remain effective. 'I dread the thought that something different might be the temptation to play like Rodney Marsh and become more of a showman,' he said damningly, shortly after leaving Anfield. But he explained, 'People had become content just to stop me … my game has to develop.'[710]

In the meantime, Paisley, with an eye on a potentially Keegan-less future, had broken the club transfer record to sign England forward David Johnson from Ipswich Town for £200,000. 'Selecting a player for Liverpool is a carefully thought-out business,' he said. 'I look for character, also ability to think quickly as well as skill.'[711]

Johnson soon came to appreciate Paisley's deep thinking about all matters. 'He never missed a trick,' he said. 'Someone had a bit of a bad back, and he said, "What have you done different? Changed your car? Different seat?" He was right.'[712]

He also appreciated quickly that patience was another important Anfield virtue, a lesson learned by McDermott, who had been signed for £180,000 a few months after facing Shankly's team for Newcastle in the 1974 FA Cup Final. Born in Liverpool, it was a dream homecoming for the midfielder who'd grown up as a fan. But in two years at Anfield he had barely registered. Initially overawed by the superstars in the dressing-room, he'd failed to play enough games to earn a Championship medal in the most recent season. But as he had done with Kennedy, Paisley chose his moment to make a previously discouraged McDermott a feature of the side, rewarding him for a good pre-season with an extended run in the first team.

With every move, the links to Shankly were being loosened. Liverpool were evolving towards a more thoughtful method of possession, a system where players understood their geography on the field and had total trust in each other. 'I see Ray going forward on the left flank with the ball, Jimmy and Terry see him, too, and I notice that they begin to move towards the centre,' Neal explained. 'The opposition send men to close them down. That is the signal for me to go. By closing down space round the ball, our opponents leave space off the ball. As I run forward, Ray delivers a beautiful ball. By this time Jimmy and Terry and Ray himself are in attacking positions.' Describing the way he, Case and McDermott 'move up and down as a triangular unit', Neal added, 'There is nothing complicated about our play,' and quoted a favourite saying of Paisley's. 'If the ball's controlled, keep it controlled.'[713]

Games of one-touch five-a-side were designed to improve everyone's decision-making, while peer pressure was a more effective monitor than the risk of disapproval of coaches. 'You were scared you were going to lose [the ball] because of the bollocking you used to get off the players,' Fairclough explained.[714] It added up to a system that earned a second consecutive League Championship, Liverpool finishing a point ahead of Manchester City but without the last-game drama of the previous season.

It was the other end of the table that provided controversy on the final night, when Coventry City, Bristol City and Sunderland sought to avoid the last relegation place. Coventry chairman Jimmy Hill delayed the kick-off of his team's game against Bristol City for 15 minutes because of supposed crowd congestion, meaning that the teams knew a draw would save them both when scoreboard operators were instructed to post news of Sunderland's defeat to Everton. With the score 2-2, *The Guardian* noted that 'what had been an intensely physical contest dissolved farcically' and Sunderland dropped to the Second Division with Stoke City and Tottenham Hotspur.

Back at the top, Liverpool's eight defeats were more than they would have liked, but they could be excused for being somewhat distracted as they attempted to become the first English team to win a treble of League, FA Cup and European Cup – the very challenge that had seen Leeds United fall short on all fronts seven years earlier.

In the FA Cup, they reached the final by beating neighbours Everton in a controversial semi-final. McDermott's chipped goal – voted the best seen on BBC all season – contributed to a 2-2 draw at Maine Road, but Everton were denied a winner when Clive Thomas ruled that Bryan Hamilton had been offside when diverting Duncan McKenzie's header into the net. 'I was satisfied,' Thomas said subsequently, 'that he was offside.' He added, 'If I had not blown for offside, I would still have disallowed the goal for handball.'[715]

But Everton captain Mick Lyons claimed, 'The linesman who was on duty that day, he actually said that Clive Thomas came in and said "Listen, lads, we better get our story straight about this one." I think he robbed us.'[716] And team-mate Bob Latchford would say of Thomas, 'He thought more of himself than any other referee I ever encountered. I've never known a referee who liked the focus on him like he did. He made decisions that defied comprehension.'[717] Even Hughes said two decades after the game that he'd met Thomas on holiday and he'd admitted his mistake. 'Everton should have won the game because they played better than us,' Hughes conceded.[718] Their chance gone, they lost the replay 3-0.

As the climax of the campaign approached, Keegan became agitated that no transfer had been finalised. Struggling to deal with the death of his father in December, he told the chairman that he was losing patience with the club's apparent stubbornness in holding out for a transfer fee that no one appeared willing to pay. Real Madrid, Barcelona and Bayern Munich had all ruled themselves out. Meanwhile, perhaps remembering the difficulties players such as Jimmy Greaves and Denis Law had experienced when making moves overseas in the previous decade, Paisley suggested, 'Kevin is a determined boy with his head screwed on, but you wonder what he is considering with his career.' He feared that Keegan would miss the support system that was such a part of the Anfield environment.

When a deal to SV Hamburg appeared to have collapsed over the weekend of the FA Cup Final, it was assumed to have contributed to Keegan's distracted ineffectiveness as Liverpool's ambitions of the treble ended with a 2-1 defeat to Manchester United. Yet Hamburg's general manager Peter Krohn reported himself 'impressed' with Keegan once more. By the time Liverpool arrived in Rome to face Borussia Moenchengladbach in the European Cup Final four days later, negotiations between the clubs were well advanced. Keegan would take the field determined to prove that he was 'worth the fee Liverpool had put on my head; and to crown my career with Liverpool with an exhibition that would repay the club and everyone connected with it, including the marvellous fans, for the six wonderful years at Anfield.'[719]

That Keegan was able to sign off his Liverpool career in Rome was due in part to events in what came to be considered one of the greatest nights in Anfield history. After losing the first leg of their quarter-final 1-0 against St Etienne, Liverpool survived a fraught, tension-filled home leg for which thousands more than the official 55,000 were thought to have squeezed into the ground after a gate was broken on the Kemlyn Road side. The Kop had never seemed more alive, more integrated into what was happening on the field. Players admitted to being distracted during the game because their attention was drawn to the pulsating mass of humanity around them. 'There was such an atmosphere I got a feeling something special was about to happen,' said Fairclough. 'There was something different about it.'[720]

Keegan scored early on, but the previous season's runners-up replied through Dominique Bathenay's long-range effort early in the second half. Liverpool now needed to score twice. Kennedy found the net as the hour mark approached, but with no further breakthrough Fairclough was sent on with 16 minutes left. Only six minutes remained when he chased after Kennedy's hopeful knock forward, chested the ball ahead of him and beat the goalkeeper with an early finish. Anfield erupted and Fairclough disappeared under a pile of red shirts, being told to stay down to waste more time by Keegan, who said later, 'We came off feeling as though we had won the final itself.'[721]

After such drama, a straightforward victory in the last four against FC Zurich seemed anti-climactic. But nothing could diminish the significance of the club's first European Cup Final, 12 years after they had lost to Inter Milan in their previous semi-final. Not even the disappointment of Wembley defeat four days earlier. As the Liverpool players sat in gloomy silence in the losers' dressing-room, Clemence had broken the ice by announcing that he intended to get pissed. By the time the squad arrived back in Liverpool, spirits and confidence were high once more. Smith felt that the loss of the treble meant that pressure had been relieved, while Hughes sensed that it enabled the players to play down the occasion ahead of them.

Paisley had allowed fear of a delayed FA Cup Final replay** to affect his team selection at Wembley, sacrificing Callaghan in midfield for an extra striker, Johnson – Toshack's season having ended through an

** International commitments meant that the FA were forced to name 27 June as the date of a replay, six weeks after the original game and two weeks before clubs were due to begin training for the next season. An offer by United and Liverpool to decide the game on penalties if necessary was declined. 'I'm not intellectual enough to find words to express my disgust at this stupidity,' said Paisley, while Docherty quipped, 'We'll have to take our holidays on the Costa del Stretford.'

Achilles tendon injury. Callaghan was back for the European final, while Thompson's late-season injury meant another survivor of the 1965 campaign, Smith, had regained his place for the closing weeks of what he intended to be his last season.

For the Liverpool manager, there was additional poignance in the selection of the Stadio Olimpico as the venue for the final. As a member of Montgomery's Eighth Army in the Second World War, Paisley had been part of the liberation of Rome in June 1944. The heat and humidity made some question the suitability of the venue selection, but it did not deter 30,000 Liverpool supporters making the trip, outnumbering the German fans by an estimated four to one. 'The hills of Rome are alive to the Liverpool sound,' was how BBC commentator Barry Davies described the setting. Among the Liverpool fans, one banner stood out, in tribute to the hard-tackling full-back Jones: 'Joey ate the Frogs' legs, made the Swiss roll, now he's munching Gladbach.'[††]

Paisley's intention was to match Borussia's patience and to take advantage of their opponents' plan to station veteran defender Berti Vogts close to Keegan. 'Vogts tackles best on his right foot,' he said, 'so as far as possible Kevin led him to the side of the field where he had to tackle on his weak left side.'[722] It would pay particular dividends late in the game.

Keegan sensed that Borussia's preoccupation with him displayed a defeatist attitude, their apprehension allowing Liverpool to settle quickly. Even so, it was Borussia who almost scored when Rainer Bonhof struck the post with a low shot from 30 yards. Liverpool took the lead after 28 minutes when Heighway cut in from the right and slid a pass into the box for McDermott to lift a shot over the goalkeeper. Vogts was off somewhere shadowing Keegan, yards from where the action was. Yet Borussia hit back after half-time when Danish international Allan Simonsen capitalised on a rare Callaghan misjudgement to thrash the ball past Clemence. Simonsen, destined to become one of the more unlikely signings in the history of Charlton

†† Jones was presented with the banner by the two fans who made it 26 years later, passing it on to the Liverpool FC museum.

Athletic, could have given his team the lead had he not fluffed a free header. And then Clemence spread himself to deny Uli Stielike in what he considered the most important save of his career.

Despite the scares, it was Liverpool who regained the lead after a corner on the left, delivered by Heighway and met with a thunderous header. 'Look at the delighted scorer – it's Tommy Smith,' exclaimed Davies, voicing the nation's incredulity and his colleagues' joy. As Case said, 'I couldn't have been happier: he had been my hero, my inspiration, my mentor and my friend.'[723] When Smith had practised coming up for corners during the season, the focus had been on flicking the ball on for Keegan. This time, however, he was presented with 'the greatest cross I've ever seen' and 'so much room it was untrue'.[724]

The game was secured eight minutes from time when Vogts, frustrated and dragged out to the left of the defence once more, fouled Keegan as he burst past him. 'Vogts never had a chance. Kevin was in irresistible form,' said Hughes. 'Vogts's frustration spilled over. He had been turned inside out.'[725] Neal sent Wolfgang Kneib the wrong way and the European Cup was bound for Merseyside.

Smith duly unretired, Shankly admitted to being 'bloody well jealous' and Keegan completed his £500,000 transfer to Hamburg, new holders of the European Cup Winners' Cup. 'I know in my heart I will never again experience the camaraderie of the Liverpool team and all the staff there,' he said a few weeks later.[726] Towards the Liverpool fans, however, there was a tone of ambivalence. 'The way they turned against me in the last couple of months of the season, when I had lost my consistency and needed their support proved to me that it was right for me to go,' he recorded. 'My name was chanted in Rome, when I played well again. But I had barely heard the supporters for a year. To be honest, I found it hard to forget that as I waved to them.'[727] Keegan felt flat after the final whistle and quickly consigned the game to history, moving ahead with plans to sell his farmhouse in north Wales to Everton full-back Mike Pejic.

Paisley, meanwhile, gave £100,000 to Patrick Thistle for gangly defender Alan Hansen, who admitted that he was 'about to start my football education'. But attention focused mostly on where Liverpool would spend their Keegan windfall. They did so in Glasgow – under assumed names in a hotel 30 miles outside, to be precise – buying Kenny Dalglish from Celtic for £440,000 after several weeks of pursuit. No English club had ever spent more.

Dalglish had grown up as a Rangers fan and had once had a trial week with Liverpool when 15 years old. He had gone on to score 167 goals for Celtic at a rate of one every other game, helping the club to four Scottish League titles during six years as a first-teamer. Skilful and intelligent, strong on the ball, an equal threat as scorer or provider, he was the shining light of Scottish football by the time Paisley persuaded Jock Stein to part with him. Like Keegan, Dalglish had been agitating for a new challenge and had been persuaded to remain for one final season.

Comparisons with Keegan were inevitable. Chairman John Smith said, 'We have sold one of the best and bought the best.' Paisley pointed out that Dalglish shared Keegan's flexibility in playing in different positions, while the new signing insisted, 'I am not trying to take over from Kevin, I am trying to be my own man.'

Dalglish walked into a dressing-room where, not only was he taken aback by the number of hairdryers being used by his fashion-conscious colleagues, but he needed to prove himself. 'When he first arrived at Anfield I thought there was no chance of him ever being as good as Kevin,' said McDermott. 'No one could have forecast that he would be held in the same high esteem.'[728]

As Clemence described it, Liverpool soon came to realise that Dalglish offered a 'a different dimension', being 'crafty and cunning'.[729] According to Graeme Souness, 'He wasn't the quickest, but he had that sixth sense that would tell him where everyone was all the time. He could read the game several steps ahead. His brain worked at a different level.'[730]

Dalglish found it easy to find his feet at a club that had a philosophy of keeping things simple on the field. And, coinciding with Toshack's departure – which meant no more target man – his arrival completed Liverpool's personality change from the old regime to one that was pure Paisley. If Keegan had personified the passion and energy that characterised Shankly's side, then Dalglish was the intelligent hub of Paisley's more sophisticated unit.

Even the Kop had undergone change. The terrace songs of the 1960s had been a symphony for a city enjoying full employment and finding itself at the centre of the modern world; birthplace of The Beatles and, by extension, spiritual home for millions. By the late 1970s, the chants had become cries of defiance from a population that would not go quietly into the night of urban decay, rising unemployment and the erosion of its industry. Liverpool lost an estimated 80,000 jobs between 1972 and 1982 as modern freight methods led to unemployment at the Mersey docks. Trans-Atlantic lines ceased operating from the port and the local manufacturing industry contracted by half. 'The country owed quite a lot to Liverpool,' said Liverpudlian actor Ricky Tomlinson, 'but when they've decided they didn't have much more to contribute, particularly under Heath and Thatcher: "We'll give it the elbow."'[731]

In the middle of the 1980s almost half of the city's males between the ages of 16 and 24 were unemployed – not that there was much sympathy from the rest of the country. Liverpool-born author Tony Evans recorded, 'If the unemployed were to be sneered at, those who were in work earned little more respect. When they fought for their jobs and refused to accept the terms offered by management and government, they were looked upon as troublemakers … genuine grievances were dismissed as pointless militancy and laziness by outsiders.'[732]

In the austere years after the Second World War, during which the city had suffered horribly at the hands of the Luftwaffe, it was football that had lifted spirits and provided the escapism that carried its citizens through the working week. In the 1970s, as hardship bit once more, so the sport of the working man – and of those out of work – offered hope and happiness. 'In a city cast as an outsider in its own land, battered by the deliberate economic downturns and clear-outs of the early 1980s,' wrote historian David Goldblatt, 'Liverpool Football Club was an enduring source of pride, a magnet for the energies and emotions of a public hungry for success.'[733]

Liverpool-born John Aldridge, who would play for his hometown team in the 1980s, knew better than anyone that 'this city needs football badly'. Calling it 'an outlet for the people', he said, 'They need the teams to be up there winning trophies, to help them enjoy one day a week … having a few beers with their friends, getting all the anxieties out. Over the years gone past, that's what helped the city stay on its feet.'[734]

It was why Rome, the destination of so many religious pilgrimages, had been worth days of harsh travel or the sale of whatever belongings had value or the dissolution of savings – even among those who had to be more selective about attending home games because of lack of cash. With Wembley as the venue, there was slightly less commitment required when Liverpool returned to the European Cup Final at the conclusion of Dalglish's first season.

Going into the game against FC Bruges – like Borussia, a team Liverpool had beaten in a previous UEFA Cup Final – Dalglish had scored 30 goals across the various competitions, including finding the net in his first three League games for the club. The *Liverpool Echo* had seen enough of Dalglish in a goal-scoring debut at Middlesbrough to declare, 'This lesson is clear. Give Dalglish the ball on the deck and he'll score a lot of goals.' And the Kop's love affair with 'King Kenny' began when he cleverly chipped home against Newcastle three days later.

January had brought another momentous transfer, the purchase of Scotland midfielder Souness from Middlesbrough for £352,000, completed not long after Liverpool crashed out of the FA Cup at Chelsea. Born and raised in Edinburgh, Souness's early career at Tottenham Hotspur – where he won the FA Youth Cup – was dominated by the occasion when he took himself home without permission. When Spurs suspended him, West Lothian MP Tam Dalyell questioned in the House of Commons whether the club had the right to deny a minor the right to work in his chosen profession because he was homesick. 'People only remember the bad things,' Souness said a couple of years later. 'Things that have happened in the past keep cropping up.'[735] He created a new narrative at

Middlesbrough, where he became the heartbeat of Jack Charlton's unlikely title challengers.

An instinctive, visionary passer and possessor of a fierce shot, no player since Johnny Giles brought such a stark blend of talent and terrorism to the midfield of First Division matches. 'He's one of the most fearsome players I've ever seen, but he can also create poetry with one of his perfectly-timed passes,' said Paisley. Journalist David Miller's description of him as 'a bear of a man with the touch of a violinist' takes some beating. New team-mate Case's overriding memory of his new colleague was the photograph that had appeared in the Sunday papers after Liverpool knocked Boro out of the previous season's FA Cup. Case was on his back with hands and knees raised while Souness had his left hand on his opponent's throat and his clenched right fist drawn back, ready to throw a punch.

Souness was given an early insight into the Liverpool set-up. When he approached Paisley for instructions, surprised he had not yet been given any, the gist of the reply was that when the club paid that much for someone they didn't expect to have to tell him how to play. Just as Paisley trusted his players to act responsibly away from the ground without the need for petty rules and regulations, so he believed he could rely on them to find their way on the field. Similarly, McDermott had initially been confused when Paisley kept telling him to play 'the Liverpool way'. Having asked coach Ronnie Moran what Paisley meant, he was told, 'Work it out for yourself, son.'[736]

Souness recalled, 'I knew from the outset that I would be coming into a ruthless dressing-room with a winning mentality. There would be nobody to hold your hand.'[737] After he made his debut against Birmingham, Moran bawled him out for receiving a short pass from Hughes at left-back and rolling it to Thompson. 'Don't you think our left-back, who is England captain, can pass the ball 20 yards to our centre-back, who is a regular player in the England team?' yelled Moran. 'We don't take the easy option just to get a touch of the ball. Get the ball in midfield and work.'[738] Before long, Souness was playing the role of on-field regulator, using his understanding of

Liverpool's game and his forceful personality to dictate the pattern of play. McDermott said of his new team-mate, 'What we didn't realise until we saw him close up was that, actually, he was a brilliant player. On the field he had great determination. He wouldn't exactly bollock you for a mistake, but he had that withering look, a horrible glare so you knew not to do it again.'[739]

Despite these signings, Liverpool lost nine matches in finishing as distant First Division runners-up behind Nottingham Forest and were beaten by Brian Clough's team in the final of the League Cup. A 7-1 aggregate win against Keegan's Hamburg in the European Super Cup, including a 6-0 victory at Anfield, was a mere side note. A second European Cup triumph had become a requirement if something was to be taken from the season.

After a first-round bye, Liverpool swept past Dynamo Dresden and Benfica before another meeting with Borussia Moenchengladbach in the semi-final. A 2-1 defeat in Germany did not reflect the poise and control of an outstanding performance, but it set up a 3-0 victory in the second leg. Bruges were unexpected opponents at Wembley, having beaten Juventus in the semi-final. Liverpool began as strong favourites, which might have been why the game was unmemorable to anyone who wasn't a fan of the competing teams. The Belgians appeared to have no ambition beyond stretching the game out to penalties.

Fittingly for the story of Liverpool's season, Dalglish scored and Souness created the only goal after 64 minutes. The former ran on to his team-mate's pass towards the right corner of the six-yard box, paused long enough to allow keeper Birger Jensen to commit himself, and clipped the ball over him into the far corner. Dalglish put his finish down to noticing that Jensen had previously dropped down early to deal with two shots by McDermott. From most players, that would sound like a boast delivered with the benefit of hindsight, yet Dalglish's cleverness made it entirely plausible.

With two European Cups, Paisley had not only eclipsed Shankly, he had brought English football the kind of success at the highest level it had been craving since Ramsey and Busby were achieving their knighthoods. No wonder BBC Radio Merseyide had questioned him about the position of England manager. 'I've got my own problems at Liverpool without being saddled with England's,' he'd responded. 'It doesn't cross my mind.'

FANFARE FOR THE COMMON MAN

Oh no, we won't give in
Let's go living in the past

'Living in the Past', Jethro Tull (Ian Anderson; Ian Anderson Music Ltd, Chrysalis Music, BMG Rights Management, 1969, 1972)

Don Revie and Tony Greig had defected. Tommy Docherty had been caught with his trousers down. Johnny Rotten had tried to hijack the Queen's Silver Jubilee. But when the Football Association looked to its future in the summer of 1977 they saw not chaos and anarchy, but the comfort of cardigans. Paisley, who happily wore one on the training ground and in the team hotel, had won club football's greatest prize. Virginia Wade had recently slipped into a pink one to receive the Wimbledon singles trophy from the Queen. Paisley might not have been a realistic option for the post of England manager, but he and Ginny represented the kind of reliable establishment figure that the FA needed in order to put the embarrassment of Revie behind them and show that perhaps society wasn't crumbling after all.

Ron Greenwood had been spending more time in knitwear than tracksuits since vacating the manager's job at West Ham United three years earlier. Considered in the 1960s one of the most forward-thinking brains in football, he was now a 55-year-old who had lost his love of the game. His spirit, he said, was as low as that of the national team itself. To many he was an unlikely choice to be offered the England job – albeit on a temporary basis – to see them through the final weeks of a doomed World Cup qualifying campaign. To the FA, frightened of their own shadows after Revie, he was perfect. From a reputational point of view, there was no one better.

'We've a bit of a situation and we haven't made up our minds about anything,' FA chairman Sir Harold Thompson told Greenwood.

'The image of the game is all wrong and we need a firm, stable hand immediately.'[740]

Greenwood was happy to help, believing that Revie's defection 'undoubtedly damaged the reputation and morale of our game and that was unforgiveable'. There was also an important element of self-help involved in his acceptance of the role. Missing regular contact with players, he'd felt detached from West Ham's 1975 FA Cup win – despite being the club's general manager – and had avoided the celebrations. He was as unhappy with the man in the mirror as he was about the state of the national game. Having been starved of success in his last nine years at West Ham, after winning the FA Cup and European Cup Winners' Cup, he also admitted, 'I had a hope, too, that my ideas might be better suited to international football.'[741] Greenwood was considered by many to have carried too soft, too idealistic an approach into the hardened Seventies. In 1971, *Goal* had written, 'We hope that he recognises his allegiance to high principles has gradually become an indulgence.'[742]

It was to Anfield that Greenwood travelled as he tried to apply his principles to a new environment. Having gained Paisley's permission to meet with his English players, he heard reports of a 'lack of a collective spirit'. His response was to build his team to face Switzerland in a Wembley friendly around the Liverpool side. Along with the departed Keegan, he selected Clemence, Neal, Hughes, McDermott, Kennedy and Callaghan, who had last played for his country during the 1966 World Cup. Callaghan was shocked by what he encountered on his return to the England squad. 'They start to worry about the game and the result, often before the kick-off,' he said, 'and continue to do so for 90 minutes, getting more frustrated as time goes on.'[743]

If one went along with Greenwood's Liverpool-based philosophy, you could argue that it didn't go far enough. It would have made sense to include Case to complete Liverpool's four-man midfield. In fact, when Paisley was asked why England could not play like Liverpool, his answer was, 'Simple. It's because they don't play Jimmy Case.' Instead, Greenwood picked three front men in Keegan, Trevor Francis and Mick Channon. They spent the evening getting into each other's space as England drew 0-0 in front of a sparse crowd of 42,000. It was hardly the uplifting night Greenwood hoped to deliver. Nor was a 2-0 win in Luxembourg a month later, when all the Liverpool contingent but Neal were again selected. It marked the end of the Anfield experiment.

'I decided eventually that simplicity was our best bet,' Greenwood said of his approach to a game against Italy in which only victory by multiple goals would give them a realistic chance of rescuing World Cup qualification. 'We needed to fall back on a basic pattern that was immediately understandable.'[744] By that he meant two wingers – Manchester United's Steve Coppell and Manchester City's Peter Barnes – and an old-fashioned centre-forward in Bob Latchford. Keegan would join those three debutants up front, with Francis left out by Greenwood. 'I had the feeling he wanted Kevin and me in the same team,' Francis recalled, 'but wasn't sure how to achieve it. I knew that Keegan's best position was up front. So that in the long run, it was going to be a question of whether Greenwood would change the system and play without a target man.'[745]

The midfield two were players who met Greenwood's preference for the elegant, Trevor Brooking and Ray Wilkins. It appeared that the only *True Grit* on television that night would be the movie BBC had decided to put up against ITV's live coverage from Wembley. But if there was a risk that England might have limited possession, Greenwood was prepared to accept it for the attacking options the middle two would find ahead of them.

The match programme made a brave attempt to walk the tightrope between acknowledging the national team's deficiencies and sounding upbeat. To that end, Jack Rollin was invited to pen a piece headlined, 'A sympathetic view of England's problems', which became a tortuous exercise in not upsetting anyone. 'The state of English football is such that it appears on the surface at least to be considered by the professional body of opinion to be capable of not only being able to hold itself with the world's best but good enough to overcome it,' he said, which did not exactly gel with the comments from within the game after their lesson at the hands of Holland. Aware of exactly that, he added, 'On the other hand the public impression is that our standards have fallen considerably.'[746]

At least everyone would end up happy on this night. Greenwood's selection was vindicated in the 11th minute when Wilkins and Brooking worked their way down the right with an interchange of passes before Brooking curled in the kind of diagonal near-post cross he'd practised under Greenwood at West Ham. Keegan looped a header beyond Dino Zoff to give England the lead. With 10 minutes to play, Keegan stabbed a pass through to Brooking with the outside of his foot and the midfield man netted his first England goal.

Italy might still have needed only to beat Luxembourg at home to end England's World Cup, but 92,000 at Wembley and millions watching at home had seen England's footballing pride restored, with the Keegan–Brooking partnership laying down a marker for the years to come. 'What a pair they were,' Greenwood enthused. 'They cooked up goals for England that suggested telepathy. There was a special relationship between them on the field that springs from familiarity, confidence – and something beyond my ken.'[747]

Keegan's satisfaction went deeper than the matter of restored national honour. He felt vindicated personally in the face of comments, including from Paisley, that he should not play for his country after leaving English football. 'He convinced the whole of England that I wasn't good enough to play for England,' Keegan said. 'From that day on there was a lynch out for me from the England squad. When I came back to play against Italy I phoned up [agent] Harry [Swales] and said, "I think this is the end of the road because my England place is gonna go."' But after the performance against Italy, 'I was the hero again. That was probably the changing point in my international career.'[748]

It also helped him forget the early struggles he was experiencing in Hamburg, where the resentment he encountered among team-mates dissipated only after he was suspended for several weeks and they realised what they were missing. 'Keegan had been having a terrible time in Germany,' Greenwood acknowledged. 'He fought back and that is the character of the man. He's not necessarily a better player for going abroad, but he is certainly a more alert and adaptable player.'[749]

Greenwood's caretaker tenure was up, and the moment had arrived to determine England's permanent manager. He faced opposition from three others, including Brian Clough, who was on his way to winning that season's League title with Forest. Clough had never hidden his ambition to manage his country. A few months earlier, when asked by a journalist whether he thought he could do a better job than Revie, he'd replied, 'If I didn't think that I wouldn't bother about applying for the job. I've never failed as a manager – and with the best players from the country in the team, how could I fail?' The other candidates were Bobby Robson, bound for the FA Cup with Ipswich Town; and Lawrie McMenemy, who was about to lead his former Cup winners to promotion from the Second Division.

The trio of new candidates headed to FA headquarters for hour-long interviews, with Clough telling reporters as he breezed in, 'I am just delighted to be associated with it.' While Clough was positioned by the media – and himself – as 'the people's choice', the FA's own survey of First Division captains was reported by *The Times* as having revealed 12 votes for Greenwood, twice as many as Clough garnered.

Yet how open a competition this was has always been a subject of conjecture. According to Glen Kirton, the England team press officer at the time, 'Ron Greenwood wasn't actually on the candidate list, presumably because he had already been lined up.'[750] Greenwood himself recalled his 'interview' in a manner that cast further doubt about its formality. 'I had an office at Lancaster Gate and I certainly took the few steps into the interviewing room. My interview lasted about half an hour. It was friendly, relaxed and I put all my hopes and plan to the committee.'[751]

Being England manager, even on a temporary basis, also gave him a platform to outline his manifesto to the media, calling for a 'reappraisal throughout the country, starting in the schools'. He added, 'There is a great gulf between League soccer and the international game. This is the biggest problem: finding players who can bridge the gap.' And he implicated club managers for creating a situation where games were condensed into suffocating midfield battles. His most persuasive argument, however, remained the victory over Italy.

McMenemy, who recalled that Greenwood had been absent on interview day, admitted, 'I wasn't ready [for the job] and I believe Bobby felt the same about himself. Brian was different. In his estimation he should already have been in the job.'[752] So did all four players canvassed for a feature in *Shoot!*: Ian Callaghan, West Brom captain John Wile, Middlesbrough's John Craggs and a Welshman, Terry Yorath – despite his experience of Clough at Leeds.

According to Kirton, no minutes were kept of the meeting of the electoral committee that determined the new England manager. 'Everybody was scared stiff of [Sir Harold Thompson] and very few people had the intellect or strength of character to withstand him,' he suggested. 'There wasn't a vote; the decision was made beforehand. The chairman would have said, "I want to appoint Ron Greenwood," and they would have agreed.'[753] Greenwood was, after all, a man described by Thompson on his appointment as 'a jolly decent fellow'.

Greenwood learned of his appointment on the car radio and, aware of scepticism over his West Ham record, told reporters, 'At club level, you have to make do. At international level you have the best players in the country.' He also argued that there were good players capable of representing England but 'we have destroyed them by not giving them space to work'. And he concluded with a rallying cry. 'Let's forget how defensive we were. Let's go forward.'

14

THE OUTSIDERS

MRS PARSLOW: Foreign is he?
GRANVILLE: It looks like that, Mrs Parslow.
MRS PARSLOW: Ee, don't they have some funny ways?

***Open All Hours*, 'St Albert's Day' (Roy Clarke; BBC TV, 1981)**

SOME HAD gone prepared with bags of scrap paper or had chopped up pages from phone books. Others, seeing what those around them had planned, quickly improvised by tearing newspapers or food wrappers. When Osvaldo Ardiles and Ricardo Villa climbed the steps that brought the players into view at the south-west corner of White Hart Lane, passing below the ubiquitous navy blue home-made Spurs banner, the makeshift tickertape fell about their ears in a poignant reminder of home.

It took an exaggerated stretch of the imagination to truly conjure up images of the sea of white that welcomed the World Cup-winning Argentina team every time they'd entered the River Plate Stadium in Buenos Aires during the summer but, for the Tottenham fans who had grabbed places close to the players' tunnel on this sunny August afternoon, it was their way of welcoming two men who had become the talk of English football.

'Pre-season was absolute chaos,' Villa, the less celebrated of the duo, recalled of his arrival in London. 'People seemed to gather wherever we went, in their hundreds at training.'[754] Yet it was a home game against London rivals Chelsea – the third game of the campaign – that offered most of a fascinated population their first chance to see these exotic specimens in their new habitat. Commentating for *The Big Match*, Brian Moore welcomed the players to the field by highlighting 'this amazing atmosphere' and added, 'It really is still a novelty to see those two great Argentinian players on an English field.'

There was no danger of mixing up the two men, born within two weeks of each other 26 years earlier and now firm friends. Short and slight, Ardiles, in the No.8 shirt, wore several days' dark stubble, giving him an even leaner look than usual, like a Spaghetti western villain. Villa, No.7, sported a full beard and a taller, fuller figure. Opposing them was a Chelsea side boasting experienced defenders Ron Harris and David Hay, himself a World Cup veteran, and a group of fresh-faced, mostly home-grown, forwards, including skipper Ray Wilkins.

It had been Chelsea's previous visit to White Hart Lane more than three years previously when 18-year-old Wilkins, more commonly known in those days as 'Butch', had inherited the Chelsea captaincy for the match that, as well as featuring battles on the pitch between the fans, ensured that it was the visitors who were condemned to relegation. For this game, Spurs, fresh from their own one-year sentence in the Second Division, had seen their fans gathering around Tottenham High Road since early morning in readiness for their first home Saturday of the season. At least they were intent on voyeurism rather than violence, inspired by the opportunity to see men who had reportedly cost a combined £700,000.

Both players crossed themselves as the game kicked off and Spurs centre-forward Gerry Armstrong, sporting one of several fashionable bubble perms on view, hit the first shot over the bar. Colour television was still uncommon enough in 1978 for Moore to say sorry to those monochrome viewers having trouble distinguishing the traditional Spurs kit from Chelsea's yellow shirts and green shorts, but there was nothing apologetic about the way the big blond figure of Steve Wicks bundled the ball and Villa into touch in the eighth minute. Far from clearing the danger, though, it set up a piece of Argentinian magic.

Villa dropped the throw-in at the feet of Ardiles, who took the ball down the right wing beyond his team-mate before dragging it back to his colleague with the sole of his boot. Villa powered around the outside of a desperate challenge by Gary Stanley and then back-heeled into the path of Ardiles advancing into the area. He skipped past Wicks and used the outside of his left foot to flick the ball back from the byline. After it bounced off Armstrong's chest, Scottish striker John Duncan tucked away the loose ball for a goal that was, according to Moore, 'the work undeniably, though, of the two Argentinians'. A couple of teenaged fans in cap-sleeved T-shirts ran on to hug Ardiles as the crowd took up the 'Ar-gen-tina, Ar-gen-tina' chant that had been heard so frequently during the summer.

The lead lasted less than a minute and Ardiles set about aiming to restore the advantage, clipping a shot outside the post. With half-time approaching, Villa laid the ball off to Ardiles. Progressing into the area, Villa latched on to a nicely-weighted first-time return pass from his team-mate, checked back inside Kenny Swain and presented the ball for Armstrong to drive in from near the penalty spot. 'And again the Argentinians have made it,' observed Moore, who chirped as the half-time whistle blew, 'Tottenham are beginning to get dividends from their outlay. Little Ardiles has looked so skilful, so spritely and so capable of pulling off the incredible.' He couldn't do all the defending, though, and the final score of 2-2 meant a third game for Tottenham's new acquisitions without victory.

The contribution of Ardiles was enough to encourage *The Big Match* producers to piece together a slow-motion montage, shot on film, of the Argentinian flitting around the field to the musical backing of Lindisfarne's recent top ten hit, 'Run For Home'. Wicks was rather more prosaic in his reaction. 'Ardiles could cost them a lot of goals because he doesn't get back,' he argued. 'Every time an attack broke down he seemed to be standing next to me.'

It had not been because of defensive abilities that Ardiles had found Spurs manager Keith Burkinshaw sitting with an interpreter in a Buenos Aires hotel, two weeks after Argentina had beaten Holland 3-1 in the World Cup Final. Energetic and intelligent with a sharp mind and a delicate touch, Ardiles had been one of the most important elements of the host nation's progress to what appeared pre-ordained glory. Having missed the 6-0 victory over Peru that had earned them a place in the final after suffering an ankle injury in the previous game, he was considered so vital that Argentina's medical staff gave him a series of painkilling injections to ensure that he got through 70 minutes of the final. Prompting the play from central midfield in his No.2 jersey – courtesy of his country's alphabetical distribution of squad numbers – he provided the platform for the headline-grabbing Mario Kempes. 'Half my job was to create, the other half to defend,' Ardiles explained. 'I was a pure midfielder who you rarely saw in either penalty area.'[755]

Burkinshaw's journey had been inspired by Sheffield United boss Harry Haslam, who, in conjunction with his Argentinian coaches Danny Bergera and Oscar Arce, had been tracking young players in the country, including an exciting prospect who had just failed to make the World Cup squad, Diego Maradona. Knowing that Ardiles's club, Huracan, needed more money than Sheffield United could afford, Haslam alerted Burkinshaw and arranged for Antonio Rattin, the Argentina captain infamously sent off in the 1966 World Cup quarter-final, to help broker a deal.

Ardiles had already begun imagining himself in European football, although in Spain or Italy, whose biggest games were shown on local television. 'While the Italians drooled over his skills and the Spaniards awaited developments, Burkinshaw caught a plane to the Argentine capital,' reporter Malcolm Folley explained when the *Daily Express* broke the exclusive story under the headline, 'SPURS SCOOP THE WORLD'. *Daily Mirror* chief sports writer Frank McGhee countered by claiming Burkinshaw made his move having 'studied my report that the successful Argentine team was about to break up'.

Ardiles was summoned to the Sheraton Hotel in his nation's capital. He knew little of English football and had never heard of Tottenham Hotspur; he certainly had no idea they had only just regained First Division status. Burkinshaw watched him intently while an interpreter laid out the Spurs offer. Like a prospective dog owner who chooses two puppies so that they can keep each other company, Burkinshaw had been persuaded of the wisdom of signing two Argentinians and revealed his interest in Villa, who had roomed with Ardiles during the World Cup. 'Many people think he is the best player in Argentina,' Burkinshaw said of a man who had played only twice as a substitute during the World Cup. Hence Villa picked up the telephone and heard his friend asking, 'Do you fancy playing in England?'

Once it had been explained that Tottenham was in London, Ardiles and his wife, Sylvia, took little persuading. Having begun training for a law degree before becoming a professional footballer – a curiosity most commentators couldn't resist mentioning at least once per game during the World Cup – Ardiles negotiated on behalf of both players, ensuring identical personal terms. Surprisingly, the reported combined transfer fee of £700,000 (or £750,000 in some newspapers) was weighted towards Villa; £375,000 to £325,000 according to his own recollection. Both men were to be paid a £25,000 annual salary, not a great deal more than they had received in their home country. Villa noted, though, that it was a novelty for him when his wages arrived on time. He also banked £45,000 as his percentage of the transfer fee. Additionally, Spurs gave the players a monthly allowance to call home, but as Villa's parents in Roque Perez didn't have a telephone it meant a little extra cash in his pocket.

News of the transfers stunned British football. There had been no inkling in the press that anything was in the works, no protracted negotiations in the media. And Burkinshaw, a former miner from Barnsley with a strait-laced public persona, had hardly been the most likely candidate for such a display of flamboyance and audacity. While Brian Clough's subsequent £1 million capture of Trevor Francis would be totally in character, Burkinshaw had led Tottenham back to the First Division on the back of judicious signings from Scotland or England's lower divisions. Colin Lee, a forward who scored four goals on his Spurs debut after a £60,000 move from Torquay United, was his kind of deal.

Burkinshaw, 43, had been sacked as coach of Newcastle United and relegated and promoted in his first two seasons in charge at Spurs. Suddenly he was a pioneer; someone who would stroll into a Las Vegas casino, dinner jacket draped over his shoulder, and throw down a wad of cash on red. Admitting that he 'never expected to get the pair of them', Burkinshaw added, 'It proves that Tottenham think big and want to be the best club in the country.' Burkinshaw acknowledged that the impoverished state of both Huracan and Villa's Racing Club contributed to it becoming 'the easiest deal I have ever done'. And he added, 'Sometimes we undersell ourselves. Our game still warrants tremendous respect abroad. Both players wanted to come to England and can't wait to get on with the job.'

Within five days of the deal being completed, Ardiles and Villa were bound for England for the first time. They were given a taste of the kind of winter of industrial unrest that awaited them in Britain when they were stranded for a night in Madrid by the same work stoppage of Spanish and French air-traffic controllers that was wrecking the plans of thousands of British holidaymakers. Having at last made it to London, they were taken to White Hart Lane to see the stadium, finalise contracts, meet team-mates and then be introduced to fans and photographers on a sunny Monday morning. Then came lunch, a medical and the first press conference, aided by a translator.

'Everyone has been marvellous,' said Ardiles, whose wife was expecting their second child. 'I would like the baby to have double nationality. I think London is a beautiful city and England a very beautiful country. I know about the Queen, the Thames river, Manchester, Liverpool, the Beatles and,' he added, apparently unaware of the Irish Sea, 'George Bernard Shaw.'

The state of the British economy, ubiquitous even in the minds of sports hacks, featured prominently in the exchanges. Questions such as, 'What do you know about the crippling tax system we have here?' were balanced by, 'Are you impressed by our relatively low rate of inflation?' To the latter, Villa responded, 'Yes, one year's inflation here is equal to one month's inflation in Argentina.'

The following day, the duo returned to Buenos Aires to prepare for a more permanent trip. Their transfers had in part been made possible by the European Economic Community ruling in February that a player's nationality was not a lawful reason to prevent a club signing him. Football was ordered to follow the principles of the Treaty of Rome, which allowed for workforce fluidity between member countries. Clubs should be allowed two overseas players, Brussels decided, and the Football League duly approved the measures at its annual general meeting early in June, adding that players from the Republic of Ireland would continue not to count as 'foreign'. That ruling effectively ended England's 47-year ban on overseas players. Approval for work permits would still be needed for players from outside the EEC, but on that score Burkinshaw had stated, 'The Department of Employment told me last week that there wouldn't be any problem.'

The English sporting media were happy to offer their endorsement of the new arrivals. 'All we need now is one or two foreign managers,' said David Miller in the *Daily Express*. 'Ardiles might just persuade us to ask why we have so few comparable stars. The answer is that for 15 years English soccer has crushed intelligent players under a mountain of defensive caution, intimidation and weak refereeing.'

The Guardian quickly became besotted, writing in its season preview that 'there has been something in the air at White Hart Lane' and putting it down to 'two Argentinians, one small and dapper, the other tall, handsome and of the build one would expect to see spread across the centrefold of *Playgirl*.' Yet Cliff Lloyd, the long-standing secretary of the Professional Footballers' Association, saw warning signs for his members. 'It is a situation that cannot be dismissed lightly,' he said. 'There is, of course, nothing to stop Common Market players coming here, but I am surprised Spurs say they have been assured there will be no problem about signing these Argentinians.'

A few days after Tottenham had completed their shopping, Haslam made a signing of his own for Sheffield United, spending £160,000 on uncapped River Plate midfielder Alejandro Sabella. That prompted PFA executive committee member and soon-to-be-chairman Gordon Taylor to warn, 'If the trickle of foreign players becomes a flow it would be detrimental to our members.'

Within two weeks, the Football League management committee had sanctioned the Ardiles-Villa-Sabella signings, on the same day that Southampton paid £50,000 for Partizan Belgrade right-back Ivan Golac, a Yugoslav international. Sports minister Denis Howell promptly hinted that transfers from outside the EEC could be halted. 'What we have to establish is some kind of principle,' he said. 'There is no guarantee that players from outside the Common Market will get work permits. Tottenham made no proper attempt to clarify the position before they signed the Argentinian players and the government have not yet received the official attitude of the FA.'

John Grant, the employment under-secretary, was even more explicit. 'No further permits will be issued for the employment of overseas footballers until we have urgent government discussions with the football organisations concerned,' he said. With football, for once, appearing to have a more progressive attitude than government desired, England manager Ron Greenwood complained about the authorities' 'head-in-the-sand attitude'. He said, 'They've granted three registrations and it's about time they granted 33 if necessary.'

Southampton manager Lawrie McMenemy warned that he would be 'very disappointed' if Golac was denied a work permit. In the end, the player, who was studying agricultural engineering, was signed as a non-contract player to avoid him being registered as foreign. Instead, the 28-year-old son of an army colonel was given a six-month student visa while the red tape was negotiated.

Manchester City were next to put their cat among the PFA's pigeons when chairman Peter Swales announced he had negotiated the signing of Poland's World Cup midfielder Kazimierz Deyna from Legia Warsaw. Yet the further comments of Lloyd can hardly have given McMenemy or Swales cause for optimism. 'It only needs a club to enjoy success with foreigners in their team and the rest will jump on the bandwagon,' he warned with a logic that could not be disputed.

And, sounding not unlike those who had spoken against the influx of immigrant workers in other industries over the previous three decades, he added that 'every job taken by an overseas player will mean less *(sic)* opportunities for our own' and suggested that 'we could be caught up in something that is detrimental to the game in this country'.

Manchester City's Scottish international midfielder Asa Hartford suggested that there was a need to 'safeguard the future of our own young stars'[756] yet former Derby manager Dave Mackay argued, 'I think that this is one of the bravest strokes that's ever been pulled in English football. Bring in all the best players and make it harder for our professionals. Most of them are getting fortunes in wages; let them work for it.'[757] Ardiles would develop a philosophical acceptance of his situation, having arrived in England unaware of the history he was helping to create: 'I think all processes of change start off like that. The first thing that has to shift is the cultural preconception.'[758]

There had, in fact, been various foreign players in the Football League before 1978. Walter Bowman, a Canadian of Swiss heritage, played for Accrington Stanley in the 1890s before Tottenham made German Max Seeburg the first European-born foreigner to play in the League in 1908. A small handful followed until Arsenal attempted to sign Austrian goalkeeper Rudy Hiden in 1930. His work permit was denied and when the Gunners instead went after Dutchman Gerry Keizer the following year the FA declared that all incoming foreigners would have to fulfil a two-year residency before being eligible for English football. Thus, the borders were closed, although Manchester City famously signed German goalkeeper Bert Trautmann, who had fulfilled residency requirements by spending four years in England as a prisoner of war.

Players from colonial countries continued to perform in England, by virtue of the 1948 Nationality Act, which offered right of entry to citizens of the Commonwealth. Among a steady stream of South Africans to arrive were Bill Perry, scorer of the winning goal for Blackpool in the 1953 FA Cup Final, Charlton Athletic forward Eddie Firmani and Leeds United winger Albert Johanneson. But a broader opening of the borders as a way of attracting crowds had been dismissed by Football League secretary Alan Hardaker in 1972 when he stated, 'The import of foreign stars would weaken the domestic game like water dilutes good home brewed whisky and if the dreaded foreigners were allowed in we would be in the same mess as France and Italy.' Writing in *Football Monthly*, columnist Leslie Vernon referred to Hardaker's comments as 'gross ignorance' and pointed out that crowds in those countries were increasing.[759]

There was no doubting the breakthrough moment that Ardiles and Villa represented. And, despite the dissenting voices from the PFA, there was no real suggestion at this stage that these events would herald the kind of overseas takeover of England's top flight that, three decades later, would be cited among the biggest reasons for the national team's lack of achievement. Besides, English football was already populated by plenty of players not qualified for England, thanks to a large contingent of Scots, Irish and Welsh. In 1972, one-sixth of top-flight professionals were said to be from Scotland, while *Football Handbook* studied one Saturday in October 1978 and reported that only two of 22 First Division clubs fielded a full team of Englishmen. On average there were 3.4 non-English players in each starting line-up. That season's FA Cup Final between Arsenal and Manchester United would feature only seven Englishmen among the 22 who started the game.

Greenwood felt the Argentinians' arrival 'gives the new season a tremendous boost', while the assessment of one of his West Ham protégés, Frank Lampard, a year earlier had been, 'Our football is going through a funny stage at the moment and I'm not sure it's a very good phase. There is not much individual flair coming on the field from our players, whereas if foreign players came over here that would change.'[760]

The general level of acceptance and excitement shown towards the players by fans was an interesting phenomenon, not entirely in keeping with the British public's usual approach to strangers in their midst. As *The Sweeney*'s DI Jack Regan said on hearing of a foreign colleague's problems getting through the airport, 'Oh, well that's par for Heathrow, innit? Fortress England. If Hitler was alive, they'd give him a job out there.'[761]

In his chronicle of the decade, Alwyn W. Turner observed, 'There was still a strong legacy of suspicion aimed at mainland Europe, a reluctance to get too involved ... Britain might have been late in joining the EEC but the same was also true of English football clubs entering the European Cup, or the Eurovision Song Contest and even the slapstick television game show *Jeux Sans Frontieres*.'[762] Reports such as that in *The Times* in mid-decade claiming the rabies frontier was moving 30 miles closer to England every year didn't help.

But, as Laurel Forster and Sue Harper noted in their introduction to *British Culture and Society in the 1970s*, 'The 1970s in Britain was a decade of immense complexity in almost every sphere. There were numerous contradictions.'[763] One of those, it appeared, was that football fans, used to having their sport denigrated as being backward in comparison to the supposedly more sophisticated Europeans and South Americans, took sufficient pride in the arrival of Ardiles and Villa to put aside the xenophobia that was a more typical response to any suggestion of 'foreign invasion' in other walks of life.

Portrayals of foreigners throughout the 1970s never strayed too far from the template outlined by writers Dick Clement and Ian La Frenais via the words of Terry Collier *(see Chapter 6)*. In *Fawlty Towers*, it may have been the exasperation of John Cleese at his Spanish waiter's failure to comprehend his instructions that provided many of the laughs, but Andrew Sachs's simple, if well-meaning, character played to stereotypes and ended up making life hell for the country's foreign waiters, who now had self-styled comedians screaming 'Manuel!' at them from over their Saturday-night lagers.

And between 1977 and 1979, ITV aired three series of *Mind Your Language*, in which Barry Evans played an English teacher hired to teach foreign students at night school. His class included a series of perceived national archetypes: a loud, womanising Italian chef; a Spanish bartender with a total inability to grasp the English language; and a pair of female au pairs – an efficient, hard-working German and an amorous and beautiful French girl. Endearingly, Ardiles managed to sound as though he was auditioning for a role in the show every time he referred to his new club as 'Tottingham'.

International influence had become an increasing part of British life in the 1970s, with millions taking package holidays to the Continent and French-style wine bars and Italian coffee shops becoming a feature of many high streets, even out in the provinces. 'And yet,' stated historian Dominic Sandbrook, 'exceptionalism – the belief that Britain was different and should steer its own course free from continental entanglement – died hard.'[764]

The manner in which the British public saw themselves in relation to their nearest foreign neighbours had been put to the test in 1975 in the referendum that asked the simple question, 'Do you think the UK should stay in the European Community?' The campaign was low-key on both sides, with one of the most memorable elements being the celebrities, including football figures Sir Matt Busby, Jock Stein, Don Revie and Derek Dougan*, who were recruited to urge people to vote 'Yes'. The voting took place shortly after Leeds United's defeat against Bayern Munich in the European Cup Final. When the French referee inexplicably ruled out Peter Lorimer's goal, one pro-Europe MP commented, 'My God, there goes half a million votes.'[765]

When Edward Heath had led the UK into Europe on the first day of 1973, *The Times* reported that only 38 per cent of the public were in favour, but by the time of the referendum two and a half years later, the voters' national inclination towards the status quo now weighed in favour of the pro-European campaign. The Common Market had been given enough time to become the devil people knew and, besides, did anyone really have a clear idea of what difference it made? As *Monty Python's Flying Circus* star Michael Palin noted in his diary, 'Neither decision I think involves the downfall of our nation. Once a decision is taken it will all be absorbed into the system and the country will carry on working (or not working) as it always did.'[766] The voting turnout ended up at 65 per cent – as opposed to 78 per cent in the first general election of

---

* By the latter years of his life, Dougan's views had changed sufficiently for him to appear as a UKIP spokesman on BBC TV's *Question Time* programme.

1974 – and the 'Yes' campaign scored a convincing victory with 67 per cent of the vote.

THIS IS THE MODERN WORLD

Dalglish. Johnson. And Johnson, a ball into acres of empty space for Heighway. And Heighway, a brilliant cross back … [crowd erupts]. McDermott it was who finished it, and what a classic goal. Tottenham in remnants.

Granada TV commentator Gerald Sinstadt, Liverpool v Spurs, 1978

While foreigners had either been tolerated as economic partners or laughed at as television caricatures, they were now being accepted as football imports by most fans. In September 1978 a compromise was reached where 'overseas players of established international reputation, who have a distinctive contribution to make to the national game' would be allowed in by the Department of Employment, provided clubs could prove they could not find a player of similar standard in Britain. Even after the resulting ratification of the Golac and Deyna transfers, Ipswich Town's early-season signing of Dutch midfielder Arnold Mühren and, most unlikely of all, Birmingham City's recruitment of the wild-haired Argentinian right-back Alberto Tarantini, the number of foreign players was still too low for them to be perceived as a threat to the fabric of the English game.

There were plenty of on-field stereotypes at play, though. The view prevailed that the true test of a footballer was his ability to slog through the rain on a cold winter's night, something assumed to be beyond anyone brought up with the sun on his back. Everton manager Gordon Lee said, 'I would like to see their reactions to playing on a wet and windy mid-winter evening when they are trailing 2-0 away to Blackburn Rovers.'[767]

Ardiles's response to the meteorological argument was that 'we have winters in Argentina too', but West Bromwich Albion forward Tony Brown warned, 'The big test will come when they go out and play in the snow or on a mud-caked pitch. It's not easy to play fancy football on a dodgy surface.' Brown, no mean craftsman himself, was hardly alone in believing that an elevated degree of ball skill amounted to 'fancy football' – and unrelated to results. One of the decade's biggest selling music acts, Slade, had even released a single earlier in the year containing a pay-off line to the chorus that went, 'Stop your fancy footwork now and give us a goal.'†

Lee, whose Everton team had been the top flight's leading scorers in the most recent season, had stubbornly insisted after the World Cup that 'we have nothing to learn from the continentals'. By mid-season he was even more entrenched in his views. 'When I sign a player, I want to find out all there is to know about him, down to what toothpaste he uses. I could not possibly hope to know that by snapping up somebody who had impressed me in the World Cup finals. I am challenging for the League title with my present squad. What are Tottenham doing with their imported players?'[768]

And when Dennis Tueart had stated, 'Only a small number of foreign players would last the pace of a full season,'[769] he was expressing another common concern about anyone not reared on the traditional English love of laps of the field during training. Liverpool full-back Phil Neal voiced it when he said, 'I think the thing the Argentinians find difficult is keeping up their work rate, getting totally involved in the game.'

Even the new arrivals' Tottenham team-mate, Glenn Hoddle, needed convincing. 'The thing that has really hit them over here,' he said after a month of the season, 'is the pace of the game. Ossie, particularly, doesn't find it easy to get back and cover.'[770] Which sounded a bit rich coming from a player who admitted that he and Burkinshaw frequently clashed over the amount of defensive work he needed to do.

Among fans, those able to put aside any jealousy that it was not their club making such game-changing transfers were generally excited by the arrival of visitors who seemed no less other-worldly than the alien played by Robin Williams in the series *Mork and*

† Struggling to recreate their success of earlier in the decade, Slade failed again to re-enter the charts with the football-chant styled 'Give Us a Goal'. The video for the song was shot on the terraces and pitch at Brighton and Hove Albion's Goldstone Ground.

Mindy, which reached British television screens that year. The newcomers were rarely subjected to the kind of abuse that created the gauntlet run by the growing number of black British players in professional football.

In fact, crowds flocked to see them. After one third of the season, Tottenham averaged the highest away attendance in the country, their figure of 37,289 placing them well ahead of title-chasing Liverpool, Nottingham Forest and Everton. One teenaged girl was seen on television saying of Ardiles, 'He's such a cuddly little man. I'd go anywhere to see him play.'

Just as Britain limped through economic crisis and loss of power on the international political stage during the Seventies, so English football was not exactly overflowing with self-esteem after failing to qualify for two successive World Cups. Sure, Liverpool had just won back-to-back European Cups, but even Scotland's failure in Argentina had been felt keenly by supporters of the First Division. The Scots may never have been likely to justify manager Ally MacLeod's hype that they could actually win the tournament, but with names such as Liverpool's Kenny Dalglish and Graeme Souness, Manchester United's Joe Jordan, Gordon McQueen and Lou Macari and champion Nottingham Forest's Archie Gemmill and John Robertson they were expected to make a greater representation on behalf of English club football. Defeat to Peru, an embarrassing draw against Iran and a face-saving 3-2 win against Holland, remembered for Gemmill's brilliant individual goal, had resulted in exit at the first stage. West Bromwich Albion winger Willie Johnston had gone home even earlier, found to have taken a cold treatment containing a banned drug.

English clubs could not afford to entice players from the richer domestic games in Italy, Spain and Germany, but they could at least boast now that members of the best footballing nation in the world wanted to play in the First Division. Ardiles had even turned up spouting stuff like, 'We consider that football-wise England is the great country.' Such flattery helped immunise Ardiles and Villa against any lingering antipathy towards Argentina from the 1966 World Cup or the brutal battles between that country's leading club sides and European champions Celtic and Manchester United in the World Club Championship.

This was all somewhat surprising given the typical stance of British fans to overseas opposition. While television viewers might have been laughing at comedic stereotypes, there was very little humour among terrace-goers when their teams were up against 'foreigners'. National anthems were usually a cue for crescendos of booing in British grounds, which meant journalist Christopher Davies was astonished to find how polite the Argentinians were towards their visitors during the World Cup. 'The fans were silent through the Hungarian national anthem and even applauded at the end as a mark of respect,' he wrote. 'When I commented to an Argentine journalist how unusual this was for me, he merely commented, "Only British fans show no respect for other countries."'[771]

Ipswich manager Bobby Robson had no qualms about signing 27-year-old midfielder Mühren for £143,000 after his pay dispute with Twente Enschede. 'I became so frustrated with trying to sign players in England, where I was quoted ridiculous prices,' he said. A few weeks later, Robson was predicting that 'we are going to see more [foreign players] coming in because managers can't get the players they want here'.[772] And McMenemy suggested that overseas players 'have better techniques than British players because they work harder at them as young players'.[773]

If the newspapers could have had their way, there would have been several signings every week. In the competitive world of tabloid journalism, no back page was complete without a story relating to the signing of some international star or other. Arsenal manager Terry Neill helped their cause by admitting that he was 'looking around in Holland and other parts of Europe' when asked about a rumoured £500,000 approach for the stylish, versatile Ruud Krol, captain of Ajax and Holland. The twins, Willy and René van der Kerkhoff, both veterans of two Dutch World Cup campaigns, were the next names to be linked with the Gunners.

In late August, Birmingham's Jim Smith reported that he had reached an agreement to sign Dirceu, a left-sided midfielder in Brazil's

World Cup team, for £425,000 from Vasco da Gama. 'He is willing to come,' Smith chirped. Yet he didn't. Nor did any of Arsenal's supposed Dutch targets. Another of Argentina's champions, midfielder Rene Houseman, reportedly turned down a move to Middlesbrough.

For a while, the most glittering prize potentially on offer was Johan Cruyff, Europe's finest footballer of the decade. Having achieved three European Cup triumphs with Ajax, inspired his brilliant Dutch team to the 1974 World Cup Final and enjoyed five seasons at Barcelona, Cruyff seemed tantalisingly available. He had left the Nou Camp and signed up for some exhibition games with the New York Cosmos. Yet his agent, Dennis Roach, broke the hearts of potential First Division suitors when he told the *Daily Mirror*'s Nigel Clarke, 'Johan feels that at 31 he no longer wants to get involved in that level of football.'

Remarkably, Tarantini preferred the bottom club in the First Division, Birmingham, to Barcelona or the New York Cosmos. 'I have always wanted to play in England,' he said through his interpreter. 'My ambition is to play at Wembley.' The interpreter even managed to keep a straight face.

From his PFA office, Lloyd continued to protest about loss of jobs, an argument *Daily Express* columnist Alan Thompson called 'fatuous' and 'about as watertight as a colander'. He argued that 'if 100 foreigners came in 100 players ill-equipped for the First Division would drop to the Second and so on. The Football League would get better.'

A renowned wheeler-dealer like Derby's Tommy Docherty was reluctant to miss out on all this activity and offered £250,000 for Norberto Alonso, River Plate's No.10, who had missed the World Cup through injury. The deal fell through when the player was reported to have asked for the same amount for himself. By the end of the 1978-79 season a handful more deals would be completed. From Yugoslavia, forward Bozo Jankovic and goalkeeper Petar Borota signed for Middlesbrough and Chelsea respectively, while Bristol City signed Dutch winger Geert Meijer and Finnish midfielder Pertti Jantunen.

Of course, it was only the elite few managers who could think about making the equivalent of 'booze cruise' trips overseas to see what bargains they could stash in the back of the team bus. The wording of the Department of Employment guidelines relating to players of a 'particular stature' saw to that. The days of lower-division teams packed with overseas names were still a few decades away.

Aston Villa centre-forward Andy Gray, who as a Sky Sports analyst would become synonymous with a cash-rich Premier League able to attract the likes of Gullit, Zola, Klinsmann and Bergkamp, was not too far off when he gave his vision of football's immediate future towards the end of the season. 'We have around a dozen or so foreign players in the League at the moment, but I don't believe this number will grow considerably,' he said, with a foresight that held good until Sky's money changed the landscape. 'We'll see more, of that I have no doubt, but it's unlikely continentals will come here in any great number. If they do come it certainly won't be for the money. Our wages still fall behind those of most European countries while our income tax is higher.'[774]

Unable to translate the debate going on about their presence, the biggest immediate problem for the new Spurs arrivals was adjusting to the rhythms of English life. 'Sundays were so empty,' Ardiles recalled, shocked to find that everything closed.[775] Tottenham were enlightened enough to provide him and Villa with identical houses next door to each other[‡] and provide them with the services of a secretary and an English teacher. 'Having them together made it a success,' Burkinshaw recalled. 'They looked after themselves. It was good for the younger players to see how they behaved. It was a sportsman's life, not the culture of going out and kicking back the pints.'[776] Ardiles and Villa contented themselves with soft drinks and were shocked at the amount of heavy fried food consumed by their team-mates, even on matchdays.

On the day of their Football League debuts, at champions Nottingham Forest, anticipation within football circles was

‡ Thus a staple of photo spreads in magazines such as *Shoot!* was created, with the Ardiles and Villa families frequently photographed together around the dinner table or with the players climbing into each other's cars for the ride to the training ground.

approaching the frenzied levels seen at the front of the newspapers during the summer for the release of *Grease*, the movie featuring the newest Hollywood heart-throb, John Travolta. The success of *Saturday Night Fever* months earlier ensured that the 24-year-old's face, hairy chest or latest girlfriend had rarely been absent from page one. There would be no on-screen premiere, however, for Ardiles and Villa. Brian Clough's champions against Tottenham's imports would be a game that in the modern age would dominate any Super Sunday, and several preceding days, but building work at the City Ground meant that Forest had to ask the cameras to stay away. 'The safety of the spectators must come first,' Clough explained.

At least the blackout meant Arsenal fans were spared the sight of their local rivals hogging the opening weekend's television coverage. The Gunners adopted a somewhat sniffy and superior attitude to the Spurs adventure. Neill claimed to have relinquished his first option on the Argentinian duo, while the match programme against Leeds United found chairman Denis Hill-Wood saying, 'We felt they would not fulfil our chief requirements and, furthermore, must represent something of a gamble.'[777]

By a quarter to five on that first Saturday of the season, most observers were prepared to back Tottenham's judgement. 'The gains dwarfed the losses as English soccer assessed the first 90 minutes of Osvaldo Ardiles and Ricardo Villa,' wrote Harry Miller in the *Daily Mirror*. Spurs had held the champions 1-1 and Villa had dummied Peter Shilton to score their equaliser. Four days later White Hart Lane had its first proper look at its new heroes, who were introduced on page seven of a match programme that, overall, adopted a somewhat low-key and matter-of-fact approach to their entrance – although the advert for the club shop did feature a picture of the pair laden down with a selection of merchandise. Club secretary Geoff Jones had reported that 'the telephone has been ringing non-stop' since the signings were announced and 47,892 turned up for Spurs' first home League game. But it was Aston Villa, rather than Ricardo, who stole the show with a 4-1 victory. The bookmakers who had taken enough money on Spurs to have brought their title odds down from 66-1 to 33-1 before the season began were as happy as the visitors.

The failure to hold on to two Argentinian-inspired leads against Chelsea meant three games without a win and provided a further dose of realism. Another was administered by the old warhorse Tommy Smith in Tottenham's next match, a League Cup tie at Third Division Swansea City, where player-manager John Toshack had embarked on a programme of surrounding himself with former Liverpool team-mates. Helping to guide Swansea to promotion in this season would be Ian Callaghan, Phil Boersma, Alan Waddle and Smith, the 'Anfield Iron' himself. Within a minute of kick-off, Smith clattered into Ardiles with what Burkinshaw described as a 'terrible tackle'. Speaking after his team had gained an unconvincing 2-2 draw, the Spurs manager said, 'It could have broken his leg. That is what is wrong with the game in this country; people deliberately trying to put people out of the game.'

Smith was as uncompromising with reporters as he had been on the field. 'What does he expect? This is not a kids' league. He can't expect to bring expensive players from South America and expect them to be given the freedom of the pitch.' Recalling the incident with some relish in his autobiography, Smith delighted in saying, 'Ardiles went up in the air like a Guy Fawkes rocket and came down just as ignominiously. The Vetch roared its approval. Ossie lay on the ground as if he had been hit by a bag of hammers.'[778]

With Ardiles lying prostrate on the Vetch Field pitch, Smith had bent down and announced, 'Welcome to English football.' Yet the real welcome followed four days later when Ardiles, recovered from Smith's attention, went with his new team to Liverpool. 'We softened them up for you,' Smith had told his former boss Bob Paisley.[779] What followed came to be acknowledged as the signature performance of one of English football's finest teams.

The deep wound of losing the League to Forest in the previous season clearly hurt Paisley's team; judging by the way they set about re-establishing the normal order of things at the start of 1978-79. They had already wrecked the Ipswich debut of Mühren before looking irresistible in a 4-1 win against Manchester City. The third goal was the best of all. Steve Heighway and Jimmy Case combined to give Terry McDermott room to cross from the right of the box; the spinning figure of Kenny Dalglish helped the ball on to Graeme Souness and he pushed it beyond City's covering man with his first touch before firing in low with his left foot. 'The match was Liverpool's at a purr,' Barry Davies told BBC viewers as the players left the field. 'To talk about a machine is an insult, unless you are talking about a Rolls-Royce.'

When Anfield welcomed Tottenham and their Argentinians, the vehicle Liverpool resembled was a juggernaut. Dalglish turned neatly to fire past Barry Daines and even a reshuffle caused by a 24th-minute injury to Emlyn Hughes couldn't spare the poor visitors. The second goal arrived when Case's off-target shot fell to Dalglish. A simple third resulted from McDermott delivering a long cross from the right to Ray Kennedy, who rose like the target man he used to be. 'We set out right from the whistle to humiliate as much as we could,' Neal remembered, citing the team's 'great pride in English football' as their motivation.[780]

In the second half, David Johnson followed up a saved effort to score the fourth, and the fifth went in when Dalglish slipped the ball to the onrushing Johnson after more exquisite build-up play. Phil Neal made it 6-0 with a penalty, and then came the magnificent seventh. It began with Liverpool on the defensive, the ball headed out of their own area into the path of Dalglish near the edge of his own penalty area. With one touch he pushed it diagonally right to Johnson, just inside his own half. One touch to turn inside, then Johnson sliced another long diagonal pass with the outside of his foot to Heighway marauding down the left wing in the shadow of the stand. His first-time cross, hit without breaking stride, was met by the airborne McDermott with a thumping header from just outside the six-yard box.

After the stunned cheers had died down, a crescendo of applause swept across Anfield as if acknowledging a concert-hall virtuoso. There were no more goals; and quite rightly. As when Brazil scored their wonderful fourth in the 1970 World Cup Final, to have scored again would have been an anticlimax. 'It was the most compelling performance I have seen from the best team I have ever seen,' wrote John Keith in the *Daily Express*. 'It was such perfection that any moment you felt that fantasy would end and the reality would send you tumbling down to earth with a thud.'

There had been no such release for Spurs. Ardiles would recall that 'it was as if that first game at Forest had been a mirage'.[781] *The Guardian*'s Patrick Barclay suggested that if Burkinshaw had spent his money on 'a time machine and had fielded instead of Ardiles and Villa the entire Double-winning side of 1961, the result would probably have been no different'.

In the days of restricted television coverage, the fact that Granada TV had captured it all was a favour to football historians everywhere. Interestingly, the brilliance of Don Revie's Leeds team had been memorialised by the cameras in a 7-0 win of their own, the dismantling of Southampton in the spring of 1972. Yet those respective performances had very different personalities. For Leeds, who had made a conscious effort to play more expansive and expressive football since achieving their first title, it felt like a collective 'up yours'. It might have been Southampton on the receiving end, but it was directed at those who could still not look beyond the cynicism of past seasons. And if the Leeds performance had been about justification, then Liverpool's was a statement of purpose. Consider the signature moments. The circus-like demonstration of trickery Leeds gave late in the game had been to show that they could; Liverpool's final goal was a clinical, brutal exercise in how to get the ball from one end of the pitch to the other and into the net. Paisley had no personal points to prove, merely League points to win; all part of the relentless pursuit of perfection.

Four days later, Spurs lost their replay against Swansea 3-1 and their new signings wondered what exactly they had got themselves into. Hoddle was not exactly offering effusive support when he said a few weeks later, 'We are trying to get across to them they should use their talent within the team framework. We don't want players trying to outdo each other. Other teams look at us and say, "Let's show these Argentinians we can play."'[782]

Yet it was Hoddle's name that disappeared from the line-up for the next game against Bristol City. 'I don't think I deserved to be dropped,' he immediately told reporters, these being the days when players spoke freely to media contacts without the confines of formal policing by PR departments. 'I want him to explain his reasons. I tried to see Keith after training. He said nothing to me about being dropped.' A day later, Burkinshaw probably felt vindicated by a single-goal victory, but James Lawton was unimpressed. 'What has become painfully clear,' he wrote in the *Daily Express*, was 'their inability to absorb the arrival of two of the world's most gifted players.' And, damningly, he concluded, 'All the merit of their signings will disappear if Tottenham cannot find a place for Glenn Hoddle, one of the few Spurs players capable of operating on the same wavelength.'

Hoddle, a 20-year-old from Hayes, Middlesex, had made a dramatic entrance to the First Division two and a half years earlier when he marked his first start for his club with a stunning goal at Stoke City. He had found the ball dropping towards him as he lurked outside the penalty area and whipped a fierce left-footed half-volley beyond Peter Shilton. He had launched a career that would eventually see him inducted into English football's Hall of Fame with a citation highlighting his 'sublime balance and close control, unrivalled passing and vision and extraordinary shooting ability, both from open play and set pieces'. Yet football in the 1970s had never been the most comfortable home for such individual talent, as the newcomers were discovering. Even as he was reporting that Ardiles reached the end of his debut season feeling 'very disappointed with the football', Burkinshaw complained, 'Ricky and Ossie, when they first came here, both thought that once the ball was over the halfway line and on its way towards our own goal it was up to the defence to deal with and nothing to do with them.'[783]

Along with that kind of reality, Ardiles and Villa were also learning the truth of their new team's place in the pecking order of English football. It would be hammered home in games such as their 5-0 home defeat against local rivals Arsenal, and a ten-game winless streak that ended two games before the end of the season and condemned them to 11th place in the table.

But as much as results like those against Liverpool and Arsenal hurt the White Hart Lane faithful, the greater significance of Tottenham's season was the barrier that had been broken; the levels of open-mindedness and tolerance to visitors that had been exhibited by a surprising number of people in and around the game.

And that was worth a tickertape parade of its own.

WORKING FOR THE YANKEE DOLLAR

Take a Jumbo across the water
Like to see America

'Breakfast in America', Supertramp (Richard Davies, Roger Hodgson; Universal Music Publishing Group, 1979)

The way in which Football League players spent their holidays had always offered an intriguing insight into lifestyle and taste. When *Shoot!* canvassed various men in its Summer Special edition of 1972, it discovered that Denis Law and his wife usually went to Majorca, although a week in Aberdeen was what he really looked forward to because 'the beaches up there are the best in the world'.

Gordon Banks had been to Majorca in 1971, 'but not again' he said, having spent most of his time signing autographs. He was going pony trekking in north Wales instead. Meanwhile, Derek Dougan had been to Ibiza to find half the Ipswich team booked into the same hotel, while Arsenal's Frank McLintock had ended up in the same Portuguese hotel as Don Revie. Much like the characters in that year's *Carry On Abroad*, who could find nothing but fault in their unfinished resort in 'Elsbels', it appeared that England's football community needed some convincing when it came to summers in foreign climes.

As the 1970s progressed, however, a new option appeared; one that promised sunshine in a place where they spoke English, served broadly familiar food, and offered a chance to boost pension funds. In the same summer that Ardiles and Villa were packing their bags for England, so the migration of Football League players to the North American Soccer League reached its peak.

Established at the end of the previous decade and run, for most of its existence, by Commissioner Phil Woosnam, a former Wales, West Ham and Aston Villa midfielder, the NASL had, from its inception, offered a home to journeymen overseas players at the end of their careers. The landscape changed, however, in 1975 when the New York Cosmos signed Pelé, the most famous footballer in the world – the one that even the neophyte American audience had heard of. George Best, who would play for three different American clubs, and Rodney Marsh, the face of the Tampa Bay Rowdies, followed not far behind.[§]

Attendance around the league soared, with the Cosmos attracting crowds in excess of 70,000 to matches in Giants Stadium. More teams were added and a trickle of English players had now become a veritable flood; mostly either older players who chose a transfer to America over a drop down the English divisions, or those who signed short-term contracts as part of a loan agreement with English clubs. During the summer of 1978, which had seen the NASL expand from 18 to 24 teams, around 130 British players performed on the AstroTurf fields of North America. Trevor Francis and a young Alan Brazil teamed up in Detroit; Charlie Cooke, Tommy Smith and Ron Davies were turning back the clock in Los Angeles, where Best played part of the season before moving to Fort Lauderdale; Keith Weller and Peter Simpson were among the old English contingent at New England; Alan Ball, Peter Osgood and Johnny Giles were in Philadelphia's garish orange and brown; George Graham was in California; ex-Northern Ireland skipper David Clements wore the tassled jersey of the Colorado Caribou; Steve Kember, Jon Sammels, Kevin Hector and Alan Hinton were north of the border in Vancouver. To name just a few. *Shoot!* covered the NASL on a weekly basis and most British newspapers dispatched reporters to the season finale, Soccer Bowl.

§ Best and Marsh made a return to England to team up, alongside Bobby Moore, for Second Division Fulham in 1976-77. They were at their best in a 4-1 win against Hereford United, shown on ITV, in which they performed party tricks in the manner of a testimonial and ended up trying to tackle each other.

Leicester City midfielder Steve Earle had decided that, at 32, playing for Detroit Express was preferable to life with Peterborough United, where he had played one game on loan. 'I was offered more money at Detroit than playing with Leicester and everything was laid on for us – cars and apartments. It was $35,000 to sign on and the basic wage at Leicester was £100 per week; double that over here. It was a better financial deal than Peterborough!'[784]

Filbert Street team-mate Weller headed to the New England Tea Men in 1978, returning to Leicester for the following English season before settling permanently in the United States, where he was still based when he died of cancer at the age of 58. 'It was absolutely wonderful what the owners did for you,' he said in 2003. 'Anything you needed you got. Everything they promised you got. We had days out and clam bakes, the kids all got on well and we all lived in a nice complex.'[785]

West Brom's Len Cantello, who spent the summer in 1978 with the Dallas Tornado before returning to The Hawthorns for his testimonial season, did his best to make the NASL sound like hard work when he said, 'We train harder than we do at West Brom and it's tough going in the Texas heat. It's nearly always in the 80s or 90s. There are 30 games before you get to the play-offs, which is ridiculous. Remember, an away game here can be a few thousand miles.'[786]

But even if it wasn't all barbecues and sunbathing, it was still worth it. Osgood was picking up a reported £50,000 per season with a Philadelphia Fury team whose owners included music stars Mick Jagger, Peter Frampton, Paul Simon and Rick Wakeman. Confessing to his hope of a return to the First Division, Osgood added, 'If it wasn't for the tax I'd be back tomorrow.'

Marsh, who bade farewell to Manchester City in 1976 and would subsequently characterise English football as 'a grey game, played on grey days by grey people', also admitted that his love of football in America was as much financial as philosophical. Pictured at his home in an apartment village on the northern outskirts of Tampa, he explained, 'I make at least twice as much as I did in England. It is also about 30 per cent cheaper.'[787]

According to Liverpool and England goalkeeper Ray Clemence 'a player owed it to his family' to maximise the earning potential of his career. 'In this game, with its uncertainties and insecurity, it's important to look ahead and think of ways to continue earning top money for as long as possible,' he said. 'The lifestyle in the States appeals to me and it would be marvellous to play a part in developing soccer into the big-time sport it's inevitably going to become.'[788]

It wasn't only the players who were casting their eyes at distant horizons. Dave Mackay, title-winning manager with Derby three years earlier, announced that he was leaving Walsall for Kuwait, where the Arabic Sporting Club were reportedly ready to pay him £42,000 for taking charge of 17 games over the course of two years. 'People who know me will appreciate that money really doesn't mean that much to me,' he said; an easy comment to make when that much was being thrown at you. 'I am going because the prospects there are excellent.'[789] Former Football League managers Gordon Jago, Ken Furphy and Eddie Firmani were already among the best-known 'head coaches' in the NASL, while Don Revie had taken his infamous flight to the United Arab Emirates.

The examples of Marsh, Revie and the rest highlighted the greater opportunities that existed around the world as Britain scrabbled down the back of its sofa to find the money to pay its workers. From 1973 to 1977 the percentage of people in the country who felt they were in a 'very strong' financial position had fallen from 18 to 5 per cent; those who described their circumstances as 'very weak' doubling from 13 to 26 per cent. In 1975, for the first time since records had been maintained, more people left British shores than arrived: 269,000 compared to 184,000. The pattern was repeated for the next two years and even Jim Callaghan would look at himself in the shaving mirror around this time and say, 'If I were a young man I would emigrate.'[790]

'The middle and professional classes have had their incomes and their values seemingly flung in their faces,' art historian Roy Strong noted in one of his published diaries.[791] By 1975, a married man on average earnings was paying 25 per cent of his salary in tax, while those earning more than £24,000 were taxed at 83 per cent and the super-rich 98 per cent. Arsenal secretary Ken Friar spoke for most clubs when he said he was 'hoping for some change in the taxation system that would allow us to keep our best players', discouraging them from ending their careers in overseas tax havens.[792]

So many citizens appeared determined to leave the country that New Zealand was forced to announce controls on British migrants, while Conservative Party leader Margaret Thatcher urged the government to cut taxation in order to eliminate the 'danger of a brain drain such as we have never seen before'.

Kevin Keegan had been football's obvious manifestation of that danger with his transfer to SV Hamburg. 'England can't afford to lose players of his calibre,' said friend and international team-mate Mick Channon. 'Our standards must start to drop if some start to go abroad. I can't think Kevin will be the only player to leave. Football is such a short life that you need to make – and keep – some fair percentage of the cash you earn. I think it is totally unfair to pay the rate of tax we do.'[793] Roger Davies had already left Derby for FC Bruges, where he helped his club to the 1977 title, saying that the higher wages and lower tax more than compensated for the higher cost of living.¶

Dennis Tueart became the first current England international to sign a permanent NASL deal in 1978 when Manchester City sold him for £250,000 to the Cosmos, where he would help fill the boots of the newly-retired Pelé. 'At the time I moved, my England prospects, if not bleak, were not particularly rosy,' he would explain after his first season in New York. 'I had to make my living while I'm at my peak and having thought about it I'm sure I did the right thing.'

Tueart, of course, was not the NASL's typical British recruit. It remained, in relation to its imported players, largely a country for old men. Jim McCalliog, a much-travelled Scottish midfielder who'd been Osgood's Southampton team-mate and spent a summer at the

¶ Davies also recalled that the club's one bout of running per week, on a Wednesday afternoon, was called the 'English session'.

Chicago Sting, warned, 'It might sound attractive to young kids who fancy fast cars and a lot of money but my advice to youngsters is simple: forget American soccer until the end of your career. Football in America is Fourth Division standard – no better.'[794]

Brian Talbot, Graeme Souness and Brazil were among the younger professionals who had competed in the NASL early in their careers as a way of gaining additional on-field experience. Peter Beardsley would be a notable addition. But for them America was merely a staging point on a journey to the top of English football. There was, however, a group of young English players, from the lower leagues or those unable to break into bigger clubs' line-ups, for whom America proved to be a lucrative final destination. It enabled them to forge long and successful careers, earning the kind of money, recognition and memories of famous team-mates that would have been beyond them at home.

Alan Willey, for example, toiled to establish himself in Middlesbrough's forward line before heading to the Minnesota Kicks to become the second-highest goal-scorer in NASL history and an inductee into the sport's Hall of Fame in his adopted country. 'Could I have been the same in England?' he pondered. 'I don't know. But I would not change a thing. I think I was successful because I was getting a chance to play more. The pace was not as fast as in England and there was not as much pressure in America.'[795]

Paul Child couldn't get a game at Aston Villa, but after a couple of years at the Atlanta Chiefs he became something of a legend at the San Jose Earthquakes. 'I was taken to every function, promotion and press conference so they could show me off,' he remembered. 'They put me in situations where I was very nervous; on television, speaking in front of large crowds. It taught me a lot about selling the game.' It also gave Child the kind of profile and rewards that Aston Villa reserves would never have offered. 'I caught a lot of people's attention because I was scoring goals and we were selling out stadiums. I had the chance to play against the best in the world and they pushed me to the next level; to be as good as I could be.'[796]

Former England goalkeeper Gordon Banks went to the Fort Lauderdale Strikers in 1977 to prove that he could still play professional football, even after losing the sight in his right eye in a car crash in 1972. But despite his redemption and the successful repatriation of Willey, Child and others, British footballers, for the most part, saw the NASL as an opportunity to have their American apple pie and eat it, shuttling across the Atlantic in the summer and returning with suntans and fistfuls of dollars. Generally, English teams accepted it, some of them arranging friendlies against NASL teams as part of the conditions of loan deals. Derby, for example, warmed up during the summer of 1978 by going to the United States to play Minnesota, where Charlie George was based, and New England, who had Gerry Daly in their team. 'It is far more interesting than slogging away day after day, week after week, running up and down sand hills and playing matches against local clubs,' said winger Gordon Hill, who would settle in America after his playing career in England.[797]

At the Football League, Alan Hardaker was growing increasingly concerned at the number of players departing before the end of the English season. 'What a mess if a hundred first-team players decided to do this,' he worried. 'It would embarrass and devalue the League.'[798] Nor would they always be back in time for the start of the new home campaign if their American team went deep into the NASL play-offs. When Trevor Francis was able to play for only 20 minutes as a substitute in his return game for Birmingham against Manchester United, the *Daily Express* warned, 'This is a far more serious problem to be sorted out than the worry of whether Ardiles and Villa and other foreign imports are good or bad for English football. The League has got to ensure that by 1990 the lure of the golden dollar has not eroded our standards.'

Ken Adam, an English football agent who helped place the likes of Marsh, Ball and Smith with NASL teams, admitted, 'The loan system was a major pain in the arse. It was not a very practical solution. At some point, one of the sides was going to be pissed off.' On occasions, as Adam confirmed, the NASL resorted to off-the-books payments to managers in England to ensure that a player was able to remain in the US for the final games of the campaign. The same method was often needed to ensure prompt arrivals at the start of the American summer.

According to Adam, even the eventual death of loan agreements did not prevent some unscrupulous English managers finding ways to supplement their income. 'There were many instances of a player being given a free transfer, but someone getting money as a transfer fee. The Americans were very generous with some of their expenses.'[799]

By the end of 1978, momentum was building to ban summer placements; including from within the NASL itself, whose players were becoming frustrated by the attitude of some temporary imports. 'Some players didn't really look for an opportunity to contribute,' said former West Brom defender Alan Merrick, who had settled permanently in Minnesota. 'They just came over for a giggle and to get some spending money. They were just mercenaries.'[800]

The wearisome trans-Atlantic friction between clubs had gone on long enough, although Alan Ball, a beneficiary of the system, couldn't understand all the fuss. 'It doesn't make sense for the British clubs to want to end the loans,' he argued. 'They get their players' wages paid for them in the summer and the players get the chance to make a few quid.'[801] Indeed, no one was forcing the clubs to allow their men to head to the States, although for many it was the only way to keep players from agitating for a permanent transfer that would improve their bank balance.

A club such as Liverpool had no such concerns, of course, so Paisley was able to dictate terms. 'I am only prepared to let players go to the States if it will benefit them and the club. Ian Callaghan and Tommy Smith were allowed to go after they had done their stint for us. I am convinced that a successful club cannot afford to release a player. If you are successful you are always in competitions … when summer comes your players need a well-earned rest.'[802]

The loan system's days were numbered and in the summer of 1979 Andy Gray would look across the water and decide that the League's ban was for 'the best interests of our game'. He continued, 'While it may be selfish to prevent some players earning a well-deserved summer bonus, every effort must be made to safeguard our own soccer. But if there was a ballot among players I am sure they would be against the ban. It is a short career and you can't blame anyone for wanting to better himself and collect security for his family.'[803]

Yet not everyone was looking to get out of Britain. Nor was it only the likes of Ardiles and Villa who were travelling against the flow. Birmingham-born Steve Hunt had been another of those players battling to break through in the English game when, as a 20-year-old, he was sold by Aston Villa to the New York Cosmos. 'The fact that Villa were ready to let me go after I had helped them win promotion from the Second Division really hurt,' he said. 'I had a choice between joining the Cosmos or dropping down into the Second or Third Division. I chose the Cosmos and never regretted it for a moment.'

While the likes of Willey and Child remained under the radar of most English fans, Hunt's success among the global stars of the NASL's most glamorous team made him an intriguing news angle for British journalists. The fair-haired winger was even named Most Valuable Player in Pelé's final competitive match, the Soccer Bowl win against Seattle in 1977. By the time he had won another title the following year he was ready to trade Manhattan for the Midlands, coming home to sign for Coventry City in September for £40,000 and turning down what his new manager, Gordon Milne, described as an 'astronomical offer' by his American team.

'I needed to prove to myself that I could make it in the First Division,' said Hunt, aware that many thought he was mad to exchange his dollars for pounds and swap Beckenbauer and Carlos Alberto as team-mates for Jim Holton and Donato Nardiello. 'Money isn't everything,' he said. 'I could have stayed and secured my future. It's simply a matter of professional pride.'[804]

15

COULD IT BE MAGIC

'[Brian Clough was] not my type of man. Not one I would go out for a pint with, I don't think so. But work for him? I would walk across the Sahara to work for him.'

Nottingham Forest captain John McGovern[805]

If you set out to be liked, you would be prepared to compromise on anything at any time and you would achieve nothing.

Margaret Thatcher

SHORTLY AFTER nine in the morning, Margaret Thatcher emerged from the front door of her Chelsea home and strode assertively towards the hordes of television cameras, reporters' notebooks and Conservative Party supporters waiting across the road. The rain that would fall later on 28 March 1979 had yet to arrive and the Leader of the Opposition offered a sunny smile of quiet confidence. 'Let's see what happens in about 13 and a half hours,' she warned as husband Denis placed a supportive arm on the shoulder of her checked suit.

Lowering herself into the back of her car, she set off towards one of the most dramatic days the House of Commons had ever experienced. Six days earlier the Scottish Nationalist Party had called for a vote of no-confidence in the Labour government. Now MPs would spend the next few hours debating and voting on that motion, determining the immediate future of Prime Minister Jim Callaghan, mired in his 'Winter of Discontent'. It was 10.17pm when the Welsh tones of the Speaker, George Thomas, declared defeat for Callaghan by a single vote – the Commons' equivalent of goal difference. Maggie would soon be on her way to No.10.

Barely around the corner from the Thatcher residence, at Stamford Bridge, another journey had got underway around lunchtime. Chelsea's footballers left for the Midlands, the latest group to attempt to deal with a Nottingham Forest team in the process of turning football upside down. Winners of the League Championship in their first season back in the top division the previous year, Brian Clough's collection of young stars and galvanised veterans had now set their sights on the European Cup, knocking out the holders, Liverpool, in the first round. The night before the gauntlet was thrown down to Callaghan, Clough had been celebrating his 44th birthday by watching Forest clinch a place in the semi-finals. After a decade that had seen three years of dominance by Holland's brilliant Ajax, followed by three more by West German powerhouse Bayern Munich and then Liverpool's double, a most unlikely team was poised to break the sequence of big-club supremacy. In the early years of the Seventies the idea of humble Nottingham Forest as champions of Europe would have been as ridiculous as that of, well, a woman Prime Minister. Change, it seemed, was everywhere.

The first stage of Clough's Forest revolution had been to work out which of his inherited players were worth persevering with. Youngsters such as full-back Viv Anderson and forward Tony Woodcock had obvious potential, but he also made peace with Northern Ireland midfielder Martin O'Neill and Scot John Robertson, both of whom had been agitating for transfers under previous manager Allan Brown.

Having kicked around the Forest squad for almost five undistinguished years, Robertson was an unlikely figure to become the cornerstone of a European Cup-winning team. Overweight, not particularly quick and with an unkempt grooming style that made him look even less athletic, he was proof that Clough possessed a tolerance not always shared by his peers and an ability to look beyond the superficial. The manager might have joked that he felt like 'bloody Errol Flynn in comparison' to Robertson and said that 'there were times when he barely resembled a member of the human race', but no one was more aware of what he could do with the ball.[806] He would eventually move Robertson from central midfield to the left wing and make him the focus of Forest's attacking play, issuing instructions to his team to 'keep giving it to the fat man'. Robertson was encouraged to take his time, hold on to the ball, look for openings and to make the most of what Clough called 'his extraordinary abilities to manoeuvre and deliver a ball'.

After Forest rose to eighth place in the Second Division in 1975-76, Clough's first full season at the City Ground, it was when Peter Taylor arrived that summer that Robertson's career really took off. Reunited with Clough after Brighton and Hove Albion had missed out on Third Division promotion, Taylor quickly confronted Robertson, who admitted that he 'wasn't living right'. Robertson was challenged before a pre-season game in Germany to look in the mirror and stop blaming others for his problems. 'Brian and I think you can play,' Taylor told him. According to Robertson, 'the effect was immediate'.[807]

The higher Forest rose in the football hierarchy, the more effective Robertson would become. His sharp footballing brain and his ability as a dribbler and crosser of the ball became even more marked in the less frenetic environment of the First Division and Europe. 'He couldn't run. He wasn't quick. But you couldn't believe some of the things he used to do when the ball was at his feet,' said Larry Lloyd. 'He'd put his fat arse to the right – and then, hey presto, he was off down the left.'[808]

Lloyd signed for Forest after Taylor, who had no superior when it came to identifying a need and the player to fill it, noted that Forest lacked defensive strength between the exciting Anderson on the right and former Newcastle United left-back Frank Clark, signed on a free transfer and now pushing 33. The former Liverpool man had slipped off the radar somewhat with his transfer to Coventry. But he believed he had successfully adapted his style to suit the referees' stricter application of the laws and felt he was a changed character from the man who'd frequently clashed with Tommy Smith at Liverpool. 'If Larry Lloyd could have controlled himself,' Smith wrote in 1980, 'he would probably still be at Liverpool, but he always seemed to lack something ... We used to call Larry "Albert Tatlock"* because he'd be moaning all the time.'[809]

Clough, however, didn't want him to change. 'We surrounded Lloyd with people who could play and got so much out of him that he finished up in the England team again,' he said.[810] He once pointed at him and told David Needham, whom he signed from Queens Park Rangers, 'I hate that fucking bastard over there. Absolutely hate him. And that, David, is why you are not in the team. You're not a bastard like Larry Lloyd. And son, I want a bastard in my defence.'[811]

McGovern could sense the difference in the mood as Forest's new promotion campaign progressed. 'Things clicked from the moment Peter Taylor arrived,' he said. 'It was as if Clough's confidence grew when that happened.'[812] As Clough himself said, he'd wanted him by his side 'almost as much for his ability to make me laugh as his ability as a talent spotter'. He would insist that Taylor's contribution to events at Forest could never be overestimated.

The management duo had McGovern filling in as sweeper alongside Lloyd for part of the season; Clough arguing that no one in football could read the game more clearly. Such was McGovern's value, despite being born with a missing back muscle that gave him an ungainly running style and robbed him of any pace, that Archie Gemmill would call him the best midfield man he ever played alongside. Legend has it that the only reason he did not make Scotland's 1978 World Cup squad was that manager Ally MacLeod didn't know he was Scottish.

With former Birmingham centre-forward Peter Withe top-scoring with 16 goals and Woodcock establishing himself as his partner up front, Forest did enough to stay in the promotion race for most of the season without ever convincing anyone they were certain to make

* The curmudgeonly pensioner in *Coronation Street*, played by Jack Howarth until his death in 1984.

it across the line. Victory in the Anglo-Scottish Cup was important, Clough felt, in giving them a taste of success, but for a while it appeared that he might not see the end of the campaign at the City Ground. Offered the opportunity to return to Derby, he was persuaded to stay at Forest by his sense of the clubs' different trajectories, his continued dislike of his former boss, Sam Longson, and his loyalty to Forest vice-chairman Stuart Dryden – although there were plenty who felt he had only negotiated with his former club in order to be able to snub them.

Having won the final game of their season, Forest had to wait to see whether Bolton Wanderers would gain enough points in their remaining matches to deny them promotion. They didn't. Clough was back in the First Division, but according to Lloyd, 'You didn't have to be a brain surgeon to realise that team would not have survived, and that Clough had to make some signings.'[813]

Again, Taylor identified the missing pieces. England goalkeeper Peter Shilton, signed for £275,000 from Stoke a few days into the season at a reported record £1,200-per-week salary, was an obvious choice; as was midfielder Gemmill, who had helped Clough and Taylor win the League at Derby. More surprising was the first of the targeted trio to be signed, Birmingham City centre-forward Kenny Burns, a man with a reputation as a fighter, a drinker and a gambler. Birmingham chairman David Wiseman even warned Clough, 'Don't buy him, he's trouble.' Taylor and Forest chief scout Maurice Edwards had him followed to a dog track and pub, where he was reported to have placed only modest bets and drunk little. Taylor also sensed that having to run around up front did not suit Burns's temperament, even though he'd scored 20 goals in the previous season. He saw enough skill in his new signing to play him as a sweeper alongside Lloyd. 'I visualized Burns turning into a Scottish Bobby Moore because he's as skilful as Moore and certainly more ruthless.'[814] One of Taylor's proudest moments in what would be a momentous season was when Burns collected the Footballer of the Year trophy.

As for his antics on the field, Clough was confident he could teach him restraint, although he did have to fine him early in the season for a calculated headbutt on Arsenal's Richie Powling in a defensive wall, missed by the referee but in full view of the TV cameras. Recalling the experience of playing against Burns and Lloyd, Kenny Dalglish said, '[They] would boot me all over the place but they knew there was every chance of getting kicked back, which wouldn't have bothered tough defenders like them.'[815]

Clough was confident in his dealings with strong characters because he felt he was stronger. 'They all toed the line,' he said. 'I didn't need to tell them I ran the place – they could see it.'[816] Burns, whose moustache, busted nose and jawline gave him the look of a blond Captain Pugwash, saw it as well as anyone, acknowledging there was 'something about the man, the aura of the man; he can make you do anything'.[817]

After winning at Everton on the opening day of the season and being the only First Division team to win their first three games, Forest were brought back to earth with a 3-0 defeat at Arsenal, the final game before Shilton's arrival. Having tripped up Shilton's financial adviser with his squash racquet as he walked into the negotiations, Clough then shipped off goalkeeper John Middleton to Derby as part of the Gemmill deal.

As Forest racked up the wins and maintained an unlikely position at the top of the table, Clough criticised the Nottingham public for not turning up in greater numbers. He also told those who did attend games to improve their behaviour, getting a sign erected that urged, 'Gentlemen! No swearing, please!' In his Clough biography, *Nobody Ever Says Thank You*, author Jonathan Wilson suggested, 'Attacking his own fans seemed an odd move; perhaps it was best to issue his criticism from a position of strength, but the complaint fitted a general pattern by which Clough soured the moment of triumph, almost as if he had to make sure he didn't enjoy success too much.'[818] He did find a way of getting more people to buy tickets through his much-publicised, and ultimately futile, interview process for the England job. When he suggested that perhaps Forest fans should persuade him to stay, it prompted £3,000 worth of season-ticket sales.

After nine unbeaten games following the loss at Arsenal, Forest lost two out of three, at Chelsea and, much to Clough's disappointment, on his return to Leeds. They would not lose another League game for more than a year. Their pattern of play was established, a 4-4-2 formation that saw an advanced Robertson as playmaker on the left and O'Neill as the deeper-lying workhorse on the right. Geoffrey Green's description in *The Times* of their 'peace, spirit and a vision of a wide field' captured their uncomplicated approach.

As Clough told McGovern, 'You play midfield. Go out and pass the ball to someone or I'll get someone who can.'[819] Burns remembered that 'everything we did was very, very simple', a method based around, 'You see a man, pass it to him. We just didn't practise anything.'[820]

When Clough could be bothered to attend, training often dispensed with any pretence of match preparation. On some days, Clough would take his players for a walk; on others he would send them racing around fields, full of three-foot high nettles and brambles. And when they trained in the stadium the day before the game, Clough might send them on one lap of the field before shouting, 'Last man out of sight.' That was the players' cue to clamber up into the stands to hide, the last one who disappeared knowing he would be first into the nettles next time. Only when five-a-side games were called for did intensity levels rise, with matches fought out like cup finals and Clough determined that his team would win.

'You might not have seen him every minute of every single day,' O'Neill recalled, 'but his influence was there all the time. It was his football club – and you knew that.'[821] Ian Bowyer, who had won domestic and European medals early in his career under the technical imperatives of Malcolm Allison at Manchester City, added, 'You were only ever under one pressure when Brian was the manager. If you gave your lot then that was it. He could live with people miscontrolling the ball; he could live with people shooting at goal and missing the target.'[822]

The most memorable game of Forest's unlikely title campaign took place at Old Trafford a week before Christmas, a crushing 4-0 defeat of Manchester United that, according to Anderson, 'served to magnify the mystique of Brian Clough and what he could drive his side to achieve'.[823]

Needham made his debut as cover for the injured Lloyd that day but was barely called upon once Brian Greenhoff diverted Woodcock's shot into his own goal after it hit the post. He was able to watch as Woodcock made it 2-0 before half-time and Gemmill set up Robertson and Woodcock for further goals. Capturing the moment, as he did so frequently throughout the decade, BBC's Barry Davies greeted the final whistle with, 'Manchester United – buried in their own backyard.' Typically, Clough complained that his team had failed to record 'a result of incredible proportions', but it could not prevent most reporters accepting the game as proof that Forest could actually win the League. *The Guardian*'s Paul Fitzpatrick went as far as saying, 'Observers with long memories of Old Trafford football would say they were the best side seen on the ground for many a long year.'

Meanwhile, Taylor would also remember it as the moment when – with success now on the horizon – caution became paramount, winning an obsession and defence a priority. Yet once the die is cast it takes some undoing. Just as Revie fought unsuccessfully to rid Leeds of their early image for dull cynicism, so Forest continued to project a freshness and style about their play, perhaps because their achievements were so unexpected.

The early weeks of 1978 saw them complete a blitzkrieg of a journey to the League Cup Final. Their 23 goals in six ties included a satisfying 7-3 aggregate win against Leeds in the semi-final. The prospect of facing League and European champions Liverpool at Wembley offered a perfect measure of their progress, even though they were already five points clear at the top of the table and nine ahead of Liverpool. *The Times* called it 'an ultimate eliminator; the matching of proved champions with the most remarkable of challengers'. That Forest survived to draw 0-0 was down largely to the cup-tied Shilton's 18-year-old replacement, Chris Woods, the youngest goalkeeper to play in a Wembley final.

For the replay at Old Trafford, O'Hare replaced the injured McGovern and a deeper role was assigned to Robertson. It was he who scored the only goal, converting a second-half penalty after O'Hare was brought down by Thompson – 'well and truly clobbered with malice aforethought' as team-mate Phil Neal described it.[824] Thompson was furious, not because he claimed his innocence but because he said he had deliberately committed the foul outside the box, a confession that had earned him a £300 fine for bringing the game into disrepute. Television cameras suggested referee Pat Partridge had made the wrong call, and Taylor's post-match acting was unconvincing enough to have earned him a place in *Crossroads*. 'Obvious penalty,' he said, trying to keep a straight face. 'No one's doubting it, surely?' Two years later he was happy to admit in his book, *With Clough by Taylor*, that Liverpool 'lost because of a mistake by [the] referee'.

Forest needed no such help to maintain their First Division lead and the title was clinched with four games to play in a goalless draw at Coventry City. 'We've done it the way everybody likes to do their job,' Clough told TV viewers. 'Nicely, honestly and well.' This particular match was highlighted by an incredible save by Shilton to deny centre-forward Mick Ferguson, and without signing the England keeper it is doubtful Clough would have become the third manager to win the League with different clubs.† What was different about Clough's achievement was that he had taken both Derby and Forest from the Second Division. As Wilson noted, 'To lead one modest club to promotion and the League title would be remarkable, to do it twice in the space of a decade was barely credible.'[825]

Liverpool, meanwhile, rose to finish second ahead of Everton, who for a great part of the season had been Forest's most serious threat. Having lost their first two games, Gordon Lee's team embarked on an 18-match unbeaten run that ended with a spectacular 6-2 home defeat against Manchester United – a week after United's own humbling experience against Forest. Everton's 76 goals were the most in the division, and centre-forward Bob Latchford created a late-season focal point with his quest to reach 30 of his own. Hoping to incentivise greater scoring, the *Daily Express* had put up a £10,000 prize for

† Clough emulated Tom Watson (Sunderland, Liverpool) and Herbert Chapman (Huddersfield Town, Arsenal), and was later followed by Kenny Dalglish (Liverpool, Blackburn Rovers).

any First Division striker reaching a threshold not attained since Francis Lee's 33 for Manchester City in 1971-72. 'Parochial by today's standards, it generated enormous interest,' Latchford recalled.[826] Goodison Park fans, who'd seen their team beaten by Aston Villa in a League Cup Final second replay the previous season, seized upon Latchford's quest.

Whereas Lee had converted 13 penalties six years earlier, Latchford didn't score his first spot-kick until four games from the end of the season against Ipswich Town, taking his tally to 28. Two blank games meant he still needed two in the season finale against Chelsea at Goodison Park. As the opposition crumbled, it was only in the 72nd minute that Latchford won a header to score his first goal of the day, his team's fourth. Everton scored again and were then awarded a generous-looking penalty. 'Just keep your head down and blast it,' team-mate Martin Dobson told Latchford. He did exactly that and the £10,000 was his. The terraces spent the final minutes celebrating as though they had won the League. 'I was so relieved and joyful that we'd made so many people happy,' Latchford recalled.[827]

Author Brian Viner, who was in the crowd that day as a young fan, recalled, 'The 39,504 of us inside Goodison Park … reacted pretty much as if we had each won £10,000, not just him.' Latchford's landmark 'had an effect on the Goodison crowd a bit like lifting the heavy lid of a pressure cooker. All the frustration that had been stored up since 1970, as Everton repeatedly failed to fulfil their potential and Liverpool repeatedly realised theirs, erupted in a spectacular whoosh of jubilation.'[828] The picture of Latchford on his knees celebrating his landmark goal was made into a poster that was available for 50 pence in the stadium's Toffee Shop at the start of the next season.

Ironically, Latchford's achievement ended up costing him money. Half the prize was never intended for him anyway, being gifted by the newspaper to FA and Football League charities. Of the remaining amount, he kept only £1,000 himself and put £4,000 into the Everton players' pool. He later received an Inland Revenue demand for tax on the full £10,000, which meant that long-running legal and accountancy costs put him out of pocket overall. He'd even turned down the opportunity to cash in further on a season that had seen him make his England debut, having been 'scared' when Mark McCormack's IMG proposed a marketing contract. He was not the first player to decline such an opportunity. He blamed 'naivety and not being in an environment where recognising your commercial value was normal'.[829] Not everyone could be Kevin Keegan.

The spring of 1976 had been a good one for the nation's fortunes in European competition. In April, Brotherhood of Man won the Eurovision Song Contest by imploring the audience in The Hague to 'Save Your Kisses for Me' and the following month saw Liverpool lift the UEFA Cup. The two European Cups that followed in successive seasons meant that Liverpool had gone almost four years since experiencing defeat in Europe by the time the 1978-79 campaign began. The Continent had become as much their domain as the terraced streets around Anfield.

The draw for the first round of the European Cup, pitting England's two representatives together at the earliest possible moment, was greeted by groans of suspicion within the Liverpool and Forest camps. 'We had visions of perhaps both of us appearing in the final,' said Ray Clemence. 'Not only is it a disappointment for us and our fans, but for everyone involved in British football.'[830] On the contrary, there was much smacking of lips by most of the English football public. Not since Celtic and Leeds had been paired in the semi-finals of the competition in 1970 – the 'Battle of Britain' as it was inevitably dubbed – had a meeting of British clubs in Europe been so eagerly anticipated. On that occasion, a crowd of 134,000 had been at Hampden Park to see the Scottish champions secure victory. In the biggest games since then, Chelsea had beaten holders Manchester City in the semi-final on their way to winning the Cup Winners' Cup in 1971; Leeds overcame Liverpool in the last four en route to lifting that same season's Fairs Cup; Tottenham Hotspur beat Wolverhampton Wanderers in the 1972 UEFA Cup final; and, 12 months on, it was Liverpool who prevailed against Spurs in the semi-final of the same competition. The European Cup had only once previously been contested by two English teams in the same season, making this the first time the biggest competition had featured such a battle for national honour.

Forest might have wished to ease themselves into the competition, especially with their domestic campaign tripping along like one of Dick Emery's drag characters in ill-fitting heels. Defeat had yet to befall them, but their League performances had hardly matched the promise of their 5-0 brushing aside of FA Cup winners Ipswich Town in the Charity Shield. While Ipswich manager Bobby Robson kept his team shut away for a dressing down, Forest raced to the airport for a flight to Spain, where – typical of Clough's love of the unorthodox – they would compete in a four-team tournament, despite the League season being less than a week away. It was all part of his deliberate ploy to unsettle his champions. 'We would rather have them cribbing and feeling a bit nasty instead of going out feeling complacent,' he said.

After Forest were held 1-1 by Tottenham in the opening League game, Withe left for Newcastle United in search of a better deal, swapping a European Cup campaign for the Second Division. Then Forest reeled off four goalless draws, including a League Cup tie at Oldham Athletic. Having previously stated that he would 'break the bank' to sign a top-class striker, Clough was slated by Steve Curry in the *Daily Express*, who described the situation as 'professional blindness on Clough's part to commence his defence of the title so depleted'.

Liverpool had won their first four games by a combined margin of 16-2, while Forest had managed a solitary goal in four draws, which meant that few were arguing with the pre-season poll of First Division managers in which 16 tipped Liverpool to win the League. Clough resorted to giving a debut to 16-year-old forward Gary Mills against Arsenal and offering the centre-forward slot to 22-year-old Garry Birtles, who had people digging into the *Rothmans Football Yearbook* to be reminded that he had played once, as a midfielder, 18 months previously. After a 2-1 win Clough raved, 'Birtles was a revelation. He laid on more chances than we've had in all our matches put together.'

Having grown up on the outskirts of Nottingham, Birtles had been working as a floor layer when Clough signed him for £2,000 from Long

Eaton United. His emergence as a potential replacement for Withe hadn't come a moment too soon, with Liverpool next up at the City Ground in the first leg of their European tie. Clough had no hesitation in declaring that he would retain his place. Superficial deliberation of how the game might play out centred on Forest's relative inexperience in Europe compared to a Liverpool team with more continental conquests than a lads' package holiday. Forest, it was assumed, would tackle the game as they would a domestic contest. As it turned out, it was Liverpool who, fatally, would pay for not treating Forest like Feyenoord. 'It is vital that we prepare as for a domestic cup tie,' Clemence had said, with flawed logic. Clough was characteristically playful in his assessment of the game. 'If I was to go through all their strengths we would be here all night,' he said before heading off to spend the evening before the game watching Frank Sinatra in concert.

These were the days before European games were prefaced by a pretentious fanfare, but the teams marched to the centre of the field and acknowledged the all-ticket crowd of almost 42,000. The fans cheered back from behind the kind of fences that would prove so deadly when the same two teams met in an FA Cup semi-final 11 years later. ITV's cameras lingered on the slight figure of Birtles during the warm-ups. Rubbing his hands nervously, he looked every bit a two-game novice. Until kick-off.

Forest were intent on not being bullied; snapping into tackles and denying Liverpool's fluent football of previous weeks. Meanwhile, Birtles turned Thompson in knots before testing Clemence. Then he left Thompson floundering again, forcing Phil Neal to cover. After 26 minutes, Burns knocked the ball forward from just inside Liverpool's half and Bowyer helped it into the path of Woodcock. Advancing into the area while Clemence charged to meet him, Woodcock stretched to knock the ball left for Birtles to run home with his left foot. The scorer's understated celebration of his first Forest goal was in contrast to the undisguised delight of his colleagues. He very nearly had a second when he headed into the side netting.

Greater urgency in the second half saw Liverpool applying more pressure, but their determination to cancel out Forest's lead was their downfall. Bob Paisley admitted they became swept along in approaching it as a domestic, rather than European, game – as Clemence had promised they would. They were still pressing for an equaliser when, three minutes from time, defender Colin Barrett charged down both Case and Neal near the halfway line and the ball ran for Birtles to race away from the snapping boots of Case. Thompson couldn't prevent a cross towards the penalty spot. Woodcock headed down and Barrett, who had continued his run forward, was in position to lash in a right-foot volley from six yards. 'I went chasing the game from central midfield,' Souness admitted, 'and ended up in the Forest left-back area. The ball was played into where I should have been, then back out to the left wing from where it was squared and they scored.'[831]

Inevitably, the performance of Birtles made the headlines and encouraged discussion that Forest may not need to buy a new forward. 'Birtles has had two brilliant games,' said Clough. 'We are still determined to spend the money if we can find the right player.' Nevertheless, he would go on to describe the discovery of Birtles as like 'a dying man crawling through the desert and finding a green shoot and a spring of water'.[832]

By the time the second leg arrived, Clough had seen warning signs in his team giving away a two-goal lead in a home draw against Middlesbrough. Although they were now only one game short of equalling the record 34-match unbeaten sequence of Leeds in the top flight, they were five points behind Liverpool, and Clough feared that minds were on Europe. If that was so, it ensured there was no drama at Anfield, where Gemmill played as an extra right-back and Burns and Lloyd were outstanding as Liverpool came up against a yellow wall and an in-form Shilton. Liverpool forced 16 corners, but there were no goals. In the space of six months, Forest had stopped Liverpool winning a third consecutive League title, a first-ever League Cup and now a third straight European Cup. 'We could just not break them down,' Dalglish recalled. 'We never scored the goals our possession deserved.'[833]

Despite Forest's success, Clough once more made a show of allowing another club to court him. At Derby, it had been Coventry;

a year previously, it was Derby who tried to beckon him back. Now it was Sunderland, for whom Clough had played and who had the size of stadium and fan base that made him envious. After his achievements at Derby and Forest, the status of Sunderland as a Second Division team did not appear to concern him. As was his style, rather than dismiss the speculation, Clough was happy to feed it. In his column in the *Daily Express* he boasted, 'I could become the first £1 million manager,' although he admitted he'd not yet been made an offer. If he and Taylor were being promised security for their families, he said, 'we have to think about it very seriously.' He concluded, 'I am a professional. I will go anywhere if the money is right.' But it appeared that Clough was playing his usual games. Before a week had passed he was declaring that he was about to sign a new seven-year contract at Forest, although warning that he and Taylor would step down after four and work out their contracts as consultants.

As Forest faced up to the next round of the European Cup, Clough remained frustrated that his team were still not considered likely tournament winners. 'Do we have to go 136 games without defeat before people accept we are a good side?' he asked. Hungarian legend Ferenc Puskas saw their potential, however. After his AEK Athens team had lost 7-2 on aggregate to Forest he said he could not see any team stopping them. At home, however, their 42-game unbeaten League run was finally halted at Anfield. Interestingly, Clemence observed, 'When the final whistle went I didn't detect any signs of dejection among the Forest players. I suspected their overwhelming feeling was one of relief.'[834]

It was some measure of revenge for a Liverpool team enjoying its finest League season of the decade, maybe of the ages. 'That was the best side I played in,' said Alan Hansen, eight times a League champion.[835] According to Karl Coppack, writing for *The Anfield Wrap*, 'What makes that season so great is the sheer dominance over the League. We absolutely pulverized all who stood in our wake. We were brilliant in 1988, but it was art in '79. Simply that. Art.'[836]

As well as the seven goals they put past Tottenham, Liverpool racked up six against Norwich, five against Derby, and scored at least three on

11 other occasions. Leading from start to finish, the only one of their four defeats that really hurt was when Everton's Andy King blasted the winner at Goodison Park to end Liverpool's 11-game unbeaten start – ten of those games having been won. They stayed ahead of a chasing pack of Everton, West Brom and Forest to win the title while scoring 85 goals, including 21 by Footballer of the Year Dalglish. Having seen the excitement generated by the *Daily Express*'s 30-goal individual prize a season earlier, *The Sun* responded by offering £50,000 to any First Division team averaging two goals per game. Such an amount spread around a full squad seems insignificant in an age when a modestly talented Premier League player earns that every week, but Case confirmed, 'Suddenly the realisation sank in that we could actually win the cash … the added incentive of that fifty grand provided an extra bit of motivation.'[837] More significantly, Liverpool conceded only 16, a record for a 42-game season at the top of English football.

By the time Liverpool were wrapping up their 11th League title, extending their own record, a debate had been raging for several months about where viewers might be able to watch them defending their crown the following season. On the evening of 16 November 1978, Football League officials had stepped out of a meeting at Wembley to announce that they were accepting a £5 million, three-year offer from ITV for exclusive television rights for three years. BBC, which had brought weekly televised football highlights to the nation, had been beaten in what the newspapers immediately dubbed 'Snatch of the Day', although the corporation warned that the deal violated a long-standing agreement with the League and FA that all coverage must be shared.

London Weekend Television head of programming Michael Grade had instigated the deal via an initial approach to Notts County chairman and League TV negotiator Jack Dunnett. The clubs' desire to see a substantial increase in the £420,000 per year paid by the two networks meant he found a receptive audience. League boss Alan Hardaker said, 'It was obvious that without this deal there would be no football on TV next season.'

BBC presenter Jimmy Hill, who voted against the deal as chairman of Coventry City, called it a 'back-alley approach' but didn't blame

ITV for making it. It was exactly the kind of audacious move he would have been proud of during his time as LWT's head of sport. And ITV suddenly felt bullish enough to announce an intention to go after the other jewels in the BBC sporting crown, including Wimbledon, the Grand National and Test cricket. BBC's head of outside broadcasts, the former rugby international Cliff Morgan, warned, 'If it's war they want, it's war they'll get.'

Before long, a group of MPs were calling for the deal to be renegotiated and speaking up for the BBC, which ended November by announcing that it was £17 million in the red and arguing that a £4 rise in the colour TV licence to £25 was not enough. The Department of Fair Trading began examining the implications of ITV's newly-won monopoly, although for a long while it appeared that ITV would prevail. One reader wrote to *Shoot!* to ask, 'Shouldn't they think of the public first? No thought for children who can't stay up late.' Aware of the risk of its readership becoming disenfranchised viewers, you could almost hear the sigh in the editor's reply. 'ITV have pulled off a great business deal,' he said, 'but at the expense of many supporters.'

In March, however, the picture changed again. Football League negotiators accepted a new joint £10 million, four-year package with BBC and ITV. The commercial network would still have its bragging rights, however, with the channels alternating the days of their coverage from season to season. ITV's invasion of the Saturday night schedules had partially succeeded. When the broadcasters agreed to link their annual payment to the rate of inflation, the club chairmen sanctioned the deal at the League's annual meeting.

THE WINNERS TAKE IT ALL

You been tellin' me you're a genius
Since you were seventeen

'Reelin' In The Years', Steely Dan (Donald Fagen, Walter Becker; MCA/Universal Music Publishing Group, 1972)

The early days of 1979 found Britain gripped by snow, and Jim Callaghan's Labour government struggling to escape the paralysing hold of industrial chaos. Clough was such a staunch backer of the Labour Party that, having once been asked to stand as an MP, it was now being suggested by Callaghan's advisers that his formal support should be enlisted as the critical Parliamentary vote that would determine his future loomed.

Ironically, as Callaghan tried to keep wages and inflation in check – being ravaged by the unions as a result – Clough was planning the grandest financial gesture the sport had ever witnessed. Determined to sign a new forward, he had been rejected when he asked Derby about Charlie George, so instead he set his sights on a player who had been a teenage sensation in the first year of the decade and now, in its final year, was anxious to make a move that would allow him to fulfil his potential.

The legend of Trevor Francis began with a goal on his first start for Birmingham City in the autumn of 1970. But it was the spring of 1971 that brought the 16-year-old from Devon to national attention. Offered an extended run in the first team, he scored 11 goals in a sequence of six games, including all four in a 4-0 home win against Bolton Wanderers. 'Things happened so quickly and some of the goals I scored were, I don't mind using the word outrageous,' he recalled. 'They were incredibly special days.'[838]

Playing alongside him as Birmingham looked to make their way out of the Second Division was Latchford, who recalled the emergence of Francis as 'something that happens perhaps once every generation'. He added, 'When this young lad, who had only just turned 16, stepped onto the pitch for his first appearance in training you looked at him and thought "Wow". You knew you were in the presence of somebody who was going to be really outstanding.'[839]

Birmingham's status outside the elite of the game helped Francis develop without too much further media frenzy around him, but it also meant that the highest recognition was relatively slow to come his way, with his England debut delayed until 1977. He admitted that his progress had been slowed after his explosive start simply by the fact that he still had a lot of physical development to do. As Latchford noted, he was not yet a man at the age of 16 in the way that Wayne Rooney was when he burst on the scene three decades later.

By the 1978-79 season, Francis was eager to escape a club that was about to see the end of a seven-year stay in the First Division. Even a few months with Sir Alf Ramsey as manager during the previous season had failed to galvanise them. Ramsey had wanted an unhappy Francis to be placed on the transfer list and cited the directors' refusal as one of the reasons that he resigned. Blues defender Joe Gallagher recalled, 'That was a time of uncertainty and I think Sir Alf got caught up in it. There was always talk of Trevor going to one club or another.'[840] Ramsey made no secret of how fed up he grew with the ongoing saga, announcing at one point, '[Trevor] has had his say. His wife has had her say. Now I am waiting for the dog.'

Now Birmingham had agreed to sell Francis, whose personal financial demands had been temporarily met by allowing him to play for Detroit Express in the NASL in the summer. But they wanted the game's first £1 million fee and only two clubs, Forest and Coventry City, were willing to get anywhere near it, both opening with bids of £900,000. 'With respect to Coventry,' said Francis, 'that would have been a contradiction if I'd gone there because I wanted to improve myself as a player and win things.'[841]

Clough was on the record as saying, 'A player like Francis who can score 25 goals a season is worth £2 million' – hardly the best negotiating stance, but then he'd never cared about the niceties and politics of transfer negotiations. The eventual fee, £1,150,00 when all the various taxes were factored in, represented a huge rise in the British record transfer of £516,000 that West Bromwich Albion had just paid Middlesbrough for forward David Mills. Francis never gave the impression that the fee weighed him down, but would regret that it became the defining element of his career. 'I think back at what I've achieved,' he said late in 2019, 'and this is the only thing I did? The first £1 million footballer.'[842]

While Francis posed for press photographs in his beige suit and blue tie, Clough, who had told Francis to take his hands out of his pockets when presenting him with an award in Birmingham a few months earlier, made a show of strolling around in a red tracksuit top and squash racquet in hand – 'just in case he makes a balls-up of it'. He projected the air of a man inconvenienced rather than having made football history. Francis was given further insights into Clough's methods when the manager made him turn out for the club's A team on a park pitch, told him off for not wearing shin pads and banned him from taking his own soap and shampoo to training.

Yet Francis would recall the respect Clough and Taylor commanded and had his eyes opened by their approach to running a team. 'The most impressive quality with Clough and Taylor was not in their coaching. They never took training,' he said. 'It's motivation. Sending players out in the right frame of mind.' He called it a 'stark contrast' with Birmingham, where little was said before kick-off. 'But with Clough and Taylor, the most important ten minutes of the week began at 2.45. I'd grown up to think that the game was all about coaching and tactics, which you concentrated on during the week. And that if those were done properly it will all come right on Saturday. Yet at Forest I suddenly discovered that the most important function of the manager … was getting the players to produce a consistent level of performance week-in, week-out by emphasis on mental attitude.'[843]

Newspapers estimated that Francis would earn upwards of £100,000 per year with Forest, plus a £50,000 share of the transfer fee and his money from another summer in America. All this at a time when the average annual salary for a UK worker was £6,000. Callaghan must have envied Clough's ability to indulge such extravagance.

A soft-edged figure who relied on an image of common sense rather than fire of rhetoric, Callaghan's three years as Prime Minister had been a constant battle against forces both external and within Parliament. By-election results saddled him with a government that had no working majority, forcing him into a pact with the Liberals in the House of Commons. That had expired in the summer of 1978, leaving Callaghan to scrape around for allies like a hard-up football manager scuffling for free transfers.

His Chancellor of the Exchequer, Denis Healey, had stated in July 1978 that the government intended to cap wage rises at five per cent, only for Ford Motors to give in to striking workers and offer a 17 per cent rise four months later. Public sector workers realised the power they now held, and weeks of crippling stoppages brought Callaghan to the dark place in which he found himself in late March 1979. Striking lorry drivers, along with weeks of unrelenting snow, brought food deliveries to a halt and left some shop shelves empty. Hospital workers ceased to care for the sick. Perhaps most damaging to the world's image of Britain was the refuse collectors' strike that left streets all over the country piled high with rubbish. Public parks and even London's Leicester Square became dumping grounds. The rats, offered easy pickings during the country's coldest winter for 16 years, couldn't believe their luck. In some parts of the country, strikes among council workers had meant that dead bodies were unable to be buried. Callaghan was paying dearly for not calling an election in the autumn of 1978 when the economy was in an upturn. That decision had sealed his fate.

While Callaghan would call upon every last man and woman at his disposal and still be beaten in the crucial Commons vote of no-confidence, Clough's latest recruit was surplus to requirements. Cup-tied in the League Cup and not yet eligible to play in Europe, Francis watched as Forest successfully defended their domestic trophy in between the two legs of their European quarter-final against Grasshoppers of Zurich. On the eve of their Wembley meeting with Southampton they arrived at their team hotel at 9.30pm after what Clough sensed was a nervous journey. He promptly ordered the players to the lounge and demanded that the 12 bottles of champagne he'd ordered must be finished before anyone went to bed. There were unorthodox goings on, too, at Southampton's hotel, where comedian Freddie Starr turned up uninvited and ended up sitting on the Wembley bench.

Southampton's victory over Leeds in the semi-final denied Clough the poignancy of coming up against his former team on what would have been their first Wembley appearance since he had led them out in the Charity Shield almost five years earlier. And there would have been additional irony in Leeds reaching the final in a season that had started, incredibly, with another high-profile manager lasting only 44 days at Elland Road.

It had always been popular to speculate how Jock Stein would fare in English football while he was leading Celtic to the European Cup and ten Scottish titles. Rarely did one of the prime positions in English football become vacant without his name being mentioned. After a decline in Celtic's fortunes saw him replaced by former skipper Billy McNeill in 1978, Stein took the job for which many had believed he'd been the best candidate four years previously. Had he been offered a place on the Celtic board he would have remained in Scotland; instead he took over from Jimmy Armfield as Leeds manager.

After Joe Jordan and Gordon McQueen returned with Manchester United to inflict defeat on Stein in his first match, things were moving along steadily enough by late September. That was when Ally MacLeod, unable to live down the embarrassment of Scotland's World Cup performance in Argentina after all his tartan-waving optimism, resigned after a losing start to European Championship qualifying. Stein, feeling displaced as he lived alone in a Leeds hotel, needed little persuading to answer his country's call. Like Clough, he had spent 44 days in charge. Unlike Clough, his departure was regretted by the Leeds fans, and journalist Christopher Davies, who – in an unusually stringent stance for *Shoot!* – argued, 'It was a sad day for football. How can anyone trust anyone again? Jock Stein, one of the most admired and respected men in football, has set the wrong example.'[844]

The Leeds players, particularly the large Scottish contingent, were not exactly surprised. According to Peter Lorimer, 'In my deepest subconscious I felt Big Jock was trying to force the Scottish FA's hand. [He] wanted to be the full-time manager of Scotland and when he moved to Leeds he made the SFA change their way of working and made him the most powerful manager they'd ever had.'[845]

Under former Burnley manager Jimmy Adamson, Leeds went on to miss out on a League Cup final played on a pitch surrounded by piles of dirty snow.‡ Instead, it was Southampton who took a half-time lead against Forest through David Peach. Such a situation would usually signal a Clough outburst. 'If we were playing badly or losing a match we should be winning, we would get a terrible roasting from Cloughie at half-time,' Lloyd explained. 'The yelling and shouting was ear-splitting.'[846] But instead of histrionics, Clough calmly told them to think of nothing but passing the ball to a red shirt and they duly went out and won the game. 'We played well first half,' said Peach. 'But on the balance of play they were a bit better than us.'[847] Birtles made centre-half Chris Nicholl's day a misery, stealing the ball from him to equalise and leaving him stranded for the second. Mind you, Nicholl had enjoyed his moment of glory in this competition two years ago with a thumping left-foot strike from more than 30 yards in Aston Villa's 3-2 win against Everton in the second replay of the final. That Nicholl would be a loser this time was ensured by Woodcock's first-time finish eight minutes from time, despite a late volley by Saints' Nick Holmes.

Having thrashed Chelsea on the night of Callaghan's no-confidence vote, Forest completed the double over them in Thatcher's neighbourhood on the day Parliament was formally dissolved in advance of a 3 May general election. Four days later they were caught off guard by FC Cologne's attacking intent at the County Ground, finding themselves 2-0 down after 19 minutes of the first leg of their European Cup semi-final. 'We've been dead and buried before but never quite as deeply as that,' said Clough, never one to understate anything.[848]

But Birtles pulled one back and Bowyer, the versatile, unspectacular workhorse, equalised after 53 minutes. When Robertson scored with a diving header after 62 minutes it appeared the crisis had been diverted, only for Yasuhiko Okudera to come on and make it 3-3 with

---

‡ As I mention in my biography of Alan Ball, the weather caught out the producers of *Yesterday's Hero*, a movie featuring Ian McShane as a has-been chasing one last glory. Using real clips from the League Cup Final to double as the fictitious 'Saints versus Leicester Forest' FA Cup Final was a good idea until the long winter left sharp-eyed viewers wondering why there were mounds of snow at a game traditionally played in the early summer sunshine.

a shot that slid under Shilton's dive, prompting a flurry of headlines about being sunk by a Japanese sub. O'Neill remembered the game as 'everything you thought football could be. I honestly felt when I came in that I just played in the most atmospheric game imaginable.'[849]

Clough smiled down the television cameras and warned, 'I hope anybody is not stupid enough to write us off,' while Taylor stuck £1,000 on his team to reach the final. The return of Anderson and Burns made Forest a different defensive proposition in Germany, where Clough assured his players that if they held out in the first half they would score in the second. Forest sensed the home team's uncertainty about how to approach a game in which they simply needed to avoid defeat, absorbing what pressure there was and countering with Bowyer's headed goal after 65 minutes. Then they completed the game with the ease of European veterans.

And so, May 1979 brought the two defining contests of the lives of Clough and Thatcher. The first day of the month found the *Daily Express* reporting that Thatcher 'wows them with her woman's vision' in a televised question-and-answer session in Bolton, although a National Opinion Poll published the same day showed that Callaghan still enjoyed 43.1 per cent of public support compared to Thatcher's 42.4. On the day's back pages, Bob Houghton, the English manager of Swedish European Cup finalists Malmo, refused to be fooled by the poor performance he'd witnessed in Forest's 1-0 defeat at Wolves. 'I haven't seen the best of them tonight,' he said, 'But Clough will motivate them when they meet us in Munich.'

The day before the election, the media's true colours were on display. 'Give the girl a chance,' urged the front page of the *Express*. 'You can help Margaret Thatcher make Britain really great again.' Meanwhile, the *Daily Mirror* asked, 'What would your life be like under Mrs Thatcher's broomstick?' A last-minute Mori poll predicted that the *Express* would get its wish, with Thatcher having charged to a six per cent lead in the polls and a likely 20-seat majority in the Commons. Callaghan was clinging to enough hope of a close contest that he arranged for Liberal Party leader David Steel to be flown to London if there was the possibility of forming a coalition government.

The plane stood idle; the nation put Thatcher into power by a clear margin of 43 seats.

The game in Munich was expected to be as one-sided as the ballot box. Having seen Malmo play, Taylor had reported to Clough, 'They're such a bad side I'm worried. We daren't let the lads know.'[850] Frank Clark had also been sent a report by a friend in Sweden. 'Malmo were a very, very ordinary team, but very, very well organised,' he said. 'They played this really well-disciplined offside trap.'[851] Clough and Taylor protected themselves against missing out on the £5,000 bonus they were contracted to receive for winning the European Cup by betting £1,000 each on Malmo.

Forest completed a League season in which they had to settle for second place, eight points behind Liverpool despite losing one match fewer, and then had to wait almost two weeks before facing Malmo. McGovern had been around Clough long enough to recognise his disregard and distrust of injured players, knowing he would make a point of keeping them on the sidelines for a couple of weeks after they told him they were fit. He could vouch for Clough's attitude that 'I would replace them all overnight if I could get a better side' and his reliance on 'fear and apprehension' as a method of man-management.[852] So when he went down injured against Southampton in a late-season testimonial for Lawrie McMenemy, he was quick to jump up and, like a floored boxer convincing the referee that he still had his marbles, told Clive Thomas to get on with the game.

But there were doubts over the health of Gemmill and O'Neill, both recovering from hamstring problems. As Clough considered his starting line-up in Munich, both assured him they were able to play. 'Good,' he replied. 'You'll be on the bench.' Admitting that he would have made the same plea in his days as a player, he explained, 'Hard decisions have to be taken. They're the ones that separate good managers from rotten managers.' While O'Neill said nothing, Clough recalled Gemmill's four-letter response as being 'typical of the miserable little bugger'.[853] Bowyer would play in central midfield and, in O'Neill's usual position on the right, the now-eligible Francis was offered a European debut.

As he had been before the League Cup Final, Clough was sufficiently attuned to the mood of his players to sense their nervousness. He deliberately engaged Birtles in an argument about shaving to take his mind off the game and produced beer for the players on the bus ride to the Olympiastadion. It needed the amusing sight of a young pedestrian walking into a lamppost after being distracted by the sight of the Forest party to break the tension on board. On arrival at the stadium, Clough defied UEFA officials by insisting he took his players directly to the pitch instead of the dressing-room.

A poor game would be remembered only for the moment in which it was decided. With half-time approaching, Robertson made one of his typically languid-looking runs down the left, two terrified defenders tracking him, before crossing to the far post for Francis to stoop and score with his head. 'I felt I had to justify my selection by playing at an extra level,' he said, remembering the goal as 'the best moment of my footballing career by far'.[854]

Clough acknowledged the defensive work Francis got through, as well as the jitters he gave the Malmo defence, but to make sure the glory and headlines didn't go to his head Taylor warned him, 'One goal doesn't make you a top-class footballer. You need a few more trophies and a regular place in the England team before you can think of yourself as established. Until then you're a glamour boy who hasn't produced the goods.'[855]

Addressing the relative mundanity of the game, Taylor felt that Forest had been drained by the domestic season and noted that 'Malmo showed little sign of wanting to raise the level of entertainment'.[856] At least Clough was for once full of praise for the Forest fans, 20,000 of whom were in Munich. 'It was impossible to ignore the emotion pouring from the terraces,' he said. In the dressing-room – already somewhat subdued due to the low-key manner of victory – Clough managed to dampen the mood further by ordering his players to hand in their medals. His desire to ensure training staff and additional players could receive replicas was worthy enough, but few players saw why they should relinquish their own cherished prize without a guarantee of getting it back. Among the few to comply was the disgruntled Gemmill, who was soon shipped off to Birmingham in a £150,000 transfer – not a bad return on a 32-year-old who had cost only £25,000.

The ungraciousness so often present in Clough at moments of triumph could not diminish the magnitude of the achievement in taking Forest from the Second Division to champions of Europe in two seasons. Nor could the fact that the victory lacked drama and didn't require the level of performance that Manchester United and Liverpool produced in their first finals in the tournament.

And to prove it was no fluke, Forest won the first European Cup of the 1980s, beating Kevin Keegan's Hamburg 1-0 in Madrid. For the second consecutive season, Liverpool had gone out in the first round, beaten 3-0 away at Dynamo Tbilisi. Clough's men reached the final by beating Ajax, the tournament's first dynasty of the 1970s, in the semi-final, and flew to the manager's favourite holiday destination of Cala Millor in Majorca to prepare. As the final approached, much was made of the Germans' influential international defender Manny Kaltz, but Clough promised, 'We have got a little fat guy who will turn him inside out.'

It was indeed Robertson, cutting in from the left and scoring with his right foot, who got the only goal. Over the TV pictures of celebration in Munich a year earlier, Barry Davies had described him as the man who had 'been turned from an also-strolled into an international'. Having made and scored winning goals in successive European Cup finals, Robertson had proved again that he didn't need to worry about running or physique. O'Neill, who played in the second final with Francis injured, was hardly exaggerating when he described Robertson as 'the most influential player in Europe for about three and a half years' and would later have him at his side throughout a successful managerial career.

O'Neill, a man who clashed with Clough more than most, came up with an analogy of his manager's remarkable five-year transformation of a club going nowhere in the Second Division. 'There was a change when that man stepped into Nottingham,' he told the makers of the documentary, *I Believe in Miracles*. 'It was almost like getting on a train and not getting off.'

This was, of course, the fourth such journey Clough had embarked upon during the decade. He'd managed to derail the first at Derby when the final destination was just out of reach; jumped train at Brighton; then forced others to pull the emergency cord while still stuck in the station at Leeds. Those adventures, and the adversaries he'd encountered along the way – Don Revie, the Football Association and Liverpool among them – did more than anything to shape events on English football fields in the 1970s.

Clough, the staunch socialist who had acquired a million-pound plaything, had created a body of work untouchable in the new world of financial football that awaited on the other side of Thatcherism and the 1980s. That he might well have been the most dominant British figure of the 1970s is a sign not only of his unique personality but also the place that football, for all its faults and failures, had come to occupy at the centre of the nation's culture. It had moved from the terraces and the Saturday evening pink 'uns to an unavoidable multi-media presence. The on-screen action still only consisted of a few hours of highlights every week, but rarely did a primetime television schedule run its course without some reference, in comedy shows or news programmes, to the national sport.

Even *New Musical Express* was getting in on it. As the final football season of the 1970s was wrapping up, it decided to offer a study of the nation's favourite sport, giving over the cover to a photograph of Cyrille Regis in full flight and the heading, 'The Human Face of Football'. It was a publication overlooked by most players; their taste in middle-of-the-road music seeing to that. It seemed incongruous, therefore, to find a six-page football feature alongside a review of the new album by The Cure, a feature on The Ramones' movie, *Rock 'n' Roll High School*, and an interview with Tom Waits. But writer Monty Smith, a Gillingham fan, was clearly fired up by developments in the sport since the dark days of the middle of the decade.

In his introduction, Smith posited that British football was 'entering a new era of skill and success', suggesting that 'we're beginning to get a bit cocky again'. His reasons for such a view included 'the appointment of a sensible England manager … the spread of catholic coaching techniques and reliance on more skilful players by managers who've learned to live with three-up, the three-down system; the emergence of an entire crop of indigenous black players; and the introduction of numerous foreign players, adding to the increasing list of superior ball players'.

Smith interviewed five individuals who made their living from football, starting with Duncan McKenzie, one of those players cursed by possessing a sublime and fragile talent in an era when the game desired strength and conformity. 'It's difficult for me to feel bitter when I've got a Mercedes and a Ford Granada in the driveway of a 60 grand house,' McKenzie said, even though he would soon be completing his career without winning a major honour or international cap. Any sadness he expressed was because of events he saw around the game. 'We're driving people away; people who are frightened to go on the terraces,' he said, referring to the one aspect of the sport that even the optimism of the *NME*'s premise could not bury.

Laurie Cunningham came across, as he often did in print articles, as distant and uninterested. The man who'd missed his interview with Brian Glanville all those years ago this time asked for a fee and caused White to write, 'He accepts the £10 disdainfully and I feel like the bloke who's farted in a lift.'

For his managerial subject, White selected Gillingham's Gerry Summers, whose biggest concern echoed McKenzie's about what was happening beyond the field. 'We've got antiquated grounds,' he said. 'You need £5 million to develop a stadium. The problem is when clubs do get money they spend it all on players.' Commentator Brian Moore was typically cheery in discussing 'a marvellous game with such great traditions that it can withstand any number of knocks' and even the fifth subject, David Lacey of *The Guardian*, was 'fairly optimistic, not least because skilful players are being allowed to make their own decisions on the pitch'.

Knowledge of what lay ahead for the sport in the 1980s makes it easy to look at White's 'cocky' feeling with a sneer. Yet as a snapshot of the game as a new decade approached, the *NME* piece offers a pretty accurate picture: increasing optimism based on club success in

Europe and the England team progressing toward the 1980 European Championship finals,[§] tempered by a growing anxiety about where the sport is headed off the field.

Poised to succeed Clough as arguably the pre-eminent character in British life in the 1980s, Thatcher could not have foreseen that she would be tied more closely to the sport's fortunes than any Prime Minister before her – whatever Harold Wilson might have believed. She would accompany football on to the front pages to condemn hooliganism and propose draconian counter-measures; to visit scenes of unspeakable tragedy; even to suggest England's World Cup withdrawal while the country was at war with a possible opponent.

By the time she left her post in 1990, football had suffered unspeakably, searched its soul and begun its rebirth. When Clough departed Forest nearly three years later – fighting alcoholism, the diminution of his powers and the stigma of relegation – the sport looked more like the one recognisable in the third decade of a new millennium than that which his personality had dominated in the 1970s.

§ England's 4-3 defeat in Austria in the final game of the 1978-79 season ended a 14-match unbeaten streak during which they had taken significant steps towards winning their Europa 80 qualifying group and beaten Scotland at Hampden Park and Wembley.

Postscipt

TRIAL OF THE DECADE

You've spoilt the game, no matter what you say
For only metal. What a bore!

'Make Me Smile (Come Up and See Me)', Steve Harley and Cockney Rebel (Steve Harley; Trigram/RAK Publishing Ltd, Music & Media International Inc., 1975)

WE ARE back where we began. Wembley Stadium, August 1974. Brian Clough leading out Leeds United and new England manager Don Revie watching from the stands, wondering what the hell that man was doing at the head of *his* team. Neither man knew it on that dramatic day, but the fortunes of both were set on a downward course.

Clough's was the more spectacular decline, a nosedive of violence and brevity, followed by a revivification that no one could have imagined. But when Revie had sat in the studios of Yorkshire TV and gloated over a humiliated Clough for the terrible job he'd done at Elland Road, little did he comprehend the course his own career had already taken. It was a slower descent, but one from which there was no Clough-like resurrection. A reputation that was already defined not so much by the trophies but by the manner of their winning would before long be shredded by unproven allegations of corruption and self-inflicted wounds of venality.

The first days of the 1970s had found Revie celebrating the award of his OBE and planning an FA Cup campaign that would take him to the brink of an historic treble, a glorious failure that would see him named English football's Manager of the Year. Yet the closing weeks of the decade would destroy what little was left of his standing beyond the boundaries of Leeds. Meanwhile, even Revie's old domain had taken a dark turn of its own; the city that had symbolised football in the early 1970s now synonymous with the brutality of murder as it suffered in the grip of a serial killer dubbed the Yorkshire Ripper.

After Revie's announcement of his job in the United Arab Emirates, FA chairman Sir Harold Thompson had wasted little time in declaring, 'We unanimously deplore the actions of Mr Revie.' For once, Sir Harold reflected the view of most football fans. And for once he had called him 'Mister'. Charges of bringing the game into disrepute followed, with three grounds outlined: announcing his resignation without telling the FA; asking for his contract to be paid up when he knew he was leaving the job; and making a secret trip to Dubai when he should have been with the England team in Brazil. Thompson, however, made an error in ignoring advice and appointing himself chairman of the five-man panel who heard the case in 1978. When Revie was banned from the game for ten years, despite speaking in his defence for four hours, Thompson had left the door open for an appeal on the grounds of bias.

By the time of Revie's appeal, the sport's image had been dragged through the courts a year earlier when Tommy Docherty sued his former Manchester United player Willie Morgan for calling him 'the worst manager there has ever been' on Granada Television. Docherty lived to regret that decision, admitting to me in interview years later, 'I trusted the advice I was given, and I was probably after a few quid as well.'

His case collapsed when he was forced to confess that he had not been truthful about the specifics of Denis Law's free transfer to Manchester City. When challenged that he had told 'a pack of lies to the jury' he was forced to admit, 'Yes, it turned out that way.' Docherty kept his job as Derby County manager, but was left facing £50,000 in costs, as well as perjury charges. He would be found not guilty at the Old Bailey in 1981 after claiming he'd felt 'intimidated and bullied' and had not intended to lie deliberately.

When Revie's appeal began on 26 November 1979, football's image was about to be soiled once more. Revie had a desire not only to clear his name; he had a practical need to have his ban overturned so that he could take up the offer of an eight-year £80,000 consultancy role at Leeds in the New Year. His case was that Thompson had been unfit to lead the original commission, with Gilbert Gray QC saying on his behalf, 'Sir Harold, in his own court, was effectively prosecutor, witness, judge and jury.'

But the hearing produced compelling content that went beyond that issue. Revie described the sleepless nights he had suffered as England manager; the objects thrown at him in the Wembley tunnel by fans; and complained that he and Les Cocker had been made to travel second-class by Thompson, despite what was specified in their contracts. He said he had turned down previous lucrative offers and had helped the FA make £500,000 profit during his tenure. He denied he had quit because he knew that stories were coming out in the press accusing him of attempting to fix matches. His decision, he said, had been made after being told during a conference in Bournemouth that someone else had been lined up for the role.

In the course of an eight-day hearing, wife Elsie confirmed her husband's insomnia; Jock Stein, Lawrie McMenemy, Jimmy Hill, David Coleman and Johnny Giles spoke up for Revie; and former FA president Lord Harewood told the court of Thompson's desire to fire Revie. In response, Thompson spoke of a public outcry over Revie's resignation that was 'as much as if there had been an outbreak of war'. He called him 'deceitful' and said that the FA 'tried to bend over backwards to be fair to him'. FA counsel Robert Johnson QC said Revie had brought disgrace to the sport more than once.

It was a week after the final statements that Justice Cantley returned with a verdict that Revie 'presented to football a sensational and outrageous example of disloyalty, breach of duty, discourtesy and selfishness'. And he made those comments while finding on behalf of the former England manager. It was with regret, he explained, that he was overturning the ban because the case met the legal requirement that a right-thinking person would see a 'real likelihood of bias' in the decision of Thompson's commission. 'But I will acquit Sir Harold of any bad faith,' he added. 'He is an honourable man.'

In no doubt that Revie had brought the game into disrepute, Justice Cantley delivered a character assassination as brutal as anything Leeds ever committed on the field in pursuit of victory. Of Revie's sale of his story to the *Daily Mail*, he said 'as a mode of resignation it was utterly selfish'. He called him 'deceitful', 'prickly', 'very greedy' and accused him of 'brooding on imagined wrongs'. The only consolation for Revie was that he was not there to hear the verdict. He was back in Dubai.

Until the case was heard, the most significant events in the sport up to that point of the season belonged to the narrative of the next decade: Malcolm Allison's disastrous return to Manchester City, where he'd splashed £250,000 on a 17-year-old, Steve Mackenzie; the transfer of Ray Wilkins from Chelsea to Manchester United; the early-season leadership of the First Division by a young Terry Venables-led Crystal Palace, who had created expectations high enough to have them branded 'The Team of the Eighties'.

But once Revie's proceedings began, it felt with every passing day that it was the football of the 1970s that was on trial. All those articles asking if Revie's Leeds were retarding English football or simply reflecting a new reality; the debates about the diminishing place in the game for individual skill in an age of stifling tactics; the desirability of the pursuit of victory at all costs. All seemed caught up in the question of whether the man whose methods and achievements provided the framework for much of the decade's football had brought the game into disrepute.

There was no more fitting way for the curtain to come down on English football in the 1970s. Unless Brian Clough himself had been the judge.

1970s ROLL OF HONOUR

1969-70

First Division: 1, Everton 66pts; 2, Leeds United 57pts; 3, Chelsea 55pts. ***Relegated*:** Sunderland, Sheffield Wednesday. **Second Division:** Huddersfield Town. **Third Division:** Orient. **Fourth Division:** Chesterfield.

FA Cup: Chelsea 2 (Houseman, Hutchinson), Leeds United 2 (Charlton, Jones), *after extra time.* **Replay** (Old Trafford)**:** Chelsea 2 (Osgood, Webb), Leeds United 1 (Jones), *after extra time.*

League Cup: Manchester City 2 (Doyle, Pardoe), West Bromwich Albion 1 (Astle), *after extra time.*

European Cup Winners' Cup (Vienna)**:** Manchester City 2 (Young, Lee pen), Gornik Zabrze 1 (Oslizlo).

Inter-Cities Fairs Cup: Anderlecht 3 (Devrindt, Mulder 2), Arsenal 1 (Kennedy); Arsenal 3 (Kelly, Radford, Sammels), Anderlecht 0. *Arsenal won 4-3 on aggregate.*

Footballer of the Year: Billy Bremner (Leeds United). **Manager of the Year:** Don Revie (Leeds United). **First Division top scorer:** Jeff Astle (West Bromwich Albion) 25. **Highest average League attendance:** Manchester United 49,862.*

1970-71

First Division: 1, Arsenal 65pts; 2, Leeds United 64pts; 3, Tottenham Hotspur 52pts. ***Relegated*:** Burnley, Blackpool. **Second Division:**

---

* Attendances as listed in *Football Through the Turnstiles... Again* (Brian Tabner; Yore Publications, 2002).

Leicester City. **Third Division:** Preston North End. **Fourth Division:** Notts County.

FA Cup: Arsenal 2 (Kelly, George), Liverpool 1 (Heighway), *after extra time.*

League Cup: Tottenham Hotspur 2 (Chivers 2), Aston Villa 0.

European Cup Winners' Cup (Athens)**:** Chelsea 1 (Osgood), Real Madrid 1 (Zoco), *after extra time.* **Replay** (Athens)**:** Chelsea 2 (Dempsey, Osgood), Real Madrid 1 (Fleitas).

Inter-Cities Fairs Cup: Juventus 0, Leeds United 0 *(abandoned 51 minutes, waterlogged pitch)*; Juventus 2 (Bettega, Capello), Leeds United 2 (Madeley, Bates); Leeds United 1 (Clarke), Juventus 1 (Anastasi). *3-3 on aggregate. Leeds won on away goals.*

Footballer of the Year: Frank McLintock (Arsenal). **Manager of the Year:** Bertie Mee (Arsenal). **First Division top scorer:** Tony Brown (West Bromwich Albion) 28. **Highest average League attendance:** Liverpool 45,602.

1971-72

First Division: 1, Derby County 58pts; 2, Leeds United 57pts; 3, Liverpool 57pts. ***Relegated*:** Nottingham Forest, Huddersfield Town. **Second Division:** Norwich City. **Third Division:** Aston Villa. **Fourth Division:** Grimsby Town.

FA Cup: Leeds United 1 (Clarke), Arsenal 0.

League Cup: Stoke City 2 (Conroy, Eastham), Chelsea 1 (Osgood).

UEFA Cup: Wolverhampton Wanderers 1 (McCalliog), Tottenham Hotspur 2 (Chivers 2); Tottenham Hotspur 1 (Mullery), Wolverhampton Wanderers 1 (Wagstaffe). *Tottenham won 3-2 on aggregate.*

Footballer of the Year: Gordon Banks (Stoke City). **Manager of the Year:** Don Revie (Leeds United). **First Division top scorer:** Francis Lee (Manchester City) 33. **Highest average League attendance:** Liverpool 47, 687.

1972-73

First Division: 1, Liverpool 60pts; 2, Arsenal 57pts; 3, Leeds United 53pts. ***Relegated*:** Crystal Palace, West Bromwich Albion. **Second**

Division: Burnley. **Third Division:** Bolton Wanderers. **Fourth Division:** Southport.

FA Cup: Sunderland 1 (Porterfield), Leeds United 0.

League Cup: Tottenham Hotspur 1 (Coates), Norwich City 0.

European Cup Winners' Cup (Salonica)**:** AC Milan 1 (Chiarugi), Leeds United 0.

UEFA Cup: Liverpool 0, Borussia Moenchengladbach 0 *(abandoned 27 minutes; waterlogged pitch)*; Liverpool 3 (Keegan 2, Lloyd), Borussia Moenchengladbach 0; Borussia Moenchengladbach 2 (Heynckes 2), Liverpool 0. *Liverpool won 3-2 on aggregate.*

Footballer of the Year: Pat Jennings (Tottenham Hotspur). **Manager of the Year:** Bill Shankly (Liverpool). **First Division top scorer:** Bryan Robson (West Ham United) 28. **Highest average League attendance:** Manchester United 48,623.

1973-74

First Division: 1, Leeds United 62pts; 2, Liverpool 57pts; 3, Derby County 48pts. ***Relegated*:** Southampton, Manchester United, Norwich City. **Second Division:** Middlesbrough. **Third Division:** Oldham Athletic. **Fourth Division:** Peterborough United.

FA Cup: Liverpool 3 (Keegan 2, Heighway), Newcastle United 0.

League Cup: Wolverhampton Wanderers 2 (Hibbitt, Richards), Manchester City 1 (Bell).

UEFA Cup: Tottenham Hotspur 2 (England, Van Daele og), Feyenoord 2 (Van Hanegem, De Jong); Feyenoord 2 (Rijsbergen, Ressel), Tottenham Hotspur 0. *Feyenoord won 4-2 on aggregate.*

Footballer of the Year: Ian Callaghan (Liverpool). **PFA Player of the Year:** Norman Hunter (Leeds United). **Manager of the Year:** Jack Charlton (Middlesbrough). **First Division top scorer:** Mick Channon (Southampton) 21. **Highest average League attendance:** Manchester United 42,712.

1974-75

First Division: 1, Derby County 53pts; 2, Liverpool 51pts; 3, Ipswich Town 51pts. ***Relegated*:** Luton Town, Chelsea, Carlisle United. **Second**

Division: Manchester United. **Third Division:** Blackburn Rovers. **Fourth Division:** Mansfield Town.

FA Cup: West Ham United 2 (A. Taylor 2), Fulham 0.

League Cup: Aston Villa 1 (Graydon), Norwich City 0.

European Cup (Paris)**:** Bayern Munich 2 (Roth, Müller), Leeds United 0.

Footballer of the Year: Alan Mullery (Fulham). **PFA Player of the Year:** Colin Todd (Derby County). **Manager of the Year:** Ron Saunders (Aston Villa). **First Division top scorer:** Malcolm Macdonald (Newcastle United) 21. **Highest average League attendance:** Manchester United 48,387.

1975-76

First Division: 1, Liverpool 60pts; 2, Queens Park Rangers 59pts; 3, Manchester United 56pts. ***Relegated*:** Wolverhampton Wanderers, Burnley, Sheffield United. **Second Division:** Sunderland. **Third Division:** Hereford United. **Fourth Division:** Lincoln City.

FA Cup: Southampton 1 (Stokes), Manchester United 0.

League Cup: Manchester City 2 (Barnes, Tueart), Newcastle United 1 (Gowling).

European Cup Winners' Cup (Brussels)**:** Anderlecht 4 (Rensenbrink 2, 1 pen, Van der Elst 2), West Ham United 2 (Holland, K. Robson).

UEFA Cup: Liverpool 3 (Kennedy, Case, Keegan pen), FC Bruges 2 (Lambert, Cools); FC Bruges 1 (Lambert pen), Liverpool 1 (Keegan). *Liverpool won 4-3 on aggregate.*

Footballer of the Year: Kevin Keegan (Liverpool). **PFA Player of the Year:** Pat Jennings (Tottenham Hotspur). **Manager of the Year:** Bob Paisley (Liverpool). **First Division top scorer:** Ted MacDougall (Norwich City) 23. **Highest average League attendance:** Manchester United 54,750.

1976-77

First Division: 1, Liverpool 57pts; 2, Manchester City 56pts; 3, Ipswich 52pts. ***Relegated*:** Sunderland, Stoke City, Tottenham Hotspur. **Second Division:** Wolverhampton Wanderers. **Third Division:** Mansfield Town. **Fourth Division:** Cambridge United.

FA Cup: Manchester United 2 (Pearson, J. Greenhoff), Liverpool 1 (Case).

League Cup: Aston Villa 0, Everton 0. **Replay** (Hillsborough)**:** Aston Villa 1 (Kenyon og), Everton 1 (Latchford), *after extra time.* **Second Replay** (Old Trafford): Aston Villa 3 (Nicholl, Little 2), Everton 2 (Latchford, Lyons), *after extra time.*

European Cup (Rome)**:** Liverpool 3 (McDermott, Smith, Neal pen), Borussia Moenchengladbach 1 (Simonsen).

Footballer of the Year: Emlyn Hughes (Liverpool). **PFA Player of the Year:** Andy Gray (Aston Villa). **Manager of the Year:** Bob Paisley (Liverpool). **First Division top scorer:** Andy Gray (Aston Villa), Malcolm Macdonald (Arsenal) 25. **Highest average League attendance:** Manchester United 53,710.

1977-78

First Division: 1, Nottingham Forest 64pts; 2, Liverpool 57pts; 3, Everton 55pts. ***Relegated*:** West Ham United, Newcastle United, Leicester City. **Second Division:** Bolton Wanderers. **Third Division:** Wrexham. **Fourth Division:** Watford.

FA Cup: Ipswich Town 1 (Osborne), Arsenal 0.

League Cup: Nottingham Forest 0, Liverpool 0, *after extra* time. **Replay** (Old Trafford)**:** Nottingham Forest 1 (Robertson pen), Liverpool 0.

European Cup (Wembley)**:** Liverpool 1 (Dalglish), FC Bruges 0.

Footballer of the Year: Kenny Burns (Nottingham Forest). **PFA Player of the Year:** Peter Shilton (Nottingham Forest). **Manager of the Year:** Brian Clough (Nottingham Forest). **First Division top scorer:** Bob Latchford (Everton) 30. **Highest average League attendance:** Manchester United 51,860.

1978-79

First Division: 1, Liverpool 68pts; 2, Nottingham Forest 60pts; 3, West Bromwich Albion 59pts. ***Relegated*:** Queens Park Rangers, Birmingham City, Chelsea. **Second Division:** Crystal Palace. **Third Division:** Shrewsbury Town. **Fourth Division:** Reading.

FA Cup: Arsenal 3 (Talbot, Stapleton, Sunderland), Manchester United 2 (McQueen, McIlroy).

League Cup: Nottingham Forest 3 (Birtles 2, Woodcock), Southampton (Peach, Holmes).

European Cup (Munich)**:** Nottingham Forest 1 (Francis), FC Malmo 0.

Footballer of the Year: Kenny Dalglish (Liverpool). **PFA Player of the Year:** Liam Brady (Arsenal). **Manager of the Year:** Bob Paisley (Liverpool). **First Division top scorer:** Frank Worthington (Bolton Wanderers) 24. **Highest average League attendance:** Manchester United 46,430.

Progression of highest transfer fees payed by English clubs during the 1970s:

1970 Martin Peters, West Ham United to Tottenham Hotspur, £200,000

1971 Alan Ball, Everton to Arsenal, £220,000

1972 David Nish, Leicester City to Derby County, £225,000

1974 Bob Latchford, Birmingham City to Everton, £350,000

1977 Kenny Dalglish, Celtic to Liverpool, £440,000

1979 David Mills, Middlesbrough to West Bromwich Albion, £516,000

1979 Trevor Francis, Birmingham City to Nottingham Forest, £1,150,000

1979 Steve Daley, Wolverhampton Wanderers to Manchester City, £1,450,000

1979 Andy Gray, Aston Villa to Wolverhampton Wanderers, £1,469,000

(Peters and Latchford fees included players as part-exchange).

ACKNOWLEDGEMENTS

AMONG THE biggest joys of writing my books has been the hundreds of hours I have spent talking to many of the people whose images I cut out of magazines; whose faces I swapped in the playground; and whose names I entered assiduously into my log books of Subbuteo leagues – the men who made me fall in love with football. Thank you to all of them, especially those whose interviews I have quoted in this book.

Anyone recording history is heavily reliant on those who have gone before and I am, therefore, indebted to everyone whose written and spoken words have helped me put together the story of English football in the 1970s. I have tried to list key sources in the book's notes; along with making every endeavour to identify publishers of lyrics etc. Any mistakes or omissions will happily be rectified in any future editions.

Richard Whitehead has played Don Howe to my Bertie Mee for many years, being a sounding board for most of my projects as well as doing another fantastic job of editing this one. My agent, David Luxton, continues to fill the Joe Mercer role of offering wise counsel and advice. (He is a Leeds fan, but far too nice to be compared to Don Revie.) And the team at Pitch Publishing – especially Paul Camillin, Jane Camillin, Graham Hales, Dean Rockett and designer Duncan Olner – have been the trusted 'boot room' for many of my books.

I will spare my daughters, Amy, Sarah, Laura and Karis, and my grandsons, Jacob and Oscar, any tortuous analogies that would go over their heads. They just need to know the love and pride I feel for all of them.

As for my wife, Sara, the support and love I get from her gives me the boost I imagine Liverpool's players must have felt when the Kop was willing the ball in for a late winner on a big European night. She has smiled patiently while I have accumulated just about every football annual, player autobiography, magazine and sticker album published in the 1970s, and I am sure she hopes that, to quote from one of our favourite movies, it's a case of, 'Enough now. Enough.' She may be right. But then there is always the 1980s.

ENDNOTES

Where not referenced below or identified in the main text, quotes are sourced from contemporaneous interviews and press conferences reported in national and local media:

INTRODUCTION

1 *Striker*, 16 May 1970
2 *Parkinson* (BBC TV, 1973)
3 Christian Caryl, *Strange Rebels: 1979 and the Birth of the 21st Century* (Basic Civitas Books, 2013)
4 Interview with www.thewordonthestreet.tv
5 Philip Cato, *Crash Course for the Ravers: A Glam Odyssey* (ST Publishing, 1997)

CHAPTER 1: RAGE AGAINST THE MACHINE

6 *Goal*, 1 April 1972
7 *Football Monthly*, September 1973
8 Billy Bremner, *You Get Nowt for Being Second* (Souvenir Press, 1969)
9 Rogan Taylor and Andrew Ward, *Kicking and Screaming: An Oral History of Football in England* (Robson Books, 1998)
10 *Shoot!*, 17 August 1974
11 Richard Sutcliffe, *Revie: Revered and Reviled* (Great Northern, 2010)
12 Interview with author
13 *Park Drive Book of Football 1970*
14 Leeds United player recruitment brochure, 1966
15 Marshall Cavendish *Football Handbook*, Part 30, 1979
16 *Action Replay*, September 1996
17 Taylor and Ward, *Kicking and Screaming*
18 Jack Charlton, *The Autobiography* (Partridge Press, 1997)
19 Taylor and Ward, *Kicking and Screaming*
20 Eddie Gray, *Marching on Together: My Life at Leeds United* (Hodder & Stoughton, 2001)
21 Marshall Cavendish *Book of Football*, 1972
22 Clive Thomas, *By the Book* (Willow Books, 1984)
23 Taylor and Ward, *Kicking and Screaming*
24 Rob Steen, *The Mavericks: English Football When Flair Wore Flares* (Mainstream, 1994)
25 Interview with author
26 Interview with author
27 Alan Hardaker, *Hardaker of the League* (Pelham Books, 1977)
28 *Yorkshire Evening Post*, 1 March 2018
29 Interview with author
30 *Charles Buchan's Football Monthly*, September 1969
31 Howard Kendall, *Love Affairs & Marriage: My Life in Football* (De Coubertin Books, 2013)
32 Interview with author
33 Interview with author
34 Everton FC championship brochure, 1970
35 Taylor and Ward, *Kicking and Screaming*
36 *Leeds United: The Glory Years* (BBC Video, 1988)
37 Hardaker, *Hardaker of the League*
38 *Whatever Happened to the Likely Lads?*

'Guess Who's Coming to Dinner?' (Dick Clement and Ian La Frenais, BBC TV, 1973)
39 Paolo Hewitt and Mark Baxter, *The Fashion of Football: From Best to Beckham, From Mod to Label Slave* (Mainstream, 2004)
40 Interview with author
41 Steen, *The Mavericks*
42 Interview with author
43 *Jimmy Hill's Football Weekly*, 20 February 1970
44 *Goal* magazine
45 Steen, *The Mavericks*
46 Alan Hudson, *The Working Man's Ballet* (London Books, 2017)
47 Steen, *The Mavericks*
48 *The Independent*, 15 December 2012
49 Taylor and Ward, *Kicking and Screaming*
50 Hudson, *The Working Man's Ballet*
51 Taylor and Ward, *Kicking and Screaming*
52 *Jimmy Hill's Football Weekly*, 20 February 1970
53 *Black Dwarf*, 12 June 1970
54 Taylor and Ward, *Kicking and Screaming*
55 *Football Monthly*, January 1972
56 Peter Osgood with Martin King and Martin Knight, *Ossie: King of Stamford Bridge* (Mainstream, 2002)

CHAPTER 2: WHATEVER HAPPENED TO THE LIKELY LADS?

57 *Kenneth Wolstenholme's Book of World Soccer* (World Distributors Ltd, 1968)
58 *Wolverhampton Express and Star*, 2 September 1969
59 *Backpass*, Summer 2008
60 *Goal*, 23 August 1969
61 Brian Moore and Martin Tyler, *The Big Matches: A Decade of World Soccer, 1970-1980* (Queen Anne Press, 1980)
62 Interview with author
63 *Radio Times*, 15 August 1970
64 Interview with author
65 Interview with author
66 *Inside Football*, 8 January 1972
67 *Shoot!*, 18 January 1975
68 Interview with author
69 Interview with author
70 Interview with author
71 Interview with author
72 Interview with author
73 Interview with author
74 Eamon Dunphy, *Only A Game?* (Viking, 1976)
75 *Football Monthly*, February 1972
76 Rob Steen, *The Mavericks: English Football When Flair Wore Flares* (Mainstream, 1994)
77 Geoff Hurst, *The World Game* (Stanley Paul, 1967)
78 *Goal*, 10 March 1973
79 Interview with author
80 *Shoot!* 17 May 1973
81 *Goal*, 23 September 1972
82 Interview with author
83 Mick Channon, *Home and Away: An Autobiography* (Stanley Paul, 1977)
84 *Goal*, 5/12 January 1974
85 Marshall Cavendish *Football Handbook*, Part 23, 1978
86 Stan Bowles, *The Autobiography* (Orion, 2004)
87 Steen, *The Mavericks*
88 *Shoot!*, 18 December 1971
89 *Shoot!* 30 January 1970
90 *Goal*, 10 November 1973
91 Marshall Cavendish *Football Handbook*, Part 3, 1978
92 Marshall Cavendish *Football Handbook*, Part 3, 1978
93 Interview with author
94 Interview with author
95 Goal, 7 October 1972
96 *Parkinson* (BBC TV, 3 November 1973)
97 Marshall Cavendish *Book of Football*, 1971
98 *Goal*, 22 November 1969
99 *Goal*, 6 September 1969
100 Steen, *The Mavericks*
101 Steen, *The Mavericks*
102 *Goal*, 2 August 1969
103 *Goal*, 28 July, 973
104 *Goal*, 6 September 1969
105 *Goal Annual*, 1977
106 *The Big Match*, London Weekend Television, 13 October 1974
107 Bowles, *The Autobiography*
108 Bowles, *The Autobiography*
109 Steen, *The Mavericks*
110 Marshall Cavendish *Football Handbook*, Part 14, 1978
111 Marshall Cavendish *Book of Football*, 1972
112 *Backpass*, Summer 2008
113 *The Big Match*, London Weekend Television, 22 September 1974
114 http://www.swlondoner.co.uk/football-maverick-marsh-looks-back-on-illustrious-career-at-qpr-and-fulham/
115 http://www.swlondoner.co.uk/football-maverick-marsh-looks-back-on-illustrious-career-at-qpr-and-fulham/

116 *The Independent*, 21 May 2009
117 Steen, *The Mavericks*
118 *One Hump or Two? The Frank Worthington Story*, (ACL & Polar Publishing, 1994)
119 *Shoot!* 14 April 1979
120 Interview with author
121 *Shoot!*, 25 June 1977
122 *The Guardian*, 6 December 2004
123 Russell, *Football and the English*
124 Peter Douglas, *The Football Industry* (George Allen & Unwin Ltd)
125 Steve Perryman, *A Spur Forever: My Lilywhite and Blue Life* (Vision Sports Publishing, 2019)
126 *Foul*, October 1972
127 *Foul*, May 1973
128 *Backpass*, Autumn 2009

CHAPTER 3: THE EMPIRE STRIKES BACK

129 Alan Hardaker, *Hardaker of the League* (Pelham Books, 1977)
130 *Goal*, 21 August 1971
131 *Charles Buchan's Football Monthly*, December 1969
132 Norman Burtenshaw, *Whose Side Are You on Ref?* (Arthur Baker, 1973)
133 Jack Taylor, *World Soccer Referee* (Pelham Books, 1976)
134 *Football Monthly*, January 1972
135 David Russell, *Football and the English: A Social History of Association Football, 1863-1995* (Carnegie Publishing, 1997)
136 *Goal*, 18 September 1971
137 *Goal*, 25 September 1971
138 *Goal*, 4 September 1971
139 *Goal*, 16 March 1972
140 *Football Monthly Digest*, December 1971
141 Hardaker, *Hardaker of the League*
142 Eamon Dunphy, *Only a Game?* (Viking, 1976)
143 *Shoot! Summer Special*, 1971
144 *Goal*, 21 August 1971
145 Tommy Smith, *I Did it the Hard Way* (Arthur Baker, 1980)
146 *Shoot! Summer Special*, 1971
147 *Goal*, 1 January 1972
148 *Shoot!*, 9 November 1974
149 Hardaker, *Hardaker of the League*
150 Hardaker, *Hardaker of the League*
151 Brian Moore and Martin Tyler, *The Big Matches: A Decade of World Soccer, 1970-1980* (Queen Anne Press, 1980)
152 Alan Hudson, *The Working Man's Ballet* (London Books 2017)
153 Peter Osgood with Martin King and Martin Knight, *Ossie: King of Stamford Bridge* (Mainstream, 2002)
154 *Inside Football*, 18 March 1972
155 *Shoot!*, 12 February 1977
156 Burtenshaw, *Whose Side Are You on, Ref?*
157 Interview with author
158 *Busby* (Fulwell 73 Productions, 2019)
159 *Frank O'Farrell: In the Shadow of Busby* (RTE, 2011)
160 Alex Stepney, *Alex Stepney* (Arthur Baker, 1978)
161 *Charles Buchan's Soccer Gift Book*, 1973
162 *Goal*, 13 November 1971
163 *Shoot!*, 4 December 1971
164 *Frank O'Farrell: In the Shadow of Busby*
165 John Roberts, *Fall of a Superstar* (Derek Hodgson, 1973)
166 *Frank O'Farrell: In the Shadow of Busby*
167 Ibid

CHAPTER 4: MIDDLE-CLASS HEROES

168 http://www.dailymail.co.uk/sport/football/article-1345397/Too-average-footballers-millionaires—drive-Ferraris-deserve-Reliant-Robin.html#ixzz42VlJmMMf
169 *Goal*, 20 March 1971
170 *Rothmans Football Yearbook 1970-71* (Queen Anne Press, 1970)
171 *Goal*, 20 March 1971
172 *Goal*, 9 August 1969
173 Alan Hardaker, *Hardaker of the League* (Pelham Books, 1977)
174 *Shoot! Annual 1972* (IPC Magazines Ltd, 1971)
175 Dominic Sandbrook, *Seasons in the Sun: The Battle for Britain, 1974-79* (Allen Lane, 2012)
176 Alan Hudson, *The Working Man's Ballet* (London Books, 2017)
177 Interview with author
178 Brian Viner, *Looking for the Toffees* (Simon & Schuster, 2013)
179 Hunter Davies, *The Glory Game* (Wiedenfeld & Nicolson, 1972)
180 Peter Douglas, *The Football Industry* (George Allen & Unwin, 1973)
181 Hunter Davies, *The Glory Game* (Wiedenfeld & Nicolson, 1972)
182 Interview with author
183 Alan Gowling, *Football Inside Out* (Souvenir Press, 1977)
184 Interview with author
185 Douglas, *The Football Industry*
186 *Backpass*, Autumn 2012

187 Interview with author
188 Interview with author
189 Bob Latchford, *A Different Road* (de Coubertin Books, 2015)
190 Douglas, *The Football Industry*
191 Alan Gowling, *Football Inside Out* (Souvenir Press, 1977)
192 Stephen Wagg, *The Football World, A Contemporary Social History* (The Harvester Press, 1984)
193 Match programme, Liverpool v Derby County, 20 January 1973
194 Interview with author
195 Interview with author
196 *Backpass*, Autumn 2012
197 Wagg, *The Football World*
198 *Goal*, 9 August 1969
199 *Shoot!*, 20 March 1971
200 *Football Monthly*, November 1973
201 Eamon Dunphy, *Only a Game?* (Viking, 1976)
202 Peter Cormack, *From the Cowshed to the Kop* (Black & White Publishing Ltd, 2012)
203 Interview with author
204 Duncan McKenzie with David Saffer, *The Last Fancy Dan* (Vertical, 2009)
205 Duncan McKenzie, *One Step Ahead* (Souvenir Press, 1978)
206 Jack Charlton, *The Autobiography* (Partridge Press, 1997)
207 *Jimmy Hill's Football Weekly*, 20 February 1970
208 Interview with author
209 *Inside Football*, 18 March 1995
210 Interview with author
211 Marshall Cavendish *Book of Football*, 1972
212 Terry McDermott, *Terry Mac: Living for the Moment* (Trinity Mirror Sports Media, 2017)
213 Lawrie McMenemy, *A Lifetime's Obsession* (Trinity Mirror Sports Media, 2016)
214 Terry Neill, *Revelations of a Football Manager* (Sidgwick & Jackson, 1985)
215 Interview with author
216 *Goal*, 23 November 1973
217 Interview with author
218 *Shoot!* 30 June 1979
219 *Shoot! Annual 1977*
220 *Football Monthly Digest*, June 1974
221 *Shoot! Summer Special*, 1977
222 Gordon Williams and Terry Venables, *They Used to Play on Grass* (Odhams, 1972)
223 *Bloomfield* (Richard Harris, Joseph Gross, Wolf Mankowitz; 20th Century Fox, 1971)
224 Williams and Venables, *They Used to Play on Grass*
225 Interview with author
226 *Shoot!*, 9 March 1974
227 *Goal*, 2/9 February 1974
228 Interview with author
229 Interview with author
230 *Goal*, 2 September 1972
231 Match programme, Leeds United v Tottenham Hotspur, 4 October 1974
232 Peter Douglas, *The Football Industry* (George Allen & Unwin, 1973)
233 Interview with author
234 Kevin Keegan, *An Autobiography* (Arthur Baker, 1977)
235 *Brian Moore Meets Kevin Keegan* (London Weekend Television, 1979)
236 Keegan, *An Autobiography*
237 Keegan, *An Autobiography*
238 *When Saturday Comes*, September 2003
239 *Brian Moore Meets Kevin Keegan*
240 Kevin Keegan, *My Life in Football: The Autobiography* (Macmillan, 2018)
241 *Nottingham Evening Post*, quoted in *Football Monthly*, January 1973
242 *Shoot!*, 30 January 1971
243 *Shoot!*, 27 November 1971

CHAPTER 5: SWEET TALKIN' GUYS

244 Tomas, Jonas, *The Leeds United Story* (Arthur Baker, 1971)
245 Stephen Wagg, *The Football World, A Contemporary Social History* (The Harvester Press, 1984)
246 Mark Garnett, *From Anger to Apathy: The Story of Politics, Society and Popular Culture in Britain since 1975* (Jonathan Cape, 2007)
247 Barney Ronay, *The Manager: The Absurd Ascent of the Most Important Man in Football* (Sphere, 2009)
248 *Goal*, 2 September 1972
249 Jeremy Novick, *In a League of Their Own: Football's Maverick Managers* (Mainstream, 1995)
250 Brian Reade, *44 Years with the Same Bird: A Liverpudlian Love Affair* (Pan Books, 2009)
251 Novick, *In a League of Their Own*
252 Rogan Taylor and Andrew Ward, *Three Sides of the Mersey* (Robson Books, 1993)

253 Peter Cormack, *From the Cowshed to the Kop* (Black & White Publishing Ltd, 2012)
254 Bill Shankly, *Shankly* (Littlehampton Book Services, 1976)
255 Shankly, *Shankly*
256 Interview with author
257 Interview with author
258 Brian Moore, *The Final Score: The Autobiography of The Voice of Football* (Hodder & Stoughton, 1999)
259 Interview with author
260 Interview with author
261 Interview with author
262 Interview with author
263 John McGovern, *From Bo'ness to the Bernabeu: My Story* (Vision Sports Publishing, 2012)
264 *Backpass*, Spring 2012
265 *Daily Mail*, 6 January 2018
266 *Backpass*, Spring 2012
267 *Inside Football*, 18 March 1972
268 Interview with author
269 *Match of the Seventies* (BBC, 1995)
270 *Inside Football*, 15 April 1972
271 John Toshack, *Tosh: An Autobiography* (Arthur Baker, 1982)
272 Richard Sutcliffe, *Revie: Revered and Reviled* (Great Northern, 2010)
273 John Giles, *A Football Man: The Autobiography* (Hodder & Stoughton, 2010)
274 Interview with author
275 Interview with author
276 Interview with author
277 Interview with author
278 *Goal*, 23 October 1971
279 *Goal*, 6 January 1973
280 Interview with author

CHAPTER 6: GAMES WITHOUT FRONTIERS

281 Brian Clough, *Clough: The Autobiography* (Corgi, 1995)
282 Brian Clough, *Cloughie: Walking on Water* (Headline, 2002)
283 John McGovern, *From Bo'ness to the Bernabeu* (Vision Sports Publishing, 2012)
284 Tony Francis, *Clough: A Biography* (Hutchinson, 1987)
285 *Goal*, 21 April 1973
286 *Backpass*, March/April 2016
287 *Goal*, 26 May 1973
288 *Shoot!* 8 January 1972
289 Interview with author
290 *Goal*, October 10 1970
291 Interview with author
292 Interview with author
293 *Backpass*, Christmas/New Year 2011-12
294 *Daily Mail*, 2 December 2018
295 Terry McDermott, *Terry Mac: Living for the Moment* (Trinity Sports Media, 2017)
296 *Football League Review*, Volume 5, 1970-71
297 *Goal*, 10 January 1970
298 *Goal*, 17 April 1971
299 *Backpass*, March/April 2016
300 *Rothmans Football Yearbook 1972-73* (Queen Anne Press, 1972)
301 *Football League Review*, Volume 5, 1970-71
302 Alan Hardaker, *Hardaker of the League* (Pelham Books, 1977)
303 *Shoot!*, 19 February, 1977
304 *Shoot!*, 19 February, 1977
305 Alwyn W. Turner, *Crisis? What Crisis? Britain in the 1970s* (Aurum, 2008)
306 Giles Radice, *Friends and Rivals: Crosland, Jenkins and Healey* (Little Brown Books, 2003)
307 Memorandum of conversation, Gerald R. Ford Library, 1975, quoted in Dominic Sandbrook, *Seasons in the Sun: The Battle for Britain, 1974-79* (Allen Lane, 2012)
308 Hardaker, *Hardaker of the League*
309 Interview with author
310 *Football Monthly*, June 1973
311 *Shoot!*, 7 July 1973
312 Interview with author
313 Hardaker, *Hardaker of the League*
314 *Topical Times Football Book*, 1970-71
315 *The Making of Match of the Day* (BBC TV, 1974)
316 Joe Moran, *Armchair Nation: An Intimate History of Britain in Front of the TV* (Profile Books, 2013)
317 *Goal*, 21 November, 1970
318 David Russell, *Football and the English: A Social History of Association Football, 1863-1995* (Carnegie Publishing, 1997)
319 *Football Monthly*, March 1973
320 *The Listener*, 19 December 1974
321 John Fiske and John Hartley, *Reading Television* (Methuen, 1978)
322 *Goal*, 30 January 1971
323 *Goal*, 9 December 1972
324 Marshall Cavendish *Book of Football*, 1972
325 *Shoot!* 1 July 1978

326 *Soccer Monthly Annual 1980*
327 *Inside Football*, 26 February 1972
328 *Football League Review*, 7 March 1970
329 *Inside Football*, 26 February 1972
330 Hardaker, *Hardaker of the League*
331 *Goal*, 2/9 February, 1974

CHAPTER 7: THE YEAR OF LIVING DANGEROUSLY

332 Interview with author
333 Interview with author
334 Interview with author
335 Interview with author
336 *Goal*, 13 February 1971
337 *Shoot!*, 13 November 1971
338 *Goal*, 17 October, 1970
339 Interview with author
340 Interview with author
341 *Shoot! Summer Special*, 1971
342 *Football Monthly*, April 1972
343 *Football Monthly Digest*, September 1973
344 Interview with author
345 *Shoot!* 20 November 1971
346 *Football Monthly*, June 1973
347 *Goal*, 13 May 1972
348 *Goal*, 30 December 1972
349 *Goal*, 8 July 1972
350 Kenny Dalglish, *Dalglish: My Autobiography* (Hodder & Stoughton, 1996)
351 *Shoot!* 22 September 1973
352 *World Cup Grandstand* (BBC TV, 6 June 1973)
353 Mick Channon, *Home and Away: An Autobiography* (Stanley Paul, 1977)
354 *Shoot!*, 7 July 1973
355 Interview with author
356 *Football Monthly Digest*, January 1974
357 Interview with author
358 Interview with author
359 *Goal*, 1 September 1973
360 Colin Bell with Ian Cheeseman, *Reluctant Hero* (Mainstream, 2005)
361 *Action Replay*, October 1996
362 *Goal*, 1 December 1973
363 Norman Hunter, *Biting Talk: My Autobiography* (Hodder & Stoughton, 2004)
364 Interview with author
365 Martin Chivers with Paolo Hewitt, *Big Chiv: My Goal in Life* (Vision Sports Publishing, 2009)
366 Bell, *Reluctant Hero*
367 *Goal*, January 5/12 1974
368 *Football Monthly*, July 1973
369 *Goal*, 10 November 1973
370 *Shoot!*, 17 November 1973
371 Interview with author
372 Ted Croker, *The First Voice You Will Hear...* (Collins Willow, 1987)
373 https://www.dailymail.co.uk/sport/football/article-2458091/England-v-Poland-1973-Peter-Shilton-Norman-Hunter-Allan-Clarkes-memories-heartbreak.html
374 Interview with author
375 Interview with author
376 *Goal*, 4 August 1973
377 *Match of the Seventies* (BBC TV, 1995)
378 Interview with author
379 Interview with author
380 Richard Kurt and Chris Nickeas, *The Red Army Years: Manchester United in the 1970s* (Headline, 1997)

CHAPTER 8: SATURDAY NIGHT'S ALRIGHT FOR FIGHTING

381 Richard Kurt and Chris Nickeas, *The Red Army Years: Manchester United in the 1970s* (Headline, 1997)
382 Michael Crick, *Manchester United: Betrayal of a Legend* (Pan, 1990)
383 Alan Hardaker, *Hardaker of the League* (Pelham Books, 1977)
384 *Football League Review*, Volume 4, 1969-70
385 Rob Steen, *The Mavericks: English Football when Flair Wore Flares* (Mainstream, 1994)
386 Eric Dunning, Patrick Murphy and John Williams, *The Roots of Football Hooliganism: An Historical and Sociological Study* (Routledge & Kegan Paul, 1988)
387 https://www.politics.co.uk/reference/football-hooliganism
388 Ian Stone, *To Be Someone: A Memoir About one Teenager's Obsession with The Jam* (Unbound, 2020)
389 *Goal*, 5 August 1972
390 *Shoot!*, 23 July 1977
391 *Shoot!*, 14 September 1974
392 Match programme, QPR v Orient, 26 December 1972
393 Mike Barson, *Before We Was We: Madness by Madness* (Virgin Books, 2019)
394 *Football Monthly*, November 1972
395 Terry McDermott, *Terry Mac: Living for the Moment* (Trinity Mirror Sports Media, 2017)
396 *Foul*, June 1974

397 Alan Hardaker, *Hardaker of the League* (Pelham, 1977)
398 *Professional Foul* (Tom Stoppard; BBC TV, 1977)
399 *Goal*, 4 September 1971
400 Hunter Davies, *The Glory Game* (Weidenfeld and Nicolson, 1972)
401 *Boy George's 1970s: Save Me from Suburbia* (IWC Productions for BBC, 2016)
402 Desmond Morris, *The Soccer Tribe* (Jonathan Cape, 1981)
403 Dunning et al, *The Roots of Football Hooliganism*
404 Morris, *The Soccer Tribe*
405 Roger Ingham (editor), *Football Hooliganism: The Wider Context* (Interaction Imprint, 1978)
406 Morris, *The Soccer Tribe*
407 Dunning et al, *The Roots of Football Hooliganism*
408 Dunning et al, *The Roots of Football Hooliganism*
409 Interview with author
410 Bobby Robson, *Time on the Grass* (Arthur Baker, 1982)
411 Quoted in Steen, *The Mavericks*
412 Trevor Brooking, *The Autobiography* (Pelham Books, 1981)
413 Morris, *The Soccer Tribe*
414 Stanley Cohen, *Folk Devils and Moral Panics: The Creation of the Mods and Rockers* (HarperCollins, 1972)
415 Wagg, *The Football World*
416 *The 1970s* (Dominic Sandbrook, BBC TV, 2012)
417 Peter Marsh, *Aggro: The Illusion of Violence* (Dent, 1978)
418 Russell, *Football and the English*
419 *The 1970s*
420 *Whatever Happened to the Likely Lads?* 'Guess Who's Coming to Dinner?' (Dick Clement and Ian La Frenais; BBC TV, 1973)
421 *The 1970s*
422 *The 1970s*
423 Wagg, *The Football World*
424 *Shoot!*, 6 January 1979
425 Morris, *The Soccer Tribe*

CHAPTER 9: TAKE ME TO YOUR LEADER

426 *Inside Football*, 8 April 1972
427 Interview with author
428 Peter Taylor, *With Clough by Taylor* (Sidgwick and Jackson, 1980)
429 *Goal*, 29 September 1973
430 Taylor, *With Clough by Taylor*
431 *Match of the Seventies* (BBC TV, 1995)
432 Don Shaw, *Clough's War* (Ebury Press, 2009)
433 Emlyn Hughes, *Crazy Horse* (Arthur Baker, 1980)
434 *The Fall and Rise of Reginald Perrin* (David Nobbs; BBC TV, 1976)
435 Phil Rostron, *We Are The Damned United* (Mainstream Publishing, 2009)
436 Kevin Keegan, *An Autobiography* (Arthur Baker, 1977)
437 Hughes, *Crazy Horse*
438 Tommy Smith, *I Did It the Hard Way* (Arthur Baker, 1980)
439 John Toshack, *Tosh: An Autobiography* (Arthur Baker, 1982)
440 Bill Shankly, *Shankly* (Littlehampton Book Services, 1976)
441 *Clough* (ITV, 2009)
442 Rostron, *We Are the Damned United*
443 Match programme, Leeds United v QPR, 21 August 1974
444 *Clough*
445 Match programme, Leeds United v Luton Town, 7 September 1974
446 *Backpass*, Christmas/New Year 2011-12
447 *Topical Times Football Book*, 1972-73
448 *Football Monthly Digest*, June 1974
449 Smith, *I Did It the Hard Way*
450 Keegan, *An Autobiography*
451 Keegan, *An Autobiography*
452 *Shoot!*, 17 August 1974
453 *Shoot!*, 31 August 1974
454 Bill Nicholson, *Glory Glory: My Life with Spurs* (Macmillan, 1984)
455 Rob Steen, *The Mavericks; English Football when Flair Wore Flares* (Mainstream, 1994)
456 Steen, *The Mavericks*
457 Stan Bowles, *The Autobiography* (Orion, 2004)
458 *Goal*, 1 August 1970
459 Nicholson, *Glory Glory*
460 *Goal*, 9 December 1969
461 *Radio Times*, 5-11 May 1973
462 *Shoot!*, 26 February 1977
463 *Goal*, April 4 1970
464 *Goal*, 3 March 1973
465 Alan Hardaker, *Hardaker of the League* (Pelham Books, 1977)
466 Hardaker, *Hardaker of the League*
467 *Shoot!*, 21 May 1977
468 *Shoot!*, 26 February 1977
469 *Shoot!*, 24 August 1974

470 Jonathan Wilson, *Brian Clough: Nobody Ever Says Thank You* (Orion, 2011)
471 Rostron, *We Are the Damned United*
472 John Giles, *A Football Man: My Autobiography* (Hodder & Stoughton, 2010)
473 Match programme, Leeds United v Sheffield United, 21 September 1974
474 Richard Sutcliffe, *Revie: Reviled and Revered* (Great Northern, 2010)
475 *Clough*
476 Bill Shankly, *Shankly* (Littlehampton Book Services, 1976)
477 Bob Latchford, *On A Different Road* (de Coubertin Books, 2015)
478 *Backpass*, Spring 2010
479 *Shoot!*, 14 September 1974
480 *Clough*
481 *I Believe in Miracles* (Baby Cow Productions, 2015)
482 Viv Anderson, *First Among Unequals* (Fullback Media, 2010)
483 Brian Clough, *Cloughie: Walking on Water* (Headline, 2002)
484 *I Believe in Miracles*
485 Dominic Sandbrook, *Seasons in the Sun: The Battle for Britain, 1974-79* (Allen Lake, 2012)

CHAPTER 10: WE CAN BE HEROES

486 Jimmy Case, *Hard Case* (John Blake, 2014)
487 *Shoot!*, 21 May 1977
488 Brian Barwick, *Watching the Match: The Inside Story of Football on Television* (Andre Deutsch, 2013)
489 *Shoot!*, 22 January 1972
490 *Goal*, 19/26 January 1974
491 Brian James, *Journey to Wembley: The Story of the 1976-77 FA Cup Competition and Liverpool's Bid for the Treble* (Marshall Cavendish, 1977)
492 *Shoot!*, 11 January 1975
493 *Backpass*, Spring 2011
494 *The Guardian, Football Weekly Podcast*, 30 March 2020
495 *Goal*, 16 December 1972
496 Dennis Tueart, *My Football Journey* (Vision Sport Publishing, 2011)
497 Malcolm Allison, *Colours of My Life* (Everest, 1975)
498 *Shoot!*, 7 April 1973
499 Interview with author
500 Lance Hardy, *Stokoe, Sunderland and '73: The Story of the Greatest FA Cup Final Shock of All Time* (Orion, 2009)
501 *Sunday People*, 3 January 2015
502 Tueart, *My Football Journey*
503 Hardy, *Stokoe, Sunderland and '73*
504 *Shoot!*, 25 August 1973
505 *Bobby Charlton's Football Scrapbook* (Sky Sports, 1997)
506 Hardy, *Stokoe, Sunderland and '73*
507 *Goal*, 2 March 1974
508 *Shoot!*, 1 February 1975
509 *Backpass*, Summer 2008
510 *Shoot!*, 22 February 1975
511 *Shoot!*, 22 February 1975
512 https://www.afcwimbledon.co.uk/news/2019/january/dickie-on-creating-fa-cup-history-44-years-ago/
513 Interview with author
514 Interview with author
515 https://www.thegoalhanger.co.uk/blogs/news/john-motson-my-favourite-goal-1
516 *The Observer*, 28 January 2007
517 *The Observer*, 28 January 2007
518 *The Observer*, 28 January 2007
519 *The Observer*, 28 January 2007
520 Brian Moore and Martin Tyler, *The Big Matches: A Decade of World Soccer, 1970-1980* (Queen Anne Press, 1980)
521 Ricky George, *One Goal, One Horse* (Pen Press Publishers, 2001)
522 *Inside Football*, 26 February 1972
523 *Football League Review*, Volume 7, 1972-73
524 *The Observer*, 28 January 2007
525 *Football Flashback* (Tyne Tees TV, 2003)
526 *Football Flashback*
527 Marshall Cavendish *Book of Football*, 1972
528 *Shoot!*, 17 August 1974
529 *Shoot!*, 18 January 1975
530 Tony McDonald, *West Ham In My Day* (Football World, 2007)
531 McDonald, *West Ham In My Day*
532 Trevor Brooking, *The Autobiography* (Pelham Books, 1981)
533 Interview with author
534 Lou Macari, *Football: My Life* (Bantam Press, 2008)
535 Interview with author
536 Lawrie McMenemy, *A Lifetime's Obsession* (Trinity Mirror Sports Media, 2016)
537 Interview with author
538 Interview with author
539 Interview with author
540 Interview with author
541 *Football Monthly*, November 1972
542 *Jimmy Hill's Football Weekly*, 12 December 1969

543 Bobby Robson, *Time on the Grass* (Arthur Baker, 1982)
544 *Foul*, June 1974
545 *Shoot!*, 1 January 1977
546 *Shoot!*, 9 April 1977
547 *Shoot!*, 1 November 1977
548 *Shoot!*, 21 May 1977
549 Terry Neill, *Revelations of a Football Manager* (Sidgwick & Jackson, 1985)
550 Robson, *Time on the Grass*
551 Neill, *Revelations of a Football Manager*

CHAPTER 11: ENGLAND'S DREAMING

552 *Featuring the Champions* (Leeds United publication, 1974)
553 *Goal*, 29 September 1973
554 *Featuring the Champions*
555 *Goal*, 18 May 1974
556 Richard Sutcliffe, *Revie: Revered and Reviled* (Great Northern, 2010)
557 Sutcliffe, *Revie: Revered and Reviled*
558 *Shoot!*, 19 February 1972
559 Interview with author
560 Interview with author
561 *Match of the Seventies* (BBC TV, 1995)
562 Stan Bowles, *The Autobiography* (Orion, 2004)
563 Bowles, *The Autobiography*
564 Frank Worthington, *One Hump or Two? The Frank Worthington Story* (ACL & Polar Publishing, 1994)
565 Alwyn W. Turner, *Crisis? What Crisis? Britain in the 1970s* (Aurum Press, 2008)
566 *Shoot!*, 2 November 1974
567 Interview with author
568 *Shoot!*, 23 November 1974
569 Kevin Keegan, *An Autobiography* (Arthur Baker, 1977)
570 Trevor Brooking, *The Autobiography* (Pelham Books, 1981)
571 Malcolm Macdonald with Colin Malam, *Supermac: My Autobiography* (Highdown, 2003)
572 *Shoot! Annual*, 1976
573 *Titbits*, September 1974
574 Rob Steen, *The Mavericks: English Football When Flair Wore Flares* (Mainstream, 1994)
575 Macdonald, *Supermac*
576 Turner, *Crisis? What Crisis?*
577 *Shoot!*, 22 March 1975
578 *Professional Foul* (Tom Stoppard: BBC TV, 1977)
579 Emlyn Hughes, *Crazy Horse* (Arthur Baker, 1980)
580 Interview with author
581 Brooking, *The Autobiography*
582 Interview with author
583 Sutcliffe, *Revie: Revered and Reviled*
584 Sutcliffe, *Revie: Revered and Reviled*
585 *Shoot!*, 11 June 1977
586 *Shoot! Annual*, 1979
587 Interview with author
588 *Backpass*, Summer 2008
589 *Shoot!*, 12 February 1977
590 Keegan, *An Autobiography*
591 Keegan, *An Autobiography*
592 Hughes, *Crazy Horse*
593 Brooking, *The Autobiography*
594 Rod Stewart, *Rod: The Autobiography* (Century, 2012)
595 *Shoot!*, 9 July 1977
596 Sutcliffe, *Revie: Revered and Reviled*
597 Interview with author
598 Interview with author
599 Sutcliffe, *Revie: Revered and Reviled*
600 *Shoot!*, 6 August 1977
601 *Shoot!*, 25 June 1977
602 *Shoot!*, 15 March 1975
603 *Shoot!*, 1 October 1977
604 Sutcliffe, *Revie: Revered and Reviled*
605 Hughes, *Crazy Horse*
606 Interview with author
607 David Tossell, *Tony Greig: A Reappraisal of English Cricket's Most Controversial Captain* (Pitch Publishing, 2011)
608 Turner, *Crisis? What Crisis?*
609 *The Home That Two Built* (BBC TV, 2014)
610 Christopher Booker, *The Seventies* (Penguin, 1980)
611 Sutcliffe, *Revie: Revered and Reviled*
612 *Shoot!*, 20 August 1977
613 Interview with author
614 Interview with author
615 Interview with author
616 Interview with author
617 Eamon Dunphy, *A Strange Kind of Glory: Sir Matt Busby & Manchester United* (William Heinemann, 1991)
618 Interview with author
619 Tommy Docherty, *The Doc: My Story* (Headline, 2006)
620 Dunphy, *A Strange Kind of Glory*

CHAPTER 12: YOUNG, GIFTED AND BLACK

621 *Shoot!*, 13 November 1971
622 *Football League Review*, Volume 6, 1971-72

623 *Goal*, 12 February 1972
624 *Shoot!*, 25 April 1970
625 Clyde Best, *The Acid Test* (De Coubertin Books, 2016)
626 http://www.thefa.com/news/2018/oct/30/viv-anderson-black-history-month-301018
627 Brian Belton, *EastEnd Heroes, Stateside Kings* (John Blake Publishing, 2008)
628 *Jimmy Hill's Football Weekly*, 20 February 1970
629 Best, *The Acid Test*
630 Best, *The Acid Test*
631 *Shoot!*, 12 February 1972
632 Dominic Sandbrook, *Seasons in the The Sun: The Battle for Britain, 1974-79* (Allen Lane, 2012)
633 *Election 70* (BBC TV, 1970)
634 Interview with author
635 Interview with author
636 Colin Babb, *1973 and Me: The England v West Indies Test Series and a Memorable Childhood Year* (Hansib, 2020)
637 Dermot Kavanagh, *Different Class: The Story of Laurie Cunningham* (Unbound, 2017)
638 Kavanagh, *Different Class*
639 *First Among Equals: The Laurie Cunningham Story* (ITV, 2013)
640 Kavanagh, *Different Class*
641 *Sunday Times Magazine*, 21 March 1976
642 Paul Rees, *The Three Degrees: The Men Who Changed Football Forever* (Constable, 2014
643 *Sunday Times Magazine*, 21 March 1976
644 *Shoot!*, 4 June, 1977
645 Kavanagh, *Different Class*
646 Viv Anderson, *First Among Unequals* (Fullback Media, 2010)
647 Anderson, *First Among Unequals*
648 Anderson, *First Among Unequals*
649 Cyrille Regis, *My Story: The Autobiography of the First Black Icon of British Football* (Andre Deutsch, 2010)
650 Dave Bowler and Jas Bains, *Samba in the Smethwick End: Regis, Cunningham, Batson and the Football Revolution* (Mainstream, 2000)
651 Rees, *The Three Degrees*
652 Regis, *My Story*
653 *Backpass*, New season 2014-15
654 *The Observer*, 16 December 2018
655 Rees, *The Three Degrees*
656 Rees, *The Three Degrees*
657 Regis, *My Story*
658 *Shoot!*, 23 April 1977
659 Rees, *The Three Degrees*
660 Anderson, *First Among Unequals*
661 https://www.theguardian.com/music/2008/apr/20/popandrock.race
662 Rees, *The Three Degrees*
663 https://www.thepfa.com/news/2018/10/23/former-qpr-player-bob-hazell-on-the-game-he-loves
664 Quoted in *Socialist Review*, October 1999
665 Regis, *My Story*
666 *Backpass*, Winter 2011
667 Bowler and Bains, *Samba in the Smethwick End*
668 *Shoot!*, 4 June 1977
669 *Backpass*, November 2017
670 https://www.thepfa.com/news/2018/10/23/former-qpr-player-bob-hazell-on-the-game-he-loves
671 *Whites v Blacks: How Football Changed a Nation* (BBC TV, 2016)
672 *Whites v Blacks: How Football Changed a Nation*

CHAPTER 13: THE LIVERPOOL WAY

673 Kevin Keegan, *An Autobiography* (Arthur Baker, 1977)
674 Ian Herbert, *Quiet Genius: Bob Paisley, British Football's Greatest Manager* (Bloomsbury, 2017)
675 *Shoot!*, 5 April 1975
676 Peter Cormack, *From the Cowshed to the Kop* (Black & White Publishing, 2012)
677 Bill Shankly, *Shankly* (Littlehampton Book Services, 1976)
678 Shankly, *Shankly*
679 Cormack, *From the Cowshed to the Kop*
680 *The Guardian*, 15 February 1996
681 *Goal*, 11 May 1974
682 Phil Neal, *Attack from the Back* (Littlehampton Book Services, 1981)
683 John Toshack, *Tosh: An Autobiography* (Arthur Baker, 1982)
684 David Fairclough, *Supersub: The Story of Football's Most Famous Number 12* (De Coubertin, 2015)
685 Cormack, *From the Cowshed to the Kop*
686 Cormack, *From the Cowshed to the Kop*
687 Kenny Dalglish, *Dalglish: My Autobiography* (Hodder & Stoughton, 1996)
688 Herbert, *Quiet Genius*
689 Fairclough, *Supersub*

690 Terry McDermott, *Terry Mac: Living for the Moment* (Trinity Mirror Sports Media, 2017)
691 *Shoot!*, 21 May 1977
692 Marshall Cavendish *Football Handbook*, Part 37, 1979
693 *Shoot!*, 12 August 1978
694 Tommy Smith, *I Did it the Hard Way* (Arthur Baker, 1980)
695 Keegan, *An Autobiography*
696 Keegan, *An Autobiography*
697 Stan Bowles, *The Autobiography* (Orion, 2004)
698 Bowles, *The Autobiography*
699 Interview with author
700 Bowles, *The Autobiography*
701 *Action Replay*, October 1996
702 Rob Steen, *The Mavericks: English Football When Flair Wore Flares* (Mainstream, 1994)
703 *Shoot!*, 8 January 1977
704 Keegan, *An Autobiography*
705 Keegan, *An Autobiography*
706 Brian Reade, *44 Years With the Same Bird: A Liverpudlian Love Affair* (Pan Books, 2009)
707 Smith, *I Did it the Hard Way*
708 *Brian Moore Meets Kevin* Keegan (London Weekend Television, 1979)
709 Emlyn Hughes, *Crazy Horse* (Arthur Baker, 1980)
710 Keegan, *An Autobiography*
711 *Shoot!*, 3 September 1977
712 Rogan Taylor and Andrew Ward, *Three Sides of the Mersey* (Robson Books, 1993)
713 Phil Neal, *Attack from the Back* (Littlehampton Book Services, 1981)
714 *The Independent*, 14 January 2016
715 Clive Thomas, *By the Book* (Willow Books, 1984)
716 *Howard's Way* (Toffee Films, 2019)
717 Bob Latchford, *A Different Road* (de Coubertin Books, 2015)
718 *Match of the Seventies* (BBC TV, 1996)
719 *Shoot!*, 25 June 1977
720 John Keith, *Bob Paisley: Manager of the Millennium* (Robson Books, 2001)
721 *Shoot!*, 9 April, 1977
722 *Shoot!*, 3 September, 1977
723 Jimmy Case, *Hard Case* (John Blake, 2014)
724 Smith, *I Did it the Hard Way*
725 Hughes, *Crazy Horse*
726 *Shoot!*, 25 June 1977
727 Keegan, *An Autobiography*
728 McDermott, *Terry Mac*
729 *When English Football Ruled Europe* (ITV, 2018)
730 Graeme Souness, *Football: My Life, My Passion* (Headline, 2017)
731 *Kenny* (Pitch International Films, 2017)
732 Tony Evans, *Two Tribes: Liverpool, Everton and a City on the Brink* (Bantam Press, 2018)
733 David Goldbatt, *The Ball is Round: A Global History of Football* (Penguin, 2007)
734 Taylor and Ward, *Three Sides of the Mersey*
735 *Goal*, 19/26 January 1974
736 McDermott, *Terry Mac*
737 Souness, *Football: My Passion, My Life*
738 Herbert, *Quiet Genius*
739 McDermott, *Terry Mac*
740 Ron Greenwood, *Yours Sincerely* (Harper Collins, 1984)
741 Greenwood, *Yours Sincerely*
742 *Goal*, 13 February 1971
743 *Shoot!*, 22 October 1977
744 Greenwood, *Yours Sincerely*
745 Trevor Francis with David Miller, *The World to Play For* (Sidgwick & Jackson, 1982)
746 Match programme, England v Italy, November 16 1977
747 Greenwood, *Yours Sincerely*
748 *Brian Moore Meets Kevin Keegan*
749 Marshall Cavendish *Football Handbook*, Part 46, 1979
750 *Clough* (ITV Sport, 2009)
751 Greenwood, *Yours Sincerely*
752 Lawrie McMenemy, *A Lifetime's Obsession* (Trinity Media Sports Media, 2016)
753 *Clough* (ITV)

CHAPTER 14: THE OUTSIDERS

754 Ricky Villa, *And Still Ricky Villa: My Autobiography* (Vision Sports Publishing, 2010)
755 http://www.fifa.com/fifa-tournaments/players-coaches/do-you-remember/people=174354/index.html
756 *Shoot!*, 20 January 1979
757 *Shoot!*, 20 January 1979
758 Ossie Ardiles, *Ossie's Dream: The Autobiography of a Football Legend* (Transworld Digital, 2010)
759 *Football Monthly*, December 1972

760 *Shoot!*, 22 October 1977
761 *The Sweeney*, 'Visiting Fireman' (Troy Kennedy-Martin; Thames Television, 1976)
762 Alwyn W. Turner, *Crisis? What Crisis?: Britain in the 1970s* (Aurum Press, 2008)
763 Laurel Forster & Sue Harper (editors), *British Culture and Society in the 1970s: The Lost Decade* (Cambridge Scholars Publishing, 2010)
764 Dominic Sandbrook, *Seasons in The Sun: The Battle for Britain, 1974-79* (Allen Lane, 2012)
765 Philip Goodhart, *Full-Hearted Consent* (Davis-Poyner, 1976)
766 Michael Palin, *The Python Years: Diaries 1969-79 Volume 1* (Weidenfeld & Nicolson, 1976)
767 *Shoot!*, 23 September 1978
768 *Shoot!*, 17 March 1979
769 *Shoot!*, 22 October 1977
770 *Shoot!*, 30 September 1978
771 *Shoot!*, 15 July 1978
772 *Shoot!*, 4 November 1978
773 *Shoot!*, 4 November 1978
774 *Shoot!*, 7 April 1979
775 Ardiles, *Ossie's Dream*
776 *England Their England*, Nick Harris (Pitch Publishing, 2003)
777 Match programme, Arsenal v Leeds United, 19 August 1978
778 Tommy Smith *Anfield Iron: The Autobiography* (Bantam Press, 2008)
779 Smith, *Anfield Iron*
780 Taylor and Ward, *Three Sides of the Mersey* (Robson Books, 1983)
781 Ardiles, *Ossie's Dream*
782 *Shoot!*, 30 September 1978
783 Marshall Cavendish *Football Handbook*, Part 51, 1979
784 Interview with author
785 Interview with author
786 *Shoot!*, 1 July 1978
787 *Shoot!*, 1 July 1978
788 *Shoot!*, 7 December 1978
789 *Shoot!*, 16 September 1978
790 James Callaghan, *Time and Chance* (Harper Collins, 1987)
791 Roy Strong, *The Roy Strong Diaries 1967-87* (Weidenfeld & Nicolson, 1997)
792 *Shoot!*, 6 January 1979
793 *Shoot!*, 23 July 1977
794 *Shoot!*, 3 March 1979
795 Interview with author
796 Interview with author
797 *Shoot!*, 5 August 1978
798 Alan Hardaker, *Hardaker of the League* (Pelham Books, 1977)
799 Interview with author
800 Interview with author
801 *Shoot!*, 9 September 1978
802 *Shoot!*, 10 March 1979
803 *Shoot!*, 14 July 1979
804 *Shoot!*, 11 November 1978

CHAPTER 15: COULD IT BE MAGIC

805 Clough (ITV Sport, 2009)
806 Brian Clough, *Walking on Water* (Headline, 2002)
807 *The Guardian*, 19 October, 2015
808 Daniel Taylor, *I Believe in Miracles: The Remarkable Story of Brian Clough's European Cup-Winning Team* (Headline, 2015)
809 Tommy Smith, *I Did it the Hard Way* (Arthur Baker, 1980)
810 Clough, *Walking on Water*
811 Taylor, *I Believe in Miracles*
812 *Backpass*, Christmas/New Year 2011-12
813 Taylor, *I Believe in Miracles*
814 Peter Taylor, *With Clough by Taylor* (Sidgwick and Jackson, 1980)
815 Kenny Dalglish, *Dalglish: My Autobiography* (Hodder & Stoughton, 1996)
816 Clough, *Walking on Water*
817 *Clough* (ITV)
818 Jonathan Wilson, *Brian Clough: Nobody Ever Says Thank You* (Orion, 2011)
819 *Backpass*, Christmas/New Year, 2011-12
820 *Clough* (ITV)
821 *Clough* (ITV)
822 *I Believe in Miracles* (Baby Cow Productions, 2015)
823 Viv Anderson, *First Among Unequals* (Fullback Media, 2010)
824 Phil Neal, *Attack from the Back* (Littlehampton Book Services, 1981)
825 Wilson, *Nobody Ever Says Thank You*
826 Bob Latchford, *A Different Road* (de Coubertin Books, 2015)
827 Latchford, *A Different Road*
828 Brian Viner, *Looking for the Toffees* (Simon & Schuster, 2014)
829 Latchford, *A Different Road*
830 *Shoot!* (September 15, 1978)
831 Graeme Souness, *Football: My Life, My Passion* (Headline, 2017)
832 John Lawson, *Forest: The 1979 Season* (Wensum, 1979)

833 Dalglish, *My Autobiography*
834 *Shoot!*, 20 January, 29
835 Rogan Taylor and Alan Ward, *Three Sides of the Mersey* (Robson Books, 1993)
836 *The Anfield Wrap*, 25 February, 2015
837 Case, *Hard Case*
838 *Backpass*, Winter 2020
839 Bob Latchford, *A Different Road* (de Coubertin Books, 2015)
840 *Backpass*, Winter 2011
841 *Backpass*, Winter 2020
842 *Backpass*, Winter 2020
843 Trevor Francis with David Miller, *The World to Play For* (Sidgwick & Jackson, 1982)
844 *Shoot!*, 28 October, 1978
845 *The Scotsman*, 28 March, 2009
846 Larry Lloyd, *Hard Man, Hard Game* (John Blake, 2009)
847 Interview with author
848 John Lawson, *Forest: The 1979 Season* (Wensum, 1979)
849 *I Believe in Miracles*
850 Wilson, *Nobody Ever Says Thank You*
851 Wilson, *Nobody Ever Says Thank You*
852 *Football Monthly*, November 1972
853 Clough, *Walking on Water*
854 *I Believe in Miracles*
855 Taylor, *With Clough by Taylor*
856 Taylor, *With Clough by Taylor*

INDEX

C
AN GOUD